WORSHIP AND THEOLOGY
IN ENGLAND

WORSHIP AND THEOLOGY IN ENGLAND

WORSHIP
AND THEOLOGY IN
ENGLAND

FROM ANDREWES

TO BAXTER AND FOX, 1603-1690

BY HORTON DAVIES

PRINCETON, NEW JERSEY
PRINCETON UNIVERSITY PRESS
1975

Publication of this book has been aided by
the Whitney Darrow Publication Reserve Fund
of Princeton University Press.

HORTON DAVIES is currently the Henry
W. Putnam Professor of the History of Christianity at Princeton University. He was born
in Wales, became an honors graduate in both
Arts and Divinity at Edinburgh University,
and obtained his Doctorate of Philosophy at
Oxford University. Mr. Davies has served successively as minister of an English Congregational Church in London, Dean of the Faculty
of Divinity at Rhodes University in the Union
of South Africa, and Head of the Department
of Church History at Mansfield and Regent's
Park Colleges at Oxford University. In 1970
he was awarded the Doctorate of Letters of
Oxford University for the first three volumes
of this series to be published.

This book was composed in Linotype Monticello
Printed in the United States of America
by Princeton University Press, Princeton, New Jersey

ACKNOWLEDGMENTS

IT WOULD HAVE BEEN impossible to complete these five volumes and over fifteen years of research in the libraries of Britain and the United States without the help of several institutions and persons to whom I tender my thanks: to Princeton University for leaves of absence, and to its Committee for Research in the Humanities and Social Sciences for grants for summer travel and support as well as for typing; to the John S. Guggenheim Memorial Foundation of New York City for two Fellowships; to the Henry E. Huntington Library and Art Gallery of San Marino, California, for a Grant-in-aid; to the Princeton University Press, its Director, Herbert S. Bailey, Jr., and to several of its editors; and to my colleagues past and present of the Department of Religion at Princeton University for their encouragements, despite their ironical references to my "pentateuch."

The Bibliography owes much to the help I received from David Moessner of the Class of 1971 at Princeton, now reading theology at Mansfield College, Oxford. My companion and helper in so much of this research, which delayed her own research into the English Renaissance, is my wife, Marie-Hélène, to whom I owe more than words can convey. Other expressions of my indebtedness will be found in footnotes, in the List of Illustrations, and, of course, in the Bibliography.

HORTON DAVIES

CONTENTS

PART THREE: THE HISTORY AND FORMS OF WORSHIP

ILLUSTRATIONS

Following page 32

WORSHIP AND THEOLOGY
IN ENGLAND

INTRODUCTION

T HIS VOLUME concludes my study of the history and theology
of Christian worship in England from the Reformation and
Counter-Reformation until the present. I began liturgical
research as a graduate student in the University of Oxford thirty-
five years ago and thirty-three hundred miles away from Princeton
University where I have the honour to teach amid Neo-Gothic
buildings with all modern conveniences. The present series of five
volumes has used up almost all of my spare time for thirteen years.
My greatest regret is that it is so long, especially as I detest prolixity. It seems supremely ironical that an account of Christian
worship in a single nation should be longer than the Old and New
Testaments combined. It would be some mitigation if this introduction were to prove the briefest I have written.

My sub-title bears three symbolic names: *From Andrewes to
Baxter and Fox: 1603-1690*. They direct attention to the fact that
the most creative religious thinking and living in the seventeenth
century was the achievement of the Anglican Caroline divines, the
Puritan pastors, and the new Religious Society of Friends, or
Quakers.

Lancelot Andrewes, who had twice turned down Queen Elizabeth's proposals to make him a Bishop, was Dean of Westminster
Abbey when our history begins. He fathered an important tradition of Biblical and Patristic scholarship, a knowledge of and fondness for liturgiology, a love of the Eucharist and of appropriately
high ceremonial. He was a brilliant "Metaphysical preacher," a
distinguished apologist of the Church of England, as well as the
author of *Preces Privatae* which raided the liturgies of the East
and West as a monarch, and demonstrated his own reverence for
God and sensitivity to human needs. This remarkable Father-in-
God (who died as Bishop of Winchester) gave Anglicanism its
direction for at least a century to come, as it distinguished itself
from both Rome and Geneva. He let Anglicans see that their
church was firmly built upon the traditions of the primitive church
of the first five centuries. He was followed by Cosin, Wren, Hammond, Bramhall, and Laud, as well as by many others. His authorities were, so he stated, "one canon, reduced to writing by God himself, two testaments, three creeds, four general councils, and the
series of Fathers of that period—the centuries, that is, before Constantine and two after—determine the boundary of our faith."

Baxter, the second name, who, like Fox, died at the end of our period, symbolizes the Puritans at their least political and most spiritual. The author of the classic concept of the Reformed ministry, *Gildas Salvianus, the Reformed Pastor*, as of the Reformed liturgy, he was the leader of the "Presbyterian" divines at the Savoy Conference with the Anglicans in 1661, who had written a sensitive treatise on the cultivation of the spiritual life, *The Saints Everlasting Rest*, an incisive autobiography, and a comprehensive textbook on casuistry, *The Christian Directory*. Not a university man, he was one of the most learned men of his time, and he possessed a spirit that admirably reflected his highest loyalties.

The third name is, of course, that of the century's most persistent quester for religious truth, George Fox, who finally created his own religious burrow. After trying both conventional and unconventional forms of Christianity in the fantastic Commonwealth laboratory of experimental sectarianism, he founded, what the Quaker apologist, Barclay, called a third type of Christianity. This denied all external formal religion, repudiated the sacraments and sacerdotalism, that all Fox's friends might be ministers and receive the inner illumination and warmth of the Holy Spirit.

Theologically, the three names and the traditions for which they stand, represent three different understandings of religious authority. Andrewes stands for the triple cord of Scripture, the Catholic heritage of the first five centuries in doctrine, polity, and liturgy, as well as reason. Baxter, as a Puritan, though with Arminian leanings, stands for the supremacy and sole domination of sacred Scripture, with an experimental emphasis on the empowering of the Holy Spirit which illuminates Scripture. Fox represents the primacy of the Holy Spirit in the hearts of men and women, with Scripture as a subordinate check on experience. Their names are an indication of the importance and variety of the major traditions of belief, behaviour, and worship in England.

This particular volume is planned differently from the others. In the first place, instead of providing separate studies of Anglican, Roman Catholic, and Dissenting theologies, as I did in Volume I, I have given up this idea. One reason was that there is little basic theological change between the sixteenth and the seventeenth centuries, apart from the growing Arminianism and pragmatism of the Church of England[1] and among the General or Non-Calvinist

---

[1] Furthermore, the main task has already been undertaken by others. These include H. R. McAdoo in *The Spirit of Anglicanism*, J.H.A. New in *Anglican*

Baptists. A more compelling reason was that it might prove more intriguing to derive the theology from the architecture which was its outward and visible expression. Hence Part One, "The Context of Worship," begins with Chapter I: "Church Architecture: Its Theology." This considers the differing nature of the holy communities worshipping in Anglican, Roman, Puritan, and Quaker churches, chapels, or meeting-houses. It also asks how important the following factors were in determining church architecture: symbolism, functionalism, social prestige, and economics.

After the theological and theoretical considerations, it seemed desirable to see what in fact had been built, so Chapter II was inevitably styled, "Church Architecture: Achievements." It documents the "Gothic survival" type of architecture in Anglicanism before the Great Fire and the "Wrenaissance" that followed it, and the domestic simplicity of the first Puritan meeting-houses and the domestic elegance of the later ones.

While still considering the background of worship, it is clear that the patterns of private and family devotion or spirituality are of great importance. Public worship is likely to be no more than a formal nod to God unless it is engaged in by praying households of faith, whether these be monasteries and convents or families about the domestic hearth. Chapter III is entitled, "Spirituality: Preparation for Public Worship." It examines the brilliant spirituality of the Counter-Reformation in Spain, Italy, and France, as these manuals filtered through in the English translations to the many religious houses of English exiles in the Low Countries and to the Recusants in England. It also glimpses the household altars of Anglicans, Puritans, and Quakers.

The fourth and last chapter of the first part deals with preaching. The seventeenth century was the golden age of preaching in England, with Andrewes, Donne, Jeremy Taylor, Bunyan and Baxter, to mention only the brightest luminaries in a great galaxy. What George Herbert said (and exemplified) of the country parson could be said of almost every preacher of this century, that he "preacheth constantly, the pulpit is his joy and throne." This was the case even when the congregation wished he would abdicate, as

---

and Puritan, the Basis of Their Opposition, 1558-1640; and Gerald Cragg in *Puritanism in the Period of the Great Persecution* and in *The Church and the Age of Reason, 1648-1789*. However, a synoptic and detailed account of the institutional and intellectual developments of Roman Catholicism in seventeenth century England is needed to fill out David Mathew's *Catholicism in England* which was published in 1936.

probably the Presbyterian hearers of Dr. Manton did when he preached the 190th successive sermon on a single Psalm. The title of Chapter IV is self-explanatory: "Preaching: Stimulus and Supplement to Worship."

Part Two, "Cultic Controversies," mirrors the extraordinary theological wrangling that riddled the seventeenth century. It is reflected in the bitter but often ingenious titles of lengthy pamphlets like William Prynne's *A Brief Survay and Censure of Mr. Cozens His Couzening Devotions* (1628), and more seriously and tragically in the Civil War that tore England asunder and deserves, at least in some respects, Trevelyan's title for it, the "Metaphysical War." The four chapters in this section deal with four major and continuing problems in worship. Chapter V treats the question of the most appropriate "Style in Worship: Prestigious or Plain?" It is concerned with whether prayer, vestments, and ceremonial should be highly stylized or austerely simple. Chapter VI contrasts the Roman Catholic and Anglican retrospective Calendar of Christological and Sanctoral Days, with the contemporary Puritan Calendar of Sabbaths and Days of Thanksgiving and Humiliation. Its title over-simplifies the issue as that of "Calendary Conflict: Holy Days or Holidays?" The truth in it is that Puritans wanted a weekly holy day, the Sabbath, while the Anglicans wanted an element of festivity and holiday hilarity. They and the Roman Catholics would have agreed more readily with Herrick, vicar, poet, and propagandist for the jollity of Church feasts:

> For Sports for Pagentrie and Playes,
> Thou hast thy Eves and Holydayes . . .
> Thy Wakes, thy Quintels, here thou hast,
> Thy May-poles too with Garlands grac't:
> Thy Morris-dance; thy Whitsun-ale;
> Thy Sheering-feast, which never faile.
> Thy Harvest home; thy Wassaile bowle,
> That's tost up after Fox i' th'Hole;
> Thy Mummeries: thy Twelfe-tide Kings
> And Queenes; thy Christmas revellings.

Chapter VII, entitled "Sacred Music: Splendid or Scriptural?" reviews the issues raised in Chapter IV in a different context. Here Anglicans insist that in cathedrals and other great churches

there is value in offering chants, verse anthems sung by professional choirs, and organ music and string symphonies or interludes, as men's best music to God. The Puritans stake the claim
of metrical psalmody as an apter expression of the priesthood of
all believers with rhymed and easily memorable jingles to easy
tunes, so that even the illiterate can join in God's praise.

The last Chapter in Part Two is Chapter VIII. It describes and
analyses the different theories of the presence of Christ: corporal
presence, real spiritual presence, or memorialism in the Mass, Holy
Communion, or Lord's Supper. It also asks which religious group
values the Eucharist most. Its title is: "The Chief Sacrament:
Means of Grace or Mnemonic?"

Part Three deals with "The History and Forms of Worship,"
and it requires less explanation than the other two parts.

Chapters IX and X tell the story of the ups and downs of the
Anglican Prayer Book. It was loved by the Caroline divines,
loathed as an instrument of tyranny by the Puritans and proscribed
by them, secretly used during the Commonwealth and Protectorate,
restored with the king in 1660, and revised conservatively in 1662
and very slightly later. Chapter IX is titled, "The Anglican Prayer
Book Admired and Rejected: 1603-1659," and Chapter X is
styled, "The Prayer Book Restored and Revised: 1660-1689."

The next two chapters deal respectively with Puritan and Nonconformist Worship. Chapter XI, "Puritan Prayer Books," concentrates on the Westminster or Parliamentary Directory of 1644
and on Baxter's Savoy or Reformed Liturgy of 1661. Both are
viewed in the light (or dark) of the criticisms of their contemporaries. Chapter XII, "Nonconformist Worship: Presbyterians and
Independents, 1662-1690," deals with their worship chiefly during the shadows of persecution.

Chapter XIII moves away from the Anglican-Puritan struggle
which dominated the century to consider the secret and forbidden
worship of the English Roman Catholics or their rare open worship
in the chapels of embassies in London or in the royal chapels of
Catholic queens in England.

Chapter XIV goes in the opposite direction to consider "Radical
Worship: The Baptists and Quakers."

The final Chapter XV, a summation of the entire book is entitled, "A Concluding Survey and Critique."

In this acrimoniously partisan century one is grateful that on both the Anglican and Puritan sides there were ecumenical spirits. The Puritan Baxter was happy to call himself a "meer Catholick" regarding party labels as mere libels. The droll Anglican church historian, Dr. Thomas Fuller, wrote: "For those who endeavour to make the way to heaven narrower than God hath made it, by prohibiting what he permits, do in event make the way to hell wider, occasioning the committing of such sins, which God hath forbidden." One's sympathies are entirely with Jeremy Taylor when he complained: "How many volumes have been writ about angels, about immaculate conception, about original sin, when all that is solid reason or clear revelation in all these three articles may be reasonably enough comprised in forty lines? And in these trifles and impertinences men are curiously busy, while they neglect those glorious precepts of Christianity and holy life which are the glories of our religion, and would enable us to a happy eternity."

This is a century of apparently implacable hostility, of fratricide between Christians, of almost unbearable prolixity in pen and pulpit, of deliberate misrepresentation of one's theological opponents, of damnable dogmatism even in speculative matters, and of hideous intolerance. It is, at the same time, like lilies growing in manure, an era which produced the brilliant sermons of Andrewes and Donne, those exemplary and complementary pastors Herbert and Baxter, the two religious epics of the Biblical visions and musings of Milton and Bunyan, and the greatest constellation of religious poets England has ever seen. The same century saw the beginnings of distinguished Patristic scholarship, a sense of social justice as the correlate of the Christian faith, and in the Society of Friends the tiny embodiment of that reconciliation which the era needed on a vaster scale. To have lived in that time must have led men and women to dream wild dreams and to waken to the wilder nightmares of reality. But the seeds of hope were already planted even in the cracked earth of disillusionment. They would eventually blossom into toleration, a reasoned faith, and that charity which leads to ecumenical appreciation. Even if one would not wish to have lived in their century, one cannot withhold admiration for their faith, their zest, and their endurance. The famous and the humble invite us to make the seventeenth century pilgrimage; to steal quietly inside their churches or meeting-houses or homes, to join in the liturgy or to listen to extemporary prayers, to sing their metrical psalmody, to hear and take notes of their sacred oratory, and to share, above all, their ornate Eucharist or simple Lord's Supper. In all these experiences, the curtain of the centuries is pulled back, and Christ encounters his elect, whether Roman Catholic, Anglican, Puritan, Baptist, or Quaker. The spectrum of their many-coloured worship refracts the white radiance of eternity.

PART ONE
THE CONTEXT OF WORSHIP

CHAPTER I

CHURCH ARCHITECTURE:
ITS THEOLOGY

GEORGE HERBERT, the poetical rector of Bemerton, celebrated the Church of England as the happy medium between the splendour of Roman Catholicism and the squalour of Puritanism, and succeeded in being unfair to all three traditions. Counter-Reformation church architecture in England was, with the exception of the royal chapels of Stuart queens and of King James II, and certain foreign embassy chapels in London, exceedingly restrained. Puritan architecture had its theological reasons, irrespective of its aesthetic tastes, for its simplicity which was far from squalour. And Anglican architecture itself was demonstrating an intriguingly distinctive quality of "Gothic survival" almost until the time of Wren. Most serious, however, was the assumption by Herbert that architecture, ceremonial, and fittings of churches are matters of subjective choice between aesthetic richness or imaginative poverty. His spurious and simplistic conclusion is, therefore, inevitably:

> A fine aspect in fit array,
> Neither too mean, nor yet too gay,
> Shows who is best.[1]

The aim of this chapter is to show that the selection of church architecture and fittings is a complex of at least five interrelated

---

[1] "The British Church," *The Works of George Herbert* (ed. F. E. Hutchinson, Oxford, 1941), p. 109. Archbishop William Laud expressed the median position of the Church of England with felicity. "Truth usually lies," he averred, "between two extremes and is beaten by both, as the poor Church of England is at this day by the Papist and the Separatist." (Cited in E.C.E. Bourne, *The Anglicanism of William Laud* [1947], p. 79.) John Donne, a former Roman Catholic, is deeply concerned by the problem of the intermediate role of the Church of England. It is anguished in the sonnet which begs:

> Show me, dear Christ, thy spouse, so bright and clear.
> What! is it She, which on the other shore
> Goes richly painted? or which rob'd and tore
> laments and mourns in Germany and here?

In *Satire* III Donne shows Mirreus seeking true religion at Rome, "because hee doth know/ That shee was there a thousand yeares agoe,/ He loves her ragges so." The rags are the unhappy additions to Rome's pristine purity. In reaction Crantz goes to the opposite extreme, following what "at Geneva is call'd/ Religion, plaine, simple, sullen, yong,/ Contemptuous, yet unhansome."

factors, which help to account for the differences (and partial similarities) in the four traditions under consideration. That is, these factors have helped to make Anglican, Roman Catholic, Puritan, and Quaker sacred buildings what they are.

One basic factor is the nature of the holy community envisaged by the worshippers of the church, chapel, or meeting-house. A second is where the dominant foci of worship are: on sacraments or on sermons, on praises or prayers, or on a combination of each? A third determinant of architecture and fittings is whether the sacred space is planned functionally or with a view to its numinous or symbolic quality? A fourth is socio-political. Is the church or meeting-house built to show by its external impressiveness and its interior richness the social prestige of the donors or worshippers, or by its simplicity their sense of the irrelevance of such considerations? And are churches or meeting-houses in England (and Europe) in the politically polarized seventeenth century a reflection of the views of its strongest supporters, whether the absolutism associated with ecclesiastical Baroque architecture or the simpler republicanism or democracy of the meeting-house? A fifth is the closely related economic consideration in architecture. What resources are available to the architect in finance and materials? How significant in the motivation of his patrons is the desire for grandeur, or the love of simplicity? Or, how far is sheer economic necessity responsible for design?

Furthermore, all these factors involved in ecclesiastical architecture and furnishings will also reflect the way the architect or builder and his patrons or customers understand the nature of God and the ceremonial style appropriate for the approach to the Divine.

1. *The Nature of the Holy Community*

For the Anglican worshippers the Church expresses the deep sense of the English nation on its knees, united by its Prayer Book and linked with its cousins across the Atlantic in Virginia, or gathering in English embassies in European capitals, owing allegiance to their sovereign who is both king and supreme governor of the church. Church and nation were coextensive for the Anglican, despite the fact that Recusant Catholics and dissenting Puritans denied the Erastian equation. This link was clearly expressed verbally in the Prayer for the King, and visually in the royal arms that so often replaced the figures of the rood in the days of Catholicism. It was the constant and not always convincing argument of the Anglican apologists that the Anglican church rightly held on to the fanes of the medieval church because they had been built and served by Englishmen, irrespective of the change of religious allegiance. To make that claim to continuity visible it was necessary that Anglican architecture should be "Gothic *survival*," rather than revival. And the liturgical changes that came about made little modification in the architecture, except for the removal of some statuary and stained-glass that naively represented God or the Holy Trinity, or proclaimed too obviously the intercession of the saints.[2] On the other hand, the dedication of the parish churches to particular saints, and the retention in the Anglican calendar of the major festivals of Christ, of the Virgin and the apostles, as also of other New Testament saints, and their representation in the stained-glass or on the choir stalls, kept a sense of the communion of saints alive in the Anglican Communion. In a more restricted sense also, the tombs and gravestones of the ancestors in the nave or in the graveyard kept alive a sense of continuity of Christians through the generations.

The union of throne and altar was vigorously propounded by John Bede in 1612: "Of all the creatures of the Universe, none draweth nearer to the Creator than man; neither any degree of men, so much as doth the King. . . . As the face of Moses descending the Mount from God, shone bright and glorious: so the Maiesticke looke of a King (reflecting divine beames, received from the King of Kings) daunteth the most proud and savage hearts of inferiors."[3] Thus the dominant conception of the church held by Anglicans was that of the subjects of the heavenly and earthly Kings united in prayer and sacrament, a "mixed multitude" to their Puritan detractors, but to them a devout nation.

For the Roman Catholics the holy community was the international body of Christians owing allegiance to the Pope in the Petrine succession and outnumbering all others through the centuries (voting, as G. K. Chesterton said in our own century, by tombstones). The church militant on earth was united with the church triumphant in heaven, and the experience, concern, and intercession of the great saints of the past were available for the

2 The sixteenth-century modifications are described in Horton Davies, *Worship and Theology in England* (Princeton, N.J., 1970), Vol. I, pp. 356-65.
3 *The Right and Prerogative of Kings, Against Cardinal Bellarmine and Other Jesuits* (1612), p. 1. I owe this reference to the kindness of the Rev. Belden C. Lane of Princeton Theological Seminary, as also those in footnotes 4 and 9.

spiritual strengthening of the faithful of the present. All representations of that mystical unity were not only lawful but encouraged in Roman Catholic chapels, and the relics of a saint were included in every altar, and each day in the Catholic calendar honoured the memory of some distinguished imitator of God, while statuary, woodcarvings, and glass were aids to the memory of the pious. On the roods that survived, the central crucifix spoke eloquently of the suffering and sacrifice of the Saviour, between the grieving Virgin Mother and the beloved disciple John. The greatest contemporary theologian the Catholics had was Cardinal Bellarmine (1542-1621), whose books were translated into English and secretly read by the Recusants. He defined the church as comprising "a convocation or congregation of men which are baptized and make profession of the faith and law of Christ under the obedience of the chief Bishope of Rome."[4]

For the Puritans the holy community was conceived as the covenanted fellowship of the households of faith, the saints (in the sense of those in the process of being sanctified), the local outcropping of the hidden *coetus electorum*, the members of which were only known to God. Yet for practical purposes, those who owned the covenant acknowledged its obligations to walk in all the ways God in Christ had made known to them and who lived in ethical conformity with such expectations, were acknowledged as "visible saints." As Perry Miller has shown, the very idea of covenant meant not only that the "saint" had bound himself to God, but that God had also bound himself to be his God. The fundamental point, so he insists, is that the undertaking had a voluntaristic basis. "Where two parties do stand mutually obliged one to another in a voluntary Agreement, there is a Covenant."[5] Involved in this covenant on the part of men and women chosen by God was the responsibility for fellowship and mutual encouragement and oversight (or discipline).[6] The same emphasis on expressing outward-

---

[4] *An ample declaration of the Christian Doctrine* (English trans., 1604), p. 65. It was a frequently reprinted exposition of the Creed, Lord's Prayer and Decalogue.

[5] *The New England Mind: The Seventeenth Century* (Boston, 1961), p. 375. It should be noted that the unmodified Calvinist position insisted on the unconditonal sovereignty and freedom of God, without contractual obligations, on God's mysterious unpredictability in election, and, consequently on the impossibility of any human, linear tradition of succession. For a study of the origins of the Puritan covenant idea in the Rhineland and its exponents, including Oecolampadius and Bucer, as well as William Tyndale in England, see Leonard J. Trinterud, "The Origins of Puritanism" (*Church History*, XX, 1951, pp. 37-57).

[6] These aspects of the covenanted life are admirably analysed and illustrated in Geoffrey F. Nuttall's *Visible Saints* (Oxford, 1957), pp. 74ff. John Owen's *Eschol, or Rules of Direction* (1648) affirms that true Christians are to exhibit

ly the inner light, the illumination and grace of the Holy Spirit, marked the tightly knit, deeply committed, suffering and witnessing early Quaker communities that sprang up in the days of Commonwealth turbulence to give their testimony for peace. They, too, though without taking a formal covenant, were bound to God and to one another in loving fellowship, but they were a potentially universalistic communities in the way that Puritans were not, for while the Calvinist doctrine of providence was retained by them, they abhorred and rejected the doctrine of double predestination and reprobation. But the meeting-houses of both Puritans and Quakers are testimonies to simplicity, the fear of the idolatrous eye, and to the nature of "gathered churches" out of the world. But chiefly, these meeting-houses are, as their very titles indicate, *domestic*. They are homes for the people of God to meet in,[7] not houses of God. The true altar for the Puritan as for the Quaker is the prepared human heart, where the Holy Spirit dwells, and so all places are sacred, and therefore special places are only conveniences not necessities.

Thus the nature of the holy community, whether international as in Roman Catholicism, national as in Anglicanism of this period, or local, is reflected in the character of the architecture appropriate to express these ecclesiologies.

2. *Foci in Worship as Functional Factors in Architecture*

If ecclesiastical architecture is partly determined by the nature of the holy community, it is even more strongly influenced by the community's understanding of the high points of its worship, its foci of major interest. This is as basic as it is obvious, for whatever else a church or meeting-house may be used for, its primary function is liturgical.

At first glance, it is clear that the church will eloquently, if silently, express the character of the worship (and the worship-

---

"affectionate sincere love" and "vigilant watchfulness over each others conversation" [latter term means "way of life" in seventeenth-century and Biblical usage]. (Cited by Nuttall, *op. cit.*, p. 74.) The purpose of this intensity and exclusiveness was to try to preserve the purity of church membership. John Robinson, pastor of the Pilgrims in Holland, claimed that "only saints, that is, a people forsaking all known sin of which they may be convinced, doing all the known will of God, increasing and abiding ever therein . . . Of such only, externally, and so far as man can judge, the true church is gathered." (*A Justification of Separation from the Church of England*, 1610, *The Works of John Robinson*, ed. J. Ashton, II, p. 10.)

[7] George Fox's *Journal*, I, 8 states: "The Lord showed me clearly that he did not dwell in these temples which men had commanded and set up, but in people's hearts."

7

pers) from its exterior and its interior. Its exterior will indicate whether it is world-affirming in its splendour and triumphalism or world-denying in its simplicity and even its fugacity, as in the days of persecution, for Huguenots in France and Nonconformists in England after 1662. Its interior, too, if it is formal, grand, ornate, will bespeak the use of a liturgy, or if it is domestic the appropriateness of the spontaneity and directness of free prayer in the family.

Such general considerations apart, church architecture will be largely determined by the worshipping community's priorities in worship. In the Church of England, the holy table (if one were of Puritan or Latitudinarian leanings) or the altar (if one were a high churchman of the Laudian or Non-Juror tradition) predominated. Not only was it the centre—to which the aisles and the steps of the chancel (and the central opening of the screen in some cases) directed one's gaze and feet, but it was railed by Laudian fiat to mark its great sacredness and dignity. If the chancel were more sacred than the nave, the most sacred part of the chancel was the altar. But there were also other liturgical foci, marking the great, if subordinate, importance of the pulpit, and the prayer-desk, as well as the font. George Herbert, as Izaak Walton reminds us, determined in the rebuilding of Leighton Bromsgrove, a project shared with the neighbouring Ferrar family, on two pulpits of equal height so that "they should neither have a precedency or priority of the other; but that prayer and preaching, being equally useful, might agree like brethren, and have an equal honour and estimation."[8]

The Caroline divines certainly stressed the primacy of the church as a place of devotion,[9] and Herbert is typical in this respect. His *Country Parson* shows the parson entering the church and "humbly adoring, and worshipping the invisible majesty and presence of Almighty God." In his other book, *The Temple*, a poem entitled "The Church Porch" endorses the view:

[8] It should be noted, however, that Herbert was more of a liturgical and architectural innovator than is commonly recognised, and so this view of the equal importance of prayer and preaching may be untypical. This insight I owe to Professor John Schnorrenberg's unpublished paper, "George Herbert, Poet and Churchman," delivered to the Philological Club of the University of North Carolina at Chapel Hill in January, 1966. On the other hand, Herbert's view has many supporters in the Restoration Church.

[9] In our own day Professor Mascall ties the centrality of devotion in the Church of England to the role of its liturgy: "The Church lives neither by tradition alone, nor by the Scriptures directly. The Church lives day by day by her liturgy, which is her living tradition but of which the Scriptures are both constituent and normative." (*Toward a Church Architecture*, 1962, p. 198.)

Though private prayer be a brave design
Yet publick hath more promises, more love;
And love's a weight to hearts, to eies a signe.
We are all but cold suitours; let us move
Where it is warmest. Leave thy six and seven
Pray with the most: for where most pray is heaven.

The other focus of worship was provided by the font, almost always at the west end of the church, symbolizing the entry into the Christian community through Baptism.[10] The principle on which the Gothic churches inherited by the Anglican church were organized was that of "two rooms." That is, the chancel was used as the centre for Holy Communion, the communicants receiving at the altar rail, and the nave was used as the centre for prayers and preaching and psalmody in the services of morning and evening prayer.[11] The Book of Common Prayer helped to instruct the builder engaged in additions, or alterations that the church building was primarily a place of common prayer, including sacramental devotion.

For the Roman Catholics, in England as well as elsewhere, the Sacrament of the Altar, and therefore the altar itself, was the most sacred part of the sacred space. But during the seventeenth century, as a result of the spread of the ideals of the Counter-Reformation in which the Jesuit Baroque churches of Italy, Spain, and France took the lead, the pulpit occupied an increasingly important role and position in worship. It was, however, only in the chapels of foreign embassies in London, or in those of a Catholic queen in England or of the Catholic aristocracy in the country that members of the old faith were likely to get a glimpse of the new architecture and ornaments, and the growing importance of the pulpit. From

[10] Yet the font was most awkwardly placed, if it was intended that the congregation should share in the sacrament of initiation, for they had to turn round. This fact of itself must have encouraged the separation of Baptism from the regular congregational services of the Church of England, and encouraged the unfortunate practice of private Baptism, often with socially elite godparents rather than Christian sponsors.

[11] The Anglican modifications of Roman Catholic fanes for worship are duly described in G.W.O. Addleshaw and Frederick Etchells, *The Architectural Setting of Anglican Worship* (1948), p. 45. On the Continent, there were three types of adaptation, including losing the nave and moving into the choir (at the cathedral of St. Pierre, Geneva), closing the choir and moving into the nave (as at Basel), and the two chamber arrangement by retaining the ancient choir-screen followed by the Church of England and also used in St. Bavo's Church, Haarlem. See André Biéler, *Architecture in Worship* (Edinburgh and London, 1965), pp. 57-60 and Donald J. Bruggink and Carl H. Droppers, *Christ and Architecture: Building Presbyterian/Reformed Churches* (Grand Rapids, Michigan, 1965), p. 86.

9

Gunpowder Plot to the Titus Oates Conspiracy, the Catholics espoused a forbidden and hidden faith and were apparently a doomed and therefore desperate minority, a people fleeing the light (*gens lucifuga*, as Cardinal Newman described them two centuries later). It must have been small consolation to them that every cathedral and practically every parish church they saw in England was a mute testimony in its cruciform shape and Gothic style to the faith of their ancestors, however much the interiors might have been simplified together with the ceremonial. England remained Gothic as far as its church buildings were concerned until the first waves of Renaissance work in Inigo Jones reached its shores and the flood tide came with Sir Christopher Wren. Some private Anglican chapels or college chapels (like those of Peterhouse, and Emmanuel College in Cambridge or Lincoln, Exeter, and Pembroke Colleges at Oxford) were the few exceptions. They, however, as we shall see later, are mixed Gothic-Renaissance creations.

The only alternative to Gothic architecture in England (Wren's classicism excepted) was the austere, scrubbed and domesticated simplicity of post-Restoration Puritan or Quaker architecture. Puritan and Quaker meeting-houses resembled the middle-class houses of the later seventeenth century, with large and long windows, allowing the unstained light to pass through them. They were, in the most literal sense of the words "house churches." Since all, as led by the Holy Spirit could preach, or rather, speak in the meeting, there was no need for a pulpit in Quaker meeting-houses and the building reflected a complete egalitarianism where all the Lord's people were prophets, both men and women. Since Sacraments, on the Quaker interpretation, were individually renewable experiences of the Holy Spirit which dispensed with the outward means such as water, bread, and wine, no altar was needed.[12] All was simplicity and the streamlining of spirituality to the Quakers, if iconoclasm to their critics. The name of the edifice, "meeting-house" (as contrasted with Roman Catholic and Anglican dedications to the Holy Trinity, St. Michael and All Angels, and the like) indicated that here was the meeting-place of God's people with their God, not in any sense a "house of God."

The Puritans, of course, used the same term for the same reason, but they emphasized the co-ordinate importance of the Word and Spirit, so that the preaching of the Word and the celebration

12 See Robert Barclay's *Apology for the True Christian Divinity* (1678) Chaps. XII and XIII for the exposition of this viewpoint.

of the "Gospel Sacraments" (Baptism and the Lord's Supper) required in Puritan assemblies for worship a centrally placed pulpit, usually on the long wall of the rectangular-shaped church, and beneath it a Communion table centrally placed surrounded by a pew in which the elders or deacons sat, and a font (usually rather inconspicuous). Apart from these fittings, both Quaker and Puritan meeting-houses gave the same family-at-worship appearance— a study in black and white etching, rather than the coloured and multi-textured appearance of Anglican and the highly dramatic and even theatrical Baroque effect of Counter-Reformation Catholic churches on the Continent, of which their English analogues (when visible and not hidden for reasons of persecution) were restrained adaptations.

In both Catholic and Anglican churches the primacy of the altar or Communion table was to be seen, with a strongly subordinate emphasis on the pulpit, for the Mass or Holy Communion was primary in both forms of worship. In Puritan meeting-houses the primacy was given to the pulpit with its central position and high stairs, often one on each side, and a subordinate position was given to the Communion table, though not as secondary as is often supposed. In the meeting-houses of the Society of Friends (as also in the first meeting-houses of the Baptists), we see the expression of Cistercianism in Dissenting worship, and the egalitarianism[13] of benches as opposed to pews which developed from the fourth to the tenth decade of the seventeenth century to great lengths in the Church of England.[14]

3. Numinosity or Functionalism?

Already the importance of functionalism in sacred architecture has been considered. In addition, however, there is a grand general distinction to be made between Catholic-Anglican and Puritan-Quaker places of worship. This depends upon the decision of

---

[13] While the statement about the egalitarianism expressed in Quaker architecture is substantially true (and applies with equal relevance to early Baptist churches, in each case deriving, as H. L. Short suggests from their common Mennonite background in Holland), it should also be recognised that both Quakers and early Baptists had a pew respectively for "elders" and "messengers," who were lay leaders of their religious communities, and in many cases these benches were raised up a little. H. L. Short of Manchester College, Oxford, made the suggestion in an article in the *Listener*, March 17, 1955, pp. 471f., "Changing Styles in Nonconformist Architecture."

[14] Sir Christopher Wren was aesthetically averse to filling a church with pews, especially the high-backed variety, but he also desired for greater space so "that the poor may have room enough to stand and sit in the alleys, for to them equally is the Gospel preached." (See Stephen Wren, *Parentalia*, 1750, pp. 319f.)

whether to employ symbolism and ornamentation, or whether to adhere strictly to functional considerations. To begin with, recognition must be given to the fact that both Roman Catholics and Anglicans give a value to symbolism and ornamentation which the Puritans and Quakers deny for theological, cultural, and economic reasons.

Hooker speaks for the medieval view (and therefore for both Roman Catholic and Anglican viewpoints) when he argues that the Church Fathers claimed that "the house of prayer is a Court beautified with the presence of the celestial powers; that there we stand, we pray, we sound forth hymns to God, having his Angels intermixed as our associates."[15]

Hooker is also aware of the importance of atmosphere in a church, for he insists that "the very majesty and holiness of the place where God is worshipped hath in regard to us great virtue, force, and efficacy, for that it serveth as a sensible help to stir up devotion, and in that respect no doubt bettereth even our holiest and best actions in this kind."[16] A Roman Catholic could go even further and claim that the stained-glass windows and the statues were a notable teaching device; in short, the Bible and church history of the poor. It would be possible to make the same claim if Laud's views had prevailed in the Church of England, and certain Oxford and Cambridge College chapels in the 1630s have fulfilled Laud's reverential and didactic intentions by their images in windows, and wood, as by their splendid ceiling bosses. If one seeks pedagogy in glass, he has only to think of the remarkable east window in Lincoln College Chapel, Oxford, with its typological exegesis as constituting an astonishing sermon on the Old Testament anticipations of New Testament fulfillments, as seen, for example, in Adam's creation as foreshadowing the nativity of Christ the second Adam, or of Jonah's three-day stay and deliverance from the "great fish" presaging Christ's resurrection after three days in the tomb.[17]

Indeed, the differing views on church architecture and worship as between the Caroline divines (from Lancelot Andrewes to Archbishop Laud and his friends, John Cosin and Matthew Wren)

---

[15] *The Laws of Ecclesiastical Polity*, Bk. v, Chap. 25, Para. 2.

[16] *Ibid.*, Bk. v, Chap. 16, Para. 2.

[17] As another example of the astonishing veneration of the Carolines for King Charles I, even before what they considered as his "martyrdom" at the hands of the regicides, it should be observed that the east window of Lincoln College shows Christ with a Vandyke beard, bearing a clear resemblance to the royal "saint." The window is dated 1631.

12

and the Puritan divines (aided by the fierce parliamentarian Prynne) were the cause of a furious controversy. It is not too much to claim that this controversy helped to polarize the nation into irreconcilable factions and thus was one of the causes of the Civil War. It was, in part, a fight between the iconophiles and the iconoclasts, between a reverence that might lead to mere formality and a spontaneity that could degenerate into casualness, and an aesthetic as against an ethical test of worship.

Archbishop Laud's views were stated with the greatest clarity and vigour before the Star Chamber in a speech made on June 14, 1637, at the censure of John Bastwick, Henry Burton, and William Prynne, "concerning pretended innovations in the Church."[18] The Archbishop began by stating that he worships with his body as well as his soul, and that even if there were no holy table in the church he would still revere God on entering it as it is God's House, and even if no stone were left in Bethel, he would still worship wherever he came to pray. The misery of the present is, he asserts, that it is accounted "superstition nowadays for any man to come with more reverence into a church than a tinker and his bitch come into an ale-house." He then shrewdly pointed out that the Lords of the Garter bowed towards God's altar in their great solemnities because it is "the greatest place of God's residence upon earth." He continues with great conviction and emotion:

> I say the greatest, yea, greater than the pulpit; for there it is *Hoc est Corpus meum*, "This is My Body"; but in the pulpit it is at most but *Hoc est verbum meum*, "This is My Word." And a greater reverence no doubt is due to the Body than to the Word of Our Lord. And so, in relation answerably to the throne where His Body is usually present, than to the seat whence the Word useth to be proclaimed. And God hold it there at His Word."[19]

This vivid expression of Laud's view is indistinguishable from the Roman Catholic viewpoint and expresses a strong belief in the "Real Presence" in the Eucharist. Moreover, it is interestingly defended by images derived from the sovereign and the nobility, just as Hooker had urged the earthly court as an image of the heavenly court of the King of Kings. (By a complete contrast, it will be seen that the Puritan Fifth Monarchist, John Archer, defends

[18] Laud's *Works* (Library of Anglo-Catholic Theology), VI, Pt. 1, pp. 56f.
[19] *Ibid.*

the sitting posture at the service of the Lord's Supper precisely because Christ had called His disciples to be friends, not serfs of a sovereign.) A Puritan might also have argued that the Archbishop was undervaluing the transforming power of the Word of God which was also and equally evidence of His presence.

The Laudian view of the importance of the church as housing the very Body of Christ in the Eucharist was expressed in the canons issued by the Convocation of 1640, which had continued to meet by the royal warrant after the closure of the Short Parliament, one of which required the Communion table to be placed under the east window and railed to avoid profanation. It is declared that the purpose is to encourage reverence, "because experience hath shown us how irreverent the behaviour of many people is in many places, some leaning, others casting their hats, and some sitting upon, some standing and others sitting under the Communion table in time of Divine Service. . . ."[20] One of Laud's most enthusiastic disciples, Foulke Robarts, Prebendary of Norwich, even argues for the enclosure of the font with rails.[21] William Hardwick, curate of Reigate, cites St. John Chrysostom's description of a church in his own rather free translation: "The Church is no Barber's or Apothecary's Shop; it is no Westminster or Guildhall but the place of Angels, the Court of Heaven, yea, Heaven itself."[22] He urges that those who are afraid of superstition, should beware its opposite, profaneness. He then provides two vivid companion pictures of reverence and disrespect for God:

For my part, when I come into a Church and there behold a poor sinner kneeling upon his knees, weeping with his eyes, and with a humble and lowly reverence, both petitioning and hearing his God, my charity bids me think the best, as how that these shews are not without substance, because I know no other—it being a peculiar privilege and prerogative of Almighty God to be καρδιαγνώστης, a knower, a Searcher of the heart. But again, let me see a man here sitting in his Master's

20 *Ibid.*

21 *Gods Holy House and Service according to the primitive and most Christian forme thereof* (1639), pp. 45-46: "And if (as in some Churches it is) the font were decently with rayles enclosed: it were (I speake under correction) more suteable to the reverence due thereunto."

22 The Latin source which Hardwick cites (itself a translation from the Greek original) reads: *Non est Ecclesia tonstrina aut unguentaria taberna aut officina forensis; sed locus Angelorum, Regia Coeli, Coelum ipsum.* William Hardwick, *Conformity with Piety requisite in God's Service* (1638), cited in P. E. More and F. L. Cross, eds., *Anglicanism, the Thought and Practice of the Church of England* (2nd ed., 1957), p. 606.

14

house in his Master's presence, as if he were rather God Almighty's fellow than His servant, seldom uncovering his head, seldomer bending the knee, or saucily lolling on his elbows; let such a man make never so many protestations that his heart is upright to Godward, I shall never be brought to believe him.[23]

Prebendary Robarts insisted that it was an act of piety to build houses of worship for God, especially as the men of noble houses and of wealth outtopped the poor church with their "Patrons' Pyramids." Otherwise, the impiety of the affluent would be seen in the "poore Church . . . [which] standeth cringing behinde, as ashamed to be seene, so tattered without in her roofe, walls and windows: so dusty, sullied, and forlorn within, as that the stone doth answere it."[24] He maintained that many individual men in a parish each spend more on their own house than they combine to "lay out on the house of God." The same author argued that the required raising of the altar or holy table was so that it "should provoke in you a desire for that blessed food."[25] Clearly then, the splendour of God's house is an indication of the piety of those that build, furnish, or repair it, and of the impiety of those who neglect it or abuse it. Further, the fittings of the church, whether altar, font, windows, or royal arms serve a didactic or monitory purpose.[26]

One of the most learned defences of the view that Christians ought to use special places for worship and had in fact even in early days done so was the work of the great writer on eschatology in the seventeenth century, Joseph Mede, Fellow of Christ's College, Cambridge, a notable centre of Puritanism. At any rate at this stage in his life, Mede was both a believer in the sacrificial interpretation of the Eucharist, and a defender of the view of the

---

[23] *Ibid.*
[24] F. Robarts, *Gods Holy House and Service* (1639), p. 33. Before Laud's advent to power, the fabric of churches had been allowed to deteriorate in sad fashion. For one example of slow but steady improvement, see F. W. West, *Rude Forefathers* (1949), pp. 10-14.
[25] Robarts, *op. cit.*, p. 45.
[26] Robarts's didacticism is plainly to be seen in his comments on the windows and the king's arms above the chancel arch of the church: ". . . what meane those images and pictures which are in the glasse? They are not there for any matter of worship of either God, Saint or Angell; but for history and ornament" (*ibid.*, p. 46). The Royal Arms are set "to professe the subjection of every soule to the higher power. For as the written sentences upon the walls by letters, so these Scutchions by their expressions do put us in minde of that *Defender of the Faith* and of our duty to him who is *next and immediately under God* supream governor over al persons and causes as well Ecclesiasticall as Temporall in all his Majesties Realmes & Dominions" (*ibid.*, p. 46).

appropriateness of erecting churches, or, as his title implies, *Churches, that is, appropriate Places for Christian Worship both in and ever since the Apostles Times* (1638). He sets out to repudiate the view held by "most of our Reformed writers" that when in early days the church "lived under pagan and persecuting emperors Christians had no oratories, or places set apart for Divine Worship, but that they assembled here and there promiscuously and uncertainly as they pleased, or the occasion served in places of common use. . . ."[27] The very appropriate text that he uses is I Corinthians 11:22: "Have ye not houses to eat and drink in? Or despise ye the Church of God?" He demonstrates that Augustine and Basil, Chrysostom and Theodoret interpret this text the same way as he does, and learnedly traces the development of the idea of the place where the church assembles through the Fathers of the second and third centuries. He also shows the development of the church from a convenient room in a house (usually a *coenaculum* or upper room) of a disciple to a mansion donated by a wealthy Christian for his numerous fellow Christians to worship in, until finally, as the multitude of believers grew, "they built them structures of purpose, partly in the coemiteries of martyrs, partly in other publique places."[28]

It is significant how far the sense of the inherent holiness of a church had developed under the impetus of Archbishop Laud and his supporters by the end of the fourth decade of the seventeenth century, as our citations and references have shown. This can be verified further by contrast from the sermon preached by John Prideaux, only fourteen or fifteen years before, at the consecration of the Exeter College Chapel, Oxford,[29] which looks like a diminutive Sainte Chapelle. Prideaux, then Rector of Exeter, Regius Professor of Divinity, and Vice-Chancellor of the University of Oxford, argued from the text, Luke 19:46 ("My house is the house of prayer") that there was a warrant for churches and for their consecration, and provided directions for their chief uses. But it is especially interesting that he would not argue for the inherent sanctity of the building, since this was the contention of Cardinal Bellarmine in *De Cultu Sanctorum*, which he expressly repudiates and to which his printed sermon makes reference in the margin: "Not for the inherent sanctity of the place (which our Adversaries

---

27 Mede, *op. cit.*, pp. 2-3.   28 *Ibid.*, pp. 15-16.

29 See *A Sermon preached on the Fifth of October 1624: at the Consecration of St. Iames Chappel in Exeter College* (Oxford, 1625).

presse too far) but through the obiective Holinesse adherent to it, by Christs promises, sacred meetings, united devotion, ioynt participating of the Word and Sacraments, lively incitements through others examples."[30] Thus from Hooker to Laud there is an increase in the claims made for the churches; they are not merely convenient, or their fittings didactically valuable, or the encouragements from the example of others worshipping, or even the place where angels join with humans in worship, but they are the places of God's presence and most fully in the Body and Blood of Christ in the Eucharist centred on the elevated and enclosed altar.

The fullest confirmation of the high evaluation placed upon churches by the Caroline divines, however, is to be found in their Orders for the Consecration of Churches, from that of Jesus Chapel, Peartree, Southampton by Bishop Lancelot Andrewes in 1620 to that of Sir Ranulf Crewe's private chapel in Crewe by Bishop John Bridgman in 1635. In Andrewes's first Prayer of Consecration the purposes for which the church was erected are declared to be, "as an habitacion for thee, and a place for us to assemble and meete together in, for the observacion of thy divine worship, invocation of thy great great name, reading, preaching and hearing of Thy heavenly Word, administring thy most holy Sacraments, above all, in this place, the very gate of heaven upon earth, as Jacob named it, to do the work of heaven, to sett forth Thy most worthie praise, to laud and magnifie thy most glorious Maiestie for all Thy goodness to all men, and especially to us that are of the household of faith."[31] The second Prayer of Consecration in the same order includes the petition, "consecrate it to the invocation of thy glorious name: wherein supplications, prayers, intercessions, may be made for all men; thy sacred word may be read, preached, and heard; the holy sacraments, the laver of regeneration, the commemoracion of the precious death of Thy deer sonne, may be administered; thy praises celebrated and sounded forth, thy people blessed by putting thy name upon them." If the first prayer expresses in part the numinous aspect of worship as aided by church architecture, the second stresses more its liturgical functionalism.

The consecration of the private chapel of Sir Ranulf Crewe, the judge, by the Bishop of Chester fifteen years later demonstrates

---

30 *Ibid.*, C 3 *recto*. The marginal reference is to "*lib.* 3, *cap.* 5" of Bellarmine's book.

31 J. W. Legg, *English Orders for Consecrating Churches in the Seventeenth Century* (Henry Bradshaw Society, Vol. XLI, 1911), p. 57.

through the prayer of consecration a stronger sense of the Communion of Saints, a more vivid and fresh use of the image of the sovereign and the court (God's "Whitehall") and the king by implication the supreme governor of the Church of England, and the increasing importance of music in the worship, while it has also its intriguing commercial metaphor, which makes one wonder whether this was for the special benefit of the well-to-do Sir Ranulf. The prayer begins:

> Theise houses are the Courts of thyne Audience where thou dost sitt to heare our prayers and supplications unto thee, they are that Royall Exchange where thou and we doe meete. And as it were comerce and trade together, for thou dost bring thy graces when we bring our devotions hither. They are parte of thy heauenly Quire, for here our Cryings make an Eccho to thyne Angels singinge (for they rejoyce when we repente) when we cry Peccavi here on Earth, they answere Halleluuiah aboue in heauen, O let our Musique be as sweet to thee here on the ground, as is that Angels descant in their full harmonie and heauenly Sound.[32]

It continues and concludes:

> 'Tis true, o Lord, Heauen is thy glorious Temple, thy *Whitehall*, thy dwellinge house, the Earth also is thyne, and the whole round world and all that is therein, This is thy Outhouse, thou art the good Husbandman which thy sonne speaks of, who so beautifyest those vpper roomes where thy Saintes doe lodge, as thou dost dispise theise meaner receptacles of thy Servantes. Accept therfore this slender and poore habitacion and accept it not according to ye worth of the guifte but the harte and desire of those that giue it or rather accordinge to thy wonted loue and favour to thy Children.[33]

While the spirit of the later consecration orders is clearly that of Archbishop Laud, greatly dependent on the theology, patristic knowledge, devotion, and example of Lancelot Andrewes, there is only one church that Laud is known to have consecrated, namely that of St. Catherine, Cree, on Sunday, January 16, 1630/1, when he was Bishop of London. There is no order extant for this consecration, but there is an account of it from the vitriolic pen of William Prynne. Prynne is particularly caustic in describing the

---

[32] J. W. Legg, *op. cit.*, p. 202. [33] *Ibid.*

prostrations which Laud made towards the altar, as indicating his great reverence for it, however overdone the ceremonial gestures were in Prynne's rather jaundiced eyes. Prynne leaves nothing to the imagination in his description of what is to him an artificial, idolatrous, and frenetic imitation of Roman ceremonial. Thus the ensuing report is both an account of Laud's gestures of reverence and of a Puritan's intense dislike of them:

> . . . when the Bishop approached neare the Communion Table, he bowed with his nose very neare the ground some six or seven times; Then he came to one of the corners of the Table, and there bowed himselfe three times; then to the second, third and fourth corners, bowing at each corner three times; but, when he came to the side of the Table where the bread and wine was, he bowed himselfe seven times, and then, after the reading of many praiers by himselfe and his two fat chaplins (which were with him, and all this while were upon their knees by him, in their Sirplisses, Hoods, and Tippits) he himself came neare the Bread, which was cut and laid in a fine napkin, and then he gently lifted up one of the corners of the said napkin, and peeped into it till hee saw the bread (like a boy that peeped after a bird-nest in a bush) and presently clapped it downe againe, and flew backe a step or two, and bowed very low three times towards it and the Table: when he beheld the bread, then he came neare and opened the napkin againe, and bowed as before; then he laid his hand upon the gilt *Cup* which was full of wine, with a cover upon it; so soone as he pul'd the Cupp a litle neerer to him, he lett the Cupp goe, flew backe, and bowed againe three times towards it: then hee came neere againe, and lifting up the cover of the Cupp peeped into it, and seing the wine, he let fall the cover on it againe, and flew nimbly backe and bowed as before: After these and many other Apish Anticke Gesturs he himselfe received, and then gave the Sacrament to some principall men onely they devoutly kneeling neere the Table, after which more prayers being said, this Sceane and Enterlude ended.[34]

For Roman Catholic and High Anglican alike, objects could be consecrated as well as people because of their dedication to God's service. For Quakers and Puritans, however, consecrated people

[34] *Canterburies Doome* (1646), pp. 114f.

19

alone were God's true temples. The difference of attitude is concisely expressed in a poem of 1664, in which the Puritan exclaims:

> I love no such triumphant Churches—
> They scatter my devotion; whilst my sight
> Is courted to observe their sumptuous cost,
> I find my heart lost in my eyes. . . .

The Churchman replies:

> But I love Churches mount up to the skies,
> For my devotion rises with their roof;
> Therein my soul doth heav'n anticipate.[35]

The Puritan objections to the sumptuous and numinous edifices of the Church of England were precisely to their sumptuousness and what we today would call their "triumphalism" the distraction of ornaments in worship ("I find my heart lost in my eyes"), and the idolatry involved in the representation of divine persons as forbidden in the Decalogue. Also, the conviction grew (*pace* Joseph Mede's claims to the contrary), especially after St. Bartholomew's Day, 1662, when Puritan ministers became Dissenters and were ejected from their livings, that the most faithful companies of Christians in the apostolic and early days of the persecuted Christian church convened in rooms and houses or in the open air in great simplicity and fervour.

Furthermore, it was a great comfort to the Dissenting divines and their secretly gathered congregations, while smarting from the five-stringed whip of the Clarendon Code, to recall that the Epistle to the Hebrews lauded the faithful who lived in caves and dens of the earth "of whom the world was not worthy."[36] In the same way they recalled that the Christ whom they tried to imitate had been buried in a borrowed grave, had lived in no settled home since Nazareth, and had warned his disciples of the danger of riches and of the subtler danger of the Pharisaism that desires its piety to be seen of men.

In short, the simplicity of Puritan architecture and fittings was a matter of choice, since the Puritans preferred an unsumptuous worship. Bernard Manning, a modern historian belonging to that tradition, has rightly pointed out that to enter into conversation

---

35 "Philonax Lovekin" (probably a pseudonym for J. Wilson, *Andronicus* [published 1664]), and cited by E. F. Carritt, *A Calendar of British Taste, From 1600 to 1800* (1948), p. 61.
36 Hebrews 2:38.

with the living God is so transcendent an experience and so momentous in its consequences, that it renders all human artifice merely meretricious. In his words, "To call upon the name of God, to claim the presence of the Son of God, if men truly know and mean what they are doing, is in itself an act so tremendous and so full of comfort that any sensuous heightening of the effect is not so much a painting of the lily as a varnishing of sunlight."[37]

Behind the simplicity and even iconoclasm of Puritanism, there lay a simple and profound truth known to Judaism, and Islam, as well as to St. Bernard of Clairvaux and the Cistercians, together with the Quakers: that is the great danger of idolatry. The worst feature of idolatry is that it will try to limit, to fix, and even freeze the living God by our human concepts or representations of him. It is this fear of what may be called the absolutisation of the finite, whether in art or in credal confinement, that controls this simplicity in all the cases mentioned. It is the recognition that God must be sovereign, and cannot be "boxed in," since He is the Holy Spirit who blows as invisibly, freely, unpredictably, and mysteriously as the wind, whether as zephyr or cyclone, that lies behind this tradition.

There is a further reason for Puritan simplicity, apart from the economic which will be considered later, and that is the great fear that the aesthetic will distract the people of God from the ethical. Its classical expression in the Bible is given in the monition: "For all that is in the world, the lust of the flesh, and the lust of the eyes, and the vainglory of life, is not of the Father, but of the world."[38] In Puritan worship there were no stained-glass windows to lure the eye as the light shone full upon the pages of Holy Writ and upon the faces of the people of God being sanctified by the Holy Spirit who made them His temple. This worship was an etching; while Anglican and Catholic worship were oil-paintings.

Its rationale is a profound sense of the universality and ubiquity of the Spirit of God, taught so vividly by Psalm 139, and felicitously expressed by John Rainolds, one of the translators of the King James Version of the Scriptures, and reaffirmed by George Gillespie when the Laudian-Puritan controversy was at its height in 1637: "How much more soundly do we hold with J. Rainolds, That unto us Christians no land is strange, no ground unholy; every coast in Jewry, every house is Sion; and every faithful

---

[37] *Christian Worship* (ed. Nathaniel Micklem, Oxford, 1936), p. 162.
[38] I John 2:16.

21

company, yea, every faithful body a Temple to serve God in . . . whereas the presence of Christ among two or three gathered together in his Name (Matthew XVIII.20) maketh any place a Church. . . ."[39] Their simplicity of architecture and fittings was a matter of conviction, but it was also a matter of economic necessity.

4. *Social Prestige as an Architectural Factor*

A fourth element will help to account for the differences between the churches or meeting-houses of seventeenth-century religious groups. This is the factor of social prestige, by which the exterior and interior of religious buildings will be a mark of the standing in society of their donors and to some extent those who worship in them. To this extent elegance and sumptuousness will mark the sanctuaries of the monarch and the nobility, and simplicity and even poverty will distinguish the buildings for worship erected by the persecuted or the underprivileged.

As might be expected on this basis, the most splendid new church buildings in England during the seventeenth century were the royal chapels of the Stuart kings or their queens, and none more splendid than the short-lived transformation of the Tudor Royal Chapel of Windsor at the request of the Roman Catholic James II by the combined talents of Hugh May, Grinling Gibbons and Verrio, respectively architect, sculptor, and painter. Evelyn, good Anglican that he was, found himself greatly impressed by such splendour.[40] From the time of James I, the Stuarts lost no opportunity by their aesthetic commissions (whether royal portraits or decoration of their audience chambers, and even of their own or their Catholic queen's chapels) or in their high-handed actions of regarding Parliaments mainly as existing to vote them monies, of asserting in the strongest way their belief in the divine right of kings. Moreover, as "supreme governors" of the Church of England, they counted on the unwavering support of the archbishops and bishops. James I at the Hampton Court Conference had informed the Puritans, who had hoped that the Presbyterians in Scotland had taught him to distrust prelates, that in fact it was their opponents he most distrusted. Succinctly, even abruptly,

---

[39] The citation is not from the 1637 but the 1660 edition of Gillespie's *Dispute Against the English Popish Ceremonies*, p. 123. It should, however, be noted that the Puritans in avoiding the visual images were not protected from the auditory images of the Scripture lessons or the illustrations in the sermons of their preachers, but these, being transitory, were less likely to have permanent features of "idolatry."

[40] *Diary*, October 18, 1685, which is cited in full in Chap. II, Sect. 4.

James insisted on the common interest of hierarchy in state and church: "no bishop, no king."

Since in Italy, France, Spain, Flanders, and Portugal, Baroque architecture and art were used for the glorification of absolute monarchy and the assertion of the claims of the post-Tridentine Church,[41] it naturally appealed to the Stuarts, and especially those who had married Roman Catholic queens,[42] and, most of all to James II who openly avowed his Catholicism, while still head of the Reformed Church of England. Its allure was increased after the sojourn of the future Charles II and James II in the brilliant court of France, and the English court of the Restoration copied the French fashions in taste, morals, and politics. Consequently, another feature of Baroque, its marriage of many arts, such as architecture, sculpture, painting, and carving, together with vocal and instrumental music, was immensely popular in secular and sacred gatherings. This was seen earlier in the century in the masques staged with many elaborate changes of scenery by Inigo Jones, England's earliest Renaissance-type architect, and in the later part of the century in the opera and stage plays, as well as in the elaborate services in royal chapels or in the London embassy chapels of Catholic countries.

These services in royal chapels and embassies were splendidly theatrical attempts to enthrall all the senses. By ingenious *trompe l'oeil* devices, the eye of the spectator would be swept up into the ceiling which pierced the dome to reveal a sky of Italianate blue,[43] as he followed the ascension of Christ or of the saints.[44] The processionals and recessionals—with the monks and priests wearing

[41] See Margaret Whinney and Oliver Millar, *English Art, 1625-1714* (Oxford, 1957), Chap. XII, especially p. 285.

[42] Queen Henrietta Maria's Chapel at Marlborough Gate, built about 1627 from Inigo Jones's design, had departed from the "Gothic survival" tradition which was Archbishop Laud's preference for English ecclesiastical architecture, by the choice of a semi-Palladian style, with three long windows at the east end divided by pilasters, the middle one being round-headed and itself surmounted by the royal coat of arms, and it had a richly panelled reredos and a barrel roof with gilded stucco bosses (*ibid.*, illustration 3). The apotheosis of Queen Catherine of Braganza, consort of Charles II, was depicted by Verrio who shows her, in a painting in the Queen's audience chamber, proceeding in a triumphal car in the clouds to the Temple of Virtue. Whinney and Millar (*ibid.*, p. 298) claim that there "can have been few more wholly Baroque iconographies in Europe than the glorification of the English Crown with which ceiling after ceiling at Windsor was concerned."

[43] Such was the ceiling painting of Verrio in the Royal Chapel of Whitehall described by Evelyn (*Diary* entry for October 18, 1685).

[44] *Il Gesù* at Rome and other distinguished Jesuit churches often depicted the triumph of St. Ignatius and the martyred Jesuits who ascended in a spiral into the empyrean of Heaven.

23

their dramatic habits or richly embroidered vestments, the angels on the bosses of the roof suggesting the closeness of the court of heaven to the earthly court, the many gestures of adoration and obeisance in various parts of the Mass, the perfume of the incense, and the richly encrusted golden chalice and the reliquaries, not to mention the honeyed eloquence of the preacher and in anthems and voluntaries, the contrapuntal music of the voices, organs, and instruments echoing and re-echoing—were a consort of ecstasies. All this splendour was the acme of social prestige as well as of aesthetic tribute to God, and his vicegerent the monarch. On September 21, 1662, Pepys crowded into Queen Catherine of Braganza's chapel and was greatly impressed by the elegance of the fittings, where he "saw the fine altar, ornaments, and the fryers in their habits, and the priests come in with their fine crosses and many other fine things." For social prestige fineness is all.

Nowhere did the Church of England seem more to be the *via media* than when, after the Great Fire of London, her churches in the city underwent a classical renaissance. There is neither theatricality, nor anything gaudy or tawdry in the architecture or fittings of Wren's churches. There is a decent, sober suitability, dignity, and orderliness, as well as inventiveness, in almost all of Wren's work. These "auditory" churches were built in part to meet the needs of as many worshippers as could be accommodated within sound and sight of the preacher.[45] The undramatic nature of the altars, as compared with their Roman Catholic counterparts on the Continent, and the restricted expenditure possible depending upon the coal tax which financed these churches and St. Paul's Cathedral, together with the Protestant emphasis on the pulpit which was of growing importance in Restoration Anglicanism,[46] and the fact that these churches would be used predominantly by merchants of the City of London and their wives and servants, tended to make for elegant simplicity, but of course, not for Puri-

[45] The younger Christopher Wren as cited in *Parentalia* (p. 318) makes it clear that for Wren a "convenient auditory" is one in which "everyone should hear the Service and both hear and see the Preacher." Thus the altar was not, as in the Counter-Reformation continental churches the focal point of the entire design, emphasized by plan, lighting, and decoration. But the altar itself had to be against the east wall, safeguarded from profanation by rails, and sufficiently unhidden (as had been the case in apse or chancel in Gothic type churches) to be visible to all who would participate in the Holy Communion.

[46] One cannot fail to notice the importance of the pulpit in this period in the frequent references to sermons by the Presbyterian sympathiser Pepys and the loyal Anglican Evelyn in their diaries. Another indication of its importance would be the variety of pulpits designed by Wren, and their impressive sounding-boards.

tan austerity. It is also significant that Wren designed many galleries, for which there were medieval precedents, not forgetting their prevalence in the churches of both Huguenots in France[47] and Jesuits in northern Europe,[48] two communities which emphasized preaching strongly.

The open, well-lit interiors of Wren's churches have a functional simplicity, and an absence of ostentation which would please not only the government but, one supposes, also the city merchants, who were not admirers of extravagance. On the other hand, the fittings, while not usually elaborate, were often panels that were richly carved, especially in the later decades of the century. These panels were sometimes framed by pilasters and sometimes bore, especially in St. Stephen's, Coleman Street, delicately carved flowers and fruit. Grinling Gibbons, at his richest, is to be found in the marvellously varied cherubs and festoons of the choir stalls of St. Paul's Cathedral. But these fittings were the exception. The general impression was of quiet good taste such as pleased the bourgeoisie.

Puritan (strictly Nonconformist) meeting-houses built during the last decade of the seventeenth century were also examples of unostentatious good taste, especially those built in London and the larger provincial towns such as Ipswich and Norwich, Bury, St. Edmunds, and Taunton. The earlier Puritan chapels of the century were of two kinds. Either they were simplifications of Anglican churches in the Commonwealth period, or they were built during a short lull in the sixteen-year period of persecution which lasted from 1662 to 1688, and then they were often only private houses or cottages or public rooms used for Puritan worship.[49] In any case, they are domestic architecture for the

---

[47] Salomon de Brosse built the Huguenot Temple at Charenton in 1623, which Wren must certainly have visited when he was in Paris. It is illustrated in Margaret Whinney's *Christopher Wren* (1971), p. 32.

[48] One might give as an example the Jesuit Church in Antwerp built between 1625-1631, and burnt in 1718. (Whinney and Millar, *English Art, 1625-1714*, p. 156.)

[49] King Charles II published a Declaration of Indulgence in 1671/2 allowing non-Anglican places of worship to be used. Twenty-five hundred licences were issued during this shortlived lull in the persecution, but it is doubtful if even a handful of new Puritan sanctuaries was built. It is far more probable that private houses were more openly equipped for worship or that even public halls were used. It is in the final decade that, under the toleration encouraged by William III, 2418 buildings were registered for public worship by Presbyterians, Independents, and Baptists, besides scores of Quaker meetings. It is in this final decade that the typical Puritan meeting-houses emerge. See the list of surviving chapels from this time in Martin S. Briggs, *Puritan Architecture and Its Future* (1946), p. 23.

gathering of the families of God, never houses of God. While they do not express any sense of social prestige, still less do they symbolize social servility. They express a quiet confidence in the promises of God and an integrity of outlook that is as uncomplex as a white wall.

The same lack of triumphalism, save the triumph of simplicity, would have been found in the fittings of Anglican churches where there were Puritan incumbents. One such church, complete with its Puritan fittings, survives from the seventeenth century, almost untouched by the restorer's hand. This is Langley Chapel, near Acton Burnell between Bridgnorth and Shrewsbury. This chapel has avoided any Augustan or Victorian change of its interior, partly through the disappearance of the neighbouring hall and the depopulation of the village, and the virtual disuse of the chapel since the beginning of the nineteenth century.

It is a simple rectangular one-room building, with a three-light east window and two doors on the southern wall. It is filled with Jacobean pews. It has a pulpit on the south side and opposite this is a box-pew containing a reading-desk, all constructed of unpolished oak cut in the simplest designs. Its liturgical arrangements, however, are most intriguing and worthy of detailed consideration.[50]

There is no structural separation of the chancel from the nave, but a distinction is made by a slight raising of the level of the chancel floor. The simple Communion table (measuring 41½ inches long by 25¼ inches wide by 34 inches high) is surrounded on the north and east sides by a bench, and may originally have had a further bench on the west side of the holy table. The north bench is 44½ inches distant from the table and the east bench is only 29 inches distant. The most interesting feature of all is the kneelers or footrests attached to and below the seats of the benches. These are usually described as kneelers, since this is the almost invariable Anglican posture for prayer and the reception of Holy Communion. On examining them, however, this writer thinks it

[50] The date 1601 appears in the roof timbers, but the pews are almost certainly a decade or two later. Information on the history of this chapel will be found in the *Victoria County History of Shropshire*, Vol. 8 (1968), p. 145 and there is a photograph of the interior opposite p. 144. My own drawing appears as illustration no. 7 of the present volume.

I wish to thank the Reverend D. W. Gould, the Rector of Acton Burnell, for his great kindness in arranging for me to visit Langley Chapel and for answering various queries.

highly probable that they are footrests not kneelers. My first reason is that they are almost impossibly uncomfortable to serve as kneelers, though some might argue that this very masochism might identify them as Puritan for this reason. In fact, however, the declivity from the back to the front of the lower rest being 3¼ inches meant that the knees would slip off the rest while the foot could remain comfortably on it. Furthermore, it is only 22 inches from the front of the seat to the nearest point of the kneeler or footrest, diagonally, which is uncomfortable for kneeling but convenient for sitting. Finally, it should be remembered that the Puritans (along with John Knox who is reputed to be responsible for the last-minute inclusion of the "black rubric" in the 1552 Prayer Book) objected most strongly to receiving the Communion kneeling, for they considered this a "noxious ceremony" countenancing idolatry. Why, then, should Anglican Puritans erect kneelers when footrests for those who were invited guests at Christ's Table seemed the most appropriate gesture at what they called The Lord's Supper? Whether my theory is right or wrong, it is intriguing to see the survival of the Puritan treatment of the holy table as a table, by surrounding it on two if not three sides with benches and not as an altar. One kneels before an altar, but one sits at a table.

In any case, the single-room chapel, the plain unstained windows, and unpolished oak furnishings, the functional benches and uncomplicated holy table, speak of the simplicity of Anglican as well as of Nonconformist Puritanism in our period. Neither sought the good opinion of the great, but only to fear God and to worship Him in the ways commanded in his ordinances in Holy Scripture. To the holders of such convictions social and political prestige and all its external trappings, however impressive, were only an impudent irrelevance in the eyes of God.

5. The Economic Factor in Building

It is obvious that social prestige in architecture is dependent upon having the finance to support it, when it is desired. But it is still true, social and political prestige apart, that economy will have a considerable impact on architecture and fittings. For example, it costs much less to build in brick than stone, to leave a wall white-washed or painted in monochrome than to panel it, to erect a simple pulpit or choir stall without the elaborate festoons of fruit and flowers and cherubs that are the distinctive mark of Grinling Gibbons' work or to have a flat ceiling rather than a barrel-vaulted one with golden bosses or to use plain rather than stained windows.

The old Catholic aristocracy paid dearly for the recusancy of its members. One has only to contrast the splendour of the Baroque Catholic chapels in Europe in noblemen's houses, with the disguised domesticity of their English counterparts, where perhaps the most distinctive feature of their architecture were "priests' holes" where the hunted celebrants of Mass might hide once the *poursuivants* came close. If this was the case for the Roman Catholics, it was equally so for the Nonconformists during the reigns of Charles II and James II, when they, too, met in private cottages or in the open air, and designed pulpits that closed like cupboards. In the case of the former and latter, it was necessity that drove them to simplicity; but had theirs not been a forbidden faith there is little question that the wealthier Catholics, at least, would have erected ornate and splendid chapels for the celebration of the mysteries.

The greatest architect of the age was also limited by financial considerations. Sir Christopher Wren's fifty-two churches in London were built to replace the eighty-seven churches destroyed or damaged by the Fire of London.[51] The fittings were to be paid for by the individual parishes and the more richly fitted ones often indicated the wealth of one of the City companies that financed them, or the affluence of a particular Croesus in the neighbourhood. The fabric of all the churches was, however, to be paid for out of the tax on "sea coal"; that is, from a tax paid on all the coal that entered London. This is one reason why the spires of churches were often added fifteen or twenty years after the rest of the buildings had been completed.[52] It also accounted for his use of galleries as a means of greatly adding to the size of the congregation without adding proportionately to the cost of the building. A further evidence of the economic element was the fact that Wren used the same medieval foundations wherever possible, and since these had often been cheek by jowl with houses and shops (rapidly rebuilt by their owners) he had often only a front façade to provide. This financial factor, in his case at least, was not always a disadvantage. On the contrary, it made him use his considerable

---

51 St. Clement Dane's, St. James's, Piccadilly, and St. Anne's Soho, were also Wren's work, but these were erected to the west of the city proper.
52 Margaret Whinney, *Wren* (1971), p. 67.

ingenuity in varying his single-room church plans, and encouraged the inventiveness employed in his splendid and varied steeples.[53] This twofold preoccupation of Wren's mind, functional and economic, can be seen in his memorandum written after 1708 in which he gave advice on how the newer churches to the west of the city of London should be built: "in our reformed Religion, it should seem vain to make a Parish church larger than all who are present can both see and hear. The Romanists, indeed, may build larger Churches, it is enough if they hear the murmur of the Mass, and see the Elevation of the Host, but ours are to be fitted for Auditories."[54] His uncle Bishop Matthew Wren would have loved to extol the mystery of religion in rich architecture and splendid ceremonial. Wren was typical of his age in preferring explanation to mystification, the simple to the symbolical, and the functional to the fantastic.

The complex of five factors—the nature of the religious community, the foci of worship, numinosity or functionalism, social and political prestige, and the degree of financial support—is involved to a greater or lesser degree in all the religious buildings erected during the seventeenth century.

Moreover, all testify to the differing definitions of the church which each tradition holds and transmits to the future. For the Anglican the church is the house of God's presence, both convenient and symbolical, where the English people of God gather for prayer, preaching and Holy Communion. For the Roman Catholic it is the sacred place where God re-enacts the daily miracle of Transubstantiation in the presence of the people, the angels, and the saints. For the Puritans it is the place where the covenanted holy community ("visible saints") are gathered to hear the oracles of God expounded and the Lord's Supper shared. For the Quakers, who regard dedicated personalities as the only true temples of the Holy Spirit, who illumines them with inner light and garrisons them with interior peace, only the simplest and least distracting of buildings is suitable for silent worship.

Roman Catholics and Anglicans are aware of the numinous element in architecture, while Puritans and Quakers stress the functional and pragmatic considerations. Roman Catholics and Angli-

---

[53] *Ibid.*, pp. 47, 66. They evidently impressed Canaletto for in 1746 he painted several views of the Thames, and in each of them showed the steeples like the masts of great stranded stone ships, piercing an unusually Italian skyscape.

[54] Cited from the *Parentalia* by the younger Christopher Wren in Margaret Whinney's *Wren*, p. 48.

cans emphasize the historical continuity of the Christian faith and the hierarchy in the style and symbolism of their sanctuaries, while Puritans and Quakers concentrate on the contemporaneity of divine providence and the direction of the Holy Spirit. Roman Catholic churches or chapels (whenever permitted) and new Anglican churches are impressive, while Puritan and Quaker meeting-houses are expressive. The danger of Roman Catholic churches or chapels (especially on the Continent) during this Baroque era is theatricality and idolatry. The danger of Laudian Anglican churches or their fittings is that beauty may prove a substitute for ethical duty. The danger for Puritan and Quaker meeting-houses is that colour-blindness and poverty of the imagination may be confused with simplicity and restraint, and the *tabula Domini* with a *tabula rasa*.

CHAPTER II

CHURCH ARCHITECTURE: ACHIEVEMENTS

FROM THEORETICAL and theological considerations we turn to the actual achievements in English religious architecture during the seventeenth century, from Inigo Jones to Christopher Wren. This will involve a survey of the Anglican, Roman Catholic, Puritan, and Quaker churches or meeting-houses, and their fittings and plate. Inevitably, however, it will be only a selection of distinguished church architecture or of typical meeting-houses, especially from 1660 onwards.

It has been argued that there is no denominationally or even distinctively religious architecture in this age,[1] no more than there is an Anglican mathematics or a dissenting geometry and that an age builds in a certain style without distinguishing except functionally between sacred and secular buildings. Even further, it is maintained that a "style" is seen to exist not by contemporaries, who merely build, but only by successive and troubled ages which are in the throes of a new and contrasting form of building. Such a view could be maintained by showing, for example, the likeness between Wren's London churches of the unpretentious kind and the simple meeting-houses built in 1688[2] and in the next genera-

[1] This point has been forcibly put by an architect, Ronald F. Jones, in *Nonconformist Church Architecture* (1914), pp. 8-11.

[2] A. L. Drummond, *The Church Architecture of Protestantism* (1934), pp. 36-37, claims: "Wren was the creator of the modern Anglo-Saxon Protestant church." So far so good. Then he immediately continues: "The effect of the late Puritan supremacy in moulding the English attitude to public worship and the church building could not be undone. Wren recognised the change by designing places of worship that were primarily meeting-houses; his aim was to ensure seeing and hearing." R. F. Jones, see footnote 1 immediately above, takes the same view, but neither of them does justice to Wren's preference for rectangular over square ground plans, nor to the fact that Wren's altars are in the east of his churches while meeting-house Communion tables are in the centre. Finally, they ignore the further fact that Wren's pulpits though similar in shape are not located on the south walls of his edifices but against pillars and on the north. These differences are fundamental. See also H. Lismer Short's interesting suggestion that the distinctive interior arrangements of the meeting-houses derive from Calvinist precedent in Geneva, Holland, and Scotland, in the adaptation of medieval fanes, and that the transmission of these ideas was either by Marian exiles or university students going to Dutch or Scottish universities in the seventeenth century. ("The Architecture of the Old Meeting Houses," *Transactions of the Unitarian Historical Society*, Vol. 8, No. 3, 1944, pp. 98-112.)

tion, or even by demonstrating the similarities between Wren's ecclesiastical and domestic architecture.

There is, of course, considerable truth in this view. In the choice of brick rather than stone, in the use of clear rather than stained-glass windows, in the use of circular or oval windows with "cob-webbed" glass, in the porticoes, and the functional well-lit simplicity of the architecture of the period, there are parallels between sacred and secular architecture, and between a Wren church and a Dissenting meeting-house.

On the other hand, however, there are important differences between Wren's type of church architecture and a Dissenting meeting-house, as our second footnote has already demonstrated. In addition, there is a considerable difference between the sacred architecture of Inigo Jones and Wren, and also between their Italianate styles and the "Gothic survival" which Archbishop Laud favoured, and which produced some intriguing mixtures of Gothic-Renaissance chapels in Oxford and Cambridge. Furthermore, one must distinguish Wren in his early and late styles. One must also note the differences in Wren's architecture due to diverse patrons, such as James II, or the dean and canons of St. Paul's Cathedral or the state, or even when affluent guilds are providing the fittings of his churches in the City or west of the City of London.

The seventeenth century was a great period for building churches. In Elizabeth's reign by contrast only nineteen churches or chapels were built or rebuilt.[3] Between 1603 and 1662 (and Wren's most important and prolific commissions are executed after this time) at least a hundred and thirty-three churches are known to have been newly erected or entirely rebuilt on an old site, and nearly four hundred were significantly remodelled.[4]

It is of particular interest to note that these churches were built in three distinct and one mixed style of architecture. There is the "Gothic survival"[5] style so much favoured by Laud as emphasising

[3] See John M. Schnorrenberg's "Anglican Architecture, 1558-1662: Its Theological Implications and Its Relation to the Continental Background" (Princeton University Ph.D., 1964, Department of Art and Archaeology), p. 46.

[4] *Ibid.*, p. 51.

[5] Eric Mercer (*English Art, 1553-1625*, Oxford, p. 85) had argued that there were three reasons for the continuance of Gothic church architecture in England: one was to advertise by the familiar exterior the functions of the building as a church; another was to give the building an archaic air (which would link with the Laudian motive of creating a sense of continuity through the centuries); and the third was to emphasise a particular feature of the church by its Gothic form contrasting with the classical details of the ornamentation. Marcus Whiffen (*Stuart and Georgian Churches*, 1947, p. 9) argues that Gothic was still the nat-

Bee Wise as serpents
but inocent as Dous.

LXXX.
SERMONS
PREACHED BY THAT LEAR.
NED AND REVEREND DIVINE
IOHN DONNE, D.ᴿ IN DIVINITIE
LATE DEANE OF Yᵉ CATHEDRALL
CHVRCH OF Sᵗ PAVLES
LONDON.

M.Merian Iun:

1. The Frontispiece of John Donne's *LXXX Sermons*, 1640

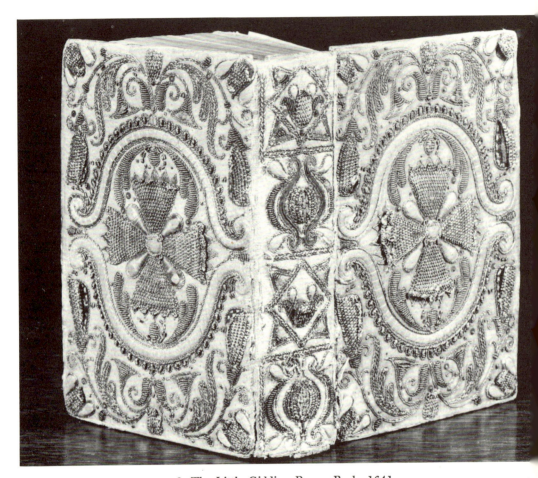

2. The Little Gidding Prayer Book, 1641

THE BOOK
OF
Common-Prayer
And Administration
Of the
SACRAMENTS,
AND OTHER
RITES & CEREMONIES
Of the CHURCH,
According to the Use
Of the
CHURCH of ENGLAND
Together with the
PSALTER or PSALMS
OF
DAVID,
Pointed as they are to be Sung
or Said in CHURCHES:
And the
FORM & MANNER
OF
Making, Ordaining, & Consecrating
OF
BISHOPS, PRIESTS,
AND
DEACONS.

LONDON,
Printed by His Ma.ties Printers
Cum Privilegio
MDCLXII

3. The Book of Common Prayer, 1662

4. The Interior of St. Andrew's, Holborn

5. The Interior of St. Stephen's Walbrook

6. St. Paul's Cathedral from the Southeast

EFFIGIES R·P· LANCELOTI ANDREWES EPISCOPI WINTONIENSIS·

See heer a Shadow from that setting SUNNE,
Whose glorious course through this Horizon runn
Left the dimm face of our dull Hemisphære,
All one great Eye, all drown'd in one great Teare.
Whose rare industrious Soule led his free thought
Through Learning's Universe, and (vainly) sought
Room for her spacious Self; untill at length
She found ỹ way home: with an holy strength

Snatcht herself hence to Heav'n; filld a bright place
Midst those immortal Fires, and on the face
Of her Great MAKER, fixt a flaming eye,
Where still She reads true, pure Divinitie.
And now ỹ graue Aspect hath deign'd to shrink
Into this lesse appearance. If you think
Tis but a dead face, Art doth heer bequeath
Look on the following leaues & see him breath.

Are to be sold by R. Badger dwelling
in Stationer's Hall. 1632.

John Payne Fecit

7. Bishop Lancelot Andrewes, 1555-1626

8. St. Nicholas' Presbyterian Meeting-House, Ipswich, Suffolk, 1700

9. Langley Chapel, Kenley, Shropshire

HEU PIETAS   HEU PRISCA FIDES

WILHELMUS LAUD. ARCHIEPISCOPUS CANTUARIENSIS.
Martyrio Coronatus 10 *January Anno* 1644.

Antonius van Dyck Eques Pinxit.   D. Loggan Excudit.

10. Archbishop William Laud, 1573-1645

11. Bishop John Cosin, 1594-1672

ÆTATIS SUÆ. LVIII.   EDWARDUS REYNOLDS SACRÆ THEOLOGIÆ DOCTOR Aº. DOM. M.DC.LVIII.

From a rare Pen there came to fill this Place
A Character too rich to sute the Face,
The Author saw't: and (to himselfe best knowne)
Admir'd the Love, durst not the Notions owne:
And for himselfe, and for his Book, he saies,
What's good is Gods, and Gods alone the praise:
Sermons take not from mens applause Renowne,
The Peoples Practice is the Preachers Crowne.

D. Loggan delin: et sculp:

12. Bishop Edward Reynolds, 1599-1676

Nos quoque floruimus, sed flos fuit ille caducus.
Flammaque de stipula nostra brevisque fuit. Ov.

ÆTATIS SUÆ 62 VERA EFFIGIES RICHARDI BAXTERI MIN: S: CLIN: OPT: ET PAT̄: FIDEISSI ET CHARITATIS AN: 1677

Thy
lovingkind:
is better
then life.
Ps: 63:3

R: White delin: et sculp:

Farewell VAINE WORLD, as thou hast bin to me
DUST and a SHADOW: those I leave with thee:
The vnseen VITALL SUBSTANCE I committ,
To him that's SUBSTANCE LIFE LIGHT LOVE to it.
The LEAVES & FRUIT are dropt, for soyle & seed,
Heavens heirs to generate: to heale and feed:
Them also thou wilt flatter and molest,
But shalt not keep from Everlasting Rest.

13. Richard Baxter, 1615-1691

14. George Fox, 1624-1691

15. The Non-Juring Bishops, 1688

16. Sir Christopher Wren, 1632-1723

the continuity of Anglicanism with the medieval Church which preceded it and the constructional techniques which had never been lost. There is, by contrast, the "Italianate" style so greatly favoured by Charles I and exemplified in the works of Inigo Jones. In Wren's work we find an "English Palladianism," which is a more domesticated Italianate style than that of Inigo Jones. The "mixed" style may be Gothic mingled with Flemish mannerism[6] (as in the Jacobean and Caroline strapwork, diamonds, obelisks, and curlicues that abound in the interior ornamentation and detail of this period). This can be seen, for example, in St. John's Church, Leeds. Or, it can be Gothic mixed with Italian details (such as cherubs, framed paintings used as a reredos, festoons of fruit and flowers), some of which are found in part in the chapels of Trinity College and Lincoln College, Oxford, or in Peterhouse Chapel in Cambridge.

1. *Anglican Architecture*

The most famous architect in England before Wren was, of course, Inigo Jones, whose court masques familiarised England with Italian *mises-en-scène*. His most famous ecclesiastical architecture includes St. Catherine Cree,[7] St. Paul's Covent Garden, the new portico of St. Paul's Cathedral, and the Marlborough Chapel.

St. Catherine Cree, built in 1628, combines Gothic elements with classical. It resembles Lincoln's Inn Chapel, since both are Gothic buildings that have Italian arcades surmounted by shouldered Gothic windows. St. Catherine's has a Gothic plan, Gothic vaulting, and Gothic window tracery while the west doorway, however, has a classical character, but the most notable classical characteristic is, of course, the Corinthian order of the nave arcading.

The more characteristically classical work is St. Paul's Covent Garden which is indubitably the creation of Inigo Jones, and which provides a kind of miniature *piazza* setting for the church. It was the first English and ambitious attempt to use the Tuscan Order according to the rules of Vitruvius.[8] It was built between

---

ural way of building in out of the way places, and so the idea of a conscious "survival," especially country districts, may be greatly exaggerated.

[6] Gerald Cobb, *The Old Churches of London* (1942), p. 8.

[7] *Ibid.*, p. 7, is doubtful whether Inigo Jones built St. Catherine Cree, London. But whether or not it is an intriguing mixture of Gothic and classical elements and of the transitional character associated with the earlier work of Inigo Jones.

[8] *Ibid.*

1631 and 1633. It has a rectangular simplicity, open interior, and a Tuscan portico, all features that spell a long farewell to Gothic.

About 1627 Inigo Jones was commissioned to build the Queen's Chapel in Marlborough Gate by King Charles I for the use of his Catholic Queen, Henrietta Maria. The vaulted and bossed roof provides a gilded ceiling that overarches the three long windows divided by pilasters, with the double-width central window with a superimposed lunette window. Below the windows is a richly panelled reredos stretching the width of the sanctuary and converging on a framed painting, in front of which is the altar. The whole effect is of restrained Baroque, with clear lighting and a single room or chamber, rather than the Gothic standard cruciform. The decoration is restricted to the panelled and embossed roof and the royal arms above the lunette of the central window. It is all the more effective because it is modest rather than heavily ornamented, as contrasted with later royal chapels in the century.[9]

The most widely seen work of Inigo Jones was the western front of St. Paul's Cathedral, which accorded with the taste of Charles I rather than that of his Bishop of London, as Laud was at the time it was projected. It was begun in 1633 and it put a classical face on the Gothic body of the old St. Paul's. In fact the restoration of the cathedral was to occupy Jones for a decade. Jones built a great portico sixty-six feet high, with a Corinthian Order of fourteen columns, while huge scrolls filled in the side angles between the high nave and the low aisles. Above the entablature there was a balustraded parapet instead of a pediment. It had pedestals set at intervals that were to receive the statues of the benefactors of the cathedral. The purpose of this portico was to be used as a public ambulatory to avoid the cathedral's interior being similarly employed, a concern very much in the forefront of Laud's mind who could not endure the desecration of edifices built for the worship of God. But if the proposer of the portico was Laud, the style was that of the bishop's royal master, and Charles I paid for it as a memorial to his father, King James I.[10]

[9] Its interior as restored, is the fourth illustration in Margaret Whinney and Oliver Millar, *English Art, 1625-1714* (Oxford, 1957).

[10] Doreen Yarwood, *The Architecture of England* (1963), pp. 191ff. The subsequent history of St. Paul's during the Commonwealth period was deplorable. The scaffolding set up to support the vaulting and tower was cut down and sold, so that much of the vault collapsed. The building was entirely secularised, the nave being used as stables and the portico as a cover for stalls and shops, while the undercroft of the chapter-house became a wine-cellar. The Great Fire of 1666 was an apocalyptic ending to the sorry state of the old Gothic St. Paul's, which rose Phoenix-like from its ashes, in Wren's new masterpiece.

2. *The Impact of Laud*

It was unquestionably Laud, a subject for distant admiration rather than close affection because of his great energy and rigour, with the unswerving support of Charles I, who left the greatest impact on Anglican architecture in the first half of the century, as did Wren in the second half. Laud had inherited the triple tradition of Bishop Lancelot Andrewes,[11] a concern to main spiritual continuity between the doctrine and discipline of the church of the first five centuries and the Church of England, a profound concern for reverence in worship, including a particularly high evaluation of the chief Sacrament, and a respect for the divine right of kings that his Puritan enemies could only consider as subservient if not servile. In these convictions Laud was supported by such a prelate as Matthew Wren, uncle of the great architect. It is this conservatism of outlook in aesthetics, combined with determination in execution that explains what must be called "Gothic survival" in the church architecture of the period.[12] For Laud, since his consecration as Bishop of Bath and Wells, on his way to the sees of London and Canterbury, not forgetting his earlier years as President of St. John's College, Oxford (1611-1621) which prepared him for the role of Chancellor of the University of Oxford (1630-1641), dominated Anglican aesthetic taste. It is clear that he had little sympathy with the Italianate fashions of Inigo Jones. Even in the semi-Baroque splendour of the Canterbury Quadrangle of St. John's, it seems as if medievalism is attempting to suppress the future. For if both open ends of the quadrangle have loggia, the façades that surmount them are medieval in shape as are the ornaments. And it is quite typical that his loggia spandrils are filled with busts of the theological and cardinal virtues and of the seven liberal arts, with half-length angels on the central arch. This was an iconographical programme "common in the ecclesiastical art of the middle ages, but it is probably unique in the secular art of the seventeenth."[13]

[11] But Bishop Lancelot Andrewes was a great preacher and a man of wit, while Laud was afraid of the latitude preaching allowed and lacked the psychological insight which produced humour.

[12] See Sir Alfred Clapham's article, "The Survival of Gothic in 17th century England," *Architects' Journal*, CVI, Supplement (1942), 44; also the unpublished doctoral dissertation of John M. Schnorrenberg, *op. cit.*, pp. 51ff.

[13] Mary Whinney and Oliver Millar, *English Art, 1625-1714* (Oxford, 1957), p. 55. The authors point out that the only concession made to contemporary taste are the larger than life bronze figures of Charles I and his Queen Henrietta Maria by Le Sueur, the King's sculptor. These were placed in the niches above the entrances.

If his secular buildings are Gothic in inspiration and iconography, how much more will be the sacred architecture he sponsored or otherwise influenced? The impact of Laud can be seen in the vigorous chapel building programme at Oxford, and, to a lesser degree, at Cambridge. A harlequin floor of black and white marble was laid in Magdalen College Chapel and there was a partial remaking of the stalls. The decoration showed a curious mingling of classical swags and pediments with Gothic style tracery and finials. More decisively Laudian was the decision of Accepted Frewen,[14] President of the College, in 1631 to substitute an altar for the Communion table, the first similar transformation since the Reformation. Despite his Puritan Christian name, the offence was made even ranker to the Puritans by the later addition of a crucifix, and the provision of painted hangings featuring scenes from the life of Christ, while from the roof there was suspended a corona of lights. By 1635, as was noted in Laud's diary, the work had been completely finished and it included the surviving brass eagle lectern and eight statues provided by the Christmas brothers.[15]

Even Lincoln College Chapel, Oxford, which was the gift of Laud's inveterate enemy, Bishop Williams, and which was consecrated in 1631, is at least as Gothic in plan and treatment as it is neo-classical. It has traceried Gothic windows and a wooden and canted roof, with small ribs that divide it into panels, even though the bosses in the panels are gilded and include cherubs and swags. The splendid east window, almost unquestionably the work of Bernard Van Linge, has a thoroughly medieval iconography, since it consists of Old Testament anticipations and the New Testament fulfilment of events central in the life of Christ and is a typical example of Patristic typological exegesis. In conception it is thoroughly medieval,[16] if not earlier, but in execution the Vandyke

14 Later to be Archbishop of York.

15 Whinney and Millar, *op. cit.*, p. 55.

16 This astonishing window deserves detailed consideration for its iconography which suggests that Bishop Williams was trying to outdo Bishop Laud at his own game. Moving from left to right, and upper light to lower light, we have the following series of themes. First, the Nativity of the Second Adam, Christ, and below it the birth of the First Adam in Paradise (both expounding I Cor. 15:45). Next comes the Baptism of Christ (Matthew 3:16) and below the dramatic drowning of the kings and soldiers presumably of Egypt (I Cor. 10:2). The third upper light depicts the institution of the Communion (Matthew 26:26-30) and the light below depicts a lamb resembling a child and illustrates Exodus 12:3. The fourth upper light shows the Crucifixion and Christ surrounded by his Mother and the Magdalen (Colossians 2:4) with its anticipation in the serpent raised by Moses in the wilderness in the light below (John 39). The fifth upper

beards of Christ and the prophets bear a distinct contemporary resemblance to royal tonsorial fashions. The arrangement of the figures is dramatic, and the colours are as fresh as they are subtle.[17] But the shape of the chapel is medieval not modern, and so is its fenestral iconography.[18]

Another Laud-inspired addition to Oxford was the new porch added to the Church of St. Mary the Virgin in 1637. As William Prynne described it, on the deposition of Sir Nathaniel Brent, it was "standing in the very heart of the University towards the street [High Street], to which Church all the University resorted."[19] It was peculiarly offensive to Presbyterian Prynne because "in front of which porch was a statue of the *Virgin Mary* cut in stone with the Picture of a child in her armes, commonly taken to be the Picture of Christ." He might have been even more displeased if he had known that the twisted columns supporting the pediment were smaller reminders, if not replicas, of the Solomonic pillars (reputedly remaining from the Constantinian basilica) of St. Peter's in Rome, which Bernini had used ten years before to construct his impressive balddachino over the High Altar.[20] The donor of St. Mary's portico was Laud's chaplain, Dr. Morgan Owen.

The College Chapel in Cambridge most clearly associated with the Laudian movement was that of Peterhouse during the Mastership of Dr. Matthew Wren, Laud's protégé. Almost all of it was built between 1628 and 1632, except for the east and west facings which were added at the charge of Dr. John Cosin, Wren's successor as Master.[21] Here again there was a mixture of Gothic and neo-classical styles. The outside combined a Jacobean frieze with

---

[17] Van Linge, a native of Emden, created the East window of Oxford's Wadham College Chapel and of Lincoln's Inn Chapel in London (1623-1624) and was associated with Christ Church Cathedral in Oxford when this was refurnished by Dean Duppa (between 1629 and 1638). The pictorial window in the N. aisle showing a sulking Jonah beneath the gourd, with Nineveh in the background is the work of Abraham Van Linge, his brother or his son. See C. Woodforde, *English Stained and Painted Glass* (1954), pp. 42ff.

[18] For details and photographs, see the report of the Royal Commission on Historical Monuments, *City of Oxford* (1939), pp. 64, 67 and plates 121-26.

[19] See *Canterburies Doome* (1646), p. 71.

[20] The four bronze twisted columns were not unveiled until June 29, 1627 and the *balddachino* was inaugurated exactly six years later. See Rudolph Wittkower, *Gian Lorenzo Bernini, Roman Baroque Sculptor* (2nd edn., 1966), pp. 189-90.

[21] Whinney and Millar, *op. cit.*, p. 57.

light illustrates the Resurrection (Acts 2:24) and below is Jonah and the great fish in which he was incarcerated for three days (Matthew 12:24). The sixth and final light (upper) depicts the Ascension (Acts 1:9) and below it is shown the burning chariot of Elijah ascending into heaven (2 Kings 2:6). In each case the inscription from the Bible is given in Latin, emphasising medievalism.

perpendicular tracery in the window. Inside there were statues of the four evangelists, the patron saint, and figures of angels and cherubim. Prynne gives us the report of a Mr. Wallis, a rather jaundiced observer, on the interior: ". . . in *Peter house* Chappel there was a glorious new *Altar* set up, & mounted on steps, to which the Master, Fellowes, Schollers bowed & were enjoyned to bow by Dr. *Cosens* the Master, who set it up; that there were Basons, Candlesticks, Tapers standing on it, and a great Crucifix hanging over it."[22] Even more sinister was the note made by the iconoclast William Dowsing, describing his work of destruction at Peterhouse, just before Christmas in 1643: ". . . we pulled down 2: mighty great Angells, with wings and divers other Angells, & the 4: Evangelists, & Peter, with his Keies, over the Chappell Dore, & about a hundred Chirubims & Angells, & divers superstitious Letters in gold: & at the upper end of the Chancell these words were written as followeth. Hic lucus [locus] est Domus Dei, nil aliud, et Portae Coeli."[23]

It is noteworthy that the fondness for cherubim and angels in the decoration of churches in the high-church tradition is more than a fancy.[24] It is rather the attempt on the part of sensitive Anglicans to visualise the heavenly context in which the liturgy is celebrated. It gives the worshippers the visual complement to the priest's vocal affirmation "therefore with angels, and archangels, and the whole company of heaven," to which the people's response is the *Sanctus*. The latter is, of course, an exact echo of the words in which the prophet Isaiah expressed the adoration of God after realising the divine presence behind the six-winged cherubim in the temple. This sense of the invisible host of saints surrounding the heavenly throne described in the Seventh Chapter of the Book

22 Prynne, *op. cit.*, pp. 73-74.

23 *The Cambridge Journal of William Dowsing*, transcribed by A. C. Moule and reprinted from the *History Teachers' Miscellany* (1926), p. 5.

24 Cosin had a notable penchant for angelology. When he was a Prebendary of Durham, Canon Peter Smart had criticised him for his introduction into Durham Cathedral of "popish baits and allurments of glorious pictures and Babylonish vestures." Cosin was also charged with setting up many images about the choir, "some of the angells, in long scarlet gowns, greene petticotes golden wings and gilded beards." Instead of the prescribed wooden altar, he had substituted "a double table very sumptuous of stone . . . upon 6 stone pillars, curiously polished, and fastened to the ground, having upon every black pillar 3 cherubim— faces as white as snow." Smart thought the high Gothic font-cover (still extant) and which he claimed cost £140 both "fantastical" and "capricious." (See Rawlinson Mss. A. 441f. 28; also *The Correspondence of John Cosin*, D.D., Surtees Society, 1869, Vol. I, p. 161.)

of Revelation, has persisted in Roman Catholicism through its sanctoral cycle in the liturgy, with special days remembering the saints and invoking their aid. Furthermore, Rome as the mother of saints has added to their number by the careful process of canonisation through the centuries, thus recognising post-Biblical eminent imitators of God. Moreover, most Roman Catholic churches have images of the saints in windows and statues.

The Anglican Communion has managed to retain the sense of the Communion of saints (the New Testament saints[25] rather than the saints of ecclesiastical tradition), through its more restricted sanctoral cycle in the Book of Common Prayer, which had the advantage of stressing the Christological feasts and fasts. This verbal remembrance of the examples of the saints was reinforced, as we have noted, by the Laudian tradition through stained-glass windows, and, even occasionally, by statues, as at Peterhouse. It is significant that the Puritans (although they had their own martyrologists from Foxe to Adam Clarke) restricted the term "saints," according to St. Paul's example in his epistles, to those in whom the Holy Spirit was indwelling, namely, the "elect," who ultimately were known only to God, though one might presume that men and women living according to the Divine ordinances were "visible saints." Far from depicting the historic saints in their places of worship, the Puritans even destroyed those represented in the national church as a fitting recompense (in their view) for the idolatry of breaking the Second Commandment.

All in all, the university chapels (especially Peterhouse in the Puritan stronghold, Cambridge) were a bold and beautiful tribute to the new respect for reverence, the sense of the primacy of the Eucharist over preaching, and the sheer aesthetic sensibilities of the upholders of the Laudian tradition. At least one contemporary felt that they rivalled the royal chapels and the cathedrals; George Garrard chaplain to the Earl of Northumberland, summed up the situation thus: "the Churches or Chapels of all the Colleges are much more beautified, extraordinary cost bestowed upon them; scarce any Cathedral Churches nor Windsor nor Canterbury, nay

---

25 One consequence of the restriction of the number and the role of the saints in Anglican worship was the paucity of opportunity for sculptors, who had in large measure to confine themselves to secular work. By contrast, the many side altars in Roman Catholic churches on the Continent provided great scope for sculptors of the saints in the ecclesiastical tradition of the west. Bernini, for example, would have been exceedingly hampered in England, and his famous St. Teresa unthinkable.

nor Paul's Choir exceeds them, most of them new-glazed; richer glass for figures and painting I have not seen, which they had most from beyond the seas."[26]

Other interesting examples of mixed Gothic and Baroque churches are to be found outside London and the ancient university cities. One of the earliest, dating from 1634, is St. John's, Leeds. Its distance from the centre probably helps to account for the fact that it is more Gothic than Baroque. In fact, it is essentially "Gothic survival." It was founded, furnished, and endowed by John Harrison, a merchant and a native of the town, whose generosity equalled his wealth.[27] It is an oblong building, divided by an arcade that runs along its length. It has twin roofs. Its exterior is in the austere late perpendicular style, but its interior, emerging relatively unspoiled from the restorer's hands, presents in its screens and pews a splendid display of Caroline decoration with carved strapwork and scrolls.

At about the same time St. Mary's, Leighton Bromsgrove (only about four miles away from the remarkable "Arminian monastery" of Little Gidding), was being built by the joint efforts of the brothers Nicholas and John Ferrar, and of the Prebendary, the poet George Herbert. John Ferrar wrote to his brother on the progress of the rebuilding of the ruined parish church in July 1632: "We have 18 Masons and Labrores at worke at Layton Church and we shall have this weeke 10 Carpenters. God prosper the worke and send mony in. Amen."[28] Apparently the plea was answered because the nave was finished that year and the neighbouring Duke of Lennox paid the cost of the rustic tower added later. The outline of the thirteenth century chancel was retained, and much of the stone was re-used. The existing church, despoiled of its original white plaster inscribed with golden texts, looks barer and starker than it was. It still retains, however, its famous canopied reading pew and canopied pulpit of identical pattern and height, thus fulfilling

[26] *Calendar of State Papers, Domestic* (1636-1637), p. 113. A late example of a College Chapel at Oxford is Brasenose (1656-1659). Like the previous examples considered, it mingles Gothic and Classical elements in its design, which incidentally is the work of a master mason, John Jackson. There is geometrical tracery in the windows, yet they have entablature above them, and at the top there is a crocketted, finialled gable. The side windows, with their pointed arches, yet have pilasters of the Corinthian order at their sides. (See Doreen Yarwood, *The Architecture of England*, 1963, p. 194.)

[27] Marcus Whiffen, *Stuart and Georgian Churches* (1947), pp. 12-13.

[28] Cited in *ibid.*, p. 12 from *The Ferrar Papers* (ed. B. Blackstone, Cambridge, 1938).

Herbert's demand that prayer and preaching should be equally esteemed.[29]

Other examples of provincial church architecture combining a Gothic shape with classical details include: Staunton Harold church, Leicestershire, built between 1653 and 1663; Compton Wynyates in Staffordshire erected in 1663.[30] Newent church in Gloucestershire, however, was classic in shape as well as in details. The change to the classical style was, of course, immensely accelerated by the Great Fire[31] of London in 1666 and the renowned examples of the work of Sir Christopher Wren in the City churches and St. Paul's Cathedral from 1670 onwards. The influence was so great that it deserves the collective noun of a "Wrenaissance."

3. The "Wrenaissance"

Wren dominated the church building of the seventeenth century in England, and for a variety of reasons. For one thing he built more churches than anyone else. For another, they were almost all concentrated in London where they were more easily visible than elsewhere, where they could easily impress the rising generation of architects and potential clients as well. They were, moreover, almost all built about the same time, largely because the Great Fire of London destroyed or damaged eighty-seven churches and made a vast scheme for rapid and economical building essential, and Wren had the energy, ingenuity, and brilliance to prove himself to be the man for this gigantic task. Moreover, his designs, whether he was building a small church like St. Mary Abchurch or a vast one like St. Paul's Cathedral, were marked by versatility in the use of often cramped sites and variety in planning both the interiors and the superb steeples of his churches.[32] He changed the entire skyscape of London. The Venetian painter Canaletto

[29] Izaak Walton's *Life of Herbert* (World's Classics edn., 1927), p. 278. Walton thought the church a "costly mosaick."
[30] Whiffen, *op. cit.*, p. 18.
[31] The two largest town churches in the provinces in the late seventeenth century owe their origin to fires. All Saints Church, Northampton, was burnt to a cinder in the autumn of 1675 and nineteen years later the same fate befell St. Mary's, Warwick. The new nave of All Saints was opened in 1680 and the striking Ionic colonnade on the west front was added in 1701. It bore above it a statue of Charles I to commemorate his gift of a thousand tons of lumber from his woods for the rebuilding of the church. In 1704 the cupola was added. The plan for the nave is a square within a square—a total departure from the Gothic. St. Mary's, Warwick, a fascinating church was not even begun in our period. (For the latter, see Marcus Whiffen, *Stuart and Georgian Architecture*, pp. 18ff.)
[32] Whiffen, *op. cit.*, p. 14 and Cobb, *op. cit.*, p. 9.

41

was obviously fascinated by the "masts" of the churches as he viewed them from the Thames-side in 1746, for he painted several views in which the masts of the ships in the river make a point that is counterpointed by the slender spires of Wren's churches as they contrast with the great rounded bulk of St. Paul's.

One is impressed by the energy and planning devoted to his great task and the speed with which he accomplished it. To say that he had to start from the ground up is an understatement, because his first task was to clear away the clutter left by the holocaust of the great fire, the melted ruins and slag and charred wood. John Evelyn reported on September 3, 1666: "I left it [the City of London] this afternoone burning, a resemblance of Sodome or the last day . . . the ruines resembling the picture of *Troy*: *London* is no more." The following day he described the enlarged fire moving to the west: "the stones of Paules flew like grenados, the Lead melting down the streetes in a streame, and the very pavements of them glowing with fiery rednesse, so as nor horse nor man was able to tread on them." Of the eighty-seven churches destroyed or seriously damaged, it was decided to rebuild fifty-two in the City and three other churches in the west beyond the City limits—St. Clement Dane's, St. James's, Piccadilly, and St. Anne's, Soho. Sixteen new churches were started in 1670, four more in 1671, and another fifteen before the end of the decade, so within ten years of commencing the Herculean effort, thirty-five churches were being or had been built under Wren's direction and responsibility.[33]

What was distinctive about these churches of Wren's? Primarily, it was the coming-of-age of classical architecture for English churches. For the long delay there was a variety of reasons. Though King Charles I and Inigo Jones were in favour of it, Archbishop Laud fought strongly against it. The unsettled religious and political climate discouraged any buildings other than those that were absolutely necessary: it was the Fire of 1666 that was the necessary urgency. Up to this time England had been well supplied with a host of medieval churches which needed repairing rather than supplanting.[34]

But Wren did much more than provide an impressive panorama of neo-classical architecture, both sacred and secular.[35] He

33 Margaret Whinney, *Wren* (1971), p. 45.
34 Whiffen, *op. cit.*, pp. 14ff.
35 His great secular buildings included: the Sheldonian Theatre, Oxford; the

knew the values of elegance and impressiveness, but his primary approach was strictly functional. That is, he asked the fundamental question: what is this church to be used for? As he was building Anglican churches there was no question that a central Communion table at the east end would be essential, but he did not feel the need to provide an apse or high steps or a balddachino to dramatise the altar. It was enough to provide a table and to ward off sacrilegious persons with a simple set of balustraded rails, and occasionally a simple reredos. What did, however, receive special treatment with Wren was the pulpit, with its sounding-board. For this was the era in which the sermon was ceasing to be a political weapon as it had been with the Puritans during Commonwealth days and by some of their inveterate foes among Anglican prelates in the last years of Laud's archiepiscopate, and was now becoming the means of reasoned discourse. Wren saw that a Protestant church, such as the Reformed Church of England appeared to him to be, needed an "auditory" where each member of the congregation could hear the exposition of God's Word and see it visibly re-enacted in the celebration of Holy Communion. He could, of course, have found and, in fact, probably saw, Jesuit churches in France during his important visit there from the summer of 1665 to the spring of 1666 (when he met Bernini and almost certainly also Mansart) where great emphasis was given to the pulpit and to Counter-Reformation preaching, but these "auditories" gave an even greater prominence to the altar.[36] Wren's churches were single-room churches that banished the Gothic distinction between chancel and nave, suppressed side chapels, and eliminated chancel screens to grant maximum audibility and visibility.

Another novelty in Wren's churches was the use of galleries. This was for both functional and economic reasons. They were included in his designs in order to gain the largest number of people in the space who could both see and hear the leader of worship in comfort. Moreover, Wren's synthetic mind probably added these to the typical neo-classical Catholic contemporary churches by seeing the possibilities in the great French Huguenot Temple in Charenton, with its three tiers of galleries.[37]

Library of Trinity College, Cambridge; Chelsea Hospital; the enlargement of Kensington, Hampton Court and Whitehall Palaces; and, supremely, the Royal Hospital, Greenwich.

[36] Whinney, *op. cit.*, pp. 48-49.

[37] *Ibid.*, pp. 32, 53 and illustration 22 opposite p. 33 in Margaret Whinney's *Wren*.

The evidence for affirming that Wren had a functional and rather Protestant conception of the nature of his churches is derived from an important memorandum which he prepared for a Commission, on which he served, which had been appointed as the result of an Act of Parliament passed in 1708 to build new churches to the east and west of the old City of London boundaries. It is an expression of his mature views gained after long experience as a builder of churches. He advocated the building of large churches, "but still, in our reformed Religion, it should seem vain to make a Parish church larger than that all who are present can both hear and see." At this point Protestant pride rides high, as he continues, "The Romanists, indeed, may build larger churches, it is enough if they hear the murmur of the Mass, and see the Elevation of the Host, but ours are to be fitted for Auditories. I can hardly think it practicable to make a single Room so capacious with Pews and Galleries, as to hold above 2000 persons, and all to hear the service and both to hear distinctly, and see the Preacher."[38] Margaret Whinney makes the very apt comment, particularly so for the Restoration era of experimentation and enlightenment, "Exposition rather than the mysteries of religion was the major concern of the Anglican Church."[39] She confirms this judgment by pointing out that the building was planned so that the altar would not be the main focal point, but that the seats of the clergy reading the service, the lectern, and supremely the pulpit must be so placed that all could see and hear.

A third novel characteristic in Wren's church architecture was the use of cupolas, which had not been seen in England even in Inigo Jones's day. The most impressive examples were, of course, to be found in St. Paul's Cathedral, with its vast central dome dominating the seventeenth-century skyline. The most miniature examples are the tops of the spires of some of his churches, such as St. Magnus Martyr and St. Benet, Paul's Wharf, and the most regal, St. Paul's Cathedral excepted, is St. Stephen, Wallbrook.

[38] Stephen Wren, *Parentalia* (1750), pp. 317ff. A. L. Drummond in *The Church Architecture of Protestantism* (1934), p. 36f., has argued that Wren conceived his churches essentially as meeting-houses, and that this functional Protestantism was derived in large measure from the late Puritan attitude predominant in the Commonwealth and Protectorate, with a streamlining encouraged by the development of the scientific spirit which wished to do away equally with clutter and mystery, and was fascinated with optics. There may, in fact, be a debt to Puritanism, but there are also many other influences, such as Vitruvius and Michelangelo, quite apart from such Baroque masters as Bernini, Mansart and Lemercier, and the Huguenot architect, Salomon de Brosse.

[39] Whinney, *op. cit.*, p. 48.

What distinguishes Wren's cupolas from those on the Continent, however, is the austerity of their decoration and lack of colouring. Least of all do they resemble *coup d'oeil* paintings that seem to transform the interior of the dome into cerulean blue in which phalanxes of saints are flying, as in the leading Jesuit churches of Europe at this time. Wren's work has an aesthetic simplicity, with reserve, probity, and lack of theatricality.

Wren's greatest resourcefulness, however, is seen in the variety of his interiors, often planned on sites of irregular shape[40] presenting considerable challenges, and in the profusion of differing steeple designs. It is part of Wren's genius that in adopting the neo-classical style of building, he recognised that this style had forgone the aspirational quality of the great verticals in the Gothic spires, and he invented classical spires to provide this missing element in classical architecture. It should also be noted that Wren's steeples all rise from the ground, and not merely from the roofs of his churches: they are therefore significant and distinctive elements of his architecture, and never extras "tacked on" even though he often had to wait for further money before he could finish them. As Wren's steeples provide the soaring and mystical element missing in classical architecture, his single-room churches with minimal chancels and absence of screens, and stained-glass windows, allow the light to pour in great floods into his buildings, banishing "storied windows, richly dight, casting a dim religious light." Both literally and metaphorically this was the ecclesiastical architecture of the Enlightenment.

Wren's church exteriors are much less interesting than his interiors, with the single important exception of the steeples. The reason for this is that many of the burned domestic and commercial buildings huddled close to the medieval churches in the old City of London were rebuilt before the churches were, and hence few churches presented any significant façade to the street. This was a disadvantage if impressiveness were being sought, but an advantage if speed and economy were the targets. So many of the exteriors are plain brick walls with stone dressings. Wren was able to use the foundations of medieval churches, and on often cramped sites, produce a variety of solutions to similar problems, so inventive was his mind. Not least resourceful was his brilliance in modi-

---

[40] The varieties of site led to varieties of interiors determined by those sites; many were rectangular, some irregular (St. Stephen, Coleman Street), coffin-shaped (St. Olave, Old Jewry), and even angular oval (St. Benet, Fink).

fying the ceilings of his interiors. One is impressed by the great variety in Wren's earlier city interiors, granted that he had committed himself in favour of an aisled and galleried type of church for the "Reformed" Church of England. It is significant that there are plans for plain rectangles with or without a single aisle. There are plans for a cross in a square with intersecting vaults or domes above. There are plans for domes on squares and domes on polygons.[41]

Another way of looking at Wren's interior plans is to divide them into two main groups, the one consisting of large oblong churches and the other of small square churches.[42] One example of the large, oblong church is St. Bride's, Fleet Street (begun in 1670), the nave and aisles of which were divided by arcades, supported by large doubled columns established on high bases. Galleries were arranged above the aisles. The nave had a large barrel vault that was plastered, and was lighted by oval clerestory windows. St. James's, Piccadilly (1682) is another example of a long oblong church that Wren himself regarded as one of his greatest successes, for he recommended its plan as being commodious, economical, convenient, and beautiful in his memorandum prepared about 1710, already referred to. A gallery, supported on square wooden piers, runs round three sides of the interior. At the level of the gallery small columns of the Corinthian order carry the barrel-vaulted roof, and each bay has a small barrel at right-angles to the main vaulting of the nave. St. James's Church has fine fittings; the carved reredos and font were the work of Grinling Gibbons. The gilded plasterwork of the ceiling, with its bosses and gilding, was richly finished.[43]

But the most triumphant solution of a difficult site problem was the planning of St. Stephen, Walbrook,[44] the most brilliant of the smaller square type of church to be built (1672-1679). The site is squat, but the plan suggests spaciousness within, so accomplished is its design. Yet the dimensions of the building do not exceed 82 by 60 feet.[45] How is this effect achieved? Although the shape of the site was oblong, he made one bay at the west into a miniature nave, thus enabling him to bring the central space into

[41] Gerald Cobb, *The Old Churches of London* (1942), p. 10.

[42] Whinney, *op. cit.*, p. 52.

[43] A church of very similar design but with even richer plastering and gilding on the ceiling, moreover one containing Wren's only apse, was St. Clement Dane's, begun in 1680.

[44] See illustration in the section following p. 30 of this book.

[45] A. L. Drummond, *op. cit.*, p. 36.

a square. In brief, the plan is a cross-in-square with a large central dome. What is particularly ingenious is the refusal to use the usual plan of bringing the square into a circle by erecting a dome on pendentives above the four arches made by the ends of the vaults. Instead of this, Wren arranged for the dome to rest upon eight equal arches carried on twelve columns.[46] The four corners have flat ceilings, and Wren inserted windows into the flat ceilings to give a maximum of light. Small sections of groined vaults cover the space between the windows, and the latter help to support the dome. The complex roof, held up by sixteen columns, with plain shafts, which contrasted with the rough and richly textured plaster-work above, is striking. Each type of ceiling is combined here: flat, groined, domical, and pendentive. Similarly, the arrangement of the columns suggests a Greek cross, a circle, and a polygon, in its complexity. It is intriguing to see how John Wesley regarded this church, as reported in his *Journal* entry for December 4, 1758: "I was desired to step into the little church behind the Mansion House, commonly called St. Stephen's, Walbrook. It is nothing grand, but neat and elegant beyond expression, so that I do not wonder at the speech of the famous Italian architect who met Lord Burlington in Italy, 'My Lord, go back and see St. Stephen's in London. We have not so fine a piece of architecture in Rome.' " Other domical churches built by Wren are St. Mary, Abchurch, and St. Mildred, Bread Street.

Wren's resourcefulness in his interiors was even exceeded in his steeples. Some were in stone, and others were of lead. While the main work of building the churches was completed by 1685, many of the steeples were added fifteen or twenty years later. By that time London had recovered its prosperity, and Wren's maturity coincided with the greater opulence that was available. So splendid was the effect of Wren's spires on the architectural silhouette of London that it almost looked "as if the shipping on the river had somehow spread itself over the lands." These heaven-pointing spears formed "a train to St. Paul's, stretching from the East up to the Cathedral, as it looked towards the setting sun, with Christ Church, St. Martin and St. Bride as forerunners."[47]

[46] Whinney, *op. cit.*, pp. 64ff.
[47] Cobb (*op. cit.*, p. 56) offers a most elaborate classification of the varieties of Wren's steeples. One group is of plain towers with pierced parapet. Another is a series of towers with parapets enriched with urns, pineapples, obelisks. A third includes towers with bell-cages or turrets (lead covered). A fourth group is of towers with bell-cages or lanterns on domes, pyramids or steps. A fifth se-ries is distinguished by elaborations of the bell-turret. A sixth group consists of

St. Mary-le-Bow is exceptional both in that it was finished at the same time as the church in 1680, and soared to the height of 225 feet. Since the true Londoner is defined as one born within the sound of Bow bells, it was a particularly important commission, rendered the more difficult by the juxtaposition of high buildings at Cheapside. Not only is the belfry emphasised by coupled Ionic pilasters at each corner, but there is an elegant arcade immediately above it which marks the transition from square to rounded shape, and the cylindrical core is surrounded by a colonnade, with another balustrade above it. The next higher story is a group of twelve inverted brackets, Wren's version of "bows," and the next higher story reverts to the square shape with small Corinthian columns. This leads to a high pyramid or obelisk, bearing a weathervane in the form of a dragon. Never before had a classical steeple of many stories been seen in England, nor would Wren have visited one in France. Its origin is Italian.[48] No other steeple of Wren's exploits so many ideas in different stories.

St. Bride's, Fleet Street[49] is about 10 feet higher than Bow steeple. It has a more unified design, with four octagonal diminishing stories and an octagonal pyramid at the top. Inside is an open stone staircase.

Christ Church, Newgate Street (1704), also has a single idea, that of a group of five diminishing squares, the middle story consisting of a free-standing Ionic colonnade of great elegance, through which the sky can be seen, and which contrasts perfectly with the solid belfry square with pilasters, two stories below.

There are more Baroque variations in steeple design. One of them is St. Vedast, Foster Lane (1694-1697), for above the rectangular belfry the stories are concave, convex, and concave again.

---

towers with built-up spires in stone, and a seventh with towers having true spires. The eighth group is of towers with octagonal trumpet-shaped spires of lead. Group nine is of towers with built-up spires mainly concave in outline. The tenth group consists of a single tower with lantern, dome and spire (St. Magnus Martyr). There are churches with Gothic stone towers forming the eleventh and twelfth groups, the former being distinguished by pinnacles and the latter has a single example (St. Dunstan's-in-the-East) of a tower with a spire on arches. This over-elaboration of categories does at least illustrate Wren's fecundity of invention. *Ibid.*, p. 41 for the steeple of St. Mary-le-Bow.

[48] Margaret Whinney (*op. cit.*, p. 72) states that the best known example is Antonio de Sangallo's model for St. Peter's, which had twin western towers of this type, showing a transition from two lower square stories to two higher round ones. The idea of multi-storied classical steeples first appeared in print, however, in Alberti's *De re aedificatoria*.

[49] This is reproduced in Horton Davies, *Worship and Theology in England* (1961), III, following p. 38.

This example is reminiscent of Borromini's more dramatic S. Ivo della Sapienza in Rome, but the pilasters are more reticent in their projection than Borromini's. Other startling steeples are St. Michael, Paternoster Royal (completed in 1713) which has columns projecting from an octagonal core, with superimposed vases, and St. James, Garlickhythe (1714-1717) which is similar except for paired columns on four of the eight faces. The most splendid of all are the western towers of St. Paul's Cathedral.

Unusual steeples include St. Magnus Martyr (completed 1705) which moves from the square belfry stage into an octagon carrying a small lead cupola with leaden lantern and small spire above. Here the borrowing seems to have come from the Jesuit church at Antwerp,[50] dedicated to St. Charles Borromeo. Another unique steeple is that of St. Martin, Ludgate, where the top story of the stone tower is octagonal, on which there is an ogee dome in lead, with a balcony below the lantern, all culminating in a very slender obelisk and ball. Here as in all Wren's work is God's plenty for variety and ingenuity.

4. St. Paul's Cathedral

His crowning ecclesiastical work was, however, St. Paul's Cathedral. Even here, however, he was far from getting his own favourite design approved, but had to settle for a compromise between his wishes and those of the dean and canons of the Cathedral.

Wren's own wish was to provide an entirely novel design in England—in the shape of a four equal-armed Greek cross, with an extension to the west. The latter, according to the Great Model plan as Wren's preferred design is known, ended in a vestibule entered by a large Corinthian portico which was to be covered with a small dome. The four arms of the cross were linked with concave walls and over the centre of the church was a dome supported by eight piers allowing complete circulation around their bases. It would have been a vast cathedral for the base of the dome would have been 120 feet, only 17 feet smaller than St. Peter's and 8 feet wider than the dome finally erected.

Wren's design was a brilliant amalgam from several sources, but united by its fine proportions and the lucid subordination of the parts to the whole. The dome's drum borrows from Bramante and the ribbed section above from Michelangelo. The Corinthian portico was taken over from Inigo Jones, while the domed vestibule

---

[50] Whinney, op. cit., pp. 77-78.

probably came from Sangallo's design for St. Peter's. The arrangement of the dome over eight piers, instead of the conventional four, was almost certainly derived from a design of Mansart's. In Wren's Great Model plan, however, the hints of borrowings are fused into a grand and noble unity.[51]

The plan, however, fell foul of the conservatism of the dean and chapter of St. Paul's. The clergy hardly considered any church a true church unless it were built according to the Latin cross plan, and they were particularly concerned to emphasize their continuity with the great church of the medieval centuries. Furthermore, they had two practical considerations in mind in opting for a two-room design instead of the vastly impressive single room that Wren was offering them. For one thing they envisaged a cathedral as providing a choir for regular daily services and a nave when larger congregations were expected, on Sundays, festivals, and state occasions. In addition, it would mean that their plan could be achieved in two separate parts, for the choir could be finished first and the nave extended as further funds became available. The Great Model plan did not have a separate choir, and all that remained of such was the area between the eastern apse and the beginning of the dome. Furthermore, it was not possible to build the cathedral in instalments. As soon as the eastern end should be completed, all eight piers would have to be erected to provide a roof for the cathedral.

Wren had no alternative but to accept a compromise, despite the impropriety of building a Renaissance church on a medieval cruciform plan.[52] His second design is known as the Warrant design, and dates from May 14, 1675, seven years after the commencement of planning for the Great Model. The Royal Warrant indicates that Wren was allowed by King Charles II "the liberty in the prosecution of his work, to make variations, rather ornamental than essential, as from time to time he should see proper."[53] The Warrant design was that of a Latin cross, with a choir of three bays and a nave of five bays. The east was to have an extra demi-bay and an apse. Each transept of three bays was to be entered through an inset porch, with a large projecting portico at the west of the nave. There was a dome carried on eight piers at the crossing. This plan would have allowed the choir to be built

[51] Ibid., pp. 89-90.

[52] See the criticisms of Drummond, op. cit., p. 36.

[53] The Royal Warrant with its designs attached is to be found in the Library of All Souls College, Oxford.

separately and used before the rest of the church was started. The most striking feature of the exterior of the Warrant design was the termination of the dome by a tall spire of six diminishing stories, similar to what he was eventually to build at St. Bride's, Fleet Street.

Yet there are considerable differences between the executed plan and the Warrant design. Wren must obviously have used the latitude allowed him by the Royal Warrant to the utmost and extending from ornamentals even to essentials. One great difference was apparent early. This was that the walls were to be taken to the height of two stories,[54] instead of merely to aisle height as shown in the Warrant design. This gave an immediate effect of grandeur and spaciousness. Furthermore, the walls had a new elegance in the execution, for the single strips of Inigo Jones were replaced by double pilasters. Among other important modifications of the Warrant plan was the reduction of the nave from five bays to three. Further, at the west end of the nave a larger bay was to be added, and this was to be covered with a small dome and on each side of it were to be chapels. Other changes were the additions of two semicircular porticos which replace the flat colonnades on the transept fronts. The great drum of the dome is a variation upon Bramante's design, but with a brilliant addition providing a solid interval between the columns at every fourth intercolumniation to prevent the contrast between the open columns in the western towers being too great.[55] The dome itself is a work of surpassing beauty as well as of technical brilliance, and it is topped by a large stone lantern, reminiscent of the west towers, and thus stressing the unity and interrelationship of the entire building. The cross at the top of the lantern is 365 feet above the ground.[56] The interior radiates with light, and would have done so even more in Wren's own day, when the windows had plain, not Victorian stained glass. The great central space makes the overwhelming impact he intended and irresistibly draws the eyes upwards.[57]

[54] Yet the impression these walls give that the aisles are raised to the height of two stories is a trick, for the upper part of each wall is false since the windows of the choir are set several feet behind it. Behind the false walls are stepped flying buttresses over the aisle roofs to help to support the dome.

[55] Whinney, op. cit., p. 105.

[56] Wren rightly rejected the six diminishing stories of the Warrant design's spire surmounting the dome. Also his complex western towers were greatly improved in the executed design. The latter also included small windows low in the walls for lighting the crypt, and the modification of the Warrant design.

[57] The impact of the central space would be greater in Wren's day because he closed the east vista from under the dome by a screen with the great organ above it. Thus he stressed the centralized planning of his Cathedral.

The greatest seventeenth-century church in England had been thirty-five years in building. The foundation stone was laid on the southeastern corner of the building on June 21, 1675, and the work was finished in 1710, when the final accounts were made up. This masterpiece had cost £738,845 5s. 2½d.[58] and the exhilarating exhaustion of its architect. It was the first cathedral England had built since the Reformation and it was in the new style.

St. Paul's is the finest example of the splendid fittings of Wren's churches. They set the standard for Restoration England and were its particular pride. The sculptural possibilities of the exterior of St. Paul's were fully utilized in a way that was not possible for the churches on their hemmed in and cramped sites, and the woodcarving of the interior and the wrought-iron were of the very highest standard.

Grinling Gibbons[59] carved the twenty-six delicate and different stone panels beneath the great round-headed windows, with their exquisite flowers, foliage, fruit, and cherubs. Jonathan Maine carved similar panels on the exterior of the west chapels. The transept fronts were also richly ornamented with their chains of fruit and flowers hanging down the sides of the central windows. Moreover, each of the pediments above has carvings set in the curved lunettes. The carving on the south transept front exhibits a phoenix rising from the ashes, a symbol alike of Christ's resurrection and of the re-emergence of the Cathedral. This is the noble work of Caius Gabriel Cibber. Gibbons's less distinguished work on the north transept front displays the royal arms flanked by two unconvincing angels. The dean's door is embellished by the elegant carvings of William Kempster, with coiling scrolls, life-like cherubs' heads, and delicate wreaths and fronds as good as Gibbons when the latter is in top form.

The wood-carving of the choir stalls and the screen behind them exhibits Grinling Gibbons at his superb best. He also carved the rich and complicated organ case. Both works have brilliantly devised scrolls, fruit, flowers and heads of cherubs or full length angels.

The ironwork of St. Paul's is splendid, especially the wrought-

[58] Whinney, *op. cit.*, pp. 97, 105.

[59] Gibbons is not well represented in London, with the exceptions of St. Paul's and his reredoses at St. James, Piccadilly and St. Mary Abchurch. Horace Walpole caught the essence of his art in the statement that he "gave to wood the loose and airy lightness of flowers, and chained them together in a fine disorder natural to each species." *Anecdotes of Painting*, II (edn. 1859), p. 552.

iron gates that are the work of Jean Tijou the Huguenot in 1698. These gates are at the east end of the choir and are a series of complex and interwoven variations on acanthus leaves. They make an exceedingly effective contrast between the gilded and plain iron-work of the gates creating a rich effect.

The dominant Protestantism[60] in the City of London, reinforced by the defection of James II to Roman Catholicism, forbade the use of paintings behind the altars or on the walls or cupolas, as well as the sculpture of saints required for the Baroque Catholic churches on the Continent. Thus Wren was prevented from imitating the most striking effects of Baroque architecture and the collaboration of the architect with painters and figure sculptors. He made up for this restriction at least in part, by encouraging the production of outstanding wood-carving, and occasionally also of high relief in plaster, and, sometimes, of wrought-iron work. Even here, however, economy as well as a dislike of flashy exuberance and theatricality restrained Wren.

The most impressive examples of fittings and furnishings in Wren's churches deserve at least a fleeting tribute. Generally, the Communion tables were simply carved. The notable exception was that of St. Stephen, Coleman Street, which was supported by four eagles and a straddling cherub.[61] Altar rails were usually of the balustrade shape. They were of richly carved and twisted wood at St. Stephen's, Coleman Street, and at St. Mary-at-Hill. Occasionally they were of wrought-iron, as at St. Mary, Woolnoth. In one single case, at All Hallows, Barking, they were of brass.[62]

Pulpits, in conformity with Wren's conception of the importance of "auditories" in which the age shared, were particularly imposing in both position and decoration. St. Mildred, Bread Street, had a polygonal sounding-board. St. James, Garlickhythe had twisted railed-in steps leading to the pulpit, and there were carved swags on the pulpit sides. The carving in St. Stephen, Walbrook, was even more elaborate, for it boasted cherubs, sea-shells, and swags on the sounding-board and enrichments on the sides of the pulpit. Full and detailed carving also marked the pulpit of St. Edmund the King, Lombard Street.[63]

[60] Resurgent national Protestantism on the part of both Anglicans and Nonconformists was expressed in great affirmations of loyalty to William and Mary and in gratitude for the re-establishment of the Protestant succession to the throne. This spilled over into architecture and ecclesiastical fittings, in part in the determination to avoid the theatricality and multi-coloured effects of Baroque Catholicism.
[61] Whinney and Millar, *op. cit.*, p. 162.
[62] Cobb, *op. cit.*, p. 74.   [63] *Ibid.*, p. 75.

Richly carved reredoses could be found at St. Stephen, Walbrook, St. Mary-le-Bow, and a most elaborate one at St. Martin, Ludgate. Gibbons carved his only reredos in the old City of London at St. Mary Abchurch, but he provided a splendid reredos for the west end church of St. James, Piccadilly, depicting a pelican feeding her young from the flesh of her own breast, an apt, if medieval, symbol of the Eucharist.[64]

Carved font covers of unusual elegance included those of St. Giles, Cripplegate (an octagonal dome surmounted by a dove), St. Margaret, Lothbury (eight heads of cherubs topped by a flaming torch), and St. Swithin, Cannon Street (a domed cover with a crown above).[65]

Organ cases, too, offered carvers great opportunities. A simple one of great dignity was to be found in St. Margaret Pattens, with which should be contrasted the impressively detailed carving of the organ case at St. Lawrence Jewry.[66]

Other opportunities for the skilled carver were the sword rests for the Lord Mayor on his Sunday pilgrimages to the various City churches, stave-heads for beadles (often bearing the figure of the patron saint of the particular church), specially enriched pews for the churchwardens, the royal arms, tablets for memorials or lists of bequests to the poor, alms boxes, lecterns, and, particularly, enriched doors.

The plasterwork was, of course, largely limited to the ceilings of the churches, with vaulting, crossvaulting, and coffering. The high relief was most impressive, as previously indicated, in St. Stephen, Walbrook, and in St. Mary-le-Bow, Cheapside. Wren's earlier plasterwork tended to be exuberant, but his later work in the same medium, though still luxurious, was more controlled in design. He well understood the importance of contrasted textures and surfaces, both in the use of brick and stone for his exteriors, and in the use of contrasted high relief and flat plaster, together with wood and ironwork in the interiors. All over England and New England he was paid the supreme tribute of imitation.

After dining him, his friend John Evelyn noted in his Diary for May 5, 1681, that Sir Christopher Wren was actually engaged in building fifty churches at that time, leading him to conclude that "a wonderful genius had this incomparable person." Yet his

[64] *Ibid.*, and Whinney and Millar, *op. cit.*, p. 162.
[65] Cobb, *op. cit.*, p. 75.   [66] *Ibid.*

splendid achievements are not without their critics, nor without flaw or blemish.

The first criticism is that his churches are not traditionally Christian either in shape or in the emblems used in their decoration. They are accused of supplanting Christian symbolism with Erastian and pagan decoration.[67] Wren unquestionably gave the lead in England on a wide scale in introducing a medley of urns, swags, scrolls, fruit, flowers, foliage, cherubs—later to be followed by willows, skulls, hour-glasses and such macabre symbols—into churches, though they were relatively commonplace features of Baroque decoration on the Continent at this time. Here the contrast with the surviving medievalism of Archbishop Laud and his party was strong, except, of course, for the Erastianism[68] displayed in the royal arms which Laud had approved as a vigorous supporter of the divine right of kings. In brief, Wren was not traditional enough in the shape of his buildings (as his struggle with the dean and chapter of St. Paul's demonstrates) or his symbolism.

The opposite criticism, that he is not contemporary enough in exploiting all the possibilities of drama inherent in Baroque architecture and art has also been made. Such a criticism contrasts the intellectual clarity, love of proportion, reserve, simplicity, restricted palette, and coldness of Wren's churches with the emotional excitement, geometrical strainings,[69] surprises, complexities and variegated colours of contemporary southern Baroque churches of the same period. The visual brilliance of the ceiling of Il Gesù combining painting and sculpture, the tension in the concave surfaces of Borromini's S. Carlo alle Quatro Fontane, and Bernini's moving statue of Saint Teresa in the jewelled casket of the Cornaro Chapel, as well as his towering and serpentine balddachino over the high altar of St. Peter's and his Cathedra Petri supported on four bish-

[67] A. L. Drummond, *op. cit.*, p. 37, expresses this viewpoint with stridency.

[68] An example of rampant Erastianism is the gateway of All Hallows, Lombard Street. As for accusations of paganism, the amorous cupids or cherubs seem more often to be devotees of Venus than angelic servants of God. The Puritans, who are sometimes blamed for this unchristian symbolism (see J. D. Sedding, *Art and Handicraft*, 1893, pp. 36-37), were iconoclasts and neither Erastians nor pagans. Moreover, with the arrival of the Restoration of the monarchy Puritanism was defeated, but Catholic tradition was not restored either doctrinally or symbolically in decoration.

[69] Here I refer to some frenetic features of Baroque architecture or sculpture, such as the alternation of juxtaposed concave and convex shapes, the columns that twist in agony, the ovals that seem to have been created by elongating circles, not to mention the eternally agitated draperies of the marble statues as if they had been carved in the cave of the four winds. (See H. W. Janson, *History of Art* [1962], pp. 410f.)

ops and surmounted by the dove of infallible truth that disappears in a blaze of golden glory—these rightly have their ardent admirers. Baroque architecture, like the angelic dart that pierced the heart of Saint Teresa, transfixes the emotions. Such admirers[70] will find Wren's architecture practically colourless (except for the contrast of gold and white in some plastered ceilings or black and gold in very rare wrought-iron, and the very common contrast between brown wood and white walls), and his geometrical harmonies of design will seem coldly intellectual. They may find his work too reserved, and even occasionally insipid. But the grandeur and glitter that these critics seek were alien to the taste and temper of England and to the reasoned and pragmatic faith of those who would worship in the fanes he built.

If Wren's work in its vastness and fertile variety is not itself the fullest refutation of both sets of critics, then it may be counted to his credit that he rebuilt all the churches of a city and its Cathedral, on restricted finances, on hemmed in and awkward sites, and that he had only spent six months out of England visiting France (but never setting foot in Italy), and that perforce much of the details of the work had to be left to less gifted subordinates. The wonder is not that he occasionally repeated an idea, though never exactly, or that occasionally his invention flagged, but rather that he accomplished a gigantic task so well and gave to Anglicanism churches splendidly equipped for the reasoned exposition of Christian faith and duty, expressing such rational pragmatism in the well-lit clarity and good proportions of his sacred buildings.

5. Roman Catholic Chapels and Churches

The history of Roman Catholic church architecture in seventeenth-century England is largely limited to royal chapels built for the three Stuart queens and the last of the Stuart kings, James II. Catholicism was a forbidden faith until James II's open avowal of it, such services as were held even in aristocratic houses forbade the use of any but a disguised chapel.[71] A fugacious worship had

[70] Margaret Whinney and Oliver Millar, op. cit., pp. 155-56 relate this viewpoint without concurring in it.

[71] Even a chapel over the border in Wales, at Abergavenny, which informers about the Popish Plot in 1679 said was fully equipped for Catholic worship, when rediscovered in 1907 turned out to be no more than a long attic on the ceiling of which were the remains of a painting of the Adoration of the Magi, and there was a Jesuit emblem above one of the windows. (See *The Catholic Record Society*, Vol. XVIII, pp. 98-235.) For stirring accounts of the maintenance of Catholic worship in noble houses in recusant times, see Godfrey Anstruther,

to make do with ordinary tables and movable altar stones, pewter chalices, and equipment that could be easily dismantled. High Mass was unthinkable, and Low Mass had to be muttered in a murmur so as not to be overheard by disloyal servants who would report such gatherings to the authorities.[72] Private citizens however noble could not run the risk of building chapels for Catholic worship. The only time in the entire century when it was possible to build Catholic churches or chapels openly was during the brief reign of James II.

The first English chapel to be built without a trace of Gothic in its form or details was prepared originally in 1623 for the probable use of the Infanta of Spain whom Charles was then courting as Prince of Wales. This match was, however, never made and eventually Inigo Jones's Marlborough House Chapel, part of the complex of buildings of St. James's Palace, was fitted out for the use of Henrietta Maria, who eventually became the Queen of Charles I. It was thought impolitic to give it an ornate Baroque façade for England was officially a Protestant nation. Nonetheless, its restrained classicism of style distinguished it from its Gothic neighbours. It had a large "Venetian" window of Palladian style at the east end. Its ceiling was richly coffered. Behind the altar was elegant panelling and a painting, and there were, it is said, large statues of prophets in the arched niches of the sidewalls.[73] Here the social elite of London's Catholics attended Mass as they might in the embassy chapels of the Catholic powers, even though it was a royal and theoretically a private chapel.

Queen Henrietta Maria, however, wanted a more impressive chapel in the capital than that of Marlborough House and one designed solely for her. Again Inigo Jones was chosen as architect for the Somerset House Chapel. Externally it was restrained, if not undistinguished except for its great length of 100 feet, with two short transepts for the altars of the private chaplains of the Queen. The interior was resplendent in its glory. The nave was in the fashionable shape of a double cube. A gallery at the west end afforded seclusion for the Queen and her attendants. The arches were round-headed or pedimented and the ceiling was coffered and

---

O. P., *Vaux of Harrowden, A Recusant Family* (Newport, Monmouthshire, 1953) and R. J. Stonor, O.S.B., *Stonor: a Catholic Sanctuary in the Chilterns* (Newport, Monmouthshire, 2nd edn., 1952).

[72] Bryan Little, *Catholic Churches since 1623* (1966), p. 23.

[73] *Ibid.*, p. 21.

brilliant with its contrast of gold and white. The screen was a masterpiece of carving, with its fluted Doric columns, herms, and crests.[74]

Queen Henrietta Maria's French Baroque taste was more fully exemplified in her Chapel at Oatlands, where she had engaged her fellow-countryman, Simon Vouet, to paint a ceiling depicting the Blessings of Faith and Love—what sinister suspicion led her to exclude Hope from the trio?—under the union of lilies and roses, symbolizing her marriage.[75]

The Civil War's ravage and the iconoclasm of the Commonwealth led to the sacking of both the Marlborough House and the Somerset House Chapels. With the Restoration of the monarch, Charles II's Queen, Catherine of Braganza, chose first to use the refitted Chapel in St. James's Palace and then the refurnished Chapel of Somerset House.

It was only at the end of the reign of Charles II and particularly in that of his successor (James II) that Roman Catholic worship in all its Counter-Reformation vigour and confidence sought for its appropriate architectural expression. Here at last was the chance that the advocates of the divine right of kings (and therefore of absolute monarchy) and of Catholic supremacy had been waiting for—to build, paint, and sculpt in the new Baroque style as was being done with such dramatic splendour in France, Italy, and Flanders.

Charles II had commissioned May as architect, Gibbons as sculptor, and Verrio as painter to transform the Tudor private chapel at Windsor Castle by creating a coruscatingly brilliant interior. On the ceiling was a tempestuous fresco of the Ascension, and the north wall exhibited a series of scenes of the miracles of Christ. There was also an elaborate colonnade and an open sky. This was the most theatrical chapel to have been built in England up to this time.[76]

Breathtaking as the new Windsor Royal Chapel was, even it could not match the almost Mariolatrous iconography of the new Royal Chapel built by the command of James II at his Palace of Whitehall by Sir Christopher Wren. The exterior was unassuming in its brick and stone, but the interior was stunning, from the

---

[74] *Ibid.*, p. 22.

[75] Whinney and Millar, *op. cit.*, p. 287.

[76] *Ibid.*, pp. 299-300. See also G. Webb, "Baroque Art" in *Proceedings of the British Academy*, XXXIII (1947) for an analysis of the fittings and architecture of this Royal Chapel.

towering altarpiece by Gennari to the superb ceiling painting of the Assumption of the Blessed Virgin into a heaven crowded with Verrio's figures, not forgetting the four marble statues by Gibbons. Its impact is unforgettably conveyed by Evelyn:

> I went to heare the music of the Italians in the New Chapel now first opened publickly at Whitehall for the Popish service. Nothing can be finer than the magnificent marblework and architecture at the end, where are four statues representing St. John, St. Peter, St. Paul, and the Church, in white marble, the work of Mr. Gibbons, with all the carving and pillars of exquisite art and great cost. The Altar-piece is the Salutation; the volta in fresca, the Assumption of the Blessed Virgin according to their tradition, with our Saviour and a world of figures painted by Verrio.[77]

A few far less dramatic churches were built for Catholic worship under the protection afforded by James II's Declaration of Indulgence of 1687. Of two erected in London, one was run by the Franciscans and it was in the west end. Two others were staffed by Jesuits, a modest one in Wigan, and a more spacious one in Newcastle-upon-Tyne. The new church on which the fullest information is available was built for Birmingham Catholics under the leadership of Father Leo Randolph.[78]

It was partly financed by the donation of 180 tons of lumber from the king's forest in Staffordshire. It was in the form of a Latin cross, but the transepts were only large enough to accommodate side chapels each 15 feet square. The nave was 80 feet by 33 feet and the sanctuary was 15 feet long by 23 feet wide, thus providing an overall length of 95 feet. The nave had no pillars to obscure the people's view of the high altar. The chief altarpiece framed by two Corinthian pillars, showed the Risen Christ appearing to Mary Magdalene. The side altars had reredoses formed by two Corinthian pillars each. One had a painting of the Virgin and the other of St. Francis. Yet, despite their Baroque elements, these churches for reasons of economy, temperament, and taste, "were closer in spirit to Wren than to the Fontanas or Borromini."[79]

---

[77] *Diary*, entry for October 18, 1685.
[78] See Oscott Mss., Introduction to Register Book of St. Peter's, Birmingham, printed in *Warwickshire Parish Registers* (1904). The information is also summarized in Little, *op. cit.*, p. 25.
[79] Little, *op. cit.*

6. *Puritan and Quaker Meeting-Houses*

The contrast between Catholic and Puritan churches could hardly be more sharp, though the furtive conditions in which both groups met in penal days were much alike. But the Catholics loved the drama and colour forbidden to Recusants, while the Puritans feared both as distractions to divine obedience and human duty.

After the Restoration the Puritans found the religious and political atmosphere unpropitious for the development of an appropriate type of church architecture. When they had been tolerated by or dominant in the religious establishment (from 1644 to 1660), there were numerous Anglican churches available for their use. In fact, they even divided some of the cathedrals for multi-congregational use. Exeter Cathedral choir, to take a notable example, was used by the Presbyterians (as "East St. Peter's"), and the nave by the Independents (as "West St. Peter's") during the interregnum.[80]

After St. Bartholomew's Day, 1662, the Nonconformists (as Puritans then refusing to accept the Restoration Settlement of Religion became known), being forbidden to worship according to their conscience were forced to gather secretly in houses and warehouses. Occasional and fitful Acts of Indulgence and the growing Protestantism of the Church of England (partly in reaction to James II's open avowal of Roman Catholicism) led the Nonconformists to hope for inclusion (or "Comprehension" in the noun of that day) in the Church of England. This tended to make the heirs of the Puritan and Calvinist tradition content with makeshift arrangements for worship. The consequence was that when it was finally realised that the hope of reunion was a delusion, the Nonconformists had become habituated to these simple and functional domestic buildings. Furthermore, when the time came for them to think of erecting their own meeting-houses in 1688 and afterwards, so many were needed (and all to be supplied at the voluntary charge of the Dissenters), that economy became a further reason for simplicity and even austerity. Thus the typical impression made by a late seventeenth-century meeting-house is that of a square with a double row of windows looking like a rather squat and wholly staid domestic building, utterly lacking any sense of the numinous. As Drummond points out, if the rectangular plan

---

[80] See John Stoughton, *Religion in England* . . . (1884), Vol. II, p. 366, and W. J. Harte, *Devonshire Association Transactions* (1937), pp. 44ff. Wells and Worcester Cathedrals were also used for Puritan services.

had been more often employed than the square, it would not have been necessary for the spacious meeting-houses to have the roofs designed in two parallel ridges with several obtrusive interior supports.[81]

The Puritan tradition was, of course, exceedingly suspicious of ostentation in general (after all, the God of all the earth could outdo man in grandeur, so why enter into competition with Him whose Son's Incarnation was in the stable of an inn?), and of colour in particular. This was to result in two distinguishing characteristics. The first was an emphasis on form, which is often lost in flashy splendour or intricacies of detail, and this expressed clarity, simplicity, and dignity. The second was a preference for sobriety in colour, which meant white or grey, with the brown of the woodwork as a contrast. There was, generally, good workmanship but little elegance. Nor would one find a contrast of textures, aspiration in steeples or towers, the curving delight of cupolas, the ingenuity and complexity of Gibbons's carved cornucopias or, least of all, the eye-deceiving skyscapes of Verrio.

There were some intriguing foreshadowings of the fully developed Independent and Presbyterian meeting-houses. Such anticipations could be found either in the sacred buildings of other radical religious groups, or in the occasional rare and now surviving Puritan chapels on the estates of the Puritan gentry. The former group were houses for worship built by the Baptists or the Quakers, who never had any hope of inclusion in any religious establishment, not even Cromwell's. For both groups, therefore, there was no reason for postponing their simple architectural needs. The buildings of the early Baptists and Quakers were very similar in style, as might be expected. They may well share a common ancestry in the stricter group of Dutch Mennonites—the Waterlanders.[82] Each religious group insisted on the importance of possessing rather than merely professing a Christian faith, as well as on the significance of the "inner light" or the indwelling of the Holy Spirit in the individual. Both groups revalued the Sacraments, and both insisted on the democratic rights of all men (and women, too, in the case of the Quakers) to testify publicly of their religious experience. Neither

[81] *The Church Architecture of Protestantism* (Edinburgh, 1934), p. 42. Wren, using a rectangle on many occasions, employed his piers to support roofs and even galleries, but far less obtrusively than in the square meeting-houses.

[82] See Bernard Picart, *Cérémonies et Coûtumes Religieuses de tous les Peuples du Monde* (Amsterdam, 1736), tome IV, p. 200, and H. L. Short's article in *The Listener*, "Changing Styles of Nonconformist Architecture," issue of March 17, pp. 471ff.

group had an ordained ministry. The latter is reflected strikingly in the absence of any pulpit in the earliest Quaker and Baptist[83] churches—a very marked difference from the dominating two or three decker pulpits of the Puritan meeting-houses. Instead of a pulpit there is a long bench, usually raised slightly above floor level, in front of which there was often a low panelled wall.[84] On such a bench the Quaker elders or the Baptist messengers sat facing the rest of the congregation as *primi inter pares*, just—to adapt Orwell's phrase—slightly more equal than others. As each could and did testify to the Spirit within, there was no need for an elevated place from which a single leader could address the assembled congregation.[85]

These simpler anticipations of the developed Puritan meeting-house had "the quality of a well-scoured farmhouse kitchen."[86] Their similarity is easily discernible if one compares the Jordans Quaker meeting-house (1688) in Buckinghamshire with Cote Baptist Chapel (1657) in Oxfordshire. The floors would be of stone or tiles, the open seats or forms of oak, the walls whitewashed, the windows of clear glass, and wainscoting on the lower part of the walls when it could be afforded. The only distinguishing mark would be the raised seat for elders or messengers. The impression is that of simplicity, sincerity, and austerity; and appropriately so, since the early Baptists and Quakers were the Cistercians of English Nonconformity.

There are also a few early Dissenting buildings, belonging to neither Baptists nor Quakers, which may also be forerunners of the fully developed Nonconformist meeting-houses. One of these is a thatched cottage at Horningsham,[87] Wiltshire, which is

[83] There is a pulpit in the seventeenth-century Particular Baptist Chapel at Tewkesbury, Worcestershire, but its exact age is difficult to determine. The interior of the chapel is illustrated in Davies, *op. cit.*, III, p. 38.

[84] Short, *op. cit.*, pp. 471f.

[85] One would expect a simple Communion table to differentiate early Baptist from Quaker meeting-houses. Since, however, one early group of English Baptists (led by Helwys the apostle of religious toleration) was deeply influenced by the Mennonites in Holland where the English had fled as refugees, and since the Mennonites of the Waterland group held the Lord's Supper only once each year, they might have copied them in this respect. If this were so, then it would be a simple matter to bring a table into the meeting-house annually. The Calvinistic or Particular Baptists, it should be emphasised, were, with the single exception of Believers' Baptism which they practised, very close to the Independents in the matter of worship, and celebrated the Lord's Supper frequently and also ordained their ministers towards the end of the century and used pulpits for their preaching.

[86] John Betjeman, *First and Last Loves* (1952), pp. 90f.

[87] Martin S. Briggs, *Puritan Architecture and Its Future* (1946), p. 14.

claimed to have been built in 1566 by Sir John Thynne for the Scots (and Presbyterian masons) who were imported for building his palatial residence at nearby Longleat. Although it has for centuries been used by Independents (later known as Congregationalists), this represents a transplanted Scottish kirk rather than an indigenous Independent chapel. There are also other chapels of the utmost simplicity for which early dates are claimed. One is the "Ancient Chapel of Toxteth" near Liverpool, supposed to have been built in 1618, but which was extensively reconstructed in 1773. There is also an ancient Independent chapel at Walpole[88] in Suffolk, built about 1647. This is certainly a likelier date than the Toxteth Chapel. Its exterior is indistinguishable from that of two twin-storied semi-detached cottages; its interior, however, has the high pulpit on one long wall, the central Communion table, and the three galleries facing the pulpit, which were probably added considerably later. Indeed, the presence of galleries and the high pulpit necessitated by them suggests that the two cottages were used in penal days for worship and that when Toleration arrived, the interiors were remodelled. In this case, then Walpole would represent an important transition between the cottage church and the meeting-house. Another claimant to distinction as a pioneering church is St. Mary's Independent Chapel, Broadstairs,[89] Kent. It is claimed that this was first equipped for worship in 1601 by the local Puritan family of the Culmers. It has been carefully restored. The existence of these and other ancient Puritan chapels,[90] and the unhampered development of Puritan architecture in New England,[91] provided the prototypes of developed Dissenting meeting-houses.

When Charles II authorised the Declaration of Indulgence in 1671/2, permitting the use of non-Anglican places of worship, over 2,500 licenses were applied for within ten months. It is very probable, however, that most of the meetings for worship were held in private houses or in public rooms. The habitual use of temporary buildings, the simplicity and functionalism of the prototypes considered, the self-supporting character or Dissenting reli-

[88] *Ibid.*, p. 17.   [89] *Ibid.*, p. 19.

[90] Another family chapel was that erected in 1647 at Bramhope by the Puritan Robert Dynely of the adjacent Hall near Ottley, Yorkshire. It has belated Gothic details, but is still a building of great simplicity.

[91] Where wood usually replaced stone, with frequent ingenuity and great elegance, and Puritan worship could be celebrated openly a generation before the establishment of the Commonwealth in England, and two generations before the Glorious Revolution of 1688.

gious communities, the urgently rapid need for many buildings simultaneously as well as for great economy in building them, and the consistently Calvinist character of the worship of Dissent— all helped to determine the shape of the fully fledged meeting-houses of the late seventeenth century. Final permission to build was granted only in 1689, after twenty-seven years of persecution, only fitfully eased by occasional Indulgences.

From that year of great relief for Nonconformity, 1689, to the end of the century, a total of 2,418 buildings was registered for public worship by Presbyterians, Independents, and Baptists, besides many Quaker meeting-houses. From that era there survive, in whole or in part, a considerable number of Dissenting meeting-houses.[92]

It would be difficult, even if profitable, to describe all these meeting-houses in detail, since they are all built very much in the same unostentatious manner. At the risk of creating a stereotype, an attempt will be made to describe a typical larger meeting-house of the period, of which those at Norwich (the Old Meeting built in 1693), Ipswich (Friar Street built in 1700), and Taunton (Mary Street built in 1721) are representative.

Their model, as has been cogently argued by Principal H. L. Short of Manchester College, Oxford, would be no new-fangled adaptation of Wren's Anglicanism—for the Anglicans were their persecutors in this period—but what they tried to do in the parish churches when they had power, namely to follow Calvin and the manner of the best Reformed churches in Europe.[93] They would now renounce all relics of pre-Reformation times in their meeting-

[92] The following list of surviving meeting-houses was made by the architect, Martin Briggs near the end of the Second World War in 1946, in *op. cit.*, p. 23. Dampier Street, Bridgewater, Somerset, is dated 1688, and Brook Street, Knutsford and King Edward Street, Macclesfield, both in Cheshire, from 1689. Box Lane, Boxmoor, Hertfordshire, was built in 1690, and St. Saviourgate, York, in 1692. Norwich Old Meeting, a distinguished meeting-house, was built in 1693, as was Dean Row, Stockport, Cheshire; and in the next year Elder Row, Chesterfield, Derbyshire, was erected. Waterside, Newbury, Berkshire and Dagger Lane, Hull, Yorkshire, date from 1697; and in 1699 the Presbyterian (now Unitarian) Chapel, Gloucester, the Watergate Chapel, Lewes, Sussex, and Doddridge Chapel, Northampton, as well as Upper Chapel, Sheffield, were all built. Another splendid chapel, Friar Street, Ipswich was built in 1700, also Tottlebank Chapel, near Ulverstone, in the Lake District. Later meeting-houses were: Rook Lane, Frome, Somerset (1707); Great Meeting, Leicester (1708); Churchgate Street, Bury St. Edmunds (1711); Chinley (1711); High Street, Portsmouth (1714); the famous Cross Street, Manchester (1715); and the elegant Mary Street, Taunton, Somerset (1721); and Crediton (1721).

[93] See "The Architecture of the Old Meeting Houses," *Transactions of the Unitarian Historical Society*, Vol. 8, No. 3 (1944), pp. 98-112.

houses, eliminating towers and spires, transepts, apses, or chancels. Most distinctive would be their arrangement of the pulpit against a long wall (north or south), with a centrally placed Communion table, with the minister presiding like a father at a meal of the family—Calvin's eucharistic arrangement at St. Pierre in Geneva and copied in the great Nieuwe Kerk in Amsterdam, familiar to most religious radicals exiled from England in Holland's hospitable and tolerant land. The pews would face the Communion table from three sides, and the holy table itself would be railed or surrounded by a Communion pew which was often occupied by the poor on non-sacramental Sundays. It was curiously conservative that they built their churches with a main east-west axis, for the absence of an altar at the east end made such orientation quite unnecessary. Equally curious was their placement of the pulpit on a south wall, flanked by round-headed clear windows through which the morning sun shone with brilliance to cause those in pews facing the pulpit extreme discomfort. The only architectural distinction that can be made between the two sets of Calvinists, the Presbyterians and the Independents concerns the fittings for the Lord's Supper. It seems that the Independents preferred a small Communion table from which the minister took the consecrated elements to the people sitting in their pews, while the Presbyterians favoured a long table at which all the church members sat, passing the bread and wine that had been blessed to each other. Galleries were provided in many meeting-houses, and there was good precedent for this in the great three stories of galleries in the Huguenot Temple at Charenton, near Paris. Galleries in meeting-houses were either single—that is, over the door and opposite the pulpit—or, on the three sides not occupied by the pulpit. These were, as in the case of Wren's churches, clearly auditory, designed for the hearing of God's Word, but also particularly designed around a central Communion table.

Their exteriors were built of good brick (Churchgate Street, Bury St. Edmunds had notable brickwork), with hipped roofs, and were covered with tiles but lacked gables. Doorways were decorated with the usual classical columns or pilasters common to the middle-class dwellings of the times. They were well-proportioned, but rarely ornate. The windows had either flat or semi-circular tops and were divided into small panes with good leadwork. The chapels at Bury St. Edmunds and Friar Street, Ipswich, as well as St. Mary's, Taunton, also had elegant oval windows. Walls were white-washed and the polished dark brown wood of the pews contrasted well with them. Similarly, a simple beauty was discovered in the contrast between the open rails or balustrading on the pulpit stairs and the solid panels of the pulpit itself, surmounted by a sturdy canopy or sounding-board. Occasionally there would be carving on the pulpit, and even, though rarely, on the gallery fronts. St. Mary's meeting-house in Taunton has exquisitely carved square Corinthian piers supporting the roof, and superbly finished brass chandeliers, consisting of stems with four spheres from which radiate S-branches and candleholders, all surmounted by a dove.[94]

The most vivid and yet accurate pen-picture of the Dissenting meeting-house is the work of the historian, Stoughton. "Your attention," he writes, "would be attracted to the pulpit, either a good large platform enclosed by wainscot sides, with a carved projection in front supporting a bookboard, or a deep narrow box . . . surmounted by a heavy sounding-board." After referring to the possibility that this canopy might bear a carved dove with an olive-branch in its mouth—the proof that God keeps His covenant promises with His people as with Noah—Stoughton continues: "Occasionally a desk for the precentor, and in front was almost always placed a table-pew . . . a large square or oblong enclosure, containing a seat running all round, with the Communion-table in the middle." It would have on it a Bible and less frequently that token of faithful Protestantism, Foxe's *Book of Martyrs*, or even a volume of sermons.[95] The poor would occupy a "table pew" except when Holy Communion was being celebrated, when they would give place to the Minister and deacons. The font would often be brought into the meeting-house and placed in a ring at the side of the pulpit. "The principal pews," writes Stoughton, "were spacious like parlours; and those appropriated to rich men[96] resembled such as were appropriated in a country church to the squire of the parish. They were lined with green baize and were often concealed behind thick curtains, whilst on the door, in a few distinguished instances, was carved either a monogram or a family crest. Two or three large brass chandeliers were in numerous cases suspended

---

[94] Illustrated in Davies, *op. cit.*, III, following p. 38.

[95] The latter was there presumably in case a visiting minister failed to arrive as preacher, and so, in a pinch, a sermon might be read to the congregation, a practice that would have horrified a first generation Puritan leader like Thomas Cartwright.

[96] See the castigation of erecting pews in meeting-houses as essentially undemocratic offered by Clement E. Pike in "Pews and Benches" in *Transactions of the Unitarian Historical Society*, Vol. 2 (1919-1922), pp. 131ff.

from the ceiling by a chain, and with a few candles they gave a winter's afternoon just enough light to make darkness visible."[97]

Stoughton's description, especially in his closing sentences, seems to fit the 1730s rather than the 1690s, for the Dissenters were not at ease in Zion in the very first decade after persecution ended. The earliest meeting-houses and even later ones in country settings were not so much indicators of rising social status as they were of simplicity, sincerity, and a costing spirituality.

These meeting-houses were the perfect architectural expression in their secluded back streets of a different conception of the church than that of the nation on its knees to which Wren's aspiring towers and spires bore witness. This was rather a retiring religion for men and women who saw the church as gathered from the world (not one to attract worldlings with an imposing site or an attractively seductive interior). These were not public buildings for all and sundry to attend: they were the quiet trysting-places of the visible church of Christ meeting there. This Calvinism which had been at its zenith so eager for a public reorganisation of the state for the sake of the saints, now insisted on a separation of the "saints" from the world.

[97] *Religion in England*, Vol. v, pp. 447-48.

CHAPTER III

SPIRITUALITY: PREPARATION
FOR PUBLIC WORSHIP

E XCEPT FOR the most isolationist of mystics, spirituality in private or family devotions, is the preparation for liturgy or public worship. It is in the "closet" of the layman, or in the cell of the monk or nun, or about the family table which serves as the domestic altar, that the interior struggle with doubt and temptation goes on and where the true sources and motives of the Christian life are to be found. No one knew this better or expressed it with greater power than John Donne in the eightieth of his *LXXX Sermons*:

> I thrust myselfe down in my Chamber, and I call in, and invite God, and his Angels thither, and when they are there, I neglect God and his Angels, for the noise of a Flie, for the ratling of a Coach, for the whining of a doore; I talke on, in the same posture of praying; Eyes lifted up; knees bowed downe; as though I prayed to God; and if God, or his Angels should ask me, when I thought last of God in that prayer, I cannot tell: Sometimes I finde that I had forgot what I was about, but when I began to forget it, I cannot tell. A memory of yesterdays pleasures, a feare of tomorrows dangers, a straw under my knee, a noise in mine eare, a light in mine eye, an anything, a nothing, a fancy, a Chimera in my braine, troubles me in my prayer. So certainly is there nothing, nothing in spirituall things, perfect in this world.

It is in the privacy of spirituality that the soul,[1] in Eliot's phrase, "swinging between Heavengate and Hellgate" re-enacts the drama of the interior Civil War. It is in the devotional life that the pattern of the religious life is known, the true icon or false idol is served in the imagination, and the springs of affection and motivation are discovered to the eye of faith. Here, when the final capture of the errant soul by Christ is acknowledged, argument ends

[1] For the first half of the century on this topic Helen C. White's *English Devotional Literature* (Madison, Wisconsin, 1931) is unequalled, needing to be supplemented only by Louis L. Martz's *The Poetry of Meditation* (New Haven, Connecticut, 1954), and by Gordon S. Wakefield's *Puritan Devotion* (1957).

68

in adoration. Then the private preparation is completed by corporate participation in worship. For worship that is unprepared by devout souls and praying households is largely an antique and meaningless mimicry. In the seventeenth century, however, Catholic, Anglican, and Puritan found private and public prayers the celestial journey of the heart in pilgrimage, Herbert's "reversed thunder" and "Christ-side-piercing spear." They believed that they were heard and answered.

The spirituality of the Catholic Counter-Reformation of the sixteenth century had been the most brilliant since the fourteenth century. Some of the influence of the new methods would be felt not only by the English Catholic exiles in the Low Countries and France, but also by the Anglican high-church divines and the meditative or metaphysical poets of the seventeenth century. The Papal approval of St. Ignatius Loyola's impressive *Spiritual Exercises*[2] in 1548 marked the high point of recognition, and there followed a flood of books of spiritual direction. Among the most influential were Friar Luis de Granada's *Book of Prayer and Meditation* (1554),[3] Lorenzo Scupoli's *The Spiritual Combat*,[4] which was equalled in European popularity only by the late medieval *Imitation of Christ*, and Gaspar Loarte's *Instructions and Advertisements*, *How to Meditate the Misteries of the Rosarie* and *The Exercise of the Christian Life* (both of which probably appeared in 1579).[5] Shortly after the turn of the century there was published the important *Introduction to the Devout Life* by St. François de Sales (1609).[6] During the *siglo d'oro* or golden sixteenth

[2] H. Watrigant, "La genèse des Exercises de Saint Ignace de Loyola," *Études*, Vol. 71 (1897), pp. 506-29; Vol. 72, pp. 195-216; Vol. 73, 199-228, shows that behind Loyola there were important methods of meditation in the Low Countries, including Mauburnus's *Rosetum exercitiorum spiritualium et sacrarum meditationum* (1494), meditations on the life of Christ by the Pseudo-Bonaventure and Ludolph the Carthusian, the exercises of Abbot Garcia de Cisneros of Montserrat, in the chapel of which Loyola had exchanged the life of a soldier for the defender of the Virgin Mother and the church, and the interior self-examination counselled by the *Imitatio Christi* and its imitators.

[3] See Helen C. White, *op. cit.*, pp. 104-109, and Maria Hagedorn, *Reformation und Spanische Andachtliteratur* (Leipzig, 1934), who both claim that Luis de Granada was far and away the most popular spiritual writer read in England at the start of the seventeenth century.

[4] This work, attributed to Scupoli, is, in fact, probably the work of a group of Theatines, according to Pierre Pourrat, *Christian Spirituality*, tr. W. H. Mitchell and S. P. Jacques, 3 Vols. (1922-1927, Paris), III, pp. 239-40.

[5] The former work of Loarte is important also because it stimulated the composing of the *Christian Directory* by the Jesuit, Robert Persons, which, in the Protestant adaptation of Bunny, converted Richard Baxter and was again adapted for Anglican purposes in 1700 by Dean Stanhope of Canterbury.

[6] This treatise was so attractive in its appeal that it superseded even Fray

century in Spain St. Teresa of Avila and her friend St. John of the Cross scaled the topmost of ecstatic heights of union with God, but before they had lived in the desolate abandonment of the dark night of the soul.[7]

English Protestantism of the sixteenth century had nothing to show worthy of comparison with these Roman Catholic maps of mysticism, probably because Anglicans and Puritans were at the foundational and very often acutely controversial stage of developing their theology and ecclesiology, quite apart from the Pelagianism the Calvinists among them detected in Catholic mystical methods.

The seventeenth century, however, exhibits a greater maturation of spirituality in both Anglicans and Puritans and leads to the production of several classics of the spiritual life. Three of them are by Anglicans. These are the *Preces Privatae* of Bishop Lancelot Andrewes, and Bishop Jeremy Taylor's companion volumes, *Holy Living* and *Holy Dying*. A fourth is a Puritan classic, Richard Baxter's *The Saint's Everlasting Rest*. (An English Benedictine also produced a classic in Augustine Baker's *Sancta Sophia*.) Setting these masterpieces aside, however, the level of serious cultivation of the spiritual life by the wayfaring Christian had perceptibly risen in quality and quantity.

1. *General Characteristics*

The first impression that is made by the devotional books so prolifically produced in this period is their strenuous and persistent earnestness, their deep and occasionally desperate seriousness. They are prepared with the complete concentration and effort of those who wrote them and tested them out in their experience. This was unquestionably the fruit of the conviction that all human affairs are constantly directed by God, so that each moment and every event is providentially determined. It lies behind their spirituality as it lies behind the belief in special providences that explains the official days of thanksgiving and humiliation. Even a Puritan tinged with Arminianism (instead of the characteristic Calvinism) exhibits this high seriousness, as in the case of Richard Baxter. His

---

Luis de Granada's spiritual handbook, as Helen C. White shows, *op. cit.*, pp. 111-13.

[7] See E. Allison Peers, *Studies of the Spanish Mystics*, 2 Vols. (1927-1930); Alois Mager, O.S.B., *Mystik als seelische Wirklichkeit* (Salzburg, 1945), pp. 144-203; Louis Oechslin, O.P., *L'Intuition mystique de sainte Thérèse* (Paris, 1946); and Jean Baruzi, *Saint Jean de la Croix et le problème de l'expérience* (Paris, 1924).

conclusion to his masterpiece of spirituality can speak for the age, as well as for himself in its monumental and moving concern:

> Thus, Reader, I have given thee my best advice, for the attaining and maintaining a heavenly Conversation. The manner is imperfect, and too much mine own; but for the main matter, I dare say, I received it from God. From him I deliver it thee, and this charge I lay upon thee, That thou entertain and practise it. If thou canst not do it methodically and fully, yet do it as thou canst; onely, be sure thou do it seriously and frequently . . . Be acquainted with this work, and thou wilt be (in some remote sort) acquainted with God: Thy joys will be spiritual, and prevalent, and lasting, according to the nature of their blessed Object; thou wilt have comfort in life, and comfort in death; When thou hast neither wealth nor health, nor the pleasure of this world, yet wilt thou have comfort: Comfort without the presence, or help of any Friend, without a Minister, without a Book, when all means are denied thee, or taken from thee, yet maist thou have vigorous, reall Comfort. Thy Graces will be mighty, and active, and victorious; and the daily joy which is thus fetcht from Heaven, will be thy strength. Thou wilt be as one that standeth on the top of an exceeding high Mountain; he looks down on the world as if it were quite below him: How small do the Fields, and Woods, and Countreys seem to him? . . . The greatest Princes will seem below thee but as Grasshoppers; and the busie, contentious, covetous world, but as a heap of Ants. Mens threatenings will be no terrour to thee; nor the honours of this world any strong enticement: Temptations will be more harmless, as having lost their strength; and Afflictions less grievous, as having lost their sting; and every Mercy will be better known and relished.
>
> Reader, it is, under God, in thine own choice now, whether thou wilt live this blessed life or not; and whether all this pains which I have taken for thee shall prosper or be lost.[8]

This sense of the providential governance of the world by God which gives Baxter and his contemporaries such a solemn temper

---

[8] *The Saint's Everlasting Rest*, Pt. IV, pp. 295-98 (3rd edn., 1652); *Works* (ed. W. Orme, 1830), XXXIII, p. 406f. This devotional classic was written by Baxter during a period of apparently irrecoverable illness. It first appeared in 1650 and reached a third edition in two years, continuing to be read by all parties in the church with undiminished popularity to the end of the century.

in their writings also has three other consequences. It generates deep fervour, in the first place. Here, again, Baxter warrants quotation, when his theme is perseverance in the life of contemplation:

> Keep it close to the business till thou have obtained thine end. Stir not away, if it may be, till thy love do flame, till thy joy be raised, or till thy desire or other graces be lively acted. Call in assistance also from God; mix ejaculations with thy cogitations and soliloquies; till having seriously pleaded the case with thy heart, and reverently pleaded the case with God thou hast pleaded thyself from a clod to a flame, from a forgetful sinner to a mindful lover; from a lover of the world to a thirster after God, from a fearful coward to a resolved Christian, from an unfruitful sadness to a joyful life.[9]

Its second result is to give time a profounder significance, and in this respect it may be contrasted with the medieval, neo-Platonic and timeless *visio Dei*. Robert Bolton in *Some Generall Directions for a Comfortable Walking with God* (1625) exemplifies this typical Puritan attitude: "Wee must bee countable for time at the dreadfull Barre of that last Tribunall, as we must be exactly answerable even for wandring vaine imaginations, idle words, and every the very least errour of our whole life . . . so must we also give up a strict account for the expence of every moment of time."[10]

The third consequence will manifest a sense of strain in this spirituality. It may take the form of making the Christian feel, at least sometimes, that he is walking the giddying path on the edge of a precipice, with the engulfing whirlpool of the frenzied enthusiasts below, and nearer the indifferent but jagged rocks of the uncaring and worldly, and wondering why the way to salvation is so inordinately narrow. This strain is demonstrated in the diatribes (even in devotions) against the enemies of God or of one's own theological position. Michael Sparke whose prayers scintillate with joy and charity begins a "Morning Prayer" with adoration of the Immortal God, yet ends it scabrously with the following petition: "We beseech thee, remember the groaning griefs of all thy Churches, in all parts. Root out, O dig up, destroy, and root out all that be not planted by thy hand, all Quakers, Shakers, Ranters, and Seekers, such as look not after thy Laws, or that live not

---

[9] *Op. cit.*, Pt. IV, p. 205.   [10] *Op. cit.*, pp. 165-66.

according to thine Ordinances, but according to their own list, and wickednesse of theire wills."[11]

Another characteristic of the books of devotion of this age is their sheer practicality. They do not fly in the spacecraft of the great Carmelites to reach mystical ardour and ecstasy; their Piper cubs of small planes get them airborne with difficulty for the most part; but even then they always remain in direct radio contact with the earth, and the directions they give are always clear.

The Protestant conviction that God is to be served not *per vocationem* (through a special world-renouncing calling) but *in vocatione* (in one's daily, secular calling) is partly responsible for this practical emphasis. This activism on the part of holders of a predestinarian faith seems curiously contradictory, as does the emphasis on good works by those who maintain that justification is by faith and not by good works. But the spiritual life was the way of making one's election sure, and devotional exercises were not the causes but the consequences of a salvation already assured. The Anglicans and Puritans alike believed in an intramundane holiness—in fight, not flight from the world. Robert Bolton claimed "An honest Calling is a Schoole of Christianity."[12] Moreover, attendance at this school was not voluntary, but compulsory. Not only so, but it was as necessary for the ennobled as the lowly. Arthur Dent in his phenomenally popular and persuasive manual, *The Plaine Man's Path-way to Heaven* (1601) permits his simple man to wonder, "But may it not be allowed unto Lordes, Gentlemen and Gentlewomen, and other great ones, to live idly, sith they have wherewith to maintaine it?" The levelling of society before God is clearly affirmed in the answer of Theologus (obviously a Puritan Teacher): "God alloweth none to live Idlely: but all both great and small, are to be imployed one way or another: either for the benefite of the Churche, or Commonwealth: or for the good government of their own households: or for the good of Townes and Parishes, and those amongst whom they doe converse: or for the succour and reliefe of the poore: or for the furtherance of the Gospell, and the maintenance of the Ministery: or for one good use or another."[13]

[11] *The Crums of Comfort to Groans of the Spirit, The Second Part* (1652), sigs. B10-B10 verso.

[12] *Some Generall Directions for a Comfortable Walking with God* (1625), p. 49.

[13] *Op. cit.*, pp. 191-92. This work, according to the early part of *Grace Abound-*

73

Moreover, this service of God in daily business and diurnal duty counterbalances the other-worldliness of seventeenth-century Christianity seen, for example, in the nostalgia of the religious English Catholic exiles in their monasteries and nunneries in France and the Low Countries, or in the Anglican "Arminian Nunnery" of Little Gidding, where the Ferrar family and friends offered unceasing adoration and praise to God through the day and the night. The this-worldly emphasis of service to God was not exclusively Anglican or Puritan. This was a central concern of St. François de Sales whose *Introduction to the Devout Life* was directed at lay folk living in the world, not at the religious who had adopted the counsels of perfection. A translation of this work issued from Rouen in 1614 for the English exiles (and also presumably for crypto-Catholics in England) makes this clear in the Preface: "Those who have treated of devotion before me have allmost all attended onelie to the instruction of persons alltogether retired from worldly conversation. . . . But my intention is particularly and principally to instruct such as live in citties and townes, busied with the affaires of their household, or forced by their place and calling to follow their princes court, such as by the obligation of their estate are bound to take a common course of life, in outward shew, and exteriour proceedings. . . ."[14] What had begun with Luther as an expression of the priesthood of all believers, had, within a century, been adopted in part by the Counter-Reformation. One might say that for Catholics the degree of holiness possible for the religious was still *summa cum laude*, but good men and women could now aspire to an honours degree—a *cum laude*—instead of merely taking the pass degree.

The high Anglican and Puritan recognition that one's daily duties could be the expression of a spiritual calling gave the common task a deep meaning, since it was work for the glory of God and the benefit of mankind. It had occasionally, however, the unfortunate consequence of assuming that material prosperity is the reward of the godly, and worse, their right and due. Michael Sparke's prayer for Monday morning petitions God thus: "Grant

---

ing, together with Bishop Bayly's phenomenally popular *Practice of Piety*, made up the totality of the dowry of Bunyan's wife, and may well have given Bunyan the idea for *Pilgrim's Progress*.

[14] *An Introduction to the Devout Life composed in Frenche by the R. Father in God Francis Sales, Bishop of Geneva, and translated into English by I. Y.* [Yakesley] (3rd edn., 1614), pp. 10-11.

we may deale uprightly & let the carriage of our Affairs be (O Lord) so pleasing unto thee, that they may draw downe thy blessings upon us; and keep us we pray this weeke following, thriving in our estates, and religious in our carriage, alwaies meditating of good for thy glory, for the Church and Commonwealth's good, so that whatsoever we lay our hands unto, thou wilt bend our hearts to do the same, so it be to thy praise and glory."[15] Hedged about as the revealing phrase "thriving in our estates" is by protestations of seeking God first, it nevertheless expresses a sense of cupboard love, of Christianity as its own reward with ten per cent profit. This was one of the dangers of the doctrine of election that it slipped easily into a concept of divine favouritism, which the prophet Amos had warned against in the eighth century B.C.

The same divine favouritism is expressed in many partisan prayers in this period for both Cavaliers and Roundheads were sure that God was on their side, the former because of their conviction of the divine right of kings,[16] the latter because of their assurance that God would honour his "visible saints." Sparke begins his "Heavenly Meditation" in celestial serenity, but he crashes to earth in his pedantic partisanship as he informs God, "It is manifest & plaine (O Lord) that *Papists* depend more upon Pharisaicall working then upon Christian believing; and it is as true that the loose Libereine [Libertine] careth little either for faith or fruits, and both these are flat enemies against the Crosse of thy deare Sonne, our alone Saviour Christ Jesus. . . ." He ends with the smug assurance, "Farre bee it from mee (deare Father) to be ensnared by either of these."[17]

Perhaps the most significant characteristic that these books of devotion share in this contentious time, when theologians were using the resources of logic, scholarship, and rhetoric for dogmatic defences of their own positions or vituperative denunciations of the views of their opponents, and at a time when extreme enthusiasm was viewed with dislike by Laudians and Puritans alike, is a recognition of the importance of the feelings in religion, or "heart work" as it was called. Increasingly there develops a deepened appreciation of the love of Christ and a responsive affection elicited by that boundless love. Moreover, what is even more remarkable

[15] *Crums of Comfort* (edn. of 1628), sigs. D3-D3 verso.
[16] Some partisan prayers offered by supporters of the Cavaliers in desperation are cited in Chap. VI on "Calendary Conflict."
[17] *Crums of Comfort* (1628), sigs. H7-H7 verso; also cited by Helen C. White, *op. cit.*, pp. 229-30.

and little appreciated is the fact that it is shared by high Anglican, Roman Catholic, and Puritan alike.

At least since the time of St. Bernard of Clairvaux, Catholic piety has made much of the humanity of Jesus, as did St. Francis of Assisi—to whom the custom of having a Christmas crib at the festival of the Incarnation is due.[18] So it was not unexpected that St. Ignatius Loyola should encourage retreat masters to get the retreatants to use all their senses, especially sight and scent, to assist Jesus of Nazareth to walk out of the pages of the New Testament into their imaginations. Nor was it surprising that the cult of the Sacred Heart should be inaugurated in the Roman Catholic church in the seventeenth century, with St. John Eudes in 1646 instituting the feast of the Holy Heart of Mary and in 1672 the feast of the Sacred Heart of Jesus, only a year before St. Marguerite-Marie Alacoque received her first revelations at Paray-le-Monial. It was a feature of the sermons of Bishop Lancelot Andrewes that they enabled his hearers in court or cathedral to visualise the Christ-child with vividness and love, but without sentimentality, and Donne's dramatic gifts were used to make the Sacred Humanity relevant to his congregation. What is perhaps less to be expected, because it is insufficiently appreciated, is that several Puritan writers should concentrate on the humanity of the Saviour, among them Preston, Rous, Sterry, and Thomas Goodwin.

John Preston had as an appendage to his *Five Sermons on the Divine Love* in the edition of 1640, which is entitled, *The Soliloquy of a Devout Soul to Christ, Panting after the Love of the Lord Jesus.*[19] One passage shows that Preston wishes not merely for a historical knowledge of Christ, but more deeply for Jesus at his heart's centre. His soul muses:

> . . . If I look to Mount Tabor, I see thee in glory, and I cannot but love thee for that. If I look to the garden, I see thee lying on the cold ground sweating drops of bloud for me, and I cannot but love thee for that. If I look to Golgotha, I see thee nailed to the Cross, and thy heart broached that I may drinke thy bloud and live, and I cannot but love thee for that. If I looke to Mount Olivet I see thee ascending farre above all

[18] A Giotto fresco in the Church at Assisi depicts St. Francis adoring the Christ Child in a Christmas crib.
[19] John Preston, *A Heavenly Treatise of the Divine Love of Christ* (1640), pp. 89ff.

heavens, and I cannot but love thee for that also. Indeed in Tabor thou hadst visible glory but it soon vanished; in the garden and Golgotha thou hadst little visible beauty why I should desire thee; and in Olivet thou wast quite carried out of my sight. If then thou liest for me nowhere else what hope have I to love thee, Oh thou to be beloved of all? Art not thou in the tents of the shepherds? Dost thou not walke in the midst of the golden candlesticks? Dost thou not dwell in the hearts of men by faith? Oh let me see thee here below in the Church and in myselfe.

Francis Rous, a Presbyterian layman who became an Independent, and had been both Provost of Eton and Speaker of the House of Commons, composed a manual on *The Mysticall Marriage* (1635) between Christ and the soul. This, to be sure, will be consummated in eternity, but there is a solemn betrothal here and now between Christ and the trusting soul.[20] The way is by ethical conformity of the human will to Christ's, since in his invasion of the soul, "the more spiritual he doth make her; yea the more he doth melt a soule in himselfe; the more he doth turne her into his will, and the more doth he increase his own image in her; and we know that his image is righteousness and true holiness."[21] The closeness of Catholic and Puritan spirituality has been said to be fully confirmed[22] by another Puritan, Thomas Goodwin, the Independent who was Cromwell's chaplain and President of Magdalen College, Oxford, and author of a work said to anticipate the Roman Catholic Cult of the Sacred Heart, namely, *The Heart of Christ in Heaven towards Sinners on Earth* (1652). This, however, as we shall see later in this chapter, has differences from the Catholic cultus as significant as the affinities with it.

Two more excerpts from devotional books, one Puritan and the other Anglican, will suffice to establish the remarkable concurrence of streams of spirituality concentrating on transformations effected by the divine love. The Platonist Puritan to be cited is

---

[20] *Op. cit.*, p. 43. The sub-title is: *or Experimental Discourses of the Heavenly Marriage between a Soul and her Saviour.*

[21] *Ibid.*, pp. 255-56.

[22] For example, the Oratorian historian of spirituality, Louis Bouyer writes: "A Number of Cromwell's chaplains figured among the eminent representatives of this vehement mystical feeling for Christ, and, surprising as it may seem, they were closer to many aspects of the Jesuits and Visitandines of the period than were the traditional Anglicans—at least as far as we can discover." (*Orthodox Spirituality and Protestant and Anglican Spirituality*, tr. in 1969 by Barbara Wall, from the French original published in Paris in 1965, p. 134.)

Peter Sterry whose book, *The Rise, Race and Royalty of the Kingdom of God in the Soul of Man* was published in 1683, eleven years after the death of this chaplain of Cromwell's. Sterry sees the divine love as "the most universal and importunate beggar" knocking at the door of every soul, not only at the soul of the elect. The divine love is experienced as joyful celebration, holy laughter: "Abide in the Father's love by spiritual joy. Joy is love flaming. One saith, that laughter is the dance of the spirits, their freest motion in the harmony, and that the light of the heavens is the laughter of angels. Spiritual joy is the laughter of Divine Love, of the Eternal Spirit, which is love, in our spirits."[23]

Philip Traherne writing *The Soul's Communion with her Saviour* in 1685 is an Anglican in the succession of Lancelot Andrewes, but his emotion is expressed with less reserve. Meditation on the nativity of Christ results in a paean of praise:

O Thou *Light of the World*, who was born in the Night, an Emblem of that dark and disconsolat Estate where into We by Transgression fell: Thou art *the Sun of Righteousness, by whose Rising upon the Earth the Peepl that walked in Darkness hav seen a great light, and upon them that dwell in the Land of the Shadow of Death hath the Light shined.* Thy glorious Appearing hath dispersed the Cloud of thy Father's Wrath, under which the whol Creation groaned, together with those unwholsom Mists of Sin, Error, and Ignorance wherin Mankind was lost and benighted: Thou hast dissolved the Everlasting Chains of Darkness which were justly prepared to bind us in Hell and Despair, and once more restored us a Day of Hope to rejoice in the Light of thy Countenance for ever.[24]

Finally, these devotional manuals or guides to spirituality, however much they differ in the methods they inculcate or in their theological emphases, all express a robust conviction of the reality of God, of the finality of Christ's revelation of his love, of the interior transformation wrought by the Holy Spirit, and the substantiality of heaven and the comparative shadowiness of earth. For the last time in modern European history we have a sense that theology

---

23 *Op. cit.*, p. 390. See V. da Sola Pinto, *Peter Sterry, Platonist and Puritan* for a biographical and critical introduction to an anthology of his voluminous writings.

24 *Op. cit.*, pp. 36-37. One is reminded by this passage of the *risus Paschalis* of the Easter Liturgy and of Paul Claudel's *le grand rire divin de l'univers*.

is in the main current of life, not an irrelevant deviation from the most serious business of living. Later piety will often seem artificial, strained, sentimental, apologetic. In the seventeenth century it is robust, and it is significant that in different decades both Puritan and Anglican piety were the expressions of those who suffered for their faith, while throughout the period the English Catholics were Recusants, leading—except when the sun of royal patronage shone—a crepuscular and clandestine life in England and a nostalgic life in Continental religious houses. The choicer souls in each of these groups had earned the promise of the last Dominical Beatitude.[25] This gave their spirituality a profound sincerity, marked by sacrifice. As Helen White has so aptly expressed it: "Here is no thin diagram of a possibility but the full round of the dominant view of the world."[26] Whether with the aid of a Catholic crucifix, an Anglican cross, or a Puritan mental image of the suffering Redeemer, this piety was so Christocentric and so cosmic that one could say of it, in a way unintended by Marlowe, "See, see, where Christ's blood streams in the firmament."[27]

2. Roman Catholic Spirituality

It is peculiarly difficult to trace Roman Catholic spirituality among the English of the seventeenth century because it is so scattered, so multiform, and necessarily so clandestine. But there is no question at all of its influence on the Recusants, whether in exile or at home, and even on Protestants. It was profound and pervasive in its old or its new forms, in its medieval or Counter-Reformation methods.

The older forms of spirituality continued to fascinate with all the tenacity of a great tradition, confirmed by the experiences of the religious orders. St. Augustine of Hippo persisted in popularity among Protestants as well as Catholics. A Catholic translation of his *Confessions* attributed to Sir Tobie Mathew, to whom we also owe a translation of the Benedictine Rule, appeared in 1620, while in 1631 there was published another translation of the same work by William Watts. There was also published a number of treatises on the Christian life attributed to him.

Only a little less popular than St. Augustine was St. Bernard of Clairvaux. In 1616 William Crashaw, the indefatigable Puritan father of Richard, the metaphysical poet and Catholic convert, extracted and translated from the Bernardine collection of devo-

---

[25] Matthew 5:10-12.   [26] *Op. cit.*, p. 236.   [27] *Faustus*, I, l. 1432.

tional works, *The Complaint or Dialogue, Betwixt the Soul and the Bodie of a damned man.* Another work, *Saint Bernard His Meditations: or Sighes, Sobbes and Teares, upon our Saviours Passion* . . . translated and edited by "W.P.," a Cambridge graduate, appearing first in c. 1610 ran to four editions. Three other treatises of St. Bernard, bound together, appeared in 1613; they were the *Golden Treatise, Joy in Tribulation,* and *the forme of an honest life.* In 1631 an anthology of St. Bernard's devotional meditations appeared in Douai with the mellifluous title, *A Hive of Sacred Honie-Combes containing most Sweet and Heavenly Counsel.* . . .

The third most popular survival of medieval devotions, which has always had its Protestant as well as Catholic admirers, was, of course, Thomas à Kempis's *Imitation of Christ* (the title perhaps better translated by the earlier Catholic versions as "The Following of Christ"). It had first appeared in Latin between 1470 and 1475. By the seventeenth century more than 280 Latin editions of the *Imitatio Christi* had appeared on the European Continent.[28] The first English translation was that of William Atkinson printed by Wynkyn de Worde in 1502, but the most popular in England was that of Thomas Rogers the sixth translator, which came out in 1580 and ran through fourteen editions in the next sixty years. Rogers, a Protestant, not only omitted the fourth book of the *Imitation*, that on the Eucharist, but substituted for it another treatise of à Kempis, providing his own translation of the *Soliloquium Animae* under the punning title of *The sole-talke of the Soule.* . . . The fishiest part of the whole proceeding, however, was his bland assumption that a better (i.e., Protestantly) instructed Thomas à Kempis would have taken this very decision. This is corroborated to the translator's satisfaction by the following words in his "Address to the Christian Reader," assuring him that à Kempis's prayer for correction "God hath heard, and discovered those things for thy benefit, and testification besides howe Kempisius, the Auctor, howsoever living in a Popish time, was yet in hart no Papist, but would like well of that which is doon, as I trust thou wilt, whose edifieing, and spirituall comforting, I have onlie aimed at."[29]

While they are not properly either devotional manuals or collections of prayers, yet the rules of the founders of medieval orders

[28] White, *op. cit.*, p. 81.
[29] *The Imitation of Christ* (tr. Thomas Rogers, London, 1592), sig. A4 verso. Cited Helen White, *op. cit.*, p. 85.

aim at the culture and discipline of the spiritual life, and so they are ancillaries to devotion.[30] The Rules of both St. Benedict and St. Francis of Assisi were Englished and translated. The former appeared in Ghent in 1632 and parts two through four comprise "Statutes compyled for the better observation of the holy rule for the use of the English Benedictine nuns at Brussels." *The rule and testament of the seraphical father S. Francis* was published in Douai in the Richard Mason translation in 1635, while eleven years earlier there had appeared in Brussels a translation by Arthur Bell of *The rule of the religious of the third order of Saint Francis . . . living together in communitie and cloyster.*

In estimating the impact of the older forms of devotion of Catholicism the continuance of the primers should not be forgotten. They were exceedingly popular in the sixteenth century,[31] and in many homes they must have been retained in the seventeenth century, however dog-eared or even tattered.

The new methods of spirituality encouraged by the renewal of the spiritual life in the Roman Catholic Church through the Council of Trent and by the founding of the Jesuits and the reform of the Carmelites and Franciscans (all of which took place in the sixteenth century) had a profound impact on seventeenth-century English devotional life. Far and away the most popular Spanish author in translation was Luis de Granada,[32] Provincial of the Dominican Order in Portugal. His *Libro de la Oracion y Meditacion* written in 1561 was translated and published in Paris in 1582 by Richard Hopkins, an exile Recusant. The edition of 1599 is an anonymous adaptation for Anglican purposes, and with it is bound up an additional work, Granada's *An Excellent Treatise of Consideration and Prayer.* In 1598 the same author's *Guia de Pecadores* was digested and translated by Francis Meres as *The Sinners Guide.* As early as 1586, however, there had appeared a most influential volume of Fray Luis de Granada, Englished as *A Memoriall of a Christian Life* "from the beginning of his conversion until the end of his conversion." This reached a fourth edition in 1625. It contained seven treatises of which the fourth is of special interest. It comprises "two principal Rules of a Christian life," the first for beginners and the second for experts. The former are described

---

[30] There should also be noted the publication in Paris in 1636 of *S. Austin's Rule . . . together with the Constitutions of the English Canonesse regulars of our B. Ladyes of Sion in Paris.* Tr. and ed. Miles Pinkney.

[31] See Davies, *op. cit.*, I, pp. 409-15.

[32] See E. Allison Peers, *Studies in the Spanish Mystics* (1927), I, pp. 33-76.

in the table of contents as "such Christians as beginne newlie to serve God, and have a desire to be saved." The latter are described as "all professed Religious persons in Monasteries, and for such other Christians as are not contented with the doinge of all such things as they know to be of necessitie for their Salvation, but will endeavour to wade further and profit more and more in the Way of vertues." It is important to recognise, however, that the spiritual method outlined by the Dominican friar was an adaptation for daily morning and evening use of the important *Spiritual Exercises* of St. Ignatius Loyola, designed to be performed in a month of spiritual intensity.

The impact of Ignatian spirituality was very strong in England because of the intrepidity of the Jesuits in the English Mission and the impact of their martyrdoms. One of their number, Robert Persons, wrote the highly popular *Christian Directory*[33] (originally called *The First Booke of the Christian Exercise appertayning to resolution* in 1582) which reached the seventh approved and authorised edition in 1633 under the imprint of the English College at St. Omer. It was also successful in the Protestant bowdlerisation by Bunny in 1584, which went through nine impressions in sixteen years. It was the Bunny version that converted that exemplary Puritan, Richard Baxter.[34] In Rouen in 1630 there appeared leaflets for those making St. Ignatius's *Spiritual Exercises*. Furthermore, Tomas Villacastin's *A Manuall of devout Meditations and Exercises, instructing how to pray mentally* was another adaptation of the Ignatian *Exercises*. It was translated by Fr. Henry More and was published at St. Omer in 1618, and two further editions were called for in 1623 and 1624. Finally, as another index of widespread Jesuit influence in spirituality, there was Michael Lancicius's biography, *The glory of the B. father S. Ignatius of Loyola, founder of the Society of Jesus*, first published in Ghent in 1628 and reissued in 1633.

---

[33] Persons owed much to the work of a Jesuit predecessor, Gaspar Loarte, two treatises of which were translated into English. The first was *Instructions and Advertisements, How to Meditate the Misteries of the Rosarie* which appeared ca. 1579, and the other, *The Exercise of a Christian Life* (1579) which resembled Luis de Granada's most popular work, and had reached four more editions by 1634. For the origin of the use of the rosary as a means of recollection see Herbert Thurston's article "Genuflections and Aves, a study in Rosary Origins" in *The Month*, Vol. 127 (1916), pp. 546-59, a reference among others I owe to the kindness of Dr. D. M. Rogers of the Bodleian Library, Oxford, an authority on English Recusant history.

[34] *Reliquiae Baxterianae* (ed. M. Sylvester, 1696), p. 3.

The extraordinary success of the Jesuit spirituality was owed to certain intrinsic qualities, not forgetting its timeliness.[35] St. Ignatius knew that the clue to the changing of the will is to be found in the imagination and his was an imagistic, pictorial spirituality, not an abstract or negative one. "Composition of place" is the technique for capturing all the senses for Christ. In the second place, he knew that the inveterate complacency and lukewarmness of the unredeemed or only partly redeemed human must be shaken loose by fear and self-analysis. Finally, he was able to enlist the resolution of his retreatants by a modern Crusade in which courage, loyalty, devotion, and manliness were all elicited. Its impact is powerfully envisaged in English literature in the poems of Southwell, Donne, and Gerard Manley Hopkins and in the Ignatian-shaped blank in James Joyce's *Portrait of the Artist as a Young Man* and *Ulysses*.

An important, though less popular, writer of devotional treatises was a Franciscan friar, St. Peter of Alcantara, who wrote a *Treatise on Prayer and Meditation* (c. 1558). This opens with a definition of devotion which derives from St. Thomas Aquinas, continues with an exhortation on the needs and advantages of meditation from the pseudo-Bonaventure, and ends with a similar one from St. Laurence Justinian, the Augustinian, thus combining the precise theology of the Schoolmen with the ardour of the mystics,[36] and making the transition from older to newer spiritual methods easier. His *Golden Treatise of Mental Prayer* was published in translation in Brussels in 1632 and the *Pax Animae* (attributed to him though almost certainly the work of another Spanish Franciscan, Juan de Bonilla) appeared in translation in Paris in 1665.

The most striking omission, while Spanish mystical treatises are under consideration, is of any of the great works of either St.

[35] Of its timeliness, Professor David Knowles, O.S.B., has written: "in the Catholic camp . . . the need for a firm and explicit grasp of doctrine, and for an active, apostolic, sacramental, apologetic reply to opponents brought about a new model of the devout life which concentrated attention upon the war against vice and ignorance, and developed the technique of spiritual exercises, regular retreats, set meditations, and methodical direction." (*The English Mystical Tradition*, 1961, p. 152.)

[36] The forerunner as author of this type of meditative treatise combining theological acuity with mystical ardour is Jean Gerson, Chancellor of the University of Paris in the early fifteenth century, with his *On the Mountain of Contemplation*. It may be of interest to note that the future Anglican Bishop Joseph Hall in *The Arte of Divine Meditation* (1606) lists the masters of meditation as follows: Origen, Augustine, Bernard, Hugh of St. Victor, Bonaventure, Gerson (Chap. 16).

Teresa of Avila or St. John of the Cross. There is, however, as a partial counterpart for this tragic loss a translation of her auto-biography by "W. M. of the Society of Jesus" which is entitled, *The lyf of the Mother Teresa of Jesus foundresse of the Monasteries of descalced or bare-footed Carmelite nunnes and fryers . . . Written by her self. . . .* Such a mountain-top view, Alpine in its chill austerity and bitter climbing through the dark nights and dazzling days, seemed perhaps impossible of attainment by English temperaments. Richard Crashaw, the Baroque poet and convert to Catholicism, however, was deeply influenced by her Christological ardours.

The most influential French writer of devotional works translated into English was St. François de Sales, the Bishop of Geneva. His impact was felt early in the century, but its fullest force was reserved for the Restoration of the monarchy in 1660 when the light ladies who returned to England with Charles II brought their French devotional books with them. It was the triumph (and failure) of St. François de Sales that he succeeded in recommending the practise of piety to the world of fashion, for this could rouse an aesthetic interest without any ethical transformation. The first English translation of *The Introduction to a Devout Life* was published in Douai in 1613 hardly five years after its original had appeared in Paris. Another edition of this translation was published in Paris in 1637, while a new edition bore the imprint of the English priests at Tournai in 1648. Thomas Carre, English exile and Recusant, published his translation of de Sales's *Of the Love of God* in 1630. It was from the eighteenth French edition of the work. It is questionable whether this actually crossed the English Channel, as also was the case of the *Delicious Entertainments of the Soule* (also by de Sales) which had been translated by "a Dame of our Ladies of Comfort" and published in Douai in 1632.

The Ignatian spirituality is a pugnacious, even bellicose one, while the Salesian devotion seems more reconciliatory. The Salesian spirit relies much less on the "terrors of the Lord"—the concentration on sin, death, hell and judgment—inculcated as a deliberate unsettlement and divine disturbance of a complacent soul by the Ignatian spirituality. It focuses rather on the love, mercy, and goodness of God, and more on the attracting power of the love of Christ than on what must be expelled by that power. As Louis L.

Martz has rightly seen,[37] for St. François de Sales all meditation and self-analysis must be performed *tout bellement et doucement*. Its typical expression is found in the following citation from John Yakesley's translation of *An Introduction to a Devoute Life* (3rd edn., Rouen, 1614): "When thou desirest earnestly to be freed from any evil, or to obtaine any good; the first thing thou must doe, is to repose thy mind, and quiet thy thoughts and affects from over-hastie poursuite of thy desire; and then faire and softly beginne to pourchase thy wishe, taking by order, one after another, the meanes which thou judgest convenient to the attaining thereof."[38] Such a spirituality must have proved increasingly attractive in the century which had known the Thirty Years War in Europe[39] and the Civil War in England.

So far it seems as if English Catholic spirituality is limited to the translation of medieval and modern European works of devotion with the Spanish influence predominating. This is largely the case, but not wholly so. During our period there are some minor indigenous treatises on the devotional life,[40] some important collections of prayers in English, one Catholic metaphysical poet of distinction (Crashaw), and one original masterpiece worthy of comparison with the fourteenth century English mystics. The selections of prayers continue the tradition and structure, if not the larger part of the contents of the primers.

A very useful and popular collection of prayers for the use of Catholics (one of a number of such) was printed first in 1583 and published most probably in Rouen.[41] Its full title was, *A Manuall of prayers newly gathered out of many and famous divers authors as well auncient as of the tyme present*. Its history is an index of the difficulties Recusants faced in publishing and disseminating copies to the faithful. It was compiled and translated by George Flinton. Another edition appeared in Rouen in 1589. Three

---

[37] *Op. cit.*, p. 149.   [38] *Op. cit.*, p. 479.

[39] In our days a play which has poignantly revealed the upheavals of the Thirty Years War is Berthold Brecht's *Mother Courage*.

[40] The reference is to Benet Fitch and Gertrude More. The former (alias Canfield) besides producing a translation of his fellow friar and Capuchin's Constantin Barbanson's the *Anatomie of the Soule*, wrote the treatise, *Of the three-fold will of God*, referred to approvingly by Augustine Baker, O.S.B., in his distinguished work, *Sancta Sophia*, I, pp. 86-87. The latter, Dame Gertrude More, published in 1657 in Paris *The Holy Practises of a Divine Lover: Sainctly Idiot's Devotions*. One is bound to guess that Sir Thomas More would have provided a very retired nook in *Utopia* for his great-granddaughter to meditate in, quite alone and utterly undisturbed.

[41] Helen C. White, *op. cit.*, p. 128.

further editions were secretly printed in England; one probably in 1593 and the two others certainly in 1595 and 1596. One other appeared in 1599 falsely claiming to be issued at Calice [Calais], but was in fact secretly printed in England. Further secret editions appeared in England between 1599 and 1604, and another definitely in 1604. There then appeared in Douai an expanded version of the work, retitled, *A Manual of prayers now newly corrected and also more augmented and enlarged.* This ran to eighteen further editions.[42] The enlarged edition of 1604 deserves a digest, both because of its inherent interest, and also because its wide popularity makes it a normative manual of English Recusant piety for at least the first half of the seventeenth century.

Chapter I consists of daily prayers, to be said at morning, noon, and night, with an exercise to be used in meditating on the Passion of Christ with aspirations and meditations on his holy wounds. The second chapter contains prayers to be said before, during, and after Mass. For example, at the elevation of the Chalice, the recommended meditation reads: "Al haile, most precious & blessed blood, flowing out of the side of my Lord and Saviour Jesus Christ, wasting away the spottes both of the old and new offences: cleanse, sanctifie, and keep my soule, I beseech thee to everlasting life."[43] There follow brief directions with prayers before and after sacramental Confession. Chapter III contains prayers for Sunday, with praises and thanksgivings directed to the Holy Trinity. Chapter IV has Monday prayers in commemoration of departed souls. Chapter V invokes saints and angels in Tuesday prayers. Wednesday prayers (Chapter VI) are for "our troubles and necessities, both spiritual and temporal." Thursday prayers (Chapter VII) deal with repentance for sins. The Friday prayers, not unnaturally, focus on the "Passion of our Saviour" (Chapter VIII), while the prayers of Chapter IX for Saturday are directed to "our Blessed Ladie." Chapter X (the last) comprises "Advertisements, with prayers and suffrages for the sick." An appendix contains the Jesus Psalter. The whole comprises 275 pages.

It is methodical, simple to follow, comprehensive, and fervent. It must have warmed the hearts of the faithful in testing times,

---

42 These editions are fully documented in A. F. Allison and D. M. Rogers, *A Catalogue of Catholic Books in English printed abroad or secretly in England, 1558-1640* (Bognor Regis, 1956).

43 *Op. cit.,* p. 50. It is noteworthy that the meditations are not based on the text of the Liturgy or on the text of Scripture. Strictly, they are extra-liturgical meditations.

and kept them loyal to the old religion, while instructing the young, and, given to both groups of Catholics the stability of tradition. It was a typical collection of prayers for the Catholic household of faith.[44]

Richard Crashaw (1603-1649), the single Catholic among the metaphysical poets, was the son of a distinguished Puritan and preacher to the Temple, and moved from the high churchmanship of a fellowship at Peterhouse, the most Laudian of Cambridge colleges to the highest of high Catholicism, a canonry at Loreto, where he died. The ardour and austerity of Catholic religion in its most Baroque forms attracted him by its captivity of the senses for spirituality. This lover of painting and music, demonstrated this in poetry that is rich with vivid word-painting and richly musical in its cadences. His spirituality is Baroque in the brilliance of its tortured sensibility, its vivid portrayal of the religous emotions of awe, ecstasy, and pity, but it easily degenerates into sentimentality or mere theatrical posturing.

The distinctiveness of his spirituality, without its extravagances, can be sensed if we compare two poems on the Nativity, Crashaw's "Sung as by the Shepherds" and Milton's great Ode. Milton ends where Crashaw begins, in visualising the scene of the Nativity, for Milton's interest is in the Redemption wrought by the power of Christ, while Crashaw's is on the Incarnation and its expression of God's love:

> See, see, how soon his new-bloom'd CHEEK
> Twixt mother's breasts is gone to bed
> Sweet choise, said we! no way but so
> Not to ly cold, yet sleep in snow.

Christ's is paradoxically a gentle Kingship that rules by affection:

> To thee, dread Lamb! whose love must keep
> The shepheards, more then they the sheep.
> To THEE, meek Majesty! soft KING
> Of simple GRACES & sweet LOVES
> Each of us his lamb will bring
> Each his pair of sylver Doves;
> Till burnt at last in fire of Thy fair eyes,
> Our selves become our own best SACRIFICE.

[44] In many ways it resembled the parallel Protestant collections of prayers such as *A Booke of Christian Prayers* (1581 and many later editions), which had originally been issued by John Daye in 1569 under another title.

Milton's theme is Redemption, announcing at the very beginning:

> This is the Month, and this happy morn
> Wherein the Son of Heav'ns eternal King,
> Of wedded Maid and Virgin Mother born,
> Our great Redemption from above did bring. . . .

The emphasis in Catholic meditation and meditative poetry is on the paradoxical gentleness of omnipotence in the Nativity of Christ, with the tribute of love responding to his love; the emphasis in Puritan poetical spirituality is on the role of Christ in power, not on his tenderness. Catholicism glories in the sacred humanity, Puritanism in the divine powers of God as man. This generalization is, however, subject to partial revision as more is learned of the mystical tendencies of some Puritan writers such as Rous, Thomas Goodwin, and Sterry.

For the man or woman who wished to advance further in spirituality, there was one masterpiece, originally prepared for a group of English Benedictine nuns in exile by their director, Father Augustine Baker, O.S.B.[45] Born in Abergavenny, South Wales, in 1575, he was educated at Christ's Hospital, Broadgates Hall (now Pembroke College), Oxford, and trained as a lawyer at Clifford's Inn and the Middle Temple. He was admitted as a Benedictine novice in 1603. After difficult, even desperate times and failures, he was reconverted in 1608, the thirty-second year of his life. There followed twelve years of tepid spiritual life after which he was reconverted again. In 1624 he was appointed to Cambrai, as auxiliary confessor to the Benedictine dames which Crisacre More, grandson of Sir Thomas More, had established for his daughter and her seven companions. Somewhere between 1620 and 1624 he gained his most faithful disciple, Serenus Cressy, the chaplain to Lady Falkland.

During the following nine years he was prolific, producing about forty treatises on spirituality, of which roughly twenty-five were original, and the rest collections from the writings of others. Four years at Douai followed, and he died in 1641 while on the English Mission in which he had been engaged for about three years. He died aged sixty-five, presumably happiest in the recollection of the

---

[45] See *Memorials of Father Baker* (ed. R. H. Connolly and Justin McCann, Catholic Record Society, XXXIII, 1933) and [Augustine Baker], *Sancta Sophia, or Directions for the Prayer of Contemplation . . . Extracted out of more than Forty Treatises written by . . . Augustin Baker and Methodically digested by . . . Serenus Cressy* (Douai, 1657).

instruction he had given in the spiritual life, for there duty and delight were combined.

His many treatises, existing only in manuscript form, were arranged most systematically by his pupil and brother in the Benedictine Order, Fr. Serenus Cressy, thus providing an encyclopedic and well-ordered account of the stages in the spiritual life. This collection, known as the *Sancta Sophia* (or *Holy Wisdom*) is distinguished by its exhaustive treatment, and by the extraordinary richness of its citations from the devotional masters and mystics of the Christian past. He recalls the Greek and Latin Fathers of the ancient church who wrote on spirituality, such as Gregory of Nyssa, Gregory Nazianzen, and Gregory the Great. He cites medieval writers such as St. Bernard, St. Francis of Assisi, and St. Catherine of Siena and the late medieval masters such as Tauler, Suso, Ruysbroeck, and Harphius, as well as the English mystics of the fourteenth century such as Walter Hilton, Richard Rolle, and the author of *The Cloud of Unknowing*. Among the moderns he is fondest of St. Teresa of Avila and St. John of the Cross, as well as the French writers, de Blois, Barbanson, and St. François de Sales, and a host of minor figures as well. His candour, moderation, common-sense, and practicality, together with a tendency towards angularity, are among his more obvious characteristics.

It is an unusual genre of devotional book, half formal treatise on ascetical theology and half personal instruction taught with urgency. The *Sancta Sophia* is over five hundred pages in length, and thus difficult to summarize. Its teaching emphasizes three means of interior enlightenment: the spiritual director, spiritual reading, and divine inspirations. It then focuses on mortification of the passions, and the cultivation of solitude and silence, as well as of the virtues of charity, patience, and humility. A lengthy chapter deals with various scruples. The final two hundred and twenty pages deal with prayer and its distractions, the three stages in meditation, acts of the will and "aspirations." It ends with an outline of the mystical life.

It is a highly impressive book, but not without errors. It is intended for those engaged in the religious life, and particularly for the "monastic contemplative life." According to Professor David Knowles, himself a Benedictine monk, it is at its best on such topics as mortification, divine inspiration (the belief that when a person can find no compelling guidance, he will be given light to see and strength to act, provided he offers his prayer in faith and goodwill), and the necessity and stages of mental prayer.[46] The same historian and critic asserts that "some of his spiritual writings, though unquestionably orthodox, are on important points confused, and at variance with what would seem to be the accepted doctrine of the great masters."[47] Fr. David Knowles makes the precise charges that he is mistaken in assuming that all would-be mystics are capable of attaining to the unitive experience, and also that his thinking is confused on active and passive contemplation, and even doubts whether Baker himself had any experience of the mystical life. So, he concludes, this prolix and melancholy book, may suffice to guide some for a very great part of their lives, but that Fr. Baker cannot communicate what he does not possess (*Nemo dat quod non habet*) and therefore will be unable to show a true contemplative the way to the summit. He may even mislead him into thinking that what is merely a foothill is the massif of Mount Carmel.[48]

On the other hand, this is a learned and creative work and one unique in English Catholic spirituality. For parallels one must look back to the English mystical writers of the fourteenth century.

One wonders how these clandestinely printed volumes of devotion ever reached the Recusants in England, for whom many copies were intended. Evidence of such secret activities is, by its very nature, difficult to discover. The successes are silent: the failures are discovered and usually punished by the law. Two lists of books of a Roman Catholic nature seized by the searchers (seventeenth-century equivalents of customs men) at Newcastle-upon-Tyne are known.[49] The first consignment was almost certainly, because of the many copies of practically every book, intended for a distributor of illegal books, especially as they were in English or Latin and no other European language. The second consignment discovered was with equal probability intended for a priest, and might well have been a travelling priest's library, for it included a little missal for travelling priests[50] and theological and devotional works

---

46 *The English Mystical Tradition* (1961), pp. 178-81.
47 *Ibid.*, p. 160.   48 *Ibid.*, p. 187.
49 Respectively to be found in *Calendar of State Papers: Domestic: Charles I*, XXIV, No. 23, III, Newcastle-upon-Tyne, "Popish Bookes taken in a Dutch Shippe the 1 of Apr. 1626" and *Calendar of State Papers: Domestic: Charles I*, XXVI, No. 16, VI, Newcastle-upon-Tyne, "A Catalogue of the Popish Bookes and Reliques of Popery seized on by the Searchers Men in searching of a Shipp in this Porte the last day of Aprile 1626."
50 *Missale Parvum pro Sacerdotibus itinerantibus.*

in Hebrew, Greek, Italian, and French, as well as the customary English and Latin.

The names of Catholic devotional books are of special interest here, presumably because the first list included commonly used books, and the second list mentioned those of special professional interest to a priest in the English Mission. The first consignment seized on April 1, 1626, included one copy of the *Breviarium Romanum*, for a member of a religious order presumably, while there were twenty-five copies of the *Jesus Psalter*, and several copies of Luis de la Puente's *Meditations upon the Mysteries of our holy Fayth, with the practise of mentall prayer*, Thomas à Kempis's *The Following of Christ*, and of Persons's *A Christian Directory*. One can, therefore, infer that the devotional life of the less educated of Catholics centred on the Rosary,[51] the stations of the Cross (though these would be difficult to hide in a hurry), and the *Jesus Psalter*[52] with its 150 petitions, with fifteen decades for the fifteen chief petitions, and further divided into three series according to the three states of the mystical life—purgation, illumination, and union.

The second consignment may indicate the kind of treatises a priest on the English mission in the first year of the reign of Charles I would be reading. They would include Bellarmine's *The Art of Dying Well*, R[obert] S[outhwell's] *An Epistle of Comfort* (1593), Diego de Estella's *The Contempt of the World*, *St. Peters Complainte* and *Mary Magdalens Tears*, an unnamed work of

[51] See Luca Pinelli, *The Virgin Maries Life*, tr. "R. G." and printed at Rouen in 1604, which was combined with *The Society of the Rosarie* in a St. Omer edition of 1624. Other similar books were: Alexis de Solo, *An Admirable Method to Love, Serve and Honour the B. Virgin Mary* (tr. "R.F.," Rouen, 1639); Thomas Worthington, *The Rosarie of our Ladie* (Antwerp, 1600); Sabin Chambers, *The Garden of our B. Lady. Or a devout manner, how to serve her in her Rosary* ([St. Omer], 1619); *The Society of the Rosary*, newly augmented ([St. Omer, possibly], ca. 1600). While there are many ways of meditating on the Rosary, the most important form is the official Dominican Rosary, comprising 150 "Aves," divided into fifteen "decades" which are subdivided for purposes of meditation into three parts of five decades each: meditation on the five joyful, the five dolorous, and the five glorious mysteries. These are, respectively, the Annunciation, Visitation, Nativity, and Finding of Christ in the Temple; Gethsemane, the Whipping of Christ, the Crown of Thorns, the Carrying of the Cross, the Crucifixion, the Resurrection, Ascension, Coming of the Holy Ghost, Assumption of the Virgin, and Coronation of the Virgin. (See Martz, *op. cit.*, pp. 101-102.) Legend is added to Scripture in these devotions, especially in the two concluding Marian mysteries. The popular piety of the laity was a combination of the Rosary and the Stations of the Cross.

[52] This was attributed to Richard Whytford, a member of the Brigittine order. An edition of 1575 bore the title, *Certaine devout and Godly Petitions, commonly called Iesus Psalter*.

Dionysius the Areopagite and another unnamed of St. Bonaventure, as well as two of Tauler's works, namely, the *De Vita et Passione Salvatoris* and *Pious Meditations upon the Beads*.[53]

John Gee's *The Foot out of the Snare* (1624) is evidence for a long catalogue of books that have been sold "by the priests and their agents" during the previous two years. He mentions a priest who has rooms full of illicit religious books for sale near the Savoy, and refers to a wealthy vintner who stores them in a church, and tells how booksellers pay copyists of banned books and get four times the regular price for them. An easier way to get such volumes, though this required wealth, was to pick them up while travelling on the Continent.[54]

However these books of spirituality were obtained, they helped to keep the embers of the devotional life of the English Catholics glowing. More, they even passed on the fire to converts like Richard Crashaw from a strong Puritan family, and gained readers in adapted versions among both high Anglicans and supposedly low Puritans, as will be seen. So well trained were some lay Catholics that they retained their contemplative zeal in the unlikeliest situation—amid the corruption and worldly ambition of the court. One such was Sir Oliver Manners, the king's carver, who had been converted by Father John Gerard the Jesuit. The latter writes of his spiritual son: "You might see him in the court of the Presence Chamber, as it is called, when it was crowded with courtiers and famous ladies, turning aside to a window and reading a chapter of Thomas à Kempis's *Imitation of Christ*."[55]

3. *The Spirituality of the Caroline Divines*

A case can be made for combining the Caroline divines and the Puritan divines in a common spirituality termed "Anglican" for the piety of their laity was very much alike.[56] This, however, would not do justice to the historical antagonism between the two tradi-

---

53 The first five items in this list are by Jesuits, which heightens the probability that this travelling library was destined for a Jesuit father, whose taste in spirituality was discriminating.

54 Helen C. White, *op. cit.*, pp. 178-82.

55 *John Gerard. The Autobiography of an Elizabethan* (tr. Philip Caraman, intro. Graham Greene, 1951), p. 367.

56 A. Tindal Hart, *The Man in the Pew 1558-1660* (1966) writes of the typical Anglican holy household that "in addition to its regular round of worship and prayer, its Bible study and the reading of countless books of devotion, of which perhaps the favourites were Foxe's *Book of Martyrs*, Lewis Bayly's *Practice of Piety*, Jeremy Taylor's *Holy Living* and *Holy Dying*, and *The Whole Duty of Man*, it inculcated habits of personal discipline and social benevolence" (p. 189).

tions which finally issued in a permanent rupture in 1662 when the Puritans left the Church of England, if they had not already left for New England, and their new name was Dissenters or Nonconformists.

The growing fissure in the Church of England was, indeed, widened by the production of one of these Caroline books of devotion, namely, the anonymously published, *A Collection of Private Devotions in the practise of the Antient Church, called, The Hours of Prayers. . . .* This was the work of John Cosin, subsequently Master of Peterhouse, Dean of Durham, and, in Restoration days, a reviser of the Book of Common Prayer and Bishop of Durham. It helped to cost his two major critics, William Prynne and Henry Burton, the one a fearless Presbyterian lawyer and the other an intrepid London Puritan divine, the cropping of their ears, and it led eventually to Cosin's going into exile after the downfall of his patron, Archbishop Laud and the death of his King, Charles I, who is rumoured to have instigated Cosin to prepare this very volume.

This notable but controversial volume is not a masterpiece of spirituality, as are most of the others we shall consider in detail. While a significant supplement to prayer, public or private, it is also an important pointer to the rapid growth of the high-church movement in the Church of England in the early years of the reign of the first Charles. Its sub-title, as if expecting opposition and trying to disarm it in advance, included, after "Hours of Praiers," the clause, "as they were much after this manner published by Autoritie of Queen ELISA, 1560," and, as a further sop, "TAKEN out of the Holy Scriptures, the Antient Fathers, and the Divine Service of our own Church."

The first edition of 1627 was followed by a second in 1655 and the ninth in 1693. Its Baroque frontispiece contained the Jesuit monogram, IHS surrounded by flames, suggestive of a monstrance, and was calculated to please royal, Catholic, and European taste, but to alienate democratic, Puritan, and English sensibilities. William Prynne in his punning title, *A Brief Survay and Censure of Mr. Cozens His Couzening Devotions*, bluntly asserted: "That booke, whose frontispiece, title, frame and method, stile, and phrases, yea, and doctrine too, is altogether Popish; must needes be meerely Popish, both in forme and matter."[57]

The contents of Cosin's book proved even more heinous in the

[57] *Op. cit.*, p. 38.

eyes of his Puritan critics. The preface reflects a strong and sarcastic anti-Puritan bias, with its scathing reference to "extemporall effusions of irksome and indigested praiers which they use to make, that herein are subject to no good order or form of words, but pray both what and how and when they list."[58] It claims that the first purpose of the book is to use the anciently approved forms of prayer of Christ's Church rather than the rude dictates which are framed by private spirits." Its second aim is to tell the world that England has neither set up a new faith nor a new church, neither has it "abandoned All the *Antient Forms of Piety and Devotion*," nor "taken away all the *Religious Exercises and Praiers of our Forefathers*," nor "despised all the old *Ceremonies*," nor have English Churchmen "cast behind us the Blessed Sacrament of Christ's Catholic Church."[59] The third value claimed for this book of devotions is that it will provide a means of private prayer for those prevented from attending public prayers who desire to practise religion. Finally, it was prepared "that those who perhaps are but coldly this way yet affected, might by others example bee stirr'd up to the like heavenly duty of performing their *Daily* and Christian Devotions, as beeing a work of all others most acceptable to his divine Majestie."[60]

This work is a return to the royal Tudor primers. Though Cosin claims his authority and example is Elizabeth's primer of 1560, this is itself largely dependent on the Reformed Catholic primer of Henry VIII of 1545. It could be legitimately argued that this is equally a briefer Breviary, with instruction on the Christian life, since it restores the prayers for the seven traditional hours of the day.[61]

This *horarium* provides practical instruction on prayer, forms of prayer, the Calendar, the Creed, the Lord's Prayer, the Deca-

[58] *Op. cit.* (edition of 1655, which is used throughout), sig. A5; the Bodleian Library copy in Oxford (shelfmark Douce C 111) is particularly interesting for its pertinent notes in the bibliographer's handwriting.

[59] *Ibid.*, sig. A6.   [60] *Ibid.*, sigs. A7-A7 verso.

[61] In fact, H. Boone Porter in an article, "Cosin's Hours of Prayer: a Liturgical Review" (*Theology*, 56, 1953, pp. 54-58) claims that the *Devotions*, since their first appearance in 1627, have been the classical English order of the Canonical Hours. Next to the various versions of the Prayer Book itself, they have been the most important Anglican liturgical compilation of the Reformation." Boone Porter further observes that "most of the classical Anglican writers urge at least a partial observation of the hours" by example or recommendation in their devotional treatises. This group and their works are: Andrewes's *Preces Privatae*, Laud's *Private Devotions*, Sherlock's *Practical Christian*, and the *Whole Duty of Man*.

logue, the Seven Sacraments (while insisting that Baptism and the Lord's Supper are "the two principal and true Sacraments"), and it lists the Spiritual Works of Mercy, and the Corporal Works of Mercy. It also contains abbreviated forms of the seven canonical hours of prayer, collects for the major festivals, the Seven Penitential Psalms, prayers before and after receiving the "Blessed Sacrament" and prayers to be used at Confession and Absolution, as well as forms for the sick and dying. Inevitably, also, prayers for the king and queen were included.

Cosin's ecclesiastical fidelity consists in keeping the Morning and Evening Offices close to those of the Prayer Book, while his originality is displayed in making Terce as an Office of the Holy Ghost and Sext and Nones as Offices of the Passion more consistently and relevantly so than in the Latin versions.

There are two major theories current as to the origin of this book. Evelyn the diarist reports a story he claimed to have confirmed from the lips of Cosin himself. This was that Charles I had commissioned the book, using Bishop White of Carlisle as his intermediary, and that the royal reason for the commission was because his Queen had remarked on the absence in the Church of England of any book of prayers to be used at regular intervals during the day like the Hours of Prayer in the church of Rome.[62] The other theory is the explanation offered by Jeremy Collier that the book was written at the request of the Countess of Denbigh (sister of Charles's favourite, the Duke of Buckingham), to offset her attraction to the Roman church.[63] The second theory is advanced three generations later than the event and *prima facie* is less likely to be true than the first. On the other hand, it is curious that if King Charles was its instigator there was no reference to this patronage in a dedication or preface, unless the King used Cosin as his stalking-horse to see how far he and Laud could move in a Catholic direction without seriously alienating a large number of his subjects. Perhaps the simplest explanation is that offered by C. J. Stranks[64] and partly suggested by the second edition, because it combines the first and second theories. Cosin says in the second edition that he compiled it for a friend's private use, without any

[62] *The Diary of John Evelyn* (ed. E. S. de Beer, Oxford, 1955), III, pp. 45-46. For another reference to this Roman Catholic taunt, see Sir Edwin Sandys, *Europae Speculum* (1673), pp. 87-88.
[63] *An Ecclesiastical History of Great Britain* (1708), p. 742.
[64] C. J. Stranks, *Anglican Devotion* (1961), p. 67.

intention of making it public, but that the friend had two hundred copies printed for his friends to avoid manuscript copying. Cosin was a collector of prayers and liturgies, and it is quite possible that he made printed copies available for both the King and the Countess.

How Catholic (as contrasted with Protestant) was Cosin's *Devotions?* Prynne felt that Cosin was cozening or cheating the English church and people. The author's sole aim, wrote Prynne, was "to introduce and usher Poperie into our Church" and he had tried to make Queen Elizabeth "the Patroness of this his Poperie" and to delude the simple people into believing she countenanced Popery.[65] He found four parallels to Cosin's work: The *Horas de Nuestra Senora* (Paris, 1556), the *Horae beatissimae Virginis Mariae secundum usum Saru* [Sarum, or Salisbury], Laurence Kellam's *Manuell of Praiers* (Douai, 1624), and *Our Ladies Primer in Latine and English* (Antwerp, 1604). He effectively demonstrated the Roman Catholic character of Cosin's sources by printing the *Devotions* and the supposed sources in parallel columns.

Cosin's other published Puritan critic was Henry Burton, the Rector of St. Matthew's Church, Friday Street, London. His work was *A Tryall of Private Devotion, or a Diall for the Houres of Prayer* (1628). His prefatory epistle deplores the inroads Arminianism and Popery have made into the Church of England in the previous seven years, observing that the most convenient and visible way of determining the degree of true religion is to visit any town or village on the Lord's Day to discover if it is treated as a holy day or only as a holiday. "That's the true touchstone of a truely religious man," since "The seventh day sanctifieth our six. . . ."[66] He contends that Cosin's book is turning the Church of England back to Roman Catholicism by reintroducing the seven Sacraments,[67] in referring to marriage as an "unnecessary avocation,"[68] by stating that the Sacraments are of the church's and not of Christ's appointment, by urging the restoration of the seven canonical hours and over-turning Queen Elizabeth's reduction of them to Matins and Evensong.[69] The crowning insult is the publication of the Jesuit emblem and symbol, IHS.[70] Burton

---

[65] *A Briefe Survay and Censure of Mr Cozens His Couzening Devotions* (1628), p. 3.
[66] *Ibid.*, sig. G2.
[67] *Ibid.*, sigs. H2-H2 verso.
[68] *Ibid.*, sig. E4 verso.
[69] *Ibid.*, sig. C4 verso.
[70] *Ibid.*, sig. C1 verso.

seems to be less choleric than the irascibly erudite and fulminating Prynne. He also marshalls his information more carefully. But he, too, can be vividly amusing in the satirical vein, as when he is protesting what he calls "Lent-relenting" and the eagerness with which the priest on Easter Day withdraws the veil which has obscured the images in the church, with the result that the worshippers "down they fall on their Maribones, beating their breasts more eagerly now than ever, as imputing it to their sinnes, that they have been so long withheld from their prettie-pettie gods."[71]

The founder of the Anglo-Catholic tradition in theology was Hooker, while in patristic scholarship, preaching, spirituality and the exalted role of a truly pastoral bishop, it was Lancelot Andrewes, although he can only be called a Caroline divine by a hair's breadth, since he died a year after Charles I came to the throne. His chief contribution to spirituality (apart from the dignity and beauty of the ceremonial with which he celebrated at the service of Holy Communion in the Prayer Book)[72] was his *Preces Privatae*, which did not appear in a complete edition until 1675, though a tolerable edition from the Greek text was translated and issued by Drake in 1648, twenty-two years after his death,[73] and twenty-one years after the first edition of Cosin's *Devotions*.

The *Private Prayers* (to translate the title) were found in manuscript after Andrewes's death, and it was said that the pages were frayed and worn away by the constant pressure of his fingers and the stains made by his copious tears. They are the index to the mind and heart of a distinguished scholar (the Pentateuch and some of the historical books of the Authorized or King James Version of the Scriptures are part of his lasting memorial), a cultivated mind, a tender spirit, and a saintly man. There are echoes in the *Preces* of his knowledge of the Greek and Latin Fathers, the medieval Schoolmen and the mystics, the great pagan classical authors such as Sophocles, Euripides, Aristophanes, Virgil, Seneca and Horace, as well as of the moderns like Erasmus. He also had an unrivalled knowledge of the ancient liturgies and other forms of prayer, and even of Knox's *Book of Common Order*, and made

---

[71] *Ibid.*, sig. I1.

[72] See the illustration of the altar arrangements and furnishings in his chapel at Winchester in P. A. Welsby, *Lancelot Andrewes* (1958).

[73] Parts of the *Preces* appeared in *Institutiones Piae* (1630) prepared by his secretary, Henry Isaacson. The best modern edition, with critical introduction, is that of F. E. Brightman, published in 1903.

use of the Roman Missal and Breviary of his day, as well as of the English Prayer Book and primers.

In structure the *Preces* are a superb example of the old type of devotional book, the manual of prayers for every day, which stretches back through Protestant primers to their Catholic medieval examples. They are written like prose poems, with broken lines, deliberately so as to suggest the rhythms and pauses of contemplative meditation. They are usually in Greek or Hebrew, but occasionally in Latin. Their concision means that they are a series of direction posts on the map of prayer, but not walking-talking guides to the terrain. In these succinct prayers there is neither garrulity nor sentimentality, but catholicity and homely practicality. The joins of this mosaic of heterogeneous sources are forgotten, so well do the individual phrases fit together. Louis Bouyer reminds us that Cardinal Newman kept these prayers of Andrewes on his *prie-dieu* where he offered his thanksgiving after Mass, and says of them: "Never has the image of a bee going from flower to flower to gather a honey of fragrant simplicity been so apt."[74]

Andrewes has four types of devotions in his *Preces Privatae*: prayers of penance; meditations on the mystery of faith (which was always a paradox that transcended reason for Andrewes who yet believed with St. Anselm of Canterbury that faith is the clue to understanding);[75] prayers of intercession for all kinds and conditions of people with a deeply practical knowledge of their needs; and throughout an inexhaustible fountain of praise for God as creator, sustainer, and redeemer of the world.

One example of these "golden zig-zag prayers," as the Abbé Brémond called them, must be given to show their skeletal structure, concise directions, and richness of allusion, yet all are articulated into an objective whole, concentrating on love to God and charity to mankind and excluding the man who is on his knees writing them or praying them. This is the concluding "Praise" of the first day's prayers:

> Let us lift up our hearts unto the Lord, as it is very meet, right, and our bounden duty, that we should *in* all, and *for* all Things, *at* all *Times*, *in* all *Places*, by all *Means*, ever, every where, every way,

[74] *Orthodox Spirituality and Protestant and Anglican Spirituality* (Paris, 1963, tr. Barbara Wall, 1969), p. 111.

[75] Anselm's famous definition of the relationship of faith and intelligence was *credo ut intelligam* (I believe in order to comprehend).

Make mention of Thee,
Confess to Thee,
Bless Thee,
Praise Thee,
Sing laud to Thee,
Give Thanks to Thee,

    Creator,
    Nourisher,
    Preserver,
    Governor,
The Physitian,   *of all*
    Benefactor,
    Perfector,
    Lord & Father,
    King & God
The Fountain of Life and Immortality
    Treasury of eternal good things:
        Whom
The Heavens, and the Heavens of Heavens,
    Angels, and all the Celestial Powers sing praise unto;
Uncessantly crying one to another,
    (and we, base and unworthy we, with them under their feet)
    Holy, Holy, Holy,
Lord God of Hosts,
    Heaven and Earth is full of the Majesty of Thy Glory,
    Blessed be the Glory of the Lord from His place.

    Divinity,
    Incomprehensibleness,
For His Sublimity,
    Dominion,
    Almightiness,
    Eternity,
    Praevision and Providence
           my God, my
    Strength and Stay,
    Refuge & Deliverer,
    Helper & Defender,
    Horn of salvation,
          and my Lifter up.[76]

[76] *A Manual of the Private Devotions and Meditations of the Right Reverend Father in God, Lancelot Andrewes* (tr. and ed. R. Drake, 1648), pp. 86-89.

This superb prayer begins with the Preface in the Prayer of Consecration in the Book of Common Prayer, then moves from duty to thanksgiving for the divine roles by which God helps men, and then into the Heaven of Heavens where the *Tersanctus* of the cherubim and the saints surrounding the throne of God allows unworthy humans to join in the chorus of adoration of God's transcendent attributes, and, by mentioning his prevision and providence prepares for the return to earth, sustained by the comfort of his stabilising, liberating, aiding, saving, and encouraging divine presence. The whole prayer is like Jacob's ladder, in that the petitions or ascriptions are like angels ascending to heaven and returning down the ladder to earth carrying the blessed booty of grace.

Helen C. White has caught the distinctive character of the spirituality of Andrewes, which, in her view resembles that of the *Imitatio Christi* and which she described as a savouring or long brooding over things first thought of by others and meditated on so thoroughly that they have become one's own, and an even deeper quality, that "intimately as they seem to spring from the heart of the writer, they have a certain austerity, a certain objective impersonality, as if in the presence of its God the soul sheds its idiosyncrasy and laying down all shadow of temperament and whim, finds in what is least personal, the fullest expression of its innermost being."[77] What is most distinctive in Andrewes, apart from his rich reading and meditation, is a profound concern for the unity of the Church of Christ throughout the world and a charity sympathetic enough to envision the plight of the world's poor in their various callings, all *sub specie aeternitatis*. His heritage was nobly possessed by Donne, Herbert, Ferrar, Jeremy Taylor, and others.

It is difficult, at the outset, to imagine a spirit and temper more unlike Andrewes than John Donne, author of *Devotions upon Emergent Occasions*, apart from their common erudition and metaphysical style of preaching. For if Andrewes was classical and objective, Donne was romantic and subjective. One cannot imagine Andrewes for all his capacity to dazzle the court with the word-play of his sermons, ever preaching like Donne in his winding-sheet, drawing attention to the man as much as to his message. It is true, at least for moderns, that they go to Andrewes for what he writes, but to Donne because of his manner of writing. Andrewes, like the last medievalist, submits to the divine gover-

---

[77] Helen C. White, *op. cit.*, p. 249.

nance with joy; Donne, like Jacob, fights with God's angel to the very break of day. He would, like his own poem suggests, be the kind of pilgrim who rides westward on Good Friday. Andrewes was a Puritan (at least on the Sabbatarian issue) before he became a high Anglican, but there never was, so far as is known, a time when he was not a Christian. Donne had been a moral prodigal and a sceptic, knowing the new philosophy that puts all in doubt. Andrewes offers a Johannine spirituality, Donne is a doubting Thomas who must fight for faith and struggle against sensuality. Andrewes is lost in God in his spirituality; Donne is lost in admiring Donne trying to be lost in God. Brilliant in his psychological penetration and wide-ranging imagination that garners from a wide direct experience, as well as from unusually exotic sources of knowledge derived from reading, Donne yet incurs a suspicion of the impure motive, of the exhibitionist.[78] His rhetoric exceeds even that of Andrewes in its sustained power and daring, but his *Devotions* seem too contrived to suit the poor in spirit. They were printed immediately after they were written; those of Andrewes were *Privatae*: the difference is significant.

It began as a kind of spiritual diary kept during a serious illness, but it tells one much more about the ways of Donne than the ways of God and it has more literary and psychological interest than spiritual. Individual prayers capture the passionate longing for God found in some of the sermons and the divine poems, but it is perhaps in the latter his finest spirituality is to be found.

There is his searing honesty:
> I durst not view heaven yesterday; and to day
> In prayers and flattering speeches I court God:
> Tomorrow I quake with the true feare of his rod.[79]

There is his passionate and paradoxical cry for God to conquer him:
> Batter my heart, three-person'd God . . .
> . . . for I
> Except you enthrall mee, never shall be free,
> Nor ever chast, except you ravish mee.[80]

There is the hope that the civil war between spirit and sense, that was forever waging in himself would be overcome in death, at once

---

[78] T. S. Eliot, *For Lancelot Andrewes* (1928), p. 20.
[79] *Holy Sonnets*, No. 19.
[80] *The Divine Poems* (ed. Helen Gardner, Oxford, 1952), p. 11.

despair to the natural man and deliverance to the spiritual, where the divine love would prove stronger than death:

I joy, that in these straits I see my West;
    For though theire currants yeeld return to none,
What shall my West hurt me? As West and East
    In all flatt Maps (and I am one) are one,
So death doth teach the Resurrection. . . .

We thinke that Paradise and Calvarie
    Christs Crosse, and Adam's tree, stood in one place;
Look Lord, and find both Adams built in me;
    As the first Adams sweat surrounds my face,
May the last Adams blood my soule embrace.

    So, in his purple wrapp'd receive me Lord,
        By these his thrones give me his other Crowne;
    And as to others Soules I preach'd thy Word,
        Be this my Text, my Sermon to mine owne,
        Therefore that he may raise the Lord throwes down.[81]

The influence of the Ignatian spirituality on this former Catholic is exceedingly strong, and it may account in part for Donne's hard gaze at the many forms of death that terrify him in order to attain to the resolution that will keep him safe with Christ and search for the stratagems to humiliate pride, as well as the severe self-analysis that make him realize his chief temptations are fear and intellectual arrogance.[82]

George Herbert (1593-1633), according to Louis L. Martz, shows greater affinity to the Salesian than the Ignatian spirituality and temper.[83] Earlier in his life than Donne he gave up the dazzle of the court and the intellectual attractions of Cambridge, where he was public orator of the university, to become an exemplary country parson, though he came of aristocratic lineage and his elder brother Lord Herbert of Cherbury was the first English Deist and his beautiful and devout mother Lady Magdalen, Sir Philip Sidney's sister, had been celebrated by Donne in the immortal couplet:

[81] *Ibid.*, p. 30.
[82] See Louis L. Martz, *The Poetry of Meditation*, pp. 38, 43-56, 106, 219-20, where it is claimed that there is strong Jesuit influence upon Donne's religious poetry. Martz's brilliant thesis is that Jesuit methods of meditation influenced Donne, the Salesian method, Herbert, and the Augustinian (via Bonaventura) Vaughan and Traherne.
[83] *Ibid.*, pp. 58, 154-59, 299, 318.

No Spring, nor Summer hath such grace,
As I have seen in one Autumnal face.[84]

Herbert[85] is widely regarded as the model country priest of the Church of England of his century, a high Anglican counterpart to the Puritan pastor, Richard Baxter. His life retold eulogistically by Izaak Walton, his own admirable handbook on the ministry, *A Priest to the Temple, or the Country Parson, His Character and Rule of Holy Life*, and, supremely, his sacred poems, all create the image. In fact, however, he had been a priest only two years as Rector of Bemerton, near to Salisbury, when he died. This hardly gave him time to warrant the encomiums poured upon him as a pastor, but it was time enough to provide us with a glimpse that was exemplary in its holiness, though we have no devotional treatise written by him.

In *A Priest to the Temple*, he insists on two basic spiritual requirements, "because the two highest points of life wherein a Christian is most seen are patience and mortification—patience in regard of afflictions, mortifications in regard to lusts and affections— . . ."[86] He expects the country parson not only to be an expert on agriculture, as well as in the Scriptures in which he will find "precepts for life, doctrines for knowledge, examples for illustration, and promises for comfort."[87] He also assumes that he will be familiar with the Fathers and the Schoolmen, and that he will make a commonplace book of divinity. He is perceptive in pointing out that the parson will fail as an interpreter of the Scriptures unless he lives a holy life and calls in the aid of prayer.

Such was the theory, but what of Herbert's practice? According to Walton, Herbert's devotion to God both public and private matched the theory. He read divine service in full from the Book of Common Prayer twice each Sunday, preaching in the morning and catechising in the afternoon, and celebrating Holy Communion about six times each year. More impressive still was his daily practice of reading Matins and Evensong at the canonical times with his whole family, namely, at 10:00 A.M. and 4:00 P.M.[88] Walton adds the touch that canonises Herbert: "and some of the

---

[84] Donne's ninth elegy, "The Autumnal."
[85] See an early edition, *The English Works of George Herbert*, 3 Vols. (ed. G. H. Palmer, Boston and New York, 1905), and *The Works of George Herbert* (ed. F. E. Hutchinson, 2nd edn., Oxford, 1945).
[86] *Works* (ed. Palmer, 1905), I, p. 213.
[87] *Ibid.*, I, pp. 215-17.
[88] Izaak Walton, *The Life of George Herbert* (ed. George Saintsbury, World's Classics edn.), pp. 301-302.

meaner sort of his parish did so love and reverence Mr. Herbert
that they would let their plough rest when Mr. Herbert's Saints'-
Bell rung to prayers, that they might also offer their devotions to
God with him."[89] Nor, according to the same authority, did he
neglect his private prayers, "nor those prayers that he thought himself bound to perform with his family, which was always a set
form, and not long. And he did always conclude them with that
Collect which the Church hath appointed for the day or week."[90]

It is in his poetry above all that Herbert's spirituality soars.
The Temple, a series of sacred poems carefully interrelated,
includes one poem at least that says more about devotion and its
potentialities than many pedestrian treatises. It deserves full
citation:

> Prayer the Churches banquet, Angels age,
>> Gods breath in man returning to his birth,
>> The soul in paraphrase, heart in pilgrimage,
> The Christian plummet sounding heav'n and earth;
> Engine against th'Almightie, sinners towre,
>> Reversed thunder, Christ-side-piercing spear,
>> The six-daies world transposing in an houre,
>
> A kinde of tune, which all things heare and fear;
> Softnesse, and peace, and joy, and love, and blisse,
>> Exalted Manna, gladnesse of the best,
>> Heaven in ordinarie, man well drest,
> The milkie way, the bird of Paradise,
>> Church-bels beyond the starres heard, the souls bloud,
>> The land of spices; something understood.[91]

Such paradoxes as "reversed thunder" Luther or Kierkegaard
would have appreciated, and such ecstasy straining the language to
its limits to express the ineffable the mystics would appreciate.
But Herbert knew that the deepest unity is reached in uniting with
the suffering Redeemer, and this he expressed with characteristic
simplicity and sincerity in the eucharistic poem, "The Banquet":

> But as pomanders and wood,
>> Still are good,
> Yet being bruis'd are better sented,

[89] *Ibid.*   [90] *Ibid.*
[91] *Works* (ed. Hutchinson, 1945), p. 51.

God, to show how farre His love
Could improve
Here, as broken, is presented.[92]

Metaphysical poets other than Donne and Herbert made their contribution to spirituality, either directly like Traherne in his *Centuries of Meditations* (1653), which had little impact in its own time and was only rediscovered in 1895, and like Vaughan in his *Mount of Olives*, or indirectly in their poems which depicted the splendour of God and the love of Christ irradiating all things, save where the shadow of sin obscured. Space forces compression and omission of all these religious poems to concentrate on treatises of devotion that were either masterpieces or had profound popular impact, or to describe unusual experiments in spirituality such as Little Gidding, the creation of Nicholas Ferrar.[93]

This consecrated spirit was a deacon of the Church of England who never became a priest, but had been a high executive of the Virginia Company and travelled widely in Germany, France, Italy, and Spain. In his travels he had found little help from the rather Quietistical Catholic circles he frequented, so he returned greatly enamoured of the piety of the Church of England. At Little Gidding, near Huntingdon and fairly near to Cambridge, he established a community of about thirty persons who shared his family monasticism. Its memory has been kept green in a Victorian novel, *John Inglesant* by J. H. Shorthouse, and in the final one of T. S. Eliot's *Four Quartets*.

The community, centred on his family and that of his brother-in-law, to which neighbouring friends came from time to time, lived a life of prayer and work according to a strict rule. At the beginning of every hour, from 6:00 A.M. to 8:00 P.M., there was an office lasting for about a quarter of an hour, in which several groups in the community took their turn. This office comprised a hymn and portions from the Psalms and Gospels, so that the entire Psalter was recited each day and the Gospels once a month. Furthermore, two or more members kept a vigil from 9:00 P.M. to 1:00 A.M. while reciting the Psalter once more. Charles I visited the community in 1633 and called it his "little Arminian Nunnery."

92 *Ibid.*, p. 181.
93 See B. Blackstone, *The Ferrar Papers* (1938), which includes a critical ed. of a contemporary life written by Nicholas's brother, John Ferrar; also A. L. Maycock, *Nicholas Ferrar of Little Gidding* (1938), and the D.N.B. life by M. Creighton, XVIII (1889), pp. 377-80, and the *Oxford Dictionary of the Christian Church* (ed. F. L. Cross, reprint of 1963), pp. 500b-501a.

The community was chiefly engaged in the adoration of God, but its members also visited the sick and the poor of the village and taught the children the Psalms. Such recreations as they had included gardening, manuscript illumination, and exquisite book-binding. The British Museum has an example of this in the cover for a harmony of the Gospels, and the Page liturgical collection at the Huntington Library in California has a prayer book of Little Gidding decorated by the community which is reproduced in the illustrations of the present volume.

Mary Collett of the community, inaccurately described in *John Inglesant* as having a love affair, consecrated herself to Christ as a virgin. The austerities of the founder, Ferrar, were also genuine. He kept the late watch in the chapel in his manor house two or three times a week and slept only four hours on other nights, and was sparing in eating and drinking. His piety was modelled upon the Bible and in a filial conformity with the canons of the Church of England. He died in 1637, but the community was not disbanded until 1646, after being the subject of several Puritan criticisms. One of these, printed in 1646, shows how its author was offended by what he thought to be the "idolatry" of the chapel, but he could not—fortunately for another age—forget it, so he wrote:

> I observed the Chapel in general to be fairly and spaciously adorned with herbs and flowers, natural and artificial, and upon every pillar along both sides of the chapel . . . tapers (I mean great Virgin-wax candles on every pillar). The half-pace [a semi-step dividing nave and east end?] was all covered with tapestry, and upon that half-pace stood the Altar-like Table, with a rich carpet hanging very large on the half-pace, and some plate, as a chalice and candlesticks . . . a laver and cover all of brass, cut and carved with imagery work . . . and the cover had a cross erected on it. . . .[94]

Here for twenty-one years could be found the Caroline Anglican holiness of beauty, the fit context for the beauty of holiness.

No Caroline divine has exhibited more beauty in his style than Jeremy Taylor (1613-1667) whose loyalty to the Church of England during the days of the Commonwealth and Protectorate were

[94] *The Arminian Nunnery, or, A Brief Description and Relation of the late Erected Monasticall Place called the Arminian Nunnery at Little Gidding in Huntingdonshire* (1641), pp. 7-8.

honoured by his consecration soon after the Restoration to the Irish see of Down and Connor, to which Dromore was joined later, the cathedral of which he built and was buried in. His *Holy Living* (1650) and *Holy Dying* (1651) are both masterpieces and yet representative of Anglican devotional writing at this time at its best. Taylor was erudite, quarrying from obscure and exotic as well as traditional mines, a distinguished casuist, a splendid preacher, a stylist of magnificence, a man combining sympathy and imagination with practicality, all directed by a pastoral heart. In the beginning of *Holy Living*, he complained that as a consequence of the Civil War religion was "painted upon banners, and thrust out of churches." He considered even more serious the fact that God was worshipped, "not as he is, the Father of our Lord Jesus Christ, and afflicted Prince, the King of Sufferings; nor as the God of peace; . . . but . . . rather as the Lord of hosts, which title He was pleased to lay aside when the Kingdom of the Gospel was preached by the Prince of Peace."[95] So distressed was the state of the Church of England in 1650, with the use of the Prayer Book forbidden, and many of the bishops silenced, that Taylor felt it to be his duty to encourage Anglicans in faith and hope. Under the onslaughts of successful Calvinism it seemed that some of them doubted whether they were saved, ironically the very problem that over-scrupulous Puritan spirits had felt some forty years earlier about their election. Taylor in one pithy paragraph enumerates twelve signs of "grace and predestination" to prove that those who have them as certainly belong to God and are His sons as certainly as they are His creatures.[96]

Holy Living is a combination of a guide to prayer, a collection of prayers, a book of meditations, and a book of general directions for living the good life, all in one literary parcel. "I thought," he wrote in the introduction as he recalled the difficulty of being loyal to the dispossessed Church of England, "I had reasons enough inviting me to draw into one body those advices which the several necessities of many men must use at some time or another and many of them daily: that by a collection of holy precepts they might less feel the want of personal and attending guides, and that the rules for conduct of souls might be committed to a book which they might always have; since they could not always have a prophet

---

[95] *The Rule and Exercises of Holy Living* (ed. A. R. Waller, 1901), p. 1.
[96] *Ibid.*, p. 3.

at their needs, nor be suffered to go up to the house of the Lord to inquire of the appointed oracle."[97]

The book has an introduction followed by four chapters. The introduction affirms that there are three instruments or helps to a holy life: "care of our time," "purity of intention," and "the practise of the presence of God." The first chapter is concerned with the right use of time, the next with the duties the soul owes to itself, the third with duties owed to others imposed by Christian justice, and the last chapter with the duties we owe to God.

It is this last and longest section that is chiefly concerned with spirituality. The primary demand is for faith, through which we believe in God's self-revelation, which motivates us to pray and enact good works, and which is also the basis of hope in God's bounty for time and for eternity. Of these the chief blessing is love, for this is to receive God himself, and it evokes the response of human love in return. But this does not, and should not in Taylor's view, lead to supernatural and ecstatic visions or trances. He insisted upon the quietness of the Divine approach: "It is sweet, even, and full of tranquility; having in it no violences or transportations, but going on in a course of holy actions and duties which are proportionable to our condition and present state."[98]

Bible reading and fasting are recommended as aids for the development of the soul. The Word of God is the foundation of Christian doctrine and duty. A soul thus nourished upon the Scriptures and prayer must serve its neighbour with superabounding charity.

Holy Dying was written for Lady Carbery, Taylor's patroness in Golden Grove, Carmarthenshire, but she died before it was completed, and at her funeral he preached the greatest panegyric of its kind in the English language.[99] His wife, to whom he had been long and happily married, died about the same time. His accustomed spirit of joyful acceptance of all that God sends is still there, but the trumpet is muted, and the shining confidence is framed in clouds. This was no academic exercise in trying to console the sick and dying and those who minister to them: this intensely sympathetic divine was describing and prescribing for his own pain.

He begins by warning against postponing repentance, the beginning of the godly life, until sickness starts, because then

[97] *Ibid.*, pp. 1-2. [98] *Ibid.*, p. 158. [99] See Chap. IV, Sect. 4.

there are lacking both mental clarity and physical vigour. He is highly critical of the church of Rome's emphasis on extreme unction, because it was often used "when the man is half dead, when he can exercise no act of understanding."

This briefer companion volume keeps to the essentials in trying to persuade the healthy that sickness and death are subjects for immediate consideration, and not to be postponed. So the opening chapter by reflection, and the second chapter by the use of religious exercises, stresses the brevity of human life and its unexpected termination. The third chapter treats the special temptations induced or increased by sickness, while the fourth deals with the special graces elicited in those who count on God's continuing goodness, turning sickness into a school of virtue. The last chapter expounds the duties of a priest ministering to the sick and closes with a moving account of the duties of relatives to the dying.

One citation from this curiously erudite and richly wrought tapestry must suffice for the many passages deserving citation. It tells magnificently of the equalising brevity of human life in the long span of the historical centuries:

> A man may read a sermon, the best and most passionate that ever may be preached, if he shall but enter into the sepulchres of kings. In the same Escurial where the Spanish princes live in greatness and power, and decree war or peace, they have wisely placed a cemetery where their ashes and their glory shall sleep till time shall be no more; and where our kings have been crowned, their ancestors lay interred, and they must walk over their grandsire's head to take his crown. There is an acre sown with royal seed, the copy of the greatest change from rich to naked, from ceiled roofs to arched coffins, from living like gods to die like men. There is enough to cool the flames of lust, to abate the heights of pride, to appease the itch of covetous desires, to sully and dash out the dissembling colours of a lustful, artificial, and imaginary beauty. There the warlike and the peaceful, the fortunate and the miserable, the beloved and the despised princes mingle their dust, and pay down their symbol of mortality, and tell all the world that when we die our ashes shall be equal to kings, and our accounts easier, and our pains or our crowns shall be less.[100]

[100] *The Rule and Exercises of Holy Dying* (ed. A. R. Waller, 1901), pp. 28-29.

This book, of the *ars moriendi* genre, was so obviously a twin of its immediate predecessor that it was soon bound up with it, and *Holy Living* and *Holy Dying* were thought of as a single book. It has had an incalculable influence on English life and even played a part in starting two of England's later great religious movements, Methodism and Tractarianism.[101] John Wesley read it while a young man at Oxford and, as a result, began to doubt if he was saved; he also attributed to it his keeping a journal.[102] Also, John Keble, whose sermon on "National Apostasy" from the pulpit of St. Mary's Church is generally accepted as marking the beginning of the Oxford Movement in 1833, studied Taylor's companion volumes sixteen years earlier, evaluating them as an epoch in his religious life.[103]

What are Jeremy Taylor's leading characteristics? First, he expresses great tenderness of devotion, but no ecstasy, no delight in tears for their own sake, no posturing. He also exhibits that sobriety and moderation which the Caroline divines thought should mark the Christian life. Taylor recaptures the spirit of medieval devotion, as in the following "Act of Desire" in a Communion meditation: "O now come Lord Jesus, come quickly; my heart is desirous of thy presence and thirsty of thy grace, and would fain entertain thee, not as a guest but as an inhabitant, as the Lord of all my faculties. Enter in and take possession, and dwell with me for ever; that I also may dwell in the heart of my dearest Lord, which was opened for me with a spear and love."[104]

Taylor, like the metaphysical poets and other Caroline divines, sees through a transparent world to its Creator, or, to change the metaphor, views all creatures as ladders leading up to God. "Let everything you see," he writes, "represent to your spirit the presence, the excellence and the power of God; for so shall your actions be done more frequently with an actual eye to God's presence by your often seeing him in the glass of the Creation."[105] Also, let the human creation prove worthy of its Creator: "Let us remember that God is in us, and that we are in Him: we are His workman-

---

101 Stranks, *op. cit.*, p. 93; also see R. Southey's *Life of Wesley* (1848), I, p. 3. I am indebted to Canon C. J. Stranks's book for this reference and for the two immediately following.

102 See *The Journal of John Wesley*, 8 Vols. (ed. Nehemiah Curnock, 1909), I, p. 42.

103 See J. T. Coleridge, *Memoir of John Keble* (Oxford, 1870), p. 68.

104 *The Rule and Exercises of Holy Living* (ed. A. R. Waller, 1901), II, p. 186.
105 *Ibid.*, I, p. 45.

ship, let us not deface it; we are in His presence, let us not pollute it by unholy and impure actions."[106]

Taylor is, also, the humanist as well as the Christian in his concern to educate people out of their follies, inconsistencies, and absurdities; in his use of illustrations to bring the truth home to them (he is a master of sustained metaphors, vivid word-painting and of simpler similes); in his use of pre-Christian classical authors; and, above all, in his rational desire to remove obscurity and paradox. All his writing is reminiscent of *l'Humanisme Dévot*, Abbé Brémond's term for the French spirituality of the seventeenth century in his monumental *Histoire du Sentiment Religieux en France*.

A closing citation from *Holy Living* on contentment will reveal Taylor's human qualities of sympathy and helpfulness that make this book break through the moulds of his religion and century in a deep understanding of the perennial human condition:

> We are in the world like men playing at tables; the chance is not in our power, but to play it is; and when it is fallen we must manage it as we can; and let nothing trouble us but when we do a base action, or speak like a fool, or think wickedly: these things God hath put into our powers; but concerning those things which are wholly in the choice of another, they cannot fall under our deliberations, and therefore neither are they fit for our passions. My fear may make me miserable, but it cannot prevent what another hath in his power and purpose: and prosperities can only be enjoyed by them who fear not at all to lose them; since the amazement and passion concerning the future takes off all the pleasure of the present possession, therefore if thou hast lost thy hand, do not also lose thy constancy: and if thou must die a little sooner, yet do not die impatiently. For no chance is evil to him that is content, and to a man nothing is miserable unless it be unreasonable. No man can make another man to be his slave unless he hath first enslaved himself to life and death, to pleasure or pain, to hope or fear: command these passions, and you are freer than the Parthian kings.[107]

All other writings on spirituality among high-church divines in this century are necessarily anticlimactic after Jeremy Taylor, and will therefore receive the briefest treatment.

---

[106] *Ibid.*, I, p. 46.   [107] *Ibid.*, I, pp. 147-48.

4. *Popular Anglican Spirituality and Liturgical Devotions*

The two most popular devotional guides in the seventeenth century were *The Practice of Piety, Directing a Christian how to walk with God*, the earliest recorded edition of which appeared in 1612, and *The Whole Duty of Man* published in 1657. Both were anonymous, but the former was soon claimed to be the work of Lewis Bayly, Bishop of Bangor in North Wales.[108] The author of *The Whole Duty of Man* is still veiled in obscurity, though he was a royalist, a loyal churchman in the days when Anglicanism was in the shadows, and probably a clergyman. Intriguingly enough all three of the names put forward as putative authors were at one time or another canons of Christ Church, Oxford: the theologian Dr. William Hammond, Dr. John Fell (Dean of Christ Church in November 1660 to which was added the office of Bishop of Oxford in 1676), and Dr. Richard Allestree (Regius Professor of Divinity at Oxford from 1663 to 1679), the most probable author.[109]

Both books were widely influential, Bayly's for four of the first five decades and Allestree's for the last five decades of the century. Bayly's was influential when Calvinism was the dominant theology, Allestree's when Arminianism was on the eve of its victory and through the era of rationalistic moralism. Though it would be inaccurate to call any bishop a Puritan, as has been done in the case of Bayly, he seems to have followed Calvin in everything except church order, and therefore his work was eagerly purchased and used in Puritan circles,[110] although dedicated to Prince Charles, afterwards Charles I. It reached its twenty-fifth edition by 1630, its fifty-ninth in 1735, and was last republished in 1848.[111] Allestree's book reached its twenty-eighth edition by 1790. While it appealed to all classes, its tone was definitely high church. Its orthodoxy, rationality, sobriety, practicality and prudence made it particularly suitable as a guide to eighteenth-century

[108] A chaplain to Prince Henry, his Puritan views brought royal disfavour, so he apparently trimmed his sails, and was appointed chaplain to James I in 1616, and later in the same year Bishop of Bangor in North Wales. The best account of him and his devotional handbook is J. E. Bailey, "Bishop Lewis Bayly and his *Practice of Piety*" in *The Manchester Quarterly*, II (1883), pp. 221-39. His contentiousness made many enemies for him, not to mention a yawning gap between profession and practice. See H. R. Trevor-Roper, *Archbishop Laud* (1940), p. 188.

[109] See Paul Elmen, "Richard Allestree and *The Whole Duty of Man* in *The Library*" (5th series), VI, pp. 19-27.

[110] See Gordon S. Wakefield, *Puritan Devotion* (1957), p. 4.

[111] It was translated into French in 1625, Welsh in 1630 (the year before Bishop Bayly's death), German in 1629, Polish in 1647, and into a North American Indian dialect in 1665 at Cambridge, Massachusetts.

piety when it was even more popular than in the seventeenth century.

Bayly in the epistle which prefaces *The Practice of Piety* provides both incentives to piety and dissuasives from its disuse: "For as Moses his face, by often talking with God, shined in the eyes of the *People*, so by frequent praying (which is our talking to God) and hearing the Word (which is God speaking unto us), we shall be changed from glory to glorie, by the Spirit of the Lord, to the Image of the Lord."[112] Piety "hath the promise of this life and that which shall never end. But without Pietie, there is no internall comfort to be .found in Conscience nor externall peace to be looked for in the World, nor any eternall happiness to be hoped for in Heaven."[113]

His work combines meditations and prayers, together with the noncontroversial elements of the Protestant conception of Christian practice. The nature of God, the misery of an unreconciled, and the blessedness in life and death of a man reconciled to God in Christ, take up the first 103 pages. The next 234 pages are concerned with seven obstacles to piety, reading the Bible beneficially once a year, and prayers for the morning and evening. Meditations and prayers for a godly householder, family prayers, graces before and after meals, a lengthy discourse on the Sabbath day, and prayers for the Sabbath occupy the next 163 pages. Fasting, giving alms, feasting, meditations on receiving Holy Communion together with a confession of sin and a soliloquy before and a prayer after reception take up the next 115 pages. Then there follows a large miscellaneous collection of directions, meditations, and prayers, for the beginning of sickness, when making one's will, "comfortable thoughts against despair," consolation for one about to die, "the last speech of a godly man dying," and a controversial set of meditations on martyrdom, attempting to prove that the martyrs of Popery cannot be found. This book of almost 800 pages ends with a colloquy between Christ and the soul about the efficacy of his Passion, and the soul's soliloquy addressed to Christ her Saviour.

Bayly provided the model for Puritan and "low church"[114] devo-

[112] *Op. cit.* (11th edn. of 1619), sig. A5 verso.
[113] *Ibid.*, sigs. A6-A6 verso.
[114] This term is anachronistic but it points to an important fact: namely, that there was a Puritan Anglicanism, that is, Puritanism *within* the Church of England until 1645, when Parliament and the Westminster Assembly of Divines established Puritanism in its Presbyterian and Independent forms as the officially

tion, by his recommendation that Bible study was as necessary as prayer and meditation. One chapter of the Bible was to be read before leaving the bedroom, another at noon, and a third at night. If this method was kept up regularly, and the part of the Psalter appointed for the day in the Book of Common Prayer, then the whole Bible would be read through once a year, six chapters excepted which could be added for December. The result of Bible reading should be a heart sorrowing for sin, and a resolve (assisted by divine grace) to amend. An hour should be given to private prayer, according to Bayly, and the same time to household prayer. Christians are then ready to do their daily work fortified by the promises of God and the directions of the Word of God. The product of such a work of piety would be perhaps excessively conscious of human sin, original and actual, but would never dare to be trivial with God, and it would seem to mould men and women of gravity and dignity, as well as intrepidity. Fearing God, they were unafraid of men. Bayly shows us the profound respect for the Bible as the guide in all aspects of living, an insistence on morality, a sense of individual responsibility before God, and the unremitting effort to justify justification by faith and make one's election sure, which was at the heart of Protestantism in its Calvinist manifestation, and especially in Puritanism.

The whole style and temper of *The Whole Duty of Man* is as different as the time in which it was written. That was a time when men were exhausted with religious controversy, and doubtful whether any reconciliation could come from the bitter factions of the supporters of either the King and the bishops, or of the Protector and his Puritan divines, some of whom were as disaffected as Richard Baxter in the final days of the Protectorate. The book, suitably written for the changing climate of theological opinion, avoided the disputatious points of theology and concentrated on morality. Its title came from the final words of the Book of Ecclesiastes, where the penetrating sceptic's thrusts are sidestepped by the impatient statement that the essence of religion is "Fear God, and keep his commandments: for this is the whole duty of man."

The full title is also a summary of the contents: *The Whole*

supported religion of England. From 1662 onwards the Puritan tradition in religion and worship continued *outside* the Church of England as Nonconformity or Dissent. The other alternative term, the "Puritan wing" is an importation from nineteenth century French politics, and this is an anachronism and an anatopism also, but it suggests something of the dynamic and shifting nature of Puritanism.

Duty of Man, laid down in a plain and familiar way for the use of all, but especially the meanest reader; divided into seventeen chapters, one whereof being read every Lord's Day, the whole may be read over thrice in the year; necessary for all families. With private devotions for several occasions. Here was an attempt on the part of a high churchman to write a book on devotion which would reach the middle and working classes, which Bayly and the Puritan writers had particularly aimed at with their plain English. Hence its determination to make this plain in the title, despite being open to the charge of snobbery in assuring "the meanest reader" that he would understand it. The book's opening paragraph makes its purpose clear: "The only intent of this ensuing treatise, is to be a short and plain direction to the very meanest readers, to behave themselves so in this world, that they may be happy for ever in the next."[115] The emphasis was to be on behaviour, less on belief, especially any speculative matters such as election and predestination. Furthermore, enlightened self-interest is the sensible man's guide here to get to the hereafter. Duty is all, and delight and imagination and vision are completely excluded from consideration. We are offered orthodoxy with blinkers, respectability without rapture, but the thrill of adventure and the daring of faith with the aid of grace are almost entirely absent.

For all the limitations of the book it has its strengths, particularly in its instruction on the two Sacraments and the due preparation for them. There is an abundance of clear and commonsense advice. And if the instruction on prayer lacks the lyricism of Herbert, there were times when the author of *The Whole Duty of Man* could express affection in his prayers and even a longing for eternity and the company of the saints, but not in this volume. In another volume, *The Whole Duty of Prayer*,[116] there is a fine extended "aspiration" which concludes: "Lord, let the hope and expectation of this eternal rest and felicity sweeten all my labours, and ease my torments, let it mitigate my afflictions, and comfort my spirits, that I faint not in my journey, nor be depressed under my burden, and hold on cheerfully and valiantly, till I arrive at the Land of Promise, and there receive the Lot of mine inheritance with the Saints in Light for evermore."[117] If there is more of Sto-

---

[115] *Op. cit.* (quarto ed. of 1684), sig. A1.

[116] The full title is: *The Whole Duty of Prayer containing devotions for every day of the week, and for several occasions ordinary and extraordinary; By the author of The Whole Duty of Man. Necessary for all Families.* All references are to this edition of 1692.

[117] *Op. cit.* (1692), p. 47.

icism than of St. Bernard's mysticism here, at least the spirit of calculation is muted.

A new type of Anglican devotion appeared just prior to and during the Restoration of the monarchy. The latter led to the restoration of the Book of Common Prayer which had been proscribed by Parliament since 1645, though its defenders had secretly used it in apocopated services or had combined liturgical and non-liturgical elements in worship as a disguise.

In 1660, however, the Prayer Book became the symbol alike of Anglican loyalty and of the overthrow of Puritanism and its despised *Directory of Public Worship*, and of the rejection of all informal and extemporaneous worship which was soon equated with anarchy or rebellion. A generation had grown up which was ignorant of the Book of Common Prayer, and so there was a need for liturgical information and devotional discipline. The new books combined to make devotions more liturgical, and less supplementary to or independent of the Book of Common Prayer.

One of the very best of these was Anthony Sparrow's *A Rationale upon the Book of Common Prayer*, the first known copy of which is dated 1657. The preface defends the Prayer Book from the contradictory charges of being "old Roman dotage" (the Puritan criticism) and "schismatically new" (the Roman Catholic criticism). Its answer was that it is primitive and reasonable, neither anachronistically irrelevant nor superstitious. "As for those that love it and suffer for the loss of it, this will show them reasons, why they should suffer on, and love it still more and more."

This work is a commentary on every part of the Prayer Book in the order in which its contents appear. It demonstrates an impressive knowledge of Scripture, the Fathers, and especially of the liturgical customs of the non-Papal Catholicism of the eastern churches. Sparrow is very fond of St. John Chrysostom, among the eastern Fathers, and of St. Augustine among the western Fathers.

His concise comments are often not merely liturgically informative, but devotionally full of insight. The versicle of salutation: "The Lord be with you" is a text for a good example of Sparrow's commentary. After remarking on its Biblical origin and its use in ancient liturgies, he explains that it means, in effect: "The Lord be with you, to lift up your hearts, and raise your devotions to his service. The Lord be with you, to reward you hereafter with eternal life." The response: "And with thy spirit," is explained as meaning virtually, "thou [the priest] art about to offer up prayers and spiritual sacrifices for us, therefore we pray likewise for thee, that He without whom nothing is good and acceptable may be with thy spirit while thou art exercised in these spiritual services, which must be performed with the Spirit, according to St. Paul I Cor. 14.14." The summary is most pithy: "Thus the priest prays and wishes well to the people, and they pray and wish well to the priest."[118]

Among several partly didactic, partly devotional commentaries on the Prayer Book,[119] the most complete are those of Thomas Comber[120] (1645-1699), who became Dean of Durham in 1691. Between 1672 and 1677 he published a series of four studies of the Prayer Book, dealing with Matins and Evensong (1672), Holy Communion (1674), the Litany and Occasional Prayers (1675), and the Occasional Offices (1677). His largest work, however, was entitled, *A Companion to the Temple; Or, a help to Devotion in the use of the Common Prayer, Divided into Four Parts* (1684). Its primary aim was to reconcile Dissenters to the Church of England services, for Comber was opposed to James II's attempt to fill Anglican benefices with Roman Catholics, and he warmly welcomed the arrival of William and Mary.

His work was prolix, thorough, accurate, and deadly dull, except when he forgot to be devotional and turned controversial. The triple advantages of this type of book which was to have many successors in the eighteenth and particularly in the nineteenth centuries,[121] were that it fostered an informed appreciation of the Prayer Book, cultivated loyalty to the Church of England, and promoted liturgical devotion as contrasted with idiosyncratic devotions that were extra-liturgical.

5. Puritans and the Devotional Life

In considering Puritan piety, we shall not analyse such "guides to godliness"[122] as the one Downame wrote with that very title in

[118] *Op. cit.*, p. 62.
[119] As examples, H. L'Estrange, *The Alliance of Divine Offices* (1659) and T. Elborow, *An Exposition of the Book of Common Prayer* (1663).
[120] See ed. C. E. Whiting, *The Autobiography and Letters of Thomas Comber* (Surtees Society, CLVI-CLVII, 1941-1942).
[121] See R.C.D. Jasper, *Prayer Book Revision in England, 1800-1900* (1954) and William Seth Adams, "William Palmer of Worcester, 1803-1885, The Only Learned Man among Them" (Princeton University, Ph.D., 1973). It is an account of him as liturgiologist, theologian and Tractarian.
[122] This title for Puritan devotional treatises and collections of prayers has been popularized by Gordon S. Wakefield, *op. cit.*, pp. 6 and 85, but it also happens

1622, nor his more famous *The Christian's Warfare* (1609), nor even Arthur Dent's highly popular *A Plain Man's Pathway to Heaven* (1601), because this has been done elsewhere,[123] and because the difference between non-high-church Anglican spirituality and Puritan devotions is negligible. This will enable us to concentrate on two masterpieces of the way to godliness, both produced by men who had never been to a university, who, like George Fox, the founder of Quakerism, were experts in the experimental knowledge of God. One was Richard Baxter, who declined the bishopric of Hereford at the Restoration, and was the leader of the Presbyterian delegation who were considering a possible ecumenical revision of the Book of Common Prayer at the Savoy Conference, with a representative group of Anglicans, and who is the author of *The Saints' Everlasting Rest*. The other is the immortal tinker and allegorist, John Bunyan, whose superb imagination extracted from his experience in the Civil Wars and from his understanding of God gained in fair weather and more often foul, created the prose epic of Puritanism, *The Pilgrim's Progress*.

Richard Baxter (1615-1691) wrote his classic devotional work, *The Saints' Everlasting Rest* at Rouse Lench when recovering from a most serious illness. It was an instantaneous success and was reprinted nine times in the decade following its first publication in 1650. It is a treatise of a familiar type in Anglicanism, namely the persuasive to a good life; but within Puritanism, as Louis L. Martz has argued,[124] it is most unusual in that it employed the Catholic techniques of meditation using the Ignatian "composition"—employing the senses usually regarded as inimical by Protestants to true spirituality, to enable the soul to concentrate more fully on Christ in his sufferings and redemption or on the joys of heaven, and the interior soliloquy as a way of preaching to

---

to be the title of a devotional treatise of Downame's, *A Guide to Godliness, or a Treatise of a Christian Life* (1622).

[123] One reason is that they do not differ greatly from the Anglican works of the period such as Bishop Bayly's, Dent's and Downame's, but also because some of the earlier works of the period have already been treated in Davies, *op. cit.*, I, pp. 317, 320, 322f., 417, 432.

[124] Louis L. Martz claims: "Baxter deliberately sets out to recover for the Puritans some of these devotional practices which had fallen away as a result of Calvinist thinking. This is perfectly clear from his constant marginal references to St. Bernard, Gerson, Cardinal Nicholas of Cusa, the Jesuit Nieremberg, and . . . Bishop Hall who was himself engaged in this kind of devotional recovery." (*Op. cit.*, p. 168; see also pp. 169-75.) This statement is correct, but it does not do justice to some of the Puritan predecessors of Baxter, such as John Preston or Francis Rous, who also had meditations on the sacred humanity of Christ.

one's self. At the same time he shares the desperate Puritan desire for assurance that he is one of the elect. Both Catholic techniques and Protestant concerns are mated in this volume.

The Saints' Everlasting Rest is, in fact, his calm assurance of salvation, his conviction that he belongs to the elect. Yet, as it is perfectly clear from Baxter's wide experience as a minister in Kidderminster and as an army chaplain, there were very many apparently God-fearing Christians who had no such assurance, but only a turbulence produced by anxiety and fear. "Why do they lack the calmness of the sense of assurance?" says Baxter. He finds two answers to his question. The first is that many Christians seem to have a false idea of grace—that one must just sit and wait for it, without making any preparation for it. The other is that many feel, knowing that many are called but few are chosen, that their chances seem infinitesimally small. The only remedy that Baxter proposes is a very practical one. That is, "to ply his duty, and exercise his Graces, till he finde his Doubts and Discomforts vanish."[125]

Baxter is addressing himself to Puritanism's central problem: how one may know for sure whether God has chosen him as a brand to be plucked from the burning? It was as acute a problem at the start of the century as at its mid-point. Dent had consoled many bruised and tender consciences by providing them with "eight signes of salvation." These all-important marks were: "A love of the children of God, a delight in his word, often and frequent prayer, zeale of God's glorie, deniall of our selves, patient bearing of the crosse with profit and comfort, faithfulnesse in our calling, and just, honest, faithful, and conscionable dealing in all our actions amongst men."[126]

The fourth part of Baxter's treatise is concerned with meditation, moving from intellectual issues to exciting the heart's affections in order to free the will for conformity to God. His defence of this is most interesting: "As the Papists have wronged the Merits of Christ by their ascribing too much to our own works, so it is almost incredible how much they [Protestants] on the other extream, have wronged the safety and consolation of men's souls by telling them that their own endeavours are only for Obedience and Gratitude, but are not so much as Conditions of their Salva-

125 *Op. cit.* (4th edn., 1653), Pt. III, p. 168.
126 *A Plain Man's Pathway to Heaven*, pp. 31-32. See also on this important point of Puritan casuistry, M. M. Knappen, *op. cit.*, pp. 348, 393-95; William Haller, *op. cit.*, pp. 88-91; and Max Weber, *The Protestant Ethic and the Spirit of Capitalism* (trans. Talcott Parsons, 1930), pp. 98-128.

tion, or Means of their increased Sanctification or Consolation."
He continues: "had they bestowed but that time in exercising holy
Affections, and in serious thoughts of the promised Happiness,
which they have spent in enquiring only after Signs, I am confident, according to the ordinary workings of God, they would have
been better provided with both Assurance and with Joys."[127]

He provides several "meditations" that are vivid word-paintings,
and "compositions" of the Ignatian type. One,[128] a lengthy meditation on the suffering Saviour, is fairly commonplace, though not
lacking in genuine fervour. Another, worthy of citation, is part of
his canvas of the Eternal City:

Thus take thy *heart* into the *Land of Promise*; shew it the
pleasant hills, and fruitful valleys; Shew it the clusters of
Grapes which thou hast gathered; & by those convince it that
it is a pleasant Land, flowing with better then milk and
honey; enter the gates of the *Holy City*; walk through the
streets of the *New Jerusalem*, walk about *Sion*, go round
about her, tell the Towers thereof, mark well her bulwarks;
consider her places; that thou mayest tell it to thy Soul . . .
What sayest thou now to all this? This is thy Rest, O my Soul,
and this must be the place of thy Everlasting habitation.[129]

This work was one of the most popular companions to the Bible
England had ever seen. It appealed to the unlettered and the let-
tered alike, because of its clarity, simplicity, practicality, and its
willingness to break new ground. For this highly original man any
label is a libel. No wonder he preferred to be called a "meer
Catholick."

John Bunyan's masterpiece also appealed to the simple and
the cultured alike and has now been translated into more than a
hundred languages. Bunyan[130] (1622-1688) followed his father's

---

[127] *Saints' Everlasting Rest*, Pt. IV, p. 5. He (Baxter) tells us that Bishop
Joseph Hall of Exeter and Norwich, who was suspended by Archbishop Laud in
1641, had taken the same step as himself, in using a method derived from Roman
Catholic spirituality, as this was documented in Hall's *Arte of Meditation* (1606).
This was itself derived from Jean Mompaer's famous *Rosetum* which was the
principal source of Abbot Garcia de Cisneros's treatise which indirectly assisted
St. Ignatius Loyola's composition of *Spiritual Exercises*. These, in Bunny's Anglican adaptation, had converted Baxter to Christianity. Hence Baxter knew the
value of such methods from experience.

[128] *Op. cit.*, Pt. IV, pp. 191-96.   [129] *Ibid.*, Pt. IV, pp. 205-206.

[130] See Henri Talon's magisterial *John Bunyan, the Man and His Works* (1931).
For a modern edition, see ed. R. Sharrock, *Pilgrim's Progress* (Oxford, 2nd edn.,
1950). There is also a combined edn. of *The Pilgrim's Progress, Grace Abounding,
and a Relation of his Imprisonment* (Oxford, 1925) by Edmund Venables.

trade as a brazier (he is loosely termed a "tinker"), fought on the parliamentary side in the Civil War, and about 1649 married a poor woman whose dowry comprised Bishop Bayly's *Practice of Piety* and Arthur Dent's *A Plain Man's Pathway to Heaven*. The Bible, Foxe's martyrology, and the two devotional treatises mentioned, appear to have constituted all his reading. Most of the years between 1660 and 1672 he spent in Bedford prison for refusing to be silent as an unlicensed preacher of the Gospel in Independent and Baptist circles. *Grace Abounding to the Chief of Sinners* (1666), his spiritual autobiography, shows that he had been in anxiety about his salvation for seven years, and that was written in durance vile, while his greatest work, *Pilgrim's Progress*, was also written during a second period of imprisonment in 1676 and printed about two years later.

This work shows life as an almost unending spiritual warfare, and salvation as the Gospel pearl of great price worth losing the whole world to gain. It depicts vividly, spiritually, and simply, and with the greatest sincerity, earnestness, and intensity, Christian's journey from the City of Destruction to the Heavenly City, through the Slough of Despond, up the daunting Hill of Difficulty, through Vanity Fair, and the Valley of the Shadow of Death, each symbolizing the pitfalls on the way to salvation. Christian's companions or persons he encounters are also vividly imagined, as helpful like Evangelist or Greatheart, or as hindrances like Mr. Worldly-Wiseman, Mr. Legality, or Mr. Facing-both-Ways. The theme has been compressed into a popular hymn, "He who would valiant be . . ." which is a modification of the heartening lines sung by the pilgrims on the way to the Enchanted Ground.

Despite the criticism of Fr. Louis Bouyer, the French Oratorian, that this is a "tedious and boring book," which has contributed much "to Puritanism's reputation as being the quintessence of boredom,"[131] it has been a perennial favourite with the English-speaking people, to say nothing of being in C. H. Firth's phrase "the prose epic of Puritanism."

It represents the values inculcated by Puritan religion, especially the doctrine of the perseverance of the saints, which was the Puritan counterpart of the Catholic pursuit of perfection. It stresses the constant need of grace to face the hardships of life. It exposes the glittering and insubstantial nature of temptations. It emphasizes the strenuous loneliness and singularity of the Christian life,

[131] *Op. cit.*, p. 160.

121

and its Calvinism is clearly revealed in the overwhelming sense of divine providence and guidance and in the acknowledgment that the gate leading to everlasting life is narrow. Yet for all its gravity, the joy of the elect pilgrims can be seen when their solemn countenances break into psalmody and praise.

What can be said generally about the nature of Puritan spirituality? Almost all commentators emphasize its dark view of human nature, its depressing pessimism, its constant self-scrutiny. But Puritans themselves would have argued that this was realism, and it was the glory of Christ that he delivered men and women from the scum and foulness of original and actual sin. Nor was this peculiarly Puritan, for it was shared alike by John Donne in his sermons and by St. Ignatius Loyola in the first part of his *Exercises* to shake the soul out of its complacency. In all fairness, however, it cannot be denied that some gentle souls have been unnecessarily frightened by being "dangled over the pit" by Calvinism. There was the notable case of Mistress Katherin Brettergh, an admirable woman, and the sister of John Bruen[132] of Bruenstapleford himself a godly man. Her long illness and her supposed temptation by Satan were a bitter and prolonged testing of her election, so much so that they occupy pages 11 to 37 of the 38 page pamphlet entitled, *A Brief Discourse of the Christian Life and Death of Mistris Katherin Brettergh . . . who departed this world the last of May, 1601* (published 1612). When she knew she was going to die, she was terrified by the thought that she would be damned. Although her minister tried to console her, and even after a Puritan posse of parsons was called in to fortify her without effect, her despair disintegrated just prior to her death, and for five hours she praised God without ceasing, being assured that she was an elect soul. "And after this, shee fell into a short slumber, and awaking said, Oh come kisse me with the kisse of thy mouth for thy love is better than wine! Oh, how sweet the kisses of my Saviour bee."[133] This echo of the Song of Songs is at once the indication of the passion of Puritan devotion, and, in this case, the desperation inflicted by such a prolonged interior scrutiny of motives and actions.

With equal certainty one can affirm that the home is the chief locus of Puritan piety, as the monastery or the convent is of Catholic piety. The flowers of Puritan piety flourished best in rich domes-

132 Described in Davies, *op. cit.*, I, pp. 428-32.
133 *Op. cit.*, p. 33.

tic loam. William Perkins calls the family "a little church,"[134] while William Gouge referred to it as "a seminary of the Church and Commonwealth, a beehive in which is the stock."[135] Baxter made the same point in the following words: "A Christian family . . . is a church . . . a society of Christians combined for the better worshipping and serving God."[136]

This home-bred holiness was nurtured by the parents, themselves taught by the Scriptures, their minister's example and exposition of the sacred oracles, as well as by stirring books such as Foxe's Book of Martyrs or guides to the good life like Bishop Bayly's or Downame's or Dent's, or later, Baxter's or Bunyan's. Richard Baxter's comprehensive and influential *Christian Directory* (1673) devotes considerable space to family worship. This should be held twice each weekday, as Scripture, experience and reason all recommend. The latter dictates: "1. That it is seasonable every morning to give God thanks for the rest of the night past. 2. And to beg directions, protection and provisions and blessing for the following day. 3. And that the evening is a fit season to give God thanks for the mercies of the day, and to confess the sins of the day, and ask forgiveness, and to pray for rest and protection in the night."[137] On the Lord's Day the head of the household has specially important duties. These begin with holding family prayers as a solemn preparation for the services of the day. Then the father leads his family to church for the public service. "After dinner," instructs Baxter, "call your families together, and sing a Psalm of Praise, and by examination or repetition or both, cause them to remember what was publickly taught them."[138] After the afternoon church service, the father is again instructed to "call your families together and first crave God's assistance and acceptance: and then sing a Psalm of Praise: and then repeat the Sermon which you have heard; or if there was none, read out of some lively profitable book; and then pray and praise God: and with all the holy seriousness and joy which is suitable to the work and the day."[139] The father's work is not yet done, for after supper he has to examine the children and servants on what they have learned about the life of a Christian during that day. The day's duties end with family prayers and praises. It was in Puritanism that the principle of the priesthood of all believers was carried out

[134] *Works* (1605), p. 865. [135] *Workes* (1627), II, p. 10.
[136] *Works* (ed. Orme, 1830), IV, p. 75.
[137] *Op. cit.*, Vol. II, Pt. III, p. 507. [138] *Ibid.*, p. 572.
[139] *Ibid.*, p. 573.

to its logical conclusion, with the father of the household acting as priest at the family table.

Private or "closet prayers" were also an important part of the Puritan spiritual regimen. This is most vividly shown in the short and exemplary life of John, Lord Harrington as recorded by Richard Stockton, Milton's childhood rector at All Hallows, Bread Street, London.[140] We are informed that "he usually rose every morning about four or five of the clock, not willingly sleeping above his six hours. As soon as he was thoroughly awake, he endeavoured religiously to set his heart in order and to prepare it for goodness all the day after, offering the first fruits of the day and of his thoughts unto God."[141] He next read a chapter of Scripture, then went to prayers with his servants in his chamber and this lasted the better part of an hour. "After this he read some divine treatise to increase his knowledge in spiritual things, and this for the greater part of an hour. He had of latter times read over in this course Calvin's *Institutions*, and he was at the time of his sickness reading the works of a reverend man now living, one Master Rogers."[142] Then he led the family devotions and returned to his closet, and "after his own private prayer disposed himself to some serious study, if some special business interrupted not his course, for the space of three or four hours."[143] After dinner, if not detained by other business, he again withdrew to his closet and there meditated "upon some sermons, which he had lately heard, for which use he retained some five or six in his mind. . . . He did ordinarily meditate and call to mind four or five in a day" even when he was travelling.[144]

Another characteristic of Puritan spirituality was a very careful self-scrutiny and scrupulous spiritual auditing. Here again John, Lord Harrington's example, is of value. Stockton's account states that "which is markable above many other things," Lord Harrington, after prayers with his servants, in the evening, "withdrew himself, and there in a book which he kept for the account of his life

[140] In *The Church's Lamentation for the Loss of the Godly* (1614), pp. 63-88, which has been republished in ed. Everett H. Emerson, *English Puritanism from John Hooper to John Milton* (Durham, North Carolina, 1968), pp. 189-98.
[141] *Ibid.*, pp. 194-95.
[142] *Ibid.*, p. 195. The "Master Rogers" referred to is almost certainly Richard Rogers, author of the popular *Seven Treatises . . . leading and guiding to true happiness both in this life and in the life to come* (1603). His diary is reproduced in ed. M. M. Knappen, *Two Elizabethan Puritan Diaries by Richard Rogers and Samuel Ward* (1930), and on pp. 7-8 diary keeping is discussed.
[143] *Ibid.*   [144] *Ibid.*, pp. 195-96.

he set down what he had done all that day; how he had either offended or done good, and how he was tempted and withstood them, and according to his account he humbled himself."[145] He also scrutinized his spiritual accounts for the whole week on Saturday evening "to call himself to a strict account how he had spent the whole week, that, according as he found his estate, he might better fit himself to sanctify the Sabbath following."[146] Stockton also reports that a great friend of Lord Harrington's told him that he did on the last Saturday of the month a monthly spiritual audit also, to see, in a good month or week, "how he had added and got more grace and strength of piety."[147] Here was one, indeed, who could say, with John Milton, though Harrington did not reach his twenty-third birthday, "All is if I have grace to use it so, as ever in my great Task-Master's eye."[148]

Puritan spirituality was Bible-centred, and therefore exceedingly suspicious in general of traditional Catholic methods of spirituality, though there were significant exceptions.[149] The suspicion has already been met in its most vitriolic form in the diatribes of Prynne and Burton against Cosin's *Devotions*. Baxter approved of mental prayer, but was critical of the inconvenient, time-wasting and health-endangering austerity of the night office.[150] The Puritans also ridiculed those who considered that continence and the virgin life were superior to the married life, and affirmed that it was the continent who achieved the greatest mystical heights. It seemed inconsistent to them to consider virginity an excellent calling and yet to call holy matrimony a Sacrament, for this was to set one Sacrament against another (holy orders against matrimony).[151]

The Bible-centred character of Puritan spirituality involved several other significant consequences. One was that the emphasis on the sole mediatorship of Christ excluded any possibility of invocation of the saints. Another consequence was that there was no unmediated union with God, least of all any absorption into God,

---

[145] *Ibid.*, p. 196. [146] *Ibid.*, p. 197.
[147] *Ibid.* [148] Milton's *Sonnet* II.
[149] It is interesting that Ambrose Isaac, Richard Baxter, and William Gouge, all Puritans, approve of mental prayer, but Owen does not; but it is typical that Gouge should justify the practice by Biblical precedents in Moses, Nehemiah, and Hannah (*Workes*, 1627, I, p. 208).
[150] *Works* (ed. Orme, 1830), IV, p. 239: "unless men did irrationally place the service of God in praying this hour rather than another, they might see how improvidently and sinfully they lose their time in twice dressing and undressing, and in the intervals of their sleep, when they might spare all that time by sitting up the longer or rising the earlier for the same employment."
[151] W. Gouge, *Workes*, II, p. 72.

apart from Christ. Moreover, that union was attainable proleptically here and now, and was not the final stage and ultimate prize of a concentrated spiritual regimen over the years. To maintain that respect for and appreciation of the Bible, Bible study was necessary (and many godly Puritans read several chapters of Holy Scripture every Sunday and also sometimes every day). Equally needed was an ear attentive to the minister's exposition of it in his Sabbath sermons. Further, there was the responsibility, if the head of a household with children and servants or a master with apprentices under him, to see that all understood and repeated the main lessons inculcated in the sermons. Such Biblical exposition could be idiosyncratic, but it was kept in check to a considerable degree in Puritanism by a ministry learned in the Biblical languages, trained in logic and rhetoric, by discussion of the spiritual life in the fellowship of the church, and the reading of reliable guides of godliness.

Another characteristic of Puritan spirituality is that it relies on experience. The fact that every father of a household could be his own priest to the family and did not need a clergyman as confessor and spiritual guide gave a welcome independence to the strong but led to anxiety on the part of the unsure, as in the case of Mistress Brettergh who was sorely tried by Satan. But it was in the daily experience of the providence of God as either blessing or threatening, that the Puritan saw the confirmation of His ways revealed in Scripture. So quite apart from the national days of thanksgiving and humiliation (to be considered in Chapter vi), Puritanism instituted private days of fasting and humiliation and private days of thanksgiving. These customs outlived the demise of the Commonwealth and the Protectorate. Oliver Heywood, a Presbyterian divine in the West Riding of Yorkshire, enters into his diary for October 7, 1679: "My wife and I rode to little Horton, we kept a solemn day of thanksgiving at Mr. Sharps for his wife delivered of a daughter a month before."[152] The following March 5, Heywood writes: "we had a solemne day of thanksgiving for my wives and sons recovery, my son Eliezer begun, Mr. Dawson, John proceeded, I concluded with preaching, prayer, we feasted 50 persons and upwards, blessed be God."[153] Heywood also reports days of fasting and humiliation that were kept by Puritan families, for the recov-

152 *Diaries*, i and ii (ed. J. Horsfall Turner, Brighouse, 1882), iii (Bingley, 1883), ii, p. 207.
153 *Ibid.*, ii, p. 110.

ery of sick persons, or in days of persecution. Our Northowram divine notes that on December 2, 1679, "I rode to Wyke, kept a solemne fast at Joshua Kersheys, he being in a consumption, God helped me in discoursing extempore on Jer. 17.13.14 and praying, it was a good day blessed be God."[154] Family feasts and fasts were far more common than might be imagined. In 1690 Heywood participated in 40 fasts and 17 days of thanksgiving; in 1691 he officiated at 37 fasts and 11 days of thanksgiving; in 1692 he was at 50 fasts and 14 days of thanksgiving; while in 1693 he presided at 35 fasts and 12 days of thanksgiving.[155]

Perhaps the most striking example of the relevance of prayer in daily life is that of Oliver Cromwell, who in the midst of his military and political duties, insisted on finding time to commend himself to God and to find in the events of the time the signs of divine approval or displeasure. The letters of this Puritan leader abound in advice to others to seek the will of God in prayer.[156] There was a celebrated occasion, when Cromwell and the other Roundhead generals were convinced that through their temporizing with the king and their consequent lack of popular support, they had earned God's disapproval, Cromwell called a special meeting of the army leaders. Its purpose was, in the words of Adjutant Allan: "To go solemnly to search out our own iniquities, and humble our souls before the Lord in the sense of the same; which, we were persuaded had provoked the Lord against us, to bring such sad perplexities upon us that day."[157] The whole day was then spent in prayer and the examination of their consciences. On the second day, following the exposition of Scripture and further prayers, Cromwell addressed them, urging them to make "a thorough consideration of our actions as an Army, and of our ways particularly as private Christians: to see if any iniquity could be found in them; and what it was, that if possible we might find it out, and so remove the cause of such sad rebukes as were upon us (by *reason* of our iniquities, as we judged) at that time."[158]

It is not commonly recognized that the Puritans, although they ridiculed Catholics for their belief in the invocation of the saints,

---

[154] *Ibid.*

[155] *Ibid.*, III, pp. 247, 254, 262, 264.

[156] *The Letters and Speeches of Oliver Cromwell* (ed. Thomas Carlyle, 1845), I, pp. 121, 167. He received similar letters, as one from Major-General Harrison which is cited in ed. Nathaniel Micklem, *Christian Worship* (Oxford, 1936), p. 185.

[157] *Ibid.*, I, p. 264.   [158] *Ibid.*, p. 265.

had their own saints. This is to go considerably beyond the statement of Gordon S. Wakefield that "the people of God in the wilderness, patriarchs and prophets, were the companions of the Puritan's way. He lived with them as intimates, as the Catholic with his saints."[159] The frequency with which Foxe's Book of Martyrs was reprinted and referred to as approved devotional reading is one pointer to their admiration for the English Protestant Martyrs in Queen Mary's reign. Yet another is the popularity of the sale of funeral sermons extolling the virtues of the godly deceased, their trials and temptations, and their exemplary public and private devotions. One among hundreds is the memoir of John, Lord Harrington, while another, also already referred to, is that of Mistress Katherin Brettergh. One interesting example is *A Pattern of Pietie, Or, the Religious life and death of that Grave and gracious Matron, Mrs. Jane RATCLIFFE, Widow and Citizen of Chester. Of whom the discourse is framed and applied so as the commemoration of the dead may best serve to the edification of the living, whether men or women, whereof part was Preached, and the whole written* (1640). Its author was John Ley, Vicar of Great Budworth and Prebendary of Chester Cathedral. The work is in part a defence of the national Church which he says has been calumniated by the Papists and Brownists "for want of holiness in those that are members of it."[160] He is exceedingly critical of the Roman Catholic conception of sainthood because of their extreme austerities, and instances a report that St. Anthony of Padua is said to have kicked his mother as a child and to have cut off his foot "for the wickednesse of the fact" and St. Catherine of Siena is commended by Catholics "for licking and sucking the sores of such as were leaprous and cankered."[161] The piety of Mrs. Ratcliffe is particularly admired and defined as "the affections of the heart as they tend towards God."[162] Moreover, five tests of her piety are given. These include: her frequent and fervent communion with God in private; her zealous and affectionate discourse of Him; her love for things that had nearest reference to Him; her estrangement from communion with the world for his sake, especially in reference to sensual delights, worldly profit, and from the desire of life itself; and, finally, her "conscionable and constant endeavour to keepe all

---

[159] *Puritan Devotion*, p. 27.
[160] *Op. cit.*, the heading of Chap. 27. This is the work of one who is more Anglican than Puritan, but the latter element is there.
[161] *Ibid.*, p. 193.   [162] *Ibid.*, p. 57.

Gods Commandements."[163] The final proof that the Puritans had their own saints, as eminent imitators of God worthy of emulation is the publication of Samuel Clarke, *A Collection of the Lives of Ten Eminent Divines* (1661), a distinctively Puritan hagiography.

All in all, Puritan spirituality is impressive by its intramundane simplicity, sincerity, relevance, and the large numbers of otherwise ordinary people who tried to live up to the high demands of the elect. It was a foul weather as well as a fair weather piety, for it gained in strength during the days of persecution following 1662. It was a secular piety exercised in the calling and duties of every day, and demanded ethical fight, not flight. It was, above all, vertebral piety.

6. *Concluding Contrasts*

Since it is the glory of the Church of England to be the *via media*, combining both Catholic and Protestant elements, its spirituality does not lend itself conceptually to the polarity and contrast that there is between Roman Catholic and Puritan spirituality. Since the opening section of this chapter stressed the common interconfessional factors in spirituality, the concluding section, avoiding the perils suggested by Ronald Knox's "Re-union All Round," will emphasize the distinctions that give these pieties shape, definition, and recognition, without denying any significant common characteristics. Some similarities will be seen to hide important differences.

To take an example of the latter, one might note the remarkable way that the Puritans, for whom all honouring of saints was a form of idolatry and therefore dishonouring of the Creator, seemed to have taken a leaf out of Catholic hagiographies in writing the lives of their own saints. This is true, however, only at a superficial level, because the Catholic saints are invoked for their aid whereas the Puritan saints are not. The Catholic saints are almost demigods; the Puritan saints are human.

Yet again, it has been argued by E. I. Watkin in his fascinating volume, *Poets and Mystics*,[164] that the Puritan Thomas Goodwin's *The Heart of Christ in Heaven towards Sinners on Earth*[165] is an

[163] *Ibid.*, p. 58.
[164] *Op. cit.* (1953), pp. 56ff. The point is also accepted by Fr. Louis Bouyer, *op. cit.*, p. 67, and was earlier remarked upon by the Abbé Henri Brémond in his magisterial *Histoire littéraire du sentiment religieux en France*, 11 vols. (Paris 1915-1932), III, p. 641.
[165] This appeared in 1652.

astonishing anticipation of the Roman Catholic cult of the Sacred Heart, as envisioned by St. John Eudes and St. Marguerite-Marie Alacoque. There are parallels, indeed: the emphasis on the affections in an age of controversy where the intellect has divided too much, the permanent disposition of Christ as loving towards sinners, and its Biblical basis in his Farewell Discourses in the Fourth Gospel. But the differences are equally significant. For the Catholic the mystical union sought in the prayer of love is one in which Neo-Platonism and Christian practice have amalgamated, and the mystic's aim is to be absorbed in the infinite God, at the end of a long process of which the prior steps are purgation and illumination. For the Puritan, however, conformity of wills is sought, not a loss of identity. Furthermore, the sense of the love of God is not a rapture at the end of a long and strenuous spiritual regimen, it is felt at the beginning of the way. Thirdly, for the Puritan there is a sense that sanctification offers a proleptic fruition in God, but there is always "eschatological distance" between the soul and the beloved in even the most rapturous and mystical of Puritans, like Thomas Goodwin, Francis Rous, and John Preston. Puritans have no sense of the "alone with the Alone"—it is always a mediated presence of God in their hearts, known in Christ, and shared with the people of God, who are incorporated into Christ in the Lord's Supper. So the notion of absorption, or of unmediated and immediate awareness of God is not part of Puritan experience. Even the Cornish layman, Rous, who wrote *The Mysticall Marriage* makes his mystical union an experience "intermediate between sinful historical existence and the pure life of the Godhead, but the union is mediated by Christ."[166] The precondition of the eschatologically consummated union is radical, no less than the death of the old husband, the old self. Rous, like St. John of the Cross, knows that the divine lover sometimes withdraws his consolations from the soul, and he is certain that "His [Christ's] best coming is his last coming . . . without any more going asunder."[167] These examples of the prayer of love in Puritanism are proof positive that its devotional life was not a cold, grey, cerebral piety, for it changed the affections and therefore transformed the wills of those who used it. But, again it must be said, this is not the same as Catholic mysticism. The distinction has been perceptively expressed by Gordon Wakefield in the observation: "For the Puritan, too, it may be said

166 Wakefield, *op. cit.*, p. 103.
167 Published 1635, the reference is to p. 56.

that there are three ways, but these are justification, sanctification, glorification. *Union with Christ is not the end but the beginning of the Christian life.*"[168]

The point need not be laboured, but it also ought not to be ignored that the locus of the life of perfection for the Catholic is the monastery or the convent, whereas for the Puritan it is in the home and at one's daily work. There is, therefore, a big difference between an extra- and an intra-mundane spirituality.

The devout Catholic is able to make effective use of the senses so that art, architecture, music, and poetry combine for the instruction in and expression of spirituality. The aesthetic approach to God as the Divine Artist is natural for the Roman Catholic and the high Anglican metaphysical preachers and poets. For the Puritans, with the possible exception of Baxter and perhaps Sterry, the ethical repelled the aesthetic, and this was a moral victory but an aesthetic defeat.

Even in the language of prayer, the differences are most noticeable. Catholic prayer uses stately language to address God, whereas Donne and Herbert use conversational and even argumentative and expostulatory approaches to God (e.g., "Batter my heart . . ."). The same filial naturalness was cultivated by the Puritans and especially the Separatists (like the Brownists and Barrowists). This reflects a different conception of God and a different idea of the community of the faithful. One cannot fail to be impressed by the Roman Catholic and high Anglican fondness for referring to God as the King to whom homage and obedience are due, and to whom it is appropriate to kneel, and who must be addressed in the language suitable to the celestial court, while His Son can be called "Prince of Peace" or, more imperially, "King of Kings." The Puritans, on the other hand, are filled with awe as they approach God, but, as their fondness for citing Romans 8:15 and 16 shows, their image of Him is that of a Father who has adopted them into His family, and their speech with him is intimate, personal, natural, and simple.[169] In some cases it was crudely simple, even boorish, but these were the exception. Thus the political preferences of the parties coloured even the language of prayer, as much as at times it did the very partisan nature of the petitions offered up.

[168] Wakefield, *op. cit.*, p. 160. The italics are Gordon Wakefield's.

[169] John Owen in *Works* (ed. W. H. Goold, 1851), IV, p. 269 wrote: "There is no more required unto prayer either way but our crying, 'Abba, Father'—that is, the making of our requests known unto him as our father in Christ—with supplications and thanksgivings, according to our state and occasions do require."

There is also a difference between the Catholic, Anglican, and Puritan concepts of the nature of the religious community and the style of approach appropriate in prayer. For the Roman Catholic there is a sense of belonging to an international community that spans oceans and overleaps seventeen centuries. For the Anglican there is a sense of the entire nation on its knees in common prayer. For the Puritan there is the sense of the gathering of several of the families of God, His elect. A stately and liturgical style of prayer is entirely appropriate for both Roman Catholics and Anglicans, while an intimate, filial, familiar style of address fits the *ecclesiola*, the context of Puritan piety and prayer.

In one respect, however, the unity among Catholics, Anglicans, and Puritans in their spiritual treatises and in their devotional depth is astonishing—and that is when they are persecuted. This is true of the prayers and Prayer Books of the English Catholics in penal times (through most of our period, except when the sunshine of monarchical favour cheered them), as of the *Holy Living* and *Holy Dying* of Anglican Bishop-to-be Jeremy Taylor writing during the darkest days of the Church of England, as also of the Nonconformists, successors to the Puritans, under the Cross of Persecution. One of the greatest of them, Richard Baxter, came reluctantly to the conviction that suffering is the Church's true *métier*, "even when there are none but formal, nominal Christians to be the cross-makers, and though ordinarily God would have vicissitudes of summer and winter, day and night, that the Church may grow extensively in the summer of prosperity and intensively in the winter of adversity, yet usually their night is longer than their day, and that day itself has its storms and tempests."[170]

The medieval cry *Intra tua volnera absconde me* is heard echoing through the seventeenth century by all who fight the good fight and are wounded for their loyalty, and who hope to share the promise that "if we suffer with Him, we shall also reign with Him."[171]

[170] Cited from *Reliquiae Baxterianae* (ed. M. Sylvester, 1694) by Alan Simpson, *Puritanism in Old and New England* (Chicago, 1955).
[171] II Timothy 2:12.

CHAPTER IV

PREACHING: SUPPLEMENT AND
STIMULUS TO WORSHIP

S ERMONS WERE perhaps never more devoutly heard nor read
with greater avidity than in the England of the seventeenth
century. The passion for preaching reached its highest peak
during the 1640s and 1650s when it seemed, to use an anachronistic analogy, that the whole of England was a Hyde Park Corner,
where every sectarian, no matter how eccentric his viewpoint,
could climb onto a pulpit and progagate his opinion. John Evelyn
wrote in his *Diary* for August 4, 1650: "I heard a sermon at the
Rolls, and in the afternoone I wander'd to divers churches, the
pulpits full of novices and novelties."

1. *Sermons in General*

During these two decades and for part of the third following
them there was the constant possibility that the daring preacher
might be fined, put into the pillory, sequestrated, ejected from his
living, or even imprisoned, as a penalty for his rashness in speaking his mind. In Archbishop Laud's case the penalty was behead-
ing. In the case of his opponent, Hugh Peters, it had been hanging, drawing, and quartering.[1] Throughout the century religion
was a central and highly controversial issue and if print provided
the wider audience, the spoken word gained the immediate impact,
and many preachers exploited both media by expanding and publishing the spoken sermon in print.

What is equally impressive about the sevententh-century sermon is its great variety of style. There is the moving naïveté and
apocalyptic expectancy of the Fifth Monarchy utterances of such
a man as Archer, or the Biblical fidelity, plainness, and compassionate pastoral urgency of Richard Baxter, in which he was emulated by so many Puritan "painful" (that is, painstaking) and
plain preachers. Or, at the other end of the stylistic scale, there
are the elegant, urbane, rational addresses of a Stillingfleet or a
Tillotson at the end of the century, mirroring the new scientific
spirit and natural mode of clear thinking and crystal expression

---

[1] Caroline F. Richardson, *English Preachers and Preaching, 1640-1670* (New
York, 1928), p. 48.

inspired by the Royal Society. Then, most important of all, there was the Golden Age of the English pulpit in the days of James I and Charles I. It glittered in the etymological analysis, far-fetched analogies and patristic learning of Bishop Lancelot Andrewes, as in the passionate and sceptical mind of Dean Donne, like Jacob, trying by sheer will to wrest a blessing from the angel of divine inspiration and holding the congregations of St. Paul's Cathedral spell-bound by his coruscating imagery, his shrewd observation of the ways of the world, and his theological acrobatics as he walked the tightrope between heaven and hell. Or, again, there was the brocaded style of Jeremy Taylor, raiding the classics, the Fathers, and the Scriptures, and emerging with his own tenderness and profoundly ethical concern, becoming—with the exception of his extreme sensitivity and his tendency to divagation like the meandering Towy River in his golden grove retreat in Carmarthenshire—a kind of English Bossuet.[2]

The uses to which seventeenth-century preaching was put were manifold. Normally, of course, the purpose of the sermon was to unfold divine revelation as recorded in the Old and New Testaments, with a view to instruction and correction of the mind, and the encouragement of the will in the ways of God. This purpose was fulfilled in many pulpits throughout the century with great fidelity. But there were other uses or abuses of preaching. In this highly partisan and controversial century one cannot fail to be impressed (or depressed) by the political tuning of the pulpit, whether by Cavalier parson or by Puritan preacher. Moreover, it is as useless to deprecate the servility of Bishop Lancelot Andrewes to his sovereign in the court sermons preached at Whitehall, as it is to disapprove of the way Puritan preachers in the pulpit of St. Margaret's, Westminster, excoriated and flattered Parliament[3] prior to and during the Commonwealth. Preaching was often propaganda, a political weapon during this period. Some sermons were for the demonstration of theological and patristic learning, and particularly to vindicate the claims of the Church of England to be true to the early church in its orthodoxy of doctrine and ceremonies without diminution or addition. Such apologetical or defensive sermons were preached by Hooker and Andrewes early in the

[2] I have in mind in particular his great funeral orations, especially the one commemorating his patroness, Lady Carbery (1650).

[3] For the most thorough and judicious analysis of these sermons see the work of my colleague, John F. Wilson, *Pulpit in Parliament* (Princeton, N.J., 1969).

century, as by Bramhall, Hammond, and Thorndike in the middle of the century, and by the irenical Stillingfleet in behalf of comprehension towards its end. Another type of sermon in which this century was prolific was casuistical preaching; that is, attending to particular ethical cases or problems that concerned the parishioners of the preachers. The Caroline divines excelled in casuistical divinity and the Anglican Puritan, Richard Baxter, was not behind them in this. After the Restoration there appeared the rational address, which was devoted to the calm and well-reasoned elaboration of a single theme. It avoided both the word-splitting exegesis of an Andrewes and the divisions and sub-divisions of the Puritan divines working on the basis of doctrine, reason, and use.[4]

This division of sermons into expository, political, apologetical, ethical and rational, is, of course, the way that a modern attempts to analyse them. Seventeenth-century men were clearly aware of the differences between "Anglo-Catholic" and Puritan sermons in topics and styles. What is, however, most interesting is the way a mid-seventeenth-century Anglican divine, writing at a time when Anglicanism was proscribed, classifies the types of preaching in his own time. This is precisely what Abraham Wright does in his *Five Sermons in Five several Styles or Waies of Preaching* (1656). This former Fellow of St. John's College, Oxford, and presumably a Laudian, cleverly insinuates his own preferences for the first two sermons of his anthology. The first is "In Bp. Andrews his Way, before the late *King* upon the first day of Lent." The second is "in Bp. Hall's Way; before the Clergie at the Author's own Ordination in Christ Church, Oxford." The third category comprises the sermons of Dr. Maine and Mr. Cartwright before the University of Oxford at St. Mary's Church. The fourth is "in the Presbyterian Way; before the *Citie at St. Pauls, London.*" And the final type is "in the Independent *Way*; never preached."[5] The earlier sermons are marked by learning, rather than the "inspirations" and "revelations" that distinguish the final sermon, with its philistine attitude towards education and its endless repetition. The Preface indicates that Wright means his work to show the importance of "humane learning," the ability to meet the needs of differing auditories, and thus "should I see an *English Clergie-man* to equal at the least the *Jesuite* or *Capuchine*, who by his exact skill in the Arts and Oratorie can command a confused Rabble (met to see an

---

[4] This triple Puritan schema will be considered fully later.
[5] Wright, *op. cit.*, all parts of the very lengthy descriptive title.

Interlude or a Mountebank) from their Sport to a Sermon, and change this *Theater* to a *Church*; having a greater power over the passions of their *Auditorie*, then the Actor hath upon the *Stage*; being able to turn even the *Player* himself into a *Monk*, and the *Mimical Jester* into a religious Votarie."[6] The book's chief present interest, however, is its recognition that the Anglican sermons whether "metaphysical" or moral are marked by the use of rhetoric and Patristic and classical lore, while the Presbyterian sermons are distinguished by the schema of reason, doctrine, and use, as well as by elaborate analysis and definitions, whereas the Independent sermon which he prints is characterized in its ultra-Calvinistic form, by an affirmation of grace which involves a refusal of all learning and natural gifts, by several cant phrases, and by a desire for spiritual states beyond those produced by the ordinances and Scripture itself. This is, in fact, a complete caricature of the kind of sermon that John Owen or Thomas Goodwin would have preached, and Wright has the honesty to admit that he invented it. Throughout the century, however, the most significant change is from the *oration* as found in the metaphysical divines like Andrewes, Adams, and Donne, to the *address* or urbane lecture, as exemplified by Tillotson, Stillingfleet, Burnet, and the Latitudinarian divines of the Restoration and afterwards, and to which oddly enough the Puritan "plain" style, the thematic concentration of the preachers at the French Court, and the scientific functionalism of the time, all contributed. Bishop Burnet signalled the change in 1692 in his *Discourse of Pastoral Care*, in which, after referring to the return to "plain Notions of simple and genuine Rhetorick," he claims:

> The impertinent way of dividing Texts is laid aside, the needless setting out of the Originals, and the vulgar Version, is worn out. The trifling Shews of Learning in many Quotations of Passages, that very few could understand, do no more flat the Auditory. [Here Bishop Andrewes must have turned in his grave] *Pert Wit* and *luscious Eloquence* have lost their Relish. So that Sermons are reduced to the plain opening of the meaning of the Text, in a few short illustrations of its Coherence with what goes before and after, and of the Parts of which it is composed; to that is joined the clear Stating of such Propositions as arise out of it, in their Nature, Truth,

6 *Ibid.*, sig. A3 verso.

and Reasonableness; by which, the Hearers may form clear
Notions of the several Parts of Religion, such as are best
suited to their Capacities and Apprehensions: In all which
Applications are added, tending to the Reproving, Directing,
Encouraging, or Comforting the Hearers, according to the
several Occasions which are offered.[7]

Apart from the Whiggish smugness of the citation and the influence of Locke in the emphasis on the clarity of ideas, one can detect
most clearly the difference between the older "hard-sell" technique
and the newer "soft-sell" approach in preaching. Anglican preachers by metaphysical wit or *recherché* lore, and Puritan preachers
by Biblical fidelity, pastoral psychological insight, and the urge to
sanctification had made a determined effort to change their listeners into ardent partisans. The preachers of the new mode were
much less concerned to please and delight their hearers;[8] they were
more detached and less enthusiastic in outlook; less reliant upon
tradition (whether Scriptural or Patristic) and more on reason and
common-sense; less urgent and more urbane. After the hot, not to
say fevered, intensity of the earlier decades, the cooler approach
must have come as a relief. At least it offered an armistice after a
prolonged theological civil war, even if it came at the cost of dis-
solving supernatural mystery in natural explanation, and of substituting prudence for going the sacrificial and ethical second mile.

2. *Anglican and Puritan Sermons Compared*

If sermons were of great importance[9] alike for Anglicans and
Puritans, yet they were not so to an equal degree. The Puritans
valued preaching more highly than the Anglicans. Hooker, as the
leading Anglican apologist against the Puritans, and himself a
most competent composer of sermons, derides the Puritans for
implying that these are the only roads that lead to God, reminding them that conversation in the bosom of the church, "religious
education," "the reading of learned men's books," "information

7 *Op. cit.* (3rd edn. of 1713), pp. 192-93.

8 Rapin in his *Réflexions sur l'Eloquence de la Chaire* (1672), so greatly admired by English imitators of the new rational style of French preaching, declared:
"L'éloquence de la chaire aime la pureté, sans rechercher l'élégance: elle veut estre
forte, sans se soucier d'estre agréable." (Cited in J. Fraser Mitchell, *op. cit.*,
pp. 121-22.)

9 This conviction was gleefully expressed by Vavasor Powell in his *The Bird and
the Cage* (2nd edn., 1662, p. 9) when he asked: "Hath any generation since
the Apostles days had such powerful preachers and plenty of preaching as this
generation?"

received by conference," as well as the public or private reading of the Scriptures, all are avenues to God. In his view it is far too restrictive to tie the term "God's Word" to sermons alone, and even to sermons preached apart from a book.[10] His irony is scathing as he refers to the Puritan claims: "How Christ is by Sermons lifted up higher, and made more apparent to the eye of Faith; how the savour of the Word is made more sweet, being brayed, and more able to nourish, being divided, by Preaching, than by only Reading proposed; how Sermons are the keys of the Kingdom of Heaven, and do open the Scriptures, which being but read, remain in comparison still clasped. . . ."[11] Laud and his followers tended to depreciate sermons in order to elevate the sacraments. Archbishop Laud himself had dared to argue that the preacher only presents the Word of Christ in the sermon, while the priest represents the very Body of Christ in the chief sacrament.[12] Laud insisted that all altars should be railed: he had never thought of railing off the pulpit. He was far more likely, as Archbishop of Canterbury, to have eliminated all pulpits that he could not tune, so alert was he to the danger of deviation from theological or political orthodoxy.

The greater Puritan estimation of sermons was due to a number of causes. The greatest unquestionably was the evidence in the pages of the New Testament that preaching had effected the conversion of the godless into the godly. It was, as St. Paul indicated, "the power of God unto salvation." By it the apostles transformed a crowd on the day of Pentecost into the first Church of Christ. One had only to preach the Word faithfully and the inner testimony of the Holy Spirit in the heart of the elect would cause it to be receptive soil for that holy seed to grow and fruit. But the seriousness with which the Puritans viewed and practised preaching can be gathered from four subordinate considerations also.

It should be noted that in the Book of Common Prayer no sermon is required for the Offices of Morning or Evening Prayers, yet it would be unthinkable for any service to be held in which Puritans did not merely read but also expounded Holy Writ. Where otherwise were men to find the revelation of the living God, except in His own Word, and its confirmation in their daily experience of His providence? No diet of worship, as they might have phrased

10 *The Laws of Ecclesiastical Politie*, Bk. v, Chap. xxi, Sect. 2.
11 *Ibid.*, v, xxii, 12.
12 *Works* (Library of Anglo-Catholic Theology), vi, Pt. i, pp. 56f.

it, would be complete without the "Bread of Life," for as their Master had taught them: "Man does not live by bread alone, but by every word which proceeds out of the mouth of God." The sermon was necessary even when they were celebrating the Lord's Supper which they recognised to be, with St. Augustine, the *Verbum visibile*, or visible Word of God. This insistence on the primacy and sovereignty of God's Word was their reason for rejecting officially written and prescribed homilies as a substitute for preaching, for in their mind there was no alternative to a godly divine's own responsibility to instruct, exhort, encourage, and correct his congregation from his own study of God's revelation and his personal knowledge of the needs of his flock based upon catechising them and on pastoral visitation. A further proof of the intense seriousness with which preaching was taken is found in the demand that heads of households and fathers of families (and their charges, whether children, servants, or apprentices) should memorize and cause to be rehearsed the main headings of the sermon on Sunday evenings at home. We are able to glimpse this in the *Memoirs of the Life of Colonel Hutchinson*, penned by Lucy, the devoted wife of this Cromwellian commander. "By the time I was four years old," she writes, "I read English perfectly, and having a great memory, I was carried to sermons; and while I was very young could remember them and repeat them exact. . . ."[13] It was, however, the great length of Puritan sermons which demonstrated conclusively the extraordinary pains taken in their preparation to say nothing of the godly endurance and patience required by the congregations who listened to them.

Two famous Puritan stories, not to mention the criticisms of Anglican opponents, are evidence of the prolixity of Puritan preaching.[14] The first of them concerns the demagogue Hugh Peters, that darling of the Puritan groundlings, who once preached for three hours on a fast day. When the hour-glass had twice been emptied, he took it in his hand, turned it, and said, "Come, my beloved, we will have the other glasse, and so we'll part."[15] Our second story proves that variety of matter and fluency of delivery

[13] *Op. cit.* (ed. C. H. Firth, 1906), p. 15.
[14] Anglicans and Quakers also erred in this respect, but not as frequently as Puritans. A great offender was the learnedly loquacious Master of Trinity, Dr. Isaac Barrow, whose sermon was once abruptly terminated by a sexton drowning him out by blowing the organ. Fox could be long-winded, for he mentions in his *Journal* (ed. N. Penney, 1924, p. 145) that while at Leominster, he "stood up and declared about three hours."
[15] *Tales and Jests of Mr. Hugh Peters* (1807), Jest No. 50.

were regarded as major qualities in the estimation of a good preacher. It appears that Cromwell wished to test John Howe as a chaplain. Summoning him to his camp headquarters, he gave him a text to study on the eve of the Sabbath. The next day, immediately after the prayer preceding the sermon, Cromwell altered the text which he had commanded Howe to expound; the worthy divine preached on the changed text until the monitory sands of the first and second hour had run out. Only when he was turning the hour-glass for the third hour was he called upon to desist.[16] One wonders how often congregations had to endure preaching marathons of this type.

Anglicans were not slow to criticise either the frequency or prolixity of Puritan preaching. Two examples deserve citation for their vividness and wit. Dr. Nicholas Andrews is reported by the Puritan divine John White as saying that "Peter's sword cutt off but one eare, but long sermons like long swords, cutt off both at once . . . and that the silliest creatures have longest eares, and that preaching was the worst part of God's worship, and that if he left out anything, he would leave that out."[17] Herbert Thorndike, a more distinguished and scholarly Anglican divine, believed that the fame of preaching among the Puritans could be proved to be merely a matter of physical endurance and observed: "I call the World to witness; is it not a work as much of lungs and sides, as an office of God's service, which takes up the time of their Church Assemblies?"[18] But these views of Anglicans, who had suffered in penal times, are tinged with bitterness rather than characterized by balance. They would not have been approved of by Andrewes or Donne. Indeed, Donne wished to insist on the co-ordinate importance of sermon and the chief sacrament, declaring that they are like thunder and lightning, since preaching is like the lightning in clearing the air of ignorance and the sacrament is the presence of Christ himself.[19] On another occasion, as if to forestall the criticism that he made too much of preaching, Donne reminded his hearers that Christ "preached long before He instituted the sacraments, and that the sacraments were instituted by Christ as subsidiary things, in a great part because of human

---

16 E. Calamy, *Continuation of the Ejected Ministers* (1727), I, p. 250f.

17 *The First Century of Scandalous Malignant Priests* (1643), p. 8.

18 *The Due Way of Composing the Differences* (1660), p. 50.

19 *The Sermons of John Donne*, 10 vols. (eds. George R. Potter and Evelyn M. Simpson, Berkeley and Los Angeles, California, 1953-1962), IV, p. 105.

infirmity who need such sensible [that is, apprehensible by the senses] aids to our understanding of divine things."[20]

Another important difference between Anglican and Puritan preaching consisted in the way in which sermons were prepared and delivered.[21] Theoretically there were four possibilities. The sermon could be read from a full manuscript. Or, it could be preached from notes or headings, as summaries or mnemonics. Or, again, it could be learned by heart and preached without manuscript. Or, finally, and most brashly, it could be preached *ex tempore*,[22] so as allegedly to be more completely the work of the Holy Spirit. (The last alternative was employed almost exclusively by the most radical sectarians and "mechanick" preachers.)

Anglican custom generally favoured the reading of the manuscript (as was clearly so in the cases of Hooker and Sanderson), or the use of notes, as in the case of Hammond or Donne, though either of the latter two could have preached sermons from memory. Izaak Walton informs us, for example, that Donne, as Dean of St. Paul's Cathedral, preached at least once a week. Moreover, "he never gave his eyes rest, till he had chosen out a new text, and that night cast his sermon into a form, and his text into divisions; and the next day betook himself to consult the Fathers, and so committed his meditations to his memory which was excellent."[23] An amusing anecdote about Dr. Robert Sanderson, former Regius Professor of Divinity at Oxford and a future bishop, informs us of that divine's practice. According to Walton, when the learned Dr. Henry Hammond tried to persuade Dr. Sanderson to trust himself to preach a short sermon without reading his manuscript so as to address a neighbouring village congregation with greater liveliness, directness, and freedom, the result was disastrous for both congregation and preacher. Hammond, who had Sanderson's sermon manuscript in his hand, saw that the latter was "so lost as to

[20] *Op. cit.*, X, p. 69. Donne spoke as if he normally preached a sermon of an hour's length. Indeed, on one occasion he indicated that each of his four divisions lasted for a quarter of an hour. (*Op. cit.*, VI, p. 64.)

[21] See the fascinating essay of John Sparrow, "John Donne and Contemporary Preachers," *Essays and Studies by Members of the English Association* (Oxford, 1931), XVI, pp. 144-78.

[22] Donne anticipated this theory by arguing, in rebuttal, that the Holy Spirit would give the preacher "a care of delivering God's messages with consideration, with meditation, with preparation; and not barbarously, not suddenly, not occasionally, not extemporarily, which might derogate from the dignity of so great a service." (*Works*, XI, p. 171.)

[23] *The Lives of John Donne, Sir Henry Wotton, Richard Hooker, George Herbert, and Robert Sanderson* (World's Classics edn., 1927), p. 67.

the matter, especially the method, that he also became afraid for him, for it was discoverable to many of that plain auditory." The upshot was that as they walked together back to Hammond's home, Dr. Sanderson said most eagerly, "Good Doctor, give me my sermon and know, that neither you nor any man living shall ever persuade me to preach again without books." A chagrined Dr. Hammond replied, "Good Doctor, be not angry; for if I ever persuade you to preach again without book, I will give you leave to burn all the books that I am master of."[24]

After the Civil Wars the Anglican custom changed decisively in favour of the use of notes only in the pulpit and schemes that could be retained in the memory of preacher and congregation, instead of the earlier preference for learning the manuscript by heart. This change tended to give sermons less of an oratorical and more of a conversational quality, and it was precisely the qualities of naturalness and clarity that previous sermons lacked. The only major exceptions to the changed rule on the part of post-Restoration preachers were Barrow and Tillotson.

For their part, the Puritans throughout the century encouraged the delivery of sermons carefully written out either from memory or from notes. A few among them went with notes into the pulpit, and may well have written the sermon out in full (with additions) for its publication in print.[25]

3. *The Metaphysical Preachers*

The two most distinguished members of this famous circle were, of course, Bishop Lancelot Andrewes and Dean John Donne, but there were others such as Bishop John King (author of the superb tribute to his dead wife, *The Exequy*), Richard Corbet, and John Hacket, and even a Puritan divine, Thomas Adams, whom some have claimed, perhaps erroneously, to be of this company. Yet even before Donne and contemporary with Andrewes there was a distinguished preacher of the same mode, Thomas Playfere.[26] So great

---

[24] Walton reports the incident in the last part of his *Lives* and it is also recorded with interesting comments in the *Works of Robert Sanderson, D.D.* (ed. William Jacobson, Oxford, 1854), VI, pp. 314-15.

[25] J. Fraser Mitchell, *English Pulpit Oratory from Andrewes to Tillotson* (1932), p. 26.

[26] Reference is made to Playfere in Davies, *op. cit.*, I, pp. 236, 245. In a sermon named "Heart's Delight" he spoke of Christ as "our heavenly Ulysses" and the cross as "the mast to which we must bind ourselves for safety." (*The Whole Sermons*, 1623, p. 8.) This reference is an incidental reminder that the metaphysical preachers used not only the Scriptures and the Greek and Latin Fathers, but the classical pagan writers also, and, in some cases, even the cabbalists.

was the attraction of the metaphysical style in preaching for the learned and witty men that were its practitioners that they were unable to give it up even when the style was no longer in the mode. Cosin, for example, continued to preach in this manner even as Bishop of Durham after the Restoration, a whole generation after its popularity had waned. And as late as 1679 Evelyn recorded: "The Bp. of Gloucester preach'd in a manner very like Bishop Andrews, full of divisions, and scholastical, and that with much quicknesse."[27]

The epithet "metaphysical" as applied to these preachers is curious to modern eyes. It cannot bè metaphysics as distinguished from logic, the two traditional major divisions of philosophy, because these men were as much concerned with dividing and subdividing their texts as their Puritan opponents. Their analytical powers were striking, but so were those of the Presbyterians. Nor could the controversial term be thought to refer to their philosophical profundity. Andrewes was, indeed, a deeply devout Christian, a mine of patristic lore, and a polylingual scholar,[28] but he was no philosopher. Nor was Donne, however penetrating his psychological knowledge of the springs of human behaviour. The term "metaphysical" can then only have been used in the loosest sense to describe preachers who emphasized the paradoxical character of the Christian revelation, who used far-fetched analogies to create surprise and interest, and whose word-play was dazzling, while their erudition and culture were wide. It was, without doubt, highly intelligent preaching of the relevance of the essential dogmas of the Christian faith to the human condition. Bishop Andrewes preached seventeen different sermons which shed light on different aspects of the Incarnation of the eternal Son of God, and Donne kept on recurring to the theme of the Life Everlasting, that stage beyond his macabre meditation on death on which his sceptical spirit sought assurance. Above all, this witty, learned, ingenious word-play was the delight of the Jacobean court before whom Bishop Andrewes preached at the request of James I, as it was the

[27] *Diary*, April 4, 1679.

[28] "His admirable knowledge in the learned tongues, Latine, Greeke, Hebrew, Chaldee, Syriack, Arabick, besides other Moderne Tongues to the number of *fifteene* (as I am informed) was such & so rare, that he may well be ranked in the first place as one of the rarest linguists in Christendom." (*A Sermon preached at the funerall of the Right Honourable and Reverend Father in God Lancelot late Lord Bishop of Winchester . . . on Saturday being the XI of November A.D. MDCXXVI.*) By Iohn late L. Bishop of Ely (p. 18). These skills were used to their greatest advantage in his translation of the Pentateuch in the Authorised (or King James') version of the Scriptures.

pleasure of the polite in St. Paul's Cathedral where Donne made every sermon on occasion.

Lancelot Andrewes was pre-eminently the preacher for great occasions (festivals and fasts in the life of the church and the nation). His collected sermons are almost all classifiable in this way; 67 sermons were preached on important days in the church year, 18 on state days, and a further 10 on widely different occasions. Further subdivisions show that Andrewes preached 18 Easter Day sermons, 17 Nativity Day sermons, 15 on Whitsunday (Pentecost), 8 on Ash Wednesday, 6 general Lenten sermons, and 3 on Good Friday. State occasions on which he preached were 8 sermons on Gowrie Day, recalling the deliverance of the King from the treachery and sedition of the Earl of Gowrie, and 10 Gunpowder Plot sermons. The miscellaneous sermons vary from those preached as early as 1590 and 1591 at Whitehall, respectively on "Justification in Christ" and on "Caesar his due" to a Coronation Day sermon in 1606 and one in time of pestilence in 1609. His most enduring sermons are, naturally, those which concentrate on the great days in the Life of Christ, for he was an exceedingly devout[29] man who has enriched his meditations with those of the Fathers in east and west.

Andrewes never ceased to be astonished by the sheer generosity of divine grace in the Incarnation.[30] On the text, "Unto us a child is born," he makes the fullest use of the inherent paradox of God made man, as he develops the themes of child and son:

> All along His life you shall see these two. At His birth: a *Cratch* for the *Childe*; a *Starre* for the *Sonne*: A company of *Shepheards* viewing the *Child*; a *Quire of Angels* celebrating the *Son*. In His life: *Hungry* Himselfe, to shew the nature of the *Child*; yet *feeding five thousand*, to show the power of the *Sonne*. At His death: dying on the *Crosse*, as the Son of Adam; at the same time disposing of *Paradise*, as the *Sonne of God*.

29 *Ibid.*, p. 21, pithily informs us that *vita ejus, vita orationis*, and that "a great part of five houres every day did he spend in prayer and devotion to God." His *Preces Privatae*, a veritable classic of Anglican devotion, was considered in our Chapter III.
30 When expounding the Prologue of St. John's Gospel and the words, "And the Word became flesh" Andrewes says: "I add yet farther: what flesh? The flesh of an infant. What, *Verbum infans*, the Word an infant? The Word, and not able to speak a Word? How evil agreeth this! This He put up. How born, how entertained? In a stately palace, cradle of ivory, robes of estate? No; but a stable for His palace, a manger for His cradle, poor clouts for His array."

If you aske, why both these? . . . But that He was a *Childe*, He could not have suffered. But that He was a *Sonne* He had sunke in His *suffering*, and not gone through with it . . . Therefore, that He might be *lyable*, He was a *Childe*; that He might be *able*, He was the *Son*: that He might be both, He was both.[31]

This is most impressive for its concision, perfect balance of Christ's two natures, divine and human, splendidly exemplified in his prose, and with a singular objectivity, and the whole ordered with such admirable planning. It is only the rather strained contrast between "lyable" and "able" that seems distracting in its artificiality.

One example of the witty etymological word-play of Bishop Andrewes must suffice: It is taken from his explanation of Isaiah 7:14.

This *Immanu* is a Compounde againe: we may take it, in sunder, into *Nobis* and *cum*: And so then have we three pieces. 1. *El*, the mighty GOD: 2. and *Anu* wee, poore wee; (Poore indeed, if we have all the world beside, if we have not Him to be *with us*:) 3. And *Im*, which is *cum*, And that *cum*, in the midst betwene *nobis* and *Deus*, GOD and Vs; to couple GOD and *us*; thereby to conveigh the things of the one to the other.[32]

T. S. Eliot has rightly insisted on the capacity of Andrewes to derive a world from a word, "squeezing and squeezing the word until it yields a full juice of meaning, which we should never have supposed any word to possess."[33] His words are like firework displays in which rockets emit one jet of sparkling chrysanthemums of fire only to be succeeded by others as beautiful. And his style, also like fireworks in this respect, springs surprise after surprise.

What were the strengths of England's first great pulpit orator since the Reformation? First, he wisely concentrated his attention on the major facets of the Christ-event which are renewed in the church year. He meditated on the extraordinary generosity of God in order to lead his hearers to admire holiness and to attempt it. His subjects were: the Incarnation in which God came closest to man that he might raise man; the Crucifixion and the reconcilia-

---

[31] *XCVI Sermons*, "Second Nativity Sermon" (3rd edn., 1635), p. 12.
[32] *Ibid.*, "Ninth Nativity Sermon," p. 77.
[33] *For Lancelot Andrewes, Essays on Style and Order* (1928), p. 25.

tion thus effected between sinful man and gracious God and the forgiveness won for man; the Resurrection and its promise of hope for the Christian; and the Pentecost with its donation of the Holy Spirit as the church's bond of solidarity and that divine empowerment that overcomes human frailty and makes holiness possible. In life he was forced to use his pen in the controversial battle between Canterbury and Rome (and, incidentally, acquitted himself well with no less an antagonist than the brilliant Jesuit, Cardinal Bellarmine), but this he avoided in the pulpit like the plague, just as he avoided such points of speculative divinity as the counsel of God in predestination, a theme which so much engaged the Puritan divines.

He it was, along with Hooker, who insisted upon the continuity of the Church of England with the church of the first five centuries. This was manifest not only in the themes of his sermons, as in the mosaic of his *Preces Privatae*, but in his extraordinary knowledge of and fondness for the Greek and Latin Fathers of the church, whom he loved to cite in the original tongues, with hints to the unlearned listener of their meanings. In the same sense that the *Patres* were Fathers of the universal church, Lancelot Andrewes was a Father of the early Anglican church, a pillar of orthodoxy and stability in doctrine, in devotion, and in the exemplary charity of his life.

His third quality is wit. This combines the most subtle word-play, the use of surprising even startling images and comparisons, and brings before the hearer's amazed eyes the treasures of exotic knowledge drawn from the distant caves of Greece, Rome, Jerusalem, the deserts of North Africa, and from Renaissance Italy or medieval Christendom. One fact or legend may come from a medieval bestiary and the next from the speculations of the *Cabbala*.

These great gifts and qualities, combined with the exacting court audience for whom his sermons were prepared, might have led Andrewes to play to the gallery. In a word, his conceits might have made him conceited. Perhaps his most astonishing quality in his apparent objectivity—his capacity to lose himself in the grandeur of his message and the splendour of the mighty acts of God to which he drew attention. In a very self-conscious situation Andrewes makes one share his God-consciousness. Here he presents a notable contrast with Donne who may have his head in the clouds like an angel, but is a man very much with his feet on the solid earth; or, to vary the image, has one eye on God and one eye on the effect he is making. Eliot claims that Andrewes's intellect and sensibility were in complete harmony.[34] Certainly, one does not feel in reading Andrewes that he is exploiting our curiosity by sensationalism or using secular bait to entrap us for holiness. Even if, as the twentieth century has taught us to believe, all motives are mixed, one has the assurance that those of Andrewes are mixed with a high concentration of consecration.

What, then, were the defects of his preaching? Probably the over-concentration on the literary craftsmanship, admirable as the rhetoric is, leads to a sense of sheer artificiality and this creates a "credibility gap." The fact is that so much contrived eloquence overwhelms conviction. The superb etymological and syllable-by-syllable analysis of texts has another defect of its quality: the style is so jerky, so staccato in its effect, that it never allows the reader to relax even for the purposes of deeper meditation on the meaning. His distinctions are frequently over nice, requiring brackets within brackets, and this is the result of a very tortuous and often fussy exegesis. Moreover, even when the exegesis does not strain at a gnat, but sustains a relevant exposition of central themes, his applications are rarely driven home to hearer or reader.[35] This may well be related to the fact that while Andrewes had a great knowledge of the Fathers, he was no expert in human psychology; in this respect he was far inferior to John Donne. The result was that while he was admired in polite and aristocratic society for his brilliance, learning, and devotion, he had his critics in his own day and since. Some have despised what they consider his playing less to the gallery than the royal box,[36] and certainly his respect for the divine right of kings seems to tread between the verges of servility and idolatry. Others have felt that his word-play made folly of preaching. The serious Richard Baxter averred "when I read such a book as Bishop Andrews *Sermons*, or heard such kind of preaching, I felt no life in it: methought they did but play with holy things."[37] A Presbyterian Lord had made much the same observation to King James at Holyrood: "No doubt your Majesty's bishop is a learned man, but he cannot preach. He rather plays with his text than preaches on it."[38] These are over-censorious judgments

[34] *Ibid.*, p. 20.
[35] F. E. Hutchinson, "The English Pulpit from Fisher to Donne," *Cambridge History of English Literature*, IV, Chap. 12, p. 238.
[36] Charles Smyth, *The Art of Preaching* (1952), p. 122.
[37] *The Safe Religion* (1657), the epistle to the reader.
[38] *Op. cit.*, ed. F. E. Hutchinson, IV, p. 239. George Herbert would have been sympathetic to this viewpoint as he complained of those who practise "crumbling

and one wonders what success Baxter would have had in court or cathedral circles with his plain, urgent, pathetic Puritan style.

Though both Donne and Andrewes are classed as metaphysical preachers, they are read today for different reasons. Those who value theology will read Andrewes despite his style, while those who love Donne read him less for the theology than the style, capable of splendidly ascending climaxes, of wilting satire, of surprising paradoxes and amazing images, of macabre concentration on death, or of conscience-piercing directness, and always the vivid index of a mind that is curious and a personality that is passionate, and a memory that is served by rapacious reading. Donne seemed in his day a second St. Augustine, the voluptuous rhetorician (or poet) converted whose sermons sometimes assumed the form of the *Confessions*, a direct address and even argument with God for man's sake.

On his mother's side, Donne was descended from the courageous humanist, St. Thomas More, and was ever haunted by the Catholicism[39] that had formed him and from which he had never entirely dissociated himself. It was only at the age of forty-three that the minor diplomat and courtier took holy orders in the Church of England, that is in 1615. A year later he was appointed Reader in Divinity to Lincoln's Inn, the major professional training-centre for lawyers who admired his preaching for its brilliance and profundity. On November 19, 1621, he came to his rightful throne—the pulpit of the old Gothic St. Paul's Cathedral in London. Learned and simple, the merely curious and the sincere enquirer, the lover of learning and the collector of quips and witticisms, the godly and the godless flocked to listen to him, and knew—especially after the death of Bishop Lancelot Andrewes in 1626—that there was no finer preacher in England.

Walton, who had been his parishioner, shows us what his contemporaries admired in Donne, who preached

---

a text into small parts. . . ." (*Works of George Herbert*, ed. F. E. Hutchinson, Oxford, 1941, pp. 234f.)

39 It is not easy to determine why Donne left his ancestral faith. It may have been the difficulty of a secular career as a Recusant in Protestant England. In his sermons, Donne quarrels with Rome ostensibly because he disapproves of her additions to fundamental primitive and patristic doctrines, as also of her rather theatrical ceremonialism, calling her a "painted Church." (Cf. *Sermons*, eds. Potter and Simpson, IV, p. 106; I, p. 246.) Correlatively, he admires the Church of England because she distinguishes between essentials and non-essentials (*Sermons*, II, pp. 203f.).

the Word so, as shewed his own heart was possest with those very thoughts and joys that he laboured to distill into others: A Preacher in earnest; weeping sometimes for his Auditory, sometimes with them: always preaching to himself, like an Angel from a cloud, but in none; carrying some, as St. Paul was, to Heaven in holy raptures, and inticing others by a sacred Art and Courtship to amend their lives; here picturing a vice so as to make it ugly to those who practised it; and a vertue so as to make it be beloved even by those that lov'd it not; and all this with a most particular grace and an unexpressible addition to comeliness.[40]

He well knew the purpose of a sermon was to proclaim the saving power of God in the lives of men:

There is no salvation but by faith, nor faith but by hearing, nor hearing but by preaching; and they that thinke meanliest of the Keyes of the Church, and speak faintliest of the Absolution of the Church, will yet allow, That those Keyes lock, and unlock in Preaching; That Absolution is conferred, or withheld in Preaching, That the proposing of the promises of the Gospel in Preaching, is that binding and loosing on earth, which bindes and looses in heaven.[41]

In fact, his interesting choice of images to describe the preacher, is an indication of the variety of the duties and privileges of his divine calling. "Not only," writes William Mueller, using Donne's terms, "is the preacher a husband to his congregation: he is an archer, a watchman, a trumpeter, a harmonious charmer; he possesses the most desirable qualities of a lion, an ox, an eagle, and a man; he is an earthquake, a son of thunder, the fall of waters, the roaring of a lion."[42]

What are the strengths of this famous and engaging preacher? He offers, in the first place, an incisive meditation on the scriptural texts that he is expounding, coloured by patristic, medieval and contemporary commentaries, but above all by his own rich experience of the world. If Andrewes makes his single predominant

[40] *The Lives of John Donne* (World's Classics edn., 1927), p. 49.
[41] *Sermons* (ed. Potter and Simpson), VII, p. 320.
[42] William R. Mueller, *John Donne: Preacher* (Princeton, N.J., 1962), p. 43. This is an admirable study of Donne's theology and his rhetorical style.

theme the Incarnation (also a theme to which the paradoxical Donne is also attracted), Donne makes his *leitmotiv* the transition from death to resurrection, thus making the human tragedy end triumphantly as the divine comedy. But, and this is distinctively Donne's contribution, he faces the horror of death and dissolution to the full and in the most macabre detail, before he gives the reassurance that God will collect and resoul the scattered parts of bodies at the General Resurrection. Donne gives us the horrific nightmare of "this death of corruption and putrifaction, of vermiculation and incineration, of dissolution and dispersion" before he confidently affirms in faith that "God knowes in which Boxe of his Cabinet all this seed Pearle lies, in what corner of the World every graine of every mans duste sleeps, shall recollect that dust, and then recompact that man, and that is the accomplishment of all."[43] That is his distinctive treatment of a central Christian theme, but far from his only theme. He is concerned with the entire theme of man's fall and redemption, and particularly in his treatment of the church, he is not afraid to be a bold defender of the Church of England as the *via media* between the accretions of Rome and the nakedness of Geneva. In fact, part of his magnetism is the sense he gives that he has fought through scepticism to conviction in almost every article of Christian belief. J. Fraser Mitchell describes him as a "Tamerlane confined to a pulpit, or Faustus desiring all knowledge and vivid for sensual enjoyment, but held spellbound by the eyes of the Crucified."[44] It is because, like Augustine of Hippo before him and Francis Thompson after him, he gives the impression of having tried all other ways of life until in exhaustion he reaches Christian discipleship, that his invitations to Christian morality are psychologically insinuating and so persuasive. For him as truly as for St. Augustine, *Cor nostrum inquietum donec requiescat in Te.* Yet to stress this *taedium Christianum*, inevitable in a man who becomes a priest in middle age after a profligate youth, is entirely to forget Donne's abounding sense of the joy the devout life brings, with its conviction of the providence and protection of God. Donne found in Him the constant Love that he failed to discover in his earthly amours. God was all in all to him eventually as he implies in one passage where he speaks of God as our Father, potter, minter, sculptor, tailor, steward, physician, neighbour, Samaritan, gardener, architect, builder, sentinel, and

43 *LXXX Sermons* (1640), p. 212.   44 *Op. cit.*, p. 181.

shepherd.[45] In short, his themes were the central topics of the Christian faith and life.

Another admirable quality in his preaching was his use of striking, often esoteric, and always vivid images, which gives his prose a poetical and even dramatic quality. These images come from many walks of life or ways of observation. There are commercial, agricultural, geographical, geometrical, and marine images, and Donne is especially effective in using anatomical analogies, as we might expect from the love poems. Such is the pictorial pliability of Donne's mind that, as Mueller observes, he can use the same image of the fishing net in two different senses in two sermons: once, as when Jesus first called His fishermen disciples, as obstacles in the way of following Him, and, second, as a metaphor for the Gospel itself which catches men as a net catches fish.[46] Moreover, it is very often in the use of an apt or striking image that his considerable wit is seen. "The Devel is no recusant," he observed; "he will come to church, and he will lay his snares there."[47] How vividly he contrasts Roman Catholicism with Presbyterianism, Rome with Geneva when he says—arguing that true religion is not to be found "either in a painted Church, on one side, or in a *naked Church* on another; a Church in a *Dropsie*, overflowne with *Ceremonies*, or a Church in a *Consumption*, for want of such Ceremonies, as the primitive Church found usefull and beneficiall for the advancing of the glory of God, and the devotion of the Congregation." Donne had a most vivid artist's eye, but even this was, as M. M. Mahood[48] pointed out, almost certainly assisted by the use of emblem books, a common feature of this time. In variety and richness and originality of imagery Donne was more than a match for Andrewes.

In another respect also Donne is better than Andrewes in the pulpit. This is the way he related his teaching to the practical needs of his congregation. His preaching has about it a sanctified worldliness. His concern was not merely to move his hearers, but to move them to Christian action. He will not, for example, allow them to plead their humours or temperaments (as we might today excuse

---

[45] *Sermons* (eds. Potter and Simpson), IX, pp. 131-32.
[46] Mueller, *op. cit.*, p. 121.
[47] F. E. Hutchinson, "The English Pulpit from Fisher to Donne," p. 241.
[48] *Poetry and Humanism* (1950), p. 147. George Herbert made extensive use of emblem books for his poems, as most preachers did of commonplace books for suitable citations. There were also compilations of illustrations for sacred or secular use, as Robert Cawdrey's *A Treasure or Store-House of Similies* (1600).

our conduct or our complexes, our heredity or our early environment): "Let no man therefore think to present his complexion to God for an excuse, and say, My choler with which my constitution abounded, and which I could not remedy, inclined me to wrath, and so, to bloud; my Melancholy enclined me to Sadnesses and so to Desperation, as though thy sins were medecinall sins, sins to vent humours."[49] Donne knew that the minister must preach "for the saving of soules, and not for the sharpning of wits."[50]

Andrewes deliberately rejected controversial divinity from his sermons, while Donne accepted it as having a subordinate place in the pulpit. He seemed to be doubtful about using the double-edged weapon of irony, but when he did, it was used to devastating effect as a form of ridicule. Consider, for example, how he makes bovril out of Papal bulls and claims of infallibility by sheer ridicule; he has just observed that the Roman Catholic church has imprisoned the Holy Spirit in the bosom of the Pope: "And so the Holy Ghost is no longer a Dove, a Dove in the Ark, a Dove with an Olive-branch, a Messenger of Peace, but now the Holy Ghost is in a Bull, in Buls worse than *Phalaris* his Bull, Buls of Excommunication, Buls of Rebellion, and Deposition, and Assassinates of Christian Princes."[51] It may have been conducive to excitement, it was not to the spirit of devotion appropriate to worship.

Donne's most characteristic quality, his passionate subjectivity, has been acclaimed by some and disapproved by others. In a particularly harsh judgment, T. S. Eliot, who greatly preferred the reserve, objectivity, and "relevant intensity" of Andrewes,[52] described Donne as shadowed "by the impure motive," which added to his "facile success." Even worse, and in what one can only regard as a most unfortunate personal comparison with a stunter and exploiter in religion,[53] Eliot refers to Donne as "a little of the religious spell-binder, the Reverend Billy Sunday of his time, the flesh-creeper, the sorcerer of emotional orgy. . . ."[54] One may recognize that Donne was conscious of the various technical devices

---

[49] *LXXX Sermons* (1640), p. 390.

[50] *Sermons* (eds. Potter and Simpson), VIII, p. 42.

[51] *Ibid.*, VIII, p. 265.

[52] Mueller has countered this by claiming for Donne "existential intensity" in *op. cit.*, p. 246.

[53] One must contrast the dedication and modesty of D. L. Moody, for example, in order to understand the reprehensible self-advertising and "scalping" activities of Billy Sunday, who was a shrewd ignoramus. This makes the comparison of the learned and consecrated Donne with Sunday so inept, a mere caricature unworthy of T. S. Eliot's usual perceptive and balanced judgments.

[54] *For Lancelot Andrewes*, p. 20.

necessary for keeping his congregation awake, without charging him with entirely spurious motives. Furthermore, it could be argued that it was the lessons bitterly learned from his experience that made him so appropriate a preacher to Renaissance minds and hearts in court and law court. He was, indeed, a "personality" and a "character" but there is nothing but regret in one of the most famous passages of an autobiographical nature, which seems so moving in its sincerity, even if couched in majestic cadences:

> Let me wither and weare out mine age in a discomfortable, in an unwholesome, in a penurious prison, and so to pay my debts with my bones, and recompence the wastfulnesse of my youth with the beggery of mine age; Let me wither in a spittle under sharpe, and foule, and infamous diseases, and so to recompence the wantonnesse of my youth, with that loathsomeness in mine age; yet if God with-draw not his spirituall blessings, his Grace, his Patience, If I can call my Suffering his Doing, my passion his Action, All this that is temporall, is but a caterpillar got into one corner of my garden, but a mill-dew fallen upon one acre of my Corne; The body of all, the substance of all is safe, so long as the Soule is sage.[55]

Donne's gift was his capacity to identify with his auditory, to make their fears of death his, their hopes of amendment because of remorse his, and their longing for eternal life beyond the mutability of the age and the daily decrepitude his, and to do this, while reminding them of the power and promises and provisions of the living God. Andrewes may hide himself in his doctrine, but he is incapable of the direct and passionate address and therefore of the persuasion of Donne.

Homer nods and Donne had his faults. There is an obscurity in many of his sermons unsuitable for one whose main aim is edification.[56] It may take the form of esoteric lore,[57] or even of a coinage of new words often of a quinquepedalian length.[58]

---

[55] *Sermons* (eds. Potter and Simpson), VII, p. 56. For another passage of this kind, see II, p. 300.

[56] In *ibid.*, VII, p. 95, Donne declared: "a sermon intends *Exhortation* principally and *Edification*, and a holy stirring of the religious affections, and then *matters of Doctrine*, and points of *Divinity*. . . ."

[57] See Mary P. Ramsey, *Les Doctrines Médiévales chez Donne* (Oxford, 1917), which shows his fondness for Tertullian, Aquinas and especially Augustine. H.J.C. Grierson in *Poetical Works*, II, pp. 223-24, shows his fascination with Rabbinical and Cabbalistic writings, even in the original Hebrew.

[58] Some five-syllabled examples are the following: *contesseration, exhaeredation, immarcessible, pre-increpation, repullulation, re-efformation.*

Despite his splendid eloquence, much of his homiletical writing is dated, by its far-fetched allegorical interpretation which cannot stand up to historical criticism, not to mention the extraordinary importance on his view of the church's relation to the sovereign and the nation, inappropriate in the modern democratic and secular context of culture.

His sermon structure was more often conceived than kept. He sometimes breaks the form to great effect; more often his meandering leads to a loss of concentration and therefore of effectiveness.

Despite the need to keep the attention of both the intelligentsia and the groundlings, he sometimes degenerated into melodrama, and his final shroud sermon, though most Baroque and contemporary, is in fact to be described as Pelagian posturing, however good its motive to preach unforgettably.[59] But all in all his like has not been seen, nor will be. He was the unique glory of the English, not merely the Jacobean, pulpit.

4. The "Senecan" Preachers

From the beginning of the century until the Restoration there was a flourishing group of preachers, who used rhetorical devices without what they would consider to be the extravagances, conceits, witty word-play, esoteric knowledge, and over-fragmented exegesis of the metaphysical divines. Their pithier and more compact oratory and its powerfully ethical content, as well as their citations from classical moralists, has earned them the name of "Senecan,"[60] though this is as unsatisfactory a designation as "metaphysical" for the other group. The new group comprised such Calvinist Anglicans as the witty Puritan Thomas Adams, or the gifted Bishop Joseph Hall who held the sees of Exeter and Norwich in succession, and perhaps midway between the metaphysicals and the Senecans was the superb stylist, Bishop Jeremy Taylor, whose Patristic lore and ornate imagery link him with the former, and his moral teaching with the latter.

Thomas Adams is particularly interesting because he belonged to the Puritan wing of the Anglican church and was like Hall in being a Calvinist not an Arminian like the Laudian Metaphysicals,

---

[59] A modern secular equivalent would be the famous picture of Salvador Dali, very much alive and advertising, lying in an open, silk-lined coffin, with lilies about his head. A religious equivalent would be the annual circus service in Birmingham, England, in which the elephants are led round to the congregation with yoghurt cartons in their trunks for offertory basins!

[60] J. Fraser Mitchell, *op. cit.*, pp. 352f.

as also in making a great use of "characters," that is, descriptions of types of persons who have been carefully observed, and which are used for minatory purposes. Here are two examples of Adams's "characters" in order to drive home moral lessons. First the usurer wracked with anxiety: "And though the usurer struffe his pillow with nothing but his bonds and mortgages, softer and sweeter in his opinion then downe or feathers; yet his head will not leave aking."[61] The second is the old man, possessed by his possessions: "No man is so old but still he thinks he may live another year; and therefore lightly the older, the more covetous; and *Quo minus viae restat, eo plus viatici quaeritur*: the less journey men have, the more provision they make."[62]

Adams struck like a poniard to the conscience of his bearers. One of his most ingenious images is that of a clock's pendulum swinging from presumption to despair:

The Conscience is like the poyse of a clocke: the poyse being downe all motion ceaseth, the wheels stirre not: wound up, all is set on going. Whiles Conscience is downe, there is no noyse or moving in the heart; all is quiet; but when it is wound up by the Iustice of God, it sets all the wheels on working: tongue to confess, eyes to weepe, hands to wring, breast to be beaten, heart to ake, voyce to crie; and that where Mercy steps not in, a fatall crie, to the hilles, *Fall on us, and hide us.*[63]

For its brilliance and sustained power it is worthy of a Donne. His command of language is also reminiscent of Donne, as in the following "character" of the epicure, in which we are given his *credo*:

I beleeue that sweet wine and strong drinkes; the best blood of the grape, or sweate of the corne is fittest for the belly. I beleeue that midnight revels, perfumed chambers, soft beds, close curtaines, and a Dalilah in mine arms, are very comfortable. I beleeue that glistring silkes, and sparkling jewels, a purse full of golden charmes, a house neatly decked, Gardens, Orchards, Fishponds, Parkes, Warrens, and whatsoeuer may yeeld pleasurable stuffing to the corpse, is a very heauen upon earth. I beleeue that to sleepe till dinner, and play till supper, and quaffe till midnight, and to dally

[61] *Works* (folio ed. of 1630), p. 634.
[62] *Ibid.*, p. 684.   [63] *Ibid.*, p. 757.

till morning; except there be some intermission to toss some paynted papers, or to whirle about squared bones . . . this is the most absolute and perfect end of man's life.[64]

The success of Adams was due to such vivid characterization, to his use of the classics such as Juvenal, Horace, Martial, Seneca, Ovid, and Aesop as well as a collation of the most intriguing sections of the Scriptures, to his employment of allegories, to his relentless pursuit of the consciences of his hearers, to his use of brilliant titles for his sermons,[65] and to his capacity to sustain attention.

Joseph Hall (1574-1656) resembled Donne in his wit and in having been a man of letters before he became a divine, and won fame in 1608 for naturalising in England the Theophrastan character. Like Donne, and his nearer contemporaries, such as Ussher[66] and Burton, Hall brought back cargo from the further shores of learning, and embedded Latin and Greek citations in his sermons. But the style is natural, and pithily aphoristic. The rhetoric is there, but less obtrusive than in the metaphysicals, and it points to the type of writing that came to be admired by the Restoration writers and preachers. His qualities are exemplified in the following citation from a sermon preached on the unpromising text of Deuteronomy 33:8: "And of Levi he said, Let thy Thummim and thine Urim be with thy holy One." Bishop Hall described Moses nearing the end of his life as he prepared to ascend Mount Nebo to die:

> *Moses* will do his best for God's people; being not satisfied with his own happinesse, unlesse his charge may prosper; nor content to have been their convoy all his life except he might direct the way at his death also. 'Tis a clear sun-set that commends the day, and the chief grace of the Theater is a good com off: wherefore our Prophet reserves his best Scene for the last Act, and in the evening of his life shines most gloriously; breaking forth upon the Tribes with a double ray of counsel and blessing.[67]

[64] *Ibid.*, pp. 498-99.
[65] As examples, "Mysticall Bedlam" and "The Devills Blanket."
[66] Ussher, who became Primate of the Anglican church in Ireland, was the author of an interesting book on church order recommending a conciliar rather than a monarchical episcopate, and this "reduced episcopacy," supposedly primitive, appealed greatly to Baxter and others who disliked Independency and feared prelacy. His sermons are dull, impersonal, argumentative, and plain to the point of nudity. He was a Calvinist like Adams and Hall.
[67] Cited from Abraham Wright's *Five Sermons in Five Several Styles or Waies*

There is an easy natural flow of the diction, perfect balance of the clauses, vivid images drawn from the stage and from nature, and an affectionately drawn portrait of the faithful father in God, Moses. Like most Calvinist divines he was a most loyal and exact expositor of Holy Writ, but also much livelier than most of the others.

Bishop Sanderson also belongs to the Senecan school of divines, partly because of the naturalness of style, the use of Patristic and classical learning, a great moral concern expressed through the study of particular cases (casuistry), though unlike those we have already considered he was no Calvinist. One of the best examples of his pellucid prose is his introduction to the revised Book of Common Prayer of 1662. His style of writing and preaching is adequately described by Walton, as follows: "there was in his sermons no improper rhetoric, nor such perplexed divisions as may be said to be like too much light, that so dazzles the eyes, that the sight becomes less perfect; but there was therein no want of useful matter, nor waste of words; and yet such clear distinctions as dispelled all confused notions, and made his hearers depart both wiser, and more confirmed in virtuous resolutions."[68]

The greatest homiletician of the non-metaphysical Anglican divines was unquestionably Bishop Jeremy Taylor (1613-1667). His writing is aesthetic in style and ethical in concern. His allusions to the classics and the Fathers are the references of a well-stored mind, rather than that of a well-conned commonplace book. He has the gift of mingling Christian and pagan writers in the most natural fashion, as when he claims that the Christian hope of eternal life "will make a satyr chast, and a Silenus to be sober, and Dives to be charitable, and Simon Magus to despise reputation, and Saul to turn from a Persecutor to an Apostle."[69] No writer of sermons has been so continuously read in English than Jeremy Taylor. His spirit appealed particularly to John Keble, two centuries later, who wrote that Taylor was "so gentle in heart, and so high in mind, so fervent in zeal, and so charitable in judgment. . . ."[70]

His major collection of sermons is entitled, *Eniautos, or A*

---

of Preaching (1656), pp. 23-24. It was preached at Wright's own ordination at Christ Church, Oxford by Bishop Hall and is the second sermon included in his anthology.

[68] Walton, *op. cit.*, p. 397.

[69] "Of Growth in Sinne," Sermon XVI from *XXVII Sermons* (1651).

[70] J. T. Coleridge, *Memoir of John Keble* (1869), p. 108.

Course of Sermons for all the Sundays of the Year, fitted to the great necessities and for supplying the wants of preaching in many parts of this nation (1651). It is in two parts, the first containing twenty-seven sermons is known as "The Summer Half," and the other with twenty-five sermons is known as "The Winter Half." It is curious that there is little apparent reference to the Christian year and therefore to the life of Christ, though that subject had been elaborated theologically and devotionally before in *The Great Exemplar*. The subjects of this particular collection of sermons include prayer, godly fear, flesh and spirit, the house of feasting, the marriage ring, Christian simplicity, mercy, sin, the righteous cause oppressed, and Taylor's pet-aversion, death-bed repentance.

It has been assumed that these polished sermons cannot have been preached in this printed form, but that the originals were simpler and less learned. On the other hand, Taylor's auditory in Lord and Lady Carbery's retreat at Golden Grove in South Wales, would not be country yokels, but the aristocrats and their friends, neighbouring clergy, and servants on the estate.[71] Moreover, it was conventional for Anglican divines of the day to include Greek and Latin citations in their sermons. No one could better illustrate C. J. Stranks' contention that while Puritan sermons were plain, "the Anglicans coveted that same love of beauty which made them embellish their churches and their ritual into the enrichment of their sermons"[72] than Jeremy Taylor.

Taylor is adept at the art of a striking beginning to a sermon. One, on original sin, begins thus: "It is not necessary that a commonwealth should give pensions to orators to dissuade men from running into houses infected with the plague . . ."[73] In the beginning of "The House of Feasting" Taylor begins by citing the proverb, "Let us eat, drink, and be merry, for to-morrow we die" and comments: "This is the epicure's proverb, begun upon a weak mistake, started by chance from the discourses of drink, and thought witty by the undiscerning company; but . . . when it comes to be examined by the consultations of the morning and the sober hours of the day, it seems the most witless and the most unreasonable in the world."[74]

---

[71] C. J. Stranks, *The Life and Writings of Jeremy Taylor* (1952), pp. 118-19.
[72] *Ibid.*, p. 119.
[73] *Works*, IV, p. 356. The first sermon in a series on "The Descending and Entailed Curse cut off."
[74] *Works*, IV, p. 180.

It is, however, his images that are Taylor's chief glory and delight. The majority of them are taken from Nature in its varied seasons, its flora and fauna, dawn, and sunset. One apt example is the description of cold prayers which are like "the buds of roses which a cool wind hath nip'd into death."[75] His most quoted passages are those which are elongated similes or metaphors, as "For so I have seen a lark . . ."[76] or "But so I have seen a rose. . . ."[77] Yet it is almost always the microcosm in nature which he admires—the miniature rather than the masterful.

His jokes are very gentle gibes, as when he pokes fun at the celibate, who "like the fly in the heart of an apple dwells in perpetual sweetness but sits alone, and is confined and dies in singularity."[78] Even in his funeral oration for Bramhall, he takes a sly dig at Papal infallibility (which should be compared with the roistering mood of Donne gibing at the same claim). Taylor observes that when St. Peter came back and informed the disciples that Christ was risen, because "he was not yet got into the Chair of the Catholic Church they did not think him infallible and so they believed him not at all."[79]

His learning is, of course, immense, even rapacious. C. J. Stranks has calculated that in his collected works there are citations or references to over 1300 different authors. The list is headed by Augustine with 684, followed by Chrysostom with 286, then Cicero with 216, Seneca with 190, and Juvenal with 116.[80] His vast reading included medieval legends, chronicles, casuistry, controversy, secular and sacred histories, the Fathers in east and west, the Scholastic theologians, the Rabbinical lore, Roman Catholic books of devotion and martyrologies, apart from the classical moralists and orators. While he is usually associated with the Laudian group, they were far from subscribing to his virtualist view of the Holy Communion, and it should not be forgotten that this most tolerant of divines[81] and author of *The Liberty of Prophesying* (1647) had an early link with Chillingworth and was a

---

[75] *XXV Sermons*, Sermon v, "The Return of Prayers."
[76] *Ibid*. This image for the soul fastened itself on the retina of posterity. It was used in Baxter's *The Saints' Everlasting Rest* and by Henry Smith's "A Caveat for Christians" in *Sermons and other Treatises* (1675).
[77] *Holy Dying*, cited by J. Fraser Mitchell, *op. cit.*, p. 250.
[78] *Works*, IV, p. 278.   [79] *Works*, VIII, p. 398.   [80] *Op. cit.*, p. 129n.
[81] Taylor claimed that the best ways of uprooting error are "by preaching and disputation (so that neither of them breed disturbance), by charity and sweetness, by holiness of life, assiduity of exhortation, by the work of God and prayer." (*Liberty of Prophesying, Works*, V, p. 354.)

close friend of Henry More, the Cambridge Platonist.[82] Perhaps one should expect this of a divine who enjoyed reading Plato and Descartes, as Taylor did.

His qualities as a preacher are many. His sermons were as graceful in their delivery as in their craftsmanship. He stirred up the holy affections by his proclamation of the God of Nature and of Grace, and distilled a love for the continuity of the Anglican church with the early centuries in its doctrine and ceremonies. He knew that the genuineness of Christianity was to be found in a consecrated life, and so he helped others along the path that led to the beauty of holiness. He taught that theological roots must bear ethical fruits. In the beauty of his images, in the wide range of his learning, in the charity and joyfulness of his spirit, and in the loyalty to his church, he set an excellent example in difficult days.

His three weaknesses as a preacher were related. His style sometimes failed of its effect because it was too ornate, too contrived, and because his well constructed sentences were too long and moved at so leisurely a pace that they lost the attention of his congregation. Second, all that literary lore gives his written sermons at least a grievously impersonal and remote air. Finally, because his had been a sheltered life, even in penal days, his experience of life was restricted to university, court, and other polite society, and this prevented him from being in the best sense a popular preacher. The Civil War had interrupted his start as a parish priest, and so he had no message for the shop or the cottage, but only for those who lived in the Hall.[83] It is in this respect that the Puritans have the advantage over him in observation, directness of approach, and psychological insight. But these are charges that could with equal justice be made against many high churchmen of his day. His most valuable legacy in an age of fevered and embattled partisanship was the demand for tolerance and an insistence that only the essentials, not speculative matters, were worthy of loyalty. In a plea that links him with the Great Tew Circle of his own time and with the pragmatism of the post-Restoration preachers, but expressed in his own incomparable prose, he addresses the future:

> How many volumes have been writ about angels, about immaculate conception, about original sin, when all that is

---

[82] *The Autobiography of Richard Baxter* (ed. J. M. Lloyd Thomas, Everyman edn.), p. 177.
[83] This point is most effectively made by C. J. Stranks, *op. cit.*, p. 280.

solid reason or clear revelation in all these three articles may be reasonably enough comprised in forty lines? And in these trifles and impertinences men are curiously busy, while they neglect those glorious precepts of Christianity and holy life which are the glories of our religion, and would enable us to a happy eternity.[84]

5. Puritan Preaching

No one who is looking for a "ghost in marble" style (such was Coleridge's brilliant description of Taylor's), should read Puritan sermons. By a self-denying ordinance the Puritan preacher, especially in the days of the Commonwealth, hid his literary lore and his rhetoric so that he might transmit the light of the Gospel more transparently. His was, by choice, a plain and unadorned style for another reason: it was understood by the simple people. We look in vain, therefore, for the Patristic learning[85] of the Laudian school, because it seemed to Puritan divines out of place in the pulpit though very much in place in the study or in controversial writings with Roman Catholics. We shall find images, not as extensive set pieces in Taylor, but as brief illustrative devices to clarify the meaning rather than to adorn. We shall find occasional flashes of humour and aphorisms and proverbs. We shall also discover denunciation. Above all there will be directness of approach and application, and the sermon will have a precise structure, while throughout it will be clear that the preacher's task is to expound the oracles of God. If the Puritan preacher does not regard himself as under the divine orders of the Word, he is impudently overreaching himself. Hence these sermons will often seem no more than a mosaic of Biblical texts, but they come to the congregation with the authority of God Himself. That is why faithful Scriptural exegesis is the prime requirement of Puritan preaching, and, close after it, a sense of urgency, perfectly captured in Richard Baxter's couplet:

[84] *Works*, v, p. 359.
[85] For the Puritan disapproval of citing from the Fathers in sermons, see Perkins, *Works* (1631), ii, p. 664, and Richard Baxter's *Works* (1707), iv, p. 428. For the Puritan preference for the plain style, see the preface to Bunyan's *Grace Abounding*, where he observes that he might "have stepped into a style much higher than this. . . . But I dare not. God did not play in convincing of me, the devil did not play in tempting of me, neither did I play when I sunk as into a bottomless pit, when the pangs of hell caught hold of me; wherefore I will not play in my relating of them, but be plain and simple, and lay the thing down as it was."

I preach'd as never like to preach again
And as a dying man to dying men.

Its third great quality was its practical character: to tell the hearers not only what they should think (where Andrewes and Donne had excelled), how they should feel (Taylor's forte), but also exactly what they should do.

Preaching was primarily then for revelation of the divine love and will and for the conversion of the soul. William Bradshaw spoke for all Puritans in the statement: "They hould that the highest and supreame office and authoritie of the Pastor, is to preach the gospell solemnly and publickly to the Congregation, by interpreting the written word of God, and applying the same by exhortation and reproof. They hould that this was the greatest worke that Christ & his Apostles did." The compilers of the Parliamentary *Directory*, three decades later, make the high claim again: "Preaching of the Word, being the power of God unto salvation, and one of the greatest and most excellent works belonging to the ministry of the Gospel, should be so performed that the workman need not be ashamed, but may save himself and those that hear him."[86] For the Puritan, who never forgot the vast and yawning chasm that separated puny and sinful man on earth from the almighty and holy God in highest heaven, it was infinitely more important that God should descend in revelation and redemption than that man should ascend in prayer and praise. Perhaps the finest definition of the awesome responsibility of preaching was penned by Baxter: "It is no small matter to stand up in the face of a congregation, and deliver a message of salvation or damnation, as from the living God, in the name of our Redeemer. It is not easy matter to speak so plain, that the ignorant may understand us; and so seriously that the deadest hearts may feel us; and so convincingly, that contradicting cavillers may be silenced."[87] With such a view of the august significance of preaching, the Puritan preacher mounted the meeting-house stairs to the pulpit as if he were a modern Moses of the New Dispensation ascending Mount Sinai as the friend of God.

The preacher was not in the pulpit as a scholar to impress with his learning, nor as a wit to tickle the fancy of men about town or court, nor to gain tributes to his eloquence. On the contrary, he

[86] *Reliquiae Liturgicae*, ed. Peter Hall, III, *Directory*, p. 35.
[87] *The Reformed Pastor* (London, edn. of 1860), p. 128.

was the man of God, the prophet who denounced the people for
their sins without fear or favour, the preacher who unfolded the
"mystery" of the Gospel, revealing the whole plan of salvation,
under compulsion to bring men to the parting of the ways that
lead to salvation or damnation. What might be labelled "enthusiasm" by his critics, as if it were mere emotional energy, was in
reality the expression of his sense of urgency. By his proclamation
of the Gospel he was, under Christ, binding or loosing the souls of
his congregation. Thus, in the words of Thomas Goodwin, Commonwealth President of Magdalen College, Oxford, preaching produced "experimental, saving, applying knowledge." It was equally
far removed from didacticism as from subjectivism. In teaching,
the Puritan preacher imparted not human knowledge which might
make him and his charges proud but divine knowledge which
humbled the recipients. If he referred to his own experience, it was
only by way of illustrating what God had done for the undeserving
in His mercy. The preaching of the Word of God, as the Puritan
interpreted his task, was neither a moral homily nor a philosophical
disquisition, but the authoritative declaration of the will of the
blessed God from the written Word and twin Covenants or Testaments of God.

A Puritan type of sermon had already been specially constructed
that would be a faithful exposition of Scripture, that would go
plainly and directly and urgently to the doctrines as a straight
arrow to its target, and that would apply the doctrines for the use
of the hearers with the utmost daily relevance. The lineaments of
it are found in Perkins's *Arte of Prophesying* (1607), which
enjoyed a magisterial reputation among the Puritans. Its conclusions may be given in the author's own summary:

1. To reade the Text distinctly out of the Canonicall Scriptures.
2. To give the sense and understanding of it being read, by
   the Scripture it selfe.
3. To collect a few and profitable points of doctrine out of
   the naturall sense.
4. To apply (if he have the gift) the doctrines rightly collected, to the life and manners of men in a simple and
   plaine speech.[88]

[88] *Works* (1631), II, p. 673. Perkins, while insisting that "humane wisdom"
should be concealed because the preacher is declaring the divine, not the human

163

Such functional clarity was evidence of the impact of Ramus in the Cambridge University whence this preaching advice came. It is significant that Ramus wrote important textbooks in logic as well as in rhetoric, both of which had seminal influences on English education. This scheme advocated by Perkins, and the vogue for the rest of the century and beyond first for Puritans and then for Dissenters, was simplified even further in the triple schema—by which all Puritan sermon-structures are identified—of "Doctrine, Reason, and Use." It is interesting that, although he does not use the terms, yet John Wilkins (1614-1672), a founder of the Royal Society, and future Bishop of Chester, uses the concepts in his frequently reprinted, *Ecclesiastes: or a Discourse concerning the Gift of Preaching*, which had reached its eighth edition by 1704. Wilkins says that the chief parts of a sermon are: Explication (which corresponds to Doctrine), Confirmation (which corresponds to Reason), and Application (which corresponds to Use).[89]

The Parliamentary *Directory* made official the Puritan sermon-structure in the following instructions to the preacher according to the triple schema: "In raising doctrines from the text, his care ought to be, First, that the matter be the truth of God. Secondly, that it be a truth contained in, or grounded on, that text that the hearers may discern how God teacheth it from thence. Thirdly, that he chiefly insist upon those doctrines which are principally intended, and make most for the edification of his hearers."[90] Clearly, the first aim of the sermon was evangelical instruction. Such doctrines then have to be explained to the congregation and their contraries refuted. Thus the second division of the sermon was a logical defence of the assumptions of the first section. Then the *Directory* urges: "The arguments or reasons are to be solid; and, as much as may be, convincing. The illustrations, of what kind soever, ought to be full of light, and such as may convey the truth into the hearer's heart with spiritual delight."[91] The third section of the sermon was intended to drive home the practical

---

message, yet is adamant in denying that he means by this that barbarism should be brought into the pulpit: "hee must understand that the Minister may, yea and must privately use at his libertie the arts, Philosophy, and variety of reading, whilest he is in framing his sermon: but he ought in publike to conceale all these from the people, and not to make the least ostentation." (*Ibid.*, p. 670.)

[89] *Ecclesiastes* (8th edn., 1704), pp. 6-9.
[90] *Reliquiae Liturgicae*, ed. Peter Hall, III, *Directory*, p. 37.
[91] *Ibid.*

advantages of belief in the particular doctrine being expounded. It usually concluded with admonitions and encouragements. Thus, doctrine, reason, and use might be regarded as the declaration, the explanation and confirmation, and the application of the Christian faith. The first two sections should convince the reason, while the last section warmed the heart into acceptance of the doctrine.

Plain the Puritan sermon might be, but it was purposefully streamlined. It proceeded from informing the mind and stirring up the affections—there was a considerable element of Christ-mysticism in Puritanism as Chapter III has shown—to effect the transformation of the will. The structure of the Puritan sermon was the perfect instrument for its purpose.

Where then, since historical lore and rhetoric were forbidden, was there room for ingenuity? First, in the careful exposition of texts and contexts, and the collation of doctrines from the remoter parts of the Old Testament, not forgetting those who were living exemplars of them. Secondly, ingenuity was needed in applying these lessons to the condition of the congregation, and, as we shall see in the case of Richard Baxter, was likely to be more effective when the pastor regularly visited the people in their homes. Thirdly, there was room for intelligence in the determining of the spiritual condition of the preacher's patients and in prescribing for their soul's healing, their psychiatry. Puritan preachers were particularly gifted in this regard.[92] Fourthly, there was the deep well of human experience and observation and reading to draw upon in the search for analogies, similes, metaphors, any and all kinds of illustrations to bring home the lessons to the preacher's charges. A fifth place for ingenuity was provided by the often excessively lengthy series of Puritan sermons on the same theme or on a book or even a chapter of a book of the Bible. Anthony Burgess preached, for example, 145 sermons on John 17, which he published in 1656 and Manton preached 190 sermons on Psalm 119; while George Trosse spent several years preaching a Marathon series on the attributes of God. One congregation, however, became so exhausted by their minister preaching for four months on Joseph's coat of many colours that they called him "Eternal Bragge."

It would be the gravest error to attribute the Puritan plain style to dullness of mind, ignorance of rhetoric, or servility of

92 See Davies, op. cit., I, pp. 319-24, for Puritan sermons that are studies in the psychology of religion.

spirit. Baxter, a man of broad culture and critical mind, said: "The plainest words are the profitablest Oratory in the weightiest matters. Fineness is for ornament, and delicacy for delight; but they answer not *Necessity*."[93] The great demand for self-discipline imposed by the Puritan plain style is admirably exemplified in John Cotton, who after being convinced of the truth of Puritanism gave up his erudite and ornate style of preaching for one much simpler. It is recorded in Cotton Mather's *Magnalia Christi Americana*, along with the plain sermon on repentance which Cotton preached and caused the conversion of Preston. Here is the record of the incident:

> Some time after this Change upon the Soul of Mr. *Cotton*, it came his turn again to preach at St. *Maries*; and because *he* was to preach, an High Expectation was raised throughout the *whole University*, that they should have a Sermon, flourishing indeed, with all the *Learning* of the *whole University*. Many difficulties had Mr. *Cotton* in his own mind now, what Course to steer. On the one side he considered, That if he should preach with a Scriptural and Christian *Plainness*, he should not only wound his own *Fame* exceedingly, but also tempt Carnal Men to revive an Old Cavil, *That Religion made Scholars turn Dunces*, whereby the Name of God might suffer not a little. On the other side, he considered, That it was his Duty to preach with such a Plainness, as became the Oracles of God, which are intended for the Conduct of Men in the *Paths of Life*, and not for Theatrical Ostentations and Entertainments, and the Lord needed not any *Sin* of ours to maintain his own Glory. Hereupon Mr. *Cotton* resolved, that he would preach a plain Sermon. . . ."[94]

That this simplicity in other Puritan divines was deliberate, is amply proven. One more example must suffice. Arthur Dent, in the Preface to his *Sermon of Repentance* of 1637, apologizes for not having produced it in a high-flown style: "Let no man therefore be offended that I have not strained my selfe to flie an high pitch, to fome [foam] out the froth of mans wisedome, and to make a great show of learning, by blowing the bladder of vanity, till it burst with swelling; but it is not my use: I seek especially the

---

[93] Cited in F. J. Powicke, *A Life of the Reverend Richard Baxter* (1924), p. 282.
[94] This comes from the introduction to the reprinted Repentance sermon in *Magnalia*, in a section entitled, "Cottonus Redivivus."

salvation of the simple and ignorant: and therefore stoope down to their reach and capacity."[95]

One of the most popular Caroline Puritan preachers was John Preston (1587-1628), a favourite of Charles I's favourite, Buckingham. He had been Preacher at Lincoln's Inn and Chaplain to the King. After his death, there was published a tri-partite volume of sermons, entitled, *The Golden Sceptre held forth to the Humble, with the Churches Dignitie by her Marriage, and the Churches Dutie in her Carriage* (1638). The first part comprised sermons delivered in Cambridge in 1625 for the weekly Fasts, and the other two consisted of two series of sermons preached at Lincoln's Inn. What is particularly interesting about this volume is the table of contents because it so clearly marks the structure of the Puritan sermon and illustrates it in skeletal form:

Doct[rine]	1.	God afflicts his owne people.	3.
Reas[on]	1.	Because he loves them.	4.
	2.	That his name be not blasphemed.	*Ibid.*
	3.	He will be sanctified in those that draw neare him.	*Ibid.*
	4.	He walks among them.	5.
Vse.	1.	To feare the Lord.	6.
	2.	Want of feare provoketh God.	13.
	3.	Gods severity to wicked men.	18.
	4.	Not think strange that God afflicts his.	19.
Doct.	2.	God pities his people in affliction.	20.
Reas.	1.	He is slow to afflict.	21.
	2.	He sustains them in affliction.	*Ibid.*
	3.	He brings them through affliction.	25.
Vse.	1.	Not to be Discouraged in affliction.	32.
	2.	To come to God when we have offended him.	35.
	3.	To lead us to repentance.	37.
	4.	To choose the Lord for our God.	41.
	5.	To confirme us in that choice.	45.

To give flesh to one "Use," the last one on our list, Preston's historical and contemporary application must also be cited: "God hath been mercifull to it [the church] in all ages, and is so still; so he saith, *I have been her habitation*, that is a house for the

95 *Op. cit.*, A3 recto and verso.

Church to dwell safely in . . . looke on the Church when it was in the worst condition, take the Church of God, even when it seemed to be cut off, as in that great massacre in *France*, yet then was the Lord an habitation to it, a company was kept alive, that grew greater than the former. So the Church in Queen *Marie's* time, he suffered the storme to overtake them a little, but it was soone blowen over, he was an habitation to keepe off the storme from destroying them, and so he hath been, and will be to *Bohemia*, and the *Palatinate*, but so he hath beene found to be to our Church above all the rest, for our Nation hath been like *Gideon's Fleece*, when all about us have been wet and wallowed in blood, we have been dry. . . ."[96] There was the strength of steel in Puritanism because it was prepared for affliction, and it did so in the conviction that it was called upon to suffer for Christ's sake, because its members were the elect. Preston's next passage shows that the great strength of Puritanism lay in the conviction of being an elect people, in the bond of God's covenant with his people, "so that it seems—there is a certaine match between them, a mutuall agreement and relation, as there is betweene a husband and a wife, a father and a sonne; so if thou beest one who is married to Christ, and hee hath changed thy heart, and begotten thee anew by his Word, and art dedicated to his service as his temple; then art thou called by his Name."[97]

Another sermon, preached almost fifty years after Preston's, will serve as an indication of the weaknesses of this mode of preaching. This was preached in London in October 1682—during a lull in persecution of the Dissenters—at a morning exercise of the Nonconformist ministers in London. Such an "exercise" was rather like the "prophesyings" of Elizabethan Puritanism, ultimately derived from Zwingli's Zurich. The subject is: "Whether it be expedient and how the Congregation may say *Amen* in publick Worship." The text is Nehemiah 8:6: "And Ezra blessed the Lord, the great God, and all the People answered, Amen, Amen." It is virtually a sermon on the single word, *Amen*. The Doctrine taught is "That it is a lawful and laudable practice for people at the conclusion of publick prayer or praysing God to pronounce an *Amen*." Then follows a series of definitions of *Amen*: 1. "*Amen*

---

[96] *Op. cit.*, pp. 46-47. This was a Puritan historical commonplace apparently, because the same instances in almost the same words are used by Thomas Jackson, Prebend and Lecturer in Canterbury Cathedral in his book of sermons, *The Raging Tempest stilled* (1623), p. 127.
[97] *The Golden Sceptre held forth to the Humble* (1638), p. 48.

Substantive" (God himself); 2. *"Amen* Affirmative" (verily); 3. *"Amen* Optative";* and 4. *"Double Amen."* This is succeeded by a statement of the Uses of the Doctrine: first, "it is connatural to Prayer and Praise"; secondly, it has the authority of both testaments; thirdly, *"Amens* after Prayer and Praise, is the mans consent, judgment and approbation of what is offered unto God"; fourthly, "This vocal *Amen* is the . . . summ of all our petitions and praises to God"; fifthly, "it involves a strong faith"; sixthly, it is "an assurance that God will accept our Praises and Answer our Prayers"; lastly, "this unanimous *Amen* of Faith strikes terror into the enemies of the Church, whether Devils or men."[98] And such prolixity, one fears, produces torpor in the friends of the church! It has ingenuity in discovering seven different uses for the doctrine, but the definitions of *Amen* are exceedingly pedantic, and the entire sermon is wanting in proportion. This is Puritan prolixity, pedantry, and poverty of the imagination at its worst. For the best Puritan sermons one must look to the wit of Thomas Adams, the warmth of Richard Sibbes, the spiritual insight of John Downame, the clear analysis and strong contemporary applications of Preston, and the spirituality linked with scholarship of John Owen, Thomas Goodwin, Richard Baxter, Matthew Henry, John Howe, and William Bates.

It may well be, of course, that Puritan sermons seem much duller than they were only because we are reading them rather than listening to them. Not only was the tone of the Puritan preacher urgent, but often his gestures were vehement. This was one ground of Anglican ridicule of Puritan preaching. One such critic writes: "How often have you seen a Preacher heat himself beyond the need of any vestments? Throwing off his Cloak, nay and his Gloves too, as great impediments to the holy performance, squeeking and roaring beyond the example of any Lunatick? Sometimes speaking in a tolerable tone, and presently again crying out as if under some immediate distraction?" The result is that the Puritan congregation "have gaped upon him, and when he hath finished, given him this honourable Encomium, Well, hee's a rare man, a man mighty zealous for the Lord, a powerful preacher, and one that hath taken abundance of pains that day. . . ."[99]

[98] Sermon XXI in *A Continuation of Morning Exercise Sermons,* ed. Samuel Annesley, John Wesley's grandfather on the distaff side (1683).

[99] *A Free and Impartial Inquiry into the causes of that very great Esteem and Honour that the Nonconforming Preachers are generally in with their followers* (1673), pp. 118f.

The popularity of Puritan preaching cannot be accounted for alone in terms of the accumulation of factors already considered, such as fidelity in scriptural exposition, the plain style intelligible to the simplest, the urgent sincerity of the minister, or even the political daring of some preachers[100] and especially during the apocalyptic excitement associated with the impending reign of the saints—though the latter is an important factor. There is one essential missing element: it is the pastor's intimate knowledge of his people obtained by regular visitation of them. Possibly because the Anglican parish priest adopted other priorities, perhaps through disinclination, probably because many priests had too vast parishes for anything except sick visitation, the fact remains that it is not the Laudian clergy, but the Puritan ministers who made a conscience of spiritual as opposed to social visitation on a regular basis, going from house to house. This is true whether we take as our example Richard Baxter, the Anglican Puritan,[101] at Kidderminster in Worcestershire during the Commonwealth and Protectorate, or Oliver Heywood in Northowram in Yorkshire in Restoration penal times for Presbyterians. In an earlier day George Herbert was a true pastor of his flock, but he seems to have been the exception that proved the Laudian rule.

Baxter's parish at Kidderminster was a market town with about twenty villages, consisting of about three to four thousand souls, or eight hundred families, and about eighteen hundred were of age to be communicants. Most went to church to hear him preach because the law required it, but there would be only about six hundred souls serious about religion. The town had a bad reputation from its drunkards who raged weekly before the minister's

100 Some idea of the political excitement may be obtained from the following probably biassed and exaggerated report on the controversial Hugh Peters, who, "having shaken hands with his Text and raised himself upright in his Pulpit, with his Hand laid across his Breast, thus roars out, O Joab, Joab, *thou faithful Counsellor to David; I love thee* Joab, whom weepest thou for? David! *a Boy, a bloody Cavalier, a Prince Rupert, a plundering Cavalier. Come forth* David, *speak kindly* to thy Servants . . . *Come to thy Parliament, King Charles, wilt not come? I swear unto thee by the Lord, it will be the worst thing hath befallen thee from thy youth until now.*" (*From What has been, maybe again, or an instance of London's Loyalty in 1640, &c* . . . [Anon], 1710, p. 7.)

101 Baxter was sick of ecclesiastical party labels, which he thought were more often libels. At the end of his life he wrote: "You could not (except a Catholic Christian) have trulier called me, than an Episcopal-Presbyterian-Independent." (*A Third Defence of the Cause of Peace*, 1681, Pt. 1, p. 110, cited in Geoffrey F. Nuttall's learned and vivid *Richard Baxter* [1965], p. 84.) For Baxter as visitor, see A. S. Langley, "Richard Baxter—Director of Souls," *The Baptist Quarterly*, Vol. 3 (1926-1927), pp. 71-80.

door.[102] In estimating the change that had come over the town through his long and faithful ministry there, Baxter is honest enough to admit that the Civil War took off the most notorious enemies of godliness. A real change had taken place: "When I came hither first, there was about one Family in a Street that worshipped God and called his Name," but "when I came away there was not past one Family in the Side of a Street that did not do so." "On the Lord's Day there was no disorder to be seen in the Streets, but you might hear an hundred Families singing Psalms and repeating Sermons, as you passed through the Streets."[103] By his love for these people, by his regular catechising of them and visiting them in their homes, by his detailed and individual knowledge of each of them, and by his earnest preaching based upon such pastoral insight, he was, under God, the agent for the transformation of the carpet-weaving town. The congregation responded so well to his evident concern for them that "we were fain to build five Galleries"[104] in the church. One who knew him in his old age, and indeed, edited the *Reliquiae Baxterianae*, Matthew Sylvester, said of his speaking what may well have characterized his preaching, that "He had a moving πάθος [pathos] and useful Acrimony in his words; neither did his Expressions want their Emphatical Accent, as the Matter did require. And when he spake of weighty Soul-Concerns, you might find his very Spirit Drench'd therein."[105] To all who met him, with the exception of Judge Jeffreys, his spirituality was transparent. As Edmund Calamy said, near the time of Baxter's death, "He talked in the pulpit with great freedom about another world, like one that had been there, and was come as a sort of express from thence to make a report concerning[106] it." That one might expect of the author of both the devotional classic, *The Saints' Everlasting Rest* and the celebrated manual on the pastoral ministry, *The Reformed Pastor*, and he set an enduring example for Puritan ministers as George Herbert did for Anglican priests.

The frequency of the demand for sermons is perhaps the best indication of the value in which preaching was held by the Puritans. Baxter tells us: "I preached before the Wars twice each

---

[102] Nuttall, *op. cit.*, pp. 46-47.
[103] *Reliquiae Baxterianae* (ed. M. Sylvester, 1696), I, Pt. 1, Sect. 137, Para. 15.
[104] *Ibid.*, I, Pt. 1, Sect. 136.
[105] Cited by G. F. Nuttall, *op. cit.*, p. 49.
[106] E. Calamy, *Historical Account of my own life* (ed. J. T. Rutt, 1829), I, pp. 220f.

Lord's Day; but after the War but once, and once every Thursday, besides occasional sermons."[107] This was, however, far from exhausting his duties. He spent two entire days of each week catechising families. He also met a group every Thursday evening at his home "and there one of them repeated the Sermon, and afterwards they proposed what Doubts any of them had about the Sermon, or any other Case of Conscience."[108] One other night each week was given over to teaching his young people to pray. Also he met with his fellow ministers for discipline and disputation once a month and presided over the monthly meeting for parish discipline. On national days of humiliation also he preached to his congregation. His ardour and seriousness were indefatigable.

An equally significant series of testimonies is given to the importance of preaching by the northern divine, Oliver Heywood. Reviewing his work in 1689, when he had reached the age of sixty, he claims: "I doe find that I had travelled 1358 miles, preacht 131 times in weekdays, kept 34 fasts, 8 days of thanksgiving, baptized 21 children &c."[109] He records in the following year that he has preached 135 times on weekdays, as well as twice each Lord's Day. Even in his seventieth year, despite asthma and needing two men to carry him to Northowram chapel in a chair, he asserts "yet was enabled when I got into the pulpit to preach audibly—baptized 8 children, kept 8 conferences, preacht on week-days 23 times, writ 7 treatises, 4 short for Warly-people, 104 letters, observed 14 fasts, 3 days of thanksgiving, 2 books printed viz. the two worlds and Christs intercession—my dear Lord was with me all along."[110] On an average this Puritan pastor preached five times a week; no itinerant, he was minister to the Dissenting community at Northowram near Halifax. He was also an author of some note. To have preached so often in the midst of a busy life, is itself an enthusiastic testimony to the high opinion in which preaching was held by the sons of the Puritans.

But even they fell behind the Puritans of the 1640s. The peak of the Puritan appreciation of preaching was surely reached when the clergymen of the Westminster Assembly spent the larger part of the day on Monday, October 16, 1643, preaching and praying, with psalms for relaxation. The occasion was a solemn fast day. Lightfoot relates how the time went:

[107] *Reliquiae Baxterianae*, p. 83.   [108] *Ibid.*
[109] *The Reverend Oliver Heywood, B.A., 1630-1702: His Autobiography, Diaries, Anecdote and Event Books* (ed. J. Horsfall Turner, Bingley, 1883), III, p. 238.
[110] *Ibid.*, p. 285.

First Mr. *Wilson* gave a picked psalm, or selected verses of several psalms, agreeing to the time and occasion. Then Dr. *Burgess* prayed about an hour: after he had done, Mr. *Whittacre* preached ypon Isa. xxxvii. 3, 'This day is a day of trouble,' &c. Then, having had another chosen psalm, Mr. *Goodwin* prayed; and after he had done, Mr. *Palmer* preached upon Psal. xxv. 12. After whose sermon we had another psalm, and Dr. *Stanton* prayed about an hour; and with another psalm and a prayer of the prolocutor [Dr. Twisse], and a collection for the maimed soldiers . . . we adjourned till tomorrow morning.[111]

These learned Puritan preachers were in their and our own sense of the term "painful" preachers; they took pains and they gave pain to all but the most diligent and devoted of their persuasion.

For all their qualities, Puritan or Dissenting sermons had their faults. It was all very well to insist that true art hides the artifice of rhetoric and avoids the ornate style; this is morally good but literarily dull. Without question, the Anglican preachers, whether metaphysical or Senecan, produced sermons that must have been more interesting to hear as they certainly are to read.

The first charge against a great deal of the apolitical preaching of the Puritans, is that it was dull. A combination of prolixity, pedantry, and an atomistic splitting up of the text into divisions and subdivisions after the manner of the more scholastic of the Calvinists like John Owen and Thomas Goodwin, combined with intensity in delivery, guaranteed exhaustion except for the most obdurate or masochistic listeners. Anglicans could be prolix and pedantic, as indeed the famous Isaac Barrow was,[112] but he avoided dullness by his superb flights of rhetoric. Puritans prevented divagation but also delight through banning most rhetorical aids. The stories of John Howe's preaching test by Cromwell and of Peters' "second glass" are reminders of the long-windedness of Puritan preachers.

Every preaching style of a theological party soon develops its own jargon. The Puritans were no exception. Both Robert South and Simon Patrick hugely enjoy themselves by poking fun at the Puritan sermon structure, delivery and jargon, which took the form

[111] Ed. J. R. Pitman, *The Whole Works of the Rev. John Lightfoot, D.D.*, 13 Vols. (1825); Vol. XIII contains "The Journal of the Proceedings of the Assembly of Divines, from January 1, 1643 to December 31, 1644," see *ad loc.*

[112] Caroline F. Richardson, *English Preachers and Preaching, 1640-1670* (New York, 1928), p. 2.

of "Covenant" talk, based upon their recognition of the covenant-relationship between God and his elect, and therefore a fondness for legal and marital metaphors.

South in his brilliant sermon of 1660, *The Scribe instructed to the Kingdom of Heaven* had wittily excoriated the pedantry of Andrewes, after which he gave the Puritan divines in general, and John Owen in particular, a drubbing. The entire passage begins with urbanity, proceeds by exaggeration, and ends with blasphemy.

> I hope it will not prove offensive to the Auditory, if, to release it (could I be so happy) from suffering by such Stuff in the future, I venture upon some short Description of it; and it is briefly thus. First of all they seize upon some Text, from whence they draw something (which they call a *Doctrine*), and well may it be said to be *drawn* from the Words; forasmuch as it seldom naturally flows, or *results* from them. In the next place, being thus provided, they branch it into several Heads; perhaps, twenty, or thirty, or upwards. Whereupon, for the Prosecution of these, they repair to some *trusty Concordance*, which never fails them, and by the Help of that, they range six or seven Scriptures under each Head; which Scriptures they prosecute one by one, first amplifying and enlarging upon one, for some considerable time, till they have spoiled it; and then that being done, they pass to another, which in its turn suffers accordingly. And these impertinent, and unpremeditated Enlargements they look upon as *the Motions and Breathings of the Spirit*, and therefore much beyond those *carnal Ordinances of Sense and Reason*, supported by Industry and Study; and this they call *a saving Way* of Preaching, as it must be confessed to be a way to save much Labour, and nothing else that I know of. . . . But to pass from these Indecencies to others, as little to be allowed in this sort of Men, can any tolerable Reason be given for those strange new Postures used by some in the Delivery of the Word? Such as *shutting the Eyes, distorting the Face, and speaking through the Nose*, which I think cannot so properly be called *Preaching*, as *Toning of a Sermon*. Nor do I see, why the *Word* may not be altogether as effectual for *the Conversion of Souls*, delivered by one, who has the Manners to look his Auditory in the Face, using his own Countenance, and his own native Voice, without straining it to a lamentable

and doleful *Whine* (never serving to any Purpose, but where some religious Cheat is to be carried on). . . . For none surely will imagine, *that these Men's speaking, as never Man spoke before*, can pass for any Imitation of Him. . . .[113]

So well had the criticisms of Puritan preaching been received by the Cavalier congregation that South returned to the attack a year later, in the sermon, *False Foundations Removed*: "Some you shall have amusing their Consciences," so he tells his Oxford congregation, "with a Set of fantastical new-coin'd Phrases, such as *Laying hold on Christ, getting into Christ, and rolling themselves upon Christ*, and the like; by which if they mean any Thing else but obeying the Precepts of Christ, and a rational Hope of Salvation thereupon (which, it is certain that generally they do not mean), it is all but a *Jargon* of empty, senseless Metaphors; and though many venture their Souls upon them, despising *good Works* and *strict Living* as meer *Morality*, and perhaps as *Popery*, yet being thoroughly look'd into and examined, after all their Noise, they are really nothing but *Words* and *Wind*."[114] The jargon was there, but the doctrine of justification by faith is far too superficially dismissed as mere antinomianism by South, and this is a charge that misses the intensely serious Puritans among the Westminster divines, and may only hit some of the "mechanick preachers" of the time.

These Puritan clichés are amusingly satirised by Simon Patrick also. In *A Friendly Debate between a Conformist and a Non-Conformist* (1668), we are informed that "one man comes to tell them of the *streamings* of Christ's *Blood freely* to Sinners: another bids them *put themselves upon the stream of Free grace*, without having any foot on their own bottom." [The latter was a contortion presumably of which even the most agile Puritan was incapable.] "A third tells them how they must *apply Promises*, absolute Promises. A fourth tells them there is a special Mystery in looking at the *Testamentalness* of Christ's *Sufferings*. . . ."[115] This has the authentic character of exact reporting, especially the awkwardness in the term "*Testamentalness*." Patrick, in a work of a year later, *A Continuation of the Friendly Debate*, castigates the fad for a "Covenant" phrase, however indelicate its associations: "When a Preacher, for instance, from that text, *David served his Genera-*

[113] Robert South, *Works* (Oxford, 1823), III, pp. 34-37.
[114] *Ibid.*, II, p. 346.   [115] *Op. cit.*, pp. 25-26.

tion by the will of God, raised this impertinent Observation; *That it is our duty to mind Generation-work*; instantly all Pulpits sounded with this Doctrine of *Generation-work*. That was the phrase in those days: In so much that you should hear both Minister and people bewailing it in their prayers, that they had not minded *Generation-work* more. Which made some good innocent souls, that were not acquainted with the secret, blush when they first heard it, and wonder what they meant."[116]

Puritan preaching, however, survived the artillery of abuse. The sincerity of its preachers during the penal days of the Clarendon Code was without question, and the style dropped its splintering divisions. In the work of the Presbyterian divine, William Bates (1625-1699) there is, besides plainness a pleasing fluidity, and a selection and development of topics that is, in this respect, like Tillotson. One citation from his work must suffice as an index of the whole. It is typical in its rationalism, its concentration on Creation rather than on Grace, and on natural rather than revealed theology, as well as in its urbane approach to an intelligent congregation. Its subject is the first man and his reflections upon God:

> And as by contemplating the other works of God, so especially by reflecting upon himself, *Adam* had a clear sight of the Divine *Attributes*, which concurr'd in his Creation. Whether he considered the lowest part, the Body, 'twas formed of the Earth, the most artificial and beautiful piece of the *visible* world. The contrivance of the parts was with that proportion and exactness, as most conduc'd to Comeliness and Service. Its stature was erect and raised, becoming the Lord of the Creatures, and an observer of the Heavens. A divine Beauty and Majesty was shed upon it. And this was no vanishing *ray*, soon eclips'd by a Disease, and extinguish't by Death, but shin'd in the countenance without any declination. The *Tongue* was Man's peculiar glory, being the interpreter of the mind and capable to Dignifie all the affections of the Soul. In short, the Body was so fram'd as to make a visible discovery of the Prerogatives of his Creation. And when he reflected upon his Soul, that animated his dust, its excellent endowment, wherein it is comparable to the Angels, the capacity of enjoying God himself for ever, he had an internal

---

[116] *Op. cit.*, p. 81. See also John Eachard, *Grounds and Occasions of the Contempt of the Clergy* (1671).

and most clear testimony of the glorious perfections of the Creator. For Man, who alone admires the works of God, is the most admirable of all.[117]

If, with the Restoration, composers of sermons were to drop pedantry of all kinds, avoid the more elaborate forms of rhetoric as artifice, and cultivate plainness of style and lucidity in exposition, and attempt to be as practical as possible, some portion at least of the change is to be attributed to Puritanism for these were the strengths of its manly and direct preaching.

6. *Restoration Preachers*

The plain and functional style of Puritan preaching was only one factor helping to account for the change of style of preaching in Restoration days. Another cause was the influence of the preachers at the French court, such as Massillon, Bossuet, and Bourdaloue, whom many Englishmen had heard during the years that the remnants of the English court sought refuge in France. This constellation of French preachers were exemplars of a sacred oratory of a Ciceronian kind, in which their Scriptural quotations and ethical exhortations were adopted to illustrate a topic and adorn a theme rather than to apply the comfort and criticism of the Gospel. Divorced from the liturgical context (not being expositions of the lessons of the day), and honoured by the presence of the great, whether king or nobility, they praised the dead in their *oraisons funèbres* and maybe flattered the living by easing their consciences in their Lenten sermons. It is rarely that these French sermons reach the height of the prophetic, however sublime their rhetoric and their meditations on mutability. They not infrequently breathe the desiccated air of moralism and despite protestations to the contrary, that practical deism of the remoteness of God[118] which marks the enlightenment. Charles II, in particular, wished to encourage this kind of preaching which found the perfect context in the most baroque and absolutist of courts.

An equally significant but wholly English influence was that of the Royal Society, and the immediate need for the exact, clear, and denotative language suitable for describing experiments in natural science. Thomas Sprat, himself a Bishop of Rochester as well as

---

[117] *Harmony of the Divine Attributes* (1674), Discourse I, pp. 7-8.

[118] John Howe epitomised Deism perfectly in its exaggerated doctrine of the Divine transcendence, by asserting that its *credo* was: "There shall be a God; provided He do not interfere."

the author of *The History of the Royal-Society of London, For the Improving of Natural Knowledge* (1667), remarked that the fellows had adopted "a close, naked, natural way of speaking, positive expressions, clear senses, a native easiness, bringing all things as near the Mathematical plainness as they can, and preferring the language of Artizans, Countrymen, and Merchants, before that of Wits and Scholars."[119]

There was also, it must not be forgotten, a change of spirit in the nation and in Europe, which demanded a change of style. Thoughtful people were tired of extravagance, of unprovable speculations, of notions that were merely fantastic, of enthusiastic extremes, and sought—especially in religion—for a faith and way of living that were rational, practicable, and useful. Pope, in his *Essay on Man*, was to give perfect expression to these deliberately limited objectives and values in life:

> For modes of faith let graceless zealots fight,
> His can't be in the wrong whose life is in the right.
> In Faith and Hope the world will disagree
> But all mankind's concern is Charity.
> All must be false that thwart this one great end,
> And all of God that bless mankind or mend.[120]

The new pulpit style did not easily or rapidly convert those who admired the ornate eloquence of Jeremy Taylor, and who imitated him poorly in what John Eachard called "high-tossing and swaggering preaching,"[121] in strained similitudes and far-fetched metaphors, aiming at ingenuity rather than simplicity and relevance, and discussing remote theological matters rather than down-to-earth concerns. This criticism in turn evoked James Arderne's *Directions Concerning the Matter and Stile of Sermons* (1671),[122] which is an excellent summary of what the Dean of Chester admired in the contemporary pulpit and its shining lights of whom Tillotson was the most stellar.

Arderne recommended the young deacon whom he is instructing in homiletics to select plain and practical parts of the Scrip-

---

[119] *Op. cit.*, Pt. II, Sect. XX.   [120] *Op. cit.*, Bk. III.

[121] John Eachard's *The Grounds and Occasions of the Contempt of the Clergy* (1670) reduced the causes of unpopularity to two: poverty and ignorance, and regarded inept preaching as due to ignorance.

[122] This work has been re-issued under the editorship of John Mackay as No. 13 of the Luttrell Reprints (Oxford, 1952). Subsequent references are to the pagination of this reprint.

ture to expound and apply, and "not to chuse obscure passages, or sublime controversies, or nice speculations to be propounded to any in publick, much less to the uncapable multitude."[123] The practical doctrines to use as sermon topics are: "the Attributes of God's Holiness, Justice, Soveraignty, All-Sufficiency, Faithfullness, Mercie, Infinite Knowledge, and the rest of the Divine perfections: furthermore from the dictates of Nature, and testimony of Conscience, and loveliness of Vertue, and deformitie of Vice, from the obligation of a created being, and edification of others, and vanity of the World, and the hazard of miscarriage."[124]

The structure the Dean recommends to the neophyte is the old Puritan one rephrased by Wilkins, which Arderne calls in his triple analysis "Proposition, Confirmation and Inference."[125]

Reason is to be satisfied by relevant arguments, as we have seen, but the emotions require other persuasives. The motivation which Arderne proposes are appeals to reputation, equity, piety, gratitude, safety, prudence, delight, "demonstrating that Religion is a way of pleasantness, and that Mortification it self brings joy as its fruit to those who make it their exercise."[126]

The diction should avoid the dangerous extremes of either "high flights enthusiastick and giddy" or "by a groveling stoop to clownish phrases"[127] both of which are unsuitable to the practical seriousness of the subject-matter. The gestures, too, are to be grave and decorous "free from apish postures and distorted looks."[128] The pronunciation is to be clear and manly, with a slight inflexion in the voice to avoid dulness. In all things moderation is recommended, as befits the exemplars of the Anglican middle way, which is intended to be sensible, practical, prudential, and useful. These are all valuable ends for preaching, but are not by any means the only aims and qualities that count.

Furthermore, there was a new theology, of which the Great Tew Group and their friends were the forerunners, aided in part by the Cambridge Platonists, the theology of the Latitudinarian movement. Its teachings were characterized by plainness and directness, and it was believed that the essential content of the Christian Faith was summed up in the Fatherhood of God and the duty of benevolence in man. These divines were fully persuaded of the divine beneficence of the Creator and argued that the chief duty of men

---

[123] *Op. cit.*, p. 3.
[124] *Ibid.*, pp. 13-14.
[125] *Ibid.*, p. 9.
[126] *Ibid.*, p. 15.
[127] *Ibid.*, p. 16.
[128] *Ibid.*, p. 30.

was to imitate the divine charity by good works. Religion thought of in these terms required no abstention from innocent social life. On the contrary, it required involvement rather than renunciation, and regarded this involvement in the earthly kingdom as the best preparation for the heavenly city. Inevitably, in the popular mind there was the convenient notion that religion supplies an extra bonus in a course of moderation and virtue.

The dominance of theology up to 1660 was succeeded by the increasing dominance of the natural sciences, and its impact was to be found not only in the style, but also in the content of preaching. Within this period both the telescope and the microscope were invented, the one enabling the vastness of the universe to become recognized more fully, and the other showing the marvellous "contrivance of the parts . . . with that proportion and exactness" of which, as we have seen, Bates had spoken, as if Adam's self-reflection was that of a rather junior Fellow of the Royal Society. Now it became the fashion to think of God in his work of Creation, rather than in the paradoxical and mysterious communication of Himself in Grace. While there are two admirable preachers in the satirical South and eloquent and erudite Isaac Barrow, the man most suited to express the new style was a former Presbyterian turned Anglican, John Tillotson (1630-1694), who was to become Archbishop of Canterbury.

Robert South (1634-1716) is more important as a barometer, perhaps, than as a bringer of light and rain to the parched territory of the sermon. He served his function chiefly as warning the Anglican church of stormy weather, of what to avoid in the pulpit. While his wit can be brilliant, it can also be scurrilous. As in his famous 1660 sermon he had warned against the pedantry and over-subtle etymological divisions of texts in Andrewes and the Biblical battery of the Puritans, so in 1668 he had attacked the luscious if not over-ripe metaphors of Jeremy Taylor, and pleaded for plainness, naturalness, and familiarity in language used in the pulpit. It is enough to say that South seemed more of a pulpit journalist than a theologian in the pulpit; he could even degenerate into being an Anglican Hugh Peters, as when, on a notorious occasion, he described Cromwell as an impoverished and dirtily dressed impostor, who killed one king and banished another, who "wanted nothing of the state of a King but the changing of his hat into a crown."[129] W. Fraser Mitchell says justly of him, "all that a great

129 *Works*, Vol. I, Sermon VIII, p. 213-14.

technician could do, he did; but it remained for the finer and more sympathetic personality of Tillotson to invest with charm a manner excellently calculated to impress, but at times too truculently employed to convince or persuade."[130]

Isaac Barrow (1630-1677) was a greater scholar and a more eloquent preacher than South. He was a considerable mathematician and theologian, who drank deep of the Pierian spring, for his favourite authors were Sophocles, Demosthenes, and Aristotle, as well as St. John Chrysostom. He succeeded best with a learned auditory, for his sermons, which issued from the "loads of learned lumber in his head," were said to be of three hours' duration, making it impossible for an ordinary congregation to endure them. There is a legend that his sermon preached in Easter Week 1671 at the Spital "On the Duty and Reward of Bounty to the Poor" took three and a half hours to deliver (and that this was an apocopated version), the Court of Aldermen desired the preacher to print his sermon with whatever further material he had prepared to deliver at that time.[131] The original folio edition of his works allotted thirty-nine pages to this sermon, so there may be some exaggeration in the story. His subjects were treated in too great detail and at too great length, but they were nothing if not thorough. He had some superbly sustained passages of oratory, dazzling but required great endurance from his auditory.

Far less spectacular in eloquence than Barrow or the South of the pyrotechnic denunciations, but far more influential in becoming the new exemplar of preaching for a century to come, was John Tillotson. The latter had a style that combined the seriousness of the Puritans, the rationalism of the Cambridge Platonists, the arrangement of his homiletical material as discourses on certain themes as exemplified by the French preachers, and a warm pragmatism that was all his own.

By his parentage as his training (at Clare Hall, Cambridge where his tutor was Clarkson, and in his fondness for the sermons of Thomas Hill, the Parliamentary Master of Trinity), Tillotson had been strongly influenced by Puritanism and hardly less so by the Cambridge Platonists. His rational amiability in personality as in sermons took him to the deanery of St. Paul's Cathedral, where he would happily have remained for the rest of his life, but for a summons to Canterbury, the primatial see, which he held for only

---

130 *Op. cit.*, p. 321.
131 Henry Wace, *The Classic Preachers of the Church* (1877), p. 29f.

three years. It is from the vantage point of the present day exceedingly difficult to understand his renown. In brilliance he would have been eclipsed by the French sacred orators of his day. There seems to be little stimulus in either his lucid and candid style, or in his rational moralism. One can only suppose that his success comes from his correct anticipation of the prevailing religious and homiletical taste of the century succeeding his own. He was an Augustan ahead of his century: in that sense alone could he be said to be a prophetic preacher. Nor was he a liturgical preacher: he does not preach upon the lessons of the day, nor are there anything except the most occasional references to the Christian year in his sermons. His great strength lay in a transparent arrangement of his subject matter, with stated theme, and simple, logical development, often in three parts. This essay-type sermon of which he was the most cultivated English exponent was notable also for the lucidity and naturalness of the style, the balance of the cadences, the classical simplicity of the illustrations, and the quiet amiability of the personality of this candid preacher which tepidly warms his discourses.

He can only be fully appreciated if entire sermons of his are read, where the effect is slowly and surely created of admiration for his sound reasoning and pellucid explanation of the advantages of belief in and service to God and men. Perhaps the dominant impression is that of the reasonableness of a moral life, in which both the moralists of antiquity and Christ, the great teacher of Christianity, concur. His appeal is to the best morality of all times and in the natural theology which is presupposed in the writings of Cicero, Juvenal, Seneca, Plutarch, Epictetus, and Plato. His style is lofty and luminous, and he proposes for his hearers a simple, relevant and practical piety which will issue in the fruits of goodness and kindness. Its spirit can be easily grasped in the following citation from Sermon CLII:

> I would by no means encourage men to be over censorious to others, there is too much of that Spirit already in the World: but it is not amiss that Men should be strict and severe towards themselves. And I would to God Men would bring themselves to the test, and examine the truth and sincerity of their Religion not by the Leaves of an outward profession, but by the Fruits it produceth in their lives. Every man that will take the pains to look into himself, and to

observe his own actions, may by comparing the temper of his mind, and the general course of his life and practice with the Rules and Precepts of Religion, easily discern what power and efficacy Religion hath in him. A man may as easily know himself, and make as sure a judgment of his state and condition toward God this way, *as a tree is known by its fruit.* Therefore let us not flatter ourselves: for if we indulge any lust, or irregular passion in our Souls, and do not endeavour to mortify and subdue it; if we allow in ourselves with an opinion of our Godliness and whatever the *shew* and *appearance* we may make of Religion, we are certainly destitute of the *power* of it.[132]

Even a slight acquaintance with this passage enables one to realise that it creates an impression of conversational naturalness, candid manliness, good common-sense, and a concern for the hearer or reader that is far from a merely polite interest, in a desire that he may find integrity through unity of profession and practice in the pragmatic Dominical proof of virtue.

Even more famous is Tillotson's sermon on the text, *His Commandments are not grievous.* He began with the aim of showing "that the laws of God are reasonable, suited to our nature, and advantageous to our interest; that we are not destitute of sufficient power and ability for the performance of them; and that we have the greatest encouragements to this purpose." How are Divine commandments advantageous to our interest? "Two things make any course of life easy; present pleasure and the assurance of future reward. Religion gives part of its reward in hand, the present comfort and satisfaction of having done our duty; and for the rest it offers us the best security that heaven can give. Now these two must needs make our duty very easy; a considerable reward on hand, and not only the hopes but the assurance of a far greater recompense thereafter."[133] After analysing this sermon, Norman Sykes justly observes: "It was plain that every means had been adopted to temper the demands of Christianity to the infirmities of unregenerate human nature, and to promise the consolations of religion to the weakest of its professors."[134] Here is an unequalled

---

[132] Tillotson, *Two Hundred Sermons and Discourses*, II, p. 336; cited by W. Fraser Mitchell, *op. cit.*, p. 339.

[133] *Ibid.*, Vol. I, Sermon VI, pp. 152-73.

[134] *Church and State in England in the XVIII Century* (Cambridge, 1934), p. 262.

combination of eudaemonism, utilitarianism and Pelagianism, masquerading as authentic Christianity. It was left to the men of latitude to conceive of a contradiction, Christian discipleship without the taking up of a cross.

No other age would surely have presumed to give Jesus Christ a testimonial of good character, or so deftly to remove the "scandal of the Cross" from the record. Here is Tillotson's transformation of Jesus into a gentleman with a tie-wig who is the very soul of moderation in all things: "The Virtues of his Life are pure, without any Mixture of Infirmity and Imperfection. He has Humility without Meanness of Spirit; Innocency without Weakness; Wisdom without Cunning; and Constancy and Resolution in that which was good without Stiffness of Conceit, and Peremptoriness of Humour: In a word, his Virtues are shining without Vanity, Heroical without anything of Transport, and very extraordinary without being in the least extravagant."[135] One can only offer the comment of Dr. Samuel Johnson when he heard of women preachers: "Sir, a woman's preaching is like a dog walking on his hinder legs. It is not done well; but you are surprised to find it done at all."[136] However admirable the new Tillotsonian style is, and however popular (the counting of noses does not make it right or wrong), its content reduced Christianity to rationalism and moralism, the former diluting faith and the latter abandoning grace. For all their word-splitting pedantry and scraps of classical and Patristic learning, the metaphysical divines were expounding the adamantine orthodoxy of the Fathers. For all their forcing of texts into the Procrustean bed of a triple scheme of reason, doctrine, and use, the Puritan preachers were faithful exegetes of the faith of the New Testament in the Holy Trinity, and not any convenient reduction of it. As a result, the homiletical journey through the century has taken us down the precipitous slopes of an anticlimax: from the twin peaks of Donne and Andrewes, through the plains of Jeremy Taylor and the greater Puritan divines like Baxter, to the foothills of Tillotson, until we reach the muddy margins of the lake below, where his imitators paddle. Their ancestors breathed a rarer air. It is in the high mountain air of adoration that oracles and oratories best flourish and in which sermons are indeed the supplement of and stimulus to worship.

---

[135] Tillotson, op. cit., Vol. II, Sermon CXXXVII, "The Life of Jesus Christ consider'd as our Example," pp. 241f.

[136] Boswell's Life of Johnson (L. F. Powell's revision of G. B. Hill's edn., Vol. I, p. 463).

PART TWO
CULTIC CONTROVERSIES

CHAPTER V

STYLE IN WORSHIP:
PRESTIGIOUS OR PLAIN?

O NE OF the most acute controversies between the Anglicans and Puritans of the seventeenth century was concerned with the most appropriate style in which to approach God—in prayer, in gesture, and in vesture. Was it fitting, the Anglicans asked, to approach the most high God, Creator and Sovereign Ruler of the Universe, with casual and unpremeditated prayers, when one would not address an earthly monarch without careful preparation, appropriate etiquette, and elegant diction? For these reasons divine worship was appropriately expressed in a liturgy in which dignity, formality, and order were the leading characteristics. Similarly, it was asked, could one act as God's representative to the people, His ambassador, as it were, without using the appropriate ceremonies and gestures, such as bowing and kneeling, the sign of the Cross, and other forms of reverence and respect? And, finally, inquired the Anglican, could one be God's servant-priest without the fitting livery, or vestments that indicated the high dignity of the office of serving the King of Kings and Lord of Lords? The Anglican answer was to judge the Divine Majesty as desiring and demanding forms of address, gesture and ceremonial, as well as vesture, appropriate to the greatest potentate; to offer less seemed to them to slight Almighty God.

By contrast, the Puritan argued that Christ had taught men that it was not servility but sonship that was to characterize the new relationship with God for his disciples. Had not Christ himself insisted that he called his own "not servants, but friends," and had He not forbidden his disciples to exercise lordship as the rulers of the Gentiles did? Moreover, had not Christ given his disciples an acted parable of the new dispensation by performing the humblest duty of washing his disciples' feet at the Last Supper? All this made it superfluous to try and flatter the God who saw through human pretensions and who desired to be loved as adopted sons love their father, and who wished to be approached in the filial manner—that is, naturally and spontaneously in free prayer. He also desired the disciples of His Son to be marked by the simplicity

187

(not the pomp) of the Gospel, a sincere and natural (not artificial and contrived) ceremonial, and, above all, by a simple, unostentatious vesture.

Perhaps the easiest way to illustrate the difference between the Anglican and Puritan styles of worship is to contrast the views on ceremonial held by Archbishop John Bramhall of Armagh with those of an anonymous Puritan writing in 1640 who was a contemporary of the Archbishop. Bramhall enthusiastically eulogizes ceremonial. "Ceremonies," he affirms, "are advancements of order, decency, modesty, and gravity in the service of God; expressions of those heavenly desires and dispositions which we ought to bring along with us to God's house; adjuments of attention and devotion, furtherances of edification, visible instructors, helps of memory, exercises of faith, the shell that preserves the kernel of religion from contempt; the leaves that defend the blossoms and the fruit."[1]

For the Puritan, however, ceremonies suffocate rather than stimulate religion. They are, by contrast, thought to be the shell not the kernel of religion, its shadow not its substance. Prebendary Peter Smart of Durham attacked excessive ceremonial in an anti-Laudian outburst of a sermon which cost him four years in gaol. He asked in the course of it, ironically, whether religion consisted in "altar-decking, cope-wearing, organ-playing, piping and singing, crossing of cushions and kissing of clouts, oft starting up and squatting down, nodding of heads, and whirling about till their noses stand eastward, setting basins on the altar, candlesticks and crucifixes, burning wax candles in excessive numbers when and where there is no use of light; and what is worst of all, gilding of angels and garnishing of images, and setting them aloft. . . ." He answered his own question: "if, I say, religion consists in these and such like superstitious vanities, ceremonial fooleries, apish toys, and popish trinkets, we had never more religion than now."[2]

The Anglican viewpoint was one that preferred a prestigious, the Puritan a plain style in worship. And on this basic difference between the Anglican desire for splendour and the Puritan desire for simplicity, much of the seventeenth-century controversy on worship turned. We shall follow it as it is expressed in prayers, gestures, and vestments.

In the matter of prayer, the issue was argued as offering a sim-

---

[1] Cited from Bramhall in *Hierurgia Anglicana* (ed. Vernon Staley, 1902), I, p. viii.
[2] Smart's Sermon of 1628, pp. 23-24, also cited in ed. Staley, *op. cit.*, I, p. 187.

ple choice between set forms or spontaneity. That is, a liturgy or license for the minister to conceive his own prayers in his own words.

By the mid-seventeenth century liturgical prayers and spontaneous prayers became the symbols and party-badges respectively of the Anglican Cavaliers and the Puritan Roundheads of the Civil War era and later. The importance of the debate is not measured by the heat that it engendered, but by the significant issues it raised. It has more than a historical interest in a day like our own when the Roman Catholic church is engaged creatively in the revision of the liturgy, and when the proponents of the "underground church" argue vociferously for the introduction of spontaneous and even silent prayer into the liturgy.

1. *The Puritan Critique of Liturgical Prayer*

The Book of Common Prayer of the Church of England, an amalgam of Catholic and Protestant traditions of worship, is the only surviving vernacular liturgy of the Reformation period to have remained in continuous use for over four centuries. Moreover, it has also been welcomed by the various provinces of the Anglican Communion in the British Commonwealth of nations and in the United States of America. It is furthermore unique as a Prayer Book which combines the priest's part with that of the people. In these circumstances it may excite surprise that it should have been subjected to such a sustained barrage of criticism from the Puritans, who included in their number both Presbyterians and Independents, as well as those that a later age would denominate "low churchmen" or "evangelicals."

The Presbyterian opposition, in particular, calls for explanation precisely because the original Calvinist tradition favoured a set liturgy, such as Calvin's *La Forme des Prières Ecclesiastiques* (Geneva, 1542), which contained not only a set order of items of worship, but set prayers as well, though it also allowed the minister to frame the prayer for illumination before the sermon in his own words. The change within British Presbyterianism from what the Scottish church knew as *John Knox's Genevan Service Book* to the acceptance of a manual of worship consisting only of general directions and topics for prayers, such as *A Directory of the Public Worship of God in the Three Kingdoms* (1644) requires an explanation. The summary answer is that the Independents (later to be known as Congregationalists) in the Westminster Assembly

189

of Divines persuaded the Presbyterian majority to accept this compromise, partly on the strength of their Biblically based arguments, and partly because the Independent support was strongest in Cromwell's Ironsides. The Independents, however, were using arguments that had been provided by the Separatists and proto-Puritans of Queen Elizabeth's days.

A second occasion for surprise might be that one could find in the Bible any precedents for spontaneous prayer. John Robinson, the pastor of the Pilgrim Fathers in Leyden before they set sail for North America, freely admitted that the Psalms and the Aaronic blessing in Numbers were admirable Old Testament forms for praise and prayer, but he held that these were not binding on members of the new dispensation. If one affirmed that the Lord's Prayer was clearly intended to be repeated, Robinson was ready with two answers. The first was that St. Paul had insisted that only the pastor's voice was to be heard in public prayer to which the people were to give their concurrence by the single word, *Amen* (I Cor. 14:14, 16). His second reply was that the use of set prayers was a "quenching of the Holy Spirit" and a denial of the necessary dependence upon the Holy Spirit, for, according to Romans 8:26: "the Spirit helps our infirmities for we know not what to pray for as we ought." Robinson's ironical comment on this verse, assuming the Anglican reply was: "Yes, Paul by your leave, right well; for we have in our prayer-book what we ought to pray, word for word, whether the Spirit be present or not."[3]

Other Puritans would argue that the introduction to the Lord's Prayer in St. Matthew's Gospel ("After this manner pray . . .") could best be interpreted as offering a model on which to compose their own prayers rather than a set prayer. Yet others argued that the longer and shorter forms in the Gospels of Luke and Matthew were proof that the words were not sacrosanct and not to be repeated literally. The Anglicans, of course, regularly used the Lord's Prayer in worship, while the left-wing Puritans and Separatists did not. The Presbyterians in the Westminster Assembly prevailed upon the Independents to use it, but their own practice in the latter part of the century veered between the Anglican and Puritan views.

On the larger issue of whether a liturgy was desirable or not, both groups of theological contestants argued their own interpreta-

[3] John Robinson's *Works*, 3 Vols. (ed. Robert Ashton, 1852), III, pp. 21f.

tion of Christian antiquity. The Laudian Anglicans contended that the early church had used liturgies in such centres as Rome, Jerusalem, Alexandria, and elsewhere. The Puritans, however, insisted that this was chiefly a product of fourth-century dominance of the church by the state and a departure from the relative freedom of the earliest church. The Puritans, using Robinson again as a representative, cited Tertullian's *Adversus Gentes*: "We pray, saith he, without any to prompt us, because we pray from the heart."[4] This *de pectore, sine monitore* citation became a commonplace of the Puritan apologetic. But in this logomachy we have not penetrated to the heart of the Puritan position. The enemies of the Puritans might accuse them of having a dervish's notion of prayer, but they were affirming the sovereign freedom of the Creator Spirit whose invisible power is known in the stormy wind and tempest, whom liturgists and liturgiologists try to trap and tame in a net of words. They were so afraid of the dullness of repetition, and the staleness that is bred by indifference. They had learned in the love of Christ to speak to God as a Father, and it seemed to the Puritans as if the Anglicans wanted to approach Him only in a chill and distant court etiquette. Others might affirm God's majesty; they were amazed at His mercy. Anglicans might approach God with the words, "Your Majesty"; they would only say, "Abba, Father."

Barrow, a proto-Puritan, expressed the positive value of spontaneous prayer in the following definition. "Prayer," he wrote, "I take to be the confident demanding which faith maketh, thorow [through] the Holy Ghost, according to the will of God for their present wants, estate, etc."[5] Such spontaneous prayer was characterized by assurance, simplicity, naturalness, intimacy, and a moving directness in the approach to God. Its great abuse in practice was a tendency towards prolixity, diffuseness, disorder, and a chain reaction of clichés.

There were, in fact, five chief arguments advanced by the Puritans against liturgical prayers (or "stinted forms" as they called them). First, there was the insistence that the constant use of set forms of prayer deprived both minister and people of the desire to devise prayers for themselves. As a result, Dr. John Owen, the Puritan Vice-Chancellor of Oxford University in the days of the Cromwellian Protectorate, averred: "we daily see men napkining

[4] *Ibid.*
[5] *A Brief Discoverie of the False Church* (Dordrecht, 1590/1), pp. 64-65.

their talents until they are taken from them."[6] The point was expressed even more roundly by the anonymous author of *The Anatomie of the Service Book* (1641) in his sarcastic questions: "What, we pray you, is the procreant and conservant cause of dumbe dogges that cannot barke [Anglican clergymen]; idle shepheards, saying Sir Johns; mere Surplice and Service-Book men, such as cannot do so much as a Porter in his frocke; for he doth Service, and the Priest onely sayes service; is it not the Service Book?" The Puritan clergy anticipating their ejection from the Anglican church in 1662 affirmed the year before: "We cannot believe that it is lawfull for us at all times, by submitting ourselves to a Form of Prayer, to smother the Gift of Prayer, given (we hope) to some of us, or to cool the heat and fervency of our hearts in Prayer, or the Affections of them that hear us."[7] In short, for a minister or church member to remain satisfied with set prayers instead of his own, is like a man who, using crutches when he is lame, refuses to give them up when his legs are healthy again.

A second criticism of liturgical prayers was that they could not meet the varying needs of different congregations and occasions. While the Book of Common Prayer was comprehensive in its appeal, it lacked the particularity and immediate relevance of spontaneous prayer. Isaac Watts, a son of the Puritan tradition and the father of English hymnody, wrote in his admirable *Guide to Prayer* (1716) that it was impossible to produce forms of prayer perfectly adapted for all occasions, since "we have new sins to be confessed, new temptations and sorrows to be represented, new wants to be supplied." Moreover, he added that "every change of providence in the affairs of a nation, a family, or a person, requires suitable petitions and acknowledgments. And all these can never be well provided for in any prescribed composition." He further maintained that the weakness of set prayers is that they are so general in character that they do not warm the souls of those participating in worship.[8]

The third argument the Puritans advanced against a liturgy was that it was an abridgement of Christian liberty in that its prescription persuaded the people that it was an absolute necessity, thus equating a human composition with divine revelation, and

6 *Works* (ed. W. H. Goold, Edinburgh, 1862), XV, p. 52.
7 *A Sober and Temperate Discourse concerning the Interest of Words in Prayer* by H.D.M.A. (1661), p. 96.
8 *Works* (ed. Russell), IV, pp. 92-97.

leading to uncharitable censures on the churches that did not use a liturgy. Representative spokesmen for this standpoint were John Owen and that ecumenical spirit in an age of impassioned partisanship, Richard Baxter.[9]

A fourth Puritan criticism of liturgical prayers was that their constant use led to hypocrisy, mere lip-service. The result was that worshippers were often tempted to use unsuitable forms and expressions of prayer simply because they were at hand.

The fifth and final argument was one which was only too bitterly true in Restoration England when the approximately two thousand ministers who had found it impossible to affirm that the Book of Common Prayer was in all things conformable to the Word of God were deprived of their livings in universities and parishes. John Owen spoke for all the ejected Nonconformist ministers of 1662 when he accused the imposers of liturgies of bringing "fire and faggot into the Christian religion." He had been anticipated by the anonymous author of *The Anatomie of the Service Book* (1641) who declared that "the Hierarchie and the Service-Booke are resembled already to Mother and Child, so may they be to two twins, begotten and born of Pride and Superstition, nursed and brought up in the lap of Covetousnesse. . . ."[10]

Apart from these criticisms of liturgical prayer, the Puritans had a very rich understanding of the potentialities of Scriptural prayer.[11] They were familiar with the Bible—in the strictest sense they *were* Bible men and women. The Bible was the most thumbed volume in their homes, regularly used each morning and evening in family prayer. There was little other popular reading material to compete with it or to distract them from its message. The young had heard it read by their parents and had themselves learned passages of it by heart. They had heard their elders discuss it and argue over the interpretations of various parts of the Bible as they touched on the great issues of the day. This was the language that Christian people were most accustomed to hear, so it provided the natural diction, rich in associations, for the approach to God.

[9] For fuller treatment of these themes, see John Owen, *A Discourse concerning Liturgies and their Imposition* (1662) and *A Discourse of the Holy Spirit in Prayer* (1662); also Richard Baxter, *Five Disputations of Church Government and Worship* (1659) and *A Christian Directory* (1673).

[10] *Op. cit.*, p. 61.

[11] See A. G. Matthews, *Mr. Pepys and Nonconformity* (1954), pp. 115-20 for an illuminating exposition of Puritan Scriptural prayer from which I have borrowed.

Not only so, but the Scriptural prayers of the Puritan ministers and fathers of households at home were deeply emotional and affecting. However austere the outward mien of the Puritan, he unbent in his religious duties, for he expected "meltings," "enlargements," and "quickenings" when he approached God in prayer. These were the tokens of the Spirit bearing witness within his spirit, and the Holy Spirit inspired him with love, joy, and peace. What fitter words to approach God in than a selection from His Word? The language of Scripture had an incantatory power of communication, creating the moods of adoration, penitence, or aspiration. Admirers of the prayers in the Book of Common Prayer often forget that they are, in fact, admirable mosaics of Holy Scripture.

Furthermore, Scriptural prayer—that great ideal of the Puritans—gained the ready concurrence of those called to join in it. For prayer to have the effectual and fervent spirit appropriate to evangelical supplication, it must be the result of whole-hearted consent. On these three grounds, Scriptural prayer moved by the Spirit, was the simple but august Puritan alternative to liturgical prayer.

2. *The Anglican Critique of Spontaneous Prayer*

The Anglicans, who had a profound knowledge of and respect for the *traditio quinquesaecularis* of the early and undivided church, were not silent under these Puritan provocations. They gave as good as they got. Their representative spokesmen included such distinguished Bishops as Dr. Jeremy Taylor, the English Chrysostom, and Dr. William Beveridge, as well as Dr. Henry Hammond, Patristic scholar and apologist, but not a bishop.

Four major arguments were used against spontaneous or extemporary prayers. First, it was argued, that they might be less the product of the Holy Spirit than of mental laziness. Secondly, it was urged that the glib tongues that utter such prayers tend to ostentation rather than edification. Thirdly, it was denied that any spontaneous prayer was able to gain the full assent of any congregation since no time was allowed for its testing. Finally, it was claimed that the Puritan assumption that all ministers are able to express themselves as felicitously as fluently in divine worship is sheer folly.

Bishop Jeremy Taylor's most extensive critique of extemporary prayer and apologia for liturgical prayer is his *An Apology for*

194

Authorized and Set Forms of Liturgies against the presence of the Spirit (London, 1649).

His answer to those who urge the superiority of spontaneous prayer is to present them with a question: "Whether it is better to pray to God with consideration or without? Whether it is the wiser man of the two, he who thinks and deliberates what to say, or he who utters his mind as fast as it comes?" He also insists that the gifts of the Holy Spirit to the church "are improvements and helps of our natural faculties, of our art and industry, not extraordinary, miraculous, and immediate infusions of habits and gifts." He denies that the desire for variety in prayer is necessarily good, claiming that this is reminiscent of the children of Israel during the Exodus who "cry out that *Manna* will not nourish them, but prefer the *onions of Egypt* before the *food of Angels*," hence it is important to transform the men rather than to change the liturgical arrangements of the church.[12]

Taylor makes a further charge against spontaneous prayers, namely, that they are so variable and contradictory, depending on the viewpoint of the sectarians who offer them, that no man can in conscience "say *Amen* to their prayers that preach and pray Contradictories."[13] He also accuses the Puritans of inconsistency in approving written sermons while disapproving written prayers. He rebuts the charge that set prayers limit the Holy Spirit by reminding the Puritans that their Westminster *Directory* makes the same error by prescribing the matter if not the words to be used in public prayers. Most serious of all—to Taylor's mind—is his conviction that the absence of a liturgy officially approved means that there is no instrument for the expression of the union of Christians in belief, behaviour, and worship. The result is that in many places "Heresie and Blasphemy, and Impertinency, and illiterate Rudenesses" are "put into the Devotion of the most solemne Dayes, and the most publick Meetings, . . . and that there are diverse parts of the Lyturgie; for which no provision at all is made in the Directory; and the administration of the Sacrament let so loosely, that if there be anything essentiall in the Formes of Sacraments, the Sacrament may become ineffectual for want of due Words, and due Administration. . . ."[14] In short, private men are not to be entrusted to represent the people before God in public,

---

[12] *Op. cit.*, pp. 4, 8, 41.   [13] *Ibid.*, p. 70.
[14] *Reliquiae Liturgicae* (ed. Peter Hall, Bath, 1847), III, p. 90.

"for the people in *such Solemnities*, in matters of *so great Concernment*, where the *Honour of God, the benefit of the People, the interest of Kingdomes*, and the *Salvation of Soules* are as much concerned as they are in the publick Prayers of a whole national Church."[15]

Beveridge, who declined the see of Bath and Wells in 1691 only to accept St. Asaph in 1704, had the distinction of preaching the best known defence of the Prayer Book in a frequently reprinted sermon. It was entitled, *A Sermon on the Excellency and Usefulness of the Book of Common Prayer* (1682). In it Beveridge argued for an authorized liturgy on the following grounds: the Pauline demand for decency, order, and edification in the worship of the church at Corinth; the custom of the earliest provincial churches of Christendom; Our Lord's own prescription of the Lord's Prayer; and the value of repetition for true learning. The latter pragmatic point is strongly stressed because a set form of prayers will so imprint on the mind of the worshippers what they must think and do as Christians "that it will be no easy matter to obliterate or rase them out; but, do what we can, they will still occur on all occasions; which cannot but be much for our Christian edification." Further, he argues that one can be ductile to a known prayer, but that an entirely new prayer requires a critical challenge and not the obedience of faith. In sum, the Book of Common Prayer contains the prayers of the entire national church, "which are common to the ministers and people, to ourselves, and to all the members of the same Church, so that we have all the devout and pious souls that are in it concurring and joining with us in them; which cannot, surely, but be for the edifying not only of ourselves in particular, but of the Church in general, than any private prayer can be."[16]

The most devastating Anglican critique of Puritan prayers is that contained in the anonymous *Eikon Basilike, The Portraiture of His Sacred Majesty in His Solitudes and Sufferings* (1648), which may owe something to the "martyred" King Charles I, but probably owes more to John Gauden. Free prayers are accused of every possible spiritual and rhetorical fault, for they are charged with "affectations, emptiness, flatness, levity, obscurity, vain and ridiculous repetitions, senseless and often blasphemous expressions (all these burdened with a most tedious and intolerable length)"

15 *Ibid.*
16 Beveridge's *Works*, 12 Vols. (ed. J. Bliss, 1843-1848), VI, pp. 370-73.

which "do sufficiently convince all men but those who glory in that Pharisaic way." The objections are possible, but not compossible. On the other hand, the advantages of a set and authorized liturgy are succinctly stated. They include: soundness of doctrine (while avoiding heresy); comprehensiveness (instead of the favourite themes and limited experience of the prayers of private persons); order (instead of wanderings around the universe such as characterize some long pastoral prayers); gravity (instead of accidental levity); and, finally, unity (instead of sectarianism).

It is not to be assumed, however, that because the Anglicans stated their viewpoint with such vigour and clarity, the Puritans were left without any answer to the Anglican critique. On the contrary, the Puritans answered the Anglicans point by point.

One of the most vivid and idiomatic rejoinders is that of the anonymous author of *The Anatomie of the Service Book* who replies in particular to the Anglican arguments against the removal of the Book of Common Prayer when anti-Laudian opposition to it as an engine of tyranny was at its height in 1641. If the antiquity of the Prayer Book is urged against its removal, our Puritan author replies: "Antiquity without truth is no better than a custome of errour, *Et nullum tempus occurrit Deo*, there is no prescription to the King of Kings."[17] If it be urged that the Prayer Book was approved and used by many of the godly, our Puritan responds: that we can see further than those of the early reforming days and we ought to do more in the way of reform ourselves. If the claim is made that the Prayer Book has much that is good in it, our Puritan retorts, "so do the Alcoran, the Talmud, and the Apocrypha, but they are not therefore to be included in Christian worship."[18] If the Anglican maintains that it is better to revise than to rescind the Book of Common Prayer, the Puritan avers that no State has ever prospered in cleaning "the Pope's leprous stuffe" and that God's method is to command the pulling down of idolatry.[19] Finally, when the Anglican insists that the Prayer Book was legally established by an Act of Parliament introduced by the King, the Puritan answers with a wickedly apposite anecdote. When a Scottish nobleman was asked if it were legal to base prelacy on an Act of Parliament, he replied: "It never went well with them since their Churchmen laboured more to be versed in the Acts of Parliament than in the Acts of the Apostles."[20] The obduracy

---

[17] *Ibid.*, p. 69.
[19] *Ibid.*, pp. 70-71.
[18] *Ibid.*, p. 70.
[20] *Ibid.*, p. 71.

of the Puritan opposition to the Liturgy and the conviction of the superiority of conceived prayer inspired by the Holy Spirit and saturated by Scripture, was ultimately due to the belief that God had so ordered it in His Word—and neither King nor Parliament had any authority in the celestial court.

In the same year John Cotton stated the point plainly: "Wee conceive it also to be unlawful to bring in ordinarily any other Bookes into the publique worship of God, in the Church, besides the Book of God. . . ."[21] This was his reason for rejecting both Prayer Book and Homilies. Another Independent minister, Jeremiah Burroughes, was to insist that only that type of worship which had warrant in the divine Word was acceptable to God. Here he trumpeted the basic Puritan liturgical contention: "That in God's worship there must be nothing tendered up to God but what hee hath commanded: Whatsoever we meddle with in the worship of God, it must be out of the Word of God."[22]

3. Prayers as Reflections of Ecclesiastical Concepts

The two notions of prayer, liturgical and spontaneous, reflect two different concepts of the church and its relation to the state. The Anglicans held a national and parochial view of the church, while the Puritans thought of the Christian community as "gathered" out of the world and comprising committed Christians. While at the outset Puritanism worked for a national establishment of religion, the ejection of the Puritan divines of all persuasions from the national church in 1662 and the failure to include them in 1689, led the Nonconformists, whether Presbyterian or Independent, to adopt the Congregational conception of the church. The earliest definition of a "gathered church" was that of Robert Browne, which stated: "The Church planted or gathered is a company of Christians or believers, which, by a willing covenant made with their God, are under the government of God or Christ, and

21 John Cotton, *A Modest and Cleare Answer to Mr Balls Discourse of set formes of Prayer. Set forth in a most Seasonable Time when this Kingdome is now in Consultation about Matters of that Nature, and many godly long after the Resolution in that Point* (1642), p. 5.
22 *Gospel-Worship or the Right Manner of Sanctifying the Name of God in generall* (1648), p. 8. Exactly the same point is emphatically made by John Barnard in *A Short View of the Prelatical Church of England* (1641, reprinted 1661), p. 21: "That nothing be allowed in God's service which cannot be proved by some *warrant* out of Gods word; for the Scriptures are a perfect Rule for any thing necessary, either in substance or circumstances, in and about the holy word of God."

keep his laws in one holy communion. . . ."[23] Here is a repudiation of all inherited, nominal, birthright ideas of Christianity in the emphatic demand that the true Church of Christ shall consist only of the redeemed who, by an act of will as expressed in a covenant they have signed, have recognised God's calling of them and gathering of them out of the world for salvation. This was the concern for intensity in religion which stressed holiness above Catholicity, charity, and unity.

Such a concept of the nature of the church will demand prayers that presuppose the warmth, intimacy, spontaneity, and even informality of a gathering of friendly families, well known to each other. It also presupposes a minister who is the under-shepherd of his little flock, who has baptized their children, catechized them, married them, and admitted them to the fellowship of the holy table, and in his visitations "rejoiced with them that do rejoice, and wept with those that weep." It also assumes that the free and spontaneous and spirit-directed prayers of their minister will not scruple, if need be, to speak of their peculiar circumstances, even mentioning them by name in the petitions. There is little place for formality or uniformity in such a view of the church or of prayer appropriate to it. Its distinguishing marks are, therefore, freedom, particularity, flexibility, and the intimacy of fellowship—all expressed in sincere and spontaneous prayers. Such prayers in the mouth of a devout, learned and fluent pastor could seem the re-enactment of a miniature Pentecost, but it was too much to expect for every Christian community and every minister without such gifts.

The Anglicans still held the medieval view, restated with vigour by their leading apologist Hooker, that church and state are essentially co-extensive bodies, and that as a child is born a member of the English nation so he should be baptized as a member of the Church of England. Thus for the Anglicans the prayers of the local church are a reflection of the prayers of the entire national church. It is clear that for a type of worship which is to be comprehensive enough to include the entire nation, saints and sinners alike, beginners and mature Christians, which is to stress continuity with the church of the centuries, and which is to maintain unity by imposing uniformity of devotion, doctrine, and discipline, the Book of Common Prayer is the admirable medium and instrument.

[23] *A Booke which sheweth the Life and Manners of all True Christians* (Middelburg, 1582), C3 recto.

In our ecumenical days these two conceptions of the nature of the church are seen to be complementary, not competitive, as viewed in the seventeenth-century perspective. Our age can see that liturgical prayers may be enlivened by the inclusion of more personal, contemporary, and newly created prayers (not unlike the spontaneous prayers of the Puritans, but carefully composed). Thus the uniformity, comprehensiveness, order, dignity, and tradition that characterize liturgical prayer, with the corresponding defect of impersonality, may be combined with the flexibility, contemporaneity, and spontaneity of free prayers which, without a liturgical framework, may become diffuse and amorphous, and leave no more trace than footprints in the sand overwhelmed by the incoming sea. This was a possible compromise undiscerned by the seventeenth-century controversialists.

4. Ceremonies

Another hotly contested issue in worship was the question of the appropriateness or inappropriateness of elaborate or simple ceremonial and gesture in worship, not to mention setting. Once again, the Anglicans were cast in the role of defending dignity and splendour in ceremonial, while the Puritans were the protagonists of simplicity and plainness.

If in prayer the Puritan tended to equate the formal with the insincere, in ceremonial and furnishings he tended to equate spirituality with immateriality and the lack of sensuousness. The Anglican, by contrast, appreciated the senses as the conduits of communication. The Puritan seemed to think of a congregation at worship exclusively in terms of discarnate spirits, and even when considering the sacraments regarded them as divine accommodations to human necessity. The Puritan asserted the ethic only to banish the aesthetic. While valuing the doctrine of redemption, he ignored the doctrines of creation and incarnation which give a status to the senses as the avenues of divine communication to the psycho-physical personality of man; instead he depreciated them as earthly allurements and distractions.

It was not, however, insensitivity to the aesthetic dimensions of life, which resulted in the nakedness of Puritan ceremonial and furnishings. It was rather the conviction that this was the will of God in His Word. To worship God in ways other than He had commanded was the height of arrogance and disobedience.

It seemed to the Puritan theologians who discussed the matter in some detail that the Second Commandment which forbade the making of "graven images" demanded the removal from churches of all representations of the Divine Majesty in stained-glass windows or carvings in wood or stone. An interesting pamphlet of this century, entitled *The Blindness of the Unhappy Jews*, stated that there were three current interpretations of the Second Commandment. One prohibits the secular as well as the sacred use of images, and this is the attitude of Moslems. A second view holds that images may be used in secular life, but not in sacred life. A third view maintains that images may be used in churches provided they are not worshipped. The second view is the Puritan, and the third is the Anglican position. The author himself took the second position, arguing that images waste money that should be spent on the poor who are God's true images, that they give false impression of God, and that they are expressly forbidden in the Bible.

Perkins, the Nestor of Puritan theologians, discussed images in his important work, *A Reformed Catholike* (1603). He approved the civil use of images in buildings and on coins, and the historical employment of them in sacred or profane books used in private. He even allowed that images might denote the presence of God as in the case of the brazen serpent erected by Moses or the cherubim placed over the mercy-seat in the Temple, but only because they were positively required by God. The true images of the New Testament, said Perkins, are the doctrine and preaching of the Gospel, "hence it follows that the preaching of the Word is as a most excellent picture in which Christ with his benefits are lively represented unto us."[24] In conclusion, he insisted that images in divine worship were forbidden as idols, as strictly as Israel's golden calf ever was.

Thus the celebrated iconoclasm of William Dowsing, the Parliamentary visitor to the churches of Cambridgeshire and Suffolk in 1643 and 1644, becomes a less puzzling phenomenon than it otherwise might seem to be. He was no aesthetically deficient barbarian pulverising images in stained glass or stone. He was simply the Puritan government's agency for removing traces of superstition and idolatry.

Furthermore, while representations of the Virgin Mary or of other saints were not vetoed by Holy Scripture, they were pro-

[24] *Works* (1605), p. 705.

hibited by the Puritans as a potential danger to the "weaker brethren." They were the monuments of an older religion, "the badges of Anti-Christ," and their very existence might revive the abuses they brought to memory. But more than this, they were often agents in promoting abuses. For they bore testimony to the medieval prayers offered to the Virgin and the saints. The apostle Paul's injunction to "avoid the appearance of evil" was at the root of iconoclasm such as Dowsing's.

Simplicity seemed more in keeping with the religion of the Christ who had declared that "foxes have holes, the birds of the air have nests, but the Son of Man has nowhere to lay his head," and who, in death, was laid in a borrowed sepulchre. The relative bareness of the chapels of the Dissenters (with a similar ceremonial), when the danger of a resurgence of abuses had passed, was mainly the result of economic necessity. The impoverished Nonconformists were unable to afford lavish ecclesiastical edifices, even if they had wished to erect them.

It is also worth recalling that the Puritans never valued their meeting-houses in the way the Anglicans esteemed their churches. If the clergy of the establishment thought of the church as an edifice, the Puritans meant by the same concept the *sancta plebs*, the people of God indwelt by the Holy Spirit.

The differing attitudes towards edifices of worship can be seen in a comparison of the views of Richard Hooker, the chief Anglican apologist, and of George Gillespie, a Scottish Presbyterian divine, who was the youngest member of the Westminster Assembly. For Hooker the church is a sacred building, with hallowed associations and symbols that lead the worshipper to thankfulness and aspiration; for Gillespie the sanctity rests in the "saints," under the inspiration of God's Holy Spirit. Hooker writes: "the very Majesty and holiness of the place where God is worshipped, *hath in regard of us*, great virtue, force and efficacy, for that it serveth as a sensible help to stir up devotion; and, *in that respect*, no doubt, *bettereth* even our holiest and best actions in this kind."[25] Gillespie, on the contrary, writes:

How much more soundly do we hold with J. Rainolds, That unto us Christians no land is strange, no ground unholy; every coast is Jewry, every house Sion; and every faithful company, yea every faithful body a Temple to serve God

[25] *Ecclesiastical Polity*, Bk. v, Chap. xvi, Sect. 2.

in . . . whereas the presence of Christ among two or three gathered together in his Name (Matthew XVIII. 20) maketh any place a Church, even as the presence of a King with his attendants maketh any place a Court.[26]

Hooker's conviction led to the creation of churches which would aim at being houses of God, honouring His presence, and reminders to the people that they were also the gates of heaven. Gillespie's view led to the erection of meeting-houses as simple, functional, and utilitarian as possible.

There was a deep sense in which ceremonial and elaborate furnishings were superfluous for the Puritans. They needed no such stimulants for the imagination: their imagery was mental, elicited by the Bible. As Shakespeare relied on few artificial aids as spurs to the imagination, substituting the transcendental imagery of his verse for the fictitious help of artificial scenery, the Puritans rejected the ecclesiastical "scenery" of the medieval church for the symbolism and imagery of the Bible. For them the four Gospels and the Book of the Apocalypse provided a more vivid background to faith than human manufactures in glass, wood, or stone could do. This conviction of theirs has been admirably expressed by a twentieth-century historian of Dissent, Bernard L. Manning: "To call on the name of God, to claim the presence of the Son of God, if men truly know and mean what they are doing, is in itself an act so tremendous and so full of comfort that any sensuous or artistic heightening of the effect is not so much a painting of the lily as a varnishing of sunlight."[27]

That metaphor "varnishing" is exactly the term used by John Owen, the Atlas of Independency, to express his utter disgust at the fussy, meretricious, mock-Catholic ceremonial propagated by the Laudians, a conviction that he shared with Peter Smart, Cosin's enemy in Durham Cathedral. Preaching before Parliament in 1646, Owen explained why he had to leave the Queens' College, Oxford, in 1637, because of his abhorrence of the Laudian ceremonies in the chapel: "Now such were the innovations of the late hierarchists. In worship, their paintings, crossings, crucifixes, bowings, cringings, altars, tapers, wafers, organs, anthems, litany, rails, images, copes, vestments, what were they but Roman varnish,

---

[26] *Dispute against the English Popish Ceremonies obtruded upon the Church of Scotland*, originally issued in 1637, this citation is from the reprint of 1660, p. 123.
[27] *Christian Worship* (ed. N. Micklem, Oxford, 1936), p. 162.

an Italian dress for our devotion, to draw on conformity to that enemy of the Lord Jesus?"[28] It was not that the Puritans disliked art; it was simply that they loved religion more.

Another telling Puritan criticism of Anglican ceremonialism was directed against its fussy distraction in worship. This was well expressed by "G.F." the author of *The Liturgical Considerator Considered* (a reply to Gauden's tract on the liturgy) which appeared in a second edition in 1661. He argues in "The Epistle to the Reader" that the desires of the church ought to be expressed "seriously and composedly," asserting that this demands that the worshipper must be "sequestered from all other acts and businesse, set and intent with all seriousness," to mention those desires before God "in a fixed posture of body and mind." It is essential for this purpose, he contends, that there be no "unnecessary variation of place, or gesture, from Desk to Table, now kneeling, anon standing, and therefore transient salutations, affectionate friendly Christian wishes, quickening versicles, desultory short options, by leaps and starts" and these "cannot square with the more serious and composed frame of solemn prayer."

Humphrey Smith made the same point with greater vividness and vigour. He considers the rubrics in the Prayer Book that require the minister to change his voice, his posture, and his place, make him appear ridiculous. As to the posture, Smith asserts, "besides the *windings, turnings, and cringings*, his face must be sometimes towards the People, and sometimes his back."[29]

The Anglican viewpoint had many capable exponents besides Hooker. One of the most distinguished of them was Bishop Lancelot Andrewes, whose main concern was to inculcate reverence in worship through its appropriate ceremonial expression. Worship, he said, ought not to be an "uncovered and bare-faced religion." We would not dare to come before the meanest prince as we do before the King of Kings. Ceremonial, so Andrewes teaches, is based upon the threefold foundation of the nature of man and his

---

[28] *Works* (ed. W. H. Goold, Edinburgh, 1850-53), VIII, p. 28. It was evidently the Laudian ceremonies which stuck in the throats of the Puritans for John Barnard in his *Short View of the Prelatical Church of England* (1641, reprinted 1661), in his Sect. VII *Of The Prelatical Service* (p. 20) criticises the "long wearisome Liturgie" taken from three Romish books, the unedifying singing and piping on organs, and "superstitious crynging to the name *Jesus* towards the Altar, towords the East," and he particularly objects to "a formal observation of Habits, Surplesses, Hoods, Copes, variety of gestures, and ceremonious devotions devised by men."

[29] *Forty-Four Queries . . . propounded to all the Clergymen of the Liturgie* (1662), p. 29.

activities, as soul and body and as having worldly goods. Man must worship with each of these instruments. The result is "if all our worship be inward only, with our hearts and not our hats as some fondly imagine [a palpable hit at the Puritans!], we give him but one of three."[30] Naturally, Andrewes rejects sitting at worship, wittily explaining that God will not have humans worship Him like elephants, as if they had no joints in their knees. He recognises that ceremonies can be unnecessarily multiplied, so he advises that they be few, necessary, for edification, for good order, and for decency.[31]

Andrewes, as we saw in an earlier chapter, gave beauty a coronation in his private chapel at Winchester, and Archbishop Laud always regarded these furnishings and the ceremonial as an Anglican ideal, which he promoted with his zeal and considerable powers. This advancement of ceremonial and ornaments found its best expression theologically and liturgically in the Consecration of Churches, services that became a new feature of Anglicanism in the seventeenth century.[32]

The new Canons of 1604 made official the Anglican conviction that the chief purpose of ceremonial was to provide opportunities for paying homage to God and encouraging reverence in divine worship. This is quite explicit in Canon XVIII on the reverence and attention that are to be used within the church in time of divine service. It begins by insisting that reverence is according to the apostle's rule, "Let all things be done decently and according to order." Kneeling is prescribed for the General Confession, the Litany, and other prayers, and standing for the Creed. It is further enjoined, "and likewise when . . . the Lord IESVS shall bee mentioned, due and lowly reverence shall be done by all persons present as it hath been accustomed: testifying by these outward ceremonies and gestures, their inward humilitie, Christian resolution, and due acknowledgement that the Lord Jesus Christ, the true and eternall Sonne of God, is the only Saviour of the World. . . ."

One of the most important Anglican treatises of the period on worship is Herbert Thorndike's *Of Religious Assemblies and the Publick Service of God: A Discourse according to Apostolic Rule*

---

[30] *Sermons*, I, p. 162, cited by P. A. Welsby, *Lancelot Andrewes*, 1555-1626 (1958), p. 126.

[31] *Sermons*, II, pp. 334f., cited by Welsby, *op. cit.*, p. 127.

[32] See J. Wickham Legg, *English Orders for Consecrating Churches in the Seventeenth Century* (Henry Bradshaw Society, XLI, 1911), and my citations from them in Chap. I, Sect. 3, *supra*.

and Practice (Cambridge, 1642). This has been curiously ignored by later interpreters. Apart from being a learned defence of liturgies from Patristic sources, and a supporter of the view that prayers are more important than sermons, it provides a most interesting discussion of the function of ceremonies. Thorndike sees their primary function, whether military, political, or religious, as making the common people respect the functions performed by their leaders, a clearly hierarchical conception of the nature of society, both religious and secular. He writes: "The circumstances and ceremonies of Public Service is indeed a kind of Discipline and Paedagogie, whereby men subject to sense are guided in the exercise of godliness."[33] He goes on to describe ceremonial as "the apparell of Religion at the heart which some think, like the Sunne, most beautiful when it is most naked," except that men do not consist of minds without bodies. But "as long as our bodily senses are managed to our souls advantage, the heat within will starve without this apparell without."

Thorndike insists that the external forms of worship help even those minds which are least in tune "to corroborate their reverence and devotion at the Service of God, by their exercise of it," while the thoughtful persons present will be greatly impressed "by the example of the world practising the Service of God in an orderly and reverent form."[34] He cites Augustine to the effect that the primary purpose of special gestures in prayers is "not used so much to lay the mind open to God to whom the most invisible inclinations of the heart are best known, as to stirre up a man's own mind to pray with more humble and fervent groans."[35] Thorndike clearly approves Augustine's conviction that "the affection of the heart antecedent to the doing of these [gestures], by the doing of them gathers strength." The use of special garments in Divine worship, according to Thorndike, is to make the service seem more solemn. They procure "inward reverence to that work which it maketh outwardly solemn, to represent to our own apprehensions, and to convey it to other mens, the due respect and esteem which it ought to bear in our hearts."[36]

One cannot avoid noticing the careful attention paid to human psychology by Anglican apologists for worship whether it be Hooker pleading for collects as arrow-like prayers requiring a short time span, or Thorndike showing how reverent gestures

33 *Op. cit.*, p. 299.   34 *Ibid.*, p. 298.
35 *Ibid.*, p. 306.   36 *Ibid.*, p. 305.

beget reverence on the part of even the half-attentive. Puritan writers on worship seem to ignore the human dimensions in asserting the divine demands.

Returning to the hierarchical aspect of ceremonial, so prominent in Thorndike, these considerations carry considerably less force in a society as unhierarchical as that of the twentieth century, which is increasingly suspicious of outward forms, and finds greater sympathy with the spontaneity, sincerity, and informality of Puritanism than with the conjoint hierarchical union of church and state in seventeenth-century Anglicanism. Nonetheless, the Anglican concern for a splendid style in worship has great affinity with the medieval religious tradition, the Tudor love of pageantry, which has never died in English life, an appreciation of the doctrines of creation and incarnation, and a deeper understanding of human psychology: Puritanism with its colour-blind iconoclasm had few links with tradition or taste. Moreover, the Anglican view offered a stimulus to creativity to the painter, glazier, and carver, whereas the Puritan merely domesticated these imaginative activities so that they produced works for the council chamber or the home, but not for the house of God.

The Puritans had special reasons of long standing for taking exception to both the gestures and vestures of the established church. From their perspective, the most controversial gestures were those required by the Prayer Book at the two major sacraments, Baptism and the Lord's Supper. They took particular exception to the requirement of kneeling as the only permitted posture for the reception of Communion.

The Anglican viewpoint is finely expressed by George Herbert. Reverent himself, he insists that the country parson administers Communion to none except the reverent. While the Holy Supper is a feast, yet man's unpreparedness for such a privilege requires kneeling. Hence, "he that comes to the Sacrament, hath the confidence of a Guest, and he that kneels confesseth himself an unworthy one, and therefore differs from other Feasters. . . ." This is an excellent exposition of the Anglican posture, but it is followed by an intriguing denunciation: "but hee that sits or lies puts up to an Apostle: Contentiousnesse in a feast of charity is more scandall than any posture."[37] What has elicited Herbert's vehement accusa-

---

[37] *Herberts Remains, or Sundry Pieces of that Sweet Singer of the Temple, Mr. George Herbert, sometime Orator of the University of Cambridge* (1652), pp. 92-93.

tion of presumption in the sitting gesture? At this time it was the Independents and the Fifth Monarchists (apart from the few remaining Separatists) who used this gesture at Communion. It was, however, rightly interpreted by Anglicans as an exceedingly revolutionary and democratic gesture.

Since the time of Knox's inclusion of the "black rubric" without Parliamentary permission in the Second Prayer Book of 1552, there had been strong Calvinist objections to kneeling at the Supper, for this implied acceptance of the Roman Catholic doctrine of Transubstantiation and hence seemed to be countenancing the adoration of the elements. It was one of the three *nocent* ceremonies objected to in all the long line of Puritan critiques of the Book of Common Prayer.

In the course of the seventeenth century, however, there developed a strong positive Puritan case for sitting as the appropriate Communion gesture. It was, of course, nearer the posture of Christ and His apostles at the Last Supper. However, in connection with the growing importance of the sanctification of the Sabbath Day for the Puritans, there was an increasing recognition that this commemorated God resting after the six days of Creation, and looked forward to the future eschatological rest of the people of God. Sitting symbolized such rest perfectly, and where was this most fittingly displayed, than at the Communion table?

The revolutionary implications of the sitting posture at the Communion table were first expounded by John Archer, Independent minister and flaming Fifth Monarchist, in his radical volume, *The Personal Reigne of Christ upon Earth, in a treatise wherein is fully and largely laid open and proved, That Jesus Christ, together with the Saints, shall visibly possesse a Monarchicall State and Kingdome in this World* (1642). The Fifth Monarchy would be Christ's (following on the kingdoms of the Assyrians, Persians, Greeks and Romans). In this treatise Archer stresses the importance of Christ *sitting down* with His disciples (Luke 22:14) at the Last Supper. He claims the sitting posture has a double significance. The first is that as Christ had served the disciples with bread and wine, they should not strive who should be the greatest. Thus, this was an exemplary act of humility on Christ's part. But the second meaning was one full of consolation for the future and for the immediate future, too, since "by his admitting them to sit and eate of that his Supper and Table, he did show and seale to

them the fellowship which they should have in his Kingdome."[38]
Yet this was not a foretaste of a future heaven that Archer was
talking about. Quite the contrary, Archer affirms that it is a sign
and seal "of our Rayning with Christ in his Kingdome in this
World."[39] Here then was the supremely religious democratic symbol, a token of the equality of the saints and their sharing in the
Christocratic rule shortly to be established in England as the consummation of the divine purpose through all the ages. There, with
a vengeance, was the promised end of hierarchy in both state and
church!

The other ceremony 'to which the Puritans took such great
exception was the signation of the Cross in Baptism. It was
objected to first as the making of an additional sacramental sign
for which there was no authority in the New Testament. Query 95
of *A Survey of the Booke of Common Prayer* pertinently asks:
"Whether the childe be not received againe by and with Crossing,
and so may seeme to be a Sacrament as well as Baptism for that
cause . . . as if regeneration were by baptisme and incorporation by
crossing?"[40]

It was also scrupled as a Roman Catholic custom borrowed by
the Prayer Book, and as seeming to glorify the power of the priest
administering Baptism. The Anglicans, however, if Herbert may
be taken as their representative spokesman, gloried in the signation with the Cross. The country parson, says Herbert, "willingly
and cheerfully crosseth the Child, and thinketh the Ceremony not
only innocent but reverend."[41]

Nevertheless, the Canon XXX cautiously safeguards the Crossing from misinterpretation, insisting that the church has ever
taught that the sign of the Cross is not a substantial part of the
Sacrament, and the infant is received as a member of Christ's flock
by virtue of Baptism itself and before the signation with the Cross.

Controversy over the signation led to some ugly squabbling in
parish churches in our period. On April 8, 1642, in Radwinter
church at the Baptism of one Richard Clark's daughter, Alice,
one of the congregation, John Traps, confronted the curate "by
coming up close and standing in a daring manner by him, told
him that he should not have her out of the godmother's arms, nor

---

[38] *Op. cit.*, p. 17.   [39] *Ibid.*
[40] Frere and Douglas, *Puritan Manifestoes* (1907), p. 90.
[41] *Herberts Remains*, pp. 89-90.

sign her with the sign of the cross; and to that end flung the cloth over the face of the child, keeping his hand upon it, and saying, 'It is the mark of the Beast.' " About the same time Thomas New-comen, Rector of Holy Trinity, Colchester, finding himself forced by threats to give up making the sign of the cross in Baptism, used to parody the Prayer Book words of admission and say: "We do not receive this child into the congregation of Christ's flock, neither do we signe it with the signe of the crosse, in token that it shall hereafter be ashamed to confesse the faith of Christ crucified."[42] So objectionable was this custom of crossing to Puritan ministers, that if it were required of them, they sometimes used an ingenious escape, by not touching the infant's forehead with their fingers, but only making a pretence of doing so.[43] It is not surprising to learn that public Baptism went out of fashion during the Commonwealth and Protectorate, so that Josselin wrote in his diary for October 5, 1656: "Sacrament of Baptisme administered this day in publique, which was not for a long time before in Colne," and children were entered into the Register as "borne" not "baptized."[44]

The Puritans had similar scruples against using the ring in Marriage, the third of the *nocent* ceremonies. They argued that there was no warrant for the use of the ring in the Bible, whereas its requirement in the Prayer Book service of Holy Matrimony was to make it an additional sacramental sign. Besides, one Robert Johnson of Northampton rightly asked, whether the Anglicans were consistent: "Wee would knowe why you do reiect *hallowed beades*, and yet receyve *hallowed Ringes*?"[45]

We have seen that ceremonial and gestures are accepted by Anglicans as suited to the mixed spiritual-sensuous nature of man, as reminders of the homage due to the King of Kings, as pedagogical incentives to adoration, confession, or aspiration, and as means of encouraging the common people to respect their leaders in civil, and religious life. For tne Puritans, who are already feeling the iron hand in the soft lawn sleeves of the Laudian prelacy about their throats, the hierarchical argument is a dissuasive from prestigious ceremonial. But chiefly, they will accept the minimum of

[42] A. Tindal Hart, *The Man in the Pew, 1558-1660* (1960), p. 136.

[43] Ronald A. Marchant, *The Puritans and the Church Courts in the Diocese of York, 1540-1652* (1960), p. 103.

[44] *The Diary of the Rev. Ralph Josselin 1616-1683* (ed. E. Hockcliffe, Camden Society, 3rd series, 1908), xv, *ad loc.*

[45] *A Parte of a Register*, Ms., *circa* 1590, in the Dr. Williams's Library, Gordon Square, London, p. 104.

ceremony and gestures since these are the externals of religion, and only when these are dictated by God's Word. Furthermore, Puritans think that simplicity and sincerity are closely allied, as pomp and pretence are.

5. Vestments

We have already noticed the hierarchical element in the Anglican interest in ceremony: it is also present in the Anglican preference for distinctive vestments for the celebrants of divine worship. It can be seen in the Canons of 1604 which require those administering Communion on principal festivals in cathedral and collegiate churches to wear copes, while surplices and hoods are to be worn in such churches when there is no Communion (Canon XXIII), and students in the Oxford and Cambridge Colleges are to wear surplices in time of worship (Canon XXV). It was believed, as Thorndike maintained, that if the leaders in worship dressed solemnly, this would encourage the worshippers to believe in the great importance of honouring God in worship.

The Puritans cherished a long tradition of criticising the Anglican vestments and the fact that Archbishop Laud "dressed up" rather than "down" made them less likely to change their minds on this issue. They were especially critical of the surplice and the cope. In the early seventeenth century, when Susan Cook of Little Baddow, Essex, a Puritan stronghold, was charged with "laying her linen in the church to dry," she replied insolently that "she might lay her rags there as well as the surplice."[46] Archbishop Parker's *Advertisements* of 1566 had already sparked the Vestiarian Controversy in the Church of England and the rigour with which the policy was enforced had caused some notable "Genevans" such as William Whittingham, Dean of Durham, to lose their livings.

The Puritans rested the case against distinctive vestments on the following grounds. First and foremost, the insistence upon a particular vesture was an infringement of Christian liberty; the church which had been freed by Christ from the bondage of the law was now attempting to infringe the crown rights of Christ the Redeemer by introducing new sartorial burdens on the conscience.[47] This was especially foolish when the Anglicans them-

---

[46] A. Tindal Hart, *The Man in the Pew*, p. 175.
[47] Cf. *A Parte of a Register*, p. 41: "if it be abolished and *Christ* bee come in steede, then a great injurie is done to Christ for manie causes. The one is,

211

selves admitted that such matters were *adiaphora*, or in the realm of indifferent things. Secondly, the vestments were disliked because of their association with Roman Catholicism, and so were thought of as "badges of Anti-Christ," upholding the priesthood of the clergy and denying the priesthood of all believers. (Again, we observe the democratic and anti-hierarchical emphases in Puritan apologetic.) Thirdly, these vestments were symbols of pomp and grandeur, ill-befitting the humility with which all men should approach God, and contrary to the simplicity of the first disciples and apostles of Christ, they should be done away with, even if indifferent, for the sake of the weaker brethren.[48]

Anglicans desiring to retain the vestments argued that this national Church of England was autonomous and need not abolish vestments because other national Reformed churches did so.[49] Its teachings were evangelical and this minimized any danger accruing from the retention of traditional vestments. Furthermore, these vestments were not forbidden in Scripture. Indeed, they were decent and becoming, and the early church had favoured the use of distinctive vestments for those who discharged a public function. The surplice was to be retained for the sake of a uniform decency.

Our brief survey of the controversial difference in styles of worship between Anglicans and Puritans is reaching the end. It is clear that there was a radical dichotomy of viewpoint held on each side with equal definiteness and certainty, if not with obstinacy. The Anglicans believe in the holiness of beauty, and in the order, dignity, uniformity, and decent splendour of a liturgy, ceremonial, and ornaments that glorify God by giving Him man's best artistic creations and which thereby impress the ordinary people with the extraordinary. Ceremonial and gesture solemnise worship and lead the people to make the appropriate gesture of kneeling, for example, so that they may feel the contrition and sorrow that the liturgical action symbolizes. The acts of homage, such as bowing

---

that those ceremonies which Christ by his passion did abolishe, should in contempt of him and his passion be taken agayne."

[48] *Ibid.*, pp. 43f.: "for foure causes ought the surplisse, the coape, the Tippet, and other popish ceremonies to be taken away and removed out of God his Church. 1. First, that Christ may more clearly shine and appear in his Gospell, without the darkness of mans devyces. 2. Secondly, that papistrie may appeare more to be hated and detested. 3. Thirdlie, that the offence of the weake may be taken away. 4. Fourthlie, that contention amongst brethren might cease."

[49] A point developed by Hooker in the *Ecclesiastical Polity*, Bk. V, Chap. XXIX.

(what the Puritans call "cringing") and kneeling, are the religious equivalents of the civil courtesies, and if appropriate in an earthly court, they are thought to be even more so in the presence chamber of the King of Kings, which is what Anglicans claim the church is.

By contrast, the Puritan believes that God sees through all the posturing to the hearts of His worshippers, and prefers to be worshipped, not as King of Kings and Lord of Lords, but as "the God and Father of our Lord Jesus Christ" and "Our Father." He requires filial familiarity, not servile fear from His worshippers, and greatly prefers simplicity and sincerity to splendour and theatricality.

It sometimes seems as though the contending parties prayed to a different God—the Anglicans to a majestically transcendent Deity, and the Puritans to a familiarly immanent God. It is almost to be expected, therefore, that a Puritan should make this very accusation against the Anglicans, that they seemed to him to worship, like the Athenians, an "Unknown God." He felt that his opponents had framed this Deity according to their own rich fancy as "some carnall man, whose senses are delighted with such service; as his ears with organs, his eyes with goodly images, curious wrought copes, rich palls, fair gilded plate; his smell with sweet incense, his Majesty with sitting upon your stately high altar as upon his throne, and to keep his residence in your goodly cathedral as in his Royal Court."[50]

Equally, the Anglican might well have retorted to the Puritan, that he worshipped a colour-blind Creator, and an Eternal Son who had never become incarnate but was always the speaking Word, and a Holy Spirit who had inspired prophets and preachers, but never artists, and that the Puritan himself was an insensate and discarnate spirit, not a man.[51]

Each of the controversial parties saw the truth, but not the whole truth. They were right in what they affirmed, wrong in their dogmatic denials. Each saw in a mirror darkly, blinded by their prejudice and blinkered by their obduracy, mistaking the segments of truth which they apprehended for the whole circle. A later age

[50] *Reply to a Relation of the Conference* (1640), pp. 102, 104, cited in *Hierurgia Anglicana* (ed. Vernon Staley, 1902), I, pp. 194-95.
[51] The same charge might with perhaps greater accuracy have been made against the members of the Society of Friends who carried the principle of immateriality so far as to eliminate sermons and sacraments and sacerdotalism, but that is another story told in Chapter XIV on "Radical Worship."

may see that spontaneity can add a personal element to the liturgy otherwise missing, and that the potency and promises of Anglican ceremonialism and vestments needed the Puritan warnings that have come full circle in our age which has finally turned its back on triumphalism.

CHAPTER VI

CALENDARY CONFLICT:
HOLY DAYS OR HOLIDAYS?

CONTROVERSY over the sacred calendars of Catholics, Anglicans, and Puritans was woven into the fabric of the common life of our period. It is referred to casually in the thirty-eighth of R. Chamberlain's collection of *Conceits, Clinches, Flashes and Whimsies newly studied* (1639). This reads: "One said to another that his face was like a popish almanack all holydayes because it was full of pimples." On the same analogy the Anglican's complexion was clearer, while the Puritan's face was unspotted except for a Sabbatarian blush every seventh day.

The seventeenth-century people of God shared in the political ups and downs of the events of their own exciting century, and in the return of the natural seasons, but they also lived in sacred time, marked by their Christian calendars. That is, as members of churches, they were communities of memory and hope, celebrating the Christ-event, retrospectively and prospectively. However they differed in the emphasis they placed on the tenses of time in their calendar conflict; Catholics, Anglicans, and Puritans alike were conscious of living in "the fulness of time"—in the interval between the first and second Advents of Christ. Thus for them all the Incarnation was the hinge of history, dividing the recorded past into before and after Christ, the old and the new covenants, prophecy and fulfilment. As Christians they gratefully believed that they had been delivered from time's tyranny as sheer meaningless duration and boredom, because Christ had come to demonstrate beyond guessing the nature of God, and the origin and end of human destiny. Thus each minute of each day was lived with the backdrop of an eternal destiny which gave significance to the strivings of each human soul, and the further assurance from the Gospel itself that the humble in time might be exalted in eternity in the divine reversal of human evaluations, so that the first shall be last and the last shall be first.

Furthermore, by their celebration of sacred feasts and fasts (in which all three religious groups participated, though differently), any tendency to the humdrum and dully repetitive was overcome by the exuberant joy of thanksgiving or the rueful sadness of penitence. Perhaps more important still was a consolation rarer in our own secular age, but one which was theirs in great measure. This was the conviction that as Christ had conquered sin and suffering, so also he had taken away the worst horror of time—the threat of extinction. For these Christians saw the Resurrection of Christ as the death of death, even though paradoxically their shorter spans of life and the frequency of women dying in childbirth, and the many tombstones of infants and children meant that they had seen death and were more familiar with it than our own age which trains undertakers to cosmeticise the dead. It is important to recognize this unity in recalling the saga of God's acts in Christ accomplished and to come which characterized Catholics, Anglicans, and Puritans, because it could so easily be forgotten in their more typical relations as adversaries during this embattled century of religious wars.

Indeed, as will only be too obvious, calendary conflict is a vivid mark of distinction between the three groups.[1] Differing sacred calendars are vivid symbols of the religious differences between Anglicans and Puritans, and the attempt to enforce a particular way of celebrating sacred time, whether by the king and the bishops or the Puritans and Parliament, is an attempt at a form of social control.

The Anglican calendar is of course much closer to that of the Roman Catholic church than to Puritanism's system of calculating sacred time. Both churches, Roman and English, keep the Christian year as a cyclical remembrance and renewal of the most important events in the birth, life, passion, resurrection and ascension of Christ and the coming of the Holy Spirit, except for the Roman Catholic extension of the Marian feasts and its considerably fuller cycle of commemoration of the saints. The most radical difference is to be found between the annual Anglican and Roman celebration of the Christological calendar (with a particular emphasis on Lent) and the iconoclastic reductionism of the Puritan calendar which rejected the Christian year and substituted the Sabbath as its sole regularly recurring festival. There will also be calendary differences of hardly less significance than these to be noticed, but it may prove most intriguing to discover that there were often

[1] This chapter owes much to the research of Professor Howard Happ whose Ph.D. at Princeton University on the theme of late Tudor and early Stuart Calendary Conflict I have had the honor of supervising.

political, economic, and social factors almost as important as the clinching theological reasons that were advanced for the differing calendars.

The three distinctive ways of marking sacred time will be examined, by noting the history of the conflict among them (recalling that England will not have a distinctive Roman Catholic calendar, but that the remembrance of certain saints in English history will be ways of "naturalising" the international church in England, and also that in our century it is a fugitive and clandestine faith, so it will not openly enter the lists of calendar conflict). The concentration will inevitably, then, be on the conflict between the religious calendars of the Cavaliers and of their opponents the Roundheads. Of the proponents of both calendars a series of questions will be asked.

Do feasts or fasts predominate? Such a question will reveal whether there is a prevailing sense of joy which can degenerate into laxity, or a dominant sense of religious intensity which can deteriorate into gloom and vindictiveness, and the confusion between being the elect and the élite. Sir Toby Belch's question of the Puritan Malvolio: "Dost thou think because thou art virtuous, there shall be no more cakes and ale?" is an illustration of calendar conflict.[2] It was the reversal of roles in the masques and merriment that ended on the twelfth night after Christmas and in maypoles on May Day, and the indiscretions at the Whitsun and harvest ales that the Puritans disliked because of their encouragement of beery buffoonery, bawdiness, idleness, and profanity. The same occasions were regarded by Royalist Anglicans as occasions of relatively harmless fun and games, providing intervals of jollity in the otherwise uneventful lives of the "lower orders." In fact, both King James I and King Charles I issued their *Book of Sports*[3] as a counterblast to the Puritan Sabbatarianism, which seemed to them to turn smiles into snarls.

Another question will be: Is the predominant tense of the festivals past, present, or future? The point of such a question is that if the religious stance is conservative it will be mainly retrospective, but if intense it may be contemporary as recognising the continuing revelation of God as holy in days of judgment and loving

---

[2] *Twelfth Night*, act II, scene iii.

[3] James issued the *Book of Sports* in 1618, after recommending its provisions to the magistrates of Lancashire the year before. Charles, his son, reissued it in 1633.

217

in days of thanksgiving for deliverance. Or, again, if the religious stance is radical it may well stress the apocalyptic and imminent future as the most important tense in its calendar as well as being a fantasy of the future to compensate for present dissatisfaction.

A third question will demand whether the festivals relate to cosmic, national, ecclesiastical party, or private history? The presumed value of the answers to such a question will be that they will indicate whether God is conceived as universal deity or as a tribal totem, or a combination of both.

Moreover, in all cases, the religious values presumed to be in each competitive calendar will be investigated for possible political, social, and economic components, whether acknowledged or not. These latent or overt factors will help to explain the ferocity with which the calendars were attacked or defended. Nor should it be forgotten what a large part of the time of the men and women of the seventeenth century was taken up in festivals and fasts. Davenant in the middle year of the century attested to this in the preface of his play, *Gondibert*: Divines . . . are Tetrarchs of Time, of which they command the fourth Division, for to no less the Sabbaths and Daies of Saints amount, and during these daies of spiritual triumph Pulpits are Thrones, and the People oblig'd to open their Eares. . . ."

1. *The Roman Catholic Calendar*

Consideration of the Roman Catholic calendar will be brief because it did not differ significantly in England as the faithful moved from the sixteenth to the seventeenth century, though it became increasingly difficult for the Recusants to celebrate their festivals with the pomp and circumstance thought appropriate in countries such as France or Spain where Counter-Reformation Catholicism prevailed. In England, especially after the discovery of the Gunpowder Plot, late in 1605, supposedly aimed at both king and both Houses of Parliament, the patriotism of all Catholics was suspect and their priests led a hunted life as fugitives, except when protected as court chaplains of Catholic queens. To practise Roman Catholicism was forbidden, and Recusants were fined for their unwillingness to attend service according to the Book of Common Prayer. However, simply and secretly, except in royal or embassy chapels or in the houses of the nobility distant from London, the Catholic year was maintained as it had been with little change from the pre-Reformation days, according to the Use of Sarum.

Nonetheless, it is crucial to consider its essential character, not only because of its historic importance and influence as the calendar of the largest church in Christendom, but also as a standard with which the Anglican calendar can be compared and the Puritan calendar contrasted.

Essentially it is marked by three leading characteristics. It is cyclical, Christological and sanctoral. That is, each year it recalls the same major events in the life of Christ, his Virgin Mother, and also the saints and martyrs who bridge the centuries between Biblical times and the seventeenth century, many of them being contemporaneous with Christ, but many also belonging to the medieval "ages of faith." Precisely because the calendar is cyclical, repeating itself each year, it is strongly retrospective in character, and inevitably so because Christianity is a historical religion affirming that "God has visited and redeemed his people." The proof of that redemption is found not only in that divine revelation contained in the Scriptures of the Old and New Testaments, but also in the facts of the Incarnation, and its consequence, the church, created to be the salvific community, and in its holiest representatives, the apostles, saints, and martyrs, who show that grace can make the ordinary extraordinary. These were all helped by the Christian year and its sacred festivals—each of which is a separate segment of the circle of the Incarnation encouraging profounder focus and concentration on the meaning of each—to meditate and mould their lives on the example of Christ, God as man.

The Roman calendar also wisely makes provision for "naturalising" (strictly speaking, supernaturalising) the international faith in each of the nations to which it has brought the Gospel by remembering the contributions of its holy men and women. Thus England's Catholics rejoice that Alcuin of York, the great Benedictine scholar and adviser of Charlemagne, was an Englishman and Hilda, the great Abbess of Whitby, was an English woman, and that, although he was brought up in the Anglo-Norman abbey of Bec, that Italian expatriate, St. Anselm the innovative philosopher-theologian was England's chief religious adviser as Archbishop of Canterbury. But the saints are not restricted to the company of monks and nuns: kings such as St. Louis of France and lay women such as the martyrs in the Roman arena, Perpetua and Felicitas, span the social chasm and consecrate different secular callings. Thus there was variety in sainthood.

Our age mistakenly regards the saints as misanthropes and despisers of this world, concentrating on what they have given up. The saints themselves, however, counted the world well lost for the love of Christ and his company of the blessed, and they stressed rather what they had gained—a rich increase in the theological virtues, faith, hope, and charity. However painful the resurgence of temptations, they were striving for the prize of eternal life, and heaven seemed only a little higher than the gilded *flèche* atop the roof of the cathedral. The medieval saints had a holy hilarity, and earth resembled heaven in this respect at least that it was a place of festivity. Whatever criticisms may be brought against the medieval church, it certainly encouraged in its feasts, "the capacity for genuine revelry and joyous celebration" because it related men and women to the "parade of cosmic history, or to the great stories of man's spiritual quest." Not only so, but even a calendar so rooted in the past, still encouraged fantasy, the dream of the future establishment of the Kingdom and City of God. Such joyful occasions put work in its proper subordinate place, for like contemplation and loving, festivity was seen to be an end in itself, not a means to an end unlike modern ideas of relaxation which are only frenetic "times-off" from work, unrelated to the history of the cosmos and incapable of effecting a social transformation. The sanctoral calendar, as well as the Christological cycle, provided such opportunities for festival and, more rarely, for the fasting that alternated with the feasting.[4]

In the northern hemisphere there was a particular fitness in the celebration of the most joyful mystery of the Incarnation during the darkest and coldest days of the year, when spirit and body would otherwise be numb. Equally apt was the general coincidence of the festival of Christ's Resurrection at Easter with the spring of the year, and the freshest green of ferns is ready coiled. As the coldness of winter was warmed by the festivities that lasted twelve

[4] Harvey Cox has written most imaginatively of the resources of festivals, both retrospective and prospective, in *The Feast of Fools* (Cambridge, Mass., 1969). His own summary of his major thesis is the following: "Festival occasions enlarge enormously the scope and intensity of man's relation to the past. They elevate his sense of personal worth by making him part of an epic. Fantasy offers an endless range of future permutations. It inevitably escalates man's sense of his powers and possibilities. Therefore, the cultivation of celebration and imagination is crucial to religion and to man himself, if the Biblical estimate of his status ("a little lower than the angels") has any validity" (p. 18).

days, so the austerities of Lent were concluded by the good cheer and roast beef of Easter Day. The Roman Catholic calendar was intimately related to the natural seasons, at least in the northern hemisphere. That suggests how entirely appropriate it was for those who lived by tilling the land.

It also suggests that with the growth of a desire for rationalising manufacture in the cities and towns, there would be an objection on the part at least of the manufacturers and their ambitious apprentices that the Roman Catholic calendar, and even its Anglican modification, would be an excessively interrupted calendar, offering too many holy days and holidays, encouraging indolence, and increasing the danger of social turbulence and the difficulty of maintaining public order when hundreds of single young apprentices, sailors, carriers and others were at a loose end day after day.[5] What had been instituted in part as safety valves by the authorities, and which served their old function in the rustic environment, became potential sources of danger in the enlarging cities of the seventeenth century. Thus pragmatic factors, as well as purely theological considerations, played a part in the revision of the Catholic calendar by the Church of England, and its abolition by the Puritan alternative calendar.

2. Calendars as Symbols of Conflict

The political importance of the calendars, especially those of Anglicans and Puritans, is that they are the symbols of different bases of power in the state, and that the prerogative of authorising or modifying the official calendar and regulating the use of these holidays by law is hotly contested by the king and the church, on the one hand, and by the Parliament and its Puritan members, on the other. A brief recounting of the history of this conflict provides illumination on the meanings of the differing Anglican and Puritan systems of marking sacred time.

The conflict was particularly marked on the issue of how most appropriately to celebrate Sunday, which the Puritans called, on the authority of the Fourth Commandment, the Sabbath, and which the high-church Anglicans called the Lord's Day, recalling that the early church had changed the day from the Jewish Sabbath to

---

[5] In Spain the holidays took up five whole months of the year, so the charge of encouraging indolence is not unfounded. As for turbulence and violence, it is known that May Day in 1517 was to be devoted almost entirely to the intended wholesale slaughter of Frenchmen in London.

221

honour it as the day of the Lord's Resurrection. The scrupulous keeping of the Sabbath, with all the appropriate religious exercises, was the immediately visible badge of Puritan allegiance. The more relaxed spending of Sunday after attending Morning Prayer, and engaging in various games, on the authority of the royal *Book of Sports*, was the equally visible sign of the royalist, Laudian, high-church position.

The issue was raised by two incidents that involved animosity (followed by legal proceedings) between clergy in Suffolk and local gentry in Somerset. The first concerned John Rogers, chaplain to Archbishop Whitgift, who had been hurt by his rejection from a fraternal gathering of Suffolk clergy and who vented his spite on one of them, Nicholas Bownde, by attacking his recently published book, *The doctrine of the Sabbath, plainely layde forth, and sundly proved* (1595). The book was banned in 1599, and in 1600 the Lord Chief Justice Popham ordered the remaining copies of the book to be burned. Immediately the book became a *succès de scandale*, its price doubled, and its teachings were enthusiastically adopted by all opponents of the religious and civil settlements.[6]

In the second case two gentlemen of Somerset who took opposed views of the propriety of holding a church ale forced the issue into court. Sir Robert Philips and John, Lord Paulett, were the persons involved whose disagreement in a case in the quarter sessions made it necessary for the matter to be referred to the Assizes, at which Mr. Justice Richardson gave his judgment. Archbishop Laud, fearing that an ecclesiastical matter such as a church ale having come under the authority of the civil courts might be a wedge for the further diminution of churchly authority, overruled Richardson, severely reprimanded him before the council, and had him demoted to the Essex Circuits, and two years later he died. Twenty-one justices of the peace were alienated by Laud after he and Bishop Pierce of Bath and Wells had collected statements favouring church ales from sufficient clergymen in the diocese to offset the petitions of the justice for the abolition of church ales. This incident gave Laud the opportunity to persuade Charles I to republish James I's *Book of Sports*, which contradicted the tenaciously

[6] See Wilfrid Barnett Whitaker, *Sunday in Tudor and Stuart Times* (1933), p. 64, and Patrick Collinson, "The Beginning of English Sabbatarianism," in C. W. Dugmore and Charles Duggan, eds., *Studies in Church History* (1964), I, pp. 219-220.

maintained Puritan viewpoint on the keeping of Sundays, and to order it to be read from every pulpit in the land.[7]

The issue became a matter of greater political than religious significance, and the promoters respectively of the relaxed and serious spending of Sunday were engaged in a struggle to see who was to hold the reins of power. From the time of Elizabeth onwards, bills had emerged from Parliament proposing the reform of the Sabbath. Each one had been consistently rejected by the crown, particularly by James, for it was increasingly clear that Parliament wished to increase its power and lessen that of the crown and church.[8] In 1621 Parliament had tried to overrule James's imposition of the *Book of Sports*, for it viewed this as the crown's attempt to determine the religion and morals of the kingdom, and to mock Puritan intensity in religion with the excuse that the traditional customs, however abhorrent to Puritan bluenoses, must be maintained. With the increasing influence of the Puritan clergy and justices of the peace, it was evident that power would meet countervailing power.[9] Christopher Hill has observed that the Somerset church ale's case made it abundantly clear that the church preferred the common man to disport himself at the tavern rather than be edified by attending a Puritan religious lecture.[10]

The latter policy was clarified when the crown, strongly backed by the church, issued in 1629 a Proclamation, which forbade the giving of lectures on Sunday afternoons, which was one of the main media for the transmission of Puritan influence. These lectureships constituted a network of Puritan religious power operating independently of the centrally controlled ecclesiastical system. The right to them was purchased by merchants sympathetic to Puritan ideals and opposed to the increase of royal and ecclesiastical prerogatives.[11]

Thus the Sabbatarian controversy is only one, though dramatic, way of showing how the calendar conflict reflects the political struggle for power reaching its zenith in the third and fourth decades of the century. It is therefore time to consider the distinctives

[7] See Thomas G. Barnes, "County Politics and a Puritan Cause Célèbre: Somerset Church Ales, 1633," in *Transactions of the Royal Historical Society* (1959), pp. 112-18.
[8] See Christopher Hill, *Society and Puritanism in Pre-Revolutionary England* (2nd edn., New York, 1967), pp. 160-61.
[9] *Ibid.*, pp. 194-95.   [10] *Ibid.*
[11] See S. R. Gardiner, *The Personal Government of Charles I, 1628-1637* (1877), pp. 163f.

of first the Anglican and then of the Puritan calendar in much greater detail.

3. *The Anglican Calendar*

The Protestantism of the Anglican calendar is seen in its dominant Christological cycle (omitting the exclusively Marian feasts), and its reduction of the sanctoral cycle to the saints of the New Testament who, with the exception of Paul, were eye-witnesses to the Resurrection of Christ. Its Catholicism is seen (if it is contrasted with Calvinistic Protestantism) in its retention of a cyclical calendar at all, in its focus on Lent as a period of special spiritual discipline, and in its devotion to the Incarnation and the festival of Christ's nativity, which is so deep and tender a trait of Caroline sermons and spirituality. Apart from the rich ecumenical potentiality of this partly Protestantized Catholicism, it shares the retrospective look and the cosmic concentration of Roman Catholicism.

Its second major characteristic is its royalism, peculiar to a national church whose head was at once sovereign of the nation and its ecclesiastical leader. This sense of the divine right of kings was exaggerated by the high-church divines (beginning with Lancelot Andrewes whose almost fawning subservience to his king is his least likeable attribute), with the effect of alienating all those who like the Puritans objected to Stuart absolutism with its minimum of Parliamentary devolution. It reached its zenith in the virtual apotheosis of King Charles I as martyr of the Anglican church, who indeed loved the national church and went to his death as one calmly resigning this world for the next. This, of course, emphasized the retrospective nature of the Anglican calendar, though admittedly, its commemorations of royal accessions or deliverances were of events of fairly recent history.

A third characteristic is shared, though not to the same degree or with the same intensity, with Puritanism; namely the provision of officially appointed fast days of humiliation or thanksgiving to mark some national emergency or deliverance, the former to be days of repentance and the latter days of thanksgiving. These were recommended in the Book of Homilies.[12]

---

12 The Second [Elizabethan] Book of Homilies (1571), has the sixteenth homily "On Fasting" and a twentieth homily "Of the Time and Place of Prayer." For the mode of and authority for public fasting, reference is made to Leviticus, Chaps. 16 and 23, and the fast is to be on the 10th day of the 7th month, while Zechariah (Chap. 8:19) says there are to be three more fasts in the year. The ends of the fast, according to the homily, are: "to chastise the flesh" and tame it for the

The reduction of the many saints' days in the Roman Catholic calendar had the effect of making the major events in the life of Christ stand out with greater significance. The sanctoral foothills in the Roman Catholic calendar took away some of the solitary grandeur of the peaks of the Christological cycle. Furthermore, though the red-letter days were fewer, those retained were all holidays, and the black-letter days kept ceased to be holidays. The fasts called for national emergency were few, and so the ecclesiastical festivals predominated over the fasts in numbers and mood. The result was that, apart from Roman Catholics, and others who were tenacious of all the older mores in a day of rapid social change, and the less industrious apprentices, the Anglican calendar was fairly popular because it was more joyful and merry than the one it replaced. The sense of jollity in the Anglican calendar is expressed incidentally by that vivid recorder of London life, the dramatist Dekker. Firke, an apprentice cobbler, speaks for all the gentle craft when he hails the prospect of Shrove Tuesday, with its promise of venison pasties, fritters and pancakes, chickens and oranges, custard tarts, and the headiest of ale, crying: "Every Shrove Tuesday is our year of jubilee. And when the pancake bell rings, we are as free as my Lord Mayor. We may shut up our shops and make holiday."[13]

THE CHRISTOLOGICAL CYCLE

The Anglican emphasis on the Christological cycle was, of course, the inheritance from Cranmer, as also the celebration of the days of the Biblical saints.[14] In the days of the Puritan overthrow of the Anglican calendar, it is interesting to read John Doughty's reasons for defending the chief Anglican festivals. He claims that the saints whose days are retained are at least historical, not legendary, and that being Christological and apostolical in

---

Spirit; to encourage the spirit to be "more earnest and fervent to prayer" and as a sign before God of our inward contrition. The twentieth homily, stresses the importance of Sabbath keeping, since God worked for six days and rested the seventh, so must his obedient people, and give themselves "wholly to heavenly exercises of God's true religion and service" commanded by God and even exemplified by Him through the paradigm of the Creation of the world.

[13] Thomas Dekker, *The Shoemaker's Holiday*, Act v, Scene 2, ll. 220-23. Shrove Tuesday is, of course, the day before Ash Wednesday, the beginning of the season of Lent. The play reflects life in 1599. This reference I owe to Marie-Hélène Davies, my wife, as also the opening citation of this chapter.

[14] It should be noted that there was an unofficial celebration of the red-letter days of the English Protestant martyrs marked by Foxe.

character, they are not merely traditional, but foundational. "I mean," he writes, "not such *Dayes* the Papists celebrate, for the most part *dedicated* to Saints that ne'er were *men* or had a *being*; Again, to them whose names it is to be feared may sooner be found written in the *Rubrick*, than in *Heaven* . . . I understand *dayes* of *solemnity* instituted on *good grounds* in honour of *Christ* himself in the first place, in *memoriall* of those *speciall Saints*, the *Apostles, Evangelists etc.*"[15]

Since the Puritans argued that the only festival for which there was an explicit Biblical warrant was the Sabbath, on the basis of their belief that what the Scriptures did not command they impugned, the Anglicans were forced to defend their retention of the major feasts of the Christian year on grounds beside church tradition. It is interesting, for example, that Bishop Lancelot Andrewes, who had been a strict Sabbatarian in his earlier days in Cambridge, takes the highest ground by defending Lent on the example of the forty days of fasting undergone by Christ in the wilderness. Lent is to inculcate repentance as a fruit of fasting and penance, "for Repentance is the agonie, the bloodie sweat, the Cross of every Christian; whereby he dies into sin, and is crucified with his Saviour. Each circumstance then of Christ's Passion, each bloodie Scene in this Tragedie must be re-enacted on our own bodies. . . ."[16] The Christological cycle was clearly to encourage the *imitatio Christi*. Bishop Thomas Ken of Winchester appeals on the same firm foundation. The purpose of Lent is for the Christian to be identified with Christ in his sorrows and Resurrection. Hence, "a devout soul . . . fastens himself to the Cross on Ash Wednesday, and hangs crucified by contrition all the Lent long" so that he may sympathise with all the anguish and desertion "which God Incarnate endured when He bled upon the Cross for the sins of world; that being purified of repentance and made comformable to Christ crucified, he may offer up a pure oblation at Easter and feel the power and the joys and triumph of Saviour's Resurrection."[17]

As there had been controversy over the Sabbath, so the celebration of Christmas became a fighting issue between Anglican and

[15] I. D. Phil-Iren-Alethius, *Velitationes Polemicae or Polemicall short Discussions of certain particular and select Questions* (1651), pp. 202-203.

[16] See his sermon on "Holy Days" reprinted by Abraham Wright, *Five Sermons in five several Styles; or Waies of Preaching* (1656), pp. 19-20.

[17] *A Sermon Preached at the King's Chapel at Whitehall in the Year, 1685.* (*Prose Works*, ed. W. Benham, pp. 85f.)

Puritan contestants. Christmas in successive years falls one day later in the week, whereas Easter and Whitsun are both Sundays; thus the Anglican and Puritan controversy over Easter and Whitsun was not so acute for the Puritans celebrated the Sabbath while the Anglicans celebrated the pivotal events of the Christian saga. Christmas falling irregularly and only about once every seven years on a Sabbath raised the theological issues most acutely, though the arguments advanced for its celebration or negation apply equally well to the other Christological events.

On the positive side, the Anglicans increasingly affirm the psychological argument that one cannot celebrate everything on one day, and the need for continuity with the primitive church, as well as urging the claims of reason. Nor are they above using the *tu quoque* charge against the Puritans that while the authority of Scripture is claimed for the Sabbath alone as a red-letter day, the Puritans inconsistently observe the fifth of November as Gunpowder Plot Day for which there could not be any specific divine mandate. These abstractions will take on life in the vivid arguments of the Anglican defenders of the Christological cycle.

Dr. Henry Hammond writing in 1644 marshalls his Patristic learning[18] to support the argument for the claim that Christmas is authorised on the basis of "the practice of the Primitive Universal Christian Church." He concludes, with typical carefulness, that Christmas "appears to be at the least an ecclesiastical institution, very early received over all the West and the far greatest part of Christendom, and within four hundred years universally solemnized."[19]

Even more interesting is Bishop Joseph Hall's apologia, *A Letter for the Observation of the Feast of Christ's Nativity*, because he is a Calvinist answering the objection of Calvinist Puritans. Hall begins by arguing that if this nativity was "the best tidings of the greatest joy that ever was or ever could be possibly incident to mankind," its celebration should be correspondingly joyous. His critic is assumed to reply that a set anniversary day is needless, because "every day we should, with equal thankfulness, remember this inestimable benefit of the Incarnation of the Son of God."

Hall cleverly uses the Puritan argument of the Sabbath as the

---

[18] The authorities he cites are the *Apostolical Constitutions*, Origen, and Cyprian.
[19] Henry Hammond, *A Practical Catechism*, Chap. II, Sect. 12 (ed. Library of Anglo-Catholic Theology, 1847-1850, pp. 193-96). The first edition appeared anonymously in 1644, the second with the author's name in 1646, and the twelfth in 1683.

high peak of the week, but turns it against the Puritans by reminding them that the creation and the deliverance from Egypt should be daily recalled, but that God ordained one special day of the week "for the more special recognition of these marvellous works." Special days, he then argues, are a remedy for human forgetfulness. Otherwise, one might well say, why keep a single day of remembrance, let it be the work of the whole year. Hence it is for concentration and focus that special days were authorized by the primitive church "no doubt, by the direction of the Holy Ghost."

He then deals with a second criticism: that we are probably ignorant of the exact day of the nativity of Christ, that it may possibly not even have been in the month of December and that "it is purposely not revealed, that it might not be kept." In reply, Hall admits to some uncertainty, but considers the objection irrelevant, since what matters is "that it hath pleased the Church for many hundred years to ordain this day for the commemoration of that transcendental blessing." Further, if God had intended to keep that day a secret to avoid a celebration of it, where is this prohibition revealed? Also, "why did not the same God with equal caution conceal the day of the Passion, Resurrection, Ascension of our Blessed Saviour, and of the Descent of the Holy Ghost?"

To the third objection that there is "Popery and Superstition" in keeping that day, Bishop Hall replies that this is to slander God's saints in primitive times and the Fathers of the church.

The fourth and final Puritan criticism asserted that the seventh day is enjoined for rest, but that otherwise Christians are forbidden to observe days and times as part of the pedagogy of the old dispensation. Hall's rebuttal says that first, this is *permissive* rather than *preceptive* and second, the requirements of the Judaic ceremonial law are no longer binding on Christians.

He ends by citing St. Gregory of Nazianzen on the proper mode of celebrating Christmas Day, which Hall accepts in the last analysis because it is "so ancient and received a custom in the Church of God."[20]

The major function of the Anglican calendar, as of the Roman Catholic calendar, was clearly to encourage the imitation of Christ by meditation through the Christian year assisted by appropriate Gospels, Epistles, and Collects in the Book of Common Prayer. It also had two subordinate purposes. One was to provide an alterna-

---

[20] *Works* (ed. Peter Hall, 1837), x, pp. 126-31.

tion of feasts and fasts. The other was to serve as a medium for the expression of the religio-political unity of the nation under the sovereign who was also head of the church.

The value of the alternation of the festivals and fasts, with the former more numerous, as well as the insistence upon the more relaxed spending of Sunday than the Puritans allowed, was to provide a release of emotional tension, which the Puritan Sabbath tended rather to exacerbate, especially for those not Puritans.[21] When Charles I republished his father's *Declaration on Sports* in 1633, the introduction states that James had "found his subjects debarred from lawful recreations upon Sundays after evening prayers ended, and upon Holy Days," and that he "prudently considered that if these times were taken away from them, the meaner sort who labour hard all the week should have no recreations at all to refresh their spirits." Lawful recreations are defined as "dancing, either men or women, archery for men, leaping, vaulting, or any other such harmless recreation . . . May-games, Whitsun-ales, and morris dances, and the setting up of May-poles, and other sports therewith used. . . ." Illegal sports are defined as "bear and bull-baitings, interludes, and at all times in the meaner sort of people by Law prohibited, bowling."[22] It was also assumed that there should be church ales at the patronal festivals of local parish churches.

The opportunity for sports after church on Sundays and on red-letter days were not the only accommodations to human need in the Anglican calendar. Lent, for example, represented six weeks out of fifty-two of renunciation for repentance, which focussed on Christ's temptations and victory over them for the benefit of the Christian, but this was focussed more clearly in Holy Week, and most brilliantly on the holy weekend from Good Friday to Easter Day. With this should be contrasted the rigorous spiritual regimen required by Puritanism for the Sabbath, which would have wound up the average man as intensely as a coiled spring, but seemed to serve the Puritans well.

---

[21] E. Cardwell, *Documentary Annals of the Reformed Church of England*, II, pp. 188-93.

[22] Michael Walzer has suggested that the Puritans found release in aggression, but this seems not to accord with the mysticism of such Puritans as Sterry and Baxter, as well as Sibbes. (See his *The Revolution of the Saints*, Cambridge, Mass., 1965, Chap. VIII.) Another possibility is that the work ethic for six days provided relief in contemplation on Sunday for a member of the elect and that this was a kind of austere adaptation of an intramundane Benedictinism.

ROYAL AND STATE SERVICES

The third component of the Anglican calendar was known as the "state services." They were intended to inculcate veneration for the king and thus social stability, with subordination and satisfaction for each man in his own station of life. Such special services included anniversaries of the accession of the sovereign to the throne (March 24 for James I and March 27 for Charles I) as well as commemorations of any signal deliverance of the king (also representing the nation). Each year Gowrie Day was observed on August 5, recalling James's deliverance while King of Scotland from the conspiracy of the Earl of Gowrie and his brother, and his further deliverance and that of his Parliament was recalled each November 5, the date of the discovery of the Gunpowder Plot.

No provision for an accession service was made in the 1559 Prayer Book, but about 1571 Dr. Cooper, Vice-Chancellor of Oxford University, began holding a "public celebrity" of Elizabeth's accession. This example was widely imitated and in 1576 and 1578 a special service order was issued by royal authority in commemoration of the Queen's "entry in to her reign."[23] No such service was bound up with the Prayer Book, but copies were kept for use on the anniversary each year, it can be presumed, since no further impressions appeared during the Queen's reign. Her successor, James I, according to Frank Streatfield,[24] seemed to be satisfied with two opportunities for the expression of the loyalty of his subjects and their commendation of him to God—that is, with the Gowrie Day and Gunpowder Day anniversaries—so that no form of accession service was issued during his reign. It was, however, revived by Charles I in 1526 and confirmed by Convocation fourteen years later. Since Charles II was legally restored on the day of his father's martyrdom, which was therefore declared to be a day of fasting, he had to choose his birthday and *de facto* day

[23] See *Liturgies and Occasional Forms of Prayer set forth in the Reign of Queen Elizabeth* (ed. W. K. Clay, Parker Society, Cambridge, 1851), pp. 453, 548.

[24] See his *The State Prayers and other variations in the Book of Common Prayer* (1950), p. 31; but he appears to be unaware of *Great Britaine's litle Calendar or triple Diary in remembrance of three dayes, viz. the 24 of March the day of his Maiesties proclamation; the fift of August the day of Gowries Conspiracy; the fith of November the day of our deliverance from the Gunpowder treason, whereunto is annexed, a short dissuasive from Popery*, written by Samuel Garey, which is listed on pp. 6-7 of *A Catalogue of such English Bookes, as lately have bene and now are in Printing for Publication, from the ninth day of October 1618 untill Easter Terme, next ensuing.*

of accession as the occasion for a special service, on May 29, but this changed the character of the occasion. James II, however, revived the Accession Service, explaining why his brother had allowed it to fall into desuetude, and it was called "The King's Day." William III preferred to mark the day of his landing at Torbay and his consequent guaranteeing of the Protestant succession of the crown, by merely causing a few prayers to be added to the regular service for November 5.[25]

A Fourme of Prayer with Thanksgiving, to be used of all the Kings Maiesties loving suiects every yeere, the 24 of March: Being the day of his highnesse entry to this kingdom which is the Order for Morning Prayer of the English Prayer Book, modified for the anniversary of the royal succession, was reissued in 1640 with March 27 as the day of the accession of Charles I. It is interesting for its emphasis on the divine right of kings and its conception of their responsibilities to the church. The first lesson is taken from Joshua 1, and recounts the death of Moses and Joshua's appointment as the leader of the people to convey them over the river Jordan to the promised land.[26] Unquestionably England's king is viewed not merely as the secular ruler, but as God's vice-gerent. The second lesson from Romans 13 stresses the necessity for showing due respect and obedience to the powers that be. The "Prayer for the Kings Maiestie" describes James I as "Shepheard, Captain, our dread Soverreigne, and Angel sent from thee [God]. . . ."[27]

A fourme of prayer with thanksgiving, to be used every yeere the fift of August, being the day of his highnesse happy deliverance from the bloody attempt of the Earle of Gowry first appeared in 1603, but there were later editions of 1606, 1618, and 1623. In the second edition thanks are offered to God for protecting King James "from the cruell and bloody treacheries of desperate men, and especially as this day from the wicked designments of those blood-thirstie wretches the Earle Gowry, with his brother, and their desperate Confederates." Loyalty to the sovereign takes the form of the ferocious petition: "Smite his enemies upon the cheekebone, breake their teeth, frustrate their counsels, and bring to nought all their devices."[28] A later prayer again emphasizes the horror of treason and the certainty that divine justice will prove inexorable to all such desperate men who plan to kill the Lord's

---

[25] See Streatfield, *ibid.*, for information, and also J. H. Blunt's *Annotated Book of Common Prayer* (1866), pp. 578ff.
[26] The alternative lesson is II Chronicles 1.
[27] Sig. C3. [28] Sig. E2 verso.

representative; so that they had received "the due revenge of such treasonable attempts, spilling their blood who thought to spill the blood of thine anoynted, and leaving their slaughtered carkcises a worthy spectacle of thy dreadfull judgements, and their most impious designes."[29] This was political propaganda under the guise of theological diction, though the distinction is one that might well be denied by a sovereign who was also head of the national Church in England, Scotland, Ireland, and Wales.

The supreme service of royal commemoration in this century was, of course, that of the death of King Charles I on January 30 [12. Car.II, c. 30] which was prepared in 1660 and was chiefly the work of Bishop Brian Duppa. It was issued in 1661. It was revised by Sancroft and a proclamation concerning this version was made on January 7, 1662. A third revision, the product of a joint committee of Convocation, was annexed to the Prayer Book. On the accession of James II, a version nearer Sancroft's than any other replaced it until the withdrawal of all three versions with the accession of William and Mary. It is this particular service that preserved the high-church image of Charles I as the English church's martyr.[30]

He had almost been "canonised" while living by his high-church prelates, such as Archbishop Laud and those of his school. This seems especially to be the case in certain royalist prayers when the king's situation grew desperate in the Civil War. One "Prayer for the King" printed at Oxford in 1644, petitions God: "Take, we beseech thee into thy immediate hands and Divine protection thine annointed servant the King, that no sacrilegious prophane hand may come neere to touch him. . . ."[31] The same prayer refers to the "Sonnes of Violence" who "have joyned Nation to Nation, Covenant to Covenant, Army to Army, to pull down Him whom Thou hast exalted, and to roote that Religion which thine own right hand hath planted."[32] A second prayer, printed together with the first, pleads for the preservation of the University and City of Oxford. It asks God to "Save this City, this Nursery of thy Church" and of their oppressors that He will "set thy hook into their nostrills, to turn them back or confound them, according to thy good pleasure and secret wisdome by which thou disposest all Events

29 Sig. G2 verso.   30 Streatfield, *op. cit.*, p. 33.
31 *Two Prayers, One for the Safety of His Majesties Person; The Other For the Preservation of this University and City of Oxford to be used in all Churches and Chappells* (Oxford, 1644), p. 1.
32 *Ibid.*, p. 2.

beyond the meanes and reach of man."[33] Perhaps if the king's court had not consisted of so many flatterers and if his prelates had warned him rather than encouraging him in the belief that the king can do no wrong just because he is the Lord's anointed, Charles might have lived to be the unifier of the nation rather than the iconic property of the high-church party of the Church of England. Would that the bench had included an episcopal Nathan to warn another David!

Other services which preserved the image of the sovereign as anointed by God and given peculiar miracle-making powers were those known as "at the healing." On these occasions the sovereign's cure of the sick by touching, popularly known as "the King's Evil,"[34] was exercised. The service had been originally prepared in Latin for King Henry VII and modified from time to time, but it was never published until the reign of Anne, when it was appended to the accession service in the Prayer Book. It persisted in editions of the Prayer Book until 1732.[35]

The Latin form for Henry VII was printed in 1686, and another smaller edition in English. The English form is found regularly as an appendix to the Accession Service of the Prayer Book in Queen Anne's time. It is intriguing to see the nature of this service from the quarto edition of 1707, especially as one recalls that it was used by the Stuart kings in their royal chapels, and that Queen Anne "touched" the infant Samuel Johnson for scrofula.

After the collect, "Prevent us, O Lord . . . ," and the Gospel [Mark 16:14ff., including as a sign of the Gospel for those that are believers," "they shall lay hands on the sick, and they shall recover"], the three-fold Kyrie, and the Our Father, there follows an important rubric. It reads: "Then shall the infirm persons, one by one, be presented to the Queen on their knees, and as the Queen is laying her Hands upon them, and putting the Gold about their Necks, the Chaplain that officiates, turning himself to Her Majesty, shall say these words following: 'God give a Blessing to this Work; And grant that *these* Sick *Persons* on whom the Queen lays Her Hands, may recover, through Jesus Christ our Lord.' "

There follow four brief versicles and responses, a prayer for "these thy servants, that they being healed of their Infirmities, may give thanks unto thee in thy holy Church, through Jesus Christ our Lord, *Amen.*" The Chaplain then says to those who

33 *Ibid.*   34 See *Macbeth.*
35 Streatfield, *op. cit.*, p. 42.

come to be healed: "The Almighty God, who is a most strong tower to all them that put their trust in him . . . be now and ever-more your defence, and make you to know and feel, that there is none other Name under heaven given to man, in whom, and through whom, you may receive health and salvation, but only the Name of our Lord Jesus Christ. *Amen.*" The healing service ends with the Grace.

Although all references to the sovereign are capitalized, as well as all the possessive adjectives relative to her, yet the possessive adjectives and pronouns relative to God are in the lower case, still there is little in the service, at least by the time of Anne, to indi-cate that it is the Queen who has wonder-working powers. The healing is unambiguously attributed to God, through Jesus Christ, for faith, and in the Name of "holy Church." Earlier forms of the "At the Healing" were celebrated with greater Baroque pomp and circumstance with ceremonial representing absolutism. Anne was a "tamed" monarch, and the service represented a less authoritarian conception of the sovereign's rule. She was less a *"reine soleil"* than a *"reine éclairée."*

The most interesting of the royal and state commemorations is that of the discovery of the Gunpowder Plot on November 5, 1605, precisely because of its ambivalence. It began as an occasion of national thanksgiving for the delivery of King James and Parlia-ment and the English Reformed church from the machinations of Roman Catholic plotters. As the Stuart dynasty assisted by the Caroline divines emphasized more fully the Catholic element in the Catholic-Protestant compromise of the Anglican *via media*, and Stuart kings found Roman Catholic wives, who brought their priest-chaplains to court, and celebrated the Mass with splendour, the celebration of the fifth of November became a rallying festival for Parliament and the Puritans, especially during the days of the Commonwealth and Protectorate, until it became so exclusively associated with Protestantism and anti-Catholicism that, as has been noticed, William III, summoned to share the English throne with Mary, was seen as the guarantor of the Protestant succession to the throne and the defender of the independence of the Church of England from Papal interference.[36]

Parliament had instituted an observance of November 5 [3 Jac.I, c.I] soon after the event, but that only made provision for the reading of the Act during regular Morning Prayer. A special

36 *Ibid.,* p. 33.

form of service was drawn up by the bishops and issued by royal authority in 1606.

Two features of the service are of particular interest. One is the appositeness of the selection of II Samuel 22 as the Old Testament lesson. It is King David's song of gratitude to God for his deliverance from the hands of Saul and all his enemies. The eighth verse is reminiscent of the intended results of the Plot, "then the earth shook and trembled . . . and there went up a smoke out of his nostrils and fire out of his mouth devoured: coals were kindled by it." The divine vengeance on the rebels is characterized in verse 15: "And he sent out arrows and scattered them; lightning and discomfited them." Towards the end the chapter expresses the king's gratitude to God: "Thou hast delivered me from the strivings of my people," while the final verse sums up the providential interpretation of the saving of the Lord's anointed and of the royal house: "He [God] is the tower of salvation for his king; and sheweth mercy to his anointed, unto David, and unto his seed for ever."

The other feature of this commemoration of November 5 of interest is the fact that the second lesson in the Jacobean edition was the not entirely appropriate twenty-fourth chapter of the Acts of the Apostles, which was changed in the first Caroline edition by the king's episcopal advisers. This chapter gives an account of St. Paul's defence of his conduct and preaching before the Roman Governor, Felix. It is an admirable example of the Pauline persistence in defending the faith in Christ before Felix a Roman Governor. It was probably chosen because it contrasts an old and superseded faith (Judaism) with the new and true faith (Christianity), while expecting the expositor or reader of the passage in the English context to substitute Roman Catholicism for Judaism, and Protestantism for the Christianity of the New Testament. In a service which attempts to exalt a ruler as God's anointed who deserves the loyalty of his people it has at least one serious defect: it depicts a ruler trembling before a preacher. The politically offensive verse reads: "And as he [Paul] reasoned of righteousness, temperance, and judgment to come, Felix trembled. . . ."[37] Charles I might have needed such a preacher, a Nathan of a prophet declaring the immediately hurtful but ultimately healing truth, but assuredly he did not want one, nor to hear such commended in the lessons of the church of which he was the head. Furthermore, the conclusion of the chapter shows a ruler being unjust to, instead

[37] Verse 25.

of the protector of, the greatest exponent of primitive Christianity after Christ.

It is for such reasons, it may be guessed, that the bishops who advised Charles I, substituted Matthew 27 for the inappropriate lesson in their revision of the service in 1625, which was printed by Bonham Norton and John Gill. Theologically the account of the crucifixion of Christ and of his Resurrection was much superior to the lesson from II Samuel, but politically its brief account of the repentance and suicide of the arch-traitor of the Bible, Judas Iscariot, seemed an appropriate reminder of the grim consequences of conniving at the betrayal of God's supremely anointed, great David's greater Son, Christ. Another revision, at the time of the Restoration, was the characteristically careful work of Bishop Cosin of Durham.[38]

Other occasions which brought royalty to the attention of the public in the form of requiring special prayers, but not entire services or significant parts of services, were those "for the Queen's safe deliverance" (1605),[39] or "for the safe Delivery of the Queene" (1628, 1631, 1633, and 1636).[40] But, apart from such occasional prayers and the far more important annual anniversaries previously considered, the King and the members of the royal family were regularly commended to the divine protection in the Sunday and daily services of the Prayer Book. James I told the Puritans at the Hampton Court Conference, when they urged a greater parity of ministers according to the Presbyterian pattern of Geneva, "no bishop, no king." These royalist services we have considered in detail made plain that for the Anglican church throughout the century (with the exception of the Puritans who remained within it until 1662) it was a case of "no king, no church." All these occasions served to emphasize the importance of the crown as the symbol of the union between state and church in his person, and the desirability for loyalty on the part of his subjects both as members of the nation and the national church.

Nor should the state services, not specifically of a royal character, be forgotten, for the Church of England also observed other occasions of national urgency or emergency, on which the people were called to prayers to celebrate with due gratitude days of deliverance from war, plague, or other calamity. Such were gen-

---

[38] Streatfield, *op. cit.*, p. 33.
[39] Pollard and Redgrave, *Short Title Catalogue*, No. 16535.
[40] *Ibid.*, No. 16549.

erally known as days of thanksgiving. An example is *A Short Forme of Thanksgiving to God for staying the contagious sicknesse of the Plague: to be used in Common Prayer on Sundayes, Wednesdayes and Fridayes* (1625). One prayer vividly recalls death as the leveller, thanking God for deliverance from death and preservation from "that noysome pestilence, which not long since raged in the Land, sweeping away the rich with the poore, the aged with the young, leaving whole houses desolate, and filling all places with dead bodies."[41] Another prayer in the same service indicates that the plague is being recalled that the worshippers may "learne thereby, both to fear thy dreadfull Judgements against Sinne and so by true Repentance to turne unto thee from our wicked Wayes, lest a Worse Plague fall upon us; and also to put our whole trust in thy Mercy. . . ."[42] One might have thought that a repentance introduced by fear would be hardly likely to lead to entire confidence in a God who had stricken a country with one plague, and was now beseeched not to threaten his people with a deadlier one. But this does give a clue to the doctrine of special providence, by which every event is believed to be either determined by God or permitted to happen by his will.[43]

There were also national days of fasting or humiliation in which the people were summoned to church to hear the divine judgment upon the nation and the call to repentance expressed in the special prayers of the day. Such occasions were a fast for the drought (1611) and for the floods (in 1613 as in 1666, to take only two examples), and frequent fasts for "staying the plague" (as, for

---

[41] Sig. B4. [42] Sig. C2.

[43] The kindlier form of this doctrine is found in Matthew 5:45 ("for he [God] maketh his sun to rise on the evil and the good, and sendeth rain on the just and the unjust"), while the severer aspect of it can be illustrated from a prayer I once heard a Calvinist theologian of eminence offer in a college chapel, beseeching God to "succour those that are this day appointed to die." An ugly example of this would be the "cursing prayers" offered by each side in the Civil War. They believed that if they succeeded in defeating their enemies it was because God was making the victors the instruments of chastening the vanquished; if they lost a battle it was because God was chastising them for overconfidence or some other sin. An example of the latter can be found in the following excerpt from *A Collection of Prayers and Thanksgivings used in His Majesties Chappell and in His Armies* (Oxford, 1643): "we know, o Lord, that affliction cometh not forth out of the dust, neither doth trouble spring out of the ground, but it is thou that with rebukes dost chasten man for sinne." The same prayer later pleads with God to mark "We are become a reproach to the foolish people, and Servants bear rule over us, the mean Man is risen against the Honourable, and the fire out of the Bramble devoureth the lofty Cedars . . ." (pp. 13-14), a classic and moving example of conservatism's inability to cope with revolutionary change.

237

example, in 1604 and 1625).[44] It is often assumed that such days of thanksgiving and humiliation, accompanied by fasting, were Puritan innovations in worship, only because they were kept by them with such frequency and at what may seem to moderns inordinate length. In fact, however, they are recommended in the Elizabethan Book of Homilies, and it is of special interest that "A fourme of the Order for the generall Fast" issued in 1563[45] offers a rationale for the custom with examples drawn from both the Old Testament and the primitive church. Under both dispensations, "the people of God hath always used generall Fastyng, both in times of common Calamities, as Warre, Famine, Pestilence, &c. and also when any wayghtie matter, touchyng the estate of the Churche or the Commonwealth was begun or intended." This practise has been much neglected but is now to be remedied. So the Queen thought it suitable "in this contagious time of sicknes and other trouble, and unquietnes, accordying to the examples of the Godly Kyng Josaphat, and the Kyng of Ninive, with others, a generall Fast should be ioyned with generall Prayer, throughout her new Realme; and to be observed of all her godly subiectes. . . ."[46] It was further ordered that each Wednesday should be the appointed day of the fast and that all persons between sixteen and sixty years of age ("sicke folkes, labourers in the harvest or other greate labourers" excepted) are to eat only one competent and moderate meal each fast day, avoiding variety of meats, spices, confections, and wines, and only what is necessary, suitable, and healthy. The rich are told to eat more simply than usual so that by diminishing the costliness of their fare they can "increase therwith theyr liberalitie and almes towards the poore." The day is to be spent "in Prayer, studye, readyinge or hearying of the Scriptures, or good exhortations, &c." By a typical royal accommodation to human necessity, it is stated that when "any dulnesse or werynes shall aryse," the time is to be occupied in other godly exercise. This is rather in the spirit of the future *Book of Sports*,

[44] Other examples are listed in Pollard and Redgrave, *Short Title Catalogue*, nos. 16557 and 16559, both occurring before 1640. Another similar type of special service was *The Commemoration of the Fire of London* of 1666, which appeared in some copies of the Prayer Book towards the end of the reign of Charles II, but was discontinued in St. Paul's Cathedral only in 1859.

[45] *A Fourme to be used in Common Prayer twyse aweke, and also an order of publique fast to be used every Wednesday in the weeke, durying the time of mortalitie.* Its shelf-mark in the Bodleian Library of the University of Oxford is: 4° P 4 Th.

[46] *Op. cit.,* Sig. Cii.

238

until one reads "But no parte to be spent in plays, pastymes, or ydlenesse, muche lesse in lewd, wicked or wanton behaviour."[47]

In concluding the survey of the Anglican calendar, one is impressed again with its nature as a complex entity, combining Catholic, Protestant, and royalist elements. Its dominant tense was past in both its Christological-sanctoral cycle, as in its royalist commemorations. Its political significance was immensely influential, especially when a subservient church was manipulated in the interests of royal absolutism conveniently cloaked by the doctrine of the divine right of kings and the reality that the English sovereign was ecclesiastical as well as political leader by law. The regular prayers for the king and members of his household in the services of the Prayer Book, together with such annual commemorations as accessions, Gowrie Day, and the Gunpowder Plot, not forgetting the special prayers for the safe delivery of the Queen and the safeguarding of the succession to the throne, all reminded the people of the royal privileges and responsibilities, in the sacred as well as the secular realm, and of their own duties as loyal subjects. Socially, the Anglican calendar led to the sanctification of stratification. Its Erastianism made this inevitable, and, of course, it encouraged almsgiving by the rich towards the poor and concern for apprentices by their masters, and promised to all the consolations of eternity. But for any conception of social justice whether divinely or humanly introduced one must turn to the radical Puritans, the Diggers, and Levellers, and to the Fifth Monarchists (the latter a much larger group than hitherto recognized, as John F. Wilson has shown conclusively in his *Pulpit in Parliament*). The crown used the church as a medium of social control, along with the magistrates, even when, in opposition to Puritan Sabbatarianism, it proclaimed the necessity for a more relaxing observance of Sunday to make what it called "the meaner sort of people" happier with their lot, with the blissful escape of ale, and the lenitive of sports. The more aristocratic game of bowls, as it then was, came under the royal veto, presumably because it would make the ordinary man aspire to be extraordinary, and therefore socially "above himself." So he had better stick to archery. Economically, the Anglican calendar reduction of the Roman interruptions of work caused by frequent saints' days was advantageous, but there was still considerable waste in the holidays

[47] *Ibid.*, sig. Ciii.

permitted, together with the indolence and intoxication encouraged on these occasions. The work ethic of Puritanism with its insistence upon the divine prescription of six days of work and a seventh of rest, demanded more working days and provided greater theological incentives for work than the Anglican calendar, though its strenuousness rejected by the nation, tired after the blood-letting of the Civil War and the vagaries and visions of the saints, proved its own undoing. For sixteen years the Anglican calendar was rejected in favour of the Puritan calendar: after what the Royalists had referred to as the "usurpation" came to an end, it was welcomed with relief.

1. The Puritan Calendar

The single most notable characteristic of the Puritan calendar was its iconoclasm. Turning first to the theological considerations, it is clear that its proponents rejected the Christological cycle because they found no explicit command to keep Christmas Day or Easter Day or the rest, whereas they saw that the Sabbath alone was a Scripturally demanded day, a special seventh and sacred day. This was the pattern not only prescribed in the Decalogue, but it was the cosmic scheme. For had not God, according to the Book of Genesis, created the world in six days, and rested on the seventh? So must man labour for six days, and on the Sabbath rest (this rest also prefigured the eternal rest of the elect in eternity), he must honour God in worship and in all the exercises prescribed for edification. Hence the Sabbath was the divinely appointed sacred time Scripturally authorized, whereas the Christological cycle was only of ecclesiastical and therefore of human appointment.

The same argument *a fortiori* eliminated the saints' days. Furthermore, the Puritans used the term "saints" in the New Testament manner rather than in the traditional Roman Catholic interpretation. That is, they reserved the term not for the perfect whom the churches of the centuries in the East and West had chosen to honour as worthy of imitation and capable of interceding on behalf of their admirers, but for their fellow Christians in the process of sanctification, being made holy by the Holy Spirit. As Paul had written to "the saints that are in Rome" (meaning his fellow Christians), they restored the term to its former and most primitive usage, and so had no need for a sanctoral cycle. Once again it was Scripture they were obeying and not ecclesiastical tradition; also they believed that the claim that the saints interceded for the living was utterly idolatrous and derogating from the sole mediator-ship of Christ. In short, the Puritan believed that each Sunday or Sabbath was the Christological cycle in summary form, that each day should be a Lent (otherwise a temporary first-class Christian-ity must be equated with hypocrisy for the rest of the year), and that each of the elect should be a "saint" by the use of the religious exercises that kept his mind informed of God's Gospel and com-mands, his heart tender to God, and his resolution firm.

Puritan calendar iconoclasm is further seen in the radical dis-junction its theology makes between history and nature, with his-tory having the primacy. This had the effect of disenchanting the Puritans with the days of celebration associated with the natural seasons, especially important for an agricultural community. They disliked the dancing round the Maypole on the first of May, as well as the harvest ales, as occasions in which bawdiness and buffoon-ery, profanity and idleness predominated. They made a radical distinction between holidays and holy days, the latter being Sab-batarian and dedicated to the service of God. Their dislike of idle-ness is as economic as it is a theological factor. Indeed, they were inseparable, for it was God who commanded them to work for six days and God who commanded them to rest on the seventh day, but these arrangements because of their predictableness, their regularity, made rational planning possible for masters of crafts and merchants, however unpopular they were with unambitious apprentices.[48]

It is now important to recognize the positive emphases of the Puritan calendar, both in the "Sanctification of the Lord's Day,"

[48] For the political, social, and economic aspects of the Anglican-Puritan calen-dary controversy see the masterly chapter, "The Uses of Sabbatarianism" in Christopher Hill's *Society and Puritanism in Pre-Revolutionary England* (2nd edn., New York, 1967), esp. pp. 149-56. On the theological side, the Anglicans prepared a massive rebuttal, in which counter-offensive the big guns were Bishop White of Ely, Heylin the historian, Sanderson the future Bishop, and Gilbert Ironside. Between them they make the following points: that the Puritan conten-tion that the Sabbath was an eternal ordinance of a moral and not a ceremonial character cannot hold because it was not observed before the time of Moses and was often poorly observed by the Jews after the giving of the Decalogue; that the apostles had changed the day on which the Sabbath was observed from that which the Jews had kept; and that it was kept by the early Church as a day of festival, whereas the Puritans keep it more like a fast. Most significant, however, is the move on the part of Anglican apologists from Biblical and traditional grounds to rational, psychological, and more humane considerations. The kindly Sanderson argues that charity should urge the Puritans to judge their brethren who as "the ruder sort" need "loud and boisterous" exercises for recreation, while gentlemen can be made happy by walking. (*A Sovereign Antidote against Sab-batarian Errors*, 1636, p. 26. I owe this reference to Howard Happ's research.)

and in the special days of "Public Solemn Fasting" and of "Public Thanksgiving."[49]

The Lord's Day was celebrated, so the Puritans were convinced by divine command, authenticated by the Word of God, Scripture. That was the strength and stay of the Puritan claim.[50] The major exponent of the Puritan understanding of the Sabbath was Nicholas Bownde, who was indebted, as Everett H. Emerson[51] has shown, to his father-in-law, Richard Greenham, minister of Dry Drayton, author of *A Treatise of the Sabbath*, and both, as M. M. Knappen has demonstrated,[52] ironically were indebted to the early work of Lancelot Andrewes, *A Pattern of Catechistical Doctrine*.[53]

How, then, was this red-letter day (almost the only regularly celebrated one in the Puritan calendar) to be spent? Greenham exhibits the intra-mundane asceticism which was developing in Puritanism, for excepting his insistence that plays and unlawful sports should be prohibited on Sundays, he would ban all recreation of any kind. Apart from attendance upon divine worship and attentive listening to the preaching, he recommends participation in religious conferences so that this may be a means of stirring up their affections. Further, he insists that as businessmen scrutinize their accounts once each week, so should the Christian spend the eve of the Sabbath in spiritual self-accounting.[54]

The discipline of the Sabbath is described in greater detail by

---

[49] These terms are all taken from *A Directory for Publike Worship in the Three Kingdoms*, where they are headings of important sections of this work prepared by the Assembly of Divines at Westminster meeting in 1644 and 1645. It will be briefly referred to hereafter as the "Westminster Directory."

[50] Richard Byfield (*The Doctrine of the Sabbath Vindicated*, 1631, p. 134) explodes with Puritan horror at the thought that holy days are only matters of State (therefore of human) appointment, "then also the Feasts of Christ's Nativity, of Easter, of Witsontide, &c. are of equall authority with the Lords Day, which thing what eares can heare with patience?"

[51] See E. H. Emerson's essay in the vol. he edited, *English Puritanism from John Hooper to John Milton* (Durham, N.C., 1968), p. 147.

[52] See "The Early Puritanism of Lancelot Andrewes" in *Church History*, 2 (1933), pp. 102-103. For this and the immediately preceding reference my thanks go to Howard Happ, friend and former student.

[53] See, for an accessible modern edition, *A Pattern of Catechistical Doctrine and other Minor Works* (Oxford, 1846). Andrewes calls the day of rest, which he believes to be a moral and eternal institution, the Sabbath, insists that only light and necessary work be done, requires simplicity and frugality of fare, and emphasizes the importance of hearing preaching by "persons fit . . . such as are able to do more than read and speak" and even calls for Sabbath conferences on Scripture with teachers, social equals and servants. (*Ibid.*, pp. 162-65).

[54] *A Treatise of the Sabbath* in *Works* (1601). This circulated in Ms. form for three years before it was published in 1592. Greenham further insists that the Lord's Day includes all special days, rendering the latter otiose: "Our Easter Day, our Ascension Day, our Whitsuntide is every Lords Day." (*Works*, p. 159.)

Nicholas Bownde. Heads of households are urged to rise early themselves and to see to it that the entire family arrive in ample time to enjoy all the benefits of the public worship of God. Spiritual discipline involved careful preparation by meditation, prayer, and self-examination, to hear the sermon and prayer after the service for a love of God comfortable to the knowledge of God just received. Sermon summaries were to be copied down by apprentices and children, and both were required to recapitulate the sermon's main points for the heads of households, as masters or fathers. He was critical of the general Anglican keeping of sacred days, especially of Christmas, which was marked by distractions rather than devotions. His complaint is that "when they would seem to be most devoutly keeping the remembrance of. . . the *birth and incarnation* of *Christ* . . . they doe celebrate the feast of the *drunken god Bacchus.*"[55]

One classical picture of the Puritan seriousness in the spending of Sabbath is provided by Richard Baxter in his autobiography, testifying to it as a proof of great earnestness in religion:

> In the village where I lived the reader read the Common Prayer briefly and the rest of the day even till dark night almost, except eating-time, was spent in dancing under a may-pole and a great tree not far from my father's door, where all the men of the town did eat together. And though one of my father's own tenants was the piper, he could not restrain him or break the sport. So that we could not read the Scripture in our family without the disturbance of the tabor and pipe and noise in the street. Many times my mind was inclined to be among them, and sometimes I broke loose from conscience and joined with them; and the more I did the more I was inclined to it. But when I heard them call my father Puritan it did much to cure me and alienate me from them; for I considered that my father's exercise of reading the Scripture was better than theirs, and would surely be better thought on by all men at the last. . . .[56]

The Westminster *Directory* prescribed how the Puritan Sabbath should be spent when the Puritans came to power. It was, in

---

[55] Bownde, *op. cit.*, pp. 133-34.

[56] The substance of the original *Reliquiae Baxterianae* (ed. M. Sylvester, 1696) has been re-edited by J. M. Lloyd Thomas in an Everyman edn., titled, *The Autobiography of Richard Baxter* (1925), p. 6.

the first place, to be prepared for, so that "all worldly business or our ordinary callings may be so ordered, and so timely and seasonably laid aside, as they may not be impediments to the due sanctifying of the day when it comes." Secondly, the entire day was to be sanctified, both publicly and privately, with "a holy cessation, or resting all that day, from all necessary labours; and an abstaining, not only from all sports and pastimes, but also from all worldly words and thoughts." Thirdly, the diet for that day is to be so arranged "as that neither servants be unnecessarily detained" from worship, "nor any other person hindered from the sanctifying of that day." Fourthly, every person and family must prepare for the Sabbath by prayer for themselves and the divine assistance for the minister, and for a blessing of his ministry; "and by such other holy exercises as may further dispose them to a more comfortable communion with God in his public ordinances." Worship is to be so organized that the whole congregation is to be in time for the beginning and stay to the end of the service, and "with one heart solemnly join together in all parts of the public worship." The time before and after public worship is to "be spent in reading, meditation, repetition of sermons; especially by calling their families to an account of what they have heard, and catechising of them, holy conferences, singing of psalms, visiting the sick, relieving the poor, and such like duties of piety, charity, and mercy accounting the Sabbath a delight."[57]

We have seen earlier how there was an acute and complex Sabbatarian controversy between the Puritans and the high Anglicans, with important political as well as religious and economic implications. One further political aspect must be referred to, and that is the fact that the Puritan insistence upon keeping of the Sabbath strictly sometimes led to a matter of pitting the individual conscience against the social or religious hierarchy. Should an apprentice, for example, insist on the scrupulous keeping of the Sabbath in the most ascetical manner, while his master requested him to spend it, as the law of the land approved, in pleasurable activities? Or, again, who was to be the authoritative interpreter of God's will, the learned bishop, or the learned minister? To keep the Sabbath strictly was, therefore, to be a political and religious radical. To spend it in a relaxed way after attending worship was to belong

[57] All the citations in this paragraph come from the Directory's section headed "Of the Sanctification of the Lord's Day." (*Reliquiae Liturgicae*, ed. Peter Hall, Vol. III: *The Parliamentary Directory*, Bath, 1847, pp. 58-60.)

to, or be loyal to the royal and ecclesiastical establishment. In fact, the sixteenth of Archbishop Laud's *Visitation Articles* for 1635 in the diocese of Winchester is directed against Puritan tendencies in the ministry by specifically enquiring: "Hath your minister taken upon him to appoint any public or private fasts, prophecies or exercises, not approved by law or public authority, or hath used to meet in any private house or place with any person or persons, there to consult how to impeach or deprave the Book of Common Prayer, or the doctrine or discipline of the Church of England?"[58] He clearly recognized that the Puritan gauntlet had been thrown down in public challenge, for he listed the chief activities enjoined by the Puritans for use on the Sabbath, and intended as a counterblast to the re-issue of the *Book of Sports* by Charles I, as well as being godly "exercises" in their own right.

As the antagonism between high Anglicans and Puritan Anglicans grew more bitter, Henry Burton tried to reinforce the observation of the Lord's Day by collecting a group of "divine tragedies" or striking cases of divine retribution on Sabbath-breakers for their defiance of the law of God, resulting in death or injury. Seven cases are noted of those who were involved in maypole festivities, four for participating in Whitsun and two other church ales, four cases of superfluous bell-ringing, four cases of swimming accidents, and two for skating on thin ice, and one case each for serving a *subpoena*, frequenting a brothel, keeping company with young women, scoffing at the Sabbath, and feasting in celebration of the *Book of Sports*.[59]

The Sabbath was the great, regular red-letter day of the Puritan calendar, which looked both backward to the Creation and forward to the consummation of Creation in the eternal delight and rest of God's elect in heaven. Yet, in addition, this calendar had a strongly contemporary emphasis based upon the Puritan's reading of God's special providence revealed in events. This can be documented as clearly in the diary of Oliver Cromwell, whether as general of the Ironsides or as Lord Protector of England,[60] as in the diary of Samuel Sewall, the judge who presided over the notorious

[58] Found in P. E. More and F. L. Cross, *Anglicanism* (edn. of 1957), pp. 702-15.

[59] [Henry Burton] *A Divine Tragedy Lately Enacted* (Amsterdam, 1636), passim.

[60] See the three volume edition of *The Letters and Speeches of Oliver Cromwell* (ed. Thomas Carlyle, 1904), passim, and the admirable theological biography, *The Lord Protector* (1955) by Robert S. Paul.

witchcraft trial in Salem, Massachusetts. It was indeed part of the Protestant tradition in England to note special providences, from the time of Foxe the martyrologist, who had learned it from the pages of Calvin's *Institutes*. This tradition affirmed that every event was a disclosure of the mysterious divine will in judgment or mercy. This providential interpretation had been given official acceptance by the national church when it summoned the people to prayer in Elizabeth's reign. For example, two special days of prayer were proclaimed in 1565, and for each a form was prepared; one a thanksgiving "for the delivery of the Christians that are now invaded by the Turke." Although the doctrine had been inserted in the Book of Homilies, it was Puritanism that made it prominent.

What, then, was distinctive about the Puritan days of special providence? Two features seem to mark their days of humiliation and thanksgiving from the previous national special days. One is the great solemnity, intensity, and length, with which they were kept, lasting most of the day, and filled with exhortations, sermons, prayers, and psalm-singing, and with only a minimal concession to the needs of the body. The other feature is that such observance of days of special providence were also kept within Puritan family life: indeed, they were encouraged so long as they did not conflict either with the Sabbath or with nationally appointed special days when the latter were decreed by Puritanism in the seat of power.

Undergirding these observances was a strong Calvinist theology of special providence, which the increasing Arminianism of high-church Anglicans found to be too sure about "the secret counsels of God"; but it meant that the rational elements in their own theology lacked the dogmatic certainties of Puritanism, the immense assurance of the elect that can rapidly recover after disaster. ("Who can lay anything to the charge of God's elect? . . . If God be for us, who can be against us? . . . Nay, in all things we are more than conquerors through him that loved us. . . .")[61]

This conviction was first widely spread among Puritans by their favourite early writer, William Perkins in 1607. He observes: "God hath sundry times sent his iudgments among us; generally by plague and famine; and particularly on sundrie families and persons; but who regardeth them?" His answer is that contemplation on God's judgments is essential to avoid their repetition, and

[61] These are, of course, citations from the Epistle to the Romans 8, a favourite commonplace of Puritan theology.

for this three things are requisite. "First, we must carefully observe, marke, and remember them. . . . Secondly, . . . we must apply them to our own person in particular, so as the thought thereof may make use of Gods iudgments that light upon others by applying them to ourselves."[62]

The Westminster *Directory* supplies the official theological rationale of these days and directions for their careful observance. The days of humiliation, for example, are no exercises of faith followed by fun. They are to last the entire day, and fasting requires "total abstinence, not only from all good . . . but also from worldly labour, discourses and thoughts, and from all bodily delights and such like (although at other times lawful), rich apparel, ornaments, and such like, during the fast. . . ." Each family and person is to prepare privately apart and be early at the congregation. Further, "So large a portion of the day as conveniently may be, is to be spent in public reading and preaching of the Word, with singing of psalms, fit to quicken affections suitable to such a duty." Prayer is given the highest priority on such occasions and ministers are charged to aim at "melting" the hearts of the people (and their own), "especially with sorrow for their sins, that it may be indeed a day of deep humiliation and afflicting of the soul." A special choice of Scripture lessons and texts for preaching are to be made as will most dispose the people to repentance and lead them to reformation: "Before the close of the public duties, the minister is, in his own and the people's names, to engage his and their hearts to the Lord's, with professed purpose and resolution to reform what is amiss among them, and more particularly such sins as they have been more remarkably guilty of, and to draw near to God, and to walk more closely and faithfully with him in new obedience, than ever before."[63] Thus, the heart prepared by grace, is to be melted to end in the resolution to renew the personal, familial, congregational, and national covenant with God.

There are several striking illustrations of such day-long fasts leading from thorough group self-criticism to repentance and reso-

---

[62] *A Treatise of Man's Imagination* (Cambridge, 1607), pp. 198-200. It was published five years after the author's death.

[63] All citations are from the Westminster *Directory*'s Section, entitled "Concerning Public Solemn Fasting" (*Reliquiae Liturgicae*, ed. Peter Hall, Vol. III, *The Parliamentary Directory* [Bath, 1847], pp. 73-78). See also John F. Wilson's "The Program of Humiliation and Thanksgiving," which is Chap. iii of *Pulpit in Parliament* (Princeton, New Jersey, 1969).

lution, on the part of the Westminster Assembly of Divines and of the Puritan Army Debates at Putney.[64] Lightfoot, one of the Scottish commissioners at the Westminster Assembly, tells how the Assembly spent Monday, October 16, 1643, the occasion being a solemn fast:

> First Mr. *Wilson* gave a picked psalm, or selected verses of several psalms, agreeing to the time and occasion. Then Dr. *Burgess* prayed about an hour: after he had done, Mr. *Whittacre* preached upon Isa. xxxvii.3, "This day is a day of trouble," &c. Then, having had another chosen psalm, Mr. *Goodwin* prayed; and after he had done, Mr. *Palmer* reached upon Psal. xxv.12. After whose sermon we had another psalm, and Dr. *Stanton* prayed about an hour; and with another psalm and a prayer of the prolocutor [i.e. Dr. Twisse], and a collection for the maimed soldiers . . . we adjourned till tomorrow morning.[65]

This particular occasion lasted from 9:00 A.M. to 4:00 P.M. and the collection for maimed soldiers reached £3 15s.[66]

It would seem to be a heroic endurance test of preaching and praying only lightened by psalm-singing, and possibly unique. On the contrary, though the quality of the preaching was certainly higher in the Assembly with such a galaxy of Puritan divines than it would be at any other gathering, yet the occasion was far from being unique even at the Westminster Assembly. Parliament had sought Charles I's permission to have a fast on the last Wednesday of each month (a technical error on his part in view of the political use of such occasions that would later be made against his interests), and it became statutory by 1641. There had been a notable fast day on Monday, September 25, 1643, when the Commons and the divines took the Solemn League and Covenant, meeting in St. Margaret's Church, Westminster, which remains the parish church of the House of Commons.

When on September 9, 1644, the woeful news came of the

---

[64] For the Army Debates see *Puritanism and Liberty*, ed. with an introduction of great value by A.S.P. Woodhouse (1938).

[65] Ed. Rev. John Rogers Pitman, *The Whole Works of the Rev. John Lightfoot*, 13 Vols. (1825), XIII, containing "The Journal of the Proceedings of the Assembly of Divines," from Jan. 1, 1643 to December 31, 1644," *ad loc.* October 13, 1643. It is also cited in W. Fraser Mitchell, *English Pulpit Oratory from Andrewes to Tillotson* (1932), pp. 255-56.

[66] S. W. Carruthers, *The Everyday Work of the Westminster Assembly* (Philadelphia, 1943), p. 65.

defeat of Lord Essex's forces in the West, with Waller's Army in no position to relieve Essex because his infantry had surrendered at Lostwithiel, Burgess suggested that the Assembly should hold a fast, and they then and there discussed the causes of the divine disapproval seen in the military disaster, as it applied to their own conduct as divines.

The details of this clerical group exercise in self-criticism may be of interest. Valentine said zeal had been shown for depriving scandalous ministers, but not for rebuking scandalous people. Whitaker mentioned the breaches of the Solemn League and Covenant, such as divisions among those who professed to be religious, and falsehood. Walker mentioned neglect of justice. Gillespie said that religion was subjugated to political ends.[67] Palmer spoke of slack attendance, arriving late, leaving early, impetuosity or slowness of speech, and unhappy differences. Burgess spoke of insolence and bloodthirstiness on the part of the enemy, of the gasping condition of Ireland, of the divisions in Manchester's Army; and the deliberate fomenting of sectarianism. The analysis seems to have been comprehensive, if rambling, and it was not sparing in candour.

The other providential day in the Puritan calendar was spent more cheerfully. That was the public day of thanksgiving. Here, again, the Westminster *Directory* provides a rationale and description. Such days might be occasioned by a notable victory[68] in the field, of deliverance from some impending disaster like the plague or drought or flood. When a day of public thanksgiving is held, the minister is to "make some pithy narration of the deliverance obtained, or mercy received,[69] or of whatever hath occasioned that assembling of the congregation, that all may better understand it, or be minded of it, and more affected with it." Psalm-singing was enjoined as the fittest medium for the expression of sacred joy. The minister is to exhort the people about the signal instance of God's mercy, to read appropriate passages of Scripture, and to pick a text pertinent to the occasion. After the sermon is ended, he is also to

[67] One is reminded of Milton's disaffection with the Assembly by his description of it as being riddled "with plots and packing worse than Trent."

[68] An example of such is the Assembly's day of thanksgiving for the surrender of the king's forces at Worcester, in July of 1646. See S. W. Carruthers, *op. cit.*, p. 85.

[69] It must be recalled that thanksgiving days could be held in families and divine mercies would include gratitude for the safe delivery of a mother in childbirth, as for the gift of children, or the recovery from a serious illness, or for spiritual mercies such as reformation of life.

pray, remembering the necessities of king, church, and state, enlarging on "former mercies and deliverances; but more expecially for that which at the present calls them together to give thanks: With humble petition for the continuance and renewing of God's wonted mercies, as need shall be, and for sanctifying grace to make a right use thereof." He is also to admonish the congregation "to beware of all excess and riot, tending to gluttony or drunkenness . . . and to take care that their mirth and rejoicing be not carnal, but spiritual, which may make God's praise to be glorious and themselves to be humble and sober." Two such gatherings of the congregation on that day are expected and at one or both "a collection is to be made for the poor . . . that their loins may bless us and rejoice the more with us." Finally, the people are to be exhorted at the end of the second meeting, "to spend the residue of that day in holy duties, and testifications of Christian love and charity one towards another, and of rejoicing more and more in the Lord; as becometh those who make the joy of their Lord their strength."[70]

One can hardly fail to be impressed not only with the seriousness and solemnity of these days of thanksgiving, and with the humility that accepted weal (and even woe on days of fasting) as a divine gift for the training of the elect, without much presumptuous expectation or overt murmuring. Considering the stereotypes of Puritanism that have been widely disseminated by the Elizabethan playwrights[71] and Lord Macaulay's *History of England*, who would have guessed that joy characterized Sabbaths and days of thanksgiving, and that so much time after worship was spent in "the testifications of Christian love and charity towards one another"?

There was only one regular annual day of thanksgiving which the Puritans celebrated, and that was the fifth of November. It became increasingly interpreted as the supremely Protestant national event, given double significance for their successors the Nonconformists, through the discovery of the conspiracy of Titus Oates, a doubtful Catholic,[72] and the joining to the celebration the arrival of William of Orange in England to safeguard the English

[70] All citations in the paragraph up to this point are from the section of the Westminster Directory, headed "Concerning the Observation of Public Days of Thanksgiving." (See *The Parliamentary Directory*, ed. Peter Hall, Bath, 1847, pp. 78-81.)

[71] The references are to Malvolio in *Twelfth Night* by Shakespeare, and to Zeal-of-the-Land-Busy in Jonson's *Bartholomew Fair*.

[72] The events of this time are brilliantly interpreted in the cryptogrammatic narrative poem of Dryden, *Absolam and Achitophel*.

throne for Protestantism. Nonetheless, they needed all their considerable powers of exegetical elasticity to justify this celebration from the Word of God, as Anglicans were not slow to remind them. But its political and religious value to them was immense.

Apart from the regular and special sacred times we have mentioned, there was also an unofficial Puritan calendar, to which Samuel Pepys alludes in his diary. The entry for September 3, 1662, reads: "Mr. Coventry told us how the Fanatiques and Presbyters that did intend to rise about this time, did choose this day as the most auspicious to them in their endeavours against monarchy: it being fatal twice to the King, and the day of Oliver's death. But blessed be God! all is likely to be quiet, I hope." Certainly Cromwell considered the third day of September the most fortunate of his life because it marked his victories at Dunbar and Worcester. It was also remarkable for the vast storm that occurred at the time of his death, and also it was the day on which the Fire of London in 1666 raged with the greatest fury. But the fact that it marked Cromwell's success and time of death are proof sufficient of the ambiguity of events and the great theological, apart from scientific difficulties, in interpreting their significance.

In summation, one notes the strongly contemporary thrust of the Puritan calendar, as contrasted with the retrospective emphasis of the Anglican and Roman Catholic cyclical calendars. But one ought not either to ignore the emphasis on the future inherent in the Sabbath, and more directly envisaged on that day by the radical Puritans, who, in that day of rest from manual labor, were freed to contemplate in the freest fantasy the religious *bouleversement* that would come with the establishment of God's Fifth and final Monarchy, the kingdom of the saints. Here, indeed, and imminently, God would, as already foreshadowed in the *Magnificat* throw down the mighty from their seats and raise up the humble and meek. The Puritan calendar is acknowledged to be a rigorous and intensive one: it is more rarely realised that it was an exciting series of sacred days fraught with religious and political promise. Only the future would show that the intensity was too great for the majority of human beings to bear, and that the political promises were doomed, as Milton shows so movingly in *Samson Agonistes*.

Its economic importance, because of Christopher Hill's researches, is now widely recognized. The Puritan week was the perfect medium for the Puritan conception of calling, involving strenuous work for six days and a seventh for rest and holy exercises. John Boyes expressed the Puritan work ethic admirably in the words: "Every Christian should have a sweating brow and a working braine. . . ."[73] Such working was institutionalised by the Puritan Sabbath and made the rational planning of the industrialist and merchant possible, whereas the traditional Roman or Anglican calendars were too irregular, and too frequently interrupted by holidays for economic purposes. In this respect we see that it was also of social importance, for aristocrats[74] and their dependents who lived to a large extent on the land, with the squires and yeomen farmers, and they warmed to the traditional celebrations of church and the natural seasons, while the Puritans were men of the cities, merchants and masters. Certainly the Roman Catholic and Anglican calendars were more humane then and they may in the end prove to be as religious as the Puritan calendar. But if sincerity, and intensity of devotion (rather than accommodation of religion to human needs and the recognition of the claims of the earth and of the need for a reversal) are the criteria of judgment, the Puritan calendar was a heroic failure. The Restoration showed that the moderation of the *via media* in this as in most other respects suited the majority of the English nation.

[73] "The First Sunday" from his work, *An Exposition of the Dominical Epistles and Gospels used in our English Liturgy throughout the whole yeare* (1609), p. 9.

[74] Hill's *Society and Puritanism in Pre-Revolutionary England*, points out that the Court notoriously had masques, plays, and even revels on the Lord's Day (p. 160), that the Council met on Sunday mornings regularly until the reign of Charles I (pp. 163-64), whereas Parliament refrained from meeting on Sundays except under the most urgent necessity and then apologized (pp. 164-65).

CHAPTER VII

SACRED MUSIC:
SPLENDID OR SCRIPTURAL?

OUR TITLE for this chapter is an oversimplification. There was not one issue in this controversy, but a complex of interrelated ones. Indeed, it was a temptation to head the chapter "Sacred Music: Magnificent or Minimal?" in order to point out the difference between the rich Anglican tradition of cathedral music, on the one hand, and the austere Puritan restriction of sacred music to metrical psalmody, on the other. There could hardly be a greater contrast than that of the cathedral tradition inherited from the medieval church, reaffirmed by Tallis and Byrd in Tudor days, and developed in the Italian manner in the *stile nuovo* in Restoration times, with verse anthems sung in many parts, with soloists and the full choir alternating, and with a concert of violins playing in the vocal intervals, and its opposite—the sometimes solemn but often dreary simplicity of Puritan metrical psalmody lined out in common metre.

That would have been a justified contrast, because Cavaliers and Roundheads were differentiated in part by their preferences in sacred music. That is made clear by Anthony Wood who reports that at the Restoration organs were put back into the Oxford Colleges to counteract the popular interest in preaching, praying, and psalm-singing: "And that they might draw the vulgar from the aforesaid praying and preaching which was still exercised in some churches and houses, they restored organs at Christ Church, Magdalen, New and St. John's College, together with the singing of prayers after the most antient way: to which places the resort of people (more out of novelty I suppose than devotion) was infinitely great."[1]

Nonetheless, to have retained the alternative title for this Chapter would have implied that the difference between the Puritan and Anglican attitudes to sacred music was only a matter of taste, temperament, or cultural preference, a kind of choice between "penny plain" and "tuppenny coloured."

[1] *The Life and Times of Anthony à Wood* abridged from A. Clark's edition by L. Powys (1961), p. 313; cited by Christopher Dearnley, *English Church Music, 1650-1750* (1970), p. 157.

The ultimate difference between Anglican and Puritan and Non-conformist concepts of sacred music, however, cannot be resolved or explained in this simple fashion. In the first place, as Percy Scholes has established,[2] the Puritans were not the musical kill-joys of the stereotype made fashionable by Lord Macaulay's claim that in Commonwealth days "it was a sin to touch the virginals. . . . The solemn peal of the organ was superstitious."[3] John Milton, like Spenser, an exemplar of the rich culture of Puritanism, had an organ in his home and expressed in prose as well as in *Il Penseroso* his ecstatic delight in organ music: "while the skilful *Organist* plies his grave and fancied descant, in lofty fugues, or the whole symphony with artful and unimaginable touches adorn and grace the well studied chords of some choice composer."[4] Opera, it should be remembered, was imported into Britain in Puritan times.[5] Playfair published his *English Dancing Master* (1651) at the height of the Puritan regime, and dancing was encouraged by Cromwell, celebrated by Milton in *L'Allegro*, and formed an essential part of the education of the family of one of Cromwell's army commanders, Colonel Hutchinson. Puritans privately encouraged music, dancing, and portrait painting. If they were unable to encourage the use of organs and orchestras in divine worship, it was not that they disliked art, but that they loved religion more.

It is for the latter reason that we have labelled this Chapter's controversy that of the debate between splendour (and by implication medieval and royalist tradition) and Scripture. The Anglicans followed the Lutheran view of Scripture and tradition, which argued that what was not forbidden in Scripture and had the authority of tradition behind it was permissible in the church, and which had made possible the use of the hymnody of Luther and Gerhardt and the great tradition of oratorios and the sublime organ music of Johann Sebastian Bach. The Puritans, and their successors the Nonconformists, on the other hand, demanded a Scriptural warrant for every part of worship, believing it to be a repudiation of the doctrine of original sin for man to assume he was capable of deciding what was appropriate in the service of God, and arrant impudence to legislate for himself when God had already decided for him in the Word of God in the Holy Scriptures. The inflexible Puritan motto was: *Quod non iubet, vetat*. As we shall see later, it

---

[2] *The Puritans and Music* (1934).
[3] *The History of England* (1848), Chap. I.
[4] Scholes, *op. cit.*, p. 151.   [5] *Ibid.*, p. 195.

was the conviction that metrical Psalms were the Word of God while hymns were human compositions, that restricted their praise to the paraphrases until the last decade of the century.

Furthermore, Puritans were acutely critical of cathedral music on other grounds. The complexities of polyphonic compositions, the obscurities of Latin motets and anthems, the requirements of well-trained professional choirs to perform such elaborate music— all parts of the medieval cathedral tradition of music maintained to some degree in England—sinned against two of the major Puritan doctrines, namely, the primary need for "edification" or building up in the faith (so that, according to the Pauline injunction one could sing with the understanding) and the priesthood of all believers. Complexity and obscurity defeated the aim of edification and a professional choir stole the rights of the congregation as God's elect to sing His praises.

The Puritans were not slow to make their voices heard in criticism of elaborate cathedral and church music. John Northbrooke in 1577 wrote:

> First we must take heed that in music be not put the whole sum and effect of godliness and of the worshipping of God, which among the Papists they do almost . . . think that they have fully worshipped God when they have long and much sung and piped. Further, we must take heed that in it be not put merit or remission of sins. Thirdly, that singing be not so much used and occupied in the Church that there be no time, in a manner, left to preach the Word of God and holy doctrine; whereby it cometh to pass that the people depart out of Church full of music and harmony, but yet hunger-baned and fasting as touching heavenly food and doctrine. Fourthly, that rich and large stipends be not so appointed for musicians that either very little, or, in a manner, nothing is provided for the ministers which labour in the Word of God. Fifthly, neither may that broken and quavering music be used wherewith the standers-by are so letted that they cannot understand the words, not though they would never so fain. Lastly, we must take heed that in the church nothing be sung without choice, but only those things which are contained in the holy scriptures, or which are by just reason gathered out of them, and do exactly agree with the Word of God.[6]

[6] *A Treatise Wherein Dicing, Dauncing, etc. Are Reproved* (1577), reprinted by the Shakespeare Society, ed. Collier (1843), pp. 113-14.

255

Northbrooke does not mention the need for a professionally trained choir to perform the music, but he thinks of the cost of maintaining choristers and their choir-masters and organists. He recalls that Roman Catholic worship stinted the time allowed for preaching. He also emphasises the "broken and quavering music" which makes it difficult for the congregation to understand the words. Naturally he concludes that the primary liturgical criterion is Biblical.

Robert Browne, himself a competent lutenist and lover of music, objected to the antiphonal singing of the psalms by the two sides of a cathedral choir. It seemed to him to mock the solemnity of worship: "Their tossing to and fro of psalmes and sentences is like tenisse plaie, whereto God is called to Judg who can do best and be most gallant in his worship; as bie organs, solfaing, pricksong chanting, bussing and mumling verie roundlie on divers handes. Thus their have a shewe of religion, but in deed thei turne it to gaming, and plaie mockholidaie with the worship of God."[7]

William Prynne empties his fiercest vial of rhetoric on contemporary church music, but his main point is that this music diverts the attention from instruction in divine doctrine:

> As for the Divine Service and Common Prayer, it is so chaunted and minsed and mangled of our costly hired, curious, and nice Musitiens (not to instruct the audience withall, nor to stirre up mens mindes unto devotion, but with a whorish harmony to tickle their eares:) that it may justly seeme not to be a noyse made of men, but rather a bleating of bruite beasts; while the Coristers ney descant as it were a sort of Colts; others bellowe a tenour, as it were a company of oxen: others barke a counter-point, as it were a kennell of Dogs: others rore out a treble like a sort of Bulls: others grunt out a base as it were a number of Hogs; so that a foule evill favoured noyse is made, but as for the wordes and sentences and the very matter it selfe, is nothing understood at all; but the authority and power of judgment is taken away from the music and from the eares utterly.[8]

It is most significant that he recognises only two values in sacred music: instruction and the creation of a devotional atmosphere in worship. It is inconceivable to him that a skilfully performed

---

[7] *True and Short Declaration* (1583), cited by P. Scholes, *op. cit.*, p. 217.
[8] Cited by Scholes, *ibid.*, p. 218.

anthem or chant might itself be an act of worship, as well as creating a desire for worship in others.

It must be acknowledged that there was, at least on the part of some Puritans, an insensitivity to subtle or profound religious music. That is the only conclusion that can be drawn from the delight of John Vicars that organ music and elaborate singing were now silenced in 1649 in Westminster Abbey, both being replaced by a daily sermon. This is sheer iconoclasm:

> the most rare and strange alteration of things in the *Cathedral Church of Westminster*. Namely, that whereas there was wont to be heard nothing almost but *Roaring*-Boyes, tooting and squeaking *Organ Pipes*, and the Cathedral catches of Morley, and I know not what trash; now the Popish Altar is quite taken away, the *bellowing organs* are demolisht and pull'd down; the *treble* or rather *trouble* and base singers, Chanters or Inchanters, driven out; and instead thereof, there is now a most blessed Orthodox Preaching Ministry, even every morning throughout the Weeke, and every Weeke throughout the whole yeare a Sermon Preached by the most learned grave and godly Ministers.[9]

The crudest and most literal kind of Puritan iconoclasm is reported by Bishop Hall in the spoiling of his cathedral of Norwich in 1643:

> Lord, what work was here, what clattering of glasses, what beating down of walls, what tearing up of monuments, what pulling down of seats, what wresting out of irons and brass from the windows and graves, what defacing of arms, what demolishing of curious stone work that had not any representation in the world but only the coat of the founder and the skill of the mason, what toting and piping upon the destroyed organ pipes, and what hideous triumph on the market day before all the country, when, in a kind of sacrilegious and profane procession, all the organ pipes, vestments, both copes and surplices, together with the leaden Cross which had been newly sawn down from over the green yard pulpit, and the service books and singing books that could be had, were carried to the fire in the marketplace, a lewd wretch walking before the train, in his scope, trailing

[9] Cited by Jocelyn Perkins, *Westminster Abbey: Its Worship and Ornaments* (1952), p. 111.

in the dirt, with a service book in his hand, imitating, in an impious scorn, the time, and usurping the words of the Litany, used formerly in the Church; near the public cross all these monuments of idolatry must be sacrificed to the fire, not without much ostentation of a zealous joy in discharging ordinance to the cost of some who professed how much they had longed to see that day. Neither was it any news, upon the Guild day, to have the Cathedral now open on all sides, to be filled with musketeers, waiting for the major's return, drinking and tobaccoing as freely as if it had turned ale-house.[10]

Such desecration caused not only the loss of historical artifacts, but, as far as music was concerned, the most serious destruction was of music libraries and part-books, and the disbanding of choirs and the loss of traditions which it had taken many years to create. Much of the music would have been in sets of handwritten part-books, comprising a series of services and anthems collected by the choir-master. Music copying was both expensive and laborious, with the result that one set only, sufficient for the choir, would exist. Unless any of the parts of these services and anthems happened to be used by other churches, the loss of a set would be permanent. Furthermore, there were few extant printed part-books and they were sold in limited editions. Their widespread destruction by the Puritans led to the entire disappearance of some works and to the survival of damaged or incomplete sets of others. The result is that John Barnard's *The First Booke of Selected Church Musick* (1641), a typical compilation, which was issued in ten separate part-books, has nowhere survived in its entirety.[11]

1. Cathedral Music

If such were the criticisms, whether moderate or merely negative and destructive, by the Puritans of English church music in cathedrals and peculiars, what was to be said in its defence? Actions speak louder than words. Thus the best apologia for such elaborate music will be our later consideration of the sacred music actually composed by a galaxy of luminaries in the seventeenth century, including Tompkins, Weelkes, Gibbons, Lawes, Humphrey, Blow, and Purcell. Nor should the high standards set by the Royal

---

10 Cited by Kenneth R. Long, *The Music of the English Church* (1971), p. 205.
11 The information in this paragraph was drawn from Long, *op. cit.*, pp. 206-207.

Chapel in London or in Westminster Abbey (not ignoring provincial cathedrals), especially during the reign of King Charles II, be forgotten.

The conflict between Anglican and Puritan over the nature of church music raised issues which are still acute and relevant. If the Puritan claim is made that music must be straightforward and so simple that all can join in, then the only rights recognised are those of edification and the priesthood of all believers. In rebuttal, however, the Anglicans can claim that this will mean a very limited repertory of music, and prevent the humble worshipper from ever hearing most of the sublimest religious music ever composed or performed, for the highest music is complex and elaborate and must be performed by professionals. To demand that the music sung in church must be capable of being performed by everyone, is to require music restricted in range, elementary in rhythm, easily memorised, and often obvious in the extreme. By the same token such music will be irksome and restrictive to those with more advanced musical tastes, for it seems to be the case that the more musical people are, the more their taste turns towards richly decorated or elaborate music.

Then there is a second argument in favour of cathedral type music, as against popular music. Is it essential that the whole congregation should join in all the music offered in worship? Puritans said, "Yes." The Anglicans said, "No." The latter were able to point out that, in fact, the congregation does not join in audibly in a considerable part of divine service—in the Epistle, the Gospel, other lessons, prayers, collects, and the sermon. There is no reason therefore why a considerable part of the sacred music should not be delegated to the musical experts, the organist, choir-master, and choir. Nor, indeed, can a congregation join in splendid architecture, stained-glass windows, mosaics, tapestries, intricate wood-carving or wrought ironwork, although all of these are aids to devotion, raising the minds and hearts of the worshippers from the secular world to the spiritual, and creating the atmosphere conducive to the adoration of God. Music has the same capacity in the highest degree, whether without words, as in an organ voluntary, or with words that are difficult to hear, as in a complex polyphonic motet, or are not understood, as in a Latin anthem.

Not only so, but—provided there is a secure place for hymnody—even though the congregation cannot join in vocally with the elaborate music, this does not prevent them from active participation in heart and mind.

Even more significantly it can be argued that the best cathedral music is more than a stimulus to devotion; that it is, indeed, an act of worship in and of itself providing, as in expressionist art, an inspiring and moving setting, to the words it illustrates, whether the mood be that of pathos and sadness, as at the Cross, or the mourning for our sins, or of joy and triumphant jubilation as at the Resurrection and the contemplation of the Communion of saints.

It can even be argued that, in general, the parish church could realise the dreams of the Reformers in a service that is musically "understanded of the people" while the cathedral or abbey church delegates its musical offering to be provided by the experts.[12]

It will be interesting to consider seventeenth-century justifications of cathedral music. John Barnard, writing in 1641, considered it a sufficient apologia for music that it "could civilise the rough and boystrous fancies of a Nation, that is esteem'd of many to be naturally somewhat of the sourest."[13] Presumably a dyspeptic nation could not have too much music to cure its melancholy and morose temperament. In 1720, however, Thomas Besse makes some very high-flown claims for cathedral music, including its honouring of God, the example it sets to all Reformed churches, its promotion of spiritual happiness in the members of a cathedral choir (conveniently oblivious of their occasional quarrelsomeness), its benefit to the entire nation, and its offering of worship on behalf of every parish in the diocese.[14]

Yet one could also select other authors to give an entirely different impression. Christopher Dearnley, for example, claims that at the time of the Restoration music's chief use was for the glory of God and His divine service, as well as for the solace of humanity. By the beginning of the eighteenth century, the same writer contends that its function was to refresh mankind and to supply an antidote against temptation; while in the middle of the same century its main values were to provide for entertainment and to give an inducement to charity. Not only the motives for music, but also its techniques followed a similar process of secularization.[15]

12 *Ibid.*, p. 37 for comparison.
13 From the introduction to John Barnard's *First Booke of Selected Church Musick* (1641).
14 *A Rationale on Cathedral Worship* (1720), pp. 52-62.
15 Dearnley, *English Church Music* (1970), pp. 15f.

But, we may ask, what was the kind of musical provision made in seventeenth-century cathedrals in England? The first point is that fully choral services are sung in cathedrals on weekdays as well as on Sundays and festivals. Furthermore, far more music is customarily sung in a cathedral than in a parish church, and it is of a generally advanced type which it would be too difficult for parish choirs to attempt. Then, again, the sung parts of the prescribed services, which remain unchanged from day to day, including the ordinary of the Holy Communion, the responses and canticles, are sung to fully composed settings, several of which are highly intricate. Moreover, the set Psalms for the day are sung in full, usually by way of antiphonal chanting, verse by verse or half-verse by half-verse. The *Te Deum* and *Benedictus* in Morning Prayer and the *Magnificat* and *Nunc Dimittis* in Evening Prayer are provided usually with anthem settings.

An anthem, furthermore, is considered almost obligatory in a cathedral after the third collect (although it was introduced as an option in 1662). The type of anthem sung in a cathedral is usually longer and more elaborate than those sung in parish churches. It is this series of weekday and Sunday musical duties in worship which maintains the cathedral tradition in England.[16]

Dearnley has pointed out with the utmost clarity and conviction that it was only when a sung Eucharist was placed at the centre of Sunday worship that there was any true incentive for composers to produce their greatest work. Previously, the Holy Communion, so far as music was concerned, was regarded as a mere appendix to Morning Prayer: indeed, it was called only the "Second Service" for most of the seventeenth century. Dearnley affirms that "A cropped little Sanctus threaded in between the Litany and Ante-Communion and matched by a bobbed Creed cannot stand comparison with the wonderful tapestry of the sixteenth century settings of the Mass adorning the Liturgy, and throwing into prominence its rich symbolism."[17] It was such a noble centre that had inspired the work of Byrd and Palestrina. Morning Prayer was a poor substitute, and it is greatly to the credit of English composers that they made good use of the devotional treasury of the Psalter and found there a variety of religious affirmations and moods on which to exercise their creative gifts.

If we consult the work of Edward Lowe, organist and choirmaster of Christ Church Cathedral, Oxford, at the Restoration, and

---

[16] Long, *op. cit.*, pp. 39-40.   [17] Dearnley, *op. cit.*, pp. 96-97.

of James Clifford, a minor canon of St. Paul's Cathedral, London, during the same period, we will obtain a good idea of the sacred music performed in cathedrals shortly after the Restoration.

Lowe's *Short Direction for the Performance of Cathedrall Service* (1661) shows that the task he set himself, possibly on account of the dislocation of cathedral music in Puritan days, was unambitious, to say the least. Morning Prayer began with a monotoned introduction and Responses, except that there was a four-part setting for festal use. The *Venite* followed and the Psalms for the day were sung antiphonally to one or two simple unison tunes, one for weekdays and the other for Sundays and festivals. Three four-part tunes were provided for the following canticles; namely, the *Te Deum* and *Benedictus* (or *Jubilate*) at Morning Prayer, and the *Magnificat* and *Nunc Dimittis* at Evening Prayer. Then the Apostles' Creed and Lord's Prayer were chanted in monotone. Unison responses followed and the choir sang "Amen" to each of the three succeeding collects.

Lowe's directions for the "Second Service" are hardly more inspiring. The celebrant begins the Lord's Prayer, reading it in a deep tone, and then the Decalogue in a higher tone, to which the choir responds similarly, unless they sing a setting with organ accompaniment. Prior to the Epistle the collects are read to which the choir sings "Amen." The Gospel follows, the choir singing, "Glory be to Thee, O Lord." Then the priest (or choir) says or sings the Nicene Creed, but as no music is provided, it is presumed to be a simple harmonised setting or a unison version. The account finishes inconclusively, leaving the reader to suppose that the choral part of the service ended before the Communion, or that the choir remained in position but was not used. It seems significant that mention is made of neither anthems nor Psalms.

James Clifford made good the latter deficiency in his *Divine Services and Anthems* (1663), which contained a collection of the words of anthems sung at St. Paul's Cathedral. The following year an enlarged second edition was issued. Lowe's very brief list of chanting tunes for Psalms and canticles is considerably augmented by Clifford who provides thirteen unison melodies and four harmonised chants in his preface. Also, the alternative canticles, *Benedicite* at Morning Prayer and *Cantate Domino* and *Deus misereatur* at Evening Prayer are included by Clifford. Interestingly, he informs us that an organ voluntary followed the Psalms at both Morning and Evening Prayer, and that another was played after the Litany and before the "Second, or Communion Service." As for anthems, two were sung in the morning (one after the third collect, and the other after the sermon), while in the evening there were two anthems in exactly parallel positions. St. Paul's appears to have had no psalmody at all.

It is noteworthy that neither Lowe nor Clifford refers to either a *Sanctus* or a *Gloria* being sung. One can only suppose that the earlier practice of restricting the Communion music to settings of the Creed and the Responses to the Decalogue continued after the Restoration at least for a few years. It was not long before a place (though not the correct one) was found for both of these Eucharistic hymns. The *Sanctus* became a kind of introit to the Communion Service, taking the place of the organ voluntary, while the *Gloria* acted as an anthem concluding the choral part of the service.

A complete choral Eucharist was celebrated in many churches only on "Sacrament Sundays," which were sometimes limited to four times a year. Even churches that celebrated weekly had a choral Communion only once a month.

2. *The Masters of Cathedral Music: Gibbons, Purcell, Blow*

Despite the liturgical limitations under which the English composers worked, their achievements were highly competent and, in several cases, notably those of Gibbons, Purcell, and Blow, even distinguished and brilliant. For this accomplishment—as it affects Purcell and Blow—some credit must be given to King Charles II for his encouragement and for the high standard of music set by the Chapel Royal. The Restoration led to a reaction against austerity, drabness, and propriety in both life and music; instead there was a demand for pomp and circumstance, for pleasure and mirth. The services in the Chapel Royal were musically superb, drawing the most talented composers, organists, and singers in the nation. They were attended by the famous, the fashionable, and the cultured. They were audiences rather than congregations, who were attracted by the new instrumental music, as by the excitingly brilliant solos demanding vocal pyrotechnics from their favourite singers, and sacred programme music in which words and actions were illustrated and imitated by the music—a theatrical gift in which Purcell in particular excelled. The Chapel Royal choir included thirty-three gentlemen singers, twelve children, and three organists. The men of the Chapel Royal were England's nearest equivalent to Italy's opera stars, delighted to display their vocal gymnastics in florid solos.

The most popular development encouraged by the Chapel Royal was the verse anthem with strings. The older contrapuntal and polyphonic music now gave way to an air supported by a single bass part, its brilliant effects created by contrasting the soloist with the choral ensemble, while the stringed instruments played a dramatically independent role which added cohesion, contrast, and colour. Following the example of Louis XIV, King of France with his "vingt-quatre violons du roi," Charles II gave his twenty-four violins (strictly, violins, violas, and cellos) the additional responsibility of taking part in the services of the Chapel Royal. The string band improved the interest in the verse anthems by its symphonies and *ritornelli*. Pepys heard the new combination of strings and voices on September 14, 1662. His report was: "This first day having vialls and other instruments to play a symphony between every verse of the anthem." On December 21, 1662, that other diarist of fame, John Evelyn, attended the Chapel Royal and noted: "Instead of the ancient grave and solemn wind musique accompanying the organ, was introduced a Consort of 24 Violins between every pause after the *French* fantastical light way, better suiting a Tavern or Play-house than a Church. This was the first time of change, and now we have no more heard the cornet which gave life to the organ, that instrument quite left off in which the English were so skilful." But innovative as was the use of stringed instruments, even more significant was the use of the solo song, foreshadowed in Gibbons, but used fully as recitative by Purcell.

Orlando Gibbons (1583-1623), despite his short life, was organist of the Chapel Royal and also of Westminster Abbey. Part of his genius was that, along with Byrd, he anticipated later developments in music. In his dramatic and declamatory style of composing Gibbons is seen not only as at the climax of Renaissance music but also as a forerunner of the Baroque style, "prospecting a new path which is to lead to Blow, Pelham Humfrey and Purcell."[18] His unusual theatrical quality can be heard to advantage in the full anthem, *Hosanna to the Son of David*, especially if this setting is compared with that of Thomas Weelkes. The latter makes all his voices together shout "Hosanna" twice in massive clarity, thus implying that the curious in the crowd had turned to

18 *Tudor Church Music*, Vol. IV: *Orlando Gibbons* (eds. Buck, Fellowes, Ramsbotham and Townsend Warner, 1925), p. xxii.

worship the Messiah. Orlando Gibbons, in contrast, suggests all the excitement of a jostling, hurrying crowd, with their individual acclamations tossed backward and forward as they press to see Jesus, and quieted momentarily by the vision of eternal peace. Weelkes suggests united worship, but Purcell mounting excitement. Gibbons is humanistic as Purcell after him. Neither is a contemplative, preoccupied with mystical adoration, or even with dogma or liturgy. They exploit human situations and emotions, especially when these are expressed in action.

Of Gibbons's forty anthems (two-thirds are verse anthems), his *Lift up your heads and O clap your hands*, together with the previously mentioned *Hosanna* are among his most impressive works. His tenderness is finely exhibited in *Behold Thou hast made my days*, which was written for Dean Maxie of Windsor in 1618 when he knew that he was dying. It requires a counter-tenor soloist and a five-part choir. More impressive still is the anthem, *See, See, the Word Incarnate*, the lengthy text of which covers the birth, ministry, crucifixion, and resurrection of Christ, and is a *tour de force* of surging and driving music. His short Morning and Evening Services have never lost their popularity.

The other master composer was Henry Purcell (1659-1695), whose life was even shorter than that of Gibbons. Like his father and uncle he had been a chorister in the Chapel Royal under the direction of the masterful Captain Cooke. He studied under Blow, whom he followed when only twenty as organist of Westminster Abbey, and in 1687 he also became one of the three organists of the Chapel Royal.

Purcell's anthems are of three types.[19] The first group is composed in the older style and may be sung without accompaniment. Two admirable examples are: *Hear my prayer* and *Remember not, Lord, our offences*. A second category comprises those with an organ accompaniment. A third type of verse anthem was written for string accompaniment with symphonies and *ritornelli*. This class includes Purcell's most impressive work, yet most of these anthems are excluded from a cathedral repertoire because of their length, the special occasions for which they were written, the need for extraordinarily well-trained voices of great range, and because no organ can adequately substitute for strings. Yet these full ceremonial anthems with solo voices, trios, and quartets, with sections

[19] The classification is that of Edmund Fellowes, *English Cathedral Music* (5th rev. edn. by J. A. Westrup, 1969), p. 163.

for full choir, and intervals for strings, provide Purcell with his greatest opportunities and which his talent took to the full.

The largest, most impressive, and most important of all Purcell's verse anthems is *My heart is inditing*, which was written for the coronation of James II on April 23, 1685, and required eight verse soloists, an eight-part choir, and strings—providing the latter with an overture lengthy enough to stand as a separate work. The polyphonic chorus leads into a brilliant Allelujah coda and united shouts of acclamation. It was as dramatic and colourful as the occasion for which it was composed.

Another splendidly resounding anthem of Purcell's is his *Blow up the trumpet in Sion*. His most moving anthem is *Thou knowest, Lord, the secrets of our hearts*, which was written for the funeral of Queen Mary in 1695.

A less famous anthem, *Praise the Lord, O my soul*, will be analysed to show how elaborate verse anthems had grown since the Restoration. It has a dozen separate sections. The first is an orchestral overture beginning in common time and then becoming faster. The second section has six-part verses for *Praise the Lord* (with high voices responding to the low voices, and then all together). The third section is an orchestral interlude. The fourth is another six-part verse, starting as if it repeated the second section. The fifth section is another orchestral interlude. The sixth section is a slow verse trio: *The Lord is full of compassion and mercy*. The seventh section is a tenor solo: *He hath not dealt with us*. The eighth is a *ritornello*, repeating the second section of the overtures. Section nine is a bass recitative: *For look how high the heaven is*. The tenth section is a six-part verse, *O speak good of the Lord*, with the high voices answered by the low voices, and then all together. The eleventh section is another *ritornello*, deriving from the fifth section. The twelfth and final section is the full chorus singing, *Praise thou the Lord*. Such anthems could take as long as twenty minutes to perform.

Purcell's genius is found in the variety and quality of his music (he wrote more secular than sacred music), his ability to rise to a great ceremonial occasion, his brilliance of matching accompaniment to dramatic words,[20] and the over-all inventiveness of his effects.

For more mystical or meditative music (and less theatrical bril-

---

[20] For examples, the music to "the singing of birds" and "the voice of the turtle" in Purcell's *My beloved spake*.

liance) one would have to turn to the compositions of John Blow (1649-1708), most of whose work was sacred music. A prodigy,[21] at nineteen he was appointed organist of Westminster Abbey, after being a chorister in the Chapel Royal of which he became Master of the Children in 1674. About three years later he also became one of the three organists of the Chapel Royal, and in 1687 he also became Master of the Children at St. Paul's Cathedral. In 1695, on Purcell's death, he succeeded his pupil, becoming again the organist of Westminster Abbey. He was easily the most experienced organist and choir-master of his century.

This prolific, but unequal, composer produced nine complete services, eleven Latin motets, and ninety-six English anthems (twenty-eight with orchestral symphonies), and several settings of canticles.

He is inevitably compared with his contemporary Purcell, and few can stand the comparison as well as he. Certainly his contribution to James II's coronation service, *God spake sometimes in visions*, is a noble parallel to Purcell's *My heart is inditing*, composed for the same occasion. Each represents the acme of English Baroque sacred music.

Blow's outstanding gift was the ability to provide settings expressive of sadness, tenderness, penitence, nobility, resolution, and desperate grief. *O Lord, I have sinned*, an anthem prepared for General Monck's funeral in 1670 is outstanding in its evocation of sympathy. He is, however, not as successful in expressing gratitude, jubilation, or contentment.

Yet he is equalled only by Byrd in his poignant and mystical empathy with Christ's sufferings as in his *My God, my God, look on me*, which plumbs the depths of the Saviour's cry of dereliction insofar as a human can, and which expresses the quintessence of pity. It is one of the most moving anthems in the English language.

Other full anthems of great power are his eight-part works, notably *God is our hope and strength* and *O Lord God of my salvation*. Their rich concentrated contrapuntal harmonies are as subtle as the iridescence on a butterfly's wing caught in a shaft of sunlight, but as powerful in thrust as a lion. His Latin anthems also are inspiring. The five-part setting of *Salvator Mundi* is gloriously sonorous. It reaches perfection in a passage of ethereal beauty, *auxiliare nobis*, pleading humanity's desperate need of God's power

[21] Three of his compositions were included in Clifford's collection of 1663, when he was only fourteen years of age.

and holiness, following the choir's singing of *qui per crucem et sanguinem redemisti nos*. At such points Blow's mysticism becomes luminous.

This necessarily sketchy account of three great composers has at least shown the extraordinary riches in sacred music available to the English cathedrals in the seventeenth century. Admittedly, we have concentrated on the Chapel Royal at Whitehall, Westminster Abbey, and St. Paul's Cathedral. But we may assume that the cathedral tradition at Salisbury was well maintained or George Herbert would not have walked twice a week from Bemerton to attend worship there. Wise, its organist and choir-master, was paid an unconscious tribute when Herbert averred that the time he spent in prayer and at cathedral music elevated his soul and was his heaven upon earth. Lichfield Cathedral choir, too, had almost as high a reputation after the Restoration.

The real musical importance of verse anthems in cathedral music, however, was the opportunity it gave for full expression to the evolving musical style of the seventeenth century. This has been defined with great clarity by Christopher Dearnley as "the departure from many-voiced music to an air supported by a single bass part, from a continuous interweaving to the clear-cut definition of sections with cadence and modulation, and from the inner intensity of polyphony to the dramatic contrasts obtainable from the juxtaposition of various combinations of solo and ensemble."[22] An exclusive dependence upon metrical psalmody's music would have been a narrow groove indeed, if not a grave.

It is difficult to understand how cultured Puritans, many of whom were music-lovers, could have jettisoned this rich tradition of sacred music unless they were convinced that the Word of God refused to countenance it.

Already we have seen that cathedral music violated by its obscurity and its complexity two strong tenets of the Reformed faith, those of edification and the priesthood of all believers. We have yet to realise the importance of the alternative, sung with such gusto by the Puritans, Scriptural paraphrases in metre and rhyme.

3. *The Attractions of Metrical Psalmody*

Superficially, to choose metrical Psalms as a musical diet in preference to verse anthems seems like selecting Shakespeare's "remainder biscuit" after the voyage in lieu of a five-course dinner.

---

[22] Dearnley, *op. cit.*, p. 41.

Yet there were attractions in this rhymed psalmody more than met the ear.

In trying to evaluate it, one must not make the mistake of considering it only as poetry. The awkward inversions of style, the doggerel to which it often descended, the largely unvarying boredom of the predictable stresses of common metre, the obvious diction and the forced rhymes, only mask the secret of its attraction, which is almost exclusively theological in character. The Puritans and many of the common folk of England who were not Puritans loved them because they were *God's own Word at one slight remove*.

Foxe's *Book of Martyrs* kept the English Bible before the imagination of the English people as a volume sanctified by the blood of the English Protestant martyrs, and reminded them that England continued an independent nation only because it had broken the thralldom of Rome after Queen Mary's death and had defeated the Catholic Spanish Armada. The Bible and the Protestant succession on the throne were intimately interrelated so that the Bible was in a peculiar sense the Book of England's destiny, quite apart from its intrinsic religious merits.[23]

This popularity of the Bible was greatly increased by the Scriptural exclusiveness of the Puritan movement from 1570 to its apex in the years following 1643, when all traditions in church and state were tested by the Biblical rule, and only Scripture was allowed in divine service as the vehicle of praise.

Furthermore, during the struggle with the Cavaliers the Roundheads, who were Puritans, adopted many metrical Psalms as their battle-songs.[24] These Old Testament thought-forms suited them admirably, with faith hammered out on the anvil of difficulty, the unyielding controversy with God's enemies, the sacred invective and vivid vituperation, and in the glare of the Psalms they saw themselves as the elect army fighting under the banner of Christ the King and Son of David against King Charles. Psalmody was the song of wrath and war.

The most renowned stories associated with the metrical Psalms are not about those revered today, such as Psalms 23 and 84; rather they concern the fighting Psalms such as Psalms 68, 74,

23 This theme is carefully worked out in William Haller's *Foxe's Book of Martyrs and the Elect Nation* (New York, 1963).

24 Erik Routley in *Hymns and Human Life* (1952), p. 59, writes: ". . . there was the more primitive and human fact that the Puritanism of seventeenth century England found in the Psalter just what it wanted."

269

and 124.[25] The most famous story of all concerns Psalm 117. Cromwell's force of 11,000 men defeated Leslie's army of 23,000 at Dunbar. The Ironsides surprised the Scottish army at five in the morning in the pale gleam of the moonlight, and Cromwell's cavalry and infantry shouted their watchword, "The Lord of Hosts." A complete rout followed as the Scottish horsemen broke and fled, crushing the undisciplined thousands of infantry behind them. The pursuit of the fugitives continued for eight miles until Cromwell halted and ordered his men to sing Psalm 117. "It was but a brief respite. Practical in his religion as in all else, Cromwell chose the shortest psalm in the book."[26]

One could well believe that the Psalms were the iron-rations of Cromwell's Ironsides, so thoroughly was their chief commander's thought and vocabulary nourished on them. R. E. Prothero rightly observed that the spirit of the Psalms governed him in supreme crises, that he cited from them at the most dramatic stages of his career, while in his public despatches and private letters, as in his speeches before Parliament, he made their phraseology entirely his own.[27]

It is exceedingly difficult for us to imagine how almost universal the use of the psalter was. Psalms were sung at the Lord Mayor's feasts at city banquets; soldiers sang them on the march or beside camp fires; ploughmen and carters whistled or sang them at their tasks; and pilgrims sought a new continent in which to gain liberty to sing only the Psalms. Far from being the songs of the sour-faced, they were sung by ladies and their lovers.

The translation of the Psalms into the vernacular is not to be attributed to Calvin, but to Clément Marot, the court poet of Francis I. He began by translating Psalm 6 into French verse in 1533; seven years later his translation of the Psalms were highly popular throughout the French court, and by 1554, the year of Marot's death, he had fifty metrical Psalms to his name. The enthusiasm for the rhymed Psalms is finely depicted by Prothero, who writes:

> When Marot's Psalms first appeared they were sung to popular tunes alike by Roman Catholics and Calvinists. No one delighted in the *sanctes chansonettes* more passionately than the Dauphin. He sang them himself. . . . To win his favour the gentlemen of the court begged him to choose for

25 See R. E. Prothero (Lord Ernle), *The Psalms in Human Life* (1903), pp. 194-95 and 134, for stories about the 68th and 124th metrical psalms.
26 *Ibid.*, p. 194.   27 *Ibid.*, p. 189.

270

each a Psalm. Courtiers adopted their special Psalms, just as they adopted their particular arms, mottoes, and liveries.[28]

It was to Calvin's credit that he moved these metrical Psalms from their secular milieu into the worship of the French Reformed church in Strasbourg. While they were as yet unpublished, he introduced twelve of them into his first psalter, the *Aucun Pseaumes et Cantiques mys en Chant* (1539). These were popularised in English translation by William Whittingham, a refugee in Geneva from the Marian persecution and future Dean of Durham, in the Anglo-Genevan Psalter of 1556. Their popularity was assured when they were matched with popular, catchy tunes known as "Genevan jigs," though the Genevan tunes of Bourgeois were joyously solemn.

Proponents of the metrical Psalms encouraged Psalm-singing in the hope that they would drive out bawdy ballads. The preface to the 1562 edition of the Old Version states that it was intended "to be used of all sorts of people privately for their solace and comfort: laying apart all ungodly songs and ballads which tend only to the nourishing of vice and corrupting of youth." Nor was the devil to have all the best tunes!

The relevance of the metrical Psalms to seventeenth-century Puritanism may perhaps best be appreciated if we consider, following Sir John Hawkins's suggestion,[29] the treatise which they prefixed to their earliest impressions of the metrical Psalms and which was attributed to St. Athanasius. The following citations from it should indicate how apt it seemed to the circumstances of the fighting and God-fearing Roundheads:

> If thou seest that evill men lay snares for thee, and therefore desirest God's eares to heare thy praiers, sing the 5 psalme.
>
> If thine enemies cluster against thee, and go about with their bloody hand to destroy thee, go not thou about by man's helpe to revenge it, for al men's judgments are not trustie, but require God to be judge, for he alone is judge, and say the 26, 35, 43 psalmes.
>
> If they press more fiercelie on thee, although they be in numbers like an armed hoast, fear them not which thus reject

---

[28] *Ibid.*, p. 51.
[29] In his *General History of Music* (1776), Chap. CXVI.

thee, as though thou wert not annointed and elect by God, but sing the 27 psalme.

If they yet be so impudent that they lay in wait against thee, so that it is not lawful for thee to have any vocation by them, regard them not, but sing to God the 48 psalme.

If thou hast suffered false accusation before the King, and seeest the Divel to triumph therat, go aside and say the 50 psalme.

The Psalms were the creeds and battle-songs of the Puritans. In them they found a supernatural sanction for their conduct and comfort in perplexity and danger. Through them *Vox Dei* became *vox populi*, which was both solace and a spiritual danger.

One might readily assume that because of their closeness to sacred Scripture all Christians in this century would have welcomed metrical psalmody, whatever their reservations about verse anthems and orchestral interludes. Yet, despite all the attractions of the metrical Psalms, there were others, even among the dissenting religious groups, who utterly refused to use them, and for a variety of reasons.

The General Baptists, in this true to the tradition of their pioneer, John Smyth,[30] in rejecting all set forms in worship as a quenching of the Spirit, also rejected metrical psalmody. On this view the only acceptable spiritual songs in divine worship were charismatic solos. Thomas Grantham, their leader, certainly held this as his conviction. In his *Christianismus Primitivus* (1678) he rejected "musical singing with a multitude of voices in rhyme and metre," while approving that "such persons as God has gifted to tell forth his mighty acts . . . should have liberty and convenient opportunity to celebrate the high praises of God one by one in the churches of God, and that with such words as the nature of the matter and present occasion requires. . . ."[31] The controversy was still acute in 1689, for the General Assembly decided after thorough discussion that year that "it was not deemed any way safe for the churches to admit such carnal formalities [as metrical psalms sung in unison] . . . the singing of one was the same as the

---

[30] See John Smyth, *The Differences of the Churches of the Separation* (1605), p. v: "singinging [*sic*] a psalme is a parte of spirituall worship therefore it is unlawfull to have the booke before the eye in time of singinge a psalme."

[31] Cited by Spencer Curwen, *Studies in Music and Worship*, 5 Vols. (1880-1885), I, p. 95.

singing of the whole, as the prayers of the one are the prayers of the whole congregation."[32]

A closely related group, the Seventh Day Baptists, held similar views. Francis Bampfield, formerly a Prebendary of Exeter, became a Sabbatarian pastor. He claimed to have had a vision of Christ which "raised him into a higher way of Latter-Day-Glory-hymnifying, than his former way of singing by Mens Forms, read out of a Book, could reach unto."[33]

So strong was the conviction that all set forms, whether of prayers like the Book of Common Prayer, or of sermons like the Anglican Books of Homilies, or of praise like the metrical Psalms, were contrary to the ineluctable leading of the Spirit, that the early Independents in the Westminster Assembly scrupled a metrical psalter. Baillie, one of the Church of Scotland Commissioners and a hammer of sectaries, reports the views of Philip Nye, the leader of the small Independent group: "Mr. Nye spoke much against a tie to any Psalter and somewhat against the singing of paraphrases, as of preaching homilies; we *understand* will mightily oppose it; for the Psalter is a great part of our conformity which we cannot let pass until our church be well advised with it."[34] It was, however, a scruple which the Independents quickly overcame, and metrical psalmody in New England, according to the report of John Cotton, was one of their most valued ordinances: "Before Sermon, and many times after, wee sing a Psalme."[35]

Another argument against metrical psalmody used by the stricter sects was its unsuitability for a mixed or promiscuous congregation. The Psalms were the songs of God's covenanted people, the elect, and they were misused if sung by the unregenerate. The children of Israel had lamented in their Babylonian Captivity, "How shall we sing the Lord's song in a strange land?" True Christians were similarly putting themselves into the captivity of the ungodly by singing Scriptural songs with them.

Yet another negative criticism of the metrical Psalms and a powerful one was that God's Word was changed in meaning, however slight, when it was put through the straitjacket of rhyme and

[32] *Minutes of the General Assembly of the General Baptists, 1654-1728* (ed. W. T. Whitley, 1909), p. 27.

[33] *A name, an after-one; or* Ὄνομα καινοῦ, *a name, a new one, in the latter-day glory* (1681), p. 4.

[34] Benjamin Hanbury, *Nonconformist Memorials*, 3 Vols. (1839-1844), II, p. 225.

[35] *The Way of the Churches of Christ in New England* (1645), p. 66.

metre. Even when the non-Biblical words were little more than conjunctions, and were italicized to draw attention to the least departure from Holy Scripture, the fact remained that the words of the Word of God were no longer inalterably sacrosanct.

The argument of guilt by association was also used. The Roman Catholics by their antiphonal recitation of the Latin Psalms in their Daily Office in monasteries, the Anglicans by the chanting of prose Psalms in their cathedrals and their responsive recitation in parish churches,[36] both used and misused psalmody in worship. Therefore the sectarians avoided contamination by refusing to use them in worship.

During the days of persecution for the heirs of the Puritans, when they worshipped in secret conventicles, it became dangerous to sing Psalms as they might disclose their whereabouts to informers trying to trap them with the Conventicle Act. The latter held Nonconformists were forbidden to hold meetings at which more than five persons were present. At a conventicle gathered in St. Thomas's parish, Southwark, it was recorded: "1692. April 1st. We met at Mr. Russell's in Ironmonger Lane, where Mr. Lambert of Deadman's Place, Southwark, administered to us the ordinance of the Lord's Supper, and we sang a psalm in a low voice."[37] The view that it was dangerous to sing Psalms in penal times can, however, be questioned. If the conventiclers in Southwark sang in a low voice not to give the alarm, the Broadmead Baptists in Bristol sang Psalms to imply that they were a convivial group rather than a congregation at worship. It was prearranged that when intruders came in "we were singing, that they could not find anyone preaching, but all singing."[38]

A summary of these objections to metrical psalmody is provided by that arch-conservative Baptist author, Isaac Marlow, in his ominously entitled book, *Prelimiting Forms of praising God*,

[36] It should be noted, however, that while in the Prayer Book there was substituted a vernacular prose translation for the Vulgate Psalms, an extra-liturgical custom developed whereby a metrical psalm was sung before and after the prescribed order of worship. This appears to have obtained temporary official sanction early in Elizabeth's reign, and may have been due to the influence of the returning Marian exiles. The Elizabethan Injunctions to the clergy in 1559 directed: "For the comforting of such as delight in music, it may be permitted that at the beginning or end of Common Prayer, either at Morning or Evening, there may be sung a hymn or such like song to the praise of Almighty God, in the best melody and music that may be devised, having respect that the sentence of the hymn be understood and perceived."

[37] Spencer Curwen, *op. cit.*, I, p. 84.

[38] *Broadmead Records* (ed. E. B. Underhill, 1847), p. 226.

Vocally sung by all the Church together, Proved to be no Gospel-Ordinance (1691). He uses five main arguments to make his case. The first assumes that the essence of singing is the praise of God, but this is not necessarily "tunable." Secondly, women are prohibited from speaking in the assembly (I Corinthians 14:34-35), therefore promiscuous singing must be rejected. Thirdly, singing in the primitive church is no precedent for contemporary singing, since the former was made possible by the dispensation of an extraordinary gift limited to that era. Fourthly, unison singing demands precomposed forms, and these are as unwarrantable in singing as in praying. Fifthly and finally, there is no New Testament ground for believers to unite with unbelievers in singing God's praise.

Thus acute scrupulosity prevented many from using the songs of Sion, whether for Biblical, ecclesiological, or psychological reasons or excuses. The consequence was that it became necessary for defenders of the metrical psalms to provide dissuasives from such attitudes.

The apologists for metrical psalmody asked first: What is more suitable for God's praise than God's own Word? Indeed, not to use the Psalms and to prefer human compositions is an insult to the Divine Majesty as well as a denial of original sin. As David had been inspired by the Holy Ghost to compose his Psalms, we can rest assured of their acceptance with God. Furthermore, there is psalmody and hymnody in the New Testament and therefore for the people of the New Covenant.

In favour of metrical psalmody it was also argued that its simplicity in common metre made it accessible to God's people in the way that anthems were not. Hence William Whittingham issued the first Sternhold and Hopkins metrical Psalter with music in Geneva, along with *The Forme of Prayers . . . used in the English congregation at Geneva; and approved by the famous and godly learned man, John Calvyn* (1556). The preface denounces elaborate or obscure church music, and, by implication defends the metrical psalter it introduces:

> But as there is no gift of God so precious or excellent that Satan hath not after a sort drawn to himself and corrupt[ed]: so hath he most impudently abused this notable gift of singing, chiefly by the papists, his ministers, in disfiguring it, partly by strange language that cannot edify, and partly by a

curious wanton sort, hiring men to tickle the ears and flatter the fantasies, not esteeming it as a gift approved by the Word of God, profitable for the church, and confirmed by all antiquity. . . .

In conformity with this view the tunes were unharmonised and the underlay was carefully syllabic.

It was also argued that the putting of the Psalms into metre and rhyme made them much more easily memorised by the common people. This was particularly important when many folk were still illiterate. But there was the objection that metre and rhyme significantly altered the wording of the Psalms. This was countered by the ingenious but valid argument that the originals were Hebrew poetry and that it is better translation to turn them into poetry than to leave them as prose.

As for the arguments that Marlow had prepared, that a precomposed form invalidated worship, that Paul commanded women to silence in worship, and that God's praise ought not to be sung by a congregation including the unregenerate, it is significant that Benjamin Keach, pioneer Baptist hymnodist, disposed of them rapidly.[39] He saw no more reason to exclude a precomposed metrical Psalm than a precomposed sermon, and was convinced that he had the assistance of the Holy Spirit in each. If the silence of women in worship were to be absolute, how could they then give an account of their conversion before the church and be admitted to membership? He cites two passages in I Corinthians 14, where the apostle speaks of unbelievers entering the church, and argues that praise as well as preaching can instruct such in the ways of God.

Ultimately, the powerful Genevan tradition of metrical psalmody overcame any initial scruples on the part of the Puritan Independents. The Presbyterian Puritans were never in any doubt as to their value. It was not long before the Puritans were known as "the Psalm-roaring Saints." The duty of Psalm-singing was canonised in the Westminster *Directory* for both public and private worship. It encouraged psalmody strongly as unison singing and so apt for congregations, contrasted with the elaboration of anthems to be sung only by expert musicians, and it was recommended as Scriptural and non-traditional. The *Directory* urged: "It is the duty of

[39] In *The Breach Repair'd in God's Worship* (1691), a landmark in the history of English hymnody.

Christians to praise God publickly by singing of psalms together in the congregation, and privately in the family. In singing of psalms the voice is to be tunably and gravely ordered, but the chief care must be to sing with understanding and with grace in the heart, making melody unto the Lord."[40]

4. *The Metrical Versions and Their Tunes*

Many interesting poetical versions of the Psalms were published during the seventeenth century but almost all, Milton's excepted, were because of obscure language or metrical subtlety unsuitable for common praise. Partial translations of the Psalms were written by George Herbert (1632), John Donne (1633), Phineas Fletcher (1633), and Richard Crashaw (1634). Bishop Hall translated the first ten with an easy naturalness (1607), and Lord Bacon translated a few (1625). A version, with considerable poetical grace, set to the music of Henry Lawes, was that of George Sandys (1636), son of an Archbishop of York.

John Milton translated Psalms 80 to 88 in 1648 directly from the Hebrew. There could be no finer illustration of Puritanism's concern to preserve the exact meaning of the oracles of God than this, for the Hebrew words are printed in the margin, and every word not in the original is printed in italics. In addition to exactness, these versions have the sonority and syntactical subtlety that were Milton's gifts. Three of his paraphrases are the exception in outliving the generation for which they were written. They comprise: his work as a fifteen-year-old, "Let us with a gladsome mind" (Psalm 136) written in 1623; "How lovely are thy dwellings fair" (Psalm 84) and "The Lord will come and not be slow" (a paraphrase of selections from Psalms 82, 85, and 86), both published in 1648.

Other distinctively Puritan versions were the complete and rival metrical psalmodies of Rous and Barton, and the important Scottish Psalter (1650). The last mentioned provided the justly celebrated version of Psalm 23, "The Lord's my shepherd." Francis Rous's Psalter of 1641 was an attempt to meet the request of the Committee of Peers in their Report on Religion of 1640 that "the meeter in the Psalms should be corrected and allowed of publicly." Thus it was an attempt to improve on Sternhold and Hopkins, the "Old Version." A second edition was ordered to be printed by the

[40] *Reliquiae Liturgicae*: Vol. III: *The Parliamentary Directory* (ed. Peter Hall, Bath, 1847), p. 81.

House of Commons in 1643. The Westminster *Directory* (1644) required that each literate person should have a Psalm book and Rous's third edition was ordered to be printed by the Westminster Assembly of Divines, of which Rous was a lay member. He was also a Member of Parliament and Speaker of the House of Commons. The Scottish Commissioners, however, suspected him of heterodoxy and thought him too much in Cromwell's pocket to approve of his version, while they wanted their own version. The House of Lords preferred the version of Rous's rival, William Barton, minister of St. Martin's, Leicester, who had produced first and second editions of his Psalter in 1644 and 1645. The Lords submitted his revised edition of 1646 to the Westminster Assembly but it was rejected by them. The Assembly equally refused to sanction exclusively the choice of the Commons, namely Rous's version. Sternhold and Hopkins inevitably continued to reign supreme, its popularity untouched by the post-Restoration attempts at metrical psalmody made by Richard Baxter, Sir John Denham, and John Patrick.

The popularity of the Old Version was quite remarkable.[41] It lasted for 147 years. Sternhold's Psalter was first published in 1549. Sternhold and Hopkins was first published with music, as we have seen, in 1556 in Geneva by William Whittingham, which encouraged a great sale for it among Puritan households. By 1561 the Old Version became the standard English metrical Psalter. The rapid proliferation of editions underlined its popularity. Between 1560 and 1579 there were at least 20 editions; between 1580 and 1600 the number had grown to 45 editions; between 1600 and 1620 it had increased to 65 editions; and between 1620 and 1640 over 100 appeared.

It was abundantly clear that Psalm-singing with the aid of the easily memorised stanzas of Sternhold and Hopkins was regarded as the most divine part of divine service. Heylin reported that "the reading of psalms with the first and second lessons being heard in many places with a covered head, but all men sitting bare-headed when the psalm was sung."[42]

The poor quality of the poetry makes it extremely difficult to account for the popularity of Sternhold and Hopkins. Certainly there was little variety in metre or tune. Of the 150 Psalms 134

---

[41] Peter Le Huray, *Music and the Reformation in England, 1549-1660* (1967), p. 376.
[42] Cited by John Julian, *A Dictionary of Hymnology* (rev. edn., 1925), p. 864b.

were in common metre, which has a predictable jog-trot about it. The tunes were generally dull and only 47 of the Psalms had a tune of their own. The contorted, labouring, halting, and dreary monotony of the verses fully justified Fuller's criticism of them that "their piety was better than their poetry; they had drank more of Jordan than of Helicon."[43] Probably the inherent weakness of this and other versions in the same century was, as Baxter said in the preface to his own version, due to the fact that "the ear desireth greater melody than strict versions will allow."[44] Exact fidelity to the original ruled out almost all hymnody in this period; it also practically destroyed the freedom desirable within the bonds of metrical psalmody to permit poetry to be written rather than mere verse. For the illiterate or those with a poor memory these religious jingles filled a useful function, and this must be the most important single factor accounting for their success among the commonalty.

Some attempts, however, were made to provide a greater variety of tunes, but most were too elaborate to be accepted by the majority of people. Robert Tailour prepared complicated five-part settings in the contrapuntal style of Tudor anthems in 1615, and John Cosin had composed a five-part harmonised metrical psalter in 1585. It was, however, Thomas Ravenscroft with his *Whole Booke of Psalmes* (1621) with harmonised settings, who successfully provided additional new, simple, and therefore acceptable tunes.

The dreariness of metrical psalmody was compounded by the practice of "lining-out." That is, each line of the words of a metrical Psalm was first read or intoned by the minister, precentor, or clerk, then in turn taken up and sung by the congregation.[45] This meant each Psalm took twice as long and, since it was thought to be reverent by proceeding at a funereal pace, the psalmody must sometimes have seemed as tiring as an unending road. The disadvantage of the lining-out system was that the congregation concentrated so fully on what was going to be sung that they forgot what they had sung; also the sense often spilled over from one line

---

[43] Thomas Fuller, *The Church History of Britain* (1655), Vol. IV, p. 73.
[44] Julian, *op. cit.*, p. 919a.
[45] The *Directory* prescribed lining-out as a hopefully interim measure in 1645: "That the whole congregation may join herein, every one that can read is to have a Psalm-book; and all others not disabled by age or otherwise, are to be exhorted to learn to read. But for the present, where many of the congregation cannot read, it is convenient that the Minister, or some other fit person appointed by him and the other ruling officers, do read the Psalm line by line, before the singing thereof." (*Reliquiae Liturgicae*, ed. Peter Hall, III, p. 81.)

to the next. Furthermore, the clerk in the local parish church might have a defective sense of pitch and pace and rhythm. One suspects that the clerk who had served Buxted parish church for forty-three years received an obituary that might have been only too suitable for many others of his calling, "whose melody warbled forth as though he had been thumped in the back by a stone."[46]

In these circumstances it was to Ravenscroft's credit that he tried to introduce some variety in the singing of the psalter. His intriguing preface shows that his aim was to pick tunes appropriate to the character of each Psalm. He recommended singers to adopt the following rules:

1. "That psalms of tribulation should be sung with a low voice and long measure"—these included Psalms 6, 32, 38, 51, 102, 130, and 143.

2. "That psalms of thanksgiving be sung with a voice indifferent, neither too loud, nor too soft, and with a measure neither too swift nor too slow."

3. "That psalms of rejoicing be sung with a loud voice [and] a swift and jocund measure"—these included Psalms 33, 34, 47, 95, 96, 98, 99, 108, 113, 117, 135, 136, 145, 147, 148, and 150.[47]

The only other radical attempt to enliven the tunes of the Old Version was as desperate as it was disastrous. William Slatyer's *Psalmes or Songs of Sion turned into the language and set to the tunes of a strange land* (1635) was far too secular for those who admired sacred music, since he chose as settings for his Psalms the popular tunes of the day, such as "Goe from my window" for Psalms 8 and 11, and "Susan," "Sweet Robin," and "The Queen of Love" for others.[48] It was too much to hope that boudoir ballad tunes might be used to sing the praises of Calvin's august God.

In some quarters, however, Psalm-singing was not at all popular. Strictly speaking, it was illegal to mingle metrical psalmody with the Anglican liturgy in the seventeenth century, whatever Elizabethan Injunctions might have permitted. Its Genevan origins, its development into a Puritan badge of loyalty, and its intrusion into the Prayer Book services, produced frowns from the ecclesiastical hierarchy, such as Laud, Wren, and Cosin. Since,

46 Dearnley, *op. cit.*, p. 146.
47 Peter Le Huray, *op. cit.*, pp. 382-83.
48 *Ibid.*, pp. 383-84.

nonetheless, metrical psalmody had come to stay, it became necessary even for high churchmen to accommodate to it. In fact, while the Puritans and evangelical Anglicans preferred metrical psalmody sung to common metre tunes in unison, the high-church party preferred elaborate harmonised tunes such as Tailour's anthem-like settings, John Cosin's five-part settings, as well as the harmonised musicianship of Ravenscroft.[49]

Just beyond our period, in 1696, the monopoly of the Old Version came to an end, and it was replaced by Tate and Brady's *A New Version of the Psalms of David, Fitted to the Tunes used in Churches*. It appeared under the best auspices. It was sanctioned by the sovereign and recommended by the Archbishop of Canterbury and Compton, the Bishop of London. Its authors clearly wished it to be regarded as a substitute for the Sternhold and Hopkins psalter which had become increasingly disenchanting to the musical public.

It is not a distinguished publication, but it is smoother verse than the Old Version. Some of Sternhold and Hopkins was ruggedly robust and characterful in comparison with the frequent insipidity of Tate and Brady. On a few rare occasions the New Version rose to the occasion. Among those would have to be included their versions of Psalm 33 ("Through all the changing scenes of life"), Psalm 42 ("As pants the hart"), Psalm 51 ("Have mercy, Lord, on me"), and Psalm 84 ("Oh God of hosts, the mighty Lord") which have continued to appear in hymnbooks even in the twentieth century.

5. The Reluctant Birth of Hymnody

The more one studies the limitations of metrical psalmody, the sorrier one is that Protestant England did not follow the example of the Protestants of Luther's Germany in encouraging the writing and singing of hymns as freer transcripts of Christian faith and experience, without the bibliolatrous restrictions of metrical psalmody. In this matter, at least, the influence of Luther would have been better than the impact of Calvin.[50]

The reluctance of the English people to turn to hymnody can be explained by the very same factors that made psalmody so very popular. Such would include the power of the Bible in English which was regarded as the well-spring of national Reformation

49 K. R. Long, *op. cit.*, pp. 209-10.
50 See Charles Stanley Phillips, *Hymnody Past and Present* (1937), pp. 123-24.

and individual renovation of life; the fact that so much of the Bible consisted of songs and the rapturous praises of holy men and women; and, above all, the conviction that in using only the words of the Word of God men believed themselves to be secure from human error.

Despite the dominance of metrical psalmody in the seventeenth century, there were some notable exceptions to the rule. These were chiefly of two types. One was a handful of hymns written for private devotion. Such could be the free compositions of devout minds for the reading or singing of the few so inclined. One example would be Cosin's fine translation of *Veni Creator*, beginning, "Come, Holy Ghost, our souls inspire" which was to be found in his *Collection of Private Devotions* (1627), which eventually found a place in the Prayer Book of 1662. In 1623 the poet George Wither made a valiant attempt to produce and publish the first hymnbook of the Church of England entitled *Hymns and Songs of the Church*, with seven tunes contributed by Orlando Gibbons. His preface tells how he was invited by clergymen to collect and transmute into lyrical poetry the many hymns dispersed throughout the canonical Scriptures. To these he added "such parcels of Holy Writ, Creeds, and Songs" as he thought wise. Its importance is that it extended the material available for religious songs, for these included festal days, Holy Communion, and providential events in the life of the nation. He attributes its unpopularity to the attempt of the Stationers' Company to quash it, but the banality of some of its stanzas[51] might prove a complementary, if not an alternative explanation.

A second group of hymns consists of sacred poems that were written without any intention of their being used in public or private worship, but which later ages discovered as potential hymns. John Wesley,[52] for example, discovered George Herbert's and edited them unsparingly, but four of them are now popular hymns: "Let all the world in every corner sing"; "The God of love my shepherd is"; "Teach me my God and King" and "King of Glory."

[51] The following stanza from Song 13 is an example of his rendering of the First Canticle of the Song of Solomon:

> Oh, my love, how comely now,
> And how beautiful art thou!
> Thou of dove-like eyes a pair
> Shining hast within thy hair,
> And thy looks like kidlings be
> Which from Gilead hill we see.

[52] See Erik Routley, *Hymns and Human Life* (1952), p. 58.

Such modern editors as the Anglican Percy Dearmer[53] and the Free churchman Garrett Horder have also found hymns in the divine poems of the metaphysical poets, including Donne, Traherne, and Vaughan, and a recent edition of the Roman Catholic *Westminster Hymnal* includes hymns by Richard Crashaw.

Other notable hymns of the seventeenth century are Dean Samuel Crossman's "Jerusalem on high" and the delicate "My song is love unknown"; also Richard Baxter's noble hymn of faith as obedience and trust "Lord it belongs not to my care" and his seraphic song on the Communion of saints, "He wants not friends who hath thy love." During the last two decades of the century the saintly and prophetic Bishop Thomas Ken produced those masterpieces of devotion, his Morning Hymn ("Awake my soul and with the sun") and his Evening Hymn ("Glory to thee my God this night"). Both hymns end with the rhymed doxology, now famous throughout the English-speaking world, beginning, "Praise God from whom all blessings flow." It is a fitting monument to the piety and sensitive consciences of the Non-Juring divines.

The majority of these hymn-writers were clergy of the Church of England,[54] with the exception of the Roman Catholic priest, Crashaw. But what of the contribution of the Baptists or the Independents to hymnody? As we have seen, the General Baptists refused to use metrical psalmody, and therefore *a fortiori* hymnody. The Independents were, like the Presbyterians, deeply committed to metrical psalmody, and their pioneer hymnodist Isaac Watts only began to write in the last decade of the century while in his teens.[55] It was a Calvinistic or Particular Baptist minister, Benjamin Keach, who inaugurated Free church hymnody and in doing so demonstrated astonishing tact and patience in combatting entrenched religious prejudice against change, which the conservatives regarded as lusting after the garlic and onions of Egypt.

Apparently in 1673, Benjamin Keach, as minister of Horsleydown Baptist church in Southwark, persuaded his congregation to sing a hymn at the close of the celebration of the Lord's Supper in imitation of Christ and his disciples at the end of the Last Supper.

---

[53] For Dearmer's contributions to Anglican worship, see Davies, *op. cit.*, v, pp. 284f., and 110f.

[54] Yet they were very much in advance of their church, for the Church of England did not officially authorise hymns in worship until 1821. (See Routley, *op. cit.*, p. 8.)

[55] His first hymn was written to answer his father's challenge to prove he could compose something better than the current metrical psalmody. It was "Behold the glories of the Lamb," which was produced ca. 1695.

Later he extended the practice to days of thanksgivings and Baptisms, and, finally, to the regular Lord's Day worship. Writing directly to his own congregation in the preface to his *The Breach Repair'd in God's Worship* (1691) we can see what a patient gradualist he had been:

> 'Tis no small grief to me to see (since the Church in such a solemn manner agreed to sing the praises of God on the Lord's Day) to find some of you so offended; I am perswaded 'tis for want of Consideration, for you have no new thing brought in among you. Hath not the Church sung at breaking of bread always for 16 or 18 yeares last past, and could not nor would it omit it in the time of the late Persecution? . . . And have we not for this 12 or 14 years sung in *mixt Assemblies on Days of Thanksgiving*, and never any offended at it, as ever I heard?[56]

Keach composed his own hymns[57] and it is only fair to say that Baptists would rather their seventeenth-century contribution to hymnody was represented by John Bunyan's song, "Who would true valour see"[58] than by any composition of Keach's. His importance is solely that of a pioneer who points the way to the future, from Old Testament paraphrase to Christian hymnody. It will be the grand aim of Watts to cross Jordan to the promised land by the only possible path. As Watts put it himself: "In all places I have kept my grand design in view; and that is to teach my author [David] to speak like a Christian."[59]

Now that the end of the seventeenth century has been reached, it is possible to make out the various slow stages by which hym-

[56] *Op. cit.*, p. ix.
[57] A fairly typical example of Keach's pathetic doggerel is on the theme of repentance from his *Spiritual Melody* (1691), containing almost 300 hymns:

> Repentance like a bucket is
> To pump the water out;
> For leaky is our ship, alas,
> Which makes us look about. (p. 254)

The judgment of a twentieth century fellow Baptist, citing Blake's couplet, may stand for the quality of Keach's verse:

> The languid strings do scarcely move,
> The sound is forced, the notes are few.

(Adam A. Reed, "Benjamin Keach, 1640," *The Baptist Quarterly*, N. S., Vol. 10, 1940-1941, pp. 76f.)
[58] Written for Mr. Valiant-for-Truth in *Pilgrim's Progress*.
[59] *The Psalms of David imitated in the language of the New Testament and applied to the Christian State and Worship* (1719), in Burder's edn. of Watts' *Works* (1810), Vol. IV, p. 119.

nody was finally reached. They were five in all. First, there were translations of the Psalms into vernacular prose, which were recited or antiphonally chanted in the Book of Common Prayer. Next there came metrical psalmody. Thirdly, metrical versions were made of passages of the New Testament.[60] Then there was the combination and omission of different parts of New Testament paraphrases. Fifthly and finally, there was reached the hymnody of Christian faith and experience which blossomed gloriously in the early eighteenth century in Isaac Watts and in the middle eighteenth century in Charles Wesley.

Perhaps the most unpredictable issue and itself an ironic comment on the entire controversy examined in this chapter between tradition and Scripture, between intricate verse anthem and unison singing of metrical psalmody, and between high Anglican and Puritan protagonists, is that it was the heirs of the fiercest defenders of metrical psalmody who first introduced modern hymnody to their initially unwilling churches in England.

[60] Julian, *op. cit.*, pp. 345a-46b.

CHAPTER VIII

THE CHIEF SACRAMENT:
MEANS OF GRACE OR MNEMONIC?

AMONG THE major cultic controversies of the century, in addition to spirit versus form, and magnificence versus simplicity
in decor and also in praise, there was another debate. This
was: how is the chief Sacrament to be evaluated? To reduce the
complexity to a manageable issue—was the Sacrament, as most
Catholics and Anglicans believed, a means of grace, or, as many
Puritans affirmed, was it mainly a mnemonic? That is, did the sacraments act as channels of grace that fortified the Christian soul (as
bread and wine strengthen the body), or were they merely vivid
reminders of the Cross and Resurrection of Jesus Christ and the
benefits these events had brought to the faithful in the assurance
of forgiveness and the promise of eternal life?

If the former or high view of the sacraments as channels of
grace and healing is held, this high view will be described as a
doctrine of Transubstantiation by Catholics, as the "real presence"
by high Anglicans of the Andrewes-Laud-Cosin school of divines
(often accompanied with an unwillingness to define the modality
of the presence), and as "dynamic receptionism" by those Puritans
or their successors who maintain with Calvin that the Holy Spirit
"seals" to believers the benefits of Christ's Cross and Resurrection.
The lower doctrine is often described as "Memorialism" (and often
attributed to Zwingli, whether with truth is another matter).[1] If
the lower view of the Sacraments is held, then their function is to
be teaching aids and tender reminders of the Passion, Death, and
Resurrection of Christ, so that the costliness of these events is represented vividly to the conscience and compassion of the believer.
This doctrine often degenerates (though it need not) into a touching tribute to a heroic leader who died for the cause and is the
supreme martyr of Christianity. (Some Communion services of the
Dissenters have at times been so restricted to the commemoration
of the Passion and sacrificial death of Christ, without any suggestion of the liberation and joy of the Resurrection and Ascension,
that they gave precisely the impression of a defeated martyrdom.

[1] For the fullest recent treatment see F. Schmidt-Klausing, *Zwingli als Liturgiker*
(Göttingen, 1952).

The Free churches have occasionally forgotten that the Resurrection lies between the Last Supper and the First Eucharist.) The lower view of the chief sacrament frequently stresses that attendance at the Lord's Supper is a badge of the membership of the church, a kind of Christian loyalty test.

The two different theories of sacramental presence in fact lead to two very different practical sets of results. The higher view makes the altar central; the lower view gives precedence to the pulpit. The higher view appropriately demands greater splendour in the decoration and fittings of the church, for the altar becomes the throne of the presence of Christ and turns the church into the dwelling place of a king (a *basilica*, quite literally), a palace. Furthermore, the same view regards the Sacrament as virtually the extension of the Incarnation, and thus the hallowing of the five human senses, including the impressiveness of the eye-gate to the soul. This appropriately expresses the splendour of the Lord of glory. The lower view restricts the Sacrament to a didactic *aide-memoire* and reduces it to a mere abstraction, a mental construct, and such a view operates with less distraction in a plain, scrubbed meeting-house.

The high view of the Sacrament leads it to be celebrated frequently; the low view of the Sacrament is satisfied with a quarterly celebration such as Zwingli's in Zurich or those of the Scottish church.

This high view of the Sacrament expects it to be celebrated with pomp and circumstance in the ceremonial—marking out the altar by a sacred canopy or ciborium and raising it on steps above the sanctuary floor, veiling it in part by a balustrade or a wrought-iron screen, or beautifying it by frontals changing their colours with the liturgical seasons. The high-church view expects the Sacrament to be approached with deep obeisance—in crossings, genuflexions, kneelings, and prostrations. The low view of the Sacrament leads to its celebration with domestic simplicity, on a simple Communion table covered with a white cloth, and the gestures are simply standing or sitting about the table.

Finally, a high view of the Sacrament carries with it a high evaluation of the priesthood (often associating it with celibacy), a legitimation of it in the apostolical succession, and dressing up of the minister in special Eucharistic vestments such as the chasuble, alb, and cope. Such a high view of the priesthood and the Sacrament is often associated with a profound loyalty to the traditions of

belief and practice of the church of the Fathers of the first centuries. The lower view of the Sacrament, on the other hand, is content to regard the presiding minister as first a prophet expounding
the divine Word and only subordinately a dispenser of the sacraments. He is not a man of a higher status than other men; he shares
the same standing but has merely a different office.

It will be seen that a difference in the interpretation of the Sacraments, and especially of the Eucharist, leads to very different
conceptions of the essential task of the Christian church, the locus
of authority in religion, and in the understanding of the relative
importance of ethics and aesthetics. We shall see if the writings
of the contentious seventeenth century bear out the implications of
this theoretical analysis.

1. *The Roman Catholic View of the Sacrament*

As a persecuted community the Roman Catholic church in England had few opportunities for publishing defences of its sacramental doctrine. As a result it relied upon such famous catechetical
expositions as those of Cardinal Bellarmine or of St. Peter
Canisius,[2] or on the treatises written by English exiles in the Low
Countries, such as those written by two Jesuits, John Heigham
and Henry FitzSimon.[3]

Father Heigham's treatise, as we might expect, insists that in
the Mass the bread and wine are converted into the physical body
and blood of Christ. His theory of consecration is that it is Christ,
the Second Person of the Holy Trinity, who "imparted the virtue
of his holie benediction upon the bread and converted the substance
thereof into that of his pretious bodie." This was, in fact, a renewal
of Christ's action at the creation of the world, "when He ordayned
the multiplication and increase of His creatures, every one according to his kind."[4] Heigham supports these assertions by the
reminder that "never do we reade that He blessed the bread, but
that there insued some notable Miracle, as in the multiplication of
the five loaves and two fishes, whereof the fragments were twelve
baskets after the refection of five thousand souls."[5]

Father FitzSimon's exposition is a characteristic example of a

---

[2] Editions of English translations of his catechism appeared in Douai in 1578
or 1579, Paris 1588, England between 1592 and 1596, St. Omer 1622, with a
third edition in 1639.

[3] Each treatise is expounded more fully in Chap. XIII, Para. 5 *infra.*

[4] *A Devout Exposition of the Holie Masse* (Douai, 2nd edn., 1622), p. 252.

[5] *Ibid.*, p. 253.

common theological genre in this country, namely, controversial divinity, aimed at convincing Protestants of the inherent reasonableness of Catholic Eucharistic doctrine. FitzSimon insists strongly that the Roman Catholic doctrine of the real corporal presence of Christ in the Mass is that of the primitive Church in its representatives such as Cyprian, Ambrose, Augustine, John of Damascus, and Cyril of Jerusalem. Answering the Protestant objection that Christ's body is now since the Ascension in heaven and cannot be on the altar, he replies: "I aunswer with St. Damascen abouve alleaged that the assumpted bodie of Christ discendeth not from heaven, but that (without discension) the bread and wyne by the omnipotencie of his woord is transubstantiated or converted into his bodie and bloud."[6]

What, then, are the benefits of the Mass? Citing Bede, Fitz-Simon states them negatively: "The priest not lawfully hindred, omitting to celebrate, in as much as he may, depriveth the holy Trinitie of prayse and glorie; the Angels of ioye; the sinners of pardon; the iust of healp and grace; them in purgatorie of refreshment; the Church of spiritual assistance; & himselfe of medicine and remedie."[7] Manifestly, the benefits include the forgiveness of sins and eternal life, and the "medicine and remedy" of grace strengthens the soul against temptations.

Another Jesuit, John Floyd, wrote in 1624 *A Plea for the Reall-Presence*, which he defines as "to wit, the Reall Presence, or the change of bread and wine into the body and blood of Christ."[8] He summarizes the Patristic argument for a literal interpretation of Christ's words: "This is my body" and this he contrasts with the Protestant metaphorical interpretation:

> And this is the argument . . . used by the Fathers who prove the Reall Presence, because Christ being God can do it, to wit, can convert the substance of bread and wine into the substance of his body and blood. For if this literal sense be possible unto God, then it is neyther wicked nor absurd, then to be received as the true sense; if to be received as the true sense, then also to be received as an article of fayth, being the true litteral sense of Gods Wordd. Cōcerning the substāce of a most mayne mystery of Religion & consequently

---

[6] *The Iustification and Exposition of the Divine Sacrifice of the Masse* (1611, republished Menston, Yorkshire, 1972), p. 342.
[7] *Ibid.*, p. 69. [8] *Op. cit.*, p. 20.

the Protestant Metaphor that destroyes this litteral sense is an accursed Heresy.[9]

Such was the instruction given by the priests as to the meaning and benefits of the Mass to the faithful, but what did the laity, in fact, believe? We can only take one glimpse at the edge of a curtain covering the stage of a vast auditorium. This is provided on a blank leaf of an Antwerp missal which once belonged to Mary, daughter of Sir Peter Middleton of Ilkley, Yorkshire. The inscription reads: "The faythfull go to Masse they ought / to ioyne with the Priest and offer up the / Body and Blood of Christ / First For the giving supreme worship/and honour to God./ Secondly in thankes /giving for all his blessed benefits./ Thirdly new graces/ and blessings and even in Remembraunce of Christes passion."[10]

The essentially medieval interpretation of the benefits of the Mass provided even in Counter-Reformation theology can be seen in the inclusion in FitzSimon's treatise of a translation of the *Anima Christi* as if it were part and parcel of a seventeenth-century Eucharistic prayer, with its pleas for purification and forgiveness, for a permanent union with Christ, and for assurance of eternal life with all the saints.[11]

The point need not be laboured, but neither should it be ignored that the treatises of both Heigham and FitzSimon not only indicate in their full titles their interest in rites and ceremonies as much as doctrines, but they actually devote considerable attention to the symbolism of ornaments and vestments and gestures, as entirely appropriate to the high mystery and miracle of the Mass.[12]

Not only did Catholics hold a high view of the Mass, they also deplored Protestants accepting what they could only regard as a doctrine of the "real absence." FitzSimon has his imaginary Protestant interlocutor saying: "At least we can not be persuaded to believe the real presence of Christ." To this FitzSimon replies: "I know and lament to know it to be true of Calvinists and Zwinglians. . . ."[13]

The later period, during and after the Restoration sees the publication of treatises that do not materially add to our appreciation of the Catholic understanding of the Mass. In 1674 Robert Fuller

---

[9] *Ibid.*, pp. 43-44.
[10] Ampleforth Abbey MS 704, cited Hugh Aveling, *The Catholic Recusants of the West Riding of Yorkshire, 1558-1790* (Leeds, 1963), p. 250.
[11] *Op. cit.*, p. 118.
[12] See Heigham, *op. cit.* (edn. of 1614), pp. 7-8, 27-50, 52-59, 171, 217-18, and 399.
[13] *Op. cit.*, p. 343.

published anonymously his *Missale Romanum Vindicatum, or the Mass Vindicated from D. Daniel Brevent's calumnious and scandalous Tract*. Its leading idea is that the miracles claimed for the Mass do not seem improbable once one has accepted the central miracle of the real presence. Two more intriguing essays on the Mass were published in 1687 in Oxford by Abraham Woodhead, a convert while in Anglican orders, entitled *Two Discourses concerning the Adoration of our B. Saviour in the H. Eucharist*. The first affirmed that while Anglicans denied a crudely carnal doctrine of Transubstantiation such as was affirmed by Paschasius Radbertus, they nevertheless accepted a Berengarian doctrine of the real presence, such as the author himself held. Woodhead also insisted that while Anglicans rejected the view that Christ's natural body was in the Eucharist because it could not be in two places at once, yet any doctrine of a real presence is open to the identical objection. His second treatise dealt more fully with the same positions.

In summary, it can be said of the Roman Catholic view that it held to a real conversion of the bread and wine into the body and blood of Christ, while maintaining the appearance of bread and wine, that this sacrifice was acceptable to God for the remission of the sins of the living, for the refreshment of the souls in purgatory, for the strengthening of souls against temptation, and was the medicine of immortality. This set of convictions sustained and was sustained by the splendid *mise-en-scène* of the Mass in its ceremonial, ornaments, and vestments.

2. *The Anglican View of the Sacrament*

At the very outset we find that however impressed the high Anglican divines in the Andrewes-Laud-Cosin tradition are with the doctrine of the real presence as a primitive doctrine of the early undivided church, they have a serious quarrel with Roman doctrine and practice. These differences are reported with telling simplicity by a chaplain of Charles I, John Pocklington in his *Altare Christianum, or, the Dead Vicar's Plea* (1637). He cites Casaubon to the effect that "the things which the King's Majesty and our Church condemn are the celebration of the Eucharist without Communicants, the selling of private Masses, making a game of the simplicity of ignorant people, and causing them to pay more than once or twice for fetching of Soules out of Purgatory, by vertue of the Sacrifices of their Masses."[14]

[14] *Op. cit.*, p. 109.

291

The high-church divines of the Church of England rejected both Transubstantiation and Consubstantiation.[15] John Bramhall, Bishop of Derry and afterwards Archbishop of Armagh at the Restoration, rejected the Roman doctrine as contrary to common sense, asking: "Surely you cannot think that Christ did actually sacrifice Himself at His Last Supper (for then He had redeemed the World at His Last Supper; then His subsequent Sacrifice on the Cross had been superfluous); nor that the priest doth now more than Christ did then?"[16] Herbert Thorndike uses a different argument, but the ground is the same: Transubstantiation is rejected because "the substance of the elements is not distinguishable by common sense from their accidents."[17]

Even in the controversial Canons of 1640 that Laud introduced as Archbishop of Canterbury, requiring the Communion table to be railed in and that worshippers should do reverence and obeisance towards it on entering or leaving the church, he is careful to distinguish Anglican from Roman concepts of Christ's presence: "The reviving of this ancient and laudable custom we heartily recommend to the serious consideration of all good people, not with any intention to exhibit any religious worship to the communion table . . . or to perform the said gesture upon any opinion of a corporal presence of the body of Jesus Christ on the holy table, or in mystical elements, but only for the advancement of God's Majesty. . . ."[18]

The second affirmation made by all Anglican divines, both high and low, was that the Sacrament was to be received in faith by the communicants. Thus they denied the *ex opere operato* Roman doctrine. Archbishop Laud[19] was as insistent upon the requirement of faith for true reception as his most convinced Puritan antagonist. In this respect he was following Richard Hooker in rejecting both Transubstantiation and Consubstantiation, and in affirming Hooker's third alternative interpretation of the mode of Christ's presence in the Sacrament. Hooker had phrased it thus: "This hallowed

[15] See Chap. 8 of Lancelot Andrewes's *Responsio ad Apologiam Cardinalis Bellarmini*, parts of which are translated in Darwell Stone's *A History of the Doctrine of the Holy Eucharist*, II, pp. 264-66; also William Laud's *Works*, 7 Vols. (ed. W. Scott, J. Bliss, Library of Anglo-Catholic Theology, Oxford, 1847-1860), II, pp. 339-41 and III, p. 355.

[16] *Works*, 5 Vols. (ed. A. W. Haddan, Library of Anglo-Catholic Theology, Oxford, 1842-1845), I, p. 54. See also Bishop Jeremy Taylor's *Works*, 10 Vols. (ed. C. P. Eden, 1847-1854), II, pp. 637ff.

[17] *Works*, 6 Vols. (ed. A. W. Haddan, Library of Anglo-Catholic Theology, Oxford, 1844-1854), IV, p. 26.

[18] E. Cardwell, *Synodalia*, 2 Vols. (Oxford, 1842), I, p. 406.

[19] Laud, *Works*, 5 Vols. (Library of Anglo-Catholic Theology, Oxford), II, pp. 370-71.

food, through concurrence of divine power, is in verity and truth unto faithful believers instrumentally a cause of that mysterious participation whereby, as I make Myself wholly theirs so I give them in hand an actual possession of all such saving grace as My sacrificed Body can yield, and as their souls do presently need, this is to them and in them *My Body*."[20]

Hooker did not so describe it, but later theologians have applied the term "dynamic receptionism" to this doctrine, as implying both the objective reality of divine power and the subjective necessity for faith.

Another important element in the statement of Hooker, which was to be repeated throughout the century, was the stress on mystery. This has both strength and weakness. The strength was the recognition that in dealing with God, the ground of all being, humans are always dealing with mystery, with what transcends their understanding or God would not be God, and that Job's profound attempt to grapple with the concept resulted in the humble confession "these are but the outskirts of Thy ways." The weakness was that in the name of piety it was always possible to be theologically vague about the modality of the presence and therefore at a dialectical disadvantage in apologetical writings during this controversial century.

Bramhall, while insisting that "a real true presence" is confessed by every genuine son of the Church of England, typically adds that Christ did not say, "This is my body after this or that manner, *neque con, neque sub, neque trans*." He concludes that we should not presume to analyse mysteries. Assuredly, the presence of Christ was sacramental and efficacious, but "whether it be in the soul only, or in the Host also, and if in the Host, whether by consubstantiation, or transubstantiation; whether by production, or adduction, or conservation, or assumption, or by whatsoever other way bold and blind men dare conjecture—we determine not."[21]

Bishop Cosin takes a similar stand partly because he believes that precise definitions of the mystery of Christ's presence were scholastical and Jesuitical departures from the primitive church's attitude, partly because he saw no point in arguing about God's omnipotence "whether it can do this or that, presuming to measure an infinite power by our poor ability. . . ."[22] On the other hand,

---

[20] *Laws of Ecclesiastical Polity*, Bk. v, Chap. LXVII, Sect. 12; *Works*, 3 Vols. (ed. J. Keble, Oxford, 1836), II, pp. 359ff.

[21] *Works*, I, p. 22.

[22] *Works*, 5 Vols. (ed. G. Ornsby, Library of Anglo-Catholic Theology, Ox-

Cosin denied absolutely that it was necessary in affirming God's omnipotence to accept Transubstantiation as the consequence. On the contrary, he held that this was to deny the use of the ordinance as the Lord intended it, since it destroys the accidents and thus confuses the sign with the substance—the bread with the Body.

James Ussher, the future Archbishop of Armagh, preaching before the House of Commons in 1620, lamented that the Holy Sacrament ordained by Christ to be a bond of unity had become the occasion of "endless strifes and implacable contentions."[23] Rejecting the Aristotelian metaphysics of substance and accidents, he declared that the real presence must be left an inexplicable mystery.[24]

Granting the painful inadequacy of theological probings into the divine mystery, can anything further be said about the presence of Christ in the Sacrament which is neither "bold" nor "blind"? A seventeenth-century versifier (he was hardly a poet even though a president-designate of Harvard), Nathaniel Eaton expressed the difficulties inherent in being too precise in defining a presence in the Sacrament:

> . . . yet it is confest
> That when the holy Elements are blest
> By the Priest's powerful lips, though nothing there
> To outward sense but bread and wine appear,
> Yet doth there under those dark forms reside
> The Body of the Son of Man that died.
> This, what bold tongue soever doth deny
> Gives in effect even Christ Himself the lie.
> Yet this, whoe'er too grossly doth maintain
> Pulls his ascended Lord from Heaven again.
> A middle course 'twixt these two rocks to steer,
> Is that becomes the Christian Mariner;
> So to believe the Ascension as to grant
> His Real Presence in the Sacrament;
> Yet so His Real Presence there to own
> As not to make void His Ascension.[25]

---

ford, 1843-1855), IV, which includes the *Historia Transubstantiationis Papalis* which was written in 1656 and published posthumously in 1675.

[23] *Works*, 17 Vols. (eds. C. R. Elrington-J. H. Todd, Dublin and London, 1847-1864), II, pp. 246ff.

[24] P. E. More and F. L. Cross, *Anglicanism, The Thought and Practice of the Church of England illustrated from the Religious Literature of the Seventeenth Century* (1935), p. xxxvi.

[25] Cited *ibid.*, p. 467.

The problem was that the Apostles' Creed itself reminded the faithful that Christ's natural body was "dead and buried," and that his glorified body was located "at the right hand of God the Father Almighty." How, then, could Christ's body be present on the altar? On the other hand, if it was insisted that it is Christ's Spirit that is present in the hearts or souls of believers (which is indeed possible for a Spirit not bound in space or time), in what sense is it present sacramentally in any way different from its presence, for example, in the preaching of the Word? Furthermore, Christ said of the bread, "This is my Body" and not, "This is my Spirit." Equally, it is exceedingly difficult to explain a "mystical presence" of Christ in, with or under the elements in such a way as neither abolishes nor diminishes the physical elements.[26]

The author who has written most clearly on the befogging issue (and whose clarity, according to C. W. Dugmore,[27] almost certainly caused his Golden Grove neighbour, Jeremy Taylor, to drop a high view of the presence for a more moderate view) was William Nicholson, the Bishop of Gloucester at the Restoration. His views are contained in the *Plain but Full Exposition of the Church of England*, which first appeared in 1654 and in a later edition in 1663. He interpreted Christ's presence at the Lord's Supper in four ways:

> 1. Divinely, as God, and so He is present in all places. *Whither shall I flee from Thy presence? I, the Lord, fill heaven and earth.*
> 2. Spiritually, and so He is present in the hearts of true believers. *Christ dwells in our hearts by faith.*
> 3. Sacramentally, and so He is present in the Sacrament because He hath ordained the Sacrament to represent and communciate Christ's death unto us. *The cup of blessing which we bless, is it not the communion of Christ, etc.?*
> 4. Corporally, so present in Judaea in the days of His flesh.[28]

The same clarity and cogency are exhibited in Nicholson's analyses of the "real presence." He demonstrates that there are three meanings for the term "real" in this context. The first is real as opposed to pretended, imaginary, or fanciful; the second is real as opposed to figurative, barely representative, or metaphorical;

[26] Cf. C. W. Dugmore, *Eucharistic Doctrine in England from Hooker to Waterland* (1948), pp. 89-90.

[27] *Ibid.*, pp. 93-94.

[28] *Works* (2nd edn., reprint in Library of Anglo-Catholic Theology, Oxford, 1844), pp. 176-77.

and the third is "opposed to that which is spiritual, and imports as much as corporal or bodily."[29] The third meaning he rejects with reference to Christ's real presence in the Sacrament. He concludes that Christ is present in the Eucharist "divinely after a special manner, spiritually in the heart of the communicants, sacramentally or relatively in the elements, and this presence of His is real in the two former acceptions of real, but not in the last, for He is truly and effectually there present, though not corporally, bodily, casually, locally."[30] This account does not, of course, clear up all difficulties. How Christ can be sacramentally present in the elements, though not corporately, is difficult to comprehend; it would be easier if the presence were stated to be in the action as a whole, rather than in the elements.

In fact, there appear to be two positions and only two, which are to be expounded with great clarity and understanding. The one is Transubstantiation which affirms too much, and the other is Zwinglian Memorialism which affirms too little, and the Church of England desired a third mediating position, very difficult to explain. Transubstantiation was not acceptable to Anglican divines because as Eutychianism was a Christological heresy of the fourth century that denied the human nature of Christ by its overwhelming affirmation of Christ's godhead and divinity, so Transubstantiation denied the continued existence of the bread and wine except in appearance and destroyed, so to speak, its human or material substance. For Bishop Lancelot Andrewes this was Eucharistic Docetism. He had warned Cardinal Bellarmine: "There is that kind of union between the visible Sacrament and the invisible reality (*rem*) of the Sacrament which there is between the Manhood and Godhead of Christ, where unless you want to smack of Eutyches, the Manhood is not transubstantiated into the Godhead. . . ."[31]

The Zwinglian reductionism was also unacceptable to the Anglican divines because it affirmed that the Spirit of Christ represents without transmitting the benefits achieved by the Body of Christ sacrificed on the Cross, but is in no way a special Eucharistic presence, only a general presence of Christ with His own as believers.

Bishop Cosin asserts that the Roman Catholics misrepresent Anglican doctrine by affirming that they are only interested in transmitting the sign, and not the reality signified by the sign. On the contrary, says Cosin, there are represented and offered Christ's

[29] *Ibid.*, p. 179. [30] *Ibid.*
[31] *Responsio ad Apologiam Cardinalis Bellarmini*, Chap. 8.

"very Body which was crucified and His blood which was shed for us" so that "our souls may receive and possess Christ as truly and certainly as the material signs are by us seen and received." Cosin affirms a doctrine of dynamic receptionism, but he desires even more: "We do not say that in the Lord's Supper we receive only the benefits of Christ's Death and Passion, but we join the ground with its fruits, that is, Christ, with those advantages we derive from Him, affirming with Paul, that *the bread which we break* is κοινωνία, and the cup which we blesse the communion of His Blood—of that very substance which He took of the Blessed Virgin and afterwards carried into Heaven."[32]

There are, however, several clear landmarks in the cloudiness of the Anglican doctrine of the Eucharist. One is the insistence that while there is no change in the substance of the elements, there is a change in the use to which the bread and wine are put. William Nicholson, for instance (as also Bishop Cosin)[33] emphasizes this: "That which is more material to know is the change of these, which is wholly sacramental, not in substance, but in use. For they remain bread and wine, such as before in nature: but consecrate and set apart to represent our Saviour's passion. . . ."[34]

Another clear feature of Anglican exposition is the declaration that the chief Sacrament "seals" the benefits of Christ's act of atonement on the Cross to believers. A strong statement of this viewpoint (which inevitably recalls Calvin's Eucharistic theology) is offered by Archbishop Ussher. He holds that the Lord's Supper is not merely commemorative (the Zwinglian assertion), but also communicative; not a bare sign but an exhibitive sign of grace; in short, a seal as well as a sign of the Covenant of Grace.[35] The link between the Body of Christ in Heaven and the church on earth is the Holy Spirit. Ussher continues his exposition:

> If any do further enquire how it is possible that any such union should be, seeing the Body of Christ is in Heaven and we are upon earth, I answer . . . it being altogether spiritual and supernatural, no local presence, no physical or mathematical continuity or contiguity is any way requisite thereunto. It is sufficient for a real union in this kind that Christ

[32] *Works*, IV, Chap. IV, Sects. 2, 5.
[33] Cosin writes: "We own the union betwixt the Body and the Blood of Christ and the elements, whose use and office are changed from what it was before." *Op. cit.*, Vol. IV, Chap. iv, Sect. 5.
[34] *Op. cit.*, pp. 176-77.   [35] *Works*, II, p. 429.

and we, though never so far distant in pleace each from the other, be knit together by those spiritual ligatures which are intimated unto us in the words alleged out of the Sixth of *John*; *to wit*, the quickening Spirit descending downwards from the Head to be in us a fountain of supernatural life; and a lively faith wrought by the same Spirit, ascending from us upward to lay fast hold upon Him, Who having by Himself purged our sins, sitteth on the right Hand of the Majesty on High.[36]

Bishop William Nicholson also affirms that the purpose of the Communion is not only "to represent our Saviour's passion" but also to "exhibit and seal to a worthy receiver the benefits of that passion."[37]

The high Anglican divines, however closely they approximated to Calvin in some respects in their doctrine of dynamic receptionism, yet were not content to assert that the Holy Spirit united the glorified Body of Christ in heaven with the believers on earth, and communicated the benefits of Christ's Passion. They wanted to affirm even more.

Hence, there is another important element in their Eucharistic doctrine. This is the inclusion of a doctrine of sacrifice carefully formulated to avoid any idea of a repetition of the uniquely efficacious Sacrifice of the Cross, and deriving its Scriptural basis from the Epistle to the Hebrews. Essentially, the claim is that Christ eternally offers His sacrifice to God the Father for the sins of men, and that the church on earth represents that sacrifice by which Christ intercedes for the church which is also His Body. The doctrine is most comprehensively stated by Archbishop Bramhall and by Herbert Thorndike. Bramhall avers: "We do readily acknowledge an Eucharistical Sacrifice of prayers and praises: we profess a commemoration of the Sacrifice of the Cross; and in the language of Holy Church, things commemorated are related as if they were then acted. . . . We acknowledge a representation of that Sacrifice to God the Father: we maintain an application of its Virtue: so here is a commemorative, impetrative, applicative Sacrifice."[38] Henry Thorndike also defines the term "sacrifice" with great caution. He acknowledges that there is an oblation of the elements immediately prior to their consecration.[39] Furthermore, he asserts

---

[36] *Ibid.*
[38] *Works*, I, pp. 54-55.
[37] *Op. cit.*, p. 177.
[39] *Works*, I, p. 860 and IV, p. 106.

that the Eucharist is "nothing else but the representation here upon earth of the offering of the Sacrifice of Christ upon the Cross to the Father in the highest heavens to obtain the benefits of His Passion for us."[40] His conclusion is: "it cannot be denied that the Sacrament of the Eucharist, inasmuch as it is the same Sacrifice of Christ upon the Cross (as that which representeth is truly said to be the thing which it representeth) is also both propitiatory and impetratory by virtue of the consecration of it, whereby it becometh the Sacrifice of Christ upon the Cross."[41] The earlier Jeremy Taylor accepted a similar view, declaring:

> . . . as Christ is a priest in heaven for ever, and yet does not Sacrifice Himself afresh, nor yet without a Sacrifice could he be a priest; but by a daily ministration and intercession representeth His Sacrifice to God, and offers Himself as sacrificed; so He does upon earth by the ministry of His servants; He is offered to God, that is, He is by prayers and the Sacrament represented or offered up to God, as Sacrificed.[42]

There the doctrine must be left with whatever residual difficulties. The only later addition came from the Non-Jurors, who believed they had made their Eucharistic doctrine more objective, on the pattern of the Eastern Orthodox churches, by the invocation or *epiklesis* of the Holy Spirit to effect the conversion of the elements into the Body and Blood of Christ. It was a doctrine approximating to Transubstantiation, except that the agent in the transformation was not the Second, but the Third Person of the Trinity. Bishop George Bull held a doctrine not greatly differing from that of the Non-Jurors, except that it posited Christ rather than the Holy Spirit as the agent in the Sacrament. Bull explained its working thus: "by or upon the sacerdotal benediction, or a divine virtue from Christ descends upon the elements, and accompanies them to all faithful communicants, and that therefore they are said to be and are the Body and Blood of Christ; the same divinity which is hypostatically united to the Body of Christ in heaven, being virtually united to the elements of Bread and Wine upon earth."[43] Even so, considerable difficulties remain as pointed out by C. W. Dugmore.[44]

---

[40] *Works*, IV, p. 108.   [41] *Ibid.*, IV, p. 117.
[42] *Works*, II, p. 643.
[43] *The Corruptions of the Church of Rome* (1705) in *Works*, 6 Vols. (ed. E. Burton, Oxford, 1827), II, p. 255.
[44] *Op. cit.*, pp. 154-55. C. W. Dugmore points out that even the Non-Jurors

The Latitudinarians, as might be expected, preferred a less mystical and more functional and practical doctrine of Holy Communion. Their leading representative was John Tillotson (1630-1694) who became Archibishop of Canterbury. Although the *Oxford Dictionary of the Christian Church* claims[45] that his Eucharistic doctrine was Zwinglian, it was in actual fact Calvinist. It is stated in a posthumously published sermon, entitled, *A Discourse to His Servants Concerning Receiving the Sacrament*. This refers to it as "the most solemn institution of our Christian religion" and urges its frequent reception, otherwise Christ is treated with contempt. The memorial aspect is stressed, but the doctrine is more than mere Memorialism, since "it does not only represent this exceeding love of our Saviour in giving His Body to be broken, and His Blood to be shed for us, but it likewise seals to us all those blessings and benefits which are procured for us by His death and passion, the pardon of sins, and power against sin." He adds that "the benefit also of it is great, because hereby we are confirmed in goodness, and our resolutions of better obedience are strengthened, and the grace of God's Holy Spirit to enable us to do His will is thereby conveyed to us."[46]

Probably the best term for describing the Anglican doctrine of the real presence is "instrumental symbolism." The adjective indicates that there is a real communication of grace effected, and the noun emphasizes the significance of the symbolism. The latter includes the concepts of sacrifice and banquet, and it may well be that the confusion in interpretation is caused by trying to elaborate incompatible analogies drawn from different realms of discourse. For example, if the symbol of sacrifice is chosen, the altar is appropriate, but if that of a banquet, a table is more appropriate. A table-altar seems a contradiction in terms. John Pocklington saw this clearly when he wrote: "For the use of an altar is to sacrifice upon, and the use of a table is to eate upon."[47] It is possible, however, to speak meaningfully of a "table-altar" if it is recognized that a sacrificial meal is eaten thereon, giving equal significance to the adjective "sacrificial" and to the noun "meal."

---

left many ambiguities, such as how Christ is united sacramentally with the elements or what is intended by a "material sacrifice" of a "spiritual body" and why a material one is better than a spiritual one, to say nothing of the mind-boggling idea that at the Last Supper Christ offered both His natural and His sacramental body, and how they are related.

[45] *Op. cit.*, ed. F. L. Cross, p. 1359a.

[46] *Works* (ed. T. Birch, 1820), x, p. 211, cited Dugmore, *op. cit.*, p. 153.

[47] *Altare Christianum or the Dead Vicars Plea* (1637), p. 141.

It was argued at the outset that the higher the conception of the Eucharist, the richer would be its setting in the ornaments of the church, as in its ceremonial, and the more frequent would be its celebration. How far are these indications found in the Church of England in the seventeenth century?

In the matter of frequency of celebration alone, the pragmatic indication would be that there was a low doctrine of Holy Communion. But the infrequency can, in fact, be explained on other grounds, including the disruption caused by the Civil Wars and the official proscription of the Prayer Book for fifteen years. Indeed, this would itself lead to a depreciation of the chief Sacrament, except among the few high Anglican "conventicles" of the kind at which Jeremy Taylor presided and which John Evelyn attended in London. It is significant and more typical, however, that Ralph Josselin, recording his administration of Holy Communion in his parish at Earl's Colne on Easter Day, 1665, observed that "twelve of us received the Sacrament of the Lord's Supper publicly for which I bless God; I believe its 22 or 23 years since received on that day and occasion."[48] It is clear that the habit of regular attendance at the Sacrament had been lost for an entire generation. As late as 1679 a preacher in the University pulpit at St. Mary's, Oxford, complained of the disuse of the Sacrament in Commonwealth days: "Those intruders who called themselves the University of *Oxon.* from the bloudy and fateful year of 1648 to the King's happy Restoration, did not think fit so much as once to celebrate the Communion together in this Church, and a public Sacrament was not seen in several College Chapels during the same space of time."[49] The impression given is not entirely correct, however. It is credibly reported by his biographer that John Owen, no friend to the Prayer Book, the Independent Dean of Christ Church, Oxford, allowed about three hundred Anglicans to celebrate divine service according to the Church of England in the lodgings of the physician Willis in the Canterbury Quadrangle of the College and

---

[48] *Diary of Ralph Josselin, 1616-1683* (ed. E. Hockliffe, Camden Society, 3rd Series, 1908), Vol. IV, p. 146.

[49] Thomas Smith, *A Sermon about Frequent Communion, Preached before the University of Oxford, August the 17th, 1679* (1685), p. 33. Dr. Thomas Comber, future Dean of Durham, similarly observed: "If we consider how terribly this Sacrament was represented and how generally it was layd aside in the late times, we might wonder how Monthly Communions should be so well attended on by the people as they are." (*The Remains of Denis Granville*, Surtees Society, 1865, Vol. XLVII, p. 86, cited by J. Wickham Legg, *English Church Life* (1914), p. 21. However, it will be pointed out that the Puritans, even if they did not celebrate the Sacrament in the high Anglican way, celebrated frequently and valued their own Lord's Suppers.

later in Merton College Chapel "to which place admitting none but their confidants, prayers and surplices were used on all Lord's Days, Holy Days and their Vigils, as also the Sacrament according to the Church of England administered."[50]

The infrequency may be exaggerated by jeremiads, and it is notable that the Rector of Clayworth reported in 1676 to the Archbishop of York that 200 of 236 persons of age to communicate in his parish did so on Easter Day of that year.[51] The rehabituating of people to regular attendance at Holy Communion after two decades of absenteeism was an uphill task for the clergy, but they succeeded tolerably well. In any case, a lower estimate of Communion was inevitable at the end of the century, partly as a result of the unmystical pragmatic emphasis of the Latitudinarian divines, and even more because of the deistic diatribes against priestcraft and superstition.

Consequently our question now becomes: is there any evidence of symbolism in the decoration of the altar or of the church plate, or any ceremonialism that would imply a high doctrine of the Eucharist?

Pepys can be taken as a witness from ceremonial of a very high doctrine of the Eucharist during the Restoration. He was at Whitehall Chapel on Easter Day, 1666, and recorded: "I staid till the King went down to receive the Sacrament, and stood in his closett, with a great many others and there saw him receive it, which I never did see the manner of before. But I do see very little difference between the degree of the ceremonies used by our people . . . and that in the Roman Church. . . ."[52] A convinced Protestant critic of Anglican ceremonies during these years writes of the way to treat clergymen who admire high ceremonialism:

> Consequently handle him *as if he really were* a Popish Priest; his *Cope*, his *Hood*, his *Surplice*, his *Cringing Worship*, his *Altar* with *Candles* on it (most Nonsensically *unlighted* too) his *Bag-Pipes* or *Organs*, and in some places *Viols* and *Violins*, singing Men and *singing* Boyd &c. are *so very like*

[50] V.H.H. Green, *Religion at Oxford and Cambridge* (1964), p. 147.

[51] Eds. Harry Gill and E. L. Guilford, *The Rector's Book, Clayworth, Notts.* (Nottingham, 1910), p. 18. It should be noted also that Simon Patrick at Covent Garden and William Beveridge at St. Peter's, Cornhill, introduced weekly Communion. This was, of course, exceptional, but it shows that conscientious clergy made much of the Sacrament (Florence Higham, *Catholic and Reformed, a study of the Anglican Church, 1559-1662*, 1962, p. 332).

[52] See also Pepys's *Diary* entries for July 29, 1660, April 22 and October 18, 1666, for further comparisons between Anglican and Roman ceremonial.

Popery, (and all but the Vestments illegal) that I protest when I came in 1660, first from beyond Sea to *Pauls*, and *White-Hall*, I could scarce think my self to be in *England*, but in *Spain* or *Portugal* again, I saw so little difference, but that their *Service* was in *Latine* and ours in *English*.[53]

What evidence does the decoration or symbolism of altars provide for the evaluation of Eucharistic doctrine? There are two very impressive altars built and carved in important London churches at All Hallows, Lombard Street, and at St. James's, Piccadilly, both significantly employing the medieval symbol of the self-wounding pelican feeding her young with her own flesh. This, it will be noted, is a symbol that combines the element of sacrifice with that of eating, and this betokens a high Eucharistic doctrine. Evelyn records a visit to see the new altar at St. James's, Piccadilly:

> I went to see the new church at St. James's, elegantly built; the altar was especially adorn'd, the white marble inclosure curiously and richly carved, the flowers and garlands about the walls by Mr. Gibbons in wood; a pelican with young at her breast, just over the altar in the carv'd compartment and border, invironing the purple velvet fring'd with I.H.S. richly embroidered, and most noble plate were given by Sir R. Geere, to the value (as was said) of £200. There was no altar anywhere in England, nor has there been any abroad, more handsomely adorn'd.[54]

The following is a description of the altar at All Hallows, Lombard Street a few years after its construction:

> The Altar-piece is the most spacious and best carved that I have thus far met with: It is of right Wainscot, and consists of 4 Columns with their Entablature, all finely Cut with 5 Pediments of the *Corinthian* Order; viz. a Circular, and above it a Triangular, belonging to the two N[orth] Columns, and to the two S[outhward]; the Inter-Columns are the Commandments done in Gold Letters on Black, and the Lord's Prayer and Creed is done in Black upon Gold. And in the middle bet[ween] the Arching parts of the Frames for the Commandments, is a Pelican feeding her Young with her own Blood

[53] Edmund Hickeringill, *The Ceremony Monger* (1689), p. 18, cited Legg, *op. cit.*, p. 43.
[54] *Diary*, entry for December 7, 1684.

(an Emblem of our Saviour); and above the Cornish, over the Commandments, is a Glory finely painted and adorned, with an Enrichment of Carving, as Flowers, Fruit, &c. above all which is a large triangular Pediment and seven Candlesticks, representing the Seven Golden Candlesticks we read of in the Revelations; which Altar-piece, I am credibly assured, cost no less than £186. The Communion-Table is finely finnier'd, under is the Holy Lamb on a Chalice, and at each of the four feet of the Table is a Dove.[55]

These two altars, at least, manifest that the Eucharist was still thought to be highly important even in two of Wren's most distinguished churches, and "auditory" churches at that, constructed primarily for those who had come to hear preaching.[56]

It is also worth considering what evidence is provided by the Communion plate[57] of the period for the contemporary estimation of the Eucharist. Here, again, we are likelier to learn of the evaluations of the Eucharist by wealthy patrons and donors, than those of the average Anglican communicants. Without question it was Bishop Lancelot Andrewes who contributed most to the development of Communion plate in England in the seventeenth century by his example and enthusiasm, as well as his knowledge of ecclesiastical history. In enriching ritual "he became a patron of all the crafts which could contribute to the embellishment of churches."[58] However austere he was in private life, as a bishop he spent lavishly on furnishing his private chapel. His influence endured for fifty years after his death and it can be traced in the style and symbolism of English Communion plate.[59] Thanks to the accurate observation of the hawk-eyed and critical William Prynne, a prelate-baiter, who discovered in Archbishop Laud's private papers several documents relating to a richly furnished chapel (it was Andrewes's which Prynne mistook for Laud's) we have a full account of Andrewes's preferences in the matter of Communion plate.[60] These include some experiments which were not copied by

[55] A New View of London (1708), I, p. 109.

[56] For altar frontals, candlesticks, crosses, religious pictures during the latter part of our period, see Legg, op. cit., pp. 125-39.

[57] The two best recent studies are Charles Oman's English Church Plate, 1597-1830 (1957) and James Gilchrist's Anglican Church Plate (1967).

[58] Oman, op. cit., p. 145.

[59] See Thomas Fuller, Church History of Britain (1655) reissued 1868, Box XI, III, p. 391.

[60] See original plan of altar and furnishings in British Museum Harleian Ms.

others, such as a "tun" with a cradle for sacramental wine, or a "tricanale" with triple spouts for the water to be added to the wine. All the pieces on the altar were of gilt, and they included a chalice and cover, two patens, an alms basin, a ewer and basin (for ablutions), two candlesticks, a censer, and a canister for wafers, with the exotic additions already mentioned. The innovative Elizabethan chalices and covers do not continue to be produced because as a result of Puritan influence bread is preferred to wafers, and bread is too bulky to be kept on the chalice covers which also did duty as patens.

Andrewes's disciple, Bishop John Cosin, had seen the splendour of Baroque church ornaments in Paris when he was chaplain to the Anglican retinue of the exiled Queen Henrietta Maria. He was determined to return with some ecclesiastical splendour to England at the Restoration when he became Bishop of Durham. He converted the medieval great hall at Auckland into the largest bishop's chapel in England, and equipped it magnificently. His silver Communion plate included a chalice and cover, a French chalice with English cover, two patens, two candlesticks, an altar dish, and a Bible and Prayer Book, both mounted in silver. (This, it should be noted, is in contrast to a normal set of episcopal plate which comprised only a chalice, a standing paten, and an alms basin.)[61]

It is most significant that the style of chalices that prevailed among high-church divines (others merely purchased chalices that looked like the secular drinking cups of the period) was Gothic revival, and that this can be traced to Andrewes and was supported by Laud. The earliest example is a chalice of St. John's College, Oxford, dated prior to 1620, probably a gift to the College while Laud was its President. It bears the typical image of the Good Shepherd who sacrificed His life for His sheep, one that was reintroduced by Andrewes into England. The very earliest example associated with Andrewes is of 1620, for it was made for the church of St. Mary Extra, Southampton, out of the funds collected on the day of its consecration by Bishop Andrewes. It is practically identical with one made by the same "R. B." almost twenty years later for the chapel at Staunton Harold. The influence of this type of chalice was great since there are extant 71 chalices of Gothic revival style made between 1620 and 1704.[62] Chalices for the

---

3795 f. 23 reproduced in William Prynne's *Canterburies Doome* (1646), p. 122. See also Laud's *Works*, IV, p. 251.
    [61] Oman, *op. cit.*, p. 186.   [62] *Ibid.*, pp. 203ff.

Communion of the sick were first made in the last years of the reign of Charles II, and they, too, indicate a high estimate of Holy Communion.

Returning to iconography, it became a distinguishing mark of the high-church tradition to have engraved religious subjects on chalices, patens, and flagons, and the custom died out almost completely after the Revolution of 1688, when so many high-church divines left the Church of England as Non-Jurors. Almost all (with the single exception of the sacrifice of Isaac engraved on a chalice and paten of St. Botolph's, Aldgate in 1635) depicted subjects from the New Testament. Since the representation of a Crucifix was felt to be too obviously Roman Catholic a device, it is surprising to learn that there were three chalices engraved with this emblem, at Melbury Sampford Church, Dorset (1607), Weston St. Mary's church, Lincolnshire (1611), and on both chalice and paten at Kingerby, Lincolnshire (1637). Moreover, three Warwickshire churches were the recipients of covered patens inside which were engraved the Crucifix accompanied with the Instruments of the Passion. These were the gifts of Lady Dudley to Ashow, Kenilworth, and Leek churches. Other New Testament themes used to decorate chalices were: the Flight into Egypt, the Temptation of Christ, and the Last Supper.

Easily the most popular image to be inscribed on chalices was that of the Good Shepherd, which had been a common theme in the Catacombs[63] and in early Christian art, but relatively neglected by the Middle Ages. Its revival in the seventeenth century is uniquely Anglican for which there is no European parallel. The first reference to this theme (which combines the tender compassion and protection of Christ with His sacrificial death, and was illustrated by His parable) is found in an account of Bishop Andrewes's chapel, where it is recorded that there is "a Chalice having on the outside of the bowl Christ with the lost sheep on His shoulders."[64] Andrewes, as an erudite Patristic scholar, must have known that Tertullian in the *De Pudicitia* had made reference to "that Shepherd will play the patron whom you depict on your chalice."[65] The Bishop also gives an account of the Good Shepherd

---

[63] Eric Newton and William Neill, *2000 Years of Christian Art* (1966), pp. 30-31; see also Walter Lowrie, *Art in the Early Church* (New York, 1947), pp. 7, 11f., 42f., 50, 74.

[64] Andrewes, *Minor Works* (1841), II, p. 29.

[65] The Latin of the citation from Chap. X reads: "cui ille si forte patrocinabitur pastor, quam in calice depingis."

in a sermon written but not delivered on Easter Day, 1625, which shows that he was struck by this image: "You may see Him in the parable coming with His lost sheep on His shoulders. That one sheep is the image of us all. So careful He was, as He laid him on His own neck, to be sure; which is the true portraiture or representation of His ἀναγογή."[66]

The only other image on the Communion plate which is associated with Andrewes is the Star of the Wise Men which directed them to the Nativity of the Incarnate Son of God. According to Andrewes, this was "not only *Stella gentium* but *Stella majorum*, the great men's, the wise men's Star" and "in the old Ritual of the Church we find on the cover of the Canister wherein was the Sacrament of His Body, there was a Star engraven to show that now the Star leads up to His Body there."[67] Here, again, there is quite unmistakably a high doctrine of the Sacrament since the very Body of Christ is on the altar. The significant fact is that there were over seventy Gothic revival chalices made as a result of the inspiration and influence of Andrewes, and continued by Laud. As we have noted, the other chalices of the period are merely imitations of the secular wine cups of their time.[68]

A lower evaluation of the Eucharist, indeed a deliberate lowering of it, is probably the explanation of both Treen ware and of beaker-shaped Communion ware of the seventeenth century, alleged to be used in Puritan celebrations of the Lord's Supper. The earliest Treen ware cup,[69] dated about 1620, comes from Vowchurch in Herefordshire. This wooden cup is oviform on a baluster stem, rising from a circular base. The simple incised decoration consists of three birds each enclosed in a circle. Other wooden cups of this type were decorated with the royal arms of James I and with armorial beasts. It is very significant that it was Ulrich Zwingli who introduced sycamore cups into the Lord's Supper in Zurich in 1525.[70] The lengthy inscriptions carved on these Treen ware chalices suggest Puritan didacticism, with distinctive Puritan tenets such as election. One reads: "Drink well and welcome you that Christians be, you that have sure faith and sound repentance

---

[66] *Works*, III, pp. 89-90.
[67] *Works*, I, p. 247, cited by Oman, *op. cit.*, p. 227.
[68] James Gilchrist, *Anglican Church Plate* (1967), p. 73.
[69] *Ibid.*, reproduced in Plate 41.
[70] See *Liturgies of the Western Church* (ed. Bard Thompson, Cleveland and New York, 1961), p. 151. Zwingli's rubric reads: "The plates and cups are of wood that pomp may not come back again."

307

from every evil. Christ has made you free and from that last most heavy fearful sentence which driveth such into eternal fire as on the earth has every evil." This sounds as if it were part of a typical Calvinist fencing of the holy table. Another reads: "The Blood of Christ to them is drinke indeed, indeed, His Word and Spirit their soules but lively feede with joy and peace." A third inscription reads: "Behold what drink the Lord of life doth give now in this life, the assurance of salvation to his elect who holy do live, for unto them there is no condemnation."[71]

Another distinctively Calvinist custom in the Reformed churches of Europe was the use of beakers. Such a set was naturally used by the Dutch church meeting at Norwich in the seventeenth century, and is now in the custody of the Castle Museum in Norwich. There are also early seventeenth-century beakers in three neighbouring churches in the mid-Suffolk area.[72] Two other beakers[73] used in two Nottinghamshire Halls, those of Walesby and Walkeringham, also come from the beginning of the century, and it is known that Walesby was notorious as a Puritan parish. There is, at least, a very strong probability that extreme Puritans used both wooden cups and beaker-shaped metal cups to resemble less and less a Catholic or high Anglican chalice and more and more a simple cottage repast, using vessels that were entirely appropriate for placement on a simple table.

Thus both high and low views of the Eucharist or Lord's Supper had their fitting ceremonial, ornaments, and chalices or beakers. Until the advent of the Latitudinarians the Church of England had a high view of the real presence of Christ in the Eucharist. The judgment of J. Wickham Legg must therefore stand that although Archbishop Laud and King Charles had died for their then unacceptable convictions, their ecclesiology had gained a complete triumph at the Restoration. He writes:

> The aim of the Puritan was to have a moveable Communion table on tressels [trestles] brought out of the vestry for the Communion service, and set down in some vacant place in the church, the long sides facing north and south, while no rails protected it. After 1660 this struggle with the Puritan is over; the place of the Holy Table is determined to be in the place of the medieval altar, with one of its long sides against the east wall; it is covered with a decent carpet of silk;

---

[71] Gilchrist, op. cit., p. 66.   [72] Ibid., p. 67.
[73] Sidney Jeavons, The Church Plate of Nottinghamshire (1965).

there are often two candles upon it; and it is fenced with rails, at which the people no longer hesitate to communicate kneeling.[74]

The conclusion is inescapable that the Anglican high-church tradition always regarded the Holy Communion as a means of grace, but there is at least the possibility that some of the Puritans, in imitation of Zwingli, thought of it as a vivid sermon, an *aide-memoire*, a mere mnemonic. The examination of the latter charge is our next task.

3. *The Puritan View of the Lord's Supper*

A scurrilous but witty enemy of the Puritans declared that their creed was: "I believe in *John Calvin*, the Father of our Religion, the Disposer of Heaven and Earth, and in *Owen, Baxter*, and *Jenkins* his deare Sons our Lords, who were conceived of the Spirit of Fanaticism, born of Schism and Faction, suffered under the *Act of Uniformity*."[75] Their spiritual father was, indeed, John Calvin and nowhere were the paternal features of their doctrine more apparent than in their doctrine of the Lord's Supper. It will be a convenient beginning, therefore, to attempt to summarize the chief points of Calvin's Eucharistic doctrine from his *Institutes*.

It is sometimes alleged that Calvin regarded the Lord's Supper as merely offering Christ to the eye, as He was offered to the ear in preaching. On this view, the chief Sacrament would be merely a personal greetings telegram from God. Calvin can, indeed, be cited to this effect.[76] If this were all his teaching, or the brunt of it, then it could be argued that the Lord's Supper is a reminder of Christ's sacrifice, a particularly moving mnemonic. But this is to do Calvin considerably less than justice. Not only so, but in this statement he is chiefly concerned to deny that the Sacrament has any inherent efficacy of itself, and the correlative positive assertions are that objectively it is the Holy Spirit who conveys the grace in the sacraments,[77] and that subjectively they are received by faith;[78] but no Sacrament, according to Calvin is effective *ex opere operato*.

---

[74] *Op. cit.*, p. 119.

[75] "The Presbyterian Pater-Noster" (1681), a broadsheet now in the Bodleian Library, Oxford.

[76] "Let us abide by this conclusion, that the office of the Sacraments is precisely the same as that of the word of God, which is to offer and present Christ to us, and in him the treasures of his heavenly grace . . . The Sacraments . . . fulfil to us on the part of God the same office as messengers of joyful intelligence. . . ." *Institutes*, Bk. IV, Chap. XIV, Sect. 17.

[77] *Ibid.*   [78] *Ibid.*

His essential teaching, according to his own digest of it, includes three components: the signification, the substance, and the virtue, or effect. The signification consists of the promises of God interwoven with the sign (in the case of the Supper, to be the Christian's food and nourishment). The substance is Christ's sacrificial Death and Resurrection. The effect is "redemption, righteousness, sanctification, eternal life, and all the other benefits which Christ confers upon us. . . ."[79]

When it comes to defining or explaining the mode of Christ's presence in the Lord's Supper, Calvin's logic forsakes him as he stands in grateful awe before a mystery:

> If anyone inquire of me respecting the manner, I shall not be ashamed to acknowledge that it is a mystery too sublime for me to be able to express, or even to comprehend; and, to be still more explicit, I rather experience it than understand it. Here, therefore, without any controversy, I embrace the truth of God, on which I can safely rely. He pronounces his flesh to be the food and his blood the drink of my soul.[80]

Calvin may not be able to explain the mystery, but he is ready to reject what he considers to be erroneous attempts at explanation put forward by the Roman Catholic and Lutheran theorists. He considers both to be "exceedingly deceived," because they "cannot conceive of any presence of the flesh of Christ, except it be attached to the bread. For on principle they leave nothing to the secret operation of the Spirit which unites us to Christ. They suppose Christ not to be present unless he descends to us; as though we cannot equally enjoy his presence if he elevates us to himself."[81]

He here adumbrates the conviction that it is necessary to recognize that Christ's glorified body is now at the right hand of God the Father in heaven, and is not to be imprisoned in the bread (as the Roman Catholics affirm), nor should he be "deprived of his corporeal dimensions" by representing His Body as being in different places at once or given "an immensity diffused through heaven and earth" (as the Lutherans teach by their view of the ubiquity

---

[79] *Ibid.*, Chap. XVIII, Sect. 11.   [80] *Ibid.*, Sect. 32.

[81] *Ibid.*, Sect. 31. This concept of spiritual elevation is expressed in Calvin's Strassburg and Genevan Order of worship for the Lord's Supper in the conclusion of the Exhortation in words which are a kind of shadowy *Sursum corda*: "let us lift up our spirits and hearts on high where Jesus Christ is in the glory of the Father whence we expect him at our redemption. . . ." *Liturgies of the Western Church* (ed. Bard Thompson, p. 207.)

of Christ's human nature).[82] Nor, again, will Calvin accept the Zwinglian view that the Sacrament represents the benefits of Christ's Death and Resurrection, but does not present them. This would be to make the Sacrament a bare sign (*signum nudum*) not a seal (*sigillum*) of God's covenant of grace, a confirmation of His promises through Christ to the church.

Furthermore, Calvin insists that the reality of Christ's human nature is received in the Sacrament, for its efficacy is "not only to afford our minds an undoubted confidence of eternal life, but also to give us an assurance of the resurrection and immortality of our bodies. For they are vivified by his immortal flesh."[83]

The Sacrament is, therefore, for Calvin, "an external sign by which the Lord seals on our consciences His promises of goodwill towards us in order to sustain the weakness of our faith, and we in turn testify our piety towards Him, both before Himself and before angels as well as men."[84]

All these strong affirmations and equally vigorous denials will become familiar to us in Calvin's Puritan disciples. Like him they will see a Sacrament as a seal of the Gospel, the authentication of God's grace, just as the seal of the sender stamped on the back of the envelope guaranteed the genuineness of the communication, or the seal on a royal proclamation assured those who read it of the King's own will in the matter. The Sacrament of the Lord's Supper was like an amnesty to rebels. This is exactly how John Preston, Puritan divine and also Chaplain to King Charles, illustrated its meaning in a sermon: "You know, a Pirate, as long as a proclamation of rebellion is out against him, will not come in, but a pardon being promised, and advancement annexed to it, that, if anything, will bring him in: the theefe runnes away as long as he is pursued with Hue and Crie, but the promise of the pardon makes him returne back. . . ."[85]

There are hints of this in Calvin, but for its fuller elaboration— and this was the distinctive emphasis of later Puritanism—we must turn to the covenant or federal theologians, who are in a succession from William Perkins to his disciple William Ames, to Ames's disciple John Cotton who spread the doctrine in New Eng-

82 Bk. IV, Chap. XVII, Sect. 19.
83 Bk. IV, Chap. XVII, Sect. 32. The concluding phrase of the citation might have been penned by St. Athanasius.
84 Bk. IV, Chap. XIV, Sect. 1.
85 *The Cuppe of Blessing. Delivered in three Sermons upon I Cor. 10.16* (1633), p. 43.

land, and Ames's pupil in Franeker, Johannes Cocceius, whose *Summa Doctrinae de Foedere et Testamento Dei* (1648) was the most extensive treatise on the theme. The influence of covenant theology was profound in Dort, in the Westminster Assembly, and throughout New England.[86]

The best known exposition of the covenant theology in English was that by William Ames known as the *Marrow of Theology*.[87] To understand what a "seal of the covenant" is, the favourite Puritan description of the two Gospel sacraments, we must first understand the nature of the divine covenants as Ames expounds them.

For Ames God is essentially a promiser who also performs, irrespective of man's action or inaction, fidelity, or infidelity. Also it is this action of God as one who makes a covenant of grace or renews such a covenant (as contrasted with the transactionalism of a covenant of works) that is central for his theology. The New Covenant is unconditional on God's part, whereas the Old Covenant was dependent upon man's obedience. This covenant of grace is the saving promise of a God whose initiating love made him declare: "I will be their God and they shall be my people" (Jeremiah 31:33 and Hebrews 8:10). This concept and fact of covenant links both testaments (or covenants), beginning with the promise in Genesis 3 that Christ, or the seed of Eve, would overcome man's alienation from God and death. This covenant found renewed expression in the lives of many Old Testament figures, chief among them being Abraham, the father of the faithful who was told: "I will establish my covenant between me and you, and your descendants after you throughout their generations for an everlasting covenant and to your descendants after you" (Genesis 17:7). The covenant reached its climax in the New Testament with God's offering of Himself in the Life, Death, and Resurrection of Jesus Christ; and this was clearly seen as an unconditional covenant of grace in St. Paul's Epistle to the Romans, for "When we were yet sinners, Christ died for us" (Romans 5:8).

The Old Covenant was marked by external ritual and ceremonial, the New by interior spiritual obedience. The Old was characterized by fear, the New by love. The Old risked a bondage

[86] See Perry Miller, *Errand in the Wilderness* (Cambridge, Mass., 1956), and J. G. Møller, "The Beginnings of Puritan Covenant Theology," *Journal of Ecclesiastical History*, XIV (1963), p. 53.

[87] Citations will be taken from the excellently edited modern translation of the third Latin edition by John D. Eusden, entitled, *The Marrow of Theology* (Boston and Philadelphia, 1968).

to works, the New affirms liberation in faith. The Old was limited to the Jews, the New is for all people. The Old was oppressive, the New is inviting.[88]

So important was this conception of the covenant that for many Puritans covenants replaced creeds, as engagements of the heart and will, as contrasted with creeds as merely offering the assent of the top of the mind.[89] Personal covenants were made as solemn undertakings to serve God. Group covenants were subscribed by new members of Puritan church fellowships, and these vows were renewed on days of humiliation or thanksgiving. Marriages were rightly seen as enduring covenants. Moreover, the chief politico-religious engagement of the Puritans was naturally termed "The Solemn League and Covenant." It is in this richly theological and social context that the definition of a Sacrament as a "seal of the covenant" was made and it carried with it the absolute verification and authentication of the divine love, God's continuing providential concern, and His gracious care for the unworthy—a deeply devotional idea which had removed some of the harshness and austerity from the Calvinism of double predestination—that *decretum horribile*, as Calvin himself recognized.

William Ames writes of the sacraments with clear Ramist definitions. Arguing that a holy sign is either a bare sign or a seal, he makes much of the fact that a seal "not only represents, but presents something by sealing," and that "a sign sealing the Covenant of God is called a Sacrament, Rom. 4.11."[90] In consequence, "a Sacrament of the New Covenant, therefore, is a divine institution in which the blessings of the New Covenant are represented, presented, and applied through signs perceptible to the senses." Further, the "special application of God's favour and grace which arise from true faith is very much furthered and confirmed by the Sacraments."[91] The primary purpose or end of a Sacrament is, for Ames, "to seal the Covenant. And this occurs not on God's part only, but secondarily on ours, for not only are the grace and promises of God sealed to us, but also our thankfulness and obedience to him."[92]

Moving from sacraments in general to the Lord's Supper, Ames described the latter as "the Sacrament of nourishment and growth

88 *Ibid.*, Introduction, pp. 53-54 to which I am indebted.
89 See Champlin Burrage, *The Church Covenant Idea* (Philadelphia, 1904).
90 *The Marrow of Theology* (ed. Eusden), p. 197.
91 *Ibid.*   92 *Ibid.*, p. 198.

313

for the faithful in Christ." His argument against Transubstantiation is an extraordinary reminder how abhorrent the eating of flesh and the drinking of blood are to human nature.[93] The spiritual nourishment in this Sacrament does not require a change of substance, but only of the application and use of the bread and wine, and that Christ be spiritually present with those who receive Him in faith.[94]

So far is Ames from accepting a literal interpretation of the crux, "This is my Body," that he finds a threefold figure in it! There is a primary metaphor (bread used for Body); then there is a part for the whole (Body is used for the Body-soul); and, finally, Christ is a shorthand term for all the benefits the Christian derives from Him.[95]

Ames is clearly in the tradition of Calvin, but the logical rigour of his definitions, the consecutive march of his propositions like soldiers, and the general take-it or leave-it attitude, indicate that we are in a different atmosphere. In it Calvin's sense of awe, humble recognition of mystery, and sheer gratitude, have disappeared. Yet this understanding of the chief Sacrament was immensely popular because admirably clear for inclusion in the catechisms that proliferated in this century. Part of its popularity was also due to its removal of some of the divine arbitrariness inherent in earlier Calvinism's disposal of the reprobate.[96] Perkins defines a Sacrament as an external sign which exhibits and seals to the faithful man Christ's saving grace.[97] The Westminster Confession of 1647 (and it is echoed by the Independent Savoy Declaration of 1658) defines sacraments as "Holy signs and seals of the covenant of grace, immediately instituted by God, to represent Christ and his benefits and to confirm our interest in him; . . ."[98] The Westminster Shorter Catechism defines a Sacrament in words that echo Ames to perfection: "A Sacrament is a holy ordinance instituted by Christ; wherein by sensible signs, Christ and the benefits of the new covenant are represented, sealed, and applied to believers."[99]

The Puritans are as eager as the high-church Anglicans to re-

---

[93] Ibid., p. 212.   [94] Ibid.   [95] Ibid., p. 213.

[96] For the softening of reprobation in Ames, see Eusden's intro. to The Marrow of Theology, pp. 29-30.

[97] Works, I, p. 72. Perkins's doctrine of the Lord's Supper is considered briefly in Davies, op. cit., I, p. 283.

[98] Chapter 27. See Philip Schaff, The Creeds of the Evangelical Protestant Churches (1877), p. 660. The marginal Biblical references to "covenant of grace" are Romans 4:11 and Genesis 17:7 and 10.

[99] Question 71; Schaff, op. cit., p. 696.

pudiate Transubstantiation as the mode of Christ's presence in the Lord's Supper. Thomas Cartwright, for example, has six arguments against the Roman doctrine. One is that if it is accepted, "at the first institution there must be two Christs, one that giveth, another that is given." The second is that it eliminates the sign, bread and wine, and hence eliminates a Sacrament. Thirdly, for Christ to be physically present on each altar there would have to be an ubiquity of his human nature, which is contrary to the nature of a body. Fourthly, the apostles and evangelists call the elements bread and wine *after* the consecration. Fifthly, all other miracles have been apparent to the senses, so this one would be the greatest miracle in the world as it is utterly invisible. Finally, if this were true doctrine, then the wicked as well as the godly would receive Christ in the Sacrament, and even "(which is horrible to consider) mice and rats may eate the true bodie of Christ and drinke his blood."[100]

Thomas Gataker's short treatise, *A Discussion of the Papist Doctrine of Transubstantiation* (1624) covers similar ground. It ends: "Whence I conclude that since this *Corporall presence*, such as the *Church of Rome* maintaineth, hath no warrant from *Gods word*, as their own *Cardinal* [Bellarmine] confesseth; and is besides contrary to *Scripture*, to *nature*, to *sight*, to *sense*, to *reason*, to *religion*, we have little *reason* to receive it, as a *truth of Christ*, or a *principle of Christianitie*."[101] The body of the treatise also claims that the doctrine is contrary to the Church Fathers and to Reformation ancestors as well.

Edward Reynolds finds Consubstantiation, or, at least, the teaching of the ubiquity of Christ's human nature which is its Lutheran underpinning, equally unacceptable as a way of explaining Christ's presence in the Lord's Supper. His major objection is to an inherent contradiction in this view, namely, that "in a finite nature there should be room enough for an infinite attribute";[102] for it is not the nature of a body to have ubiquity, but only of God the Spirit. His own view of the mode of Christ's sacramental presence is one of "energy and power." It is a "Sacramentall, Relative, Mysticall Presence." He supplies an analogy for understanding it, thus: "The King is in his Court or Presence chamber only *locally and*

---

[100] *A Treatise of the Christian Religion, Or, The Whole Bodie and Substance of Divinitie* (1616), p. 228. It was published thirteen years after Cartwright's death.

[101] *Op. cit.*, p. 33.

[102] *Meditation on the Holy Sacrament* (1638), p. 91.

physically [as Christ's human nature is a carnal, physical, and local presence in heaven], but *representatively* he is wherever his Chancellor or subordinate Judges are, in as much as whatsoever they in a legall and judiciall course doe determine is accompted by him as his own personall act."[103] His analogy has one unfortunate flaw—that as the chancellor acts for the king in his absence, so the priest or minister acts for Christ in His absence also.

Elsewhere in this work Reynolds does make two important points: that Christ is in the action of the Lord's Supper, and it is the *whole* Christ who is present. Thus, while Christ cannot be said to be present in, with, or under the elements, as if the sacraments were automatically efficacious (which would be to deny the energising power of the Holy Spirit and the necessity for the elect to receive by faith), yet He is present in the action. Thus "the Sacrament, however by consecration it be separated from a common unto a divine life, yet is never properly to bee called the Body of Christ till Taken and Eaten, by means of which Actions (if they be Actions of Faith) that holy Bread and Wine does as really convey whole Christ with the vital influences that proceed from him unto the soule, as hand doth them unto the mouth, or the mouth unto the stomach."[104]

The Sacrament was not valued less by the magisterial Puritan divines of the Commonwealth, such as Thomas Goodwin or Richard Baxter. In fact, in two places in his writings, Goodwin, the Independent President of Magdalen College, Oxford, seems to value the Lord's Supper more than preaching. In one place, he writes:

> Many things in a sermon thou understandest not, and haply not many sermons; or if thou doest, yet findest not thy portion in them; but here [in the Lord's Supper] to be sure thou mayest. If sermons, some are for comfort, some to inform, some to excite; but here in the Sacrament is all thou canst expect. Christ is here light, and wisdom, and comfort, and all to thee. He is here an eye to the blind, a foot to the lame; yea, everything to everyone.[105]

[103] *Ibid.*, p. 94.
[104] *Ibid.*, p. 88. Cf. the parallel with Hooker's *Ecclesiastical Polity*, Bk. v. Chap. XVII, Sect. 12.
[105] *The Government of the Churches of Christ* in *Works* (ed. J. Miller, 1861), XI, p. 408.

Goodwin also believes that the Lord's Supper admits the Christian to the closest intimacy with Christ, and that Christ speaks more directly in His own words and actions than through the second-hand utterance of a preacher in a sermon. Also the Sacrament is more immediately impressive than the Word. The Word preached is of Christ, but it is nowhere called Christ, but the bread is Christ, of which the Lord says, "This is my Body." The Word preached is like the moon, variable; but the Christ of the Communion is constant, like the sun.[106]

One consistent theory of the Eucharistic presence runs constantly throughout Puritanism, whether Presbyterian or Independent. The presence of Christ is mystical and spiritual, not carnal or local, and it represents, presents, and applies to the believers the benefits of the covenant of grace, which it seals and authenticates to their faith by the power of the Holy Spirit. In the words of Matthew Henry, these benefits are: "Christ and a Pardon, Christ and Peace, Christ and Grace, Christ and Heaven."[107]

So much for the theory: what of the practice? Are these teachings we have considered really expressed in the Puritan rites? We cannot, of course, know the answers in detail, but we can examine three representative celebrations of the Lord's Supper, one Independent, and the other two Presbyterian. They are, respectively, John Cotton's account of Independent worship in New England, the Westminster or Parliamentary *Directory*'s[108] Communion Order, and Richard Baxter's *The Reformed Liturgy*[109] (sometimes called *The Savoy Liturgy* because it was prepared for the Savoy Conference of the Presbyterians and the Anglicans at the Restoration).

John Cotton had the unusual privilege in New England of showing Old England what the powerful new form of Puritanism, Independency, was like in practice, while this was an unknown quantity in England. His reputation in Boston, England, was so great before he emigrated that he was nominated a member of the Westminster Assembly though he had left for the shores of the New World, and consequently *The Way of the Churches of Christ in New England* (1645) was read with considerable excitement by Cromwell's supporters in England, and with some trepidation by

---

[106] *Of Gospel Holiness* in *Works*, VII, pp. 313-15.
[107] *The Communicant's Companion* (1704), p. 27.
[108] Analysed in the first section of Chapter XI entitled, "Puritan Service Books."
[109] Analysed in Chap. XI, Sect. 3.

orthodox Presbyterian divines such as Robert Baillie and Thomas "Gangraena" Edwards. Cotton writes:

> Ceremonies wee use none, but are careful to administer all things according to the primitive institutions. . . . The Lord's Supper we administer for the time, *once a moneth at least*, and for the *gesture*, to the people *sitting*; according as Christ administered it to his Disciples *sitting*, (*Mat*. 26. 20. 26) who also made a Symbolicall use of it to teach the Church their majoritie over their Ministers in some cases, and their judiciall authoritye, as co-sessors with him at the last Judgement, (*Luke* 22. 27 to 30.) which maketh us to looke at kneeling at the Lords Supper, not only as adoration devised by man, but also as a violation by man of the institution of Christ, diminishing part of the Counsell of God, and of the honour and comfort of the Church held forth in it.
>
> In time of *solemnization* of the Supper, the Minister having taken, blessed, and broken the bread, and commanded all the people to take and eate it, as the body of Christ broken for them, he taketh it himselfe, and giveth it to all that sit at Table with him, and from the Table it is reached by the Deacons to the people sitting in the next seats about them, the Minister sitting in his place at the Table.
>
> After they have all partaked in the bread, he taketh the cup in like manner, and *giveth thanks a new*, (blesseth it) according to the example of Christ in the Evangelist, who described the institution *Mat*. 26. 27. *Mark* 14.23. *Luke* 22.17. All of them in such a way as setteth forth the Elements, not blessed *together*, but either of them *apart*; the bread first by it selfe, and afterwards the wine by it selfe; for what reason the Lord himselfe best knoweth, and wee cannot be ignorant, that a received solemne blessing, expressly performed by himselfe, doth apparently call upon the whole assembly to look againe for a supernatural and speciall blessing in the same Element also as well as in the former for which the Lord will be againe sought to do it for us.[110]

The double prayer of blessing or thanksgiving is a distinctive custom of the Independents, almost certainly inherited from the Brownists. It was done in order exactly to reproduce Christ's

---

[110] *The Way of the Churches of Christ in New England* (1645), pp. 68-69.

actions at the Last Supper. While not strictly necessary, as Cotton implies ("for what reason the Lord himselfe best knoweth"), it was a token of total obedience to the very letter of the Scripture as God's orders. It was also a singular proof of their belief in the real presence, for in it they looked for "a supernaturall and speciall blessing." Nothing could be simpler; yet it was profound because faith expected an epiphany in the Eucharist.

The *Directory* is a series of rubrics with suggested prayers and exhortations for all the ordinances of worship, which carries the approval of the English and Scottish Presbyterians and of the English Independents; it is an important, normative, and representative liturgical document.

Does it have a high or a low doctrine of the Lord's Supper? We may note to begin with that it states "the Sacrament is frequently to be observed."[111] Next it should be noticed that the holy table is to be "fenced" or guarded against unworthy receivers who will bring dishonour to the ordinance.[112] In the third place, also to prevent attendance at the Lord's Supper becoming a mere formality, there should be self-scrutiny and instruction on the Sacrament on either the previous Sunday or during the preceding week "that . . . all may come better prepared to that heavenly feast."[113] Fourthly, the Prayer of Consecration gives God thanks "for all means of grace, the Word and Sacraments, and for this Sacrament in particular, by which Christ and all his benefits are applied and sealed up unto us"; it also includes an *epiklesis*, beseeching God "to vouchsafe his gracious presence, and the effectual working of his Spirit in us, and so to sanctify these elements of bread and wine, and to bless his own ordinance that we may receive by faith the body and blood of Jesus Christ crucified for us."[114] Finally, the Post-Communion Prayer of Thanksgiving again mentions the energising power of the Holy Spirit as it pleads "for the gracious assistance of his good Spirit whereby they [the communicants] may be enabled to walk in the strength of that grace, as becometh those who have received so great pledges of salvation."[115] On all these grounds, it must be adjudged a consistently high doctrine of the real spiritual presence of Christ in the action mediated by the Holy Spirit, and a true means of grace.

---

[111] *Reliquiae Liturgicae*, III: *The Parliamentary Directory* (ed. Peter Hall, Bath, 1847), p. 52.

[112] *Ibid.*   [113] *Ibid.*

[114] *Ibid.*, p. 56.   [115] *Ibid.*, p. 58.

What of the doctrine in Baxter's *The Reformed Liturgy*? We need do little more than recall the judgment of the late Regius Professor of Divinity in the University of Cambridge, E. C. Ratcliff. That eminent liturgiologist observed that Baxter's Eucharistic doctrine was "markedly higher than the doctrine expressed or implied in the Communion Office of the Prayer Book of 1552 or 1559" and that it was "nearer to the historic Western tradition. . . ."[116] From such a careful scholar and an Anglican priest that is a high evaluation. The Communion service itself bears out his assessment. Baxter's *The Reformation of the Liturgy* was intended to be, as its name implies, a more Biblically grounded alternative to the Prayer Book acceptable to the English Presbyterians, though it was entirely Baxter's own and not the composition of a committee. It has value, therefore, as a representative conservative Puritan production by a very distinguished pastor and writer.

Baxter had many gifts, but concision was not among them. Hence, his definitions are lengthy, but they are essential data for the evaluation of his sacramental doctrine. His introduction defines the Lord's Supper as having a commemorative and representational significance, so that the consecrated bread and wine are given "to signify and solemnize the renewal of his holy covenant with them and the giving of himself unto them, to expiate their sins by his sacrifice, and to sanctify them further by his Spirit, and confirm their right to everlasting life."[117] The Prayer of Consecration has an explicit *epiklesis*.[118] The sense of divine pardon as a benefit received from Christ is conveyed in the phrase, "Behold the sacrificed Lamb of God that takes away the sins of the world!"[119] Christ is begged "to feed us with the bread of life."[120] The virtue and efficacy of the Sacrament is attributed definitely to the Holy Spirit, not only, of course, in the *epiklesis*, but in the prayer immediately following the libation, which begins, "Most Holy Spirit," and which continues, "Sanctify and quicken us that we may relish the spiritual food and feed on it to our nourishment and growth in grace."[121] A Post-Communion Exhortation emphasizes the concept of the celestial banquet, as Baxter reminds the communicants

---

[116] *From Uniformity to Unity* (ed. G. F. Nuttall and O. C. Chadwick, 1962), p. 123.
[117] *Reliquiae Liturgicae*, IV: *The Savoy Liturgy* (ed. Peter Hall, Bath, 1847), p. 57.
[118] *Ibid.*, p. 68. [119] *Ibid.*, p. 61.
[120] *Ibid.*, p. 67. [121] *Ibid.*, p. 71.

that "we have feasted with the Son of God at his table upon his flesh and blood, in preparation for that feast of endless glory."[122] In short, in Baxter's own summary words, this is a "renewed covenant of pardon, grace, and glory."[123] It wipes out the past, gives strength or grace for the present, and prepares for the life beyond death. What more could the Sacrament do? Further, which is most unusual for Puritanism for whom the saints are visible, Baxter does not forget the Communion of saints and the church triumphant in heaven. Unquestionably he expresses a high doctrine of the Lord's Supper.

It is particularly fortunate that we have a manuscript letter of Baxter's written in March, 1657, in which he described how he celebrated the Lord's Supper at Kidderminster:

> A long table being spread, I first open the nature and use of the ordinance, and the qualification and present duty of the communicants; and then the deacons (3 or 4 grave, pious men chosen and appointed to that office) do set the bread and wine on the table; and in prayer we beseech the Lord to accept of those his own creatures now dedicated and set apart for his service, as sanctified to represent the body and blood of his Son; and after confession of sin, and thanksgiving for redemption, with commemoration of the sufferings of Christ therein, and ransom thereby, we beg the pardon of sin, and the acceptance of our persons and thanksgivings now offered up to God again, and his grace to help our faith, repentance, love, etc. and renewal of our covenant with him, etc. And so after words of institution etc. I break the bread and deliver it in Christ's general terms to all present, first partaking myself, and so by the cup: which is moved down to the end of the table by the people and deacons (who fill the cup when it is emptied); and immediately after it, each one layeth down his alms for the poor, and so arise, and the next table ful succeedeth to the last: after which I first proceed to some words of exhortation, and then of praise and prayer, and sing a psalm, and so conclude with the blessing.[124]

This description does not allow Baxter to develop his Eucharistic thought as thoroughly as in *The Reformed Liturgy*, but it is sig-

---

[122] *Ibid.*   [123] *Ibid.*, p. 77.
[124] Dr. Williams's Library: Baxter Ms. 3: 156; cited by G. F. Nuttall, *Richard Baxter* (1965), p. 53.

nificant that the role of the Holy Spirit is implicit in the sanctification of the elements, the covenant is mentioned, and, above all, the petition for "his grace to help our faith, repentance, love" means that the Lord's Supper is clearly conceived as a means of grace.

If we apply the tests of frequency of celebration, high ceremonial, and emblems on chalices, to determine whether the Eucharistic doctrine is high or low, the results will, to say the least, be ambiguous for Puritanism. On frequency the score will be high for the Independents and low for the Presbyterians. If a monthly Communion became the norm for Independents, they had followed Calvin[125] at the beginning by requiring a weekly celebration. *The Apologeticall Narration* prepared by the Independent Brethren for the Westminster Assembly stated that they celebrated the Lord's Supper every Lord's Day,[126] and John Owen's Catechism said that Communion is to be administered "every first day of the week, or at least as often as opportunity and conveniency be obtained."[127] But it soon became the custom, as John Cotton records,[128] for Independents to have the chief Sacrament "once a moneth at least." It is not safe, however, to argue that an infrequent celebration means a low evaluation of the Lord's Supper for, although the Presbyterian Church of Scotland, had a quarterly and sometimes a twice-yearly celebration, it was often attended by vast gatherings[129] that were prepared for by Communion discourses at several week-night services. It seemed only that Presbyterians gathered in larger numbers on fewer occasions for the Lord's Supper, apparently on the principle that familiarity breeds contempt.

The appropriate Puritan gestures (whether Presbyterian or Independent) for receiving the elements were standing or sitting, and certainly not kneeling. The latter was associated with Transubstantiation and had been a "noxious ceremony" objected to by the earliest Scottish Presbyterians like John Knox, who had caused the "Black Rubric" to be inserted in the 1552 Prayer Book to explain that kneeling carried no idolatrous innuendo. What had begun as a protest against kneeling, developed, as far as sitting is concerned, into a symbol in its own right, defended either as a

---

[125] *Institutes*, Bk. IV, Chap. XVII, Sect. 43: "very frequently, and at least once a week."

[126] P. 8.

[127] William Orme, *Memoirs of the Life, Writings and Religious Connexions of John Owen, D.D.* (1820), p. 308.

[128] *Op. cit.*, p. 68.

[129] William D. Maxwell, *A History of Worship in the Church of Scotland* (1955), pp. 141f.

proleptic sign of the rest of the eternal banquet which Christ will give to His faithful, or as an indication that Christ invites his "saints" to share His theocratic rule. But this is, of course, a very simple ceremony which could be interpreted as carrying no disrespect for the Eucharist, but equally as conveying no unusual respect to the elements either.

Then as we saw earlier, the domestication of the Eucharist in Puritanism by the use of simple Treen ware, or of functional beakers, such as might be used for family meals in cottages, would probably be consonant with a low, Memorialist interpretation of the Communion. This hypothesis is reinforced by the fact that Zwingli, the father of Memorialism, introduced wooden chalices and patens into the Lord's Supper in Zurich.

4. *The Subsequent History of Communions*

Although there was continuing controversy over the Eucharist in the seventeenth century concerning the mode of Christ's presence and its ornamental and ceremonial adjuncts, particularly in the days when Laud was Archbishop of Canterbury, it would be exceedingly difficult to distinguish Anglican from Puritan sacramental doctrine.

So the question remains: Which ecclesial community, Anglicans or Nonconformists, preserved the higher doctrine and the greater appreciation of the Holy Communion? The answer, even allowing for a certain lowering of the Anglican estimation of the chief Sacrament in Latitudinarian and deistic days, must be in favour of the Anglicans.[130] As Howard Hageman has shown in *Pulpit and Table*,[131] in a memorable chapter entitled, "Tale of Two Cities," there is a perpetual danger in Reformed churchmanship for a high Genevan evaluation of the Lord's Supper to deteriorate into a low Zurich diminishing of its value, as Calvin's theory and practice is replaced by Zwingli's. The Zwinglian interpretation is much less complex, therefore easier to understand than Calvin's, and to defend. This is to regard Communion as a sign of the Christian community's loyalty, and as a vivid illustration of Christ's love for His people; in a word it is a powerful mnemonic. Puritanism allowing its ministers with freedom to be inspired by the Holy Spirit in interpreting the Word of God, or equally to be inspired by the *Zeitgeist*, was unprotected in its Communion doctrine. The Church

---

130 See G. J. Cuming, *A History of Anglican Liturgy* (1969), p. 114.
131 Published in Richmond, Va. and London (1962).

of England was protected by having a set Order of Holy Communion, whereas the Puritans had only a set of rubrics.

It is unquestionably true that there were in seventeenth-century England several factors working towards a depreciation of the Holy Communion, and these were less easily resisted in Puritanism than in Anglicanism. A dualistic depreciation of the body and the senses (with a consequent diminishing of the value of sacraments) was a characteristic trend of the middle and later part of our period. It was to be found to some small extent even in Calvin[132] himself who stressed that the sacramental signs are God's accommodation to our weak nature needing sensible tokens. It was found in increasing strength among the so-called spiritual Puritans like William Dell, John Saltmarsh, and William Erbury, who, like Joachim of Fiore, proclaimed the coming dispensation of the Spirit and the end of institutions. This emphasis on dematerialisation was found in an extreme form in many of the new Commonwealth sects, such as the Seekers, Ranters,[133] and Muggletonians, and even the Socinians[134] would minimise the importance of Communion. The most important group who opposed the sacraments as unspiritual were, of course, the Quakers[135] whose insistence on the Inner Light equated outward forms with the outer darkness. The cumulative impact of all these protests against externality and hypocrisy in religion was seriously to diminish the general estimation in which the sacraments were held.

Another factor, having the same effect, as Stephen Mayor[136] has acutely observed, was the paradoxical fact that the Puritan insistence on preserving at all costs the purity and integrity of the Lord's Supper, actually endangered it. It was thought wiser to have no Lord's Supper than to have it celebrated by an unpreaching minister; and better to forgo it than to admit a "mixed multitude" of unworthy communicants along with the "visible saints." The logical absurdity of the position was evident in the attitude of a certain A. Pinchbeck who in 1654 went to become Rector of

---

132 *Institutes*, Bk. IV, Chap. XIV, Sect. 3, to take but one notable example.

133 See A. L. Morton, *The World of the Ranters* (1970), which also deals with the Joachite ideas of the Seekers (pp. 126-30; 155-57).

134 H. J. McLachlan, *Socinianism in Seventeenth Century England* (1951), pp. 317f.

135 On this topic see Hugh Barbour, *The Quakers in Puritan England* (New Haven, Conn., 1964), p. 164f.; W. C. Braithwaite, *The Beginnings of Quakerism* (Cambridge, 2nd edn., 1955), pp. 137f.; and Elbert Russell, *The History of Quakerism* (1942), pp. 49f. This is also considered in the second part of Chapter XIV, "Radical Worship: the Baptists and Quakers."

136 *The Lord's Supper in Early English Dissent* (1972).

Masbury in Essex and who refused to celebrate the Lord's Supper because in his judgment there was no true church there.[137]

Another powerful dissuasive from attending Holy Communion must have been the increasing emphasis on sin and unworthiness, especially in Presbyterian and Independent circles, and the consequent enlargement of the catalogue of sins listed in the monitory "fencing of the Table," and the whole system of ecclesiastical espionage and tale-bearing leading eventually to excommunication. The sense of liberation and joy in the earliest celebration of the Sacrament in the apostolic church, which Puritanism claimed to repristinate, had obviously been lost.

In these circumstances the Lord's Supper could all too easily degenerate into memorialism and a mnemonic. From this fate the set Order of Holy Communion of the Book of Common Prayer, the round of the festivals of the Christian year, the high-church veneration for the Fathers, and its rich sacramental tradition, delivered the Church of England, for which the Holy Communion had never ceased to be a valued means of grace. For the Puritans, largely also because of their high evaluation of preaching, the Communion, unless carefully safeguarded, might slip into being only a sermon illustration.

[137] Geoffrey F. Nuttall, *Visible Saints* (Oxford, 1957), pp. 134f.

PART THREE

THE HISTORY AND

FORMS OF WORSHIP

CHAPTER IX

THE ANGLICAN PRAYER BOOK
ADMIRED AND REJECTED:
1603-1659

THE MOST fascinating feature of the history of the Book of Common Prayer in the seventeenth century is the differing image it presents at different times to both friends and foes. It exhibits at least seven different faces (occasionally masks) to its supporters and critics.

1. *Changing Images of the Prayer Book*

Its dominant image under the Stuarts is that of its admirers by whom it is viewed as an excellent medium for the expression of the spirit of the English church and people before God. It is moderate. That is, it avoids the extremes of Popery and Presbytery, neither superstitiously nor anachronistically backward-looking, nor enamoured of innovation for its own sake. It is rational. That is, it avoids the mystical ecstasies of the Carmelites on the right, and the artificial hothouse warmth of the chaotic sermons and prayers of the sectaries on the left. This is a well-ordered worship of great dignity and decency. It is Scriptural in contents and in giving the Scripture a large place in the lectionary and in the prayers and sermons, but it also follows the doctrine and usages of the primitive church. It is a book alike for priest and people, intended for edification rather than the maintenance of mysteries, so it is in the vernacular tongue and it allows for the responses of the people in prayers, as well as in the psalmody. It is neither sacerdotally authoritarian, nor popularly indiscriminate. On this view, it is an admirable and entirely apt instrument of the Anglican *Via Media*, midway between Roman Catholicism and extreme Protestantism. This, we may suppose, was the view of the majority of the clergy and of the majority of the English people, thinking or unthinking, since it was revived at the Restoration, reviewed, and left not greatly changed.

Other faces presented by the Prayer Book were seen with equal vividness perhaps, but not over as long a time. The Crown and the hierarchy in church and state saw the Prayer Book as a very convenient expression (and engine) of political-religious conformity. Such is the unmistakable impression left by the partly negative response of King James I and the wholly negative response of the bishops to Puritan demands for changes in worship and church government at the Hampton Court Conference of 1604,[1] summed up in the angry rebuttal, "No Bishop, No King." After this James maintained the connexion between the divine right of kings and the apostolical succession, harrying the Puritans. The same impression is left by the high-church veneration of the unfortunate King Charles as "King and Martyr" of the Anglican church and Prayer Book.[2] The leaders in church and state found the Prayer Book a convenient way of cultivating the virtues of humility and acceptance of one's position in society as God-given, as well as of inculcating honour for the king by the daily prayers for his majesty and the members of the royal household included in the Prayer Book. And as long as the occasional service or parts of services commemorated the horror of treason on Gowrie Day and on the Anniversary of the Gunpowder Plot, social and religious revolution

---

[1] The Hampton Court Conference, over which James I presided, was convened to consider the demands of the Puritan Millenary Petition of 1603, supposedly backed by a thousand Puritan ministers, asking for changes in the Prayer Book, and deploring the profanation of the Sabbath. Its Puritan leader, a former Dean of Lincoln, now President of Corpus Christi College, Oxford, was Dr. John Rainolds, and the leaders among the Bishops were Richard Bancroft, Archbishop of Canterbury, and Bilson of Winchester. It was an abortive meeting for the Puritans, except for Rainolds's suggestion that a new translation of the Scriptures be undertaken, to which Bancroft reluctantly agreed, and which was to be the Authorized Version of the Bible (known also as the "King James Version") published in 1611. Bancroft saw the need for greater uniformity in worship and for discipline among Anglican clergy and to that end largely composed and saw through Convocation the Canons of 1604. Early in the new century orthodox Anglicans and Puritan Anglicans were preparing their strategies and flexing their theological muscles. See Mark H. Curtis, "The Hampton Court Conference and its aftermath," *History*, Vol. XLVI, No. 156 (Feb. 1961), pp. 1-16.

[2] Charles I, however arbitrary his rule and his character, was even in defeat unwilling to concede to his Puritan adversaries any agreement to give up episcopacy, and his inflexibility at this point made many consider him a martyr to the cause of the Church of England. In the days before his death he showed great courage, devotion to God and dignity; in Marvell's words about his execution,

> He nothing common did or mean
> Upon that memorable scene
>
> . . . .
>
> But bowed his comely head
> Down as upon a bed.

On the day of his death there appeared a hagiographical work, the *Eikon Basilike* [Image of a King], which many attributed to the King himself, but is generally thought to be the work of John Gauden, later to be Bishop of Exeter. The anniversary of the day of his execution, January 30, was kept as a day of national fasting and humiliation from 1662 to 1859.

seemed only a very distant possibility. Thus the Prayer Book fortified the joint rule of sceptre and mitre.

In the penal days for Anglicanism, so often referred to as the
"Interregnum" (to avoid recognition of the legitimacy of the Commonwealth or Protectorate), the Prayer Book had become the symbol of a secret, exciting, and prohibited worship (like the Mass
for the English Recusants), and, even more significantly, the symbol of loyalty to a suffering church. Even in palmier days, it was
never to lose this profound respect; as if it was necessary for it to
have been prohibited for it to be fully appreciated.

Yet another face was presented by the Prayer Book at the Restoration. To the Parliament of Charles II, bent on restoring English life to what it was like before the "Great Rebellion," the Prayer
Book was the very image of conservatism, of the unchanging island
in a sea of turbulence. So much was this the case that even the
most well considered and liturgically researched suggestions for
revision proposed by two bishops in particular whose loyalty to
the Church of England had been proven in exile and imprisonment, were rejected because they *were* changes. The Prayer Book
became almost sacrosanct.

Yet to experts in worship the Prayer Book was respected but
not idolised; it was improvable. For the liturgiologists, Bishops
Wren (who had been imprisoned for eighteen years in the Tower
of London) and Cosin (who had gone into exile in France with
the residue of the English court), the Prayer Book was an important symbol of loyalty, but it was not sacrosanct. In fact, it needed
bettering in several respects, notably in the Office for Holy Communion, which is what they had hoped to do with it in their
"Advices" and "Proposals." To Richard Baxter, the leader of the
moderate Puritans (or Presbyterians) at the Savoy Conference of
1661, convened to try and arrange a revision of the Prayer Book
to make it acceptable to both Anglicans and Puritans, it was also
improvable, as some of its phraseology could be more Scriptural,
and certain ceremonies offensive to tender Puritan consciences
might be made permissive or even dropped altogether.

Perhaps, however, more interesting is the fact that the Prayer
Book was seen by him as an *eirenicon*, an ecumenical and uniting
formulary. It is interesting because this is exactly how a later
Anglican, Dean Thomas Comber (1645-1699), who was a strong
supporter of the "Glorious Revolution" of William and Mary, saw
the Prayer Book as "so comprehensive, so exact, and so inoffensive

a Composure; which is so *judiciously contrived* that the wisest may exercise at once their knowledge and devotion; and yet so plain, that the most ignorant may pray with understanding. . . ."[3]

To the generality of Puritans the Prayer Book presented three masks rather than faces. The earlier Puritans of Elizabethan and Jacobean times saw it not so much as the instrument or channel of the *Via Media* as the exhibition of a cowardly compromise, a Mr. Facing-Bothways, a Laodicean unwillingness to go all the way towards a thoroughly Scriptural and Reformed liturgy, such as was used in Geneva or Zurich or Strasbourg, or Scotland[4] before 1637 when the so-called Laudian liturgy was imposed. Certainly this was the view of the Presbyterians who were far from objecting to liturgical forms. The more radical Independents viewed the Prayer Book as an idol, a creation of men which was prescribed for the people's worship, and which led to a quenching of the Holy Spirit in prayer, encouraged laziness in the clergy, and was flatly contradicted by the Epistle to the Romans 8:26, 27.[5]

Eventually all Puritans, moderate or radical, came to see the Prayer Book as the repressive instrument of despotic absolutism, the symbol of the retention of "the rags of Popery" and therefore of disloyalty to the Reformation, the sinister emblem of compromise and unreliability. By that time its fate was sealed. Parliament, as advised by the Westminster Assembly of Divines, issued the *Directory for the Public Worship of God* to replace the Prayer Book. This ordinance was passed by both Houses of Parliament on January 4, 1645, and penalties for using the Prayer Book or failing to use the Directory were imposed on August 26, 1645.

The theme of the ensuing pages will be the changing fate of the Book of Common Prayer, admired and then despised and rejected, and eventually restored. The arguments advanced by its Anglican defenders and its Puritan detractors will be considered only incidentally.[6] The successive changes proposed and accepted, the alternatives, such as the *Scottish Prayer Book of 1637* (mis-

---

[3] *A Discourse Concerning the daily frequenting the Common Prayer* (1687), p. 13.

[4] See W. D. Maxwell, *John Knox's Genevan Service Book, 1556* (Edinburgh, 1931).

[5] John Owen, Puritan Dean of Christ Church, Oxford and Vice-Chancellor of Oxford University, wrote a treatise, *A Discourse of the Work of the Holy Spirit in Prayer* which is an extended sermon on this text (see particularly *Works*, IV, 55, and *A Discourse concerning Liturgies and their Imposition* [1662] which is a formidable critique of all liturgies).

[6] These have been discussed in detail in Chap. v.

332

called the "Laudian liturgy"), and the interesting but entirely unofficial adaptations of the Anglican liturgy used by the future Bishops Robert Sanderson and Jeremy Taylor during the Commonwealth and Protectorate will be considered. All these are part and parcel of the history of the Anglican liturgy in our period. But more astonishing even than the protean images of the liturgy itself will be the discovery that in the most changing century of recent English history, the Prayer Book itself remained almost unaltered, apparently immune from savage attacks of time and revolution.

2. The Early Stuart Settlement of Worship: 1603-1645

The Jacobean settlement of worship comprised two components: the Hampton Court Conference and the Canons of 1604.

The demands of the Puritans at the Conference, following on their Millenary Petition presented so hopefully to the monarch of a fully Reformed church in Scotland now arriving in England to take up the English throne in 1603, provided a convenient summary of their critique of the Prayer Book. The Millenary Petition, while avoiding the thorny question of episcopacy to which James was known to be attached, made several requests, among which were the following: "That the cross in Baptism, Interrogatories administered to infants, Confirmations[7] as superstitious, may be taken away; Baptism not to be ministered by women, and so explained,[8] the Cap and Surplice not urged; that examination may go before Communion; that it be administered with a Sermon, that divers terms of priests and absolution, and some other used, with the ring in marriage, and such like in the book, may be corrected; the longsomeness of service abridged; church songs and music moderated to better edification; that the Lord's Day be not profaned; the rest upon holidays not so strictly urged; that there may be an uniformity of doctrine prescribed; no popish opinion to be any more taught or defended; no ministers charged to teach their people to bow at the name of Jesus; that the canonical Scriptures only be read in the Church."[9]

The matter was referred to the Conference convened at Hamp-

---

[7] Confirmation was seldom administered by the Elizabethan bishops, many of whom had vast dioceses, some of which had been kept vacant for long years by the Crown. See E. C. Ratcliff, *The Booke of Common Prayer of the Churche of England: its Making and Revisions, 1549-1661* (1949, Alcuin Club Collections XXXVII), p. 18.

[8] Provision for such was made in the new Canon 55.

[9] E. Cardwell, *A History of Conferences and other Proceedings* (Oxford, 1841).

ton Court in January, 1604. The established church was represented by eight bishops, seven deans, and two doctors of divinity.
The Puritans were limited to four spokesmen. The agenda, by
royal request, was also limited to consideration of six major criticisms made by the Puritans. These were: the general Absolution,
the Confirmation of children, private Baptism administered by
women, the inordinate brevity of the Prayer Book Catechism and
the too great length of Dean Nowell's Catechism (sometimes used
as an alternative), the inaccuracy of existing translations of the
Bible, certain inaccuracies in the Prayer Book, the inclusion of the
Apocrypha in the lectionary, and other various minor matters.

After three days of discussion, the following conclusions were
reached. The title of the Absolution was clarified by the addition
of the words "of pronouncing the remission of sins," while to Confirmation was to be added "catechising or examination of the children's faith." It was also agreed that private Baptism was to be
"by the ministers and curates," and that a "uniform short and plain
catechisme be made," as also a translation of the entire Bible without marginal notes,[10] which was to be required for all the churches
in England for use during divine service. Lessons from the
Apocrypha repugnant to canonical Scripture would "be removed
and not read." The words in the Marriage service were to be made
clearer. The signation of the cross in Baptism was retained as
being merely significative and not a "sign effective."[11]

Such were the agreements, whereas the changes actually made
as authorized in a letter from the Archbishop of Canterbury and
the bishops of London and Chichester, and enforced by a proclamation prefixed to the Prayer Book, were more favourable to the
established church than to its critics.[12]

The really important changes were the exclusion of Baptism
performed by women or laymen, and the enlargement of the catechism by two sections on Baptism and Holy Communion, the new
material being substantially based on the two catechisms of Nowell.
Four lessons from the Apocrypha were replaced by lessons from
the Old Testament. And, of course, the Authorized Version of the

[10] A palpable hit at the Genevan version of the Bible, with its tendentious
marginal notes, and much beloved by the Puritans.

[11] The point here is that the established church representatives were denying
that the signing with the cross was any sacrament, but only had symbolical or
pedagogical value.

[12] G. J. Cuming's admirable *A History of the Anglican Liturgy* (1969), to
which this chapter owes much, carefully notes the slight differences between the
agreement and the execution on pp. 138ff.

Bible was put in hand and published in 1611.[13] The most significant difference between the agreement and the execution of it was that no change was in fact made in the wording of the service of Matrimony.

The Puritans were still dissatisfied since the ring in Marriage and the crossing in Baptism (two of the three originally "noxious ceremonies") were retained and the surplice would be uniformly enjoined in the canons. There was to be an examination of intending communicants before the reception of Holy Communion, which was considered a profanation of that ordinance and an act of disobedience to the implicit injunction given by St. Paul in I Corinthians 11:27-29. They had less reason to grumble about the other additions made. These included a prayer for the royal family at Mattins and Evensong, together with a suffrage for them in the Litany. One may suppose that the provision of six prayers of thanksgiving "for diverse benefits" was very much to their liking, for Dr. Reynolds and others had complained of this lack of prayers for specific benefits in the Prayer Book. According to G. J. Cuming,[14] while this suggestion is not reported at the Hampton Court Conference, yet it may have come from Dean Overall of St. Paul's who was a member of the Conference, and he might have told it to John Cosin[15] who became his chaplain.

The Puritans were presumably glad that the discovery of the Gunpowder Plot of Guy Fawkes and the Roman Catholic conspirators with him to blow up both Houses of Parliament and destroy the King, Lords, and Commons, led to a renewed protest of Protestantism, and that this was annually commemorated on November 5 in a special service[16] added by royal proclamation to the Book of Common Prayer in 1605, which continued until 1859, thirty years after religious toleration had been granted to Roman Catholics in England. Gowrie Day, an annual thanksgiving for the deliverance of James as ruler of Scotland from an attempted assassination by the Earl of Gowrie and his brother, was of less interest, and it lapsed at James's death.

Puritan liturgical dissatisfaction was expressed in a more rigor-

[13] The most significant difference between the agreement and the execution was that no change in wording in the service of Matrimony was made, although promised.

[14] *Op. cit.*, p. 138.

[15] John Cosin, *Works*, 5 Vols. (Library of Anglo-Catholic Theology, 1843-1855), v, pp. 455-56.

[16] This service, as also the Gowrie Day commemoration, is considered in Chap. VI, "Calendar Conflict: Holy Days and Holidays."

ous form than hitherto in 1606 in *A Survey of the Book of Common Prayer*, which compared the Prayer Books of 1549, 1552, and the Canons of 1604, in order to point out in meticulous detail the inconsistencies between them, as well as their reduplications, and which argued for the substitution of *The Book of Common Order*, the Scottish Reformed Service Book, for the Book of Common Prayer, which would thus guarantee a unity of worship in England and Scotland.

The changes in worship in the reigns of the early Stuarts were due in part to differences between Anglicans and "Genevans" (as old as the Cox-Knox "Troubles of Frankfort" of 1554) which widened in this period as the gap between the Catholic and Puritan trends became an abyss. It was accentuated by the Canons of 1604 and the development of the so-called Laudian tradition of high churchmanship. This is perhaps more adequately described as the Hooker-Andrewes-Laud tradition of which Hooker was the theologian, Andrewes the liturgiologist-preacher-bishop, and Laud the fervent disciple and chief executant as Bishop of London (1628) and Archbishop of Canterbury (1633-1645).

The canons, so far as they applied to worship, established a new norm. The Common Prayer was to be said on all holy days and their eves, as appointed by the Prayer Book (Canon 13). As regards Baptism, godparents must have received Holy Communion (Canon 29), and an explanation of its meaning is included in this service. The wearing of the surplice is re-enforced (Canon 58). The furniture of every parish church is to include a stone font (Canon 87), a decent Communion table covered ordinarily with a silk carpet, but at the time of Communion with a fair linen cloth, and the table is to be placed conveniently for hearing and for communicating. Also, the Decalogue is to be inscribed on the east wall, with other chosen sentences (Canon 82). Further requirements are: a pulpit (Canon 83), an alms-chest (Canon 84), a Bible and Prayer Book (Canon 80), and a table for the prohibited degrees of marriage (Canon 99).

The lengthy morning service of the Church of England consisted of Mattins, the Litany, and the Ante-Communion with sermon, except when the Communion completed the whole. It was generally celebrated with order and dignity, as required by the canons, with greater or lesser attention to the enrichment of vestments and ceremonial, and with a shorter or longer sermon, depending on whether the rector of the parish were inclined to Laudianism or to Puritanism.

3. *The Laudian Tradition*

If, as we have suggested, the Puritans were flexing their theological muscles early in the century, the high-church or Catholic Anglicans of the Hooker-Andrewes-Laud tradition were also preparing their liturgical strategy at this time.

This tradition found its earliest expression in the enrichment of the altar and its furnishings and of the ceremonial. Bishop Lancelot Andrewes at Winchester[17] provides the outstanding early example in his private chapel, but cathedrals and chapels of the nobility were also richly ornamented. Laud, who became Dean of Gloucester in 1616, had a row with his diocesan because of moving the altar to the east end and for embellishing it, while Matthew Wren, the former chaplain of Andrewes, made glorious the Chapel of Peterhouse, Cambridge, while Master of the College. The favour that all three received at court raises the interesting question as to whether the ecclesiastical enrichment led or followed the heightened court ceremonial and elaborately artificial dress correlative to developing absolutism in the monarchy, and of which the future Sun King in France is Europe's most notable example. It is a subject worth exploring in detail, though not here, because of the link between Baroque art and architecture with absolutism and the Counter-Reformation in Europe. It would be surprising if high Anglicanism did not follow the European pattern, especially as the king was the supreme governor of the Church of England, and the Catholic wing of the church (as the Non-Jurors were to prove) accepted the divine right of kings and the bishops among them believed in the indissolubility of promises of fealty even when the particular king (like James II) broke his promise to maintain the Protestant faith of the Church of England.

Bishop Andrewes, as mentioned, set the example for the adornment of the altar. Apart from the altar coverings of silk that lapped lavishly over the corners, the two lighted candlesticks, and the finely carved altar rails, there was the higher ceremonial, the censing, together with the "mixed chalice," symbolizing the blood and water that flowed from the body of Christ on the Cross. Copes and Prayer Books were brilliantly ornamented. The very ceremonies

---

[17] See Chap. II, "Church Architecture: Achievements," above.

that the Puritans objected to were made more elaborate. Infants were not only signed with the cross in Baptism, but they were carried up to the altar.[18] Kneeling at the altar for the reception of Communion became only one of a series of genuflexions and bowings.

On the other hand, despite the common charges to the contrary, there was little inclination on Laud's part[19] to tamper with the text of the Prayer Book to make it conform to his higher doctrine. Dean Overall of St. Paul's, however, was willing to imply a higher Eucharistic doctrine than Cranmer's by using the Prayer of Oblation (as in the Prayer Book of 1549) after he had consecrated, since he believed the Sacrament was "the true public sacrifice of the Church." Andrewes, too, was an innovator. He distinguished between the contiguous words "alms and oblations" by insisting that the congregation should bring their oblations to the altar rails after the Creed, during which the celebrant read a newly devised set of Sentences in which the idea of offering was dominant. The people were to stay in the chancel until the end of the *Gloria in Excelsis*, and only then were they to return to their seats, placing their alms in the poor chest, while the priest read the Prayer Book Sentences.[20]

When he became Archbishop of Canterbury in 1633, Laud's liturgical concern was concentrated on placing the altar against the east wall of the church, fencing it with rails, and requiring the communicants to come forward to the altar to receive the sacred elements. Furthermore, he required the Ante-Communion to be read at the altar, not in the reading pew. But the custom went against the Protestantism of the population which had been long accustomed to drinking a heady cocktail of English patriotism with a dash of anti-Catholic bitters, shaken by the vivid words and images of Foxe's Book of Martyrs. The Communion table now looked like an altar against the east wall, not like a table at all. Furthermore, the gesture of kneeling for Communion (which the Puritans had always disliked since the time of Edward VI as implying a belief in Transubstantiation) was not only reintroduced, but

---

18 Cardwell, *op. cit.*, p. 234.

19 In fact, when the charges against him as Archbishop were investigated, Laud was shown to have made two very small and insignificant verbal changes in prayers. (Cf. Cardwell, *ibid.*, p. 234).

20 See Andrewes, *Works*, 11 Vols. (Library of Anglo-Catholic Theology, eds. J. P. Wilson and J. Bliss, 1841-1854), vol. entitled *Minor Works*, pp. 153, 158, and ed. Vernon Staley, *Hierurgia Anglicana*, 3 Vols. (1902), II, pp. 99-104.

became one gesture in increased genuflexions and bowings at the name of Jesus, which the Puritans had deprecated at the Hampton Court Conference.

It was of little use for Laud or any of his supporters to insist that the fencing of the Communion table was done to prevent persons profaning it, or that the Communion offered Christ's flesh to the communicant while the pulpit only offered Christ's Word, or that the most splendid furnishings and the most courtly etiquette were suitable for the audience chamber of the King of Kings. Far from avoiding any compromise with the national and religious enemy, Roman Catholicism, Laudianism seemed to embrace it by imitation. Laud was a man of devotion, discipline, erudition, and sympathy for the poor, as well as a loyal royalist and churchman, but he had no psychological understanding of the independence and invincible stubbornness of those who, with equal conviction, felt themselves as Puritans and patriots to be the defenders of the Reformed Church of England. What was tragic in this era of religious intolerance was that what was secondary in importance in doctrine or worship assumed major importance as the line between Catholic and Puritan Anglicans hardened.

What were the ideals of Laud and his followers? It is clear, to begin with, that there were now one major and two minor foci in the worship of the Church of England, as represented by the furnishings. The dominant focus was, of course, the raised and fenced in altar at the centre of the east end (with the subordinate foci of the pulpit at the side and the stone font at the front of the church). Clearly, the sacraments were being given precedence over the Word, splendid preachers as there were in the Andrewes-Laud tradition, including Andrewes himself and Jeremy Taylor.[21] The typical Laudian sanctuary had an altar on which was placed a silk or velvet carpet, the rails surrounding it were finely carved, and the floor of the sanctuary was usually paved with black and white marble squares. The roof was often embossed with emblems of church and state (mitres, crowns, angels), of which Lincoln College Chapel, Oxford, is one admirable Laudian-inspired example. The stained glass here, too, though of exceptional quality was not necessarily exceptional in its typological interpretation or choice of themes, emphasising as it did the Old Testament anticipations of the New Testament sacraments and the sacrifice of Christ.[22]

21 See Chap. IV on Preaching.
22 See detailed analysis of this window in Chap. II, footnote 16.

Two further developments of the Laudian tradition, or partly such, were to come, both of which aroused the fiercest Puritan opposition. The first, considered in detail elsewhere,[23] was John Cosin's *Collection of Private Devotions* (1627), commissioned by Charles I as a book of private prayers for the ladies of his court, like the brief offices of the French ladies-in-waiting but "with regard to the ancient forms before Popery."[24] This may well have been a trial liturgical balloon, testing whether the country was ready for a revision of the Prayer Book in a more Catholic direction. It is significant that its author was at the time the corrector of the text of the Prayer Book at the king's printers. Moreover, it is equally significant that in the *Devotions*, the Mattins of the Prayer Book service is extended by the inclusion of Terce, Sext and None, while Evensong combines Vespers and Compline as was originally the case. Most important of all, a prayer to be said privately during the Act of Consecration at the Holy Communion borrows from the canon of the First Prayer Book of Edward VI, the most Catholic of the editions. Not only so, but the same is the basis of a "Prayer and Thanksgiving for the whole estate of Christ's Catholic Church, with a Commemoration of the Saints before us."[25]

4. *The Scottish Prayer Book of 1637*[26]

The second clue to the Laudian liturgical direction is to be found in events in Scotland. James I had sought to interest the Scottish bishops in a new service book, and Charles I revived the project. The future Bishop of Ross, John Maxwell, brought to England in 1629 a draft service that had been drawn up ten years before. In 1634 he revisited England with several proposals contained in a Prayer Book known as the "Haddington Book" because it was fairly recently discovered in the library of the Earl of Haddington. This was, in fact, more a revision of the English Prayer Book than an independent book prepared for Scottish use. The only details of present interest are that the Authorized Version of the Bible was used for lessons and there was much freedom allowed in the

[23] See Chap. III on Spirituality.
[24] So John Evelyn reported in his *Diary*, October 12, 1651.
[25] The preceding paragraph owes much to G. J. Cuming's analysis, *op. cit.*, pp. 142-43.
[26] *The Scottish Liturgy of 1637* (ed. G. Donaldson) will be found in *The Making of the Scottish Prayer Book of 1637* (Edinburgh, 1937), pp. 95-247. It has an excellent historical and critical introduction to the text.

observance of saints' days. Donaldson's conclusion on the changes in the book is that they "seem to reflect the views of a small-minded and sacerdotally inclined layman rather than a churchman interested in doctrine and in other larger issues."[27]

In 1635 Maxwell again came south with a full manuscript which received royal approval, and printing began prematurely in the autumn of that year. Prematurely, because James Wedderburn, Dean of the Chapel Royal and soon to be consecrated Bishop of Dunblane, proposed other changes aimed at restoring the Communion Service to the 1549 model. After Archbishop Laud and his chief helper, Bishop Wren of Norwich, had considered these changes, the King approved this new version in 1636, and Laud entered it into another Prayer Book (the Christ Church Book).[28] It was printed in 1637.

Its introduction into Scotland, where it was widely if erroneously known as "Laud's liturgy," led to rioting and it was immediately dropped. Imprudently, it had never been submitted to the General Assembly of the Scottish church. However, because of its later influence on revisions of the Anglican liturgy in Britain and overseas, and for its expression of Laudian liturgical ideals, it merits more than a passing mention.

For our purposes the chief interest is to discover during the negotiations for the Scottish liturgy what Laud's views were on the various proposals submitted for his consideration. Of the first seven proposals put forward in Wedderburn's "Notes" the most important changes either approved or suggested by the Archbishop were: that in addition to the new Scottish Offertory Sentences, numbers 2, 4, 6-10, and 13-15 from the English Prayer Book should be retained. On his own initiative Laud volunteered the proposal that in the Communion Office the rubric preceding each prayer or action should explain these activities by a brief description of them. The order of the prayers in the Communion Office was to be radically altered on the Scottish initiative. Laud approved the transference of the Prayer of Oblation, the Lord's Prayer, and the Prayer of Humble Access, to a new position between the Consecration and the Administration. He rejected, however, the proposed change of position for the Invitation, Confession, Absolu-

27 *Ibid.*, p. 47.
28 So-called because it was borrowed from the Norwich City Library in 1719 at Archbishop Wake's request and is now preserved among his papers in the library of Christ Church, Oxford.

tion, Comfortable Words, Prefaces and Sanctus, which would have almost restored the 1549 Communion Office in toto. Laud approved of Wedderburn's suggestion that a rubric should be inserted directing the manual acts during Consecration.[29]

The clearest evidence of Laud's approval of a high doctrine of Eucharistic sacrifice is found, not only in the changed position of the Prayer of Oblation and the additional Offertory Sentences, but even more strikingly in his approval of Wedderburn's suggestion that the second Sentence of the Words of Administration in the Communion Order should be dropped.[30] Furthermore, Laud put forward an awkwardly phrased rubric in response to seeking his opinion on whether it was desirable to have a rubric directing the celebrant to use the eastward position during the Consecration.

Other changes of interest in the Scottish liturgy are the short invocation of the Holy Spirit on the water in the font which is added to the "flood" prayer, together with a blessing of the water immediately before Baptism (which seems superfluous in view of the previous addition). In the Churching of Women, Psalm 27 is added as an alternative, and Ash Wednesday is made the focal point of the Service of Commination.

The Scottish Prayer Book of 1637 was interesting generally for its series of explicit rubrics, its reordering of the Communion Office with a partial return to the structure of Edward VI's First Prayer Book, the use of the *epiklesis* (or, invocation of the Holy Spirit at the Consecration), the thanksgiving for the saints in the prayer for the church, the use of the Authorized Version Bible for the lectionary (including the Psalms), and changes introduced into the calendar for the Scottish saints.[31] Its influence was to be profound on the present Scottish liturgy of the Episcopal church in Scotland, on the 1662 revision of the English Prayer Book, and on the Communion Offices of the Protestant Episcopal church in

[29] The items hitherto listed in Wedderburn's proposals with Laud's additions are referred to in a letter from Laud to Wedderburn, April 20, 1636. Cf. Laud's *Works*, 7 Vols. (eds. W. Scott, J. Bliss, Library of Anglo-Catholic Theology, 1847-1860), VI, pp. 457-58.

[30] Laud (*Works*, III, pp. 356-57) stated that the words "Take, eat," etc. "may seem to relish somewhat of the Zwinglian tenet, that the Sacrament is a bare sign taken in remembrance of Christ's passion." Cuming, *op. cit.*, p. 144, mistakenly attributes them to Wedderburn. Laud also observed that the second sentence in the administration was not found in the 1549 Book.

[31] Donaldson, while insisting that it is highly ironical that the Scottish liturgy should go by the name of the man who pressed so hard for the introduction to Scotland of the English liturgy (*op. cit.*, p. 79), yet acknowledges that it is likely "that many of the changes made in the book of 1637 found their way into the programme of the Laudian party." (*Ibid.*, p. 81.)

the United States of America and of the Church of the Province of South Africa.[32]

The injudiciousness which had marked the imposition of a Catholic-tending liturgy on the Scottish Reformed church, fine fruit as it was of Caroline Anglican research into the liturgies of the primitive church, also characterized Archbishop Laud's attempts' to provide new canons and a pontifical for the Church of England. The religious differences in the church grew so acerbic and profound, and the storm cloud of the coming Civil War so threatening, that the House of Lords appointed a committee of lay peers and divines of moderate opinions and conciliatory attitudes to try to find the basis for a settlement. Archbishops Williams of York and Ussher of Ireland, Bishop Wren, and Dr. Robert Sanderson, represented the established church. Their *Proceedings*[33] provide some clues to the more unpopular Laudian practices and some moderate criticisms of the Prayer Book from a Puritan standpoint. Twenty-one "Innovations in Discipline" are criticized and six of them deal with the furnishings of the church, while eight others are concerned with posture and movement. Hardly any deal with textual changes in the Prayer Book. The real gravamen of the Committee's criticism is in its indication that the source of the Laudian deviation is "putting-to the Liturgy printed *secundo tertio Edwardi sexti*, which the Parliament hath reformed and set aside."[34]

In September, 1641, the House of Commons passed a series of resolutions on "divers innovations in or about the worship of God" which provide a convenient summary of the Laudian "innovations." These resolutions ordered:

> That the churchwardens of every parish church and chapel . . . do forthwith remove the communion table from the east end . . . ; and that they take away the rails, and level the chancels; . . . That all crucifixes, scandalous pictures of any one or more persons of the Trinity, and all the images of the Virgin Mary, shall be taken away and abolished; and that all tapers, candlesticks and basins be removed from the communion table: That all corporal bowing at the name of

[32] Ratcliff, *op. cit.*, p. 19. See also Peter B. Hinchliff, *The South African Liturgy* (Cape Town, 1959), and M. H. Shepherd, Jr., *The Oxford American Prayer Book Commentary* (New York, 1950). The present Communion Services of the three churches referred to will be found in *The Liturgy in English* (ed. B. J. Wigan, 2nd edn., 1964) on pp. 38-51 (Scottish), 52-61 (American), and 73-81 (South African).
[33] See Cardwell, *op. cit.*, pp. 273ff. for an account of the conclusions.
[34] Cardwell, *ibid.*

Jesus or towards the east end of the church, . . . or towards the communion table be henceforth forborne. . . . That the Lord's Day shall be duly observed and sanctified.[35]

5. The Prayer Book Proscribed and Defended

When the Puritans came into the ascendant, they had no desire to retain the Prayer Book, though the Presbyterians—the vast majority of the Westminster Assembly of Divines—did not object to a national liturgy as such, and would have preferred one using John Knox's *Genevan Service Book*[36] as its model. Of course, they disapproved of the Book of Common Prayer because of its association with political absolutism and because of certain customs and phrases in it which had none or only a dubious Biblical warrant. The Independents were unalterably opposed to liturgies in any shape and form as a quenching of the inspiration of the Holy Spirit. Between them, the Presbyterians and the Independents in the Westminster Assembly ousted the Prayer Book as the national formulary for prayer. The Long Parliament declared the Prayer Book illegal on January 3, 1645, and exactly a week later Archbishop Laud went to his execution on Tower Hill. Wren went into imprisonment for a long period, and Cosin fled to France as the chaplain to the English members of the court of Henrietta Maria, the widowed Queen of Charles I. Thus was the Laudian tradition eclipsed. The verdict of John W. Packer seems justified: "The Laudians during the Interregnum did little to allay these stresses [between the Papistical and Presbyterian parties] either by their staunch advocacy of the Book of Common Prayer or by their refusal to compromise over the outward expression of their worship. Once again it can be argued that this very refusal to compromise gave strength to the restored church, but it made a comprehensive church further away than ever."[37]

In place of the Book of Common Prayer, the *Directory of Public Worship* of 1645, the product of the Westminster Assembly of Divines appointed by Parliament, was decreed as the new national formulary of ordinances and prayers in worship.[38]

[35] *Journals of the House of Commons*, II, p. 279; printed in S. R. Gardiner, *The Constitutional Documents of the Puritan Revolution* (1889), pp. 197-98.

[36] See William D. Maxwell, *The Liturgical Portions of the Genevan Service Book* (2nd edn., 1965).

[37] *The Transformation of Anglicanism 1643-1660, with special reference to Henry Hammond* (Manchester, 1970), p. 131.

[38] This will be considered in detail in Chap. XI. The king's reply to the Parliamentary Ordinance came in the following November 13, *A Proclamation com-*

In these stormy days for the Church of England there were two possible strategies for Anglicans who wished to remain loyal. The one was literary counterattack. That is, the use of the considerable literary and historical talents of the Caroline divines was brought to bear in criticizing the Parliamentary *Directory*, and in defending the use of set liturgies from primitive precedent, and on rational and functional grounds. The other strategy was evasion of the law, by gathering clandestinely to worship according to the Book of Common Prayer, or an abbreviation of it, and even for the secret ordaining of priests and deacons of the Church of England.

Criticisms of the *Directory* came fast and furious. Perhaps the most learned was the work of Dr. Henry Hammond, *The View of the New Directory and a Vindication of the Antient Liturgy of the Church of England* which came out in 1645. Hammond begins his criticisms by noting what is missing in the *Directory*. His list includes: no liturgy or set forms only directions as to content, no uniformity in worship, no outward or bodily worship, no responsive role for the people, no divisions of the prayers into collects but one long prayer, and no ceremonies of kneeling at Communion, Cross in Baptism, or ring in Marriage. He also notes, in comparison with the Prayer Book, that the Absolution, the Hymns (Introit, Te Deum, etc.), the Doxology, the Creeds, the Lord's Prayer, the Prayer for the King, "the observation of divers Feasts commemorative, not only of Christ, but of Saints departed" with their appropriate lections and collects, the reading of the Commandments, the order of the Offertory, are all set aside in the services of Mattins and Holy Communion. Further, he observes the entire disuse of many Prayer Book occasional services, such as private Baptism, a prescribed form of Catechism,[39] Confirmation, a Solemn Burial

---

manding the use of the Book of Common Prayer according to Law, notwithstanding the pretended Ordinances for the New Directory. Thomas Fuller, in *The Church History of Britain* (1655, edn. 1837), III, pp. 481-83 shows how fierce the intellectual war between proponents and opponents of the liturgy was in 1645, and supplies "Breviates of the Arguments" on both sides. There were nine in all. The negative arguments can be listed most briefly: (1) The English liturgy has offended many godly; (2) and many of the Reformed churches abroad; (3) Calvin disliked it as he indicated in a letter to Lord Protector Somerset; (4) the liturgy confines the Holy Spirit in prayer and its absence encourages the gift of extemporary prayer; (5) it complies with the Papists in a great part; (6) it makes an idle and unedifying ministry; (7) it is tediously long for the people; (8) it imposes many burdensome ceremonies; and (9) many faithful ministers have been disbarred from their office and their families ruined by imposing the liturgy.

39 This omission was soon to be rectified in the Assembly's Shorter Catechism with its inspired Augustinian opening, "Man's chief end is to glorify God and to

Service, thanksgiving after child-birth, the Communion of the sick, the service containing the Commination, and the observation of Lent and the Rogation.[40]

On the positive side, Hammond is convinced that the liturgies of St. James, St. Basil and St. John Chrysostom prove that the early church used set liturgical forms. Ceremonial gestures (or "bodily worship" as he calls them) are authorized by the precedent of Scriptures and early liturgies. He favours uniformity of liturgy rather than the unpredictability of "leaving all to the chance of men's wills."[41] He claims that the English liturgy gives the people a large part in worship by responses in the prayers, as in the hymns, and in encouraging them to read the alternate verses in the Psalms, while the Litany gives them a very large part to say. He replies to the common charge of the unnecessary repetition of the Lord's Prayer in one service, that "one of the gravest and most reverend men of the [Westminster] Assembly, being asked his opinion about the use of the *Lord's Prayer*, to have answer'd to this purpose, God forbid that I should ever be upon my knees in Prayer, and rise up without adding Christs form to my imperfect petitions."[42]

Hammond rebuts several criticisms of the Prayer Book. The small provision made for preaching is denied by affirming the importance of catechetical teaching on the basics of faith. The entire second chapter answers the charge that the Prayer Book is largely compiled from the Roman Catholic service books. He counters: "The truth is notorious, that our *Reformers* retained not any part of the *Popish Service, reformed* their *Breviary* and *Processional*, and *Mass-book*; as they did their *Doctrine*, retained nothing but what the *Papists* had received from purer *Antiquity*, and was as clear from the true charge of *Popery* as any period in either Prayer or Sermon in the *Directory*."[43] His shrewdest thrust at the worship forms of the Assembly of Divines comes when he accuses them of contradicting their own argument by publishing "a Book just now come to my hands, called, *A Supply of Prayer for the Ships that want Ministers to pray with them agreeable to the Directory established by Parliament, published by Authority*."[44]

---

enjoy him for ever." (See P. Schaff, *The Creeds of Christendom* [New York, 4th edn., 1877, III, p. 676].)

[40] *The Workes of the Reverend and Learned Henry Hammond, D.D.*, 4 Vols. (ed. William Fulham, 1674-1684), I, pp. 135-36.

[41] *Ibid.*, I, p. 145.   [42] *Ibid.*, I, p. 150.
[43] *Ibid.*, I, p. 169.   [44] *Ibid.*, I, p. 180.

Hammond thoroughly enjoys himself in trouncing the Puritans for their inconsistencies, demonstrating that since it is a set form there can be no objection to such, especially as it is officially authorized, and that some obviously find extemporary prayer difficult, and, finally, since these are taken from the *Directory*, a Puritan minister need make no others and so can remain as lazy as his supposed Anglican brother is alleged to be. His ironical conclusion is that the *Directory* should be licensed for a trial period, and its use would lead to its own effective confutation and the restoration of the liturgy.[45]

A telling, if incidental criticism of the *Directory* and encomium for the Prayer Book was the unique and anonymously published, *Eikon Basilike, The Portraiture of His Sacred Majesty in His Solitudes and Sufferings*, which was attributed to John Gauden,[46] but which may well have been inspired and even partly written by Charles I. This argues against the Westminster Assembly as authors of the *Directory*, "That these men (I say) should so suddenly change the Liturgy into a Directory, as if the Spirit needed help for invention, though not for expressions; or as if matter prescribed did not as much stint and obstruct the Spirit as if it were clothed in, and confined to, fit words—so slight and easy is that legerdemain which will serve to delude the vulgar." The author considers that the ostentatious vanity and the frenetic search for variety in prayer are worse than the coldness attributed to set prayers. Moreover, he avers that if constant forms of prayer flatten the spirit of prayer, unpremeditated and confused variety serve as well to distract the spirit of devotion. His catalogue of the sins of free prayers charges extemporaneity with "affectations, emptiness, impertinency, rudeness, confusions, flatness,[47] levity, obscurity, vain and ridiculous repetitions, the senseless and often blasphemous

---

[45] *Ibid.*, p. 182. J. W. Packer, *op. cit.*, p. 135, reminds us that the king and leading bishops considered the idea of permitting the *Directory* for a trial period. Charles I wrote asking Bishops Juxon of London and Duppa of Salisbury for their advice. On October 14, 1646, they replied that Charles should permit the use of the *Directory*, suggesting a "temporary toleration." (See Bodleian Library's Tanner Ms. 59. II. 560 [transcript].) Charles agreed to their suggestion in November 1648, but events had moved too far by then.

[46] A former member of the Assembly of Divines, John Gauden, was consecrated Bishop of Exeter in 1660 and translated to Worcester (not to Winchester as he had hoped) in 1662. *Eikon Basilike* appeared in 1649, provoking John Milton's *Eikonoklastes* in reply. For the authorship see Christopher Wordsworth, *Who wrote* ΕΙΚΩΝ ΒΑΣΙΛΙΚΗ? (1824), and H. J. Todd, *Bishop Gauden, author of* Εἰκών Βασιλική (1829).

[47] This seems a highly improbable charge, unless extemporary prayers among ministers of an extremely restricted vocabulary became repetitious and predictable.

expressions (all these burthened with a most tedious and intolerable length)" which "do sufficiently convince all men but those who glory in that Pharisaic way." The advantages of a liturgy are soundness of doctrine, comprehensiveness, order, and gravity.[48]

If Hammond's was the most learned defence of the Prayer Book and critique of the liturgy, Jeremy Taylor's *An Apology for Authorised and Set Forms of Liturgies against the Presence of the Spirit. 1. For ex tempore Prayer, 2. Formes of Private Composition* (1649) was the better argued and expressed apologia. Taylor asserts that extemporary prayer can be the fruit of laziness (insisting that it is better to pray to God with consideration than without),[49] or even the product of ostentation rather than edification. He denies that the favourite Puritan citation—"the Spirit helpeth our infirmities"—is to be interpreted as a miraculous and immediate infusion of the Holy Spirit rather than the gift of the improvement of the natural faculties. "The summe is this: . . . this spirit of prayer . . . is to be acquired to humane industry, by learning of the Scriptures, by reading, by conference, and by whatsoever else faculties are improved and habits enlarged."[50] Otherwise, it is to ask for the multiplication of unnecessary miracles. Taylor also asks whether the man who prays *ex tempore* with God's Spirit is deprived of it if he writes the same prayer down, "Or, is the Spirit departed from him, upon the sight of a Pen and Inkhorne?"[51]

The desire for variety is not worthy, and like the Israelites on the way to the Promised Land, they are tired of the Manna of the Book of Common Prayer, preferring *"the onions of Egypt* to the *food of angels."*[52] It is the men not the Prayer Book which should be mended.

Scripture, says Taylor, abounds in precedents for set forms. Moses composed a set form of prayer and a song or hymn for the children of Israel, and David composed many for the service of the Tabernacle, which Solomon and the holy kings of Judah continued in the worship in the Temple. Hezekiah's reform required the priests and levites to use the words of David and Asaph in their praises. Since all Scripture is left for our learning, this must include the forms of prayer incorporated in Scripture. *A fortiori*, Christ's disciples begged for and were given a form of prayer, which is binding on his disciples of the future, "as a Breviary of Prayer,

---

[48] This paragraph summarizes pp. 96-100 of *Eikon Basilike* (1649).
[49] *Op. cit.*, p. 4.   [50] *Ibid.*, p. 21.
[51] *Ibid.*   [52] *Ibid.*, p. 41.

as a rule of their devotions, as a repository of their needes, and as a direct address to God."[53] The clinching consideration is this: "Now it is considerable that no man ever had the fulnesse of the Spirit, but onely the holy Jesus, and therefore it is also certain, that no man had the spirit of prayer like to him, and then, if we pray his prayer devoutly . . . do we not pray in the Spirit of Christ?"[54]

Liturgies, so Taylor insists, are symbols of union, the "ligament" of the ecclesial society, so that by a *reductio ad absurdum* this may "teach us a little to guesse . . . into how many innumerable atomes, and minutes of Churches those Christians must needes be scattered, who alter their Formes according to the number of persons, and the number of their meetings, every company having a new Forme of Prayer at every convention."[55] Further, how can members of the congregation approve by their *Amen* contradictory doctrines prayed over by contentious sectarians?[56] By contrast, public forms of prayer have great advantages "to convey an article of faith into the most secret retirement of the Spirit, and to establish it with a most firme perswasion, and indeare it to us with the greatest affection."[57] To the Puritan charge that this is to restrain the Spirit, Taylor replies that the *Directory* prescribes the matter but not the words, yet when the Spirit prescribes the Words (as in Holy Scripture), there can still be considerable liberty of meaning and interpretation.[58] The Puritans further ask why should not prayers be as unrestrained as sermons? Taylor answers that the minister offers prayers on behalf of the people and therefore they ought to know beforehand, so that if they do not like the message they may refuse to communicate. Further, he argues that liberty is more fitting in sermons than prayers, because discourses have to be adapted to the capacities of the audience, their prejudices must be removed, and they are to be "surprised that way they lie most open," and "discourses and arguments *ad hominem* . . . may more move them than the most polite and accurate that do not comply and wind about their fancies and affections."[59] Yet this technique in preaching is inapplicable in the approach to God in prayer.

[53] *Ibid.*, p. 48. [54] *Ibid.*, p. 49.
[55] *Ibid.*, p. 69.
[56] *Ibid.*, pp. 70-71. Taylor refers to the habit of Independents, Presbyterian and Baptist ministers to "pray over" the points of their sermon in a concluding prayer.
[57] *Ibid.*, p. 72. [58] *Ibid.*, p. 79.
[59] *Ibid.*, pp. 82-83.

Taylor is scathing in his criticism of Puritan long prayers. "They *make Prayers* and they *make them long*, by this meanes they receive double advantages, for they get reputation to their ability and to their piety."[60] The more eminent Puritan divines, he charges, make their prayers longer.

His final peroration is a most moving plea for the return to the liturgy of the Church of England:

> He that considers the universall difformity of Publick Worship, and the no means of Union, no Symbol of Publick Communion being publickly consigned; that all Heresies may, with the same authority, be brought into our Prayers, and offered to God in behalf of the people, with the same authority, that any truth may, all the particular manner of our Prayers being left to the choice of all men, of all perswasions, and then observes that actually, there are in many places, Heresie, and Blasphemy, and Impertinency, and illiterate Rudenesses, put into the Devotion of the most solemne Dayes, and the most Publick Meetings; and then lastly, that there are diverse parts of Lyturgie, for which no provision at all is made in the Directory; and the very administration of the Sacraments let so loosely, that if there be anything essentiall in the Formes of Sacraments, the Sacrament may become ineffectual for want of due Words, and due Administration; I say, he that considers all these things . . . will finde that *particular men* are not fit to be intrusted to offer *in Publike* with their *private Spirit, to God*, for the people, in *such Solemnities*, in matters *of so great concernment*, where the *Honour of God*, the *benefit of the People*, the *interest of Kingdomes*, the *being of a Church*, the *unity of Mindes*, the *conformity of Practise*, the *truth of Perswasion*, and the *Salvation of Souls* are so much concerned as they are in the Publick Prayers of a whole national Church. An unlearned man is not to be trusted, and a wise man dare not trust himselfe; he that is *ignorant* cannot; he that is *knowing* will not.[61]

There were, of course, other pre-Restoration defences of the Prayer Book, notably Anthony Sparrow's *Rationale or Practical Exposition of the Book of Common Prayer* of which the earliest extant edition dates from 1657. Its main purpose was to demon-

[60] *Ibid.*, p. 90. [61] *Ibid.*, pp. 91-92.

strate that the services of the Church of England were neither "old superstitious Roman dotage" nor "schismatically new." This important book, which continued to be reprinted frequently and was reissued by Newman in 1839, provided an explanation of the origins, purposes, and meanings of the different parts of the Book of Common Prayer, as, for example, the Collects, the Holy Days, the Communion Service, and of chancels, altars, and the fashion of churches. It provided no new arguments for the Prayer Book or against the *Directory*, but it promoted a love and appreciation for the Prayer Book through its historical lore and inspired rationality. One example of his writing, on the doctrinal value of the celebration of the Christian year, must do duty for the rest. It commences:

And this visible as well as audible Preaching of Christian Doctrine by these Solemnities and Readings in such an admirable Order, is so apt to infuse by Degrees all necessary Christian Knowledge into us, and the Use of it to the Ignorant is so great, *that it may well be feared* (as a Reverend Person hath forewarned) that *When the Festivals and Solemnities for the Birth of Christ and his other famous Passages of Life, and Death, and Resurrection, and Ascension, and Mission of the Holy Ghost, and the Lessons, Gospels, and Collects, and Sermons upon them, be turned out of the Church, together with the Creeds also, it will not be in the power of weekly Sermons on some Heads of Religion to keep up the Knowledge of Christ in Men's Hearts, &c.*[62]

The Prayer Book commentary is a new devotional and historical genre in theology in England, though its medieval ancestry is suggested in the title which recalls Bishop William Durandus of Mende's *Rationale divinorum officiorum*.[63] It was quickly followed by the work of a loyal Anglican layman, Hamon L'Estrange's *The Alliance of Divine Offices exhibiting all the Liturgies of the Church of England since the Reformation* (1659), which includes annotations upon each of the liturgies, "vindicating" as the sub-title indicates, "the Book of Common Prayer from the main objections of its *Adversaries*, Explicating many parcels hitherto not clearly understood, shewing the conformity it beareth with the *Primitive*

---

[62] *Op. cit.* (edn. of 1722), pp. 79-80.
[63] He was consecrated Bishop of Mende in 1285 and incidentally produced a model Pontifical.

practice and giving a faire prospect into the usages of the *Ancient Church.*" A very learned book, with a command of the Greek and Latin sources of liturgiology, it has not the spiritual insight of Sparrow's *Rationale*, yet it helped to keep alive an admiration for the Prayer Book which would openly flourish at the Restoration. Reprinted in 1690 and 1699, it laid the foundation for a serious historical investigation of the development of liturgies, which was to come to fruition in the work of the Victorian Sir William Palmer's *Origines Liturgicae* (1832) and in Dom Gregory Dix's *The Shape of the Liturgy* (1945).

Hammond, Jeremy Taylor, Sparrow, and L'Estrange, in their different ways both by their criticisms of the *Directory*, explicit or implicit, as by their reminder of the values of the proscribed Anglican liturgy, and of its maintenance of a tradition of the primitive church, kept alight the lamps of nostalgia and of hope in the Anglican darkness. Others adopted a more daring strategy, that of arranging and attending clandestine services according to the Prayer Book. Jeremy Taylor alone among the famous divines tried both strategies.

6. *Clandestine Anglican Worship*[64]

The celebration of clandestine Anglican worship must be considered from two viewpoints, that of the loyal lay member of the

[64] The Common Prayer services were more frequent during the Protectorate than is commonly supposed. In 1653 it was reported that "conventicles for Common Prayer are frequent and much desired in London." (*Calendar of the Clarendon State Papers*, ed. O. Ogle *et alii*, II, p. 234; also R. H. Bosher, *The Making of the Restoration Settlement*, New York, 1951, p. 11.) In both London and in the country, services according to the Prayer Book were being read by clergymen who, although ejected from their parishes, were kept as chaplains or tutors in various households, or by visiting clergymen, such as John Evelyn's Mr. Owen who preached in his library at Says Court and afterwards administered the Communion on October 25, 1653. Thus disregard for the law was relatively easy until the end of 1655, when a royalist attempt at a rising forced sterner compliance, requiring that on the third offence royalists who kept clergymen to preach in public or private (except to their own families) or to keep any school, or administer the sacraments, or solemnise marriages, or "use the Book of Common Prayer or the forms of prayer therein contained" would be punished by imprisonment or banishment. (See W. K. Jordan, *The Development of Religious Toleration in England* [1938], III, pp. 194f., and *From Uniformity to Unity, 1662-1962* [eds. G. F. Nuttall and Owen Chadwick, 1962], pp. 96-97.) Even under the stricter enforcement of the law, Drs. Wild, Gunning and Taylor continued to convene secret episcopalian services. Indeed, in 1657 the Council advised the Lord Protector Cromwell to send for the two latter "and require an account of the frequent meetings of multitudes of people held with them, and cause the ordinance for taking away the Book of Common Prayer to be enforced." (*Calendar of State Papers, Domestic, 1657-1658*, p. 159.)

Church of England, and that of the clergy who directed worship and celebrated the sacraments, though forbidden to do so. Our faithful and articulate Anglican lay observer will be the diarist, John Evelyn (1620-1706), whereas our clergy will be two future bishops, Robert Sanderson (1587-1663) and Jeremy Taylor (1613-1667), both of whom have left texts of their modifications of or substitutes for the Prayer Book Services.

Evelyn's *Diary* mirrors the increasing difficulty of gathering for Anglican worship during the days of the Protectorate. It seems that on festival days, in 1654, he either attended worship conducted by an "orthodox sequestered divine" in London or obtained the services of one of them in his own house. On Advent Sunday, December 3, 1654, he writes: "There being no office at the church, but extemporie prayers after the Presbyterian way, for now all formes were prohibited, and most of the preachers were usurpers, I seldome went to Church upon solemn feasts, but either went to London, where some of the orthodox sequestered Divines did privately use the Common Prayer, administer sacraments, &c. or else I procur'd one to officiate in my house, wherefore on the 10th, Dr. Richard Owen, the sequester'd minister of Eltham, preach'd to my family in my library, and gave us the holy communion." On Christmas Day of that year, he remarks: "No public offices in churches, but penalties on observers, so I was constrain'd to celebrate it at home."

On March 18, 1655, he went to London "on purpose to heare that excellent preacher Dr. Jeremy Taylor on Matt. 14:17. shewing what were the conditions of obtaining eternal life: also concerning abatements for unavoidable infirmities, how cast on the accompts of the Crosse." On the thirty-first of the same month he visited Dr. Jeremy Taylor, "using him thenceforward as my ghostly father."

It seems that the authorities had been fairly lenient up to this point, but a new severity is recorded by Evelyn on December 14, 1655. He had gone up to London to hear Dr. Wild, the future Bishop of Derry, preach. This was "the funeral sermon of Preaching, this being the last day, after which Cromwell's proclamation was to take place, that none of the Church of England should dare either to preach or administer Sacraments, teach schoole, &c. on paine of imprisonment or exile." Evelyn viewed this as the most dismal day in the life of the Church of England since the Reformation, and one that comforted both Papist and Presbyter. "Myself, wife, and some of our family receiv'd the Communion; God make me thankfull, who hath hitherto provided for us the food of our soules as well as bodies!"

The same Dr. Wild, a former chaplain of Archbishop Laud, convened a regular secret Anglican gathering for worship in Fleet Street, London. Here Evelyn went on August 3, 1656, "to receive the B. Sacrament, the first time the Church of England was reduced to a chamber and conventicle, so sharp was the persecution." They had "a greate meeting of zealous Christians, who were generally much more devout and religious than in our greatest prosperity." On Christmas Day of the same year he again received the Holy Communion at Dr. Wild's lodgings, "where I rejoiced to find so full an assembly of devout and sober Christians."

The following year, 1658, Evelyn was more circumspect in participation in clandestine worship, until on Christmas Day he and his wife were caught attending a service according to the Prayer Book at Exeter Chapel on the Strand, where Dr. Peter Gunning (1614-1684), the future Bishop of Chichester and of Ely, was directing worship. The account conveys the excitement of the occasion.

> Sermon ended, as he [Gunning] was giving us the Holy Sacrament, the chapell was surrounded with souldiers, and all the communicants and assembly surpriz'd and kept prisoners by them, some in the house, others carried away. It fell to my share to be confin'd to a roome in the house . . . In the afternoone came Col. Whaly, Goffe and others, from White-Hall to examine us one by one; some they committed to the Marshall, some to prison. When I came before them they tooke my name and abode, examin'd me why, contrarie to an ordinance made that none should any longer observe the superstitious time of the Nativity (so esteem'd by them), I durst offend, and particularly be at Common Prayers, which they told me was but the masse in English, and particularly pray for Charles Steuart, for which we had no Scripture. I told them we did not pray for Cha. Stewart, but for all Christian Kings, Princes, and Governors. They replied, in so doing we praid for the K. of Spaine too, who was their enemie and a Papist, with other frivolous and insnaring questions and

much threatening; and finding no colour to detaine me, they dismiss'd me with much pitty of my ignorance. These were men of high flight and above ordinances, and spake spiteful things of our Lord's Nativity. As we went up to receive the Sacrament the miscreants held their muskets against us as if they would have shot us at the altar, yet suffering us to finish the office of Communion, as perhaps not having instructions what to do in case they found us in that action. So I got home, late the next day, blessed be God.

The two documents which show how Robert Sanderson and Jeremy Taylor adapted the Prayer Book for secret Anglican gatherings for worship during the Commonwealth and Protectorate are of great liturgical interest. Sanderson's document is known as, *A Liturgy in Times of Rebellion*;[65] while Taylor's liturgical compilations are found in *A Collection of Offices*.[66] The former is strictly an adaptation, while the latter is either a radical reconstruction of the Prayer Book services or, more probably, an alternative to the Prayer Book, the wording and order of which it occasionally echoes.

Sanderson, having gained the favour of Laud, was made a royal chaplain in 1631 and became Regius Professor of Divinity at Oxford in 1642. However, he had to leave his chair for an obscure living in Boothby Pagnell in Lincolnshire in Commonwealth days. Izaak Walton tells us that Sanderson had hoped for privacy there, but that he was disappointed since the nation was filled with "Covenanters, Confusion, Committeemen, and Soldiers," who were defacing monuments, smashing stained-glass windows, and seeking revenge, power, or profit. A group of such soldiers "would appear and visibly oppose him in the Church when he read the Prayers, some of them pretending to advise him how God was to be served more acceptably, which he not approving, but continuing to observe order and decent behaviour in reading the Church Service, they forced his Book from him, and tore it, expecting extemporary prayers."[67] Walton then asserts that about 1650 Sanderson

[65] It can be found in *Fragmentary Illustrations of the History of the Book of Common Prayer* (ed. W. K. Jacobson, 1874), pp. 1-40.

[66] This was edited by R. Heber in Taylor's *Works*, 15 Vols. (1822), xv, pp. 237-389. The Communion Service alone is in *Anglican Liturgies of the Seventeenth and Eighteenth Centuries* (ed. W. J. Grisbrooke, 1958), pp. 183-99.

[67] Walton's *Life of Sanderson* is included in Vol. vi of William Jacobson's edition of Sanderson's *Works*; the reference is to pp. 311-12. Such interruptions of

was advised by a Parliament man of influence who befriended him "not to be strict in reading all the Book of Common Prayer, but to make some little variation, especially if the Soldiers came to watch him; for if he did, it might not be in the power of him and his friends to secure him from taking the Covenant or sequestration. For which reasons he did vary somewhat from the strict rules of the Rubric." Such is Walton's apologia for Sanderson's variations from the Prayer Book.

He was not alone in this practice of "following the Prayer Book outline, abbreviating freely, and varying a phrase here and there."[68] R. Nelson's *Life of Dr. George Bull*[69] alleges that Bull, the future Bishop of St. Davids and apologist of the Church of England, followed Sanderson's example, using it as justification for his own practice of composing his public devotions from the Book of Common Prayer when the times made it impractical or imprudent to use the liturgy constantly and regularly. Edward Rainbow, Restoration Bishop of Carlisle, when ejected from the Mastership of Magdalene College, Cambridge, selected prayers from the Prayer Book and "so gradually brought the ignorant people to affect the Common Prayers, a little transformed and altered, who disliked the Common Prayer Book itself, they knew not why."[70] Sanderson was deeply exercised at what was his duty as an Anglican clergyman who yet had to be a law-abiding citizen under the Commonwealth and Protectorate. Hence he presented his problem as a casuist in *The Case of the Liturgy Stated in the Late Times*.[71] His

---

divine service as the one Sanderson experienced at Mattins were fairly common. For example the autobiography of Sir John Bramston (published 1845) on p. 75 records: "At Chelmsford at a special Commission of Oyer and Terminer for trial of some Soldiers who had broken into the Church at Easterford-Kelvedon, burnt the rails about the Communion table, stolen the Surplice and Church Plate, or some of it." See also *ibid.*, p. 95, where Bramston records that it was his practice to frequent "St. Gregory's, Dr. Mossam's, Dr. Wild's, Dr. Gunning's or some other Congregation where the orthodox clergy preached and administered the Sacraments; but the Soldiers disturbing the Congregations it was not convenient for my father to be there." For a similar disturbance, but while at Communion, and at the hands of Baptists rather than the military, see Bishop Gilbert Burnet's *The Life and Death of Sir Matthew Hale* (1682) referred to by Jacobson, *op. cit.*, Vol. VI, p. 313, and reprinted in C. Wordsworth's *Ecclesiastical Biography*, 6 Vols. (2nd edn., 1818), VI, pp. 1-106.

[68] G. J. Cuming, *The Anglican Liturgy*, p. 147.

[69] Published 1713, p. 43.

[70] Jonathan Banks, *Life of Edward Rainbow*, p. 48, referred in Jacobson, *op. cit.*, VI, p. 312.

[71] Printed in Sanderson's *Works* (ed. Jacobson), V, pp. 37-57. It was prepared about 1652.

conclusion was that it was his duty "to forbear the use of the Common Prayer Book, so far as might satisfy the letter of the ordinance, rather than forsake [his] station."[72] He did not use the Prayer Book slavishly or word for word, partly because the book was taken from him and he had a memory like a sieve, partly also because he was now forced to abbreviate, and to change a phrase here and there, while following the outline of the Prayer Book, its order of items, and its spirit. His own description states that, since the threatening soldiers who had interrupted Mattins did not stay for Communion, he used the Prayer Book Office for Communion in full, but that after their departure, "I took the liberty to use either the whole Liturgy, or but some part of it, omitting sometimes more, sometimes less, upon occasion, as I judged it more expedient in reference to the Auditory, especially if any Soldiers or other unknown persons happened to be present. But all the while, the substance of what I omitted I contrived into my Prayer before Sermon, the phrase and order only varied; which yet I endeavoured to temper in such sort, as that any person of ordinary capacity might easily perceive what my meaning was; and yet the Words left as little liable to exception or cavil as might be."[73]

Such was Sanderson's practice before receiving a warning from a man of influence with Cromwell's regime. He then resolved on further changes which continued as his custom until a happy change of affairs would restore to him "the liberty of using the old way again."[74]

His Sunday morning service followed Mattins as far as the first lesson, where there ensued a choice of Psalms and a thanksgiving made up of Psalms and church collects "which I did the rather because some have noted the want of such a Form as the only thing wherein our Liturgy seemed to be defective."[75] The second lesson then was read, and a Prayer before the Sermon consisting of several collects "new modelled into the language of the Common Prayer."[76]

Sanderson provided his own version of the General Confession, which may be compared with the Prayer Book version, by setting them out in parallel columns:

72 The Prayer Book was declared illegal by Parliament on January 3, 1645.
73 *Op. cit.*, v, pp. 39-40. 74 *Ibid.*, p. 39.
75 *Ibid.*, p. 42. 76 *Ibid.*, p. 41.

Prayer Book Version:

Almighty and most merciful Father, We have erred and strayed from thy ways like lost sheep. We have followed too much the devices and desires of our own hearts. We have offended against thy holy laws. We have left undone the things which we ought to have done. And we have done those things which we ought not to have done. And there is no health in us. But thou, O Lord, have mercy upon us, miserable offenders. Spare thou them, O God, which confess their faults. Restore thou them that are penitent, according to thy promises declared unto mankind in Christ Jesus our Lord. And grant, O most merciful Father, for his sake, that we may hereafter lead a godly, righteous, and sober life, to the glory of thy holy name. Amen.

Sanderson's Version:

O almighty God and most merciful Father, we thy unworthy servants do with shame and sorrow confess, that we have all our life long gone astray out of thy ways like lost sheep and that, by following too much the vain devices and desires of our own hearts, we have grievously offended against thy holy laws, both in thought, word, and deed. We have many times left undone those good duties which we might and ought to have done; and we have many times done those evils, when we might have avoided them, which we ought not to have done. We confess, O Lord, that there is no health at all in us, nor help in any creature to relieve us. But all our hope is in thy mercy, whose justice we have by our sins so far provoked. Have mercy upon us, therefore O Lord, have mercy upon us miserable offenders, spare us, good Lord, which confess our faults, that we perish not; but according to thy gracious promises declared unto mankind in Christ Jesus our Lord, restore us, upon our true repentance, to thy

grace and favour. And
grant, O most merciful
Father, for his sake, that
we henceforth study to serve
and please thee, by leading
a godly, righteous, and
sober life, to the glory of
thy holy Name, and the
eternal comfort of our own
souls, through Jesus Christ
our Lord. Amen.[77]

Sanderson's version of the General Confession expands the
Prayer Book's 133 words to 235, clarifies some of the obscurer
wording, but at the cost of concision, crispness of diction, definiteness of statement, and loss of cadence. Even Jeremy Taylor, as
will be seen, master rhetorician and wordsmith as he was, could
not improve on the brevity, clarity, and felicity of Cranmer's diction. Cranmer's English, except where time has obscured the meaning of an occasional word, is best left untouched, because so very
rarely is it bettered.

Sanderson's Order for Holy Communion begins at the Exhortation, follows the order of the Prayer Book, but it omits the Comfortable Words,[78] while it inserts the Collect, "Prevent us, O Lord"
before the Blessing.

The Orders for the Churching of Women (thanksgiving after
child-birth), Baptism,[79] and Matrimony, follow the Prayer Book
closely, while that of Burial is modified, so that the service begins
with Sentences at the church gate, then moves into the church, and
ends at the graveside. The usual Prayer Book service went from
the church stile to the graveside and ended in the church, which,
while not the logical order of succession, might well be a psychological order of advantage to the mourners whose last associations
would be with the community of living Christians rather than with
the community of the dead awaiting the trumpet of the Day of
Judgement. Sanderson's Burial Service adds two Psalms (39 and

---

[77] Ibid.   [78] Ibid., pp. 40-41.
[79] He rather abbreviates than omits (as Cuming erroneously states, op. cit.,
p. 147) the Prayer of Thanksgiving (see Fragmentary Illustrations of the History
of the Liturgy, ed. W. K. Jacobson, Oxford, 1874, p. 27). Cuming also asserts
that Sanderson omits Evensong, when, in fact, Sanderson compares his "forenoon"
and "afternoon" practices at worship in Sanderson's Works, ed. Jacobson, v,
p. 41.

90) and concludes with the Grace. His exhortations have the lucidity in explanation that presages the admirable introduction that Bishop Sanderson will write for the revised Prayer Book of 1662.[80]

Jeremy Taylor was employed during the dark days of the Commonwealth and Protectorate (dark, that is, for Anglicans) as a private chaplain to the Earl of Carbery at Golden Grove in Carmarthenshire, South Wales, where he went in 1645 and where he remained for the most part until 1658. Here his leisure was put to good use in composing his two famous devotional treatises (*Holy Living* and *Holy Dying*),[81] his major work on casuistry (*Ductor Dubitantium*), and the liturgical compilation now to be considered. This is, to give it its full title, *A Collection of Offices, or Forms of Prayer in Cases Ordinary and Extraordinary; Taken out of the Scriptures and the ancient Liturgies of several Churches, especially the Greek, Together with A Large Preface in Vindication of the Liturgy of the Church of England.*

It was published in 1658, and there may well have been an earlier edition or editions.[82] It was written for Anglican use when the Prayer Book was proscribed. There is, however, a built-in contradiction in the volume, for while its preface vindicates the Prayer Book, the *Collection of Offices* makes use of "the devotions of the Greek Church with some mixture of the *Mozarabick* and *Aethiopick* Liturgies"[83] and we are led to believe, at least implicitly, that these are better than the Prayer Book. In favour of this volume, however, it can be said to have acquainted the Church of England clergy and thoughtful laity with the solemn splendour, the high reverence, and the radiance of the Resurrection that coruscates in

[80] It is, however, worth noting that Sanderson introduces into the service of Baptism a phrase which would delight the Puritans, namely, "the Covenant of Grace," but which would be abhorrent to Anglicans recalling the "Solemn League and Covenant" which led to the overthrow of the king and the liturgy.

[81] These are considered in Chap. III above.

[82] According to a letter written on January 14, 1656-1657, Evelyn pleads with the Lieutenant of the Tower of London on behalf of Dr. Jeremy Taylor, presumably a prisoner or about to be "of whom I understand you have conceived some displeasure for the mistake of his Printer." A footnote by William Bray the editor of *Memoirs of John Evelyn* (including the *Diary* and a selection of letters, 1818 first edition), declares that Jeremy Taylor had been committed to the Tower for setting the picture of Christ praying before his *Collection of Offices* contrary to a new Act concerning "scandalous Pictures" as this was called. I have, however, been unable to confirm this footnote. If true, however, it would indicate that there was an earlier edition of *A Collection of Offices* than 1658, which may well have been withdrawn.

[83] From the vindicatory Preface (W. Jardine Grisbrooke, *Anglican Liturgies*, p. 20).

these early eastern liturgies. In his preface Taylor argues that these devotions, since they are taken from ancient liturgies and the fountains of Scripture "and therefore for the material part have great warrant and great authority: and therefore *if they be used with submission to Authority*, it is hop'd they may doe good. . . ."[84]

The importance of this *Collection of Offices* is rather to be found as a quarry from which lapidary devotions can be hewed, than as any alternative to the Anglican liturgy, though its influence was probably profound. Taylor's prose is too swelling (occasionally even flatulent), too consciously rhetorical, and too slow in making its points, for regular liturgical use. Moreover, its Communion Office differed too much from the Prayer Book Eucharist in structure and order, as well as in diction (except for the Words of Administration) for it to be an acceptable substitute or alternative.

Some of his borrowings were most imaginative. Such were the substitution of the Beatitudes for the Decalogue, the two private preparatory prayers taken from the liturgy of St. John Chrysostom and from the Greek Church's Office of Preparation for the Eucharist, and also the "Denunciation" adapted from the anthem sung at the Great Entrance in the liturgy of St. James.

Taylor's prayers are written to reflect doctrine. As W. Jardine Grisbrooke demonstrates,[85] they admirably mirror and express the Eucharistic Sacrifice through which Christ the Great High Priest presents to the Father his perfect Sacrifice in which the worshippers (and their offerings) are incorporated as his Body. The richness of this concept and act can be illustrated from the prayer that begins, "O Lord God our Creator," in its petition: "grant that, with a holy fear and a pure Conscience, we may finish this Service, present a holy Sacrifice holily unto thee, that thou maist receive it in Heaven, and smell a sweet Odor in the union of the eternal Sacrifice, which our blessed Lord perpetually offers. . . ."[86] The same doctrine is also found in the post-Communion prayers, as in "Receive, O Eternal God, this Sacrifice for and in behalf of all Christian people whom thou hast redeemed with the Blood of thy Son and purchased as thine own inheritance. . . ."[87]

The *epiklesis* (or invocation of the Holy Spirit) which was in the first English Prayer Book of 1549 and missing thereafter (except in the Scottish liturgy of 1637 and in subsequent litur-

[84] *Ibid.*
[86] *Ibid.*, p. 187.
[85] *Ibid.*, p. 25.
[87] *Ibid.*, p. 197.

gies of the Scottish Episcopal church) returns in Taylor's Holy
Communion Rite. Above all in this Collection one is infected by
his enthusiastic admiration for the Biblical depth and fidelity, and
the vividly conceived personal and corporate piety of the primitive
and powerful liturgies he has raided like an absolute monarch
claiming the divine right of the King of Kings.

Our chapter ends with the Prayer Book still prohibited and the
Directory still prescribed. We began with the Prayer Book aloft
and end with it humbled but secretly read and followed as far as
may be. Already the defences of the Prayer Book such as Hammond's, L'Estrange's and Taylor's, with the increasing knowledge
and love of the primitive liturgies which they show, promise that
phoenix-like the Book of Common Prayer will rise again from its
own ashes. The stratagems of Taylor and Sanderson were desperate, but it was in the deepest darkness just before the dawn.
Such were the metaphors and images in which loyal Anglicans
saw these crepuscular years of the Commonwealth and Protectorate just prior to the Restoration of the Monarchy, the church,
and the liturgy in 1660. Loyalty to the Prayer Book reached its
zenith in that year, based on its new status as the channel of devotion of a suffering church.

CHAPTER X

THE PRAYER BOOK RESTORED
AND REVISED: 1660-1689

EVELYN PUT the capitalised heading of "ANNUS MIRA-BILIS" over his first diary entry on January 1, 1660. On May 29 his joy knew no bounds. "This day," he wrote, "his Majestie Charles II came to London after a sad and long exile and calamitous suffering both of the King and Church, being 17 yeares. This was also his birth-day, and with a triumph of above 20,000 horse and foote, brandishing their swords and shouting with inexpressible joy; the wayes strew'd with flowers, the bells ringing, the streetes hung with tapistry, fountaines running with wine." Evelyn "stood in the Strand and beheld it and bless'd God." His next entry in the diary for June 4 records that he went home, hoping to meet the English Ambassador to France, Sir Robert Browne, who, in fact, returned a few days later after an exile of nineteen years, "during all which time he kept up in his chapell the Liturgie and Offices of the Church of England, to his no small honour, and in a time when it was so low, and as many thought utterly lost, that in various controversies both with Papists and Sectaries our Divines us'd to argue for the visibility of the Church, from his chapell and congregation."

Although the new King had promised on April 4, 1660, in the Declaration of Breda "a liberty to tender consciences," and owed his return to his throne partly to General Monk and his Presbyterian supporters, and was to ask for the Savoy Conference to be convened in the hope of making it possible for the Presbyterians to be included in a wider national church, the Cavaliers in Parliament—to say nothing of the old or new members of the bench of bishops and the clergy now repossessed of their livings—were determined to restore the Prayer Book which now wore the halo of a persecuted and therefore doubly sacred book. Loyalty to the Prayer Book was sealed in the blood of King Charles the Martyr, his Archbishop, William Laud, and the thousands of Cavaliers who had died in the defence of their King and church. A triple cord bound together the restored King, church, and liturgy. So firm was the conviction that the liturgy must be retained, that

Parliament could only be restrained with difficulty from insisting that the Prayer Book as mildly revised in 1604 should be restored,[1] and would be alarmed to hear that the revision in which the Convocation would be engaged in 1661 resulted in over six hundred changes and would have to be reassured that these were merely alterations of wording, not of substance. Clearly the abolition of the Prayer Book in the abhorred days of the Commonwealth and Protectorate, and the risks that faithful Anglican priests had taken to maintain its worship, and the defences of it from Thorndike's very learned *Of Religious Assemblies, and the Publick Service of God* (1642)[2] up to Sparrow's *Rationale* (1655) and L'Estrange's *Alliance of Divine Offices* (1659) had created a great loyalty to the Prayer Book on the part of many who previously took its existence for granted. A new anxiety and even protectiveness about the liturgy was to be seen on the part of some of the bishops in their writings and in the Savoy Conference.

The outstanding exemplar of this attitude was John Gauden who was, as we have seen, the supposed author of *Eikon Basilike*. In 1661, now rewarded for his fidelity to Charles I by being appointed to the see of Exeter by Charles II, he wrote a timely treatise, *Considerations touching the Liturgy of the Church of England* (1661) while the revision of the Prayer Book was still under consideration. Right at the outset he makes it plain that the King's indulgent declaration at Breda "was not to show any *disaffection* or *disesteem* in *His Majesty* toward the ancient and excellent Liturgy of the Church of *England*, which was His companion and comfort in all His distresses, and which still is the daily rule

---

[1] On May 26, 1660, the House of Commons received the Sacrament according to the use of the 1604 Prayer Book, excepting three or four members who were suspended from sitting because of their refusal. Entirely disregarding the King's promise to consider revising the Prayer Book to accommodate the scruples of Presbyterian ministers, the Commons began measures for confirming the liturgy of the Church of England as it stood on June 25.

[2] The sub-title was characteristic of the best Caroline theology, namely, "A Discourse according to Apostolicall Rule and Practice." It was published by Cambridge University. Thorndike provided an erudite attempt to show that the Offices of the Church of England were in direct line with the development of worship in the synagogue, the nascent church of the New Testament, in accord with the descriptions of worship given by such early Fathers as Justin Martyr, Tertullian, and Irenaeus, and like the offices of the liturgies of the Apostolical constitutions, and of those of the early Roman Rite, as well as of St. James, St. Mark, and St. John Chrysostom. Incidentally, it reinterprets and confutes some of the Scriptural and Patristic proof-texts of the Puritan apologists. It has not received the attention it warrants probably because it requires close reading. It was not reprinted in the six volume edition of Thorndike's *Works* prepared for the Library of Anglo-Catholic Theology (1844-1854).

and measure of His Majesties publique Devotions; as it hath been of His *Royal Fathers* of blessed memory, and all His *Princely Progenitors* since the Reformation."[3] He continues with criticisms of Puritan prayers for their "rudeness, weaknesse and familiarity of some Ministers devotions"[4] which are bound only by their own fancies. The positive benefits of a prescribed liturgy, as he sees them are five. Such conduces much "to the more *solemne, complete, august,* and *reverent* worship of the Divine Majesty in Christian Congregations." It is, secondly, an admirable means "to preserve the truth of Christian and Reformed *Doctrine* by the consonancy of *publicke Devotions*." It is also a necessity for the expression of harmony and communion on the national level as well as on the parochial, for all Christians. Fourthly, a liturgical form benefits and comforts the well-bred and judicious type of Christian, but is also a measure that will guarantee security and "*composure* of their spirits in the Worship of God." Finally, "But above all, a constant and compleat Liturgy mightily conduceth to the *edification* and *salvation* as well as unanimity and peace of the *meaner sort of people. . . .*"[5] This warning of itself would serve notice on the Puritans of every stripe that not much should be hoped from either the Declaration of Breda or the Savoy Conference.

1. *The Savoy Conference of 1661*

From the standpoint of the Presbyterian ministers (now the dominant Puritan group) events built up to a disappointing and frustrating anti-climax. While the King was preparing to return to England, he granted these ministers an interview at Breda. They, counting on his favour, and at his suggestion, drew up "The first Address and Proposals of the Ministers" which included four prefatory demands they considered necessary before they could be happy in a wider Church of England. They asked that the various congregations may have "liberty for edification and mutual provoking to godliness"; that each congregation may also have "a learned, orthodox, and godly pastor residing amongst them"; "that none may be admitted to the Lord's Supper, till they completely understand the principles of the Christian religion and do personally and publickly own their baptismal covenant, by a credible profession

---

[3] *Op. cit.*, p. 1.   [4] *Ibid.*, p. 6.
[5] *Ibid.*, p. 7. These snobbish words were presumably meant for the Independents and Baptists who practised extemporary prayer, the members and supporters of Cromwell's Ironsides, and who often included in their midst "mechanick preachers" like the immortal Bunyan.

of faith and obedience . . . and that unto such only confirmation (if continued in the church) may be administered"; and "that an effectual course be taken for the sanctification of the Lord's day, appropriating the same to holy exercises both in public and private without unnecessary divertisements."[6] The rest of the proposals dealt with liturgy in general and ceremonies in particular. In principle the ministers approved of a liturgy "provided that it be for the matter agreeable unto the word of God, and fitly suited to the several ordinances, and necessities of the church; neither too tedious in the whole, nor composed of too short prayers, unmeet repetitions or responsals: not to be dissonant from the liturgies of other reformed churches; nor too rigourously imposed; nor the minister so confined thereunto, but that he may also make use of those gifts of prayer and exhortation, which Christ hath given him for the service and edification of the church."[7]

The ensuing paragraph contained the genesis of the idea of a comprehensive Scriptural liturgy to be agreed upon by a conference of Anglican and Dissenting divines. It reads:

> that for the settling of the church in unity and peace, some learned, godly and moderate divines of both persuasions, indifferently chosen, may be employed to compile such a form as is before described, as much as may be in Scripture words; or at least to revise and effectually reform the old, together with an addition or insertion of some other varying forms in Scripture phrase, to be used at the minister's choice; of which variety and liberty there be instances in the Book of Common Prayer.[8]

The tactful reference in the final sentence needs to be pointed out, so rare is the phenomenon. It is followed by the more typical intractableness in utterly rejecting all ceremonies for which no Scriptural warrant can be found, such as kneeling at the Lord's Supper, the crossing of the child at Baptism, the use of the surplice, the erection of altars, and desires the abolition of "such holy days as are but of human institution." The only ceremony they were prepared to retain which other Puritans had rejected was the use of the ring in marriage. This they wished to leave optional.

The Presbyterians were making only minimal concessions, such as the ring just mentioned, the acceptance of a liturgy (although

---

[6] *Puritan Documents* (ed. and intro., Peter Bayne, 1862), pp. 14ff.
[7] *Ibid.*, p. 17. [8] *Ibid.*, p. 18.

Scripturally not traditionally determined, excluding all responses and practically every ceremony and wanting to aggregate the collects into a longer prayer, and allowing many alternatives for the minister), and a willingness to accept a synodal as contrasted with prelatical or monarchical episcopate.[9] Their church order looked more Genevan than English, and the Prayer Book they had in mind seemed more like a cross between John Knox's Genevan Service Book and the Parliamentary *Directory*, since it bore little resemblance to the Book of Common Prayer.

When the Savoy Conference was eventually authorized by the King on March 25, 1661, it was to prove the Anglican representatives at least as obdurate as the Presbyterian divines. Not even the bishops were masters in their own house for although the Conference was called for a liturgical purpose, it "was managed by politicians rather than by liturgical scholars."[10] Clarendon's men, former Oxford dons and members of the Great Tew Circle of which Lord Falkland was the centre, and Latitudinarians[11] like the Lord Chancellor Clarendon himself, were Gilbert Sheldon, Bishop of London, and George Morley, Bishop of Worcester. The liturgists on the Anglican side were Laudians, Bishops Cosin and Wren, but the Latitudinarians won. The terms of the Commission reflect the intentions of those in power. The Commissioners are authorized "to advise upon and review the said Book of Common Prayer, comparing the same with the most ancient liturgies which have been used in the Church, in the primitive and purest times." While provision is made for changes, it is carefully limited to permit the Commissioners "to make such reasonable and necessary alterations, corrections, and amendments therein, as . . . shall be agreed upon to be needful or expedient for the giving satisfaction to tender consciences, and the restoring and continuance of peace and unity." Not only so, but there is a further restriction, namely, that of "avoiding, as much as may be, all unnecessary alterations of the forms and liturgy wherewith the people are already acquainted, and have so long received in the Church of England."[12] The Con-

9 They had in mind Archbishop James Ussher's "reduced episcopacy." His former chaplain, Nicholas Bernard, had issued it in 1656 after the Archbishop's death under the title, *The Reduction of Episcopacy unto the form of Synodical Government received in the Ancient Church.*

10 G. J. Cuming, *A History of Anglican Liturgy* (1969), p. 153.

11 According to B.H.G. Wormald's biography, *Clarendon* (Cambridge, 1951), p. 240, he took the view that ceremonial was "not in itself of that important value to be either entered on with that resolution, or to be carried on with such passion."

12 *Documents relating to the settlement of the Church of England by the Act of Uniformity of 1662* (ed. G. Gould, 1862), p. 109.

ference began on April 15, 1661, and met during the ensuing four months, ending on July 21, 1661.

What was the composition of the Commission? Anglicans and Puritans each had twelve representatives, selected for their moderation. The nominal leader of the bishops was Accepted Frewen, Archbishop of York, but because of the latter's advanced years the actual leader was Sheldon of London. During the Interregnum Sheldon had approved of modifications of the Prayer Book to permit it to be used without contravening the law, as had Robert Sanderson, Bishop of Lincoln, another member of the Commission. John Gauden, a convert from Puritanism, and Bishop of Exeter, was now a convinced apologist for both episcopacy and liturgy. Morley, Bishop of Worcester, and Cosin, Bishop of Durham (the most learned in liturgical lore), had been chaplains on the Continent during the Civil War and Protectorate.

Two Presbyterian ministers had been given the responsibility of selecting the Presbyterian members of the Commission. One was Edward Reynolds, the first Puritan Vice-Chancellor of Oxford University as Dean of Christ Church, who had been ejected from office because he could not accept the Engagement of 1649 (which was to prepare for a republic), and who had conformed at the Restoration and accepted appointment as Bishop of Norwich before the Savoy Conference was summoned, but was still attached to a synodical conception of his office. The other was Edmund Calamy, a Cambridge man, a strict Calvinist, a monarchist but against bishops. Other Presbyterian Commissioners were John Wallis, the Saville Professor of Geometry at Oxford, and Matthew Newcomen, a London minister, as Calamy was. The most notable member on the Presbyterian side was, however, the superb pastor, preacher, and prolific writer on spirituality, controversial divinity, and casuistry, Richard Baxter. No one on either side worked harder or contributed more to the Conference than he. Cosin knew most about worship on the Anglican side, Baxter knew most about worship on the Presbyterian side; both would eventually be disappointed for different reasons.

Sheldon's opening move was to state that the bishops were satisfied with the Book of Common Prayer as it was, and that as the Conference had been called at the behest of the Presbyterians, it was their responsibility to present both exceptions and alternatives. This policy put the onus for change on the Presbyterians and meant that the Anglican strategy would be to criticize the criticisms. It did have one unfortunate effect for the Anglicans: it meant that the Laudian hope of amending the Prayer Book in the direction of the 1549 Book of Common Prayer or even to bring it closer to the Scottish liturgy of 1637 was doomed, as Cosin must have realized though it did not prevent him (with the aid of Bishop Wren not of the Commission) from making his own liturgical revisions.[13]

Baxter reported that, "When we were withdrawn, it pleased our Brethren presently to divide the undertaken work: The drawing up of *Exceptions against the Common-Prayer*, they undertook themselves, and were to meet from day to day for that end: The drawing up of Additions or new Forms they imposed on *me alone*, because I had been guilty of that Design from the beginning, and of engaging them in that piece of Service (and some of them thought it would prove odious to the Independents and others who are against a Liturgy as such)."[14]

The Presbyterian Brethren produced a solid document of *Exceptions*, of which eighteen were general in character and seventy-eight particular. These are an admirable summary of the historic Puritan objections to the liturgy, as these had been advanced since the Elizabethan days of Cartwright, Travers, and Field, and renewed in the Hampton Court Conference and in the preface to the Parliamentary *Directory*.[15] The criticisms are of three kinds: major principles, weaknesses in wording, and ceremonies and customs.

It is proposed that the Prayer Book should be doctrinally acceptable to all Protestants; that the gift of conceived prayer should be allowed as a supplementation of the liturgy; that all readings from the Apocrypha will be eliminated (thus excluding the *Benedicite* and Offertory sentences from the Book of Tobit); that the practice of having godparents at Baptism, defunct since 1645, should not be revived; that since Baptism and Holy Communion are *the* two Sacraments, lax wording suggestive of Confirmation and Matrimony as Sacraments should be amended; the presumption that all worshippers are regenerate is a false one and this presupposition in the Baptismal and Burial Services should be removed; and, final-

[13] Their preliminary studies for Prayer Book revision will be considered immediately after the present section of the chapter.

[14] *Reliquiae Baxterianae* (ed. M. Sylvester, 1696), I, Pt. II, Sect. 175.

[15] John Wesley was to review these "Exceptions" before preparing his adaptation of the Prayer Book for the use of Methodists in North America. See Davies, *op. cit.*, III, p. 190.

ly, a stricter control of admission to Baptism and Communion should be applied to maintain discipline and the purity of the church.

In matters of wording, there is a strong objection raised against any responses of the people in prayers, since their duty is to listen reverently and, on the Pauline prescription, merely to say, "Amen." This, of course, would radically alter the Litany. "Minister" is to be substituted for "priest" and "Lord's Day" for "Sunday." No parts of the Old Testament or of the Acts of the Apostles are to be called "Epistles." The Collects need revision. The new translation of the Scriptures should be used for all lections from Scripture, and a truer version of the metrical Psalms should be made. Such obsolete words as "prevent," "depart," and "worship" should be amended.

The "noxious ceremonies," as might have been confidently predicted, reappear in the criticisms of customs and usages: kneeling for Communion, the surplice, the sign of the Cross in Baptism, and the ring in Matrimony. Neither is Lent to be kept, nor are Saints' Days. Unnecessary movement in services is to be avoided as distracting. On rainy days the entire burial service should be said in church. As Cuming points out,[16] this provoked the witty rejoinder from the bishops, "being not pretended to be for the ease of tender consciences, but of tender heads, [this] may be helped by a cap better than a rubric."

The criticisms were too thorough-going and radical to be acceptable, and they went far beyond the rather limited terms of the warrant for the Commission. Not surprisingly, therefore, even their most sensible proposals were given a curt rebuttal by the bishops. In fact, only seventeen of the ninety-six exceptions were conceded, three of them of a general and fourteen of a particular nature. The most significant was to require the Authorized Version of the Bible for all readings, which, of course, changed neither the structure nor the doctrine of the Prayer Book. Some agreement was found in the desire to avoid archaisms. But over-all Anglican obduracy overcame Presbyterian persistence.

The meagre concessions on unimportant points clearly disappointed the ministers, for in their "Rejoinder" they complain: "we find ourselves disappointed . . . as may appear both by the paucity of the concessions and the inconsiderableness of them, they

16 *A History of Anglican Liturgy*, p. 156.

being for the most part verbal and literal, rather than real and substantial."[17] They realized that the cause of comprehension in a wider national church was lost, for they take their farewell in terms that are more critical of the Prayer Book than even their detailed criticisms of it: "Prayer and humility are, indeed, the necessary means of peace; but if you will let us pray for peace in no words but are in the Common Prayer book, their brevity and unaptness, and the customariness, that will take off the edge of fervour with human nature, will not give leave (or help sufficient) to our souls to work towards God, upon this subject, with that enlargedness, copiousness, and freedom as is necessary to true fervour. A brief, transient touch and away, is not enough to warm the heart aright; and cold prayers are likely to have a cold return. . . ."[18] Here the main thrust of the Puritan tradition was finely expressed.

Their rejoinder was at its reasonable best, however, in its criticism of an exclusive dependence upon liturgical prayer, without the admixture of any extemporary prayers on the part of individual ministers. "Yet must we," the Presbyterian ministers insist, "before God and men, protest against this opium you would here prescribe or wish for, as that which plainly tendeth to cure the disease by the extinguishing of life, and to unite us all in a dead religion."[19] It is sincerity, they claim, rather than "comeliness of expression" by which prayers must be judged, and they cannot be wholly confined to a liturgy "that pretends to help the tongue" while it "hurts the heart." They saw themselves as moderates to the last: "We would avoid both the extreme that would have no forms, and the contrary extreme that would have nothing but forms."[20]

Richard Baxter's *The Reformation of the Liturgy*,[21] sometimes also known as *The Savoy Liturgy*, received equally short shrift from the bishops. The work was entirely his own composition, the work of a fortnight but, of course, using his experience in Kidderminster over many years. He wrote: "I could not have time to make use of any Book, save the Bible and my Concordance."[22] This astonishing achievement included a Lord's Day Service, Orders for Communion, Baptism, Matrimony, and Burial, with Forms for Catechising, the Visitation of the Sick (including Communion), for Extraordinary Days of Humiliation and Thanksgiving and

---

[17] Bayne, *Puritan Documents*, p. 201. [18] *Ibid.*, p. 213.
[19] *Ibid.*, p. 230. [20] *Ibid.*, p. 247.
[21] This work will be considered in detail in Chapter XI "Puritan Service Books."
[22] Sylvester, *op. cit.*, I, Pt. II, Sect. 172.

Anniversary Festivals, for Prayers and Thanksgiving for Particular Members of the Church, and for Pastoral Discipline (including Public Confession, Absolution, and Exclusion from the Holy Communion of the Church). An Appendix included A Larger Litany, or General Prayer and The Church's Praise for our Redemption both of which were to be used at discretion.[23] The surprise is the high doctrine of the Eucharist (though this was also a characteristic of the *Directory*'s Order for the Lord's Supper with its *epiklesis*), contained in "The Sacrament of the Body and Blood of Christ."[24] Though we have only the author's word for it, it was apparently well received by the rest of the Presbyterian ministers. Baxter writes: ". . . they past it at last in the same Words I had written it, save only that they put out a few lines in the Administration of the Lord's Supper, where the word *Offering* was used; and they put out a Page of Reasons for Infant Baptism, which I had annexed unto that Office, thinking it too long: and Dr. *Wallis* was desired to draw up the Prayer for the King, which is his Work (being somewhat altered by us). And we agreed to put before it a short Address to the Bishops, professing our readiness in Debates to yield to the shortning of anything that may be found amiss."[25]

Baxter's fondest hope must have been that his *Reformation of the Liturgy*, with its marginal Biblical references as proof that it was entirely according to the Word of God, would be accepted as an alternative to the Book of Common Prayer, an alternative particularly congenial to those of the Puritan persuasion. But this would have created a permanent dichotomy within the Church of England, and perpetuated not eased, the strife between orthodox and Puritan Anglicans. Bishop Gilbert Burnet of Salisbury (1643-1715), himself a former Presbyterian minister in the church of Scotland and former Professor of Divinity in the University of Glasgow, wrote that Baxter had convinced his colleagues that they

---

[23] For a text of *The Reformation of the Liturgy* by Richard Baxter, see *Reliquiae Liturgicae*, IV, *The Savoy Liturgy* (ed. Peter Hall, Bath, 1847), or *The Practical Works of the Rev. Richard Baxter* (ed. W. Orme, 1830), XV, pp. 450-527. The latter edition, however, excludes the prefatory Address to the Bishops.

[24] Baxter defines the Lord's Supper as "an holy Sacrament instituted by Christ, wherein bread and wine, being first by consecration made sacramentally, or representatively, the body and blood of Christ, are used by breaking and pouring out to represent and commemorate Christ's body and blood upon the cross once offered up to God for sin; and are given in the name of Christ unto the Church to signify and solemnize the renewal of his holy covenant with them, and the giving of himself unto them, to expiate their sins by his sacrifice, and sanctify them further by his Spirit, and confirm their right unto everlasting life." (ed. Peter Hall, *op. cit.*, p. 57.)

[25] Sylvester, *op. cit.*, I, Pt. II, Sect. 182.

should "offer everything which they thought might conduce to the good or peace of the Church, without considering what was like to be obtained, or what effect their demanding so much might have, in irritating the minds of those who were then the superior body in strength and number."[26] Baxter was proven to be no more a politician than Cosin would be and both traditions they represented were eventually rejected.

A series of events in the late spring and summer of 1661 made it appear that revision of the Prayer Book in a Laudian or a Puritan direction would be exceedingly unpopular. The Parliament consisting predominantly of Cavaliers who had lost lands and been mulcted by fines under the Puritan regime, and many of whom had been tutored by ejected Anglican clergymen in their youth, were in no mood to accommodate even the most conservative of Puritans, the Presbyterians. The House of Commons determined to burn publicly the Solemn League and Covenant on May 17. Nine days later the members of Parliament received the Sacrament according to the rite of the Jacobean Prayer Book. On June 18 the bishops were restored to the House of Lords. In entire disregard of the Savoy Conference, then meeting, the House of Commons commenced measures "for confirming the Liturgy of the Church of England." The aim was to pass a new Act of Uniformity, with the Prayer Book of 1604 annexed. This proposal was forwarded to the House of Lords on July 10, and there it stayed until January 1662. It was only the King and his government, together with a strong feeling in convocation that some rubrical and literary clarification was needed, with the need for a few additional services, that overcame the reluctance of the Commons which had been confirmed by the failure of the Savoy Conference to produce agreement.

2. *The Durham Book*

Two bishops, however, were preparing to make the best of the opportunity that might be given to the Church of England to revise its liturgy. One of them, Bishop Wren of Ely, had eighteen years in the Tower of London in which to think about improving the Prayer Book[27] and was seventy-six years of age in 1661, the

---

26 *History of My Own Time*, 2 Vols. (1723-1724), Vol. I, p. 320.

27 Wren when incarcerated considered that "Never could there have been an opportunity so offenceless on the Church's part for amending the Book of Common Prayer as now, when it hath been so long disused that not one of five hundred is so perfect in it as to observe alterations." (G. J. Cuming, *The Durham Book*,

embodiment of the Laudian tradition. The other, John Cosin, had succeeded Wren as Master of Peterhouse, Cambridge, had gone into exile in 1643, and was also a trusted Laudian; in 1660 he had been consecrated Bishop of Durham at the age of sixty-six. Wren's work is contained in a manuscript which he himself terms "Advices" and so can conveniently be called by that name.[28] Cosin probably saw the "Advices" shortly after he returned to England in 1660 and then prepared his own proposals which are contained in a paper with the heading, *Particulars to be considered, explained, and corrected in the Book of Common Prayer.*[29] This probability is based on the facts that the similarity of title, the specifying of reasons for each proposed change, and the over-riding concern for accuracy in detail, also characterize Wren's work.

It may also be conjectured that Cosin and Wren on learning that the King was proposing a conference such as the Savoy, combined their proposals for revision in the volume entitled the *Durham Book*, a Prayer Book dated 1619, in which Cosin had written in the changes and additions put forward by Wren and himself, together with much other material, the larger part of which was now added by Cosin himself. In preparing the *Durham Book*, it was obvious that a major source was Wedderburn's Scottish liturgy of 1637 which influenced the Order for Holy Communion. This can be seen in the introducing of a thanksgiving for the departed, rearranging the canon, restoring the *epiklesis* and the commemoration of the Passion, Resurrection and Ascension of Christ, which is "now represented" to God the Father. There is no reference to Christ's death, without the addition "and sacrifice." "Christ's Church militant here upon earth" is changed to "Christ's Catholic Church." Andrewes's Offertory Sentences reappear and the alms are first to be presented upon the holy table, and afterwards the elements. There are both epistoller and gospeller, in addition to the celebrant. The Creed and *Sanctus* may be sung, but the *Agnus Dei* is required to be sung as also the added Post-Communion Sentences. The 1549 Prayer Book was used, but Wedderburn was given the preference.

1961, pp. 287-88.) Cuming, *ibid.*, p. xv, writes of Cosin that "yet, he remains with Wren, the most copious contributor to the Prayer Book since Archbishop Cranmer."

[28] The text can be found in Cuming, *ibid.*, and in *Fragmentary Illustrations of the History of the Book of Common Prayer* (ed. W. K. Jacobson, 1874), pp. 43-109.

[29] Cuming, *A History of the Anglican Liturgy*, p. 150.

Other sources for the *Durham Book* are the Prayer Book itself. Several proposals are modifications of materials from other parts of the book, while others involved the changing of rubrics into phrases and sentences. The Canons of 1604 and even the Elizabethan *Injunctions* and *Advertisements* are occasionally consulted for rubrics. Cosin's *Devotions* is the source of some small changes. G. J. Cuming[30] emphasizes the caution with which they approached debatable matters, for they never refer to the Scottish liturgy associated with Laud, nor do they mention the requirement of Laud that the people should come up to the altar rails to receive Communion, for the words "Draw near" are diluted to read "Draw near with a true heart in full assurance of faith." But of the Laudian character of their proposed revision there is no question. This is evident not only in the changes borrowed from Wedderburn (which were approved by Laud as Archbishop of Canterbury), but also in the blessing of the water in Baptism, as in the emphasis on bodily gestures for the honouring of God in the Catechism, both objectionable to the Puritans.

Cosin, as we have seen, had been a member of the commission of the Savoy Conference, which ended July 25, 1661. He then returned to his diocese of Durham, and his chaplain, William Sancroft, took charge of the *Durham Book*. First, he added the concessions made at the Savoy Conference. Then he revised the book in thoroughgoing detail, with the result that the rubrics were clarified in about eighty cases, and the printed text was restored in sixty-six cases. Many of these revisions were mere minutiae, and about a dozen of them came from Wren's materials, little, if any, from Cosin's. Next follows new material of importance, including an Ember Collect composed by Cosin. Also the Presbyterians' request that the Sentences from Tobit be rejected as apocryphal material not in the canon of Scripture, was acceded to and entered, and their other request that the sick man receiving Communion shall be absolved, not as a matter of course, but "if he shall humbly and heartily desire it."

Hitherto, the *Durham Book* had been a private, unofficial attempt by two liturgically learned Laudian bishops to suggest Prayer Book revisions. About the beginning of September, 1661, the contents were to be considered by authority in the person of Sheldon, Bishop of London and ecclesiastical adviser to the government, for Sheldon and Wren wrote an urgent letter to Cosin, bid-

---

30 *Ibid.*, p. 153.

ding him return with all speed to London by the beginning of November, as he, in fact, did.[31]

The *Durham Book* was not yet complete. Cosin started to correct The Ordering of Deacons in a Prayer Book of 1634 because there was no Ordinal in the *Durham Book*, and Sancroft completed the work by writing in Wren's proposals for the improvement of the text. He then copied the contents of the *Durham Book* into the new book, which is known as *The Fair Copy*.[32] This included twenty additional rubrical improvements, twenty-eight more rejections of alterations, and there is a new and conservative edition of the Canon, besides the *Durham Book* version of the Canon, which is written out fully on a separate sheet, and which retains the old Canon intact, while allowing the *Durham Book* rubrics and Words of Administration. A laconic note added by Sancroft adds that both versions of the Canon are "left to censure." His final note in the *Durham Book* completes the account: "My lords the bishops at Ely House ordered all in the old method."[33] It is sufficient explanation as to why he then gives the outline of an order corresponding exactly to the new Canon of 1662.

Both the ceremonial and the doctrine of the *Durham Book* were higher than the Prayer Book of 1662, and on this double count were probably rejected. While rails about the Communion table were too bitter a memory and therefore too controversial an issue to raise again, yet the holy table is to stand in the upper part of the chancel, and there are to be both epistoller and gospeller at the Holy Communion, and the collection and the elements are to be presented at the altar by the celebrant. Wafers may be used, and the manual acts of fraction and libation are stressed. Though this was considerably less than the young Cosin would have liked, it was more than Convocation (or Parliament behind Convocation) would tolerate. The same was the case with the doctrine. In the bidding of the prayer for the church, the phrase "militant here upon earth" was omitted, leaving one to assume that the bidding was for the church militant and triumphant, and that was made explicit in the restoration at the end of the prayer of the thanksgiving for

[31] Cosin, *Correspondence* (Surtees Society Publication LV, Vol. II, p. 31, cited by Cuming, *A History of the Anglican Liturgy*, p. 159. The entire revisionary studies of Wren and Cosin have been described at length in Cuming's *Durham Book* and are very clearly and conveniently summarized in his *A History of the Anglican Liturgy*, both of which have proved invaluable for this section of this chapter.

[32] The text of the "Fair Copy" is to be found in Cuming's *Durham Book*.

[33] *Ibid.*, p. 180.

the dead. Convocation rejected a petition for their well-being "at the day of the generall Resurrection." Cosin also makes much of the Communion as a sacrifice, though insisting that Christ's sacrifice is unrepeatable and unique, and places the Prayer of Oblation immediately after the Prayer of Consecration. The *epiklesis*, based on the 1549 Prayer Book and the 1637 Scottish liturgy, affirming a transformation effected by the Holy Spirit, wisely avoids the subjective term "that they may be unto us." Finally, it should be noted that Cosin insisted that the Body and Blood of Christ were "sacramentally and really" but not "sensibly" present in the Sacrament. This view was strengthened by the inclusion of the 1549 phrase "these holy mysteries" and of the *Agnus Dei*, both of which were later rejected by convocation, presumably as seeming too Romanist.

If we compare the experiences of Baxter and Cosin as frustrated liturgists, each has a different but dubious consolation. Cosin's is one for the distant future, for the South African alternative form of 1929, the American Episcopal church rite of 1935, and the proposed Indian rite of *The Holy Eucharist* of 1951, all followed the Cosin proposals in general outline and intention.[34] Baxter's was a more immediate consolation, though it is doubtful that Cosin ever told him of it, namely, that in a few important respects Cosin accepted Baxter's proposals for bettering the Book of Common Prayer. The latter is the interesting conclusion of E. C. Ratcliff.[35] Baxter had criticised the Prayer Book Consecratory Prayer thus: "It is a disorder . . . to begin in a Prayer and to end in a Narrative" and urged that "The Consecration Commemoration . . . are not distinctly enough performed."[36] This first requirement was met in the *epiklesis* of the Scottish liturgy, and the second in Cosin's alternative Prayer of Consecration in which the Institution Narrative is followed by the Prayer of Oblation (a "Memoriall") containing a commemoration of the Passion, Resurrection, and Ascension of Christ. Not only so, but in the Savoy liturgy of Baxter the action in the Holy Communion Service is said to be a representation of Christ's death, and it is linked with his heavenly Intercession.[37]

[34] *Ibid.*, p. xxvi.

[35] "The Savoy Conference and the Book of Common Prayer," being Chap. 2 of *From Uniformity to Unity* (eds. Geoffrey F. Nuttall and Owen Chadwick, 1962), p. 134.

[36] *Reliquiae Baxterianae*, ed. M. Sylvester, I, Pt. II, Sect. 174.

[37] This "explication" of the Sacrament, at the beginning of Baxter's "Order of Celebrating the Sacrament of the Body and Blood of Christ" includes the following statement (*Reliquiae Liturgicae*, IV, *The Savoy Liturgy*, ed. Peter Hall, Bath, 1847, pp. 56-57): "And when Christ was ready to leave the world, and to

The point is that the English and Scottish Consecration prayers make no reference to either of these points, yet Cosin changed part of the Prayer of Consecration to read "by the Merits & Death of thy Sonne Jesus Christ, now represented unto thee, & through faith in his Bloud, who maketh intercession for us at thy right Hand. . . ." Cosin's Prayers of Consecration were never submitted to Convocation for the consideration of the two Houses. As we shall see, conservatism, moderation, and pragmatism, were the dominating characteristics of the revision, especially conservatism.

3. *The Prayer Book of 1662*

The clue to the character of the revision accomplished by Convocation in 1661 and authorized by King and Parliament in 1662 is to be found in the Preface, which was the work of Bishop Robert Sanderson of Lincoln. He wrote:

> That most of the Alterations were made, either first, for the better direction of them that are to officiate in any part of Divine Service, which is chiefly done in the Kalendars and Rubricks; Or secondly, for the more proper expressing of some words or phrases of ancient usage in terms more suitable to the language of the present times . . . ; or thirdly, for a more perfect rendering of such portions of holy Scripture, as are inserted into the Liturgy; which, in the Epistles and Gospels especially, and in sundry other places are now ordered to be read according to the last Translation.

The primary concern was to restore rather than to revise the Prayer Book, but to revise only where directions or language could be made clearer. As for the additions made, they were necessities. So Sanderson wrote of them:

> . . . it was thought convenient that some Prayers and Thanksgivings, fitted to special occasions, should be added in their due places; particularly for those at sea, together

---

give up himself a sacrifice for us, and *intercede* and exercise the fulness of his kingly power as the Church's Head, and by his grace to draw men to himself, and prepare them for his glory; he did himself institute the Sacrament of his body and blood at his last supper, to be a continued *representation* and remembrance of his death . . ." (I have italicized the key concepts). See also *ibid.*, pp. 61, 64, and especially p. 70 with its petition, "we beseech thee, by thine intercession with the Father, through the sacrifice of thy body and blood, give us the pardon of our sins, and thy quickening Spirit . . ." and p. 73 (an alternative prayer of Consecration), "and through his sacrifice and intercession give us pardon of our sins."

with an Office for the Baptism of such as are of riper years; which . . . by the growth of Anabaptism,[38] through the licentiousness of the late times crept in amongst us, is now become necessary, and may be always useful to the Baptizing of Natives in our Plantations, and others converted to the Faith.

The work of revision was not only politically restricted, but also it was rushed.[39] The Convocation of Canterbury was convened on May 8, 1661. Before it adjourned on July 31, it had completed three tasks. One was the preparation of a form of prayer with thanksgiving for the anniversary of the King's birth and Restoration on May 29. A second was the provision of a form of prayer commemorating the death of King Charles I, the anniversary of which was January 29. A third achievement was the completion of an Office for the Baptism of adults. But as yet nothing was done about a revision of the 1604 Prayer Book.

The latter responsibility was committed to Convocation when it was reconvened on November 21, 1661. The upper House appointed eight bishops to act in the name of all in the work of revision, and to maintain revision between the full sessions of Convocation. These Bishops were Cosin of Durham, Wren of Ely, Skinner of Oxford, Warner of Rochester, Henchman of Salisbury, Morley of Worcester, Sanderson of Lincoln, and Nicholson of Gloucester. It is this group (at least the six excluding Cosin and Wren) which must ultimately be held responsible for suppressing the proposals in the *Durham Book*, and it is not difficult to see how this could have been done. In the group Sheldon's strong supporters were Morley, Sanderson, Henchman, and Nicholson, while Skinner and Warner were under a cloud and needed the sunshine of Sheldon's approval. In any case, the Laudian proposals of Cosin and Wren would have been unlikely to win any support from the Latitudinarian bishops who wished to placate the Presbyterians, or from the House of Commons which was satisfied with the Prayer Book of 1604.

The debates, held in the full session of both Houses, and lasting from 8:00 A.M. to 10:00 A.M., enabled the committee to devote the rest of the day to revision. The whole work was accomplished

---

[38] A left-handed compliment to Tombes the learned Baptist who became Master of the Temple, and others, who had spread the tenets of their fellow believers, and the "licentiousness of the times" is an unintended tribute to the toleration of the Lord Protector, Cromwell.

[39] J. Parker, *An Introduction to the History of the Successive Revisions of The Book of Common Prayer* (Oxford, 1879), pp. cccix, cccx.

in twenty-two days. The work was finished on December 18, 1661. This was copied out and subscribed to by both Houses of the Convocation of Canterbury and by the upper House and the proxies of the lower House of York on December 20 and sent to the King. This rapidity (necessarily involving some superficiality of supervision) was made possible, partly by the political pressure and partly also because Cosin and Wren had done the preliminary work of clarifying archaisms in diction and obscurities in rubrics in great detail. Furthermore, the additional forms had been prepared by the previous session of Convocation and only needed pruning, while experts dealt with such technical items as the table of moveable feasts. Although many of the most far-reaching proposals of the loyal Laudian bishops were not accepted, yet the bulk of the revisions in detail in the 1662 Prayer Book were clearly derived from the improvements in wording and rubrics set forth in the *Fair Copy* combining part of the *Advices* of Wren and part of the *Particulars* of Cosin, with additional material.[40] As the work went on, a full manuscript text was prepared by several scribes. This was finally signed by the proctors in Convocation and annexed to the Act of Uniformity. It kept a number of readings which were later rejected. Some, it is conjectured,[41] derived from a source otherwise unknown, and others were innovations arising in the committee. Four can plainly be attributed to Sanderson, while Wren secured the inclusion of several suggestions in his *Advices* which had not been incorporated in the *Durham Book*, and Cosin managed to get several suggestions accepted which had been left out of the *Fair Copy*. The three most prominent men on the committee were Sanderson, Cosin, and Wren. Only one other bishop, not on the committee, Reynolds of Norwich contributed significantly to the 1662 Prayer Book, since he is the author of the admirable General Thanksgiving, excellent in its comprehensiveness as in its concise and balanced phrasing,[42] and even the Prayer for All Conditions of Men has been attributed to him.[43] It is a singular irony

[40] Cuming, *A History of Anglican Liturgy*, p. 159.

[41] *Ibid.*, p. 160. See also F. E. Brightman, *The English Rite*, 2 Vols. (1915, 1922), I, pp. cc-cci.

[42] Consider these phrases as basis for the evaluation: "humble and hearty thanks"; "our creation, preservation, and all the blessings of this life"; and "for the means of grace and for the hope of glory."

[43] Another attribution is to Dr. Peter Gunning, Master of St. John's College, Cambridge, and afterwards Bishop of Chichester (1670-1674) and of Ely (1675-1684), an active participant in the Savoy Conference. Although it is a misuse of prayer, he may have directed the petition "that all who profess and call themselves Christians, may be led into the way of truth, and hold the faith in unity

of history that a proponent of the view that a minister should supplement the liturgy with prayers of his own composition, should have contributed so much to the prescribed Anglican liturgy of 1662, and as a prelate who disbelieved in the monarchical episcopate.

What were the important changes made in the conservative revision of 1662? Sanderson's Preface was prefixed to it, and the original preface of 1549 became an ensuing chapter "Concerning the Service of the Church." Higher language indicated the more elevated status of the threefold ministry of the church. For example, the Absolution at Morning and Evening Prayer was to be pronounced by the "Priest" instead of the "Minister." Also, "bishops, priests, and deacons" was substituted for "bishops, pastors, and ministers of the Church." In several cases "church" replaces "congregation." It is possible that each of these verbal changes, as also the clear denial of parity of ministers in the new Ordinal, was aimed at the Presbyterians who had preferred the older terms.

The changed language is also a clue to the increasing reverence with which worship was celebrated. One important example was seen in the terminological changes used in the rubrics for the Holy Communion. "Consecrated bread and wine" were substituted for the former "bread and wine" and instructions were given for "reverently" replacing the consecrated elements on the altar after Communion, for covering them with a linen cloth, and consuming them immediately after the blessing, instead of the priest taking them home for consumption at the table. The fraction in Communion was restored also. Furthermore, the idea of "offering" was restored in requiring the priest to offer the alms at the altar instead of putting them in a box, with the added petition for the acceptance of "our alms and oblations" at the beginning of the intercessions immediately ensuing.

---

of spirit, in the bond of peace, and in righteousness of life" as an arrow against the Puritans. It may originally have been written for the chapel of St. John's College as a substitute for the Litany in Evening Prayer, and its prefatory petitions for the king and clergy, were eliminated by the 1662 revisers in view of the alternative provision made for them. (See Massey H. Shepherd, Jr., *The Oxford American Prayer Book Commentary*, New York, 1950, pp. 18-19.) On the other hand, G. J. Cuming in "The Prayer Book in Convocation, November, 1661" in *The Journal of Ecclesiastical History*, VIII (1957), pp. 182-92, and in "Two Fragments of a Lost Liturgy," *Studies in Church History* (Leiden, 1966), III, pp. 247-53, argues that Reynolds composed both the General Thanksgiving and the Prayer for All Conditions, but that both were thoroughly revised by Sanderson.

There were also changes which the Presbyterians could well have approved, and might have been caused by their protests backed by Sanderson. The *Benedicite* disappeared, along with plainsong. In the Office of the Communion of the Sick, the invalid is to make a confession only if moved to do so, not by requirement, while newly married couples are recommended to make their Communion the same day, but not obliged to do so. Their criticism of the disorderliness of the Collects had been taken with the utmost seriousness, with the result that several of them were given clearer direction by a Scriptural quotation or a more memorable incisive phrase, and the hands of Cosin and Sanderson can be detected in this tidying up. The four "nocent" ceremonies were retained, but there was a reference to Canon 30 as an explanation for the signing of the Cross in Baptism and the Declaration on Kneeling was restored, probably as late as the Privy Council meeting of February 24, 1662, long after the book had been signed, on December 21, 1661. The Prayer Book was annexed to the Act of Uniformity. It received the royal assent on May 19, 1662, and was to come into use no later than St. Bartholomew's Day, August 24, 1662, which also marks the beginning of orthodox Dissent from the Church of England on the part of all the Puritan ministers who could not conscientiously affirm that the same Prayer Book was in all things conformable to the Word of God. A liturgical formulary which had initially intended to unite the nation, despite critics, was now the instrument of acute religious division.

The most significant changes of all, however, have yet to be considered. Among them the chief was the improvement in the Ordinal. There was an amplification (and ensuing clarification) of the formulae for ordination and for consecration to the episcopate. The formula of ordination to the priesthood pronounced by the bishop in 1552 as also in 1559 was "receiue the holy ghost: whose sinnes thou doest forgiue, etc." It was changed in 1662 to read, "Receive the Holy Ghost, *for the Office and work of a Priest, in the Church of God, now committed unto thee by the imposition of our hands.* Whose sins thou dost forgive, etc." Similarly at the consecration of a bishop the presiding Archbishop in 1552 and 1559 pronounced the formula, "Take the holy ghost, and remember that thou stirre vp the grace of God, which is in thee by the imposition of hands. For God, etc." In 1662 this was changed to: "Receive the holy Ghost, *for the office and work of Bishop in the Church of God, now committed unto thee by the Imposition of our hands, in*

382

the Name of the Father, and of the Son, and of the holy Ghost. Amen. And remember that thou stir vp the grace of God, which is *given* thee by *this* Imposition of *our* hands, For God, etc." These amplifications of the ordination and consecration formulae was due, at least in part, to the criticism of the validity of Anglican orders made by a Roman Catholic controversialist, who had drawn attention in particular to a defect in the ordination formula. This Peter Talbot, S.J., wrote in *A Treatise of the Nature of Catholick Faith and Heresie* (Rouen, 1657): "The intention of the Ordainer expressed by generall words, indifferent and appliable to all, or divers degrees of holy Orders, is not sufficient to make one a Priest, or a Bishop. As for example, *Receive the holy Ghost*, these words being indifferent to priesthood and Episcopacy, and used in both Ordinations, are not sufficiently expressive of either in particular . . . In the words of forme, whereby Protestants ordaine Bishops, there is not one word expressing Episcopall power, and authority."[44]

The new services, the work of the summer session of Convocation in 1661, were also important. The forms for the return of the King and the martyrdom of Charles I were allocated to two committees on 16 May, and the first had been completed in time to be used on May 29. It was on the same lines as the form of thanksgiving for the delivery from the Gunpowder Plot and was probably Wren's work, and he certainly introduced it into Convocation on May 18. The service commemorating the martyrdom of Charles I probably originated from prayers issued for the Cavalier army in the 1640s, supposedly collated by Bishop Duppa of Winchester, revised by Sancroft and published for use on January 30, 1661. Its excessive and idolatrous glorification of King Charles I amounting almost to an apotheosis, rendered it generally unacceptable, and the last version of it was printed on January 7, 1662.[45]

On May 18, 1661, another committee was appointed to prepare a form of Baptism for adults. The adaptation of the existing form

[44] *Op. cit.*, p. 22. The point (with a confirmatory citation from Talbot) is made by Ratcliff, *op. cit.*, p. 137.

[45] It finally read as follows: "Blessed Lord, in whose sight the death of thy Saints is precious, We magnify Thy Name for that abundant grace bestowed on our late martyred Sovereign, by which he was enabled so cheerfully to follow the steps of his Blessed Master and Saviour, in a constant meek suffering of all barbarous indignities, and at last resisting unto blood; and even then, according to the same pattern, praying for his murderers. Let his memory, O Lord, be ever blessed among us, that we may follow the example of his patience and charity. And grant that our land may be freed from the vengeance of his blood, and thy mercy glorified in the forgiveness of our sins. And all for Jesus Christ his Sake. *Amen.*"

for public Baptism was a simple matter, and it is attributed to Lloyd, the Bishop of St. Asaph.

It is to Sanderson's selection and editing that the 1662 Prayer Book owes the new "Forms of Prayer to be used at sea," which are a choice of prayers and Psalms rather than complete forms.[46]

Among alterations made, there are small but significant changes in the Services for Baptism, Confirmation, and Burial, with a very important modification in Ordination. In Baptism, the number of godparents is specified, and the promises are made in the child's name, which was previously the case only in private Baptism; also the petition for the sanctification of the water is borrowed from the Scottish liturgy of 1637. The dislocation in the Order for Confirmation is removed, an explanatory Preface is prefixed, and the Lord's Prayer is placed so that it follows immediately on the laying-on of hands, and thus, in this respect, corresponds with the order of the other occasional offices. In the Ordinal, in addition to the major changes already considered, Cosin's translation of the *Veni, Creator Spiritus* replaces the older version. In the Burial Service the order is changed to correspond with Sanderson's practice during the Interregnum.

Other additions included the provision of Proper Psalms for Ash Wednesday and Good Friday. A Collect, Epistle, and Gospel were provided for the Sixth Sunday after Epiphany, together with an Epistle for the Purification, an additional Easter anthem, and a Collect for the eve of Easter (originating from the Scottish liturgy but improved). The section with the heading Prayers was amplified by the inclusion of a second prayer "in time of dearth" (restored from the 1552 Prayer Book and omitted in 1559), two Ember prayers (one of Cosin's composition and the other from the Scottish liturgy), a revision of the Prayer for Parliament, and Wren's thanksgiving "for restoring public peace at home." In the Visitation of the Sick there are four additional prayers in an appendix, which bear the imprint of Sanderson. But the most important prayers to be added, which, because of their use at Morning and Evening Prayer for two centuries have become classics of devotion, deserve detailed consideration.

These are, of course, "A Prayer for all Conditions of Men" and "A General Thanksgiving." Their structure is similar in both prayers in that God is approached as Creator, Preserver and Redeemer, and the benefits of redemption in Christ are sought. In "A Prayer

[46] Izaak Walton's *Life of Dr. Robert Sanderson* (1678), p. 15.

for all Conditions," these are the way of truth, the unity of spirit, the bond of peace, and righteousness. In "A General Thanksgiving," they are the means of grace and the hope of glory. It is worth observing that in the "Prayer for all Conditions of Men" the missionary note first appears in the Prayer Book ("Thy saving health unto all nations"), and may well reflect the expansion of English colonization in the seventeenth century. The second petition[47] of the same prayer mirrors the bitter divisions in the Christian Church in Britain, and the Thirty Years War made it equally applicable in Europe. The third petition for the afflicted or distressed begs for divine comfort and finishes strongly with the words, "giving them patience under their sufferings, and a happy issue out of all their afflictions."

Earlier (footnote 43) it was pointed out that while it is agreed that Edward Reynolds, Bishop of Norwich at the Restoration, wrote "A General Thanksgiving," yet it is disputed whether he wrote "A Prayer for all Conditions of Men," or whether Dr. Peter Gunning did so. On grounds of both style and content, even when allowance is made for the editorial hand of another such as the apparently omnipresent Bishop Sanderson, I find it difficult to credit these two prayers to the same author. "A Prayer for all Conditions" is characterized by a compulsion to use alternating pairs of alternative words, presumably so that there are two chances of understanding. Thus we have "all sorts and conditions," "guided and governed," "profess and call themselves," "afflicted or distressed," and "comfort and relieve." In "A General Thanksgiving," there are only two such pairs of alternatives, namely, "goodness and loving-kindness," and the second word is not necessarily the same in meaning as the first. The second couplet is "holiness and righteousness." "A Prayer for all Conditions" has a slower rhythm and a longer line of phrases before stops, while "A General Thanksgiving" is more staccato and the diction is more concise, yet it has a regularity and balance that is most felicitous for it reads like poetry. It is also evident that the former has many more direct Scriptural citations,[48] is, in fact, a mosaic of them, while the latter is fully theological but rarely[49] echoes directly Scripture. Unques-

[47] "More especially we pray for thy holy Church universal, that it may be so guided and governed by thy good Spirit, that all who profess and call themselves Christians may be led into the way of truth, and hold the faith in unity of spirit, in the bond of peace, and in righteousness of life."

[48] Notably, Psalm 67:2; John 16:3; Psalm 25:9; and Ephesians 4:3.

[49] The exceptions are "hope of glory" (from Colossians 1:27) and a fainter echo from Luke 1:75.

tionably, however, they, together with the revised Ordinal, justify the work of revision which otherwise was meagre in results, clarification excepted. And even clarification is only a poor second best to creative innovation. Although "A General Thanksgiving" is listed among the occasional prayers, it soon gained for itself an essential place in the Anglican liturgy, for thanksgiving is at the very heart of worship.

4. An Evaluation of the Revision of 1662

What can be said by way of evaluating the 1662 Prayer Book? The usual adjectives apply, and Sanderson in his Preface indicates that "Our general aim was not to gratify this or that party in any of their unreasonable demands; but to do that . . . which . . . might most tend to the preservation of peace and unity in the Church." There was to be no rocking of the ark of the Church of England, whether by Laudian pushing or by Presbyterian pulling, though their combined efforts had at least taken the Prayer Book out of the harbour of 1604. Cuming rightly observes that "Sheldon had a more accurate sense of the nation's religious temper than either Cosin or Baxter."[50] This is a conservative, middle-of-the-way, safe, prudential, logical, lucid, moderate, and modest revision. Perhaps the best that can be said of it, excepting its additions, or possibly in part because of them, is that it has lasted practically unchanged until 1928, when significant alternatives to it were proposed, and in that period of 268 years (and nine generations) it has moulded the moderate, sober, and dignified devotions of the moderate, sober, and dignified English people; and has provided liturgical living space to the general satisfaction, barring some vehement disputes, of the three different parties of the Church of England, high, low, and broad.

In recent years, however, its liturgical fare is felt to be too lacking in vitamins, as well as in variety, to satisfy the needs of modern man.[51] Nor has it been able to keep up with the generally higher

[50] *A History of Anglican Liturgy*, p. 167.
[51] See, for example, W. Jardine Grisbrooke, "The 1662 Book of Common Prayer: its History and Character" in *Studia Liturgica* (Rotterdam), I, No. 3, Sept. 1962, with its conclusion (p. 166): "—despite its virtues and its beauty, neither of which should be underestimated—it is, as the attempted revision of 1927-8 and the all but universal practice of making considerable unauthorised alterations in the services both prove, sadly inadequate as a vehicle for the worship of twentieth century congregations." The words of the late Professor E. C. Ratcliff should also be noted: "If the Anglican Churches are alive and healthy, they cannot be content with an ossified form of worship derived from sixteenth and seventeenth century England, and marked by the time and circumstances of

and more advanced trend of Anglican worship since the impact of the Tractarian Movement of the nineteenth century.

There are two indicators of the unsatisfactory nature of the liturgical provisions of the Prayer Book of 1662, quite apart from the contemporary frustrations experienced by Cosin and Wren on the one hand, and Baxter and his Presbyterian associates on the other. One indicator of dissatisfaction is the many changes proposed within the Church of England for the improvement of the 1662 Book of Common Prayer, especially in the nineteenth and twentieth centuries.[52] The other indicator is the improvements and changes introduced into other liturgies in the Anglican Communion which were unrestricted by any subservience to the state, which had the effect of hampering revision in England because of the need for the Parliamentary approval of liturgical change.[53]

Using both sources of information, it will be found that it is in five major areas that improvements are felt to be necessary. First, there is great need for supplementation. Forms of worship are required for patronal festivals and harvest festivals, as also for the institution or induction of a minister to a parish or to other types of clerical responsibility (such as a chaplaincy), and for a late evening service.

Secondly, the enrichment of existing services (and the provision for greater variety) is needed. This is evident particularly in Holy Week, which, apart from a daily Eucharist, is not treated as the culmination and climax of the long preparation of Lent, with different lections, collects, and prayers for each successive day. There is also a paucity of significant ceremonies hallowed by traditional usage at this time. These could include: palm processions on Palm Sunday, the washing of altars on Maundy Thursday; the veneration of the Cross and subsequent burial of it at the Easter Sepulchre on Good Friday, reaching a climax in the Easter Vigil and the Midnight Mass of the Resurrection. None of these customs find

---

its production. Life and worship and Liturgy must move in step." (*The Anglican Tradition* by Meredith Dewey, E. C. Ratcliff, and Norman Sykes [being Sermons delivered in Chichester Cathedral on three Sunday mornings in July, 1958], p. 26.)

[52] R.C.D. Jasper documents the dissatisfactions with the rite in the nineteenth century in his *Prayer Book Revision in England, 1800-1900* (1954). See, for example, a perceptive criticism cited on pp. 85-89.

[53] This point is interestingly documented in J. Gordon Davies's article (itself a most useful modern critique), "The 1662 Book of Common Prayer: its virtues and vices" in *Studia Liturgica*, I, No. 3, Sept. 1962, pp. 167-74. Its virtues are claimed to be: an orderly and logical arrangement; dignity and clarity of style; a strong Biblical basis in lections and in the thought and imagery of the prayers; and some provision for lay participation.

any place in the Prayer Book of 1662 and could not have done, without invoking charges of "Popery."[54]

A third need is for calendric implementation. There is little point in replacing the seventeenth century State Services[55] with modern equivalents. There is, however, a great need for commemorations of the eminent imitators of God in Britain and in the wider reaches of the Anglican Communion who, by their exemplary holiness, Christian service to humanity, or defence and exposition of the Christian faith as theologians and teachers, deserve remembrance for they bridge time and space for their Incarnate Lord, demonstrating His relevance and contemporaneity to each generation. There is no argument, of course, for diminishing the primacy and centrality of the Christological cycle in the calendar, but there is a need to expand the Sanctoral cycle beyond the saints of the first century A.D. Not to do so, despite the grave problems of selection, is to imply that God has left Himself without witness for the past nineteen hundred years.

A fourth area for improvement, especially in the light of the emphasis of the modern liturgical movement[56] on the corporate responsibility of the people of God in worship (for "liturgy" means the work of the people), is the provision of new forms of worship allowing and encouraging a greater amount of participation on the part of the people, a need, incidentally, which was even less well met in Puritan worship. It was to meet this need that hymns were composed for and sung by the congregation, though there is no rubric in 1662 to allow for this practice. The Prayer Book of 1662, apart from a few versicles and responses, is almost as priest-ridden,[57] as Puritan worship, and is a ministerial monologue.

Fifthly, the unhurried Sunday of the seventeenth century has been replaced by a rushed week (and often weekend) in which there is no time for the leisurely model of service in 1662, which envisaged in succession, Mattins, Litany, and Holy Communion. That is why in many modern parishes it has been replaced by the Parish Communion, which includes a brief sermon.

[54] This catalogue of desirable enrichments is that of *ibid.*, p. 172.
[55] These services were discussed earlier in Chap. VI, "Calendary Conflict: Holy Days or Holidays."
[56] See Chaps. I and XIII of Davies, *op. cit.*, V.
[57] J. Gordon Davies, *op. cit.*, p. 173, calculates that if the Communion Service is taken, with the third exhortation and the proper for the first Sunday in Advent, "we find that the congregation has some seven hundred words to say and the celebrant over 3500," excluding notices, banns, and sermon. He advises Litanies and an offertory procession as remedies.

Finally, as was the case with Cosin and Wren, so with many modern Anglicans there is a serious dissatisfaction with the Communion Service. When it is celebrated as part of the Parish Communion, there is an abbreviation of the Service of the Word, for there is usually no lesson from the Old Testament and the sermon becomes a sermonette.[58] Furthermore, there is an excessive priestly domination of the Office. Not least there is criticism because the structure of the Eucharist is seriously obscured because the Intercessions (now a part of the Prayer for the Church) should precede the Offertory. In addition, it seems wrong that the medieval Communion devotions should be interposed between the Offertory and the Prayer of Consecration. Moreover, the final Blessing is otiose, since the communicants are already united with Christ through the Holy Communion.

The preceding critique, it might be objected, employs several anachronisms adducing criticisms which were not made in its own day. This is not denied; but the point of the critique was to demonstrate that a more thoroughgoing revision in a higher direction might have made the Prayer Book a more adequate medium for seventeenth-century as for modern worship. It is surely not without significance that Baxter's *Savoy Liturgy*, together with the proposals of Wren and Cosin, included a prayer for the invocation of the Holy Spirit to consecrate the elements that they might sacramentally become the "Body and Blood of Christ."[59] The Prayer Book of 1662 had not advanced theologically beyond the Eucharistic doctrine of Cranmer in 1552, and that had been left behind by both the Laudians and the Presbyterians.

5. *The Ceremonial and Furnishings of the Restoration Church*

Before describing and evaluating further revisions, it might be well to consider how effectively the 1662 Prayer Book rubrics were implemented, and what the nature of Anglican worship was in fact, not merely in theory, in the aftermath of the Restoration. It is interesting that J. Wickham Legg thought that disregard for

[58] See the criticisms of A. M. Ramsey (later Archbishop of Canterbury, then Bishop of Durham) in *Durham Essays and Addresses* (1956), p. 20, and of E. L. Mascall, *Corpus Christi, Essays on the Church and the Eucharist* (1953), p. 78.

[59] E. C. Ratcliff has written that Baxter's Eucharistic doctrine is "more advanced than Laud's" and that his conception of the liturgical action of the Lord's Supper "is nearer the historic western tradition than the conception which Cranmer embodied in the Communion Service of the Prayer Book of 1522." (*Op. cit.*, p. 123.)

rubrics was a characteristic of the Anglican worship of the seventeenth century.[60] In making this charge, he doubts whether the priest placed on the holy table, after the presentation of the alms, so much bread and wine as he shall think sufficient. He very much doubted whether the curate, after the recitation of the Nicene Creed, did in fact declare to the people which fasting days of the following week were to be observed. The rubric at the end of the Holy Communion Service directed that in cathedral and collegiate churches that "they shall all receive Communion with the Priest every Sunday at the least": Legg thinks this was more honoured in the breach than in the observance. As for the requirement in the same liturgical context for the wearing of the cope at the Eucharist, this was not even insisted on in Durham where copes were provided. More seriously, attendance at Holy Communion was lamentably infrequent, except in a time of national anxiety.[61]

These charges are further substantiated by a lengthy letter sent by a young legal student in January 1683,[62] complaining of neglect in saying the daily service. He claims that "wee have yet as many severall wayes of Worshipp, as wee have Ministers, and every one that I could yet Discover, offends in some thing that is clearly contrary to Law. . . ." The excisions include: Exhortations, the *Benedictus*, the *Jubilate* (or substitution of a metrical Psalm), intrusion of part of Sick Visitation Office into public worship, prefacing the Creed with an idiosyncratic statement, telescoping first and second services, cutting off the Lord's Prayer and Nicene Creed, the Prayer for the Church Militant and the final Benediction, or the substitution of an invented Benediction. Other liberties include making the Churching of Women and Baptism into private services, which should be public. Other defects are: the reading of the Communion Service at the desk instead of at the altar; many churches have a weekly service (if that) instead of a daily one; children are often catechised only in Lent instead of throughout the entire year; conducting sacraments without a surplice and sometimes even without a gown. Particular indignation is reserved for those who break their canonical oath by "Venting a Prayer

[60] *English Church Life from the Restoration to the Tractarian Movement* . . . (1914), pp. 359-60.

[61] Evelyn's *Diary* records that on October 7, 1688, when people were afraid that Roman Catholicism might be brought back as the religion of the State, and Dr. Tenison preached at St. Martin's-in-the-Fields, "After which neere 1000 devout persons partook of the communion."

[62] The source is Bodleian Library Ms Rawlinson D. 851 (198 f.). It has also been printed as Appendix to Chap. IV of Legg, *op. cit.*, pp. 111ff.

(and sometimes I have had an impertinent one) of *Private Composure.*"[63]

Another feature of Anglican worship in the period after 1660 was the ceremonial victory won by the Laudians. Whatever might be said of Anglican Eucharistic doctrine after the Restoration, unquestionably a higher ceremonial was maintained. One who loathes high ceremonial writes of how to treat a clergyman inordinately fond of it: "consequently handle him *as if he* really were a Popish Priest; his *Cope,* his *Hood,* his *Surplice,* his *Cringing Worship,* his *Altar* with *Candles* on it (most Nonsensically *unlighted* too), his *Bag-Pipes* or *Organs,* and in some places *Viols* and *Violins,* singing Men and *singing* Boys &c. are all *so very like* Popery (and all but the Vestments illegal) that I protest when I came in 1660, first from beyond Sea to *Pauls,* and *White-Hall,* I could scarce think my self to be in *England,* but in *Spain* or *Portugal* again, I saw so little difference, but that their *Service* was in *Latin* and ours in *English.*"[64]

After the Restoration candlesticks were again placed on the altars. For example, Dr. Sancroft, Dean of York in 1664, presented a pair which had been made two years before.[65] Sancroft had also been begged by William Fuller, the Bishop of Lincoln, to procure him a splendid altar frontal for his cathedral, "one pane thereof to be Cloth of Gold, the other I thinke Damaske, of a sky colour; if it be not too Gawdy. Our Cathedrall hath a purple one of cloth paned with crimson Damaske: Mine I intend for solemne Dayes."[66]

Chancel screens were again built, which must have added an important element of mystery in a century becoming increasingly rationalistic and Latitudinarianly pragmatic.

Organs, which the Puritans liked for private and secular purposes but considered a distraction in church services, returned to the churches at the Restoration. Pepys observes on July 15, 1661: "Then to King's College chappell [Cambridge], where I found the scholars in their surplices at the service with the organs, which is a strange sight to what it used to be in my time to be here." It soon became the custom in Charles II's reign to play an organ voluntary after the Psalms.

[63] *Ibid.,* pp. 112-14.
[64] Edmund Hickeringill, *The Ceremony Monger* (1689), p. 18. See also Pepys's *Diary* entries April 15, 1666, April 22, 1666, and October 16, 1666; also for July 29, 1660.
[65] T. M. Fallow and H. B. McCall, *Yorkshire Church Plate* (Leeds, 1912), p. 4, cited Legg, *op. cit.,* p. 139.
[66] Bodleian Library, Tanner Ms. 44 (f. 66).

There was a return to celebrating the church year with its different seasons. Pepys writes in his *Diary* for December 23, 1660, that his pew was decked with rosemary and bays. This custom of "sticking of Churches" with boughs at Christmas gave them a festive look, but, according to the *Spectator*[67] one church was "over-deckt" and looked more like a greenhouse than a place of worship; the pulpit was so swathed in holly and ivy, that "a light fellow in our Pew took occasion to say, that the Congregation heard the Word out of a Bush, like *Moses*."

Crosses and religious pictures after the Restoration are commonly used in the furnishings of churches. These are recommended by Dr. Thomas Tenison (1636-1715), afterwards Archbishop of Canterbury, who argues that devotional pictures are "helps to excite memory and passion" and to deny this is to "impute less to a Crucifix than to the Tomb of our friend, or a thread on our finger."[68]

Gestures which had been recommended by the Laudians as ways of expressing reverence were commonly seen again. Such was bowing at the sacred name of Jesus, and the signation of the Cross at Baptism. There is incidental reference to such customs in a fragment of a discussion by "Prejudice" (standing for Puritanism) and "Reason" (standing for Anglicanism):

> *Prejudice*: "Have I not seen your Gravest Divines among you, at their entrance into the Church, cast their Eyes upon the Glass Windows, bow towards the Altars, worship the Pictur'd Saints, and make Leggs to the Brazen Candlesticks?"
> *Reason*: "All this is said upon the account of Bowing towards the Altar."[69]

In all these ways the dignity and beauty of worship, and the importance of reverence was stressed in post-Restoration Anglicanism, despite the fact that the rubrics were often laxly interpreted. In matters of ceremonial, it is clear that the Puritans have been utterly routed in the Church of England by the Laudians and their successors.

6. *Further Attempts at Revision or Supplementation*

This century seems to prove—in matters of liturgy at least—that those who will not learn the lessons of history must suffer for

---

[67] No. 282, Wed., Jan. 23, 1711-1712.
[68] *A Discourse of Idolatry* (1678), p. 279.
[69] *A Dialogue between Mr. Prejudice . . . and Mr. Reason, a Student in the University* (1682), p. 7.

their ignorance. There would be, once again, an unsuccessful attempt to move the Church of England towards comprehension in the hope of including the Presbyterians by meeting some of their criticisms of the Prayer Book. It did not work in 1661. Nor would it work in 1688 and 1689, although the external threat posed by the proselytising Roman Catholicism of the sovereign, King James II, was a strong inducement to present a united Protestant front.

Once again there would also be an attempt to supplement the latest Prayer Book with the usages of the 1549 Book or of the Scottish liturgy of 1637, believing that both were more faithful to the liturgies of the primitive church. This was, again, a maintaining of the Laudian tradition (as in the cases of Cosin and Wren), except that this time it would be the work of a single liturgical enthusiast, the lawyer turned Anglican priest, Edward Stephens. His supplement to the liturgy was published in 1696. Its character is clearly indicated in its title, *The Liturgy of the Ancients, as near as well may be, in English Forms.*[70] It was an heroic effort at making the Prayer Book read like a "primitive liturgy."

Both the corporate revision and the individual work of Stephens require to be set in their historical context of the Revolution of 1688. James II's Declaration of Indulgence in 1688 was a shrewd move. It appeared to offer the Nonconformists a breathing-space from persecution, and to promise the removal of their civic disabilities, while it was actually aimed at giving the Roman Catholic fellow-believers with the King a more favoured position. This was the final move that, starting with the "Popish Plot" of 1678-1681 in which Titus Oates had inflamed public opinion to believe that Charles II's younger brother James was involved in a plot to supplant him and to establish Catholicism as the religion of England, reached its culmination in this Declaration, and sealed the suspicions of Protestants. James had no alternative but to flee England, and William and Mary were enthroned as guarantors of the Protestant succession to the throne of England, and as supporters of the Anglican establishment. In 1691, however, the Non-Jurors (or those bishops and clergy who refused to swear the Oath of Allegiance to William and Mary because by so doing they would break their previous oath to James II and his successors) were deprived of their offices in the Church of England. The Non-Jurors (or Non-

---

[70] The text is to be found in W. Jardine Grisbrooke, *Anglican Liturgies of the Seventeenth and Eighteenth Centuries* (Alcuin Club Collections, No. XL, 1958), pp. 203-19.

Swearers) numbered about four hundred clergy, a few laymen, and some leading bishops. They included Archbishop Sancroft, and Bishops Ken of Bath and Wells, Turner of Ely, White of Peterborough, Lloyd of Norwich, Frampton of Gloucester, Lake of Chichester, and Thomas of Worcester. The last two died before the sentence of deprivation could be carried out, and Cartwright, Bishop of Chester, followed James II to France. Their guiding principles had included the conviction of the divine right of kings and, as its consequence, the duty of passive obedience. They also had a high view of the church as a divine society and were deeply interested in primitive and historic liturgies and in the devotional life.[71]

The difference between those bishops who were willing to swear allegiance to William and Mary and those who were Non-Jurors was deep and tragic. On the one hand, several Latitudinarian or broad-church bishops backed the "Revolution" and were eager to unite the Protestant forces in a more comprehensive Church of England, expressing its faith and worship in a Prayer Book responsive by permissive rubrics to the customs objected to by the heirs of the Puritans. They were supported by high-church bishops, such as Compton of London. The Non-Juring bishops, however, and those clergy that supported them were far more interested in remoulding the Prayer Book according to the pattern of the liturgies of the ancient and primitive church, than in accommodating it to the oversensitive consciences of the Presbyterians. In the end, they would mostly refuse to worship according to the Prayer Book of 1662 and took the step of either supplementing the Prayer Book, or even of creating their own liturgies in 1718 and 1734.

7. The Rites of Edward Stephens

These go far beyond the boundaries of our period, but at least we can examine the rites produced by the Non-Juror Edward Stephens, one consisting of "such enlargements of the Church Service as I thought most agreeable to the ancient Form" for private celebrations, another an expansion of it, and the third and most important, a form for public worship. This consisted of confining "ourselves to the Church Forms only supplying what I thought defective therein, as well I could, out of other parts of our Liturgy."[72] The

---

[71] See George Every, *The High Church Party, 1688-1718* (1956), p. 61. See also J. H. Overton, *The Nonjurors* (1902), and J.W.C. Wand, *The High Church Schism* (1951).
[72] Grisbrooke, *op. cit.*, p. 46.

rite designed for public use was published in 1696 as, *The Liturgy of the Ancients Represented, As near as well may be, In English Forms. With a Preface concerning the Restitution of the most Solemn Part of the Christian Worship in the Holy Eucharist, to its Integrity, and just Frequency of Celebration.* It warrants careful consideration.

Stephens denounced the 1552 Prayer Book as a defective liturgy because it spiritualised the concept of sacrifice and eliminated the *epiklesis*, and weakened disastrously the sense of the communion of saints, as well as omitting prayers for the dead. Furthermore, lawyer Stephens found it impossible to have a daily Eucharist in any London Anglican church, but decided with a group of fellow enthusiasts, to meet each day at 5 A.M. for Communion, to follow the example of the early Christians, to avoid offending any, especially Anglicans, and this practice continued for two and a half years.

The following description is taken from a letter by Stephens to Archbishop Tillotson:

> When we had continued it near a year, the person who did officiate being like to be called from us, that it might not fail, I took orders myself; and as soon as we obtained the favour of the Bishop of Gloucester to have the use of his Church at Cripplegate (which was as unexpected as the other), we without delay removed our meeting thither, the very next day, out of respect to the Church; as we had before, for the same reason, continued it in private under a tacit connivance, rather than make use of the late Act for Toleration. And we have now had it in public near three quarters of a year without intermission. While we had it in private, we used such enlargements of the Church Service as I thought most agreeable to the ancient Form: but when we came into Church we forebore most of that, and confined ourselves to the Church Forms, only supplying what I thought defective therein, as well as I could, out of other parts of our Liturgy. This I did before ever I had seen the book made by our Bishops, and published at Edinburgh, for the use of the Church of Scotland, in 1627, which I believe to be the best of any modern form whatever, and, therefore, when this lately came into my hand, it was no little satisfaction to me to find that I had so completely concurred in judgement with such eminent per-

sons, and had so great authority to allege for what I did, besides what I had before. . . .[73]

Stephens's public liturgy, *The Liturgy of the Ancients . . . in English Forms*, shows a detailed knowledge of English liturgies and, apart from its tendency to long-windedness, a craftsman's ability to join parts of liturgies together in a unified composition. He makes use of the Prayer Book of 1549, as of the Scottish liturgy of 1637. The liturgy of the catechumens is overloaded with anthems (the first half of both the *Venite* and of the *Benedictus*, together with *Gloria in Excelsis* and *Deus misereatur*) and there are seven collects (if the Collect of the Day is included). The Office of the Faithful begins with *Christ our Pascal Lamb* as invitatory anthem (borrowed from 1549), followed by Invitation, Confession, Absolution and Comfortable Words (all as in 1549 order). The Offertory follows, the *Sursum Corda*, a Preface derived chiefly from the General Thanksgiving, the *Sanctus*, with "The Worship of the Lamb" from the book of Revelation, which is taken from the lectionary. There follows the Prayer for the whole State of Christ's Church Militant here on earth, based chiefly on 1637, with optional and more specific commemoration of the saints and the departed, added in a footnote. The Prayer of Consecration's opening paragraph conflates 1549, 1637, and 1662, and there is one change in wording which is later followed in the eighteenth century Scottish rites. Instead of "his *one* Oblation of himself once offered" Stephens reads "his *own* Oblation of himself once offered." The Invocation or *epiklesis* precedes the Institution Narrative (as in 1549 and 1637) is a slight expansion of the 1637 form: "Hear us, O merciful Father, we most humbly beseech thee, and of thy abundant Goodness vouchsafe to bless and sanctifie with thy Word and holy Spirit these thy Gifts and Creatures of Bread and wine, that they may be unto us the Body and Blood of thy most dearly beloved Son, our Saviour Jesus Christ. . . ."[74] The Memorial, or Prayer of Oblation, follows 1637 almost word for word, except that there is a clause from 1549 in a footnote, "And command these our Supplications and Prayers to be, by the Ministry of thy Holy Angels, brought up into thy Holy Tabernacle, before the sight of thy Divine Majesty." On the conclusion of the canon, there ensues an intercessory Litany ending with the Lord's Prayer, and this is taken from the Prayer Book Litany. There then follow the

[73] *Ibid.*, p. 39.   [74] *Ibid.*, p. 214.

Prayer of Humble Access, the Communion, the Prayer of Thanksgiving, the *Gloria in Excelsis*, and the Blessing.

Stephens compiled two other rites, one having only the liturgy of the faithful,[75] and supposedly based on "ancient forms" which, of course, meant Book VIII of the *Apostolic Constitutions*, and another being a revised form of the rite, entitled, *A Compleat Form of Liturgy, or Divine Service, According to the Usage of the Most Ancient Christians*.[76] Stephens is better as a reviser than as an innovator or translator, but he deserves credit for breaking through English liturgical insularity, and marks the way forward from Laud and 1662 to a consideration of eastern liturgies as models instead of the examples of the "incorrigible Cranmerians."

It is interesting to note that while the Non-Juring bishops and clergy found it impossible to read the new state prayers, laity sympathetic to their convictions found several ways of avoiding compliance. Various modes of salving their conscience were adopted. Some refused to say, "Amen," at the end of the prayers. Others took Prayer Books to church printed before the Revolution containing the old prayers and the old names. Yet others showed their dislike of the new prayers by refusing to kneel when they were said. Some others took snuff at the appropriate moment and sneezed their disapprobation! That was a ruse not available for Non-Juring clergy.[77]

The true greatness of the Non-Jurors can be seen in the saintly life of the greatest of them, Thomas Ken, like them a man of principle and honour, but more conciliatory than most. The lasting contribution of the Non-Jurors to the Anglican liturgy will be found in the further development of the liturgy of the Scottish Episcopal church in the eighteenth century and in its impact on the American Episcopal liturgy. Their devotional spirit is nowhere better summed up than in the piety of Thomas Ken.

Brought up virtually as a ward of Izaak Walton (for he had married Ken's half sister), he was a thorough Wykehamist. A scholar of Winchester School, a scholar and fellow of New College, Oxford, and chaplain to Bishop Morley of Winchester from 1665, he became a fellow of Winchester. He then drew up for the School a *Manual of Prayers for the Use of the Scholars of Winchester College* in 1674 to counteract the rather unstructured Puritan influence which he remembered there as a boy. This related

75 This text will be found *ibid.*, pp. 223-30.
76 This text will be found, *ibid.*, pp. 233-45.
77 Wand, *op. cit.*, p. 12.

prayer to the daily life and was remarkable for its Eucharistic reference. At about the same time it is conjectured that he composed his famous Morning, Evening, and Midnight Hymns which are included in an appendix to the third edition of his Manual in 1695. Perhaps the most famous is the Evening Hymn,[78] which begins: "Glory to thee my God this night/ For all the blessings of the Light." The sincere and simple directness of the devotion and its profound dependence upon God is perfectly expressed in the verse:

> Teach me to live that I may dread
> The Grave as little as my Bed;
> Teach me to die, that so I may
> Triumphing rise at the last day.

The Hymn ends with the adoring gratitude of a Doxology which is known throughout the English-speaking world:

> Praise God from whom all blessings flow,
> Praise him all creatures here below,
> Praise him above y'Angelick host[79]
> Praise Father, Son, and Holy Ghost.

His conviction of the divine right of kings and of the duty of passive obedience did not prevent him from enacting the role of the prophet Nathan to King David. While seconded as chaplain to Princess Mary at The Hague, he remonstrated against a case of court immorality and was immediately dismissed. Yet a similarly motivated refusal of his Winchester residence to accommodate Nell Gwynne at Charles II's bidding, earned him soon afterwards the Bishopric of Bath and Wells. A faithful preacher to high and low, Charles II said he would "go and hear Ken tell him his faults." One could ring a coin on his integrity. Macaulay's verdict on his character was that it approached "as near as human infirmity permits to the ideal perfection of Christian virtue."[80]

8. *The Attempted Revision of 1689*

The final attempt in this century to revise the Prayer Book was begun by William Sancroft, Archbishop of Canterbury, with the

[78] For Ken's work as a hymnwriter, see John Julian's *Dictionary of Hymnology* 2nd edn., 1925), pp. 616b-622a.
[79] This is the original third line as printed in 1688 in the Second Book of Henry Playford's *Sacra Harmonia* (1688) which gave it wide publicity. The revised text of 1709 reads: "Praise him above ye heavenly host" which is close to the modern rendering.
[80] Cited Julian, *op. cit.*, p. 617a.

purpose of relaxing some of the ceremonies by providing permissive rubrics and by making some verbal changes that would make the Prayer Book more acceptable to Presbyterians supporting a Protestant monarchy in a wider Church of England.

Such a revision was proposed in the last clause of the Comprehension Bill, which called for the establishment of a commission of thirty representative Anglican divines to prepare the business. This included ten bishops, seven deans, four archdeacons, one head of a university college and two divinity professors, and six London clergy, five of whom later became bishops. The Latitudinarians in the commission naturally predominated, including such bishops as Burnet of Salisbury, Stillingfleet of Worcester, Stratford of Chester, and Humphreys of Bangor, and clergy such as Tillotson (Dean of St. Paul's) and Tenison (then the popular vicar of St. Martin-in-the-Fields) both of whom were future Archbishops of Canterbury. The most prominent Latitudinarians in the revisions were Burnet, Stillingfleet, Tenison, and Tillotson, together with the orientalist Kidder. The middle position was held by Compton, Bishop of London, Dean John Sharp (later Archbishop of York), and Simon Patrick, Bishop of Chichester, who had been a Presbyterian minister. Among the ten high churchmen in the commission (the highest of high churchmen being the Non-Jurors), the most influential was Archdeacon Beveridge, later to become Bishop of St. Asaph.

In trying to produce acceptable recommendations, the commission faced two ultimately insuperable obstacles. One was the difficulty of trying to satisfy the largely contrary desires of Non-Jurors and Nonconformists; the other was trying to gain the approval of Convocation, especially as about half of the high churchmen boycotted the proceedings of Convocation. Because of this double failure the recommendations were never completed and embodied in a detailed report.[81] They can be reconstructed, however, from two sources. One is an interleaved Prayer Book in the Lambeth Palace Library, and the other is a private journal kept by Dr. John Williams, later to become Bishop of Chichester.[82]

---

[81] Every, *op. cit.*, p. 47.

[82] A very rough idea of the work of revision was provided in E. Calamy's *Abridgment of Mr. Baxter's History of his Life and Times*. When the Prayer Book was discussed in Parliament in 1854, a motion for papers was carried in the House of Commons, and *marginalia* and journal were collated by William Henry Black of the Public Records Office. His copy was printed as a *Parliamentary Paper* and formed the basis of John Taylor's edition of *The Revised Liturgy of 1689* (Dublin, 1855). See Every, *ibid.*

Although the attempted revision was a failure, it is interesting to consider the liturgical views of the majority of influential broad churchmen, together with the views of some cooperative high churchmen. The reconstruction must, however, be partly conjectural.

The preparatory work for the revision was divided and begun in July of 1688. Archbishop William Sancroft seems to have been responsible for overseeing the revision of prayers, thanksgivings, the catechism, and the Orders for Baptism and Confirmation. Simon Patrick was in charge of the revision of the collects, and Macaulay said acidly of this, "whether he was or was not qualified to make the collects better, no man that ever lived was more competent to make them longer."[83] The Daily Office and the Communion Service were to be revised by a committee including Dean John Sharp and John Moore.[84]

The arrival of William of Orange in England created a new situation, precipitating the whole question of the validity of oaths of allegiance. The seven Non-Juring bishops (who believed that their original oaths of fealty to James II could not be set aside for William's benefit without them perjuring themselves and who might have been able to support him as regent but not as monarch) were sequestered for six months in the Tower of London, while one fled to France, and two died before their homage would be required. The official commission of thirty divines was not able to begin its work until October 1689. It had Sancroft's work before it as a basis and also "a complete list of all the exceptions that ever had been made to the Prayer Book, either by Puritans before the Civil War, or by Nonconformists afterwards." The latter was the compilation of Thomas Tenison. Furthermore, Richard Kidder had prepared a translation of the Psalms.

Among the proposals for revision in 1689 there were several important ones of a high-church source and character. One was to add the Beatitudes as an alternative to the Decalogue in the Communion Service, a repetition of Jeremy Taylor's proposal in his *Collection of Offices*, but with a different response from his. The Confirmation Service was expanded to include a renewal of Baptismal vows, an idea borrowed from the *Durham Book*. Sancroft wrote "A Prayer for Repentance" and another as preparation for

83 *History of England* (1856), III, p. 476.
84 Every, *op. cit.*, pp. 23-24.

receiving Communion. He may also have originated the emphasis on Ember Weeks and provided the Proper for Rogation Sunday. The influence of the high church may also be found in a Proper Preface for Good Friday, in the Prayer of Humble Access, and in the rubric recommending "that all ministers exhort their people to communicate frequently" as well as in the reference in the catechism to "the sacrifice" of Christ's Body and Blood.

On the other hand, twenty of the "Exceptions" made by the Presbyterian ministers at the Savoy Conference have been accepted, though these are chiefly verbal changes. The four noxious ceremonies are retained, but they need not be used. Any minister having scruples about using the surplice or signing with the cross in Baptism can obtain from his bishop a dispensation and the bishop can appoint a curate who does not share the minister's scruples to act in his stead. Parishioners, after raising the matter with their parish priest, need not kneel at the altar for the reception of the consecrated elements, but may receive them "in some convenient place or pew." A rubric asserts that the marriage ring is a civil pledge and ceremony and not a religious ceremony. The too easy assumption of regeneration in Baptism and the Burial Office is acknowledged and modified accordingly. The priest says to the sick man: "I pronounce thee absolved" and no longer, "I absolve thee." Godparents are optional in Baptism. Black-letter saints' days disappear from the calendar. Sentences from the Apocrypha deriving from Tobit and used at the Offertory, as well as the *Benedicite*, disappear. Psalms 8 and 134 are substituted for the *Magnificat* and the *Nunc Dimittis*. Dissenting ministers are even allowed conditional ordination, while the deacon's formula would be sufficient for the admission of continental Protestant ministers.[85] A small but important change was made in the Prayer of Humble Access. Instead of the petition "that our sinful bodies may be made clean by his body and our souls washed through his most precious blood," there was substituted "that our souls and bodies may be washed and cleansed by the sacrifice of his most precious Body and Blood." The emphasis on sacrifice would seem to be a high-church change in Eucharistic doctrine, but unquestionably the rest of the sentence was altered to meet Nonconformist criticism.[86]

[85] *Ibid.*, p. 45.
[86] According to William Clagett's *An Answer to the Dissenters Objections against the Common Prayers and some other parts of Divine-Service prescribed*

A third group of alterations would have been equally acceptable to both high churchmen and broad churchmen. Such were: the joining of the Litany and the Holy Communion and the revised order of the latter is interesting. The prayer "We humbly beseech thee" was followed immediately by the Collect for Purity, and the usually ensuing Collect for the King was left out. The Creed was followed by the General Thanksgiving, the Prayer of St. Chrysostom, the grace, the notices, the "singing Psalm," and the sermon. All these were to be said from the reading-pew. On "Sacrament Sundays" the Communion Service followed its regular course. As for Confirmation, it is directed that an exhortation is to be read on the previous Sunday; the Doxology is added to the Lord's Prayer, and a prayer and a second exhortation are interposed before the Blessing. In the Burial a sensible substitution of a lesson from I Thessalonians is allowed "in colder or later seasons."

The attempted improvement of the collects initiated by Bishop Simon Patrick was overseen by Stillingfleet, Burnet, and Tillotson. Their major amelioration consists of adding quotations from the Epistle or Gospel of the day, as had been attempted by the revisers of 1662. Bishop Burnet also tried to remodel the formula for Ordination, following the findings of Jean Marin, and was seconded by Tillotson. If approved, which it was not, it would have read:

> Pour down, O Father of lights, the holy Ghost upon thy servant, for the office and work of a priest in the Church of God, now committed unto thee by the imposition of our hands, that whose sins he does forgive they may be forgiven, and whose sins he doth retain they may be retained, and that he may be a faithful dispenser of God's holy word and sacraments, to the edification of his Church, and to the glory of his holy name through Jesus Christ, to whom with the Holy Ghost be all honour and glory world without end, Amen.[87]

Burnet also wished to omit the Athanasian Creed as too Western in viewpoint. While he failed to carry his point, this Creed was hence-

in the *Liturgie of the Church of England* (1683), p. 34, the Dissenters urged that in the unrevised petition "a greater efficacy in cleansing is attributed to Christ's body than Christ's blood." Clagett also says that the Dissenters objected to the individual reception of Communion, saying "it should be done in companies, as *Take ye, Eate ye, all of this.*" (*Ibid.*)

[87] *Parliamentary Paper* (1854), p. 87, cited in Every, *op. cit.*, p. 55.

forth used in public worship only five instead of thirteen Sundays of the year.

The failure of this revision of 1688 and 1689 meant that the Presbyterians and Independents who had shared persecution together were now practically driven into each other's arms, and the Independent view of the Anglican liturgy as an engine of compulsion rather than an instrument of union prevailed in Dissent, together with a concept of "conceived prayer" as always superior to "stinted forms." Eighteenth-century attempts at Prayer Book revision still aimed at comprehension, not of the Presbyterians, but of their successors, the Unitarians.[88]

9. A Conclusion

The century had begun with the Hampton Court Conference and the attempt of the Puritans to have some of their criticisms of the Book of Common Prayer accepted, but with little success. The Presbyterian ministers had also hoped for accommodation in worship at the Savoy Conference in 1661, but with the same dismal result. The last attempt at Prayer Book revision had been undertaken in 1689, with the professed purpose of making it less difficult for Nonconformists to accept. This too failed miserably.

Similarly, just as the two Laudian Bishops, Cosin and Wren, had proposals for revising the Prayer Book in 1661 and 1662 that would have emulated the first and most conservative Prayer Book of 1549 and the Scottish liturgy of 1637, so would Edward Stephens, a Non-Juror, argue against all later forms of the Anglican liturgy from 1552 to 1662, that they were Cranmerian treason against the historic western and Catholic rite. The "primitive" supplementation of the Book of Common Prayer by the additions of Stephens were not accepted by others, and as the Non-Jurors went out of the Church of England, their eighteenth-century alternative rites were also failures.

Indeed, the ding-dong battle between the high churchmen, on the one hand, and the Puritans, Presbyterians, or Nonconformists, on the other hand, can only lead to the inevitable conclusion that the Dissenting demand for a liturgy conformable in all things to Scripture and the Laudian and Non-Juror request for a liturgy conformable to the liturgies of the primitive church were utterly

---

[88] See Davies, *op. cit.*, III, Chap. IV, "Unitarian Worship: The Liturgy of Rationalism."

incompatible. In the *art nouveau* period at the beginning of the present century it was common to see juxtaposed outside a theatre or on its proscenium arch two masks: one laughing and the other crying. The saddest fact about liturgical revision in the seventeenth century is that it was begun each time, with the actors wearing the smiling mask of comedy, and it ended in practically every case with them wearing the mask of irritation, if not of tragedy.

CHAPTER XI

PURITAN SERVICE BOOKS

T
HE IDEA is widely prevalent in English-speaking countries
that Presbyterians and Congregationalists[1] have almost
always over three centuries practised free or extemporary
prayers and disdained a set liturgy or even the use of a manual by
their ministers. This erroneous view would have surprised their
seventeenth century predecessors. The English Presbyterians
would certainly have preferred a set liturgy for which there was
a Scriptural authority for each of the ordinances. This would have
been in line with Calvin's *La Forme des Prières* of Geneva (1542)
based upon Calvin's adaptation of Bucer's Strassburg liturgy in
1540. This was, in fact, Englished and used, with but a few insignificant alterations by the congregation of English exiles over which
Knox and Whittingham presided in Geneva. It was published in
1556 as *The Forme of Prayers and Ministration of the Sacraments,
etc., used in the English Congregation at Geneva: and approved
by the famous and godly learned man, Iohn Calvyn.* It was alike
the parent of the Scottish Book of Common Order and of four editions of an English Puritan Prayer Book,[2] which should—for the
sake of accuracy—be called Presbyterian or Reformed Prayer
Books. Further editions of the Waldegrave *A Booke of the Forme
of Common Prayers etc.*, published in 1584/5 appeared in Middleburgh in 1586, 1587, and 1602.[3] The Presbyterians, however
much they might have smarted from the imposition of a high-
church Anglican Scottish liturgy upon the Church of Scotland in
1637, had no objection in principle to a liturgy or set order and
prescribed words in worship; but the vociferous and persistent
caucus of the Independents, led by the learned and pertinacious
Thomas Goodwin, and the sense that the many Independents of
New Model Army of the Roundheads were ever drawing nearer
to the Westminster Assembly, pressured the Presbyterians into the
compromise of accepting a directory. The natural development of

[1] In 1972 the English Congregationalists and Presbyterians were united in one
denomination, the United Reformed Church.

[2] It is Peter Hall, the editor of *A Booke of the Form of Common Prayers* who
calls the Waldegrave edition of c. 1584 a *Puritan Liturgy* in his republishing of it
in *Fragmenta Liturgica* (Bath, 1848), Vol. III.

[3] See the *British Museum Catalogue*, Vol. L, 50, pp. 711-12 for their exact
titles. See Horton Davies, *Worship of the English Puritans* (1948), pp. 122-37, for
an analysis of the Waldegrave and Middleburgh service books.

Presbyterian worship was towards a prescribed form of prayers, with alternatives, and the occasional opportunity for extemporary prayers. It is significant that, once the Presbyterians had cut loose from their association with the Independents, as at the Savoy Conference of 1661, their leader Richard Baxter, with the concurrence of the brethren, composed a Biblical liturgy.

Furthermore, the Independents, who were anxious that the ministers should not lose the gift of extemporary prayer at the prompting of the Holy Spirit, were glad to join in the production of a directory which would have provided the structure, the theology, and the order of various ordinances, regular and occasional, with sample prayers but without dictating their very wording. Thus the *Directory* of 1644 produced jointly by Presbyterians and Independents was a compromise, exacting too little for the Presbyterians and too much for the Independents.

Yet the *Directory*'s importance is considerable and twofold. In the first place it demonstrates the kind of worship that the coalition of Puritans thought suitable for the entire three kingdoms when they came to power, after almost a century of being in the minority. Secondly, and of even greater importance, it formed the Free Church tradition of worship for almost three hundred years in Britain, the British Commonwealth, and the United States of America. This tradition would come to include the Baptists and Methodists, as well as the Presbyterians and Independents (or Congregationalists); in short, all who can be called a part of the Puritan-Pietist tradition. It should be made clear, however, that many ministers, even a generation after the *Directory*'s issue, might not own a copy of the work, yet the *Directory* had set the style of their long prayers (as opposed to brief collects), with their heavy emphasis on actual as well as original sin, the retrospective rather than prospective look in the Lord's Supper, the austere simplicity of the ceremonial and furnishings, the sermon as the high point and climax of the service, and its characteristic Calvinism as expressed in its Biblical obedience to the revealed will of God as the only legitimate authority, its perennial didacticism, and its congregational character.

1. *The Parliamentary or Westminster Directory*[4]

On March 13, 1644, it was ordered "by the Lords and Commons in Parliament assembled, that this *Directory*, and ordinance

[4] This has been reprinted in *Reliquiae Liturgicae*, III, *The Parliamentary Directory* (ed. Peter Hall, Bath, 1847), and by the Scottish Church Service Society,

concerning it, be forthwith printed and published. . . ." It was the official manual of worship for the English, Welsh, and Scottish people for sixteen years. Indeed, it continued in use among the Scots long after the Prayer Book was restored in England and Wales in 1662.

The Westminster Assembly, to which Parliament had delegated the responsibility for advising on the religious settlement produced a form of church government, confessions of faith (the Shorter and Longer Catechisms), and a *Directory for the Publick Worship of God in the Three Kingdoms.* The Assembly was chosen by Parliament on a county basis of representation, but the members also included ten peers, twenty members of the House of Commons, and commissioners of the Church of Scotland, in consequence of the taking of the Solemn League and Covenant. Some moderate Episcopal clergy were invited, but declined. Hence the business of the Assembly was almost exclusively in the hands of the Presbyterian divines, with only a handful of Independent "Brethren" who presented an *Apologeticall Narration* for their minority standpoint.[5]

It appears that originally all that was contemplated was a revision of the Book of Common Prayer, excising from it all those ceremonies or statements that conflicted with the Biblical mandate. This opinion is confirmed by a declaration of Parliament on April 9, 1642, to the effect "that they intend a due and necessary reformation and liturgy of the church, and to take away nothing in the one or the other but what shall be evil and justly offensive, or last unnecessary and burdensome."[6]

Even at the end of the deliberations, there were still two viewpoints. One believed in the need for a revised liturgy; the other argued for a manual or directory. This is confirmed by Robert Baillie, Principal of Glasgow University and a Scottish commissioner, in his letter of November 21, 1644, referring to the Assembly's approval of the hotly disputed Preface, "and in this piece we expected most difficulty; one party purposing by the preface to turn the Directory to a straight Liturgie; the other to make it so loose

---

The Westminster Directory (ed. Thomas Leishman, Edinburgh and London, 1901).

[5] See a recent republication edited by Robert S. Paul, *An Apologeticall Narration* (Boston and Philadelphia, 1963).

[6] *The Book of Common Order* (eds. G. W. Sprott and J. Leishman, Edinburgh, 1868), p. 261.

and free, that it should serve for little use: but God helped us to get both these rocks echewed. . . ."[7]

The rough draft of the *Directory* was prepared by a small subcommittee consisting of Marshall (Chairman), Palmer, Goodwin, Young, Herle, and the Scottish commissioners. The composition of this subcommittee, which included only one Independent, Goodwin, helped to account for the Scottish character of the *Directory*, which bears a close structural resemblance to the Scottish Book of Common Order, a near relative of John Knox's *Genevan Service Book*, while Goodwin's presence is presumably responsible for the several alternatives supplied and the variations from the Genevan Book.

The Preface clearly indicates the aims of the compilers. It began with a generous tribute to their "wise and pious ancestors" who produced the Book of Common Prayer which had repressed the vanity, error, superstition, and idolatry of medieval Catholic worship, and had provided a service in the vernacular tongue. Nonetheless, experience showed that the liturgy used in the Church of England has proved offensive to the godly at home and the Reformed churches abroad. "For (not to speak of urging the reading of all the prayers, which very greatly increased the burden of it), the many unprofitable and burdensome ceremonies contained in it have occasioned much mischief, as well as disquieting the consciences of many godly ministers and people who could not yield to them; . . ."[8] Meanwhile, "prelates and their faction have laboured to raise the estimation of it to such a height, as if there were no other worship, or way of worship of God amongst us, but only the Service Book; to the great hindrance of the preaching of the word, and, in some places (especially of late), to the justling of it out, as unnecessary or (at best) as far inferior to the reading of Common Prayer, which was made no better than an idol by many ignorant and superstitious people."[9] Even Roman Catholics, it is claimed, boasted that it complied with much of their service. Furthermore, "the Liturgy hath been a great means, as, on the one hand, to make and increase an idle and unedifying ministry, which contented it self with set forms made to their hands by others, without putting forth themselves to exercise the gift of prayer, with which our Lord Jesus Christ pleaseth to furnish all his servants whom he calls to that office; so, on the other side . . . it hath been . . .

---

[7] *The Letters and Journals of Robert Baillie*, 3 Vols. (ed. David Laing, Edinburgh, 1841), II, p. 240.
[8] *Reliquiae Liturgicae*, ed. Peter Hall, III, p. 14.   [9] *Ibid.*, p. 16.

a matter of endless strife and contention in the Church, and a snare to many godly and faithful ministers who have been persecuted and silenced upon occasion. . . ."[10]

The compilers believed that Providence was now calling them to a further reformation, as was made evident in the need to satisfy their own consciences, to be more comfortable to other Reformed churches, and to make public testimony of efforts at uniformity in worship as promised in the Solemn League and Covenant. All these considerations demanded a new collection of orders of worship such as the *Directory* provides.

On the positive side, they have kept three aims consistently in mind. First and foremost, "our care hath been to hold forth such things as are of Divine institution in every ordinance: and other things we have endeavoured to set forth according to the rules of Christian prudence, agreeable to the general rules of the word of God."[11] The second aim was uniformity in worship in the three kingdoms: "our meaning therein being only that, the general heads, the sense and scope of the prayers, and other parts of public worship, being common to all, there may be a consent of all the Churches in those things that contain the substance of the service and worship of God. . . ."[12] The third aim is to provide such general help for ministers as not to create a total dependence upon set forms, "and the ministers may be hereby directed in their administrations, to keep like soundness in doctrine and prayer; and may, if need be, have some help and furniture, and yet not so as they become hereby slothful and negligent in stirring up the gifts of Christ in them; but that each by taking heed to himself and the flock of God committed to him, and by wise observing the ways of Divine Providence may be careful to furnish his heart and tongue with further or other materials of prayer and exhortation, and shall be needful upon all occasions."[13]

It is clear, then, that the *Directory* hoped to combine in a way never previously achieved, the advantages of a Prayer Book without its attendant disadvantages. It was to be Scripturally authenticated in every ordinance, comprehensive, and orderly. But it was not to obtain these benefits at the cost of suppressing the creativity of the minister's own wording of the prayers. It would, in brief, try to match order and liberty, form and the spirit, unity and variety, hitherto deemed incompatible and certainly estranged.

The most distinctive changes introduced were supposed improve-

---

[10] *Ibid.* [11] *Ibid.*, p. 18. [12] *Ibid.*

[13] *Ibid.*, pp. 18-19.

ments on the Book of Common Prayer, and they were the common-place reform proposals of Puritan liturgical apologetics. In the lections the Apocrypha writings were to be rejected; private Baptism and godparents were to be discontinued; and the sign of the Cross and the ring in Marriage, together with the administration of the Communion to the sick, were to be abolished. The Communion table was to be moved away from the east wall (where Laud had wanted it) back into the body of the church, and sitting or standing were alternative postures for the reception of the Lord's Supper, both being preferred to the Anglican kneeling gesture. All saints' days were eliminated from the calendar, as were distinctive liturgical vestments. No service was appointed for the Burial of the Dead, and none for the Churching of Women. No creed was recited, nor was the Decalogue recited by the people in worship. All these innovations had been contended for since the first years of Elizabeth's reign, while in some instances the criticisms went back to John Hooper, the iconoclastic Edwardian Bishop of Gloucester and Worcester.

While there was substantial agreement in the Puritan coalition on the *delenda*, there was considerable disagreement on the *agenda*.[14] This is mirrored in part by the different degrees of constraint or permissiveness expressed in the tenses and moods of the rubrics. As Leishman rightly observes: "The obligation to a practice is not the same when it is called *necessary, requisite, expedient, convenient*, or *sufficient*; or when in one place the minister *is to*, or *shall*, or, in another, *may* do such and such things."[15]

The close structural resemblance of the Lord's Day service in the *Directory* can be seen by comparing it with *A Booke of the Forme of Common Prayers* in the table below.

This Lord's Day service begins with the minister's "solemn calling on them [the congregation] to the worshipping of the great name of God" in a prayer that bows before the sovereign mystery of God, and affirms the "vileness and unworthiness" of the worshippers, confesses human inability, and begs for divine assistance, pardon, and for help in meditating on the Word of God. It was common Presbyterian usage to provide a separate prayer for illumination before the sermon; here the petition for illumination is part

---

[14] Thomas Edwards, *Gangraena* (1646), Pt. I, p. 31, observed that some sectaries held "that a Directory or Order to help in the way of worship is a breach of the second commandment." This was probably true of the Brownists, Barrowists, and their successors, among whom were the early Independents.
[15] *The Book of Common Order*, eds. Sprott and Leishman, p. 238.

A *Booke of the Forme of Common Prayers*	A *Directory for the Publick Worship of God (1644)*
(Reader's Service: Chapters of Scripture)	
Scripture Sentences	Call to Worship
Confession of Sins	Prayer of Approach:
	Adoration
	Supplication
	Illumination
Metrical Psalm	Metrical Psalm
Prayer for Illumination and Lord's Prayer	Old Testament Lection (one chapter)
(Scripture Reading) Text	(Metrical Psalm)
	New Testament Lection (one chapter)
	Prayer of Confession and Intercession
SERMON	SERMON
Prayer of Intercession for Whole State of Christ's Church	General Prayer and Lord's Prayer (if no Communion is to follow)
Apostles' Creed, Decalogue, and Lord's Prayer (said by minister)	
Metrical Psalm	Metrical Psalm
Blessing (Aaronic or Apostolic)	Blessing (Aaronic or Apostolic)

of the general opening prayer, and the change was requested by the Independents who claimed the authority of I Timothy 2:1 for starting with a comprehensive prayer.

Lections are confined to the canonical Testaments, excluding the Apocrypha. Also in contradistinction from the Book of Common Prayer, it was judged convenient to read at least one whole chapter from each Testament in preference to the shreds known derisively as "pistling" and "gospelling" by the Puritans. An interspersed commentary on Scripture during its reading was forbidden because too distracting. Exposition was permitted only when the whole chapter had been read. This qualified permission was also a concession to the Independents.[16] After the lections and following the Psalm, a larger confession of sin was to be made. The ideal was for the minister "to get his own and his hearers' hearts to be rightly affected with their sins, that they may all mourn in sense thereof before the Lord, and hunger and thirst after the grace of God in Jesus Christ."[17] The generalisations of the Prayer of Confession in the Anglican liturgy should be contrasted with the particularisations of the confession in the *Directory*. The same prayer then moves from Confession and Petition to Intercession. There is Intercession for the propagation of the Gospel to all nations, the conversion of the Jews, for all distressed Christians, and for the Reformed churches. The prayer intercedes on behalf of the king, for the conversion of the queen, for ministers, universities, schools, religious seminaries, for the particular city and congregation, for the civil government, for those in distress, for seasonable weather and the averting of the judgments of God in famine, pestilence, or sword. It concludes with the dedication of pastor and people to the Christian life. It is not regarded as necessary for the minister to include all these groups of people in one Prayer of Intercession. Some can be deferred until the prayer after the sermon. The inclusion of all these petitions in one prayer was yet another concession to the Independents, for Baillie calls the long prayer "a new fancy of the Independents, grounded on no solid reason, and contrair to all the practice of the Church, old or late, who divided their prayers in more small parts, and did not have any one of a disproportionable length."[18] Then followed the climax of the Sermon, the obedient listening to the oracle of God.

The directions "Of the Preaching of the Word" presuppose not only a conscientious but a learned ministry, conversant with Hebrew and Greek and "in such arts and sciences as are handmaids unto divinity." The spiritual qualifications are not less needed. The minister must "know and believe in the Scriptures above the common sort of believers." The sermon is to be constructed on the model of doctrine, reason, and use.[19] That is, the preacher is to begin with an exposition of a text or passage of Scripture, then to provide the reasons why the doctrine is to be held, and, finally, he

[16] Robert Baillie, *A Dissuasive from the Errours of the Time* (1646), p. 118.
[17] *Reliquiae Liturgicae*, ed. Peter Hall, III, p. 25.
[18] Baillie, *A Dissuasive . . .* , pp. 118f., cited in *The Book of Common Order*, eds. Sprott and Leishman, p. 332.
[19] See the careful analysis of these concepts and their exemplification in Chapter IV above.

is to apply the doctrine to the daily exigencies of life, demonstrating the practical advantages to be derived from believing it. The following adverbs indicate how the minister is to preach: "painfully" (that is, taking great pains), "plainly," "faithfully," "wisely," "gravely," "with loving affection," and "as taught by God." No directions are given on the controverted issue of whether sermons should be read or not. It is known that sermons were not usually read in Scotland, but the practice was not unknown in England. According to Baillie, Nye the Independent was unpopular with an Edinburgh congregation because he had read a large part of his sermon.[20]

The sermon ended, a prayer of thanksgiving followed. This included an acknowledgement of the benefits brought by the Gospel, "as, namely, election, vocation, adoption, justification, sanctification, and hope of glory." The advice is also offered "to turn the chief and most useful heads of the sermon into some few petitions." This points to one of the weaknesses of Puritan prayer. It was excessively edifying, missing no opportunity to preach, even in the prayer following a long and strenuous sermon. Adoration is expelled by exhortation or dehortation. The prayer concludes with a petition for forgiveness, as well it might. The Lord's Prayer is recommended not only as "a pattern of prayer" (the Independent view), but also "as itself a most comprehensive prayer" (the Presbyterian view). It is to be assumed, therefore, that the prayer after the sermon concluded with the Lord's Prayer, though this is allowed, not prescribed. The spontaneity of extemporary prayer is guaranteed for the minister at the administration of the Lord's Supper and on days of thanksgiving and humiliation. The service of the Lord's Day ends with a Psalm and a blessing.

The order for the celebration of the Lord's Supper occupied eighteen out of the seventy-five sittings of the committee. Each point was keenly contested, particularly when the Scots or Independent party felt that its own principle was at stake. Baillie referred, on June 7, 1644, to "the Independents, our great retarders."[21] In a letter written a few days later, he gives a lively impression of the intense controversy between the parties, from his own Presbyterian standpoint: "This day before noone we gott sundrie propositions of our Directory for the sacrament of the Lord's Supper past, but in the afternoone we could not move one inch.

---

[20] See *The Book of Common Order*, eds. Sprott and Leishman, p. 338.
[21] *Letters and Journals of Robert Baillie*, II, p. 191.

The unhappie Independents would mangle that sacrament. No catechising nor preparation before; no thanksgiving after; no sacramentall doctrine or chapters, in the day of celebration; no coming up to any table; but a carrying of the element to all in their seats athort the church: yet all this, with God's help we have carried over their bellies to our practise. But exhortations at tables yet we stick at: they would have no words spoken at all. Nye would be at covering the head at the receiving. We must dispute every inch of our ground; . . ."[22] The point at issue which kept them arguing the longest, that was over three weeks, was the method of communicating. Here, again, Baillie gives a vivid account of it on July 12, 1644: "The Independents and others keeped us three long weeks upon one point alone, the communicating at a table. By this we came to debate; the diverse coming up of companies successively to a table; the consecrating of the bread and wine severallie; the giving of the bread to all the congregation, and then the wine to all, and so twice coming to the table, first for bread and then for the wine; the mutual distribution, the table-exhortations, and a world of such questions, which to most of them were new and strange things." The conclusion arrived at after being "overtoyed with debate" is a most significant one: "we were forced to leave all these things, and take us to generall expressions, which, by a benigne exposition, would infer our church-practises, which the most promised to follow, so much the more as we did not necessitate them by the Assembly's express determinations."[23] A rubric in the *Directory* simply states that the Communion table is to be "conveniently placed that the communicants may orderly sit about it, or at it."[24] This allowed the Independent and Presbyterian alternatives: the Independents received the consecrated elements sitting, which were brought to them in their seats "athwart the church" (in Baillie's phrase Anglicised), and the Presbyterians sat at a table or series of tables placed end-to-end. Neither group would approve the Laudian custom of requiring the communicants to kneel at the Communion rail about the altar to receive the Sacrament. Thus the Presbyterians were insistent that the communicants should "sit at" the table, while the Independents stuck to their point that the communicants should "sit about" the table. The Scottish Presbyterians believed that only by sitting at the table they could symbolize the great evangelical truth that they were guests at

22 *Ibid.*, p. 195. 23 *Ibid.*, p. 204.
24 *Reliquiae Liturgicae*, ed. Peter Hall, II, p. 54.

Christ's table and that the Lord invited his modern disciples with the reminder "I have called you friends." The Independents did not object to the doctrine, indeed one of the most radical of them, the Fifth Monarchist Archer, argued that the seated posture at the Communion table was the proof of spiritual and political republicanism,[25] and the equality of the saints, whereas kneeling implied a monarchist posture; and they sat rather than knelt though at a distance from the table. But the Independents objected to the need for several successive companies at the table and thus the destruction of the temporal unity. The Independents might receive the elements separately, but presumably they ate the bread simultaneously, and drank the wine at the same time together. The debate seemed to resolve itself into a preference for unity of place for the Presbyterians, and temporal unity for the Independents.

The Scots differed from the Independents in two other ways. They had a single consecration prayer, whereas the Independents imitating the details of the Last Supper, had two prayers of consecration, one over each element. These two graces were rejected in the *Directory*. On the other hand, the Presbyterians thought they were imitating the order of the Last Supper more exactly in requiring their ministers to communicate first, with the rest of the communicants distributing the elements from hand-to-hand. The minister was to say, "According to the holy institution, command, and example of our blessed Saviour Jesus Christ, I take this bread; and, having given thanks, I break it, and give it to you. Take ye eat ye. This is the body of Christ, which is broken for you. Do this in remembrance of him."[26]

The all-important question of the desirable frequency of attendance at Communion was not decided at the Assembly. It was left to the discretion of each minister and office-bearers of every local congregation to arrange. The Scottish Presbyterians favoured a quarterly Communion, the Independents one monthly or even weekly. But the relative rarity of the ordinance does not argue for its depreciation in value. On the contrary, two rubrics in the *Directory* show how highly it was regarded. One directs that, when the Sacrament cannot conveniently be celebrated at frequent intervals,

[25] See John Archer's *The Personal Reigne of Christ upon Earth* (1642), p. 17.
[26] *Reliquiae Liturgicae*, ed. Peter Hall, III, p. 57. In taking the cup the minister is to say, "*According to the institution, command and example of our Lord Jesus Christ, I take this cup and give it to you.* (Here he giveth it to the communicants.) *This cup is the New Testament in the blood of Christ, which is shed for the remission of the sins of many; drink ye all of it.*"

then either on the preceding Sunday or on a day of the preceding week, "something concerning that ordinance, and due preparation thereunto, and participation thereof, be taught; that, by the diligent use of all means sanctified by God to that end, both in public and in private, all may come better prepared to that heavenly feast."[27] The second rubric is a reminder that "the ignorant and scandalous" are not fit to receive this Sacrament of the Lord's Supper.[28] Furthermore, the table is "fenced" by a lengthy exhortation forbidding "all such as are ignorant, scandalous, profane, or that live in any sin or offence against their knowledge or conscience, that they presume not to come to that holy table."[29]

The structure of the Communion Service is as follows:

1. Exhortation
2. Fencing of the Table
3. Words of Institution and Exhortation
4. Eucharistic Prayer
5. Fraction
6. Delivery
7. Minister communicates himself, the officers, and then the congregation
8. Exhortation to a worthy life
9. Post-Communion Prayer
10. Metrical Psalm
11. Blessing

If the rite is prolix and didactic, it is also comprehensive. Perhaps its most striking characteristic is the emphasis given to the Words of Institution detached from the Eucharistic prayer and the high-lighting of the prophetic symbolism of the Fraction and Libation also detached from the Eucharistic Prayer. The latter has the advantage that the eyes of the congregation will not be closed in prayer (as is supposed to be the case when the Fraction and Libation take place during the Catholic and Anglican Prayers of Consecration). The Reformed services are sparing in the use of symbolism, but it gives to these *sigilla Verbi*, or dramatic demonstrations of the Gospel, their true value for eye-gate. Another significant emphasis is that on the holiness which should characterize God's elect, as indicated in both the "fencing" or the table and in the post-Communion Prayer.

27 *Ibid.*, II, p. 52.   28 *Ibid.*
29 *Ibid.*, p. 53.

The Eucharistic Prayer itself is also comprehensive, lacking only a thanksgiving for Creation. Although it is relatively short it contains the following parts: a Prayer of Access; a Thanksgiving for all benefits, especially Redemption; an *Anamnesis* (or Memorial of the Passion of Christ); and an *Epiklesis* (or Invocation of the transforming Holy Spirit). The rubric preceding the prayer reads: "Let the prayer, thanksgiving, or blessing of the bread and wine, be to this effect," and the prayer itself follows immediately:

> With humble and hearty acknowledgment of the greatness of our misery (from which neither man nor angel was able to deliver us), and of our great unworthiness of the least of all God's mercies; to give thanks to God for all his benefits, and especially for the great benefit of our redemption, the love of God the Father, the sufferings and merits of the Lord Jesus Christ, the Son of God, by which we are delivered; and for all means of grace, the word and Sacraments, and for this Sacrament in particular, by which Christ and all his benefits are applied and sealed up unto us; which, notwithstanding the denial of them unto others, are in great mercy continued unto us, after so much and long abuse of them all.
>
> To profess that there is no other name under heaven by which we can be saved, but the name of Jesus Christ; by whom alone we receive liberty and life, have access to the throne of grace, are admitted to eat and drink at his own table, are sealed up by his Spirit to an assurance of happiness and everlasting life.
>
> Earnestly to pray to God, the Father of all mercies, and God of all consolation, to vouchsafe his gracious presence, and the effectual working of his Spirit in us; and so to sanctify these elements both of bread and wine, that we may receive by faith the body and blood of Jesus Christ crucified for us, and so (to) feed upon him that he may be one with us, and we with him, that he may live in us, and we in him and to him, who hath loved us, and given himself for us.[30]

Having considered the Lord's Day Service and the Lord's Supper, it is time to look at the *Directory*'s provisions for Baptism, Marriage, and Burial. Baptism is described in true Calvinist fashion as "a seal of the covenant of grace";[31] yet any notion of its immediate and inherent efficacy is denied in the assertion "the

---

[30] *Ibid.*, pp. 55-56.　　　　[31] *Ibid.*, p. 46.

inward grace and virtue of baptism is not tied to that very moment of time wherein it is administered."[32] Baptism, according to the prefatory rubrics, is to be administered by the minister, not a private person, in the presence of the congregation and not in a private place, and "in the face of the congregation, where the people may most conveniently see and hear; and not in the places where fonts in the time of Popery were unfitly and superstitiously placed."[33] No godparents are allowed, since God's promises are to parents and their seed, and so the father is to present the child to the minister, or in the father's necessary absence, some Christian friend. The minister begins the Sacrament by instruction to the congregation on its meaning, and exhorts the parent "to bring up the child in the knowledge of the grounds of the Christian religion, and in the nurture and admonition of the Lord: and to let him know the danger of God's wrath to himself and child if he be negligent; requiring his solemn promise for the performance of his duty."[34] A prayer follows "joined with the word of institution, for sanctifying the water to this spiritual use." The name of the child is then demanded, and the minister then baptizes the child by name using the Trinitarian formula: *I Baptize thee in the name of the Father, of the Son, and of the Holy Ghost.*[35] The manner of baptizing is "to be by pouring or sprinkling of the water on the face of the child, without adding any other ceremony" (a deliberate exclusion of signing with the Cross).[36] The final act of the Sacrament with its touching reminder of heavy infant mortality in those days includes a petition that God "would receive the infant now baptized, and solemnly entered into the household of faith, into his fatherly tuition and defence . . . that if he shall be taken out of this life in his infancy, the Lord, who is rich in mercy, would be pleased to receive him up into glory," or otherwse that he may be upheld by divine power and grace "that by faith he may prevail against the devil, the world, and the flesh, till in the end he obtain a full and final victory. . . ."[37]

There was a long dispute between Independents and Scottish Presbyterians before the order for the Solemnization of Marriage was completed. Goodwin and his fellow Independents held Marriage to be a civil contract in which the minister acted only as the delegate of the magistrate. The Presbyterians, however, repre-

[32] *Ibid.*, p. 47.   [33] *Ibid.*, p. 45.
[34] *Ibid.*, pp. 48-49.   [35] *Ibid.*, p. 50.
[36] *Ibid.*   [37] *Ibid.*, p. 51.

sented by Rutherford, distinguished between marriage, the essence of which is consent, and solemnization which is concerned with the making of vows.[38] Also, the Presbyterians argued that since Marriage is commanded by God it is therefore worthy of religious solemnization. The Presbyterians gained their point.

The Service of Marriage consists of the following parts: a prayer of confession with a petition for the divine blessing on the couple; and an exhortation, Biblically grounded, reminding them of their duties to God and to one another. Then the man and woman in turn promise fidelity to one another; the minister pronounces them man and wife, and concludes with a prayer of blessing. The entire Service is modelled on a covenant relationship, as between God and humanity in Christ, so between man and wife, and a relationship freely entered into.[39] The mutuality of the relationship is stressed in the exhortation with its reference both to "the conjugal duties which in all faithfulness they are to perform each to the other"[40] and the spiritual duties, "praying much with and for one another, watching over and provoking each other to love and good works, and to live together as the heirs of the grace of life."[41] The same emphasis is found in the vow which the wife makes: *I N. do take thee N. to be my married husband, and I do, in the presence of God, and before this congregation, promise and covenant to be a loving and faithful wife unto thee, until God shall separate us by death.* The husband's vow is identical except for the substitution of "wife" for "husband" and the addition of "and obedient" after "loving and faithful."[42] The service lacks the aesthetic richness of the Anglican setting and the lovely rhetorical cadences of the promises which go back to the medieval Sarum Service, but there is still a simple, solemn strength about the *Directory*'s Service, with its sense of Marriage as an earthly image of the engagement between Christ and His church.

As we have now come to expect, the Scottish commissioners and the Independents argued fiercely about their different understandings of the significance of the Burial of the Dead. Baillie

[38] Sprott and Leishman, *op. cit.*, p. 356.
[39] A rubric directs that "Parents ought not to force their children to marry without their free consent, nor deny their own consent without just cause." (*Reliquiae Liturgicae*, ed. Peter Hall, III, p. 61). For the Puritan understanding of love and marriage, see James T. Johnson, *A society ordained by God; English Puritan marriage doctrine in the first half of the seventeenth century* (Nashville, 1970).
[40] *Reliquiae Liturgicae*, ed. Peter Hall, III, p. 63.
[41] *Ibid.*, III, pp. 63-64.   [42] *Ibid.*, p. 64.

reported in a letter of December 6, 1644, that they had "after many sharp debates" and "with much difficultie past a proposition for abolishing their ceremonies at buriall: but our difference about funerall sermons seems irreconcileable." He asserts that in England the custom is to preach funeral sermons "to serve the humours only of rich people for a reward" and that it is often "a good part of the ministers livelyhood."[43] The Scottish church refused to have funeral sermons at all.

The *Directory* tries to take the middle way between the Presbyterians and the Independents. It excoriates superstitious customs such as praying to or by the corpse and refuses to permit praying, reading, or singing on the way to or at the grave. But it is judged convenient "that the Christian friends which accompany the dead body to the place appointed for public burial, do apply themselves to meditations and conferences suitable to the occasion: and that the minister, as upon other occasions, so at this time, if he be present, may put them in remembrance of their duty."

The *Directory* also gives help for the right way to sanctify the Lord's Day, how to make the visitation of the sick an improving occasion for them, how to observe days of solemn thanksgiving and humiliation, and of "Singing of Psalms."[44]

There appears to have been great difficulty in getting the people to accept the fact that the *Directory* was replacing the Book of Common Prayer early in 1645, not surprisingly since it had been in use almost continuously since 1549. For this reason Parliament produced an Ordinance on August 23, 1645, "for the more effectual putting into execution the Directory for Public Worship" within all the parish churches and chapels in England and Wales and for disseminating copies of it. The penalty for using the Book of Common Prayer in any public place of worship or in any private place or family in England, Wales or Berwick-on-Tweed, was a fine of five pounds for the first offence, ten pounds for the second offence, and a whole year's imprisonment for the third offence. Any minister refusing to use it is to be fined forty shillings on each occasion, and any person depraving the *Directory* is to be fined an appropriate sum, not less than five pounds and not more than fifty pounds. All copies of the Book of Common Prayer are to be

[43] *Letters and Journals of Robert Baillie*, II, p. 245.
[44] The Puritan observance of Sabbaths and solemn days of thanksgiving or humiliation is considered in detail in Chapter VI, "Calendar Conflicts: Holy Days or Holidays?"

removed by churchwardens or constables and disposed of as Parliament shall direct.[45]

2. *Critiques of the* Directory[46]

Just as the Puritans had not scrupled for the best part of a century to offer detailed critiques of the successive editions of the Book of Common Prayer, when the tables were turned the Episcopalian clergy were not slow to criticise the *Directory*. But former Anglicans were by no means the only critics of the *Directory*, for the Quakers were among the most iconoclastic writers about this service book.

Two representative examples of Anglican criticism are the brief diatribe of Judge David Jenkins and the learned and lengthy critique of Dr. Henry Hammond, one of the most erudite apologists of the century.

Jenkins's title is *A Scourge for the Directorie and the Revolting Synod, which hath sitten this 5 Yeares, more for foure shillings a Day then for Conscience sake* (1647). The length of the title compensates for the brevity and occasional scurrility of the treatment. Judge Jenkins argues that many who had approved of the Book of Common Prayer as Protestants suddenly find that it is described as an idol by the writers of the preface to the *Directory*. Further, since some country folk are very unlikely to have the means to employ a preacher, they will henceforth receive little or no religious instruction, whereas a reader of the Prayer Book would have assured them of some regular instruction in the knowledge of God's laws. To tell such folk of praying by the Spirit, "you may as well tell them a tale of the Man in the Moone."[47] Moreover, Jenkins believes that many of the Reformation fathers who had a hand in compiling the Prayer Book were indued with God's Spirit.

He then provides a description of the state of worship in England three years after the imposition of the *Directory*. Although

---

[45] The Ordinance is reprinted in *Reliquiae Liturgicae*, ed. Peter Hall, III, pp. 83-88.

[46] A common criticism, one not entirely fair, is that of Walter Lowrie the Kierkegaard scholar and American Episcopalian who wrote of the *Directory* that "it is the only liturgy consisting of nothing but rubrics." (*Action in the Liturgy*, New York, 1953, p. 220), a judgment that ignores the sample prayers and liturgical formulae. James Hastings Nichols better characterizes the *Directory* as "not a service book to be placed in the hands of all literate worshippers, but a manual for the discretionary use of ministers." (*Corporate Worship in the Reformed Church*, Philadelphia, 1968, p. 99.)

[47] *Op. cit.*, p. 1.

the account is biassed, the picture of the disorder is probably not entirely exaggerated:

> O lamentable! what times do we live in? When the Church is without true discipline, Gods Lawes quite taken from us, no Lords Prayer, no Creed, no Common Prayer allowed, but *Master Presbyter* to do as his fickle braine serves him, the Sacrament of the Lords Supper not administered once in halfe a yeare, and when it is delivered wonderfull out of order it is, the Sacraments of Baptisme celebrated as any would have it that is in fee with Master Parson; the dead body buryed with five or 6 words at the most; no decency in the Churches, no manners nor order, forgetting that God is the God of Order.[48]

He is even more critical of the Independents (whom he calls the *"New-New-England* brood"[49] or "Nondependants") than the Presbyterians, for he condemns their extemporary prayers as no more than "these puddles and light-headed fooleries" and their ranting sermons preached by "*Ananias* the Button-maker, *Flash* the Cobler, Nondependants" which he claims are mere "tongue-sermons" that harm poor souls and especially poor women more than many Presbyterian sermons do good in half a year.[50] The entire pamphlet is an appeal to return from the chaos induced by the *Directory* to the uniformity, reverence and ordered dignity of the Prayer Book.

Henry Hammond's work is entitled, *A View of the New Directory and a Vindication of the Ancient Liturgy of the Church of England; In Answer to the Reasons pretended in the Ordinance and Preface for the abolishing the one, and establishing the other.* The first edition appeared in 1645 (and was 112 pages long), and the third edition in 1646. It will be possible to give only the most rapid summary of a book which combines much Patristic lore with a good deal of common sense.

After denying the legality of the abolition of the Book of Common Prayer, he provides several grounds to establish the lawfulness of a liturgy or form of worship. These include the precedents set by God's holy men in the Old Testament, Jewish practice since the time of Ezra, the practice and precept of Christ, the practice of John the Baptist, the apostles and the eastern church (the liturgies of Saints James, Basil and Chrysostom), the practice of the universal church since that time to this, the judgment and practice of the Reformed churches in other kingdoms, the example of heathens such as Plato who took up the practice, and the "irrational concludings" of the anti-liturgical groups.[51]

It is in the latter section that he provides two very telling rational arguments against the compilers of the *Directory*. The first is that "while they in opposition to set Formes require the Minister to conceive a Prayer for the congregation, they observe not, that the whole congregation is by that means as much stinted and bound to a set Forme, to wit of those words which the Minister conceives as if he read them out of a Book."[52] He also makes much, in the second place, of the inconsistency of presuming to prescribe the matter while refusing to prescribe the words of the prayers in the *Directory*. Is not the "prescription of the matter" a stinting of the Spirit as well as the form of words?[53]

As for extemporary prayers, Hammond considers them to have often been occasions of scandal to the faithful by their indiscretions, and he thinks their fascination is superficial, namely, "to the itching eare, exercise and pleasure to the licentious tongue, and the vanity of the reputation of being able to performe that office so fluently. . . ."[54]

He concentrates his chief fire on the omissions of the *Directory*. By avoiding a set form it sacrifices uniformity, and an active vocal role for the people through eliminating responses. It removes the correspondence between external bodily gestures and the inward spirit and rejects time-honoured ceremonies, while it omits the concision of collects for a long prayer, contrary to Jewish and ancient ecclesiastical practice.

After considering these general omissions, he concentrates on particular omissions. To deny any absolution at Communion, sick bed, or death, is "barbarous inhumanity."[55] The *Directory* seems to be indifferent to music and prescribes metrical psalmody only after the sermon and on special days of thanksgiving or humiliation.[56] It rejects the three larger creeds, including the Apostles' Creed.[57] It is lacking in any sense of the Communion of saints, the mutual charity of the church triumphant in heaven with the church militant on earth, which the Prayer Book's emphasis on the "Scripture-Saints" with their days and "propers" ensures.[58] As to the often criticised repetition of the Lord's Prayer, Hammond explains it as

---

[51] *Op. cit.*, pp. 12-18. [52] *Ibid.*, p. 18. [53] *Ibid.*, pp. 18-19.
[54] *Ibid.*, p. 19. [55] *Ibid.*, p. 20. [56] *Ibid.*, p. 31.
[57] *Ibid.*, p. 35. [58] *Ibid.*, pp. 39-40.

due to the fact that they appear in different parts of the liturgy (as, for example, the Litany), which could be separate. Also he adds pointedly, "I remember to have heard one of the gravest and most reverend men of the [Westminster] Assembly, being asked his opinion about the use of the *Lord's Prayer*, to have answer'd to this purpose, *God forbid that I should ever be upon my knees in Prayer, and rise up without adding Christs forme to my imperfect petitions.*"[59]

He particularly excoriates the absence of any order for Confirmation, the miserable provisions for burial in the *Directory* and asserts the need of the living for Lessons and Prayers as "laudable Christian civilities" at a time when events make human hearts malleable through mourning.[60] He laments the absence of any thanksgiving after child-birth by which the *Directory* is effectively setting up "Schools of *ingratitude* in the Church."[61]

Hammond's art is to prove his points with historical learning and then to show the practical superiority of the Book of Common Prayer over the *Directory*. He particularly delights in demonstrating the inconsistencies of the compilers of the *Directory*. He does not fail, towards the end of his book,[62] to note that all the arguments in favour of extemporary prayer (to spread the gift of prayer, to stop idle men in the ministry, etc.) are contradicted by the issuance of *A Supply of Prayer for the Ships that want Ministers to pray with them agreeable to the Directory established by Parliament, published by authority.*

The Quaker criticism of the *Directory* can be represented by Francis Howgill who wrote *Mistery Babylon the Mother of Harlots discovered . . . in answer to a Book tituled the Directory for the publick Worship of God* (1659). It was not an appeal to historical precedent like Hammond's, nor to the practical effect of using the *Directory* rather than a uniform liturgy like the Prayer Book. Rather it accuses the proponents of a spiritual or Spirit-inspired worship, such as the Independents, of not going far enough in that direction. Ironically, he suggests that if any man says the Spirit instructs each person, then he is told this is an illusion and he needs "Hebrew, Greek, and Latin, and the original of which you should expound the Scripture."[63] If he claims Christ is his teacher he is declared a heretic for despising the ministry and ordinances of the Reformed churches, natural learning, the ancient fathers, and worst

[59] *Ibid.*, pp. 35-36. [60] *Ibid.*, pp. 50-51. [61] *Ibid.*, p. 53.
[62] *Ibid.*, p. 101. [63] *Op. cit.*, p. 7.

of all, such would "make void all our arts and parts."[64] It will be
heresy and blasphemy if any man in fact claims that Christ has
made him free of sin in this life. If any one call the church or chapel
an "Idols temple," Scriptures will be brought to prove that God
commanded a temple to be built in Jerusalem and how the Jews
used synagogues.[65] Further, if any one were to say that the Spirit
should move or inspire any one "before any Teacher, Minister, or
Believer ought to pray" then a "multitude of Scriptural arguments
and precedents will be brought to prove him wrong."[66]

With supreme irony he describes the Puritan method of praying:

> And reverend Brethrens, let us all agree not to be idle but
> diligent, read the Scriptures, and pack them up together, a
> deal of exhortations, reprehensions, admonitions, and prophe-
> cies, and read some old Authors, as *Ireneus*, *Ambros*, *Cyp-
> rian*, *Ierom*, *Bazel*, *Austin*, *Origen*, *Damazin*, and its not
> amisse we take in *Luthar* and *Calvin*, *Memno* [Menno
> Simons], *Beza* . . . and so by much reading & meditation our
> actions will be shetted up and Quikened, and those words
> which we read often will lodge in our memory, so that we
> shall be able to pray half an houre *ex tempore*, or an hour
> and a halfe upon a Fast-day . . . without tautologies, or
> reiterations. . . .[67]

He then proceeds to make observations on the *Directory* chiefly
with the intention of showing the superiority of the understanding
of worship and prayer that the Society of Friends has. He does,
however, point to one contradiction. He asks why it is that the
Directory has so much to say about Baptism effecting regeneration and yet there is also emphasis on the need to confess sins. This
he calls sheer hypocrisy![68] He can see no point in requiring prayer
and the words of institution to sanctify water to its spiritual use
in Baptism, since God the Word originally instituted the water
and hallowed it, so why does it need sanctifying again?

Again, Howgill cannot see any reason for requiring the Communion Service after the morning sermon, when it was instituted
in the evening to be a Supper; nor since the wine was already hallowed by God's creation does it need to be made holy again for the
Communion.[69] He is also critical of singing in worship, accusing
the Puritans of turning David's crying in the Psalms into a song.[70]

---

64 *Ibid.*
65 *Ibid.*, p. 8.
66 *Ibid.*, pp. 9-10.
67 *Ibid.*, p. 10.
68 *Ibid.*, p. 24.
69 *Ibid.*, p. 30.
70 *Ibid.*, p. 35.

It is clear that Howgill accepts neither tradition and Scripture, as the Anglicans, nor Scripture alone as the Puritans, but the interior guidance of the Holy Spirit as the criterion of worship. Hence he uses the *Directory* as a means of proving the superiority of Quaker spirituality, its dispensing with forms and its immateriality.

Whatever the criticisms, valid or invalid, of the *Directory*, it shaped Reformed and Free church worship for the better part of three hundred years in English-speaking countries, and even had an impact on Non-Calvinistic Methodism[71] for two hundred years. Thus, as the Anglican Communion throughout the world owes an incalculable debt to the successive revisions of the Book of Common Prayer for the forming of its spirituality, so do English-speaking Presbyterians, Congregationalists, Baptists, and Methodists, to the *Directory*.

3. *Baxter's* The Reformation of the Liturgy (*1661*)[72]

The *Directory* had been in use for only sixteen years when the Restoration of the monarchy naturally led to the desire for the restoration of the Prayer Book, but a conference was held at the Savoy to see whether the Presbyterians might not be included in a more comprehensive Church of England, if some changes were made in the Prayer Book or some alternative orders were provided which Presbyterians would not scruple. While the other Presbyterian commissioners prepared their list of Exceptions to the Prayer Book, Baxter busied himself with producing the alternative Scriptural Orders of Service. The *Reformed Liturgy* was entirely Baxter's own work, the product of an intense fortnight, in which "I could not have time to make use of any Book, save the Bible and my Concordance."[73] His colleagues refused, at first, to allow him

[71] Methodist worship is, of course, an amalgam of the Free church Lord's Day Service, with the Anglican Order for Holy Communion, and the superb hymns of Charles and John Wesley. It is interesting that Wesley's adaptation of Prayer Book for American use took note of the Presbyterian criticisms of the Savoy Conference as related in a breviate of Baxter's life (the *Reliquiae Baxterianae*, ed. M. Sylvester), by Calamy.

[72] The text of *The Reformation of the Liturgy*, or *The Reformed Liturgy*, or the *Savoy Liturgy*, can be found in *Reliquiae Liturgicae*, IV, *The Savoy Liturgy* (ed. Peter Hall, Bath, 1847), and, excluding the prefatory "Address to the Bishops," in *The Practical Works of the Rev. Richard Baxter* (ed. W. Orme), XV, pp. 450-527. The Hall text will be used for references and citations. The previous Chapter, "The Prayer Book Restored and Revised" dealt with the purpose, development and results of the Savoy Conference between the Anglican and Presbyterian representatives who convened in 1661, but not in detail with Baxter's Scriptural alternative liturgy.

[73] *Reliquiae Baxterianae*, ed. M. Sylvester, Vol. II, Pt. II, Sect. 172.

426

to specify rubrics or directions but only prayers, since they thought the terms of the Conference forbade it.[74] The final revision by his Presbyterian colleagues left Baxter's work largely unchanged, as he was delighted to report.[75]

It is a remarkable work to have been accomplished in two weeks. Baxter's work, so F. J. Powicke suggested, is accounted for "by the fact that he was but writing out and supplementing what he had practised in Kidderminster."[76] Geoffrey F. Nuttall, however, would qualify this judgment: "Of the order of service this may be true, in whole or in part; but in so far as *The Reformed Liturgy* is, as the name indicates, a reforming of the 'liturgy' of the Book of Common Prayer, it is incorrect."[77] Nuttall then cites the following passage in which Baxter writes of his practice at Kidderminster: "As to the report of my using a form, the truth is, I never used one publicly or privately since I was 17 or 18 years of age; except the Lord's Prayer, which I use most Lord's Days once; . . . and except that I used much of the public liturgy in the congregation the first year and half of my ministry. And I find myself of late disposed in secret to end with the Lord's Prayer, as having a perfect method and satisfactory comprehensiveness of all that I had omitted."[78] In the light of this evidence, it would be nearer the truth to observe that Baxter was not using any forms that he had employed during his Kidderminster ministry, but was relying on his experience in conceived prayer. Even as late as 1684 Baxter prayed without a form because he found it difficult to remember forms.[79]

The following are the contents of the *Reformed Liturgy*:

1. The Ordinary Public Worship of the Lord's Day.
2. The Order of celebrating the Sacrament of the Body and Blood of Christ.
3. The celebration of the Sacrament of Baptism.
4. Of Catechising, and the Approbation of those that are admitted to the Lord's Supper.

---

[74] *Ibid.*, Vol. II, Pt. II, Sect. 175.　　[75] *Ibid.*, Sect. 182.
[76] *The Life of the Reverend Richard Baxter* (1924), II, p. 95.
[77] *Richard Baxter* (1965), p. 50.
[78] Dr. Williams's Library, London, Ms 5:9, cited by Nuttall, *op. cit.*, p. 50.
[79] *Catholick Communion Defended against both Extreams* (1684), p. 20. Many forms of Baxter's own writing are scattered throughout his works, which were intended as "a help subordinate to the Spirits help, to those that have it but in part; as Spectacles to dark Sights, and Sermon Notes to weak Memories . . . I can truly say, that Forms are oft a help to me." (*Ibid.*, p. 19.)

427

5. Of the celebration of Matrimony.
6. The Visitation of the Sick, and their Communion.
7. The Order for solemnizing the Burial of the Dead.
8. Of Extraordinary Days of Humiliation, and Thanksgiving; and Anniversary Festivals.
9. Of Prayer and Thanksgiving for particular Members of the Church.
10. Of Pastoral Discipline, Public Confession, Absolution, and Exclusion from the Holy Communion of the Church.

In addition, there is an Appendix containing:

11. A Larger Litany, or General Prayer. to be used at discretion.
12. The Church's Praise for our Redemption; to be used at discretion.

While 12 as a Scriptural mosaic of praise of Christ is wholly new, much of the rest comprises alternative provisions to those of the Prayer Book. This is especially true of 1, 2, 3, 5, and 11. Nine has a Prayer Book parallel in the "Churching" of Women, but it has an additional prayer for women drawing near the time of child-birth, and a thanksgiving for those that are restored from dangerous sickness. Eleven consists only of general directions and 7 is the same, except that suitable Scripture lessons are suggested. Four is the Presbyterian equivalent for Confirmation, without a bishop, and 10 is the traditional Puritan process of discipline. Eight provides an alternative to the Prayer Book observance of feasts and fasts.

If the structure of the service for the Lord's Day is examined, it will be seen that the order bears a close resemblance to the *Directory*. The *Directory* has an order consisting of nine items only: a Prayer; readings from the Old and New Testaments in succession; a Psalm; the Prayer before the Sermon; the Sermon; Intercessory Prayer, and Lord's Prayer; a Psalm; and the Blessing. The *Reformed Liturgy* has seventeen items:

1. A Prayer of Approach (with shorter alternative).
2. The Apostles' or Nicene or occasionally the Athanasian Creed read by the Minister.
3. The Decalogue.
4. Scripture Sentences moving to Penitence and Confession.

5. Confession of Sin and Prayer for Pardon and Sanctification ending with the Lord's Prayer (shorter alternative provided).

6. Sentences of Scripture declarative of Absolution and for comforting the penitent.

7. Sentences of Scripture declarative of the conditions of salvation.

8. Psalm 95 or 100 or 84, followed by "the Psalms in order for the day."

9. A chapter of the Old Testament.

10. A Psalm or Te Deum.

11. A chapter of the New Testament.

12. The Prayer for the King and Magistrates.

13. Psalm 67, or 98, or other Psalm, or Benedictus, or Magnificat.

14. An extemporary Prayer for the Church and the theme for the Sermon.

15. Sermon "upon some text of Holy Scripture."

16. Prayer "for a blessing on the word of instruction" and of Intercessions for causes not mentioned in 14 above. [A set form of "General Prayer" is provided, or the "Larger Litany" may be used at this point.]

17. Blessing.

The dominating characteristic of this order is, of course, its Biblicism. Two years before the composition of this liturgy, Baxter had conceived of a liturgy entirely composed of Scriptural materials. He wrote: "The safest way of composing a stinted Liturgie, is to take it all, or as much as may be, for words as well as matter out of the Holy Scriptures."[80] His grounds for such a conviction are three: the infallibility of Scripture; its ecumenical advantages; and "there is no other words that may be preferred before the words of God, or stand in competition with them."[81]

A second outstanding quality is its flexibility. It contained shorter alternatives to all the longer prayers, which the 1662 Book of Common Prayer did not. Moreover, it was intended itself to provide some alternatives to the Prayer Book Orders of Service.

The needs of the congregation were very much in mind when Baxter framed the Lord's Day Service. Their part in the worship is more than doubled, for they are allotted five Psalms (compared

[80] *Five Disputations of Church Government and Worship* (1659), p. 378.
[81] *Ibid.*, p. 379.

with the *Directory*'s two), while similar prayer-material was divided into five sections in the Reformed liturgy as compared with four in the *Directory*. The proof of Baxter's psychological insight is seen in the separation of the two Scripture lessons by a Psalm, to make concentration easier.

E. C. Ratcliff has commented on the logical character of the service,[82] to which one only needs to add its completeness. It fittingly began with a prayer for the divine acceptance of the worship. It followed by a profession of obedience to God in both mind and will, in the Creed and Decalogue respectively. By a natural transition the worshipper confessed his transgressions of the Holy Law. This was made all the more relevant by the use of sentences inciting to penitence and faith. The worshipper rightly begged forgiveness through the merits of his Saviour and as a token of reliance upon Christ recited the Lord's Prayer. The minister then read sentences declarative of God's absolution and strengthening of the sinner, with a Scriptural exhortation to a godly life. This was fittingly confirmed by the congregation which now joined in a Psalm of praise. This preparation had made the people ready to receive the Word of God or divine oracle, which was now both read and preached to them. After they had said "Amen" to intercessory prayers, and sung another Psalm, they were dismissed by a blessing. Thus the service ranged over all the Christian moods of prayer: from Adoration and Confession to Petition, and from Intercession to Consecration. It included the Christian duties of belief and conduct, and particularly in the prevalence of praise the warming of the religious affections. It is worth recalling that Baxter wrote: "For myself I confess that Harmony and Melody are the pleasure and elevation of my soul, and have made a Psalm of Praise in the Holy Assembly the chief delightful Exercise of my Religion and my life."[83]

When "the Sacrament of the Body and Blood of Christ" was to be administered, the celebration was to follow the service just outlined. The minister was to begin with an "explication of the nature, use, and benefits of this Sacrament" at his discretion, using either his own words or the form provided, and an exhortation which movingly depicted the Passion of Christ in the Sacrament.[84] There

---

[82] *From Uniformity to Unity, 1662-1962* (eds. G. F. Nuttall and Owen Chadwick, 1962), p. 121.

[83] *Poetical Fragments* (1683), Epistle to the Reader.

[84] *Reliquiae Liturgicae*, ed. Peter Hall, IV, pp. 60-62. Two excerpts from this exhortation will show how direct and moving Baxter's appeals were: "You were

followed a Prayer of Confession and a Petition for Pardon. Then the elements were received by the minister if they had not previously been placed on the table. A Prayer of Consecration followed: "Almighty God, thou art the Creator and the Lord of all things. Thou art the Sovereign Majesty whom we have offended. Thou art our loving and most merciful Father, who hast given thy Son to reconcile us to thyself: who hath ratified the new testament and covenant of grace with his most precious blood; and hath instituted this holy Sacrament to be celebrated in remembrance of him till his coming. Sanctify these thy creatures of bread and wine, which, according to thy institution and command, we set apart to this holy use, that they may be sacramentally the body and blood of thy Son Jesus Christ. *Amen.*"[85] Either before or after this prayer, the Pauline warrant or Words of Institution were read, followed by the declaration that "this bread and wine, being set apart, and consecrated to this holy use by God's appointment, are now no common bread and wine, but sacramentally the body and blood of Christ."[86] There was next a prayer addressing Christ directly pleading his Atonement, and through his Intercession and sacrifice, asking for the gifts of pardon, sanctification through the Holy Spirit, and reconciliation with the Father, and "nourish us as thy members to eternal life."[87]

The consecrated bread was broken in the sight of the people with these words: "The Body of Christ was broken for us, and offered once for all to sanctify us: behold the sacrificed Lamb of God, that taketh away the sins of the world." The Libation was made in front of the congregation with the words: "We were redeemed with the precious blood of Christ, as of a Lamb without blemish and without spot."[88] There followed a prayer for sanctifi-

---

lost and in the way to be lost for ever, when, by the greatest miracle of condescending love, he sought and saved you. You were dead in sin, condemned by the law, the slaves of Satan; there wanted nothing but the executing stroke of justice to have sent you into endless misery; when our Redeemer pitied you in your blood, and shed his own to heal and wash you. He suffered that was offended, that the offended might not suffer. He cried out on the cross, 'My God, my God, why hast thou Forsaken me,' that we, who had deserved it, might not be everlasting forsaken. He died that we might live . . . See here Christ dying in his holy representation! Behold the sacrificed Lamb of God, that taketh away the sins of the world! It is his will to be thus frequently crucified before our eyes. O how should we be covered with shame, and loathe ourselves, that have procured the death of Christ by sin, and sinned against it! And how should we all be filled with joy, that have such mysteries of mercy opened, and so great salvation freely offered to us! O hate sin! O, love this Saviour!"

[85] *Ibid.*, p. 65. [86] *Ibid.*, p. 69. [87] *Ibid.*, pp. 69-70.
[88] *Ibid.*, p. 70.

cation and the administration of the elements with the minister receiving first after saying: "Take ye, eat ye; this is the body of Christ, which is broken for you. Do this, in remembrance of him." The cup was delivered with the words: "This cup is the New Testament in Christ's blood, [*or* Christ's blood of the New Testament,] which is shed for you for the remission of sins. Drink ye all of it, in remembrance of him."[89] It was left to the minister's discretion whether to consecrate the bread and wine together, or separately and severally. "And if the Minister choose to pray but once at the consecration, commemoration, and delivery, let him pray as followeth, or to this sense." A further rubric, following a slightly longer Prayer of Consecration, showed the discretionary latitude Baxter allowed the celebrant: "Let it be left to the Minister's discretion, whether to deliver the bread and wine to the people, at the table, only in general, each one taking it and applying it to themselves; or to deliver it in general to as many people as are in each particular form; or to put it into every person's hand. . . . And let none of the people be forced to sit, stand, or kneel in the act of receiving, whose judgment is against it."[90] Then followed a splendid Prayer of Adoration and Thanksgiving ending with a petition that God's redeemed people "present themselves a living sacrifice to be acceptable through Christ useful for thine honour."[91] The Communion Service ended with part of a hymn in metre or Psalm 23, 100, 103, 116, and the Blessing: "Now the God of peace. . . ."

The flexibility of the rubrics for this Communion Service makes one curious to know how Baxter celebrated the Eucharist in Kidderminster. This is, in fact, known from a letter he wrote in March 1657:

A long table being spread, I first open the nature and use of the ordinance, and the qualification and present duty of the communicants; and then the deacons (3 or 4 grave, pious men chosen and appointed to that office) do set the bread and wine on the table; and in prayer we beseech the Lord to accept of those his own creatures now dedicated and set apart for his service, as sanctified to represent the body and blood of his Son, and after confession of sin, and thanksgiving for redemption, with commemoration of the sufferings of Christ therein, and ransom thereby, we beg the pardon of sin, and

[89] *Ibid.,* p. 72.   [90] *Ibid.*   [91] *Ibid.,* pp. 74-77.

the acceptance of our persons and thanksgivings now offered up to God again, and his grace to help our faith, repentance, love, etc. and renewal of our covenant with him, etc. And so after words of institution etc. I break the bread and deliver it in Christ's general terms to all present, first partaking myself, and so by the cup; which is moved down to the end of the table by the people and deacons (who fill the cup when it is emptied); and immediately after it, each one layeth down his alms for the poor, and so arise, and the next tableful succeedeth to the last after which I first proceed to some words of exhortation, and then of praise and prayer, and sing a psalm, and so conclude with the blessing.[92]

Baxter's Eucharistic doctrine is a high one, as not only the *epiklesis* implies, but also the combination of a strong emphasis on sacrifice with the recognition that Christ intercedes with the Father for his Body, the church, through that once offered but ever-efficacious offering of himself upon the Cross for the world's ransom. While the exhortations are too many, too long, and too didactic, yet the language is always serious and dignified, and the element of adoration is far stronger than is usual in Presbyterian liturgies of this period, where it is all too often remembered that God's people are *miseri et abiecti*, and forgotten that the ransomed should also be *laeti triumphantes*.

Since Baxter's *The Reformation of the Liturgy* failed to win the approval of the Savoy Conference as a whole as an alternative to the Book of Common Prayer—itself too ambitious a hope for the work of a single liturgist—it has received little attention either at its own time or subsequently, with the exception of the evaluation of it prepared by the late distinguished liturgiologist, and Regius Professor of Divinity at Cambridge University, Edward C. Ratcliff. Although he considered that this genre of composition, in which a deft and dignified mosaic of Biblical citations was created, unlikely to appeal today, and he noted the lack of a prayer of thanksgiving corresponding to the Preface of the Consecration Prayer of the Roman Catholic Mass and the Anglican Communion Order, yet he concluded: "This failure apart, Baxter's conception of the liturgical action of the Lord's Supper is nearer to the historic western tradition than the conception which Cranmer embodied in the Com-

---

[92] Dr. Williams's Library, Ms. 3:156, cited by G. F. Nutall, *Richard Baxter*, p. 53. Nuttall asserts that the posture for receiving Communion at Kidderminster was sitting, as can be determined from a sermon of 1657, *op. cit.*, p. 55.

munion Service of the Prayer Book of 1552."[93] That was high praise.

The Reformed Liturgy was a landmark in the history of English worship. While the *Westminster Directory* was a compromise between Presbyterians and Independents, the Reformed liturgy represents the liturgical convictions of one party, the English Presbyterians, and was drawn up by one man, rather than a committee. It is a homogeneous production. It is also valuable as an indication of how the *Directory* might have turned out, had the Independents not pressed their views on the Presbyterians, though there was not complete agreement between Scottish and English Presbyterians in the Westminster Assembly. It is, unquestionably, a clear indication that, even while the particular liturgy of the Church of England—the Book of Common Prayer—was severely criticized, the Presbyterians had no objection to a liturgy on a Biblical basis, provided it were not to be imposed with no regard to tender consciences. Moreover, it presented, with the Presbyterian critique of the Prayer Book, both the denials and the affirmations of the moderate Puritans on the subject of public worship.

The rejection of *The Reformed Liturgy* by the Anglican representatives at the Savoy Conference, while politically, ecclesiastically, and liturgically understandable, had one unforeseen and disastrous consequence. It turned the moderate Puritans (the Presbyterians) after their inability to take an oath required of them before Bartholomew's Day in 1662 affirming that the Book of Common Prayer was in all things conformable to the Word of God, into permanent Dissenters in England, and they, like the Independents, thereafter became the enemies of liturgy because they had suffered deprivation of their ministerial office for one unacceptable liturgy. Henceforth the liturgical Presbyterians became proponents of free prayer, the very party which had given the Book of Common Prayer in 1662, through Edward Reynolds, one of its glories, the General Thanksgiving.

[93] *From Uniformity to Unity, 1662-1962*, eds. G. F. Nuttall and Owen Chadwick, p. 123. Ratcliff also observed that Baxter might have assumed that the element of thanksgiving was sufficiently stressed in the regular Sunday Ante-Communion part of the Service, and it is interesting that this element is there in the description Baxter gives of his service at Kidderminster in the letter of March 1657. See footnote 92.

CHAPTER XII

NONCONFORMIST WORSHIP: PRESBYTERIAN AND INDEPENDENT, 1662-1690

PURITANISM becomes Nonconformity when it is excluded from the Church of England in 1662. It is a significant fact of religious life in the seventeenth century that every denomination of British Christianity underwent persecution at one period or another. The Roman Catholics lived under penal laws for the entire period, apart from three years of the unhappy reign of James II, and his encouragement of Catholicism cost him his throne. The Anglicans suffered obloquy and displacement from 1644 to 1660. The Nonconformists, the heirs of the Puritans, suffered under the five-stringed whip of the Clarendon Code and even when that was ended from 1662 to 1688.

The Presbyterians had much to hope for at the Restoration: the Declaration of Charles II at Breda to their ministers, the Savoy Conference to enable Anglicans and Presbyterians to consider widening the liturgical formulary to include the Presbyterians in the establishment, and the offer of bishoprics to three Presbyterians, all made this abundantly clear. The Independents, most of whom had been firm supporters of Cromwell and had received patronage from him, had almost nothing to hope for at the hands of the King and his advisers. In the event, neither Presbyterians nor Independents gained anything, and lost—if they were ministers or tutors at the universities—their livings and livelihoods.

From each minister intending to stay in the Church of England there was demanded a declaration to be made in front of the congregation before the feast of St. Bartholomew in 1662 of his "unfeigned assent and consent to every thing contained and prescribed in . . . the book of common prayer" and to "the form and order of making, ordaining, and consecrating of bishops, priests, and deacons."[1] There was also to be an abjuration of the solemn league and covenant, and the requirement that all not episcopally ordained should seek episcopal ordination. The penalty for refusal was deprivation of all the spiritual offices held. Thus ministers of

---

[1] Cited by Daniel Neal, *History of the Puritans*, 5 Vols. (edn., 1822), IV, p. 335.

the Puritan tradition, both Presbyterian and Independent, were being required to renounce their serious criticism of both prelacy and the Book of Common Prayer as conditions of remaining within the Church of England. It strained their consciences to the uttermost, and in the end almost two thousand ministers found they could not in decency comply.

The consequences, as we shall see, were formidable. The Presbyterians and the Independents were driven together as comrades in suffering, and so loathed was the Book of Common Prayer as an engine of oppression that the Presbyterians who had believed in Scriptural liturgies joined the Independents in the exclusive use of free prayers, and it is impossible to judge what the effect on the national church was through the withdrawal of such a learned, conscientious, and compassionate group of deeply spiritual ministers from their community. A persecuted and convinced congeries of conventicles of Nonconformists found its personal religion and its familial piety deepened through testing in the crucible of persecution, and the best devotional books of the Nonconformists, by authors such as Alleine, were written during this period "under the Cross."

The concern of this chapter will be to try and experience along the pulse and in the anxious and hurried beating of the heart what it was to worship secretly as a Nonconformist. We shall attempt to understand the difficulties of ministers with consciences, but also with pastoral responsibilities, expected to sign the declaration of conformity, the sufferings they underwent as a result of noncompliance by way of deprivation, imprisonment, and change of occupation in many cases. We shall also consider the different stratagems of Nonconformist conventicles employed to avoid discovery, or, if found, the methods by which they sought to escape the long arm of the law and its informers. Finally, consideration will be given to the effects of persecution on personal religion and corporate worship. This, by contrast, will prepare us for the great relief of the toleration of Dissent under William and Mary in the "Revolution" of 1688, and the "Heads of Agreement" for a happy union between the Presbyterians and Independents, the forerunner of the recent formation of the United Reformed Church in England in 1972 from the union of the Congregational Church of England and Wales and the Presbyterian Church of England. Such unity in Dissent was an unintended result of the Earl of Clarendon's and

Archbishop Sheldon's policy of "thorough" towards the heirs of the Puritans.

1. *Black Bartholomew's Day and After*

Some of the Nonconformist ministers left their livings in the Church of England before August 24, as did Richard Baxter, in order to let all the ministers in England know their resolution beforehand. Many ministers in London preached their farewell sermon on August 17, the Sunday before St. Bartholomew's Day, including such leaders as Thomas Manton, Edmund Calamy the elder, Matthew Mead, and William Bates.

Pepys made a point of hearing the farewell discourses of Dr. Bates at the church of St. Dunstan's-in-the-West. His diary entry for August 17, 1662, records his eagerness to be present at what he hoped would be a dramatic and highly emotional occasion. In fact, he seems to have been disappointed that Dr. Bates made no allusion to the situation at the morning service. Nonetheless, Pepys returned for the afternoon service, for which he had to stand in the crowded gallery, and there he heard a brief and moderate statement at the very end of the service. Bates spoke to this effect: "I do believe that many of you do expect that I should say something to you in reference to the time, this being the last time that possibly I may appear here. You know it is not my manner to speak anything in the pulpit that is extraneous to my text and business; yet this I shall say, that it is not my opinion, fashion, or humour, that keeps me from complying with what is required of us; but something, after much discourse, prayer and study, yet remains unsatisfied and commands me herein. Wherefore if it is my unhappiness not to receive such an illuminacion as should direct me to do otherwise, I know no reason why men should not pardon me in this world, as I am confident God will pardon me for it in the next." Madam Turner, with whom Pepys had lunch between the services that day and who was a regular attender at Parson Herring's services, presumably gave Pepys the information which he passed on. Herring apparently offered his apologia, not in a sermon, but as a postscript to a lesson from the Acts of the Apostles which recounted how Annas and Sapphira had kept their private possessions from the common treasury of the apostolic church. Herring is then reported as saying: "This is the case of England at present. God he bids us to preach, and men bid us not to preach; and if we do, we are to be imprisoned and further punished. All I can say to it is, that I beg your prayers, and the prayers of all good Christians for us."

These two accounts are sufficient to indicate the torments of conscience posed by the King and the established church to its ministers of Puritan persuasion who could not, in the light of their known convictions, accept an unreformed Prayer Book as fully in accordance with the Word of God (their liturgical criterion), especially as a century of Puritan scrutiny of the Book of Common Prayer made them acutely aware of its defects. Yet, equally, how could they leave their flocks to the hirelings who would succeed them? The astute could only conclude that the Act of Uniformity was a ruse to rid the established church of all dissenters by driving them into open Nonconformity.

It is worth comparing the reasons for Nonconformity adduced by the Presbyterian divine, John Howe, with those of the Independent minister, John Owen. Howe's inability to conform was based on three grounds: he could not submit to re-ordination without denying the fruits of the Holy Spirit in his previous ministry nor to the absolute enforcement of ceremonies not warranted by the Word of God, and he found the Anglican church unable or unwilling to exercise a strong Scriptural discipline for the maintenance of the purity of its church members.[2] Owen confined himself, in the main, to an attack on the imposition of the liturgy. This leads, he believes, to three disastrous results: the atrophy of spiritual gifts and to "men napkining their talents" in free prayer; the uniformity of a liturgy makes impossible the application of grace to the varying needs of different congregations; it abridges the liberty of the followers of Christ in unnecessary matters. Moreover, in the past such impositions have "brought fire and faggot in their train."[3]

Some supporters of the ministers made a less dignified and more threatening protest on their behalf on St. Bartholomew's Day. Pepys is again our informant. He states that "there has been a disturbance in a Church at Friday Street, a great many young people knotting together and crying out 'Porridge!' often and seditiously in the Church, and they took the Common Prayer Book, they say, away; and, some say, did tear it; but it is a thing which appears to me very ominous. I pray God avert it."

[2] *Works*, ed. Hewlett, i, p. xviii.   [3] *Works*, ed. Goold, xv, pp. 52ff.

Apparently "porridge" was the nickname given by Dissenters to the Prayer Book at this time. A contemporary play, *The City Heiress*, includes the following conversation. Sir Anthony says to Sir Timothy, "You come to Church, too." Sir Timothy replies: "Ah! needs must when the devil drives. I go to save my bacon, as they say, once a month, and that, too, after the porridge is served up."[4] The implication is that the real meat of the service is the sermon, the porridge only a preliminary that can be dispensed with.

Almost two thousand of the most conscientious ministers in England refused to comply with the new and stringent terms of conformity and lost their livelihoods. Some were men of considerable standing (two had refused bishoprics) and all, according to the testimony of John Locke, were "worthy, learned, pious, orthodox divines."[5] The roll of honour of these men of conscience is an impressive one for it includes: Bates, Gilpin, Manton, Jacomb, John Owen, Thomas Goodwin, Burgess, Annesley (John Wesley's maternal grandfather), Baxter, Calamy, Caryl, Charnock, Gouge, Gale, Cradock, Mead, Howe, Favel, and Philip Henry among the most famous. A few eminent men of Puritan persuasion complied, including Bishops Reynolds and Wilkins.

Of the 1,603 ejected about whom there is available detailed information, A. G. Matthews has established that 1,285 had received university education. Of this number 733 had been educated at Cambridge, 513 at Oxford, 20 at the Scottish universities, 12 at Harvard, and 2 at Trinity College, Dublin; 11 heads of colleges and halls, 39 resident fellows, 3 non-resident fellows, and 3 college chaplains were removed from Oxford in 1660, while 3 heads of colleges and 4 fellows were ejected from the same university in 1662. In Cambridge 5 heads of colleges, 18 fellows, and 2 college chaplains were removed in 1660, and 1 head and 14 fellows two years later. The headmaster and 5 fellows of Eton suffered the same fate in 1660. In all, 149 divines holding academic positions were ejected at or soon after the Restoration.[6] While many of these would place their wisdom and expertise at the services of the new Dissenting academies and there write a new

---

[4] Footnote in the Everyman edn. of Pepys's *Diary*, I, p. 282, which also observes that a contemporary pamphlet entitled, *A Vindication of the Book of Common Prayer against the contumelious Slanders of the Fanatic Party terming it Porridge*, is cited in Sir Walter Scott's novel, *Woodstock* (edn., 1822), I, p. 22.

[5] Neal, *op. cit.*, IV, p. 335.

[6] For a full and accurate account of the careers of ejected ministers, see A. G. Matthews's *Calamy Revised* (Oxford, 1948).

chapter of modern English education, they were a grievous loss to religion and sound learning.

Some younger divinity students changed their vocations to law or medicine. Other ministers were not as young or as fortunate. Some few became private chaplains in noble houses. Others officiated as prison or hospital chaplains. Many became tutors or schoolmasters. Some became noted physicians or lawyers. Many had to turn to unaccustomed and rougher work.

Daniel Neal, the historian of Puritanism, reports the pathetic shifts to which some ministers had to resort. One ploughed for six days and preached on the seventh. Another was reduced to cutting tobacco for a living. Others survived on the charity of the congregations which they served and which gathered in secret. John Goodwin became the proprietor of an eating house. Many for their persistence in leading conventicles were gaoled.

False reports stated that the Nonconformist ministers were living high off the hog. Indeed, Baxter reported that the Bishop of Chichester, Dr. Gunning, had repeated the *canard* to him. Baxter told him that "he was a stranger to the men he talked of" and added: "I had but a few days before had letters of a worthy minister who, with his wife and six children, had many years had seldom other food than brown rye-bread and water, and was then turned out of his house, and had none to go to. And of another that was fain to spin for his living. And abundance I know that have families, and nothing or next to nothing of their own, and live in exceeding want on the poor drops of charity which they stoop to receive from a few mean people."[7]

What the experience meant to a conscientious and wholly consecrated Nonconformist minister can be visualised more readily in the life of a single person than in terms of generalities or statistics. The man chosen is Joseph Alleine, the Presbyterian divine whose short life ended at thirty-nine, a former scholar and tutor of Corpus Christi College, Oxford, whose writings on covenant theology and personal religion were the basis of John Wesley's innovative annual service of the renewal of the covenant. A minister in Taunton, Alleine refused to be silenced on Bartholomew's Day, 1662, and, indeed, preached with undue frequency and redoubled seriousness and urgency knowing that he would soon be stopped. His wife wrote: "I know that he hath preached four-

[7] *The Autobiography of Richard Baxter* (ed. J. M. Lloyd Thomas, Everyman edn.), p. 223.

teen times in eight days, and ten often, and six or seven in these months, at home and abroad, besides the frequent converse with souls."[8]

He received the warrant on a Saturday evening after supper in May 1663 (this was in time to prevent him preaching the next day). He immediately repaired to the justice's house, where he was charged with breaking the Act of Uniformity by his preaching. This he denied, on the grounds that he had preached neither in any church nor in any chapel, nor place of public worship, but only in his own family, with such friends as cared to join with them. He was then accused of being present at a riotous assembly, but he replied that the meeting was wholly peaceful, without threats or weapons, the only business being preaching and prayer. He was ridiculed and called a rogue and, while forbidden to preach the next day, a warrant was made out for him to go to gaol on Monday morning. He returned home at 2:00 A.M. Sunday, slept briefly and prayed during much of the night. Throughout the day friends visited him, and he advised ministers to continue to fulfil the divine commandment to preach the Gospel by breaking the human law, and the people to encourage them by their attendance. Companies of the godly from neighbouring towns came to converse with him during the day.

His wife writes of the cheerfulness of his spirits that day: "full of Admirations of the Mercys of God, and encouraging all that came to be bold and venture for the Gospel, and their Souls." He told them he did not in the least repent of his actions; on the contrary, he "accounted himself happy under that promise *Christ* makes to his in the *5th of Matthew*, that he should be doubly and trebly blessed now he was to suffer."[9]

This faithful pastor felt it his duty to exhort his flock before leaving them for prison, so he appointed them to meet him about 1:00 A.M. on Monday, and to "young and old, many Hundreds, he preached and Prayed with them about three hours," however inconvenient the time was. This, incidentally, is a remarkable tribute to the closeness of pastor and people in Nonconformity in these penal days.

In the common gaol at Ilchester, he found six other ministers committed on the same charges as himself and fifty Quakers. Soon

---

[8] *The Life and Death of Mr. Joseph Alleine, Late Teacher of the Church at Taunton, in Somersetshire, Assistant to Mr. Newton* (1672), p. 53.
[9] *Ibid.*, p. 55.

after, ten more ministers joined them in the same suffocating room. Alleine was four months in this stinking prison before he was brought to the Sessions at Taunton on July 14, 1663, but the evidence was so slender that he was not asked to testify, and so he was returned to the old prison. On August 24, he was again indicted at the Assizes, found guilty by the petty jury, and sentenced by the judge to pay a hundred marks and to lie in prison till final judgment should be made. He then spent a whole year further in gaol, except for three days. Once he was freed from gaol, his attempt to fulfil his ordination vow to preach the Gospel was made even more difficult because the Five Mile Act had been passed. His was now a wholly itinerant existence dependent utterly on the hospitality given him in the houses of supporters at which he preached. But his marvellous courage never failed, and he would say, joyfully, echoing the old Elizabethan Puritan and nonagenarian, John Dod, that he had a hundred houses for one he had parted with.[10] His faith was invincible, and it bred true courage.

Two examples of the latter can be seen in his letters. One of them urging constancy of commitment in a person of rank and title, scoffs at fair-weather friends of Christ, but argues that stormy days are the true test of discipleship. "Verily," he concludes, "it is a greater Honour to you to be vilified for Christ, than to be dignified with the highest Titles that the greatest on earth can confer: and to be call'd *Puritan*, or *Phanatique*, for the bold and constant owning of Christianity. . . ."[11] A second letter is written to a conforming divine. Beginning ominously, "Dear Friend, . . . I hear you have Parsonages," it continues by reminding him of the souls for which he is responsible before God, and ends by urging him "and it let it be seen, however others aim at the Fleece, you aim at the Flock; and that you have indeed *curam animarum*."[12]

We have not read of the way that this man of conscience conducted worship, but we have two interesting testimonies of his mode of public prayer which is the heart of worship. A former student reported his reaction to Alleine's prayers when the latter was chaplain at Corpus Christi College, Oxford, as follows: "We were not used to a great deal of Noise, vain Tautologies, crude Effusions, unintelligible Sense, or mysterious Nonsense, instead of

10 *Ibid.*, p. 65.
11 *Christian Letters full of spirituall Instructions, tending to the Promotion of the Power of Godliness, both in Persons and Families* (1672), by Joseph Alleine, pp. 140-41.
12 *Ibid.*, p. 156.

Prayer. His Spirit was serious, his gesture reverent, his words few, but premeditated and well weighed. Pithy, solid, and to the full expressive of his as truly humble, as earnest desires. He loathed the Sauciness which went by the name of holy Boldness, and drew near to God, not as if he had been going to play with his mate, but as became a creature overaw'd with the Majesty of his great Creator."[13] His colleague, the senior minister at Taunton, George Newton, spoke in the funeral sermon of his great fervency in praying and preaching: "He was infinitely and insatiably greedy of the conversion of souls, wherein he had no small success, in the time of his ministry; And, to this end, he poured out his very heart in Prayer, and in Preaching. *He imparted not the Gospel only, but his own Soul.* His supplications, and his exhortations, many times were so affectionate, so full of holy zeal, life and vigor, that they quite overcame his hearers. He melted over them, so that they thawed, and mollified, and sometimes dissolved the hardest hearts. But while he melted thus, was wasted and consumed himself."[14] Clearly, here was a candle of the Lord who burnt himself out at both ends, weakened by imprisonment, exhausted by itinerating and pleading God's cause with the greater urgency because of the threat of renewed imprisonment. And there were hundreds like him.

Perhaps the most convincing proof of the sincerity of the Nonconformist ministers came during the Plague of 1665. It is best described by Baxter:

And when the plague grew hot most of the conformist ministers fled, and left their flocks in the time of their extremity, whereupon divers Nonconformists, pitying the dying and distressed people that had none to call the impenitent to repentance, nor to help men to prepare for another world, nor to comfort them in their terrors, when about ten thousand died in a week, resolved that no obedience to the laws of any mortal men whosoever could justify them for neglecting of men's souls and bodies in such extremities, no more than they can justify parents for famishing their children to death. And that when Christ shall say, "Inasmuch as ye did it not to one of these, ye did it not to me," it will be a poor excuse to say, "Lord, I was forbidden by the law."[15]

13 *The Life and Death of Mr. Joseph Alleine*, p. 23.
14 *Ibid.*, p. 37.
15 *The Autobiography of Richard Baxter*, ed. Thomas, p. 196.

To the Anglicans of this period, such ministers were outlaws, and the meetings at which they presided for worship were drab conventicles; but for the Nonconformists themselves they were miniature Pentecosts.[16]

2. Covert Conventicles

Apart from short intervals of toleration, which the Nonconformists were suspicious of, because they usually meant a toleration of Roman Catholicism, we shall have to hunt the Nonconformists in their worship in barns, forests, fields, simple houses in the back alleys of towns, and anywhere except in churches. Their meetings are as difficult to track down as those of the Catholics in the same period and for the same reason: they were forbidden, and exposure cost their leaders and members imprisonment and heavy fines. But in both cases, the reward of attendance at such secret gatherings for worship was an experience of intense seriousness, sincerity, the courage of faith, and the sense of belonging to God's tried and trusty elect.

What was it like to be a harried congregation? George Trosse, minister, arrested in 1685 at an Exeter conventicle is the reporter:

> We were discover'd by a malignant Neighbour, who went and inform'd against us to the Magistrates, who were then at Feast with the Mayor of the City. Three Magistrates, with Constables, and some of the baser and ruder Sort, came to find us out and seize us. After they had search'd an house or two, at length they discover'd our little Meeting, and found about Twenty People, of whom Three were Aged Ministers [Trosse himself was 54 at this time], and I the Youngest of them. They gave us hard Language, and treated us as if we had been the worst of Malefactors. The Ministers were committed to the care of the Constables, to be by them sentenc'd to be sent to Gaol, unless we would take the Oath . . . [the Oxford Oath] . . . We refus'd that Oath . . . Then, they reply'd, "You must go to Prison." I pleaded, That the Act did not extend to me, because the Law expressly says: "That he must either be a Non-conformist turn'd out for Nonconformity, or one

---

[16] Conformist or Nonconformist, one can readily echo the compassionate comments of Pepys: "While we were talking came by several poor creatures carried by, by constables, for being at a conventicle. . . . I would to God they would either conform, or be more wise, and not be catch'd." (*Diary* entry for August 7, 1664.)

convicted of keeping Conventicles." Now I was obnoxious on neither of these Accounts for I never had a Benefice to be turn'd out of, neither was ever legally convicted of keeping Conventicles. But . . . yet they committed me to Prison, without any law to warrant what they did.[17]

Trosse's experience was a relatively pleasant one in gaol, compared with Alleine's, for he had well-placed friends outside. Four other ministers shared with him the liberty of walking in the common hall and garden, and the victuals that were sent daily to them in prison, because "fourteen wealthy Friends by turns sent us Dinner every day."[18]

The interruptions of worship were not always as relatively dignified as that one. On May 29, 1670, when the authorities were searching for the meeting-place of Thomas Watson's conventicle, they could not find him or his congregation but "they brake down his pulpit and the seats, and nailed up the doors, so no meeting there."[19] On the same day other representatives of the law repaired to Mr. Thomas Doolittle's London meeting, but found only his substitute, an old gentleman, but the officers were not able to get at him to apprehend him, so the report goes, "the hearers closing fast together, they called to him to leave off and come down; to which he replied he would, so soon as he had done, but had a way of conveyance, so that he was not to be seen afterwards."[20] The "way of conveyance" may well have been a secret trap-door by which the preacher escaped through the basement.

The Nonconformists in self-defence had to provide such "escape-hatches" for their preachers and themselves. Thomas Vincent, who held Nonconformist services in a Southwark secret conventicle, had a series of ingenious devices for escaping the constables and informers. On February 12, 1682, a posse consisting of leading magistrates, and all the constables, churchwardens, and overseers of the four Southwark parishes, as well as all the officers of a regiment, tried to entrap Mr. Vincent and his congregation, but found no one there. "However," the official report continues, "we went round the place and find that almost every seat adjoining the sides of the conventicle has a door like the sally port of a fireship to escape by,

17 G. Trosse, *Life* (1714), p. 93, cited in Allen Brockett, *Nonconformity in Exeter, 1650-1875* (Manchester, 1962), p. 46.
18 Brockett, *op. cit.*, p. 47.
19 *Calendar of State Papers, Domestic*, 1670, p. 240.
20 *Ibid.*

and in each door a small peep-hole, like taverns' and alehouses' doors, to ken the person before they let them in."[21]

Some of the Nonconformist worshippers proved more than equal in physical fitness to their disturbers. Such were the hardy seamen of the vicinity of Great Yarmouth on November 4, 1674. The report to the government indignantly records: "They were so rude, as I am credibly informed, meeting at one Brewster's, near Wrentham, about twelve miles hence, that, two informers coming to the house and inquiring at the door what company they had within, they within, hearing them inquire, came running out, crying, 'Thieves,' and fell upon them, knocking them down, then drew them through a foul hog sty, and from thence through a pool. One of the two is since dead by their rash handling."[22] One can spill only crocodile tears for the misfortunes of informers on men and women of conscience.

There are so tantalisingly few reports of the nature of secret Nonconformist worship, that it is good to know the informer of Great Yarmouth sent a description to headquarters, which in its brevity still leaves much to the imagination.

> Their discipline at their meeting is: their teacher first goes up into the pulpit and there prays extempore. When he has spent himself he sits down, and then they sing a psalm, which is of their own making. When done, he stands up and preaches. They never read a chapter in the Old or New Testament, nor so much as a verse, except it be for a proof in their teaching. Their meeting-house continues yet shut. If these people designed no more than their own liberty, what occasion had they to build so large a house, which is 50 foot one way and 60 the other, with a gallery quite round it close to the pulpit, with six seats in it, one behind the other, and all accommodation possible for the reception of people below. I acquainted you that there was not above 100 men that were members. I since understand by one of them that they are not above 60.[23]

There are two possible answers to the amazement of the informant that so commodious a house is used for those relatively few Nonconformists who only want liberty to worship God in their own way. One is that it might well have been constructed in the lull in

21 *Ibid.*, 1682, pp. 75-76. 22 *Ibid.*, 1674, Nov. 4, pp. 396-97.
23 *Ibid.*

persecution in 1670 for a permanent meeting-house, as the extensive gallery would seem to indicate. The other answer would be to point out that house-meetings varied very greatly in size, and could stretch the capacity of a private house. In and about Exeter, for example, there were meetings involving 90 persons at Thomas Boyland's house on July 3, 1681; 157 at John Hopping's house on February 6, 1686; and 144 at John Guswell's house on March 6, 1687. All of these were cases dealt with under the Conventicle Act of 1670.[24]

Persecution was sporadic, varying in intensity from place to place and from year to year. The Clarendon Code did not merely pass the Act of Uniformity of 1662 to dispossess ministers: on the contrary, other acts followed which harried both ministers and people in the desperate attempt to stamp out Nonconformity. The Conventicle Act of 1664 made illegal the gathering of five or more persons over the age of sixteen under the colour of religion. A fine of £5 was imposed for the first breach of the law, while for the third breach the penalty was transportation to a colonial plantation other than Virginia or New England. In 1665 there followed the act for restraining Nonconformists from inhabiting corporations, commonly called the Five Mile Act. It forbade all preachers and teachers who refused the oaths to come within five miles of any corporate town. Such persons and any who refused to attend worship at a parish church, were prohibited from teaching, under a penalty of £40, whether as schoolmasters or private tutors.

Despite the stringency of the laws and their execution, here and there they were evaded by ingenious stratagems. The combined congregation of Baptists and Presbyterians meeting at Broadmead, Bristol, hit on the device of singing Psalms; immediately they were warned of the approach of informers. Their plans were carefully laid:

And when we had notice that the informers or officers were coming, we caused the minister or brother that preached, to forbear and sit down. Then we drew back the curtain, laying the whole room open, that they might see us all. And so all the people began to sing a psalm, that, at the beginning of the meeting we did always name the psalm that we would sing, if the informers or the Mayor or his officers come in. Thus still when they came in we were singing, that they could

24 Brockett, *op. cit.*, pp. 45-46.

not find anyone preaching, but all singing. And, at our meeting, we ordered it so, that none read the psalm after the first line, but everyone brought their bible, and so read for themselves; that they might not lay hold of anyone for preaching, or as much as reading the psalm, and so imprison any more for that, as they had our ministers.[25]

Another congregation, meeting in St. Thomas's, Southwark, almost whispered the Psalms to avoid attracting attention. A report of this conventicle states: "1692. April 1st. We met at Mr. Russell's in Ironmonger Lane, where Mr. Lambert of Deadman's Place, Southwark, administered to us the ordinance of the Lord's Supper, and we sang a psalm in a low voice."[26]

When persecution became intense, however, the Nonconformists invented (necessity being their mother) some ingenious ways of defeating the constables and their informers. Some made use of architectural conveniences. Weeks' congregation of Presbyterians in Bristol divided their meeting-room by a wooden partition, so that their minister could escape behind it into another part of the house.[27] A less ambitious ruse, but equally successful, was to hang a curtain across the room so that a stranger entering could not see the preacher, while he, wearing a cloak over his dark preaching gown was able to make his escape in the confusion of interruption. The congregation of Independents ministered to by Mr. Thompson of Bristol had two lofts above their usual meeting-room; while the preacher stood in the middle loft he could be heard above and below. The door at the foot of the stairs was kept free from strangers, and if constables or others broke it down, the minister could escape from the second storey to an adjacent house.[28] Sometimes a trap-door was employed which opened onto a lower chamber; this was probably the means of escape used by Mr. Doolittle's elderly substitute who conveniently "disappeared" in the midst of the congregation. Sometimes a hatchway on the stairs could be closed at a moment's notice, and the preacher who had used the lower part as a pulpit, could escape to the upper floor and get away to a neighbouring house.[29] Thomas Jolly, of the Northern coun-

25 *Broadmead Records* (ed. E. B. Underhill, 1857), p. 226.
26 Spencer Curwen, *Studies in Music and Worship*, 5 Vols. (1880-1885), I, p. 84.
27 C. E. Whiting, *Studies in English Puritanism from the Restoration to the Revolution, 1660-1688* (Cambridge, 1931), p. 372.
28 *Ibid.*
29 G. R. Cragg, *Puritanism in the Period of the Great Persecution* (Cambridge, 1957), pp. 41-42.

ties, stood outside a door whose top half was set on hinges, so that the room could be immediately hidden from any intruder ascending the stairs, and he preached to an audience within the room itself.[30]

Simpler devices were also successful in aiding concealment. The door of a room used for worship was often hidden by moving a great cupboard against the entrance. Sometimes a table was spread with food, so that, in an emergency, a religious gathering might be made to look like a festive occasion.[31]

When the situation grew desperate, more stringent measures were taken by Nonconformist congregations. We may be sure that the Baptists of Broadmead, Bristol, were not alone in taking to a cave on Durdham Down, or in Kingswood, or other retired places, as they did in 1682 and 1683. In April of 1685 they gathered at four in the morning, while in December of the same year they held their worship meeting in thick snow in the middle of the woods.[32] Dissenters in the South Midlands used to meet near Olney at a place known as Three Counties Point, where Northamptonshire, Buckinghamshire, and Bedfordshire adjoined. If attacked from any side, it was an easy matter to escape over the border into another county.[33]

When persecution was at its fiercest, worship was held at the dead of night, in the open air, in the woods or orchards, caves or dens of the earth, in shops or barns. It was a return to the church of the catacombs. The toponomy of England in such place-names as Gospel Beech, or Gospel Oak, testifies to the resourcefulness of proscribed conventiclers in the seventeenth century.

3. Effects of Persecution on Worship and Religion

The first effect of persecution on Nonconformist worship was to make its apologists even more inflexible in the defence of free prayer than they had ever been, and the powerful influence of John

---

[30] Henry W. Clark, *History of English Nonconformity*, 2 Vols. (1911), II, pp. 67-69.

[31] *Ibid.*

[32] *Broadmead Records* (ed. Underhill), p. 268. Dissenters in the West Riding of Yorkshire used to meet in a cave on the Rawdon estate of John Hardacre; it was sheltered by a "lean-to" roof. Occasionally the Presbyterian divine, Oliver Heywood, preached there, with watchers posted on the heights of the Buckstone Rock above (*Baptist Quarterly*, III, p. 179). It is interesting that the Nonconformists at Andover in Hampshire met in a dell four miles from the town, or occasionally in a private house at night, where they barred all doors and windows, and even put the candle out to prevent even a gleam of light from attracting informers. (J. S. Pearsall, *The Rise of Congregationalism at Andover*, 1844, p. 94.)

[33] C. E. Whiting, *op. cit.*, p. 60.

Owen was pushing entirely in this direction. It will be recalled that the Presbyterians in Scotland had the Book of Common Order (sometimes known as John Knox's *Genevan Service Book*), and that the English Presbyterians at the Savoy had no objection to a liturgy as such, as long as it observed the Scriptural demands. In the common crucible of suffering under the Clarendon Code, the Presbyterians came to the Independent viewpoint on spontaneous prayer, probably very largely because the Book of Common Prayer became for both groups the very symbol of tyranny and the requirement of which had caused them to lose their livings in the Church of England. On the other hand, however, it is clear that there was much preparation for prayer in the minister's study; there was a discipline of the devotional life,[34] that prevented any slipshod or superficial spontaneity in this intimate and free approach to God. Just as persecution had endeared the Book of Common Prayer to its Anglican clergy, so did the practice of free prayer in penal days become as cherished in the minds and hearts of Presbyterians as it had always been in those of the Independents.

In other ways, of course, Nonconformist worship in the time of what Gerald Cragg calls "The Great Persecution" had learned a great flexibility. This was inevitable when one considers the hours at which they had gathered in conventicles in times of emergency, or the very places in which they had met, varying from private houses to caves cut out of solid rock. Inevitably also, Nonconformists disliked even more than before, all false dignity, pomposity, externality, and formality in worship. The values they esteemed are the values of the church as a resistance movement of the Spirit: the courage of faith, the costliness and risk of devotion, utter sincerity and total absence of pretence, the sense of God's elect being an anvil which wears out the hammers of persecution, intense loyalty, and the close family feeling of those who share danger. It would take two hundred years before the heirs of the Puritans could even conceive of the possibility that a liturgy had anything to commend it, because the one liturgy the Nonconformists knew—the Book of Common Prayer—had become an idol, lifted to the same height as the Bible in being made obligatory, and a tyrant as well. Indeed, the anti-liturgical spirit took the extreme form of recommending the disuse of the Lord's Prayer. Philip Nye, the Independent minister, expounded this iconoclastic viewpoint in *Beams*

---

[34] Cragg, *op. cit.*, p. 200. See also Thomas Manton, *Complete Works*, 12 Vols. (1870-1873), I, p. 33.

of Former Light; Discovering how Evil it is to impose Doubtful and Disputable Forms or Practices upon Ministers (1660), while the learned Baptist, Vavasour Powell, propagated the same conviction in *The Common Prayer Book no Divine Service.*

Thus there is even more than in the past a concern for interiority in worship: no psychological concessions are made, and theological imperatives continue to rule absolutely. We find this typically in John Wilson's *Cultus Evangelicus*—the sub-title stresses the dominant values—*Or, a brief Discourse concerning the Spirituality and Simplicity of New Testament Worship* (1667). The author interprets worshipping in spirit to mean "that we must not worship Him only with the *body* or *outward* man, as heathens and hypocrites used to do, but with the *soul* or *inner* man, which is that He in all holy addresses mainly looks after."[35] The divine acceptance of such spiritual worship can be counted on, says Wilson, because it is grounded on the will of God, suits the nature of God as Spirit, proceeds from the inner man and is "a Celestial *Spark*, a *beam* of light, darted from God out of Heaven," and because "until we worship Him in *Spirit* we worship Him in vain."[36] It is very significant as representative of the Nonconformist view of worship in this period, that Wilson's contrasts are between spiritual, on the one hand, and carnal, corporeal, external, on the other hand, while he also contrasts truth to what is figurative, ritualistic, and ceremonial.

Another characteristic of this worship, which was true of Puritan worship, but is even more true of Nonconformist worship, is the closeness of the bond between minister and people, which owes nothing to any hierarchical respect but everything to shared friendship in danger. We saw how close Joseph Alleine was to his people, who, when he was to go to prison for his faith, had them coming in hundreds for his farewell messages to them, and when he was homeless, vied to have him and his wife as guests in their own homes. One senses in this worship in conventicles a rare and extraordinary spirit of *camaraderie.*

In this time also we are made aware of the heightened importance of serious Biblically based preaching, dealing with the plight of man and the succour of God. The pleading characteristic becomes even more prominent in this period, and there is a deep emotional charge as of electricity in the urgency with which the messages are delivered and the desperate seriousness with which

[35] *Op. cit.*, pp. 16-17.   [36] *Ibid.*, p. 33.

they are received. Nonconformist preachers, as G. R. Cragg reminds us, "did not preach in order to parade their learning or to express their personal convictions; they were messengers and heralds, sent by the Most High to proclaim to his people his demand for repentance and his assurance of pardon."[37] Most vividly the preacher made his listeners aware of the dangers of sin, most passionately he discoursed on the dissuasives from sin, and most eloquently he urged the divine encouragements for those who would be diligent. Bunyan probably reflects the preaching of the period as well as his own practice, when, in *The Holy War*, he speaks of the preacher who was practical and cogent in applying the message to the souls of the hearers: "he was very pertinent in the application, insomuch that he made poor Mansoul tremble. For this sermon . . . wrought upon the hearts of the men of Mansoul; yea, it greatly helped to keep awake those that were aroused by the preaching that went before."[38] The Nonconformist divines not only moved their hearers to tears, but themselves also. Their emotional involvement was extraordinarily deep. Oliver Heywood, no frail flower of femininity, but a robust and virile man, writes in his diary: "I found extraordinary enlargement in prayer and praise and oh! what floods of tears were poured forth!"[39] Thomas Jolly, another Northern divine, noted that his eyesight had deteriorated after preaching for many years, and he attributed it to weeping in the pulpit, for he had never failed to drench two handkerchiefs during every service he had conducted.[40]

Perhaps the most notable impact persecution had on worship was due to its influence on personal religion. Put briefly, it excluded the hypocrites from worship, and retained only the faithful remnant. Insincerity could not bear the searching test of suffering for the sake of Christ. In these penal years, and not merely at the end of history in the Great Assize, God was separating the sheep from the goats. Those who suffered were confirmed in the truths for which they made sacrifice. They were pruned by persecution to realise how meretricious the allure of the world was and how deceitful; they sought to produce in themselves and in others for whom they were responsible, the fruits of life everlasting and the harvest of the Holy Spirit. Faith was streamlined, stripped down to essen-

---

[37] *Op. cit.*, p. 201.   [38] *Works* (ed. Offor), III, p. 329.

[39] Oliver Heywood, *Autobiography, Diaries, Anecdote and Event Books*, 4 Vols. (ed. J. Horsfall Turner, Brighouse and Bingley, 1882-1885), I, p. 113.

[40] *The Note-Book of the Revd. Thomas Jolly, 1671-1693* (Chetham Society, Manchester, 1895), p. 57.

tials, patience became more enduring, love was more other-directed, and hope was the silver lining of the storm clouds that promised a heavenly compensation for the earthly difficulties. It was consolation to remind themselves that in God's eternal kingdom the last would be first and the first last.[41] Baxter in a prolonged self-analysis during the time of persecution, claims: "The tenor of the Gospel predictions, precepts, promises and threatenings are fitted to a people in a suffering state. And the graces of God in a believer are mostly suited to a state of suffering. Christians must imitate Christ, and suffer with Him before they reign with Him; and His kingdom was not of this world."[42] John Howe writes in a similar strain: "Every sincere Christian is in affection and preparation of his mind a martyr. He that loves not Christ better than his own life, cannot be His disciple."[43]

There are two proofs of the deepening of personal religion during this period. One of them is the number and quality of the devotional treatises written under the cross of suffering. Baxter's *Now or Never*, Joseph Alleine's *Call to the Unconverted*, John Howe's *The Living Temple*, John Owen's *A Discourse of the Holy Spirit in Prayer*, and Bunyan's *Grace Abounding to the Chief of Sinners* are the by-products of persecution. This was also the time when John Milton, the great poet of Puritanism, overcame his blindness and political disappointment in the composition of *Paradise Lost* and *Samson Agonistes*. These are plummets sounding the uttermost depths of Nonconformist religious experience.

The second proof is that this is the period when Nonconformist family worship was at its deepest. At night, especially on Sunday nights, the members of the family were collected together. The children, servants, and apprentices were questioned on the sermons they had heard that day. Psalms were sung. The head of the family offered a simple spontaneous prayer and often read a sermon by an approved Puritan divine. It was these simple but profound conversations with the living God that made the Sunday conventicles gathered for worship such profoundly significant encounters with a covenant-keeping God.

Another consequence of 1662 and after was the creation of a new phenomenon in English life, the Nonconformist conscience. As

[41] See Charnock, *Works* (Edinburgh, 1864), I, p. 111. Oliver Heywood, *Whole Works* (Idle, 1837), II, p. 122, and Baxter, *An Apology for the Nonconformists' Ministry* (1681), p. 196.
[42] *The Autobiography of Richard Baxter* (ed. Thomas), p. 122.
[43] Cited in R. F. Horton, *John Howe* (1894).

David Ogg has written, "As nowhere else men acquired the habit of thinking for themselves." And the insistence upon uniformity served only to strengthen disagreement, so that to Clarendon may be attributed "some responsibility for the entrenchment in our national life of the one native institution which no foreigner can hope to copy—the nonconformist conscience."[44] Perhaps we can also trace to the Nonconformist love of liberty born in this period the fact that radical movements were never anti-clerical in England. What is unquestionable, however, is that the Nonconformist conscience led to a sturdy questioning, an ethical sensitivity which often manifested itself as a concern for the rights of others and especially of minorities in religion. It became a powerful force in the nation's life, reaching its apex in the nineteenth century. Its chief outward characteristics were a fear of God but of no man, and an integrity that could not be bought. All this would be expressed in the searing honesty of the prayers of the Nonconformists in ensuing centuries, whether in the form of intellectual honesty as in the Unitarians who sprang from the Presbyterians, or in the moral forms in the confessions and petitions of the Independents and Presbyterians. Certainly it was manifested in the Nonconformist sermons which refused to curry favour with congregations.

Another effect—a very sad one—of the persecution of the Clarendon Code was to create a religious and cultural divide between the "church" and the "chapel" outlooks.[45] The former controlling admission and the granting of degrees in the ancient universities, prevented any Nonconformists who could not accept the Thirty-Nine Articles from entering Oxford or Cambridge for two centuries, forcing them to establish their own Dissenting academies[46] in which modern languages, history (which began as the history of liberty), geography, and the natural sciences were taught with greater superiority than in the ancient universities. Moreover, in these institutions the students learned the art of self-government. This division had the serious disadvantage of giving the Anglicans an innate sense of social superiority, and of puttng the Nonconformists constantly on the defensive. It had two very bad effects on

[44] *England in the Reign of Charles II*, 2 Vols. (Oxford, 1955), I, p. 218.
[45] See G. N. Clark, *The Later Stuarts* (Oxford, 1934), p. 23: "It became one of the dividing lines in party politics, in the press, and in everything else, even in economic life."
[46] See J. W. Ashley Smith, *The Birth of Modern Education: the contribution of the Dissenting Academies, 1660-1800* (1954).

religion itself. One was that in the continuing conflict between church and chapel, the bystander was apt to forget how much in doctrine and practice the disputants held in common. The other was that this quarrel in the same English household of faith was an appalling advertisement for the Christ who, on the eve of His Atonement on the Cross had prayed that all His disciples might be one, even as He and the Father were One, that the world might believe. This bitterness, and the exclusion of the Nonconformists from both national and local government, as from becoming officers in the armed forces, gave them a chip on the shoulder which prevented them from developing to the full the grace of *agape*, the love which forgets all hurts in serving others for Christ's sake.

Perhaps the marvel is that the Independents and Presbyterians survived this period with such firm convictions as to the nature of true Christian worship being simple, sincere, and spiritual, and that they passed on that heritage to the English-speaking countries of the world where their adherents greatly outstripped in size the small remnants of both denominations in Britain.

The most immediately impressive result of persecution (apart from the deepening of the spiritual life) was the growing comradeship of Presbyterian and Independent ministers in this period. Before this time the Independents had considered the Presbyterians legalistic and rather stuffily bourgeois with their strong merchant support, whereas they retaliated by considering the Independents too sectarian, radical, and even wild. The common suffering bred a common respect that led to serious plans for a union between the two groups, of which John Howe was the leading architect.

4. The Revolution of 1688 and Its Aftermath

One of the first effects of the "Glorious Revolution" of 1688 was to guarantee toleration for the Nonconformists. They immediately made plans for either temporary or permanent meeting-houses. Between 1688 and 1690, 796 temporary and 143 permanent Nonconformist chapels were erected, while between 1691 and 1700 another 1,247 temporary meeting-houses were erected and 32 permanent ones.[47]

As we have indicated already, the Presbyterians and Independents also planned to unite. The famous *Heads of Agreement*, proposals for the effective practical cooperation of both denomina-

[47] Duncan Coomer, *English Dissent* (1947), p. 61.

tional groups gained the assent of over a hundred ministers in the City of London, and the scheme spread immediately to the provinces. Party-cries were dropped, the beating of the denominational drum was silenced, and the cooperating ministers worked together happily from 1690 to 1694 as the "United Brethren." This promising union involved concessions on both sides, of course. Presbyterianism accepted that local congregations would desire a larger part in government, while Independents recognised the advisory authority of neighbouring churches. The union disintegrated after only four years because of a doctrinal feud, in which certain Independents out-Calvinised the Presbyterians. Closer cooperation between the denominations who had suffered persecution was to bear fruit in the next century in the formation in 1732 of the body known as "The Dissenting Deputies," whose task was to defend Nonconformist civil rights and which was granted the privilege of direct access to the sovereign. The tragedy is that John Howe's ecumenical spirit was rendered ineffectual by internecine dogmatisms. His view was that "without all controversy the main inlet of all the distractions, confusions, and divisions of the Christian world hath been by adding other conditions of Church communion than Christ hath done."[48]

What was Nonconformist worship like in the warmer and more genial climate of toleration? Fortunately, this question can be answered with greater particularity than usual because of the assiduity with which a visiting minister of the Episcopal church of Scotland, the Rev. Robert Kirk, attended churches, chapels, and even a synagogue during 1689 and 1690, recording his observations in detail.[49] It is important to know his prejudices before citing his reports. He is very critical of the vagueness of Dissenting sermons, as of their repetitiousness, both faults of extemporaneity. He greatly prefers the practicality, preciseness, and learning of Anglican sermons. His favourite Anglican preacher is Stillingfleet, as his favourite Dissenting preacher is Baxter, and he admires both because they are for widening the boundaries of the Church of England.

Of the Dissenters whom he heard, he liked the Presbyterians best, and the Quakers worst. He first heard Richard Baxter in a

[48] *Works*, v, p. 226.
[49] The Ms. of Robert Kirk's small commonplace book is in the Library of Edinburgh University. A catena of the most interesting observations will be found in Donald Maclean's *London at Worship* (The Presbyterian Historical Society of England, Manchester, 1928), from which references will be made.

hall near Charterhouse Hospital on November 10, 1689, taking as his text, "Blessed are the peacemakers." Of the service we are told: "His clerk first sung a Psalm reading the line. Then the reader read 3 Ps[alms], Isaiah 5 and Matt. 22 after he had given an extempore prayer. Then the minister, reading the papers of the sick and troubled in mind and intending a journey, he prayed and preached a sermon on popery." The report continues: "Mr. Baxter prayed in general for the King and Royal Family and Parliament; for Jacobites, Grecians, and Armenians enlightening in further knowledge; for Christians distressed with burning, dislodging and oppression of merciless enemies. The congregation all kneeled or stood up at prayer."[50] Two clarifications may be made of this report. The first is that psalmody was made so much duller by the clerk reading out every line of every metrical Psalm in advance. The second is the interesting custom by which church members sought the minister's petitions for themselves or intercessions for others by writing them down and having them conveyed to him on slips of paper put into a slotted stick. It was typical of Baxter, even in a time of toleration, to remember distressed Christians across the world.

A second visit to hear Baxter gives us further information on that notable divine. One prayer of his sounded the ecumenical note. In Kirk's words: "that all ministers might have a sound mind and a quiet disposition, and for a reconciling all differences, that party nor sect be never heard any more among Protestants." Baxter repeated the Lord's Prayer and at the last blessing said, "Blessed of God are all who consider, believe, love, and obey this word."[51]

Presbyterian ministers, however, did not pray alike. Baxter used the Lord's Prayer, but Dr. William Bates did not. Nor did Bates have any reading of Scripture. "He prayed not for King or Queen nor Church; he reflected on none. . . . He, as all regular clergy, had all intercession and thanksgiving in his first prayer, where he began by beseeching that we might approach God with a filial freedom."[52]

The third Presbyterian minister he went to hear was the animated Daniel Burgess. This minister's prayer was an exceedingly independent one, for "he prayed that the Church and ministry of England might be freed of Lords over God's heritage, and that they may no more have ministers who do not preach, nor ministers that are not of truth sound. Before the blessing he said it was fit-

50 Maclean, *op. cit.*, p. 16.   51 *Ibid.*, pp. 16-17.
52 *Ibid.*, p. 17.

ting every man challenged himself quickly that he has been doing service all his life and yet knows not his master. He had many additions to the usual blessing." Mr. Kirk liked a dependable liturgy, not extemporaneous effusions in prayer or sermon. His next comment indicates his bewilderment: "Not any two Presbyterians do I find keep one way." His summation is interesting: "Mr. Baxter reads the Scriptures and preaches; Dr. Bates only has one sermon and two prayers; Mr. Burgess lectures, preaches, sings the 'Doxology,' and in his bold way speaks diminutively of the King, saying before God, 'a king and chimney sweeper are all one and death values them so, too.' "[53]

Kirk visited the meeting-house of only one Independent minister, that of George Cokayne. The congregation of about two hundred were rather crushed and Kirk noted with some disdain that "few persons of good rank were present, only two coaches or so attended the doors." There was no Psalm sung before or after the sermon. The people stood for prayer, listened to the sermon with their hats on, but took them off for prayer. There was no blessing at the end of the service, and no church at home or abroad was prayed for. But Kirk preserves one gem which is so touching in its vivid directness that it is almost an apologia of itself for spontaneous prayer. Kirk writes: "He did plead vehemently with God for a young man at the grave's mouth, the only hope and visible standing of his father's family, saying: 'Lord, 'tis rare to find a good man, more a good young man. Thou sparedst 10,000ds. of debauched youths, may not this one not dry but tender and fruitful branch escape the blast of Thy displeasure. Save his soul. Spare his body. Sanctify all to the parents seeing Thou dost it; not theirs nor ours, but Thy will be done.' "[54]

The spirit of Puritanism clearly had been resurrected in Nonconformity. The bold confidence in approaching and beseeching God, the intensity of the sincerity, the pleading pastoral concern, and above all, the final willingness to accept God's will as Christ had done in the Garden of Gethsemane in almost identical words, prove that free prayer could reach the greatest heights, and scale the walls of heaven itself.

[53] *Ibid.*, pp. 17-18.   [54] *Ibid.*, p. 21.

CHAPTER XIII

ROMAN CATHOLIC WORSHIP

IN THIS turbulent century of upsets, the Anglicans were in the saddle for the whole period except for the seventeen years when the Puritans exchanged places; the Roman Catholics, on the other hand, were never in the saddle as an established church. It was their singular misfortune, as a great international Christian community—with the exception of five years in the sixteenth and three years in the seventeenth century—to live in the shadow of persecution from 1534 to 1829. The clouds lifted for them in our period only for the three fitful and disastrous years of the reign of their champion, James II.

The contrast between Catholicism on the European Continent and Catholicism in England must have been heart-rending for the Recusants; as heart-rending as the lot of the Presbyterians in Scotland or Switzerland compared with their English fate after 1662, or that of the Independents in New England compared with their destiny in old England after 1662. There was only one difference: the Roman Catholics seemed to pin their hopes on political changes that were doomed to disappointment. Indeed, their lot was made the harder precisely because of the hotheads of their number involved in plots and conspiracies.

The era was punctuated by the rumours and the realities of Catholic plots and their expected explosions. The reign of James I had hardly begun when there were two plots on his life by Catholics. The first, the Bye plot, was a harebrained scheme of a secular priest, William Watson and his associates, to kidnap the King and force him to obey their instructions. Hard on its heels followed the more threatening Gunpowder Plot to overthrow King and both Houses of Parliament in November 1605, which was agreed to by the four main conspirators, Catesby, Winter, Percy and Fawkes, in the Spring of 1604 and who were discovered tunnelling towards the cellars beneath Parliament. The "Popish Plot" associated with Titus Oates renewed the general fear of the Catholics from 1678 to 1681. The result of these conspiracies was that they sent dense clouds of smoky suspicion in their train never to be dissipated during this century. The Gunpowder Plot, in particular, caused the Catholics irreparable harm, because the State Service of November 5 reminded the nation annually of the treasonable proclivities of Roman Catholics, as enemies of the royal family, Parliament, and the Church of England. Even the children as they prepared the image of Guy Fawkes to be burned on their bonfire, and as they begged "a penny for the guy" to spend on fireworks, were indoctrinated with the notion that Catholicism was a cruel, sinister, violent and unreliable faith. This was a formidable shadow under which they had to live. All the more was this so when the lot of Catholics in France or Spain seemed to be a life of basking in the approval of a *roi soleil*.

What a contrast there is between the theatrical Baroque worship on the continent of Europe and the furtive celebration of the Mass in barns or upper rooms in England. When one recalls the effulgence of the brilliant European monstrances, shining like miniature meteors, the domes of such churches as the *Gesù* in Rome with the spiral of Jesuit martyrs climbing to heaven, or the mystical ravishment of St. Teresa of Avila in Bernini's statue, or the imitation of the royal courts in the etiquette of Baroque worship and its splendid appurtenances, one sees the English parallel with the church of the catacombs before the advent of the first triumphalism of Constantine. Both are secretive communities running risks by merely being Recusants and refusing the official worship dictated by the state; both also by their daring are producing martyrs whose blood is the seed of the church.

Has the impact of persecution, because it was sporadic, been exaggerated? Certainly, it was minimal in the reign of Charles I, whose Queen Henrietta Maria was a Catholic. Well-to-do Catholics could then afford to have their own chaplains and be unmolested, but the poor found it difficult to interest priests in their plight. Father Thomas Greene, the ageing Archdeacon of Essex, proposed that rich families should raise funds to pay priests to minister to the poor, but warned: "A poor man's priest must be apostolical in spirit, zealous for souls and fond of hard work, and no lover of his back or belly, and diligent to instruct."[1] Yet there were such apostolical men. One of them was Father Henry Morse whose work was chiefly among the plague-stricken poor in the city of London, and who was forced to spend nine years in three prisons. The context of his prayers and the consolation of the Mass and the *viaticum* must be imagined to contrast it with the absolutist splendour of

---

[1] Cited by Martin Havran, *The Catholics in Caroline England* (Palo Alto, California, 1962), p. 78.

continental Catholicism: "In March 1637 he was incarcerated with 47 criminals awaiting death on the gallows. Their stench made him ill . . . as did their habit of slobbering their food like starving animals. Morse managed to obtain quarters in a third-storey room which proved somewhat better than the common wards below. The room had bars on the window as thick as a man's wrist, and stone walls on which the prisoners had scribbled scriptural texts, verses, and obscenities. The only furnishings were board beds, a table, and chairs black with age and rot. The jailer sold sleeping holes in the walls at high rates, advertising them free of vermin, and he charged exorbitant rates for an hour of fresh air in the prison yard."[2]

Nor was all comfortable in ancient country houses, especially immediately after the unhappy year 1605. For a companion picture one should turn to a description of Harrowden Hall when the hunt for Father Garnet, the Provincial of the Jesuits, was in full cry, and he was finally "earthed" in January of 1605-1606. Sir Henry Bromiley, the local justice who was instructed by the Privy Council to carry out the search, reported that eleven secret corners were found in which priests could hide. On the eighth day of the search Henry Garnet and his Jesuit co-priest, Oldcorn, emerged like wan ghosts from the hiding-place behind the chimney. The report mentions that "marmalade and other sweetmeats were found there lying by them, but their better maintenance had been by a quill or reed through a little hole in the chimney that backed another chimney into the gentlewoman's chamber, and by that passage cawdles, broths, and warm drinks had been conveyed in unto them." Bromiley continues his malodorous report: "Now in regard the place was so close those customs of nature which of necessity must be done, and in so long time of continuance, was exceedingly offensive to the men themselves, and did much annoy them that made entrance in upon them, to whom they confessed they had not been able to hold out one whole day longer, but either they must have squealed or perished in the place."[3] Such was the price of loyalty to Roman Catholicism, magnificently paid by the Society of Jesus. As Godfrey Anstruther[4] points out, the most eloquent testimony to the growing fear and hatred of Popery and the costliness of recusancy is found in the Recusant Rolls of Northamptonshire, an area where Puritanism was strong and from which Browne of

2 Philip Caraman, *Henry Morse: Priest of the Plague* (1957), pp. 125-28.
3 Godfrey Anstruther, O.P., *Vaux of Harrowden, A Recusant Family* (Newport, Monmouthshire, 1953), p. 336.
4 *Ibid.*

Brownist fame hailed. These were the lists of Roman Catholics convicted for non-attendance at the Protestant services, and fined £20 a month. Before the Gunpowder Plot the number in the country never exceeded twelve; by 1608 it had risen to 182, and this level was fairly well maintained until 1620. Since few were wealthy enough to pay such fines for a long period, they had the option of parting with two-thirds of their property as the price for prolonged recusancy. Such fines became a lucrative source of royal income, since the receipts for 1612 amounted to £371,000. Many faithful Catholics suffered imprisonment for their loyalty to the old religion, for we know that when James I was persuaded by the Spanish ambassador in 1622 to liberate those incarcerated for the Catholic faith, 40,000 were set free.[5]

Cromwell's regime was equally concerned to get the full value of the Recusants' fines. The death-penalty for priests or people found participating at Mass continued, parents were forbidden to instruct their own children in Catholicism, and Catholics were disfranchised and refused entry to such professions as the army or the law.

1. Catholic Life and Worship

The effect of these conditions of life was profound on their worship. In the first place, as it was illegal in England it was quite secret or at least unobtrusive. Moreover, this was at a time when the effect of the Counter-Reformation had been to emphasise the distinctive tenets of the faith and the characteristic elements of the cultus, such as the dramatic miracle of the Mass, the intercession of the saints vividly represented in statues or stained-glass, and the pre-eminence of the Blessed Virgin as first among the faithful and the Mother of God the Son. Continental Catholic worship was religion on parade; English Catholic worship was religion in hiding.

In the second place, the quality of Catholic devotion was inevitably strained, self-conscious, and sometimes strident. It was cultivated most successfully in the monasteries and convents of the English exiles in the Low Countries in the seventeenth century. As might be expected, these English "colonies of heaven" were more English than England itself, and the standard of religious life that they trained for left the laity trailing a long way behind in the

[5] Robert Julian Stonor, O.S.B., *Stonor, A Catholic Sanctuary in the Chilterns from the Fifth Century till today* (Newport, Monmouthshire, 2nd edn., 1952), p. 271.

race, and gasping. These monasteries, convents and seminaries "never regarded themselves as forming anything else but little bits of Great Britain" and were animated by "an extraordinary spirit of fervour."[6] While concentrating on the contemplative life, they often poured out commentaries on the spiritual life, expositions of the Mass, catechisms and the like, and mediated to England the rich developments of seventeenth-century French, Italian and especially Spanish mysticism and spirituality.[7] Though they were not wealthy, the worship in these religious houses would approximate that of the Continent in its Baroque expressions, though, one would suppose, with some English reserve.

In the third place, Catholic worship was inevitably marked in England by a longing for the good old days, a retrospective glance over the shoulder, not least because the Andrewes-Laud tradition of the high church in Anglicanism seemed to be taking a few leaves out of the missal and breviary, if not out of the pontifical. Even this worship must have seemed pale beside the Sarum Rite in the first third of the sixteenth century or Counter-Reformation celebrations of Mass on festivals in European cathedrals or abbeys. We can only guess how these thoughts were sparked by the sight of a precious relic, or a richly embroidered vestment, or a chalice with begemmed knop. The Benedictine Chapel of the Rosary in London which opened about 1652-1654 had among its treasures "a most glorious and wonderfully exquisite relic of the Crown of Thorns of our Saviour, kept in Catholic times in the most flourishing monastery of Glastonbury, the burying place of the noble Decurio S. Joseph of Arimathea, who had the blessing of entombing our Lord" and also "a curious piece of the most Holy Cross, which came from the most renowned and worthy John Fecknam, last Abbot of the Royal Abbey of Westminster. . . ."[8] The superlatives in the citation are themselves a clue to the exaggerated praise of the past seen through rose-tinted spectacles.

The Jesuits, too, retained some vestiges of ancient splendour in their liturgical treasures. Father Gerard's autobiography refers to their "vestments and altar furniture" as being "both plentiful and costly." Their festal vestments were embroidered with gold and pearl. Lamps hung from silver chains above the altar which bore six massive candlesticks besides some others at the side for the

6 *Ibid.*, p. 300.   7 See Chapter III above for details.
8 Dom Hugh Connolly, "The Benedictine Chapel of the Rosary in London" in *Downside Review*, Vol. LII (N.S., Vol. XXXIII), pp. 320-29.

elevation of the Host. It also had a pure silver Crucifix. Father Gerard was rightly proud of a gold Crucifix a foot high, "on the top of which was represented a pelican, while at the right arm of the Cross was an eagle, with expanded wings, carrying on its back its young ones, who were attempting to fly: on the left arm a phoenix expiring in flames, that it might leave an offspring after it; and at the foot was a hen with her chickens gathering them under her wings."[9] The subtlety of the modelling was matched by the appropriateness of the fourfold symbolism of the self-wounding pelican representing Christ who by his sacrificial death is the food of the soul; the eagle is emblematic of the persistence of faith; while the fabled phoenix dying to be reborn represents Christ and His incorporating His faithful in the sacraments to share eternal life; the hen and her chickens are reminders of Christ weeping over Jerusalem which knew not the day of her visitation and founding the New Israel whom He protects and for whom He intercedes. Such superb artistry spoke to the wondering eye, whereas perhaps a sermon might only have led to a wandering ear. Above all, such images evoked the grandeur of a diminishing Catholicism in England.

In the fourth place, there was a fairly easy way to adapt medieval practice to seventeenth-century need on the part of the Catholic gentry. It was the use of the private house-chapel and chaplain in times of persecution for the family, servants, and nearby tenantry, forming a type of "peculiar" apart from the parish church. There would be a family liturgy of morning and evening prayers based on the divine Office and supplied by a Primer or Persons' *Christian Directory* which were also used privately. In the Primer there would also be much incidental religious instruction. On this view, according to Hugh Aveling, a learned Benedictine, "the households of the gentry would have been already provided by long tradition and way of life with forms admirably suited to maintain Catholic life in small *enclaves* amidst a hostile environment and with priests in short supply."[10] He also suggests that the compromise arrangement used by the Tyrwhit family at Thornton in Lincolnshire in the 1590s became fairly common. This was to employ an Anglican

[9] John Gerard, *The Autobiography of Fr. John Gerard, S.J.* (edn., 1881), p. 383.

[10] Hugh Aveling, O.S.B., *The Catholic Recusants of the West Riding of Yorkshire, 1558-1790* (Leeds, 1963: Proceedings of the Leeds Philosophical and Literary Society, Literary and Historical Section, Vol. x, Pt. vi, pp. 191-306), pp. 246-47.

chaplain who said prayers for the conformist members of the household (including the church-Papist head) in the hall of the house. Meanwhile, the recusant members of the family and servants went off to Twigmore, one of the "citadels" of Father Holtby, S.J., to Mass and the other sacraments.[11] If a priest were in residence, then the Recusants would hear Mass in a secret upstairs room of the house.

On the other hand, when after 1660 the secular authorities were more lenient to Catholics, the gentry with a resident priest or frequent visiting priests, began to set aside a suite of rooms on the first floor as chapel, a priest's room for conferences and confessions, and a sacristy. In the West Riding of Yorkshire, this occurred in the country houses at Carlton and Quosque in 1667, at Barnbow in 1661, and at Broughton by the 1680s.[12]

In the fifth place, there was a very surprising development for a religion as hierarchical as Catholicism and which exalted the priesthood as highly as it did. It was the growth in days of persecution of a lay spirituality in which either the master of the house (as we have just seen) became a substitute for the priest-chaplain and led in prayers, or there was a desire on the part of groups of women to live informally together to promote the religious life. Evidence for the latter development is found in a document from the Stonyhurst Anglia Mss, dated October 30, 1604, titled, "An instruction and direction for the spiritual helpe of such Inglish gentelwomen as desyre to lead a more retired and recollected life then the ordinarie in Ingland doth yeald."[13] This was similar to what was going on in Italy and Spain at this time. Informal groups of women friends might live together. There was no need for habits, and vows might be taken for a time or permanently, one, two or three of them, as the individual felt able to make the promises. Some, as might be expected, took the further step of entering a religious order. This is how the Benedictine community at Brussels was founded from groups of English exiles under the leadership of Lady Mary Percy. Similarly, the creative Mary Ward organised her Institute of Women, first known as the "Daughters of St. Agnes." They took only private vows and wore no distinctive habits in order to fulfil their active life as teachers of English girls; it was such a success that they numbered over sixty by 1616 and

11 *Ibid.*, p. 248.   12 *Ibid.*, p. 249.
13 Cited by Hugh Aveling, *Northern Catholics; The Catholic Recusants of the North Riding of Yorkshire, 1558-1790* (1966), p. 254.

by 1629 they were to be found in Italy, Germany, and Austria. This lay initiative was remarkably akin to that shown by their opposite numbers, the Puritans, who wanted every household to be a little church, while the Catholics desired every household to be a little monastery. This was a remarkable flourishing of the Counter-Reformation spirit and spirituality.[14]

2. *High Baroque Worship and Ornaments*

The unrestrained Baroque ceremonial of Catholic worship was to be found only in the London chapels of the ambassadors of Catholic countries, or in the chapels of the Stuart Catholic queens, namely, Henrietta Maria, consort of Charles I, or of Catherine of Braganza, consort of Charles II, or, grandiosely, in the chapel of King James II, open in his avowal of Catholicism. These were the great exceptions, but they are important as showing what ordinary Catholic worship lacked and would love to have, had the law and the funds permitted such opulence.

Queen Henrietta Maria's Chapel at Somerset House was completed in 1635, being the work of Inigo Jones, the Surveyor-General and himself a Catholic. Its exterior did not call the Anglican world to notice that this was the fane of a prohibited faith. But the structure and decoration of the interior proclaimed the splendour of Catholicism without any false modesty. The dome was forty feet high, suspended over the altar. The latter was raised on three broad tiers of steps and was separated from the rest of the nave by balustrades. On each side of a columned arch were niches in which there were statues of prophets or saints. Rich tapestries, silver-gilt chandeliers, and many costly vases made this a mirror of contemporary French court ceremonial in worship, although probably a little subdued for English purposes.

The Chapel of the Queen in Somerset House was served by French Capuchins, that Counter-Reformation renewal of the Franciscan Order which returned from relaxation and mitigation to the strong and simple love of the impoverished which had characterized their founder, *Il Poverello*. They laboured tirelessly among London's poor,[15] however splendid their Royal Chapel. Every Saturday the friars recited the Litany of the Blessed Virgin and held the Benediction of the Blessed Sacrament, blessing the congrega-

[14] *Ibid.*, and Hugh Aveling, *Post-Reformation Catholicism in East Yorkshire* (York, 1960), p. 36.
[15] James Lee-Milne, *The Age of Inigo Jones* (1953), pp. 86-89.

466

tion with the Sacrament reserved and exposed in the monstrance.[16] It was an extra-liturgical devotion of great popularity in the sixteenth and seventeenth century, especially among Catholic fraternities. The Capuchins would bring Communion to Catholics on sick beds or in prison, and were humbler than their Oratorian predecessors as the chaplains of the Queen.

Queen Catherine of Braganza, the consort of Charles II, had a Royal Chapel at St. James, which was served by the English Benedictines, one of whom, Father John Huddleston, preserved the life of the future King Charles II on his flight from Worcester fight in 1651 and reconciled him on his deathbed to the Catholic church. Pepys, who seemed more inclined to Presbyterianism than to Catholicism, was impelled by curiosity—seeing the Queen's coach pass by on a Sunday morning—and so, he wrote in his *Diary* for September 16, 1661, "I crowded after her, and I got up to the room where her closet is; and there stood and saw the fine altar, ornaments, and the fryers in their habits, and the priests come in with their fine crosses and many other fine things. . . . By and by, after Masse was done, a fryer with his cowl did rise up and preach a sermon in Portugese, which I not understanding, did go away, and to the King's chapel, but that was done."[17]

John Evelyn, that sturdy Anglican diarist, was more critical of Roman Catholicism at worship. Of one experience, he wrote: "I went to see the fopperies of the Papists at Somerset House and York House, where now the French Ambassador had caus'd to be represented our Blessed Saviour at the Paschal Supper with his Disciples, in figures and puppets made as big as the life, of waxwork, curiously clad and sitting round a large table, the roome nobly hung, and shining with innumerable lamps and candles: this was expos'd to all the world, all the City came to see it, such liberty had the Roman Catholics at this time obtain'd."[18]

In Evelyn's too negative judgment there are implied some of the chief criticisms that could be made of Baroque worship. Waxwork suggests something of its artificiality; "big as life" its theatricality, and the place of this chapel, in a palace, the absolutist monarchs who were its chief supporters. For all the splendour of

16 *Ibid.*, p. 147. For the history of the devotion of the Benediction of the Blessed Sacrament, see the articles of Herbert Thurston, S.J., in *The Month*, Vol. xcvii (1901), pp. 587-97; Vol. xcviii (1901), pp. 58-69, 186-93, 264-76, and Vol. cvi (1905), pp. 394-404.
17 Pepys's *Diary* (Everyman edn., 1906), I, pp. 288-89.
18 Entry for April 4, 1672.

these Royal Chapels, however, and despite the fact that they were meant to serve as the throne room of the King of Kings, Christ, they were not in the least typical of seventeenth-century English Catholic worship. The secret worship of Recusants in barns, or attics, or in remote country houses, where fines mulcted their owners and exposed them to greater risks of imprisonment, was very different, with an improvised altar and confessional, and the candlesticks, kneelers, and vestments hurriedly extracted from a cupboard, all to be rapidly dismantled as soon as a *poursuivant* was glimpsed riding in the distance.

3. *Simpler Celebrations of the Mass*

We must penetrate beyond the furtiveness, the makeshift character, and the probable shabbiness of the appurtenances of such worship, to recognise the astounding loyalty and great risks undertaken to attend or celebrate such worship and the deep sincerity that characterized it. Reports of such clandestine gatherings, where they are to be had at all, are few and short.

There is one vivid description, though all too brief, of a mission centre in the East Riding of Yorkshire in the 1620s at Osgodby Hall, the home of the Recusant family of the Babthorpes. It was frequented by many guests and visitors, and it lodged never less than two priests, and occasionally three or four. One chaplain was appointed to look after the souls of the family and household and another looked after the neighbouring Catholics. The mission centre is described thus:

> Our house I might rather count as a religious house than otherwise, for though there lived together in it three knights and their ladies with their families, yet we had all our servants Catholic. On the Sundays, we locked the doors and all came to Mass, had our sermons, catechisms and spiritual lessons every Sunday and holiday. On the work days we had for the most part two Masses, and of them the one for the servants at six o'clock in the morning at which the gentlemen, every one without fail and the ladies if they were not sick, would even, in the midst of winter, of their own accord be present; and the other we had at eight o'clock for those who were absent from the first. In the afternoon, at four o'clock, we had Evensong, and after that, Matins, at which all the knights and ladies, except extraordinary occasions did hinder them,

would be present, and stay at their prayers all the time the priests were at Evensong and Matins. The most of them daily used some meditation and mental prayer, and all, at the least every fourteen days and great feasts, did confess and communicate; and after supper, every night at nine o'clock, we had all together litanies, and so immediately to bed.[19]

Particularly in the early part of the century the Mass must have been celebrated with only the bare essentials. A manuscript book of the period which provides the missioners with advice for difficult cases of conscience observes that in cases of deep necessity the priest may use an unconsecrated table, an unblessed tin chalice, omit some of the under-vestments, use a single unblessed cloth on the altar and one oil light. Nor is a Crucifix absolutely necessary, however desirable. If the priest can remember the Mass, he need not use a missal. He may have the help of women in serving Mass, and can say Mass in necessity at any time after midnight and until an hour after midday. For a grave reason he can even say three or four Masses a day.[20]

With the distractions of the Civil War and the greater leniency of the Restoration of the monarchy after 1660, the Masses became less streamlined. At this time more permanent house chapels were furnished, and more elaborately. The Yorke family in the West Riding of Yorkshire imported fittings from abroad in the 1650s or 1660s. Their receipted bill for the order shows that they had purchased taffeta for frontals, sets of vestments, six candlesticks, Crucifixes, several holy pictures, several thuribles and an incense boat.

For most Catholics who were not gentry, Mass was celebrated simply, possibly even shabbily, but with great dignity, as can be seen from a longer account of clandestine worship—a generation after our period closes, but still in the "penal days" for English Roman Catholics. The account is of a Mass celebrated by Bishop Challoner in the 1740s to which Mr. and Mrs. Marlow Sidney, a newly married couple, came to be received into the church. Mrs. Sidney recalls the occasion many years later for the benefit of her granddaughter:

19 Hugh Aveling, *Post-Reformation Catholicism in East Yorkshire*, p. 33 citing Henry Foley, *Records of the English Province of the Society of Jesus* (1877-83).
20 Aveling, *The Catholic Recusants of the West Riding of Yorkshire, 1558-1790*, pp. 250-51.

We started from our lodgings at five in the morning to be present for the first time at a Catholic religious service, or at "Prayers" as it was generally called, for the word "Mass" was scarcely ever used in conversation. We arrived at a public house in some back street near the house at which Mr. Horne resided. I felt rather frightened, seeing some very rough-looking poor people as we passed through the entrance, though all was very quiet. These people I was told, were Irish workmen, who, with a few women, were assembled on that Sunday morning to hear "Prayers" when they could be admitted. We hurried past them; but I could not help clinging to Marlow, having a sort of undefined fear of what was going to happen, for I had no inclination to laugh then. We mounted higher and higher, escorted by a young man whom Marlow had seen at the priest's house, who had come forward at once to conduct us. When we arrived at the top, the door of the garret was unlocked, and as we entered we saw at the furthest end what seemed a high table, or a long chest of drawers with the back turned towards us. A piece of carpet was spread before it by the young man, who, after he had placed a few chairs and cushions in order, pointed us to our seats. In a few minutes, the door opened, and the Venerable Dr. Challoner, accompanied by Mr. Horne and another priest, entered the garret, the door of which was secured inside by the assistant, who then proceeded to unlock some drawers behind what I found was to be used as an altar, and take out vestments and other things requisite for the Church service. Water was brought to the Bishop, and from his hands we received our conditional Baptism, which had been fully explained to us. We then, one after the other, entered a sort of closet with the door open, and kneeling, received Absolution, having previously made our confession to Mr. Horne. After returning to our seats, the Bishop put on a vestment and a mitre, and gave us a short and excellent exhortation. We then knelt before him, and he administered to us the Sacrament of Confirmation . . . Soon afterwards we heard the door-key turn, and several rough foot-steps entered the garret; then some gentle taps, and words were exchanged between a powerful-looking Irishman, who kept his post close to it, and those outside, which were pass-words of admission. The key was again turned each time anyone entered, and just before the Bishop vested himself to say Mass, bolts were drawn also, and no one else could pass into the garret. In the meanwhile, the young man in attendance had prepared all that was required for Mass, taken from behind what was used as the altar, which was covered with a linen cloth. A crucifix and two lighted candles were placed on it, and in the front was suspended a piece of satin damask, in the centre of which was a cross in gold lace. The ceremonies of the Mass had been explained to me by Marlow, who seemed to follow the Latin prayers as if he had been used to them all his life. We received the Holy Communion when notice was given to us, both the priests holding before us a linen cloth.

When all was over, and I was praying to God to increase my faith, I heard the door-key turn once more, and all the rough foot-steps leaving the garret. The Bishop having unvested, remained kneeling before us while the people departed. The two priests, assisted by the young man in attendance, replaced the vestments, candlesticks and all that was used at the Mass, behind the altar, locking all up carefully, and leaving the garret an ordinary one in appearance, as before. Mr. Horne then requested us to follow him to the house where he was staying and breakfast with the Bishop. After breakfast we asked his blessing and took our leave; and so ended, that to us, most important morning on which we had received five sacraments of the Catholic Church. During the remainder of our stay in London we heard Mass every Sunday, either in the same garret, or at one of the ambassadors' chapels. Mass was rarely said on weekdays for a congregation.[21]

This report is valuable for its length and its detailed descriptions. It shows us that Catholic worship drew both middle-class and working class to the same service, and the authenticity of the description is proven by the presence of the "bouncer" as comfortable, it would seem, guarding the door at a celebration of the Mass as he would be beside a tavern door. The sense of secrecy and arcaneness for the neophytes, the improvisation of furniture, the simplicity of the ornaments, the dignity and reverence of the service, and the fidelity of the congregation, are most moving

21 E. H. Burton, *The Life and Times of Bishop Challoner* (1691-1781), 2 Vols. (1909), I, pp. 139-41, also cited in Michael Richards, *The Liturgy in England* (1966), pp. 8-10.

in their combined impact. These were the attractions of an unthe-atrical worship in the Baroque Age. Sincerity makes a scenario superfluous.

The paucity of evidence from penal days makes the temptation to generalise difficult to resist, dangerous though it is. Yet it is not even known how public or private the worship of the Recusants had to be during the different decades of this century, except in the first decade when persecution was fierce and during the eighth decade when it was almost non-existent. Lest we should imagine heroics where compliance was possible, it should be recalled that there was a great gulf between theory and practice in persecution; there were vagaries in royal policy, exceptions were made for rela-tives, officials were often venial and occasionally humane, and a good lawyer could exploit the complexities of the legal system.[22]

What was the strength of Catholicism in this dark century? The most reliable source of information for the country comes from a report of Gregoris Panzani, Papal envoy to the English court from 1634-1637, *Breve raguaglio di alcuni abusi introdotti nella Chiesa anglicana, delle Cause di esse el modo estirparli dal quale si rac-cogli il miserissimo stato de Catholici in Inghilterra suiche savanno senza Vescovi.*[23] Panzani estimates that there are about 600 priests of whom only 100 are in first-class positions. The latter are lodged by approximately one-fifth of the peerage (24 lords out of 130) or by perhaps 75 of the lesser nobility or gentlemen. Many of them are concentrated in London which harbours too many hopeful priests in search of generous patrons. In many of the remoter parts of England, many Catholics die without receiving the sacraments. The religious orders take in more postulants than they can afford to maintain.

Two-thirds of the priests were secular, and about one-third were members of orders. In 1632 there were 164 Jesuit fathers,[24] and a year later there were 63 Benedictine priests[25] in the English congregation.

Panzani's report casts some light in the liturgical darkness of the period in its recounting of abuses, caused in part by the com-petitiveness of the priesthood. For example, we learn that some

22 Aveling, *Post-Reformation Catholics in East Yorkshire*, p. 38.

23 Archives of the Sacred Congregation for the Propagation of the Faith, Rome, *Anglia*, I, pp. 99-143. It is summarised by Philip Hughes, *Rome and the Counter-Reformation in England* (1942), pp. 409-12.

24 *Records of the English Province of the Society of Jesus* (ed. Henry Foley, 1875-1883), I, pp. lxxiii-lxv, cited by Philip Hughes, *op. cit.*, p. 336.

25 *Catholic Record Society*, Vol. XXXIII (1933), p. 265.

priests, in order to maintain their dependence on more than one family, did not hesitate to celebrate two or three Masses on the same Sunday. A list of twenty priests is given with their irregularities in worship. Some of them allow children to be baptized in the parish church. Others admit parents to the sacraments who permit their children to attend heretical services. Others make an alteration in a will a condition of granting Absolution to the dying. Three, it is alleged, are married and continue to act as priests, and one of them is a bigamist. It is a melancholy record of desperation and an indication of the great difficulties in "the most pitiable state of the Catholic in England."

But if these are the black threads in the tapestry, there is also the crimson of martyrdom. As Philip Hughes reminds us,[26] the very same years exhibit such saintly Jesuits as Edmund Arrowsmith and Henry More, Benedictines as holy as John Roberts and Ambrose Barlow, seraphic Franciscans such as Henry Heath and Arthur Bell, and heroic seculars such as William Ward and John Southworth. Each of these prepared for the crown of the martyrs by lives of consecration and danger, and made the sensitive worshippers to whom they administered the sacraments aware of the sanctoral succession which transforms a squalid conventicle into a Pentecostal palace of the Holy Spirit. It was, in these penal years that Father Augustine Baker, the Benedictine monk, was preparing his masterpiece of devotional theology *Sancta Sophia, or, Holy Wisdom*.[27]

The mention of Father Baker's name is sufficient to recall the importance of the Benedictine ideal maintained steadily during these years. Father Baker himself thought the period had exaggerated the importance of the role of the spiritual director, and he modestly conceived of himself as only "God's usher." Furthermore, he claimed an important place for affective prayer as a stage in prayer distinct from meditation and distinct also from the extraordinarily difficult forced acts of the will.[28] A tribute to his teaching is the spiritual life of the Benedictine nun, Dame Gertrude More,[29]

[26] Hughes, *op. cit.*, p. 429.

[27] It appeared posthumously in 2 Vols. in 1657. See *Memorials of Father Augustine Baker and other Documents relating to the English Benedictines*, ed. J. McCann and [R.] H. Connolly (*Catholic Record Society*, Vol. XXXIII, 1933), pp. 1-154. His spirituality is discussed in the chapter of that title in this present volume.

[28] See David Mathew, *Catholicism in England* (1936), p. 273.

[29] See Augustine Baker's *The Inner Life of Dame Gertrude More* (ed. Benedict Weld-Blundell, 1911), and H. Lane Fox, *The Holy Practices of a Divine Lover* (1909).

a woman of wit and spirit, and of austere dedication, who was a worthy descendant of St. Thomas More. A postulant at the English Benedictine congregation at Cambrai in 1623, her distress caused by scruples and fierce temptations was removed under the direction of Fr. Baker, and her reputation for sanctity caused her to be made abbess at twenty-three. She died four years later, but not without bequeathing to the future her *Confessiones Amantis* which defend her way of prayer and contain "affective meditations of considerable beauty."[30]

Such spirituality is the austere and visible tip of the shining iceberg, the vast and invisible depths of which are submerged, and strong. These depths were the English religious communities abroad. If Elizabethan Catholicism was "red martyrdom" (with its prodigal effusion of martyrs' blood), then Jacobean and Caroline Catholicism was marked by "white martyrdom" (the efflorescence of spirituality in the monasteries and convents of the English abroad). At the beginning of the reign of Charles I an English Catholic travelling on the Continent could have visited a community of Augustinian Canonesses at St. Ursula's in Louvain with a group of twenty-two English nuns, and an English daughter-house would be founded in the same city three years later (St. Monica's). He would also have found English houses of Poor Clares at Gravelines, Franciscans and Benedictines at Brussels, and Carmelites at Antwerp.[31] These communities were sustained by the Mass and the Daily Office. Their life was vigorous. They abounded in vocations, and by their examples of a life dedicated to holiness encouraged members of their own natural families in England to emulate their holiness. By 1642 there were some seventeen completely English convents belonging to eight different orders, besides an unknown number of English nuns or postulants in foreign communities.

There were also over forty religious communities for men, eventually six seminaries for the theological training of priests, and a few secular colleges in the Low Countries in the middle decades of the seventeenth century. The tide of Counter-Reformation spiritual life was running high. One striking example of it comes from the West Riding of Yorkshire, where from an adult Catholic community of only 1,500 there was produced among the men, 33 Benedictines, 6 Carthusians, 5 Franciscans, 1 Dominican, and 35

---

[30] *The Oxford Dictionary of the Christian Church*, ed. F. L. Cross, p. 923b.
[31] Mathew, *op. cit.*, p. 72.

Jesuits, 80 in all.[32] Among these sacred refuges of the English pride of place must be given to Douai because it was in that great seminary founded by Cardinal Allen that many of the martyrs and missionaries were trained. There, too, was the principal school for the sons of English Recusants, and there, also, British Benedictine monks gathered themselves together into a community again. This was a power-house of devotion, discipline, and learning, as well as of publishing.

4. Baptisms, Marriages, and Burials

It was to be expected that the first service book for the use of post-Reformation English Catholics would be published at Douai in 1604. Its title was: *Sacra Institutio Baptizandi, Matrimonium Celebrandi, Infirmos Ungendi, Mortuos Sepelandi, ac alii nonnulli ritus ecclesiastici juxta usum insignis Ecclesiae Sarisburiensis* and it was republished in 1610 (Old Style), but with another title, namely, *Manuale Sacerdotum, hoc est Ritus administrandi Sacramenta Baptismi.* This title served as a reminder that it was substantially a re-arrangement of portions of the old Sarum *Manuale.* It provides us with a picture of the celebration of Baptism and of Marriage before the introduction of the official *Rituale Romanum*, identified with Pope Paul V, which appeared in 1614.

In Baptism, the rubrics of the Sarum *Manuale* made it crystal clear that infants were invariably baptized, apart from rare exception, by immersion. The priest was to stand at the western side of the font, take the child (presumably nude) from the godmother and holding it by the sides, with the infant's face away from him,[33] he dipped it into the water three times, the infant's head always pointing to the east, and thus in the direction of the altar. The priest first plunged the child into the water, right side downwards so its face was toward the north, saying, *N. ego baptizo te in nomine Patris*, next he immersed it, face downwards, so its face was towards the south, saying, *et Filii*, and lastly face downwards, saying, *et Spiritus Sancti, Amen.* Priests in penal times must have found it difficult to employ Baptism by immersion requiring the use of a capacious font. Yet the rubrics were retained because this

[32] Aveling, *The Catholic Recusants of the West Riding of Yorkshire*, p. 237.
[33] Herbert Thurston, S.J., "English Ritualia, Old and New" in *The Month*, Vol. CXXVI, No. 613 (July 1915), pp. 61-62. The Latin reads: "Deinde accipiat sacerdos infantem per latera, in manibus suis . . . et mergat eum semel versa facie ad quilonem et capite versus orientem, etc."

was a hallowed English tradition, but the *Rituale Romanum* which displaced the Sarum *Manuale* and its derivatives assumed that infusion would replace immersion as the mode of Baptism.

The first edition of the *Rituale Romanum* of 1614, which the English *Ordo Baptizandi* of 1626 and subsequent editions follows exactly, provides the following directions: "Then the god-father, or the god-mother, or the two together (if it be a case in which there are both) holding the child, the priest takes baptismal water from a vessel or ewer and pours some of it over the head of the infant in the form of a cross, and pronouncing the words at the same time, says once, distinctively and attentively, *N. ego baptizo te*, etc."

Although the Council of Trent required that there should be only one sponsor, whether godmother or godfather, or at the most both, the Douai *Manuale* consistently speaks of *patrini* and *matrinae* in the plural, but places a limit at three persons. There are two brief addresses to the godparents (one printed in English) which are both taken from the earlier Sarum books.

The supposed benefits of the Sacrament of Baptism are listed in the celebrated *Short Catechisme of Cardinall Bellarmine illustrated with Images* and Englished in 1614. The distinguished Jesuit theologian asks: "What effect doth Baptisme work?" and the answer he provides reads: "It maketh a man become the Child of God and heire of Paradise; it blotteth out all sinnes and filleth the soul with grace and spirituall gifts."[34]

Recusants faced great difficulties in arranging for Catholic Baptism for their children. This is evident from the problems of missioners when their charges pleaded the case for exceptions. The theory is, of course, that Catholic children are not to be baptized by Anglican clergymen. In practice, however, permission was given for Catholics under the tutelage of Anglican relatives on whom they depended financially to have their children baptized at Anglican fonts. They were also allowed to have them first secretly baptized by a Catholic priest and then proceed to an Anglican Baptism. Moreover, they were even permitted to bribe the Anglican clergyman to enter the names of their children in the parish register that he may give it out falsely that he has baptized them.[35] These equivocations dishonour the persecutors as much as they do the victims.

[34] *Ibid.*, p. 73.
[35] Hugh Aveling, *The Catholic Recusants of the West Riding of Yorkshire*, pp. 250-51.

The most important revision of the Douai *Manuale* was that of 1626, which incorporated the changes brought about in the *Rituale Romanum* of twelve years before. The most important change in the Marriage Service was the substitution of a simple Roman form of consent for the complex medieval promises of bride and groom. The bride's promise to obey her husband, though still retained as late as 1662 in the Anglican Prayer Book, was abolished in the Roman order.[36]

It has been seen that in cases of great difficulty a certain latitude was allowed for Baptism by Anglican clergy. No such leniency was permitted in the case of Marriage by Anglican clergy, for that was always regarded as apostasy from Catholicism. Recusants, therefore, had to be married before a Catholic priest and witnesses, if a priest could be found. According to the medieval canon law, which was still valid in this matter, a clandestine marriage, whether by the two parties alone or before witnesses, was regarded as valid by the Roman Catholic church and if a priest could not be found, it was also lawful. All Catholic couples in penal times were in danger of being delated to Anglican ecclesiastical courts for contracting secret marriages and the priest who had married them would also be endangered.[37]

Extreme Unction, or the Viaticum, continued to be a highly important Sacrament. It could not be received in the Baroque setting, with which the rite was dignified in France, as for example, in Picart's illustration. The latter shows the dying man supported beneath a canopied bed, while the elegant priest bends gracefully over to offer him the Host. In the foreground are members of the family devoutly kneeling, the men with tricorned hats held carefully in the crook of their left arm and shoulder and hands piously clasped, while the women meekly kneel with upward pointed hands, and the several bewigged priests are crossing themselves. A richly carved side table bears a Crucifix and two long candlesticks, and in the columned doorway partly hidden by rich hangings, men bearing torches can be seen.[38] It is clearly an important social as well as religious occasion.

For the English Recusants the receiving of the Viaticum was not a social, but only a religious event of importance. The Jesuit,

---

36 Thurston, *op. cit.*, p. 73.

37 Aveling, *The Catholic Recusants of the West Riding of Yorkshire*, p. 251.

38 Bernard Picart, *Les Cérémonies et Coutûmes Religieuses de tous les peuples du monde* (Amsterdam, 1723), II, pp. 74-76, with appropriate accompanying illustration.

Father John Gerard, has left an account of the great efficacy this Sacrament was believed to possess at this time. The person receiving the Viaticum was the married sister of his host, the latter being Sir Philip Wodehouse of Kimberley who had been knighted for his services under the Earl of Essex in the Cadiz voyage. Father Gerard writes:

> I must not omit mentioning an instance of the wonderful efficacy of the Sacraments as shown in the case of the married sister of my host. She had married a man of high rank, and being favourably inclined to the Church, she had been well prepared by her brother, that it cost me but little to labour to make her a child of the Catholic Church. After her conversion she endured much from her husband when he found that she refused to join in heretical worship, but her patience withstood and overcame all. It happened on one occasion that she was so exhausted after a difficult and dangerous labour, that her life was despaired of. A clever physician was at once brought from Cambridge, who on seeing her said that he could indeed give her medicine, but that he could give no hopes of her recovery, and having prescribed some remedies, he left. I was at that time on a visit to the house, having come, as was my wont, with her brother [a notable Recusant]. The master of the house was glad to see us, although he knew well we were Catholics, and used in fact to dispute with me on religious subjects. I had nearly convinced his understanding and judgment, but the will was rooted to the earth, "for he had great possessions." But being anxious for his wife whom he dearly loved, he allowed his brother to persuade him, as there was no longer any hope for her present life, to allow her all freedom to prepare for the life to come. With his permission, we promised to bring in an old Priest on the following night: for these Priests who were ordained before Elizabeth's reign were not exposed to such dangers and penalties as the others. We therefore made use of his ministry, in order that this lady might receive all the rites of the Church. Having made her confession and been anointed, she received the Holy Viaticum; and behold in an hour's time she so far recovered as to be wholly out of danger; the disease and its cause had vanished, and she had only to recover her strength. The husband, seeing his wife thus snatched from the jaws of death,

478

wished to know the reason. We told him it was one of the effects of the holy sacrament of Extreme Unction, that it restored bodily health when Divine Wisdom foresaw that it was expedient for the good of the soul. This was the cause of his conversion; for admiring the power and efficiency of the Sacraments of the true Church, he allowed himself to be persuaded to seek in that Church the health of his own soul.[39]

Shortly after receiving Extreme Unction the recipient usually died. Burials created great difficulties for English Catholics. The law demanded an Anglican Burial Service, and Recusants being usually excommunicated by Anglicans were denied burial in Anglican churches and graveyards, and these were the only legal burying places. The only way out of this difficulty was to arrange for the secret burial of a Recusant by his or her relations at night, and this was not uncommon. In 1677 Robert Sherburne of Stonyhurst was accused of burying the corpse of a Romish priest in Mitton parish church without asking the vicar to officiate. In the more lenient 1630s there was a practice of the relatives of a dead Recusant obtaining a formal permission for ecclesiastical burial by the device of assuring the authorities that the Recusant had regretted his defection from Anglicanism when at the point of death.[40] Panzani reported that such Catholic relatives as had to accept an Anglican burial for the deceased member of their family used to bless a little earth and throw it on the corpse in the coffin, thus "Catholicising" the Anglican ceremony.[41] Apparently, some also were able to purchase immunity from excommunication as the price for a genuinely Catholic burial. It is a sad and seamy story.

In 1721, when the practice of Catholicism was less dangerous, it is intriguing to read that Elizabeth Dunbar, wife of Charles Fairfax, caught the smallpox, died, and "Prayers" (a Requiem Mass) were said for her in the Bath chapel at her burial and on the anniversary, while "the persons that said prayers for Lady Dunbar in all the chapels were forty"—the traditional number of Masses.[42]

[39] Augustus Jessop, *One Generation of a Norfolk House* (1879), pp. 206-207; the same incident can be found in a different translation from the Latin original on pp. 19-20 of *John Gerard, the Autobiography of an Elizabethan* (1951), trans. Philip Caraman.

[40] Aveling, *The Catholic Recusants of the West Riding of Yorkshire*, p. 252.

[41] Cited by G. Anstruther, *Vaux of Harrowden, A Recusant Family* (Newport, Monmouthshire, 1953), p. 453.

[42] Aveling, "The Catholic Recusancy of the Yorkshire Fairfaxes," in *Recusant History*, No. 6 (1961-1962), p. 18.

5. *The Meaning of the Mass*

Hitherto we have been concerned to discover how the Recusants worshipped in the seventeenth century; now it is of greater interest to ask how the chief means of grace, the Blessed Sacrament of the Altar, was interpreted, and how communicants were taught to regard it and to prepare to receive Communion. At different times in the history of the Christian church different facets of its many meanings have been stressed. Indeed, it is not the least of the merits of Dom Gregory Dix's remarkable book, *The Shape of the Liturgy*, that it shows that while the central actions of the liturgy in east and west have remained the same, yet their interpretation has varied from time to time. Sometimes it is the memorial aspect which is stressed; at other times it is a proleptic anticipation of the Eucharistic banquet in eternity. Sometimes it is the concept of a mystery that prevails; at other times the idea of sacrifice dominates the rite. Sometimes thanksgiving and blessing are the main concerns; at other times it is communion with God.

In the seventeenth century (as in the Counter-Reformation of the sixteenth) in sheer contrast with the emphasis on *beneficium* and thanksgiving in Luther, as in contradistinction from the memorial emphasis in Zwingli and in Calvin (though the latter's emphasis on the dynamic power of the Holy Spirit led the way to an *epiklesis* in certain Calvinian rites), the primary, if not the exclusive, Catholic emphasis was on *sacrifice*.[43] This is made plain in the expositions written by English priests during our period or translated from foreign originals by them.

Two of the most notable interpretations of the Mass are the work of Jesuits John Heigham of Douai and Henry FitzSimon of Dublin. Heigham's is called *A Devout Exposition of the Holie Masse with an ample Declaration of all the Rites and Ceremonies belonging to the same* (Douai, 1614, with an expanded second edition in 1622). His reasons for writing the exposition, apart from the general need for it, are: "the incomparable dignitie and most excellent sublimitie of this divine and dreadfull sacrifice"; the great honour and reverence which devout Catholics have always

---

[43] The missals used by missionary priests in England in the first three decades of the seventeenth century were: (1) *Missae aliquot pro sacerdotibus itinerantibus in Anglia, Ex Missale Romano reformata* (1615 [St. Omer, English College Press]); (2) *Missale parvum pro sacerdotibus in Anglia itinerantibus, Ordo etiam baptizandi & rituale . . . extractus* (1623) which was issued in two parts, and (3) *Missale parvum pro sacerdotibus in Anglia, Scotia, & Ibernia itinerantibus* issued in three parts in 1626, the third part, without a title, containing three supplementary Masses.

paid to this Sacrament; and, a true Counter-Reformation motive and motif, "the deep, mortall and cankred mallice of wicked heretics, their most execrable blasphemies in contempt of this divine sacrifice. . . ."[44]

The Mass is declared to be the most excellent of all Sacraments because of "the great and superabundant grace which it containeth," and to be both "a Sacrament and a Sacrifice," which is "the most noble, divine, and most worthy that ever was offered nor can there possibly be a greater, it being no other then the onlie, true, and eternall Sonne of God."[45] The superlatives, typical of the Baroque decking out of the Sacrament, cloy. Heigham insists that the vestments of the priest celebrating, the richness and variety of the ornaments, the magnificence of churches and altars, the plenitude of lights, and the splendour of the ceremonies have as their main aim to declare the greatness, sanctity, and power of the Sacrifice of the Mass. To emphasize this point he likens it to a man who, on entering a great palace, and observing the arras and tapestry hanging on its walls, presumes that the owner must be a personage of nobility and wealth, for poor people could never own such a splendid house. So it is in attending Mass, for wise and virtuous men would not be at such expense unless they believed that this work was the greatest to which any man can devote his attention in the world.[46] The Baroque piety, with its strong sacerdotal emphasis, reaches its apex in the claim that the priestly dignity in offering Christ as a sacrifice excels that of the Blessed Virgin, for she "once onlie, corporallie conceived the Sonne of God," whereas "Priests as his instruments are dailie the cause that the selfsame Sonne of God . . . is trulie and reallie present in the Blessed Sacrament."[47] The end of the Mass is "chieflie to honour God, by and with soe divine a Sacrifice." The Mass is also offered for the preservation of the universal church, and the propagation of the Catholic religion, and for the Pope's Holiness; also for bishops, pastors and religious persons; for peace and concord among Christian princes; for parents, friends, and benefactors; for thanksgiving to God for all his benefits; and for our temporal substance; "and generally for all manner of necessities either of soul or body."[48] Perhaps most striking, because the image is partly used unconsciously, is the constant likening of the setting of worship to an

---

44 *Ibid.*, p. 3.
46 *Ibid.*, pp. 7-8.
48 *Ibid.*, p. 17.

45 *Op. cit.*, p. 6.
47 *Ibid.*, p. 11.

earthly royal court, and worship itself is viewed as court etiquette in the presence of the King of Kings. The monarchical image conveys both the absolute obedience due to God, and the impressiveness that should characterize worship. The first fruit of the Mass, says Heigham, is "that a man is admitted into the inward familiarity of our Lord Jesus Christ, and to be neare his person, as his secretarie or chamberlaine, where he both heareth and seeth so manie devine secrets: which places and roomes in the courts of earthlie Princes, are so much sought after even by the greatest Lords and Nobles of this world, and are so highly esteemed that oftentimes they are content to serve their whole life for them without anie recompense at all in the end: whereas our Lord Jesus Christ (the King of Heaven and earth, doth never unles he be forsaken) forsake him who hath done him service, nor leaveth him without reward and recompense."[49]

If splendour indicates the "real presence" of the Divine King, bareness implies the real absence. The churches of heretics are so "utterlie destitute of all hangings, and other costlie ornamentes, yea so emptie and quite disfurnished, that to enter into them is much like as to enter into some emptie grange or barne, after all the corne, hay and strawe, is carried out of it." Some heretics travelling into Catholic countries overseas have been converted to Catholicism by the magnificence of the ornaments of their churches. They, seeing the "ornamentes, riches, and beautifull ceremonies of the Catholike Church do so greatlie wonder and admire thereat that when they do depart, they find themselves so marvelouslie delighted and comforted thereby, as if they had bin for the time in some earthlie Paradise. Yea, to some this hath bin a chief motive of their change & conversion to the Catholike faith."[50]

The second and augmented edition of Heigham's work appeared in 1622, and it is significant that its theory of Consecration expressly links the Transubstantiation of the bread and wine into the Body and Blood of Christ, with his creative power as the Second Person of the Holy Trinity. "After the giving of thankes," writes Heigham, "he imparted the virtu of his holie benediction upon the bread, and converted the substance thereof in to that of his pretious bodie. The same likewise he did at the creation of the world, when he ordayned the increase and multiplication of his creatures, everie one accordinge to his kind. Never do we reade that he blessed the bread, but that there insued some notable miracle, as in the multiplica-

[49] *Ibid.*, pp. 20-21.   [50] *Ibid.*, p. 35.

tion of the five loaves and the two fishes, whereof the fragments were twelve baskets, after the refection of five thousand soules."[51]

The other interpretation of the Mass by a Jesuit, is Henry Fitz-Simon's *The Justification and Exposition of the Divine Sacrifice of the Masse and of al Rites and Ceremonies* appeared in 1611. It was divided into two books. The first dealt with controversies, difficulties, and devotions of the Mass; the second with a vindication and detailed exposition of the action and symbolism of the Mass. What is perhaps most remarkable is the repeated double emphasis on the Mass as the presence of the King of Kings and the rich ornaments appropriate for such a celebration. The book differs from Heigham's only in being directed against the Puritans now growing increasingly powerful as an opposition to the religious establishment. The image of the sovereign majesty of God on his throne and his monarchical presence appears in widely scattered passages of a lengthy book. "I have seen," writes FitzSimon, "the ushers exact a fine in the chamber of presence, if any weare not bare headed befor the cloth of Estate, in which the only images of lions and dragons are figured: yea, and the very cushions wherupon the Deputie of Irland was to sit at time of sermon, to be borne in al wether by gentlemen bare headed; & passers by for honour therto to discover their heads. . . . I therfor can not conceave, why we Catholiks may be iudiciously reprehended for our wonted devotion toward the expresse resemblance of Christ, or his Saincts, when we passe to, or befor them."[52] The image of the throne is applied to the Virgin, by citing a Mariological passage from the liturgy of St. James with its stiff Latinity in the translation into English: "To the ô ful of grace, doth every Creature gratulat, both the troups of Angels, and al mankinde, which art the sanctifyed temple, the spiritual paradise, the glorie of virgins, from whom our God assumpted flesh, and became a childe, who was befor al time. He made thy wombe a throne, and thy bellie more broad, and ample, then the very heavens."[53]

FitzSimon, too, contrasts the richness and glory of Catholic Churches with the nakedness of heretical churches, accusing the "late reformers" of being happy to criticise the splendour of Catholic churches only because they have purloined them to make a brave show at a banquetting table and "to adorne his wives beddchamber with curtins and cushins."[54] With admirable rhetoric he

---

[51] *Ibid.* (2nd edn.), p. 252.
[53] *Ibid.*, p. 217.

[52] *Op. cit.* (1st edn.), pp. 124-25.
[54] *Ibid.*, p. 16.

demands whether "the naked Churches, the glasseles patent win-
dowes, the ruinous roofs, the razed monuments, the rotten lofts,
and unpaved flooers belonging to God, compared to their own
hauty habitations, delightsome prospects, sumptuous galeries, silke
tapistrie, cupboards plate, and all desirable commodities, demon-
strat, that their studie is turned from the ould to the new, from
God to the bellie, from devotion to dissolution, from charity to
carnality?"[55]

The expositions of both Heigham and FitzSimon, while showing
the new Jesuit emphasis on worship as an offering to the greater
glory of God, and obeisance to the King of Kings, so vividly re-
imagined in the *Spiritual Exercises* annually undergone by every
member of the Society, and emphasize the importance of Catholic
honouring of the Mass to make reparation for heretical insults
against it, also make use of the medieval allegorical explanation
of the actions and ornaments and appurtenances of the Mass.[56]

The point of the retention of the allegorical interpretation of the
actions of the Mass may be made from another Jesuit treatise, that
of the Frenchman, Nicolas Caussin, translated by T. H. [Sir
Thomas Hawkins] and printed at Paris in 1626. This insists that
one must concentrate on the signification of all the parts of the
Mass: "as at the Confession to represent yourselfe Man, banished
from Paradise, miserable, supplyant, confessing, deploring his
sinne. At the Introite, the enflamed desires of all nature, expecting
the *Messias*. At the *Hymne* of angels, Glory be to God on high, the
Nativity. At the prayers, thanksgiving for such a benefit. At the
Epistle, the preaching of the precursor, *S. Iohn*. At the Ghospell,
truth preached by the Saviour of the World, and so of the rest."
As if this were not already enough, it is stated that the Mass must
be divided into "certayne parcels" and thus "represent to your selfe
five great things in the Mystery of the Masse from which you
ought to dream of so many fruits; These five things are, Representation, Prayse, Sacrifice, Instruction, Nourishment."[57]

It was, of course, never forgotten by Catholics that the Mass
was primarily a sacrifice for the living and the dead; the common-
est term for it was the one Henry FitzSimon uses—a "propitiatory
sacrifice"—which he defines as "a reconciliation of God offended, a
defacing of the obligation to suffre punishment; the universal doc-

[55] *Ibid.*
[56] Heigham, *op. cit.*, pp. 3, 16, 28-34, 52-59, 207; and FitzSimon, *op. cit.*,
pp. 167, 187, 343.
[57] *Op. cit.*, p. 399.

trin of the Church."[58] There was also a very strong subordinate stress on the miracle and mystery of the Mass. Nowhere is this more strongly exhibited than in FitzSimon's defence of the use of Latin in the rite, primarily because this preserves the mystery of the Mass. It is alleged (quite wrongly in fact) that Jesus did not use the vernacular language when he cried out, *Eli, Eli, Lama Sabachthani.* It is further urged that the mysteries of divinity, philosophy, science, and physic, are concealed and not conveyed to the common people. Nor should the highest mysteries of religion be subjugated to the understanding of common folk. For "as *panis absconditus suavior,* the secret bread is sweeter, so the hidden mysteries are in greater respect and veneration."[59] Augustine is cited to show that it is not quickness of understanding but simplicity of believing that makes the common sort more secure, and it is argued that the safeguarding of altars with rails is a symbolic proof that the Mass was never applied to the vulgar understanding.[60] While the "elitism" of Latinity must have appealed to the sacerdotalists, and while it was argued that Latin provided uniformity in worship (among the intellectuals), and an invariability in the rite and therefore less danger of misinterpretation, it was curiously forgotten that the over-emphasis on mystery and transcendence can easily result in maintaining the divine "Otherness" at the cost of human nescience. One has the disturbing conviction that the acceptance of the vernacular tongue could not be argued on its own grounds because it would be thought to be a concession to Protestantism, just as that any emphasis on the joint participation of the people of God would have been seen as an anti-sacerdotal move. Catholics and Protestants were locked into their assailable but impregnable fortresses of faith and practice in this period. (It has taken four centuries to erode them.)

6. *Popular Devotions*

It is often forgotten that the remarkable renewal of Counter-Reformation spirituality seen most strikingly in the Spanish saints and writers on spirituality[61] such as St. Ignatius Loyola, Luis of Granada, and Sts. Teresa of Avila and John of the Cross, had a powerful if indirect impact on England through the exiles and missionary priests who followed the new methods of devotion, or

[58] *Ibid.,* pp. 87-88.   [59] *Ibid.,* pp. 90-91.   [60] *Ibid.,* p. 91.
[61] Catholic spirituality in England is treated in more detail in Chap. III, entitled, "Spirituality: Preparation for Public Worship."

who translated them into English and sent copies of these works to their relations and friends at home. While the works of the Carmelites were only for the advanced mystics, and had little effect on the day-to-day life of lay Catholics, this was emphatically not the case with Ignatian or Salesian spirituality, nor was it true of devotions of the Rosary or the cult of the Sacred Heart.

The Jesuits were the most significant missionary priests in England in our period, and they had a powerful impact on thoughtful laymen and women. In particular, the *Exercitia Spiritualia* was a form of meditation that aimed at total transformation of the inner man and which led at its conclusion into mysticism for the many. This book of instructions on how to make a successful retreat and lead to a firm resolution to be Christ's soldier, activated the intellect, the senses, and the imagination, with the aim of influencing the will to make the firm decision to order one's life according to the purpose of God and to "think with the Church." The book breathes the spirit of the new age, since it is intimately concerned with human psychology: so much so that visualization of the Christ of the Gospels and meditation on him is encouraged, not as an end in itself, but rather as a spur to the individual who uses these "Exercises" as a generous service of God *ad majorem Dei gloriam*—the motto of the Society of Jesus founded by St. Ignatius. The Exercises end with a section called "Contemplation for Obtaining Love" which is a description of the mystical life.[62] The educational work of the Jesuits ensured that many young men of ability committed their lives to Christ, and as priests of the Society they expressed its profound sense of obedience, its vitality, and its vividness in the brilliant and entrancing worship they conducted, as brilliant as the sermons they preached or the monstrances with effulgent rays in which they exposed the Host.

Another exceedingly popular writer on spirituality was Luis of Granada, the Dominican, whose *Libro de la Oracion* (1553)[63] provided a detailed method of prayer simpler to follow than the Ignatian. This stressed the value of the preparation of the heart in devotion, and provided fourteen meditations on the Passion and the Last Things. His influence was great on St. Francis of Sales whose

---

[62] The substance of this paragraph is derived in part from Hilda Graeff's *The Story of Mysticism* (1966), pp. 232f.

[63] His influence is recognized in John Gee's *The Foot out of the Snare* (1624) in a list of Catholic books for sale in England and surreptitiously published, including "Granadoes *Memoriall*, Granadoes *Compendium*, and Granadoes *Meditations*, translated" (sig. S3).

Introduction to the Devout Life[64] (1608) removed piety from the cloister to the home and the street.

Of course, the most popular Catholic devotion was that of the Rosary,[65] which commended itself by its simplicity, its mnemonic devices, and its convenience, especially when the liturgy had to be celebrated secretly and sporadically. The Mysteries of the Rosary direct attention to fifteen subjects of meditation, divided into three groups of five. The "Joyful Mysteries" are: the Annunciation, the Visitation, the Nativity of Christ, the Presentation of Christ in the Temple, and finding the Child Jesus there. The five "Sorrowful Mysteries" recall the Agony of Christ in Gethsemane, the Scourging, the Crowning with Thorns, the Carrying of the Cross, and the Crucifixion. The "Glorious Mysteries" are the Resurrection, the Ascension, the Descent of the Holy Spirit at Pentecost, the Assumption of the Virgin into Heaven, and her Coronation, providing— apart from the two final extra-Biblical events—an admirable summary of the Christ epic or events in the New Testament.

The importance of the Rosary in the seventeenth century is witnessed to by the establishment by the English Benedictines of a Chapel of the Rosary, which was probably housed in the London home of the Earl of Cardigan, the Prefect or protector of the sodality. The first Dean was Father Anselm Crowder, who was greatly devoted to the Blessed Virgin and in her honour he obtained a privilege from Pope Innocent X for an altar of Our Blessed Lady of Power. The Chapel was frequented by those who could no longer attend the Chapel Royal at Somerset House which was forbidden to Catholics during the Commonwealth and Protectorate. The opulently devout presented the chapel with important relics including one of the thorns from Christ's Crown of Thorns, and a piece of the true Cross. Dom Hugh Connolly reported[66] having seen a booklet of thirty-one pages (no longer extant) entitled, *The Method of Saying the Rosary of Our Blessed Lady, As it was ordered by Pope Pius the Fifth, of the Holy Order of Preachers, And as it is said in her Majesties Chappel at St. James* (1669). The royal sponsor

---

[64] Gee, *op. cit.* (sig. 82), also lists this work of de Sales translated by York, a London Jesuit.

[65] Gee, *ibid.*, also lists four books on the Rosary: *The Rosary of Our Lady; Meditations upon the Rosary; An Exposition of the Rosary;* and *The Mysteries of the Rosary.* See also Herbert Thurston, S.J., "Genuflexions and Aves, a study in Rosary Origins," in *The Month,* Vol. 127 (1916), pp. 546-59; also an earlier part of the same article in same Vol., pp. 441-52.

[66] "The Benedictine Chapel of the Rosary in London," in *The Downside Review,* Vol. LII (1934), pp. 320-29.

of this devotion was Catherine of Braganza, Queen of Charles II. The second Dean of the Rosary Chapel was Father Thomas Vincent Sadler who died in the monastery of Dieulouard (where he may have sought refuge during the time of the Titus Oates plot). The inventory of the effects in his custody specified as belonging to the Rosary Altar at Cardigan House in London, include the following objects of silver: statues of SS. Benedict and Joseph, a large Cross and Crucifix, six candlesticks, a lamp, two large flower pots, various important relics, together with a chalice, vestments, and "a wooden statue of our Bl. Lady & Savr., which usually was dressed in silken clothes when set upon the Altar."[67] From these hints we can visualize the splendour of the Altar of Our Lady of Power and the riches of those who supported the Benedictines.

The last new devotion of the century was that of the Sacred Heart, one that would be more directly related to the Blessed Sacrament, and aimed at the reparation of the insults against the love of Christ caused by the coldness of Catholics or the blasphemies of heretics. This was the vision vouchsafed to a Visitandine nun, St. Margaret Mary Alacoque (1647-1691) belonging to an Order of which the co-founder was St. Francis of Sales. This visionary and devout nun was directed by the Jesuit Père de la Colombière at Paray-le-Monial. It was too late in the century to have a profound impact on English spirituality in our period. It is, however, significant in having a link with England, in that St. Margaret-Mary's director was a chaplain to the Duchess of York, later the Queen and Consort of James II. De la Colombière[68] it was who preached and popularized the cult of the Sacred Heart of Jesus.

The danger of sentimentality was inherent in this cult, but far more important was its correlation with the liturgy and the Sacrament of Sacrifice. It was not a pious extra, nor a devotion for the elite. On the contrary, it encouraged Mass for the masses. Its very sentimentality can be defended in part as a challenge to the rationalistic inroads of deism which would otherwise have blighted the blossoms of devotion with the frosts of reductionism.

One can say, in conclusion, that while a secret worship lacked splendour, the clandestine character of Roman Catholic worship in England for most of our period saved it from the obvious defects

[67] *The Downside Review*, Vol. LII (1934), p. 590.
[68] This information I owe to Dr. D. M. Rogers, authority on English Recusant history, of the Bodleian Library, Oxford, in an interview of August 25, 1971.

of the Baroque, such as artificiality, theatricality, and too close an association with monarchical absolutism. At the same time, it is clear also that public worship was sustained by the private spirituality of the religious, especially by the ardour shown by the new orders of the Counter-Reformation.

CHAPTER XIV

RADICAL WORSHIP:
THE BAPTISTS AND QUAKERS

IT MUST seem curious to the present-day members of these two
highly respectable religious denominations to find their ancestors labelled, if not libelled, as "radicals." Yet this was their
reputation in the seventeenth century, which accounts for an early
Quaker historian, Gough, observing that next to the Quakers the
Baptists were the most hated and persecuted sect.[1] The more
orthodox found it convenient to confuse the Baptists with the Anabaptists, and to recall that they had in 1534 established a New
Jerusalem in Muenster in Westphalia, defended by the sword, and
desecrated by imitating the immorality of the patriarchs. It was
even harder to forget the eccentricities of their contemporary,
Nayler the Quaker, who so over-emphasised the possession of the
inner light that he ordered his enthusiastic companions to throw
branches of trees before him as he made his triumphal entry into
Bristol. In brief, the first Baptists and Quakers (ignoring the learning of Tombes or the education and social position of Penn) were
considered to be part and parcel of the gallimaufry of Commonwealth Antinomian sectarians, represented by the Diggers, Levellers, Fifth Monarchists, the Family of Love, the Ranters, the Seekers, and even the Muggletonians the only article of whose creed
was said to be:

> I do believe in God alone
> Likewise in Reeve and Muggleton.

A more exhaustive study might have discovered some intriguing
characteristics in these sects with reference to their worship. Of
all the groups omitted in this chapter, however, it would have been
most tempting to include the Fifth Monarchists because they developed some very interesting characteristics in worship, and may
well have anticipated the Quakers in interrupting the worship of
other more staid groups. They envisioned radical changes in worship when the millennium would arrive. Both ministry and church
would disappear, as Christ would be present in person. All ordi-

---

[1] *History of the People called Quakers*, I, p. 52 n., cited Supplement V, p. 141
of Daniel Neal's *History of the Puritans* (edn. of 1822).

nances would also be swept away, and even faith would be unnecessary at the advent of the truth. The saints would pay their homage to Christ in prayers and praises only.[2]

Until that time, however, their worship would not materially differ from that of the Independents and Baptists from whose ranks the Fifth Monarchists had largely been recruited. They held their services in a variety of locales, including churches, cellars, warehouses, taverns, and in the open air.[3] Like the earliest Separatists, they refused all set prayers, including even the Lord's Prayer, and rejected organs and choirs as sensuous and carnal concessions. They did, however, accept Psalms and hymns as being Scriptural. Their highly emotional services consisted almost entirely of extemporary prayers and prolix sermons, the latter sometimes lasting five or six hours and being frequently interrupted by the comments or criticisms of the congregation. One critic observed later, a little snobbishly, that the Fifth Monarchist "so hates a Gentleman, as he can't endure God shud be serv'd like one."[4] Their most distinctive contribution to worship, as we have noted elsewhere, sprang from their egalitarianism, and took the form of insisting upon the sitting posture for receiving the elements at the Lord's Supper.

It is not likely, however, that a detailed and exhaustive study of other sectarians would have yielded much novelty. This is partly because many such as the Diggers and Levellers were more concerned with social reform than spiritual reformation, and other sectarians were absorbed into long surviving denominations, such as the Seekers and Ranters in the Quakers. It seemed the wiser path to follow, therefore, to pursue the original contributions made to worship in the Free church tradition in English-speaking lands by the Baptists and the Quakers. Both Particular (or Calvinist) and General Baptists have affirmed believers' Baptisms (while denying the validity of infant Baptism), and the General Baptists have added colour to worship by practising foot-washing as an ordinance inculcating humility, and anointing the sick with oil, and they have anticipated the Methodists of England in the celebration of love-

---

[2] See H. Danvers, *Theopolis* (1672), pp. 172-75; J. Archer, *The Personall Reigne of Christ* (1642), pp. 17, 27; and T. Edwards, *Gangraena* (1646), I, p. 23. For an erudite study of radical ideas during the English Revolution see Christopher Hill, *The World Turned Upside Down* (1972).

[3] G. Lyon Turner, *Original Records of Early Nonconformity* (1911-1914), I, pp. 144, 155; T. Crosby, *The History of the English Baptists* (1738-1740), I, p. 377.

[4] R. Flecknoe, *Enigmatical Characters* (1665), p. 28, cited by B. S. Capp, *The Fifth Monarchy Men* (1972), an admirably researched account of the movement.

491

feasts. The Quakers have been second to none in their insistence upon interiority in worship, taking the negative form of eliminating the Seven Sacraments of Catholicism and Eastern Orthodoxy, as well as singing, and the positive form of silent waiting upon the God who speaks to the soul in quietude. These contributions to worship have at least the significance of survival value, and they had—when they originated—the shock values of innovation and iconoclasm.

1. *Parallels between Baptists and Quakers*

Though there are significant differences between them in worship as in the style of religious life (notably in that the Scriptures are final authority for the Baptists and the Holy Spirit for the Quakers), yet they have many striking similarities.

It is significant that both religious Communions gained their greatest accessions during the days of the Puritan Commonwealth and Protectorate and can, from one point of view, be regarded as part of the great spiritual intensification characteristic of that time of unexampled religious seriousness on the part of the masses united with great liberty for experimentation.

Both Baptists and Quakers in England had been brought up on Foxe's *Book of Martyrs*,[5] and this had taught them that true discipleship was marked with suffering. A staunch Christian, like a staunch soldier, was known by his wounds. The faithful of God were prepared even for martyrdom, if necessary. John Bunyan, the Baptist, as well as George Fox the founder of the Quakers, had proved their integrity of faith by long periods of imprisonment during the Restoration. They were both cheered and consoled by the concept so concisely expressed in the title of William Penn's classic of Quaker practice, *No Cross, No Crown* (1669). The calm and serene courage with which the Quakers in particular faced persecution was simply astonishing. Drums might be beaten to stop the meetings of other Dissenters at worship, but could do nothing against the silence of the Friends. The driving of coaches into their midst could part them, but utterly failed to disperse them. Violence could clap them in prison, but not make them lose their composure. Indeed, when a justice had, in a fit of choler, thrown the benches out of a meeting-house, he found that the Quakers had quietly taken

---

[5] William Haller, *Foxe's Book of Martyrs and the Elect Nation* (1963).

possession of them, for as one of them observed, "since they belong to us, we might as well sit on them."[6]

Both groups shared the total dependence upon divine providence that was the hall-mark of Calvinism. However much the General Baptists and the Society of Friends dissented from the doctrines of election and predestination, they acknowledged the sovereignty of the divine government of the universe, and God's care for every individual who put his trust in Him.

A third parallel between Baptists and Quakers is found in their dream of making every city and country a community of the righteous. Here, again, both had borrowed from Calvin's theocracy; and Geneva, the Commonwealth of England, and the "Holy Experiment" of Pennsylvania, were three versions of the same vision of the *sancta plebs Dei*.

The Baptists and Quakers in their form of church government, as in their worship, demonstrated a profoundly democratic faith. They believed in the common man's religious capacity to become uncommon. The following parody of the preaching of a Baptist lay preacher by a Presbyterian could have been directed with equal fairness at some of the early Quaker witnesses:

> Gainst Schooles and learning, he exclaim'd amain,
> Tongues, Science, Logick, Rhetorick, all are vain,
> And wisdom much unfitting for a Preacher,
> Because the Spirit is the only Teacher.
> For Christ chose not the Rabines of the Jewes,
> No Doctors, Scribes or Pharisees did chuse,
> The poore unlearned simple Fisherman. . . .[7]

Another common characteristic of Baptists and Quakers was a strong abhorrence of any merely formal or nominal membership of a Christian community, and their insistence on "gathering" the Christian community from the world at large. For the Baptists this was symbolized by the profession of faith on the part of the believers who then were submerged in the water of a river, as if drowning the old Adam, and re-emerged as totally consecrated to Christ. The Society of Friends also required from its members outward tokens of their inward change of heart, such as a refusal to bear

[6] Joseph Besse, *A Collection of the Sufferings of the People called Quakers,* 2 Vols. (1753), I, p. 412.

[7] John Taylor, *A Swarme of Sectaries,* cited in William York Tindall, *John Bunyan, Mechanick Preacher* (New York, 1934), pp. 72-73.

arms or to take oaths, or to doff hats in subservience to authority, but chiefly, of course, in the endurance of sufferings for the proclamation of the truth. Fox had insisted strongly on the contrast between "professors" and "possessors" of the Holy Spirit. The Baptists were also as greatly concerned with sincerity and integrity in their spiritual fellowships.

Yet, as Troeltsch so rightly insisted, this is an intramundane asceticism that William Penn clearly recognized: "The Christian convent and monastery are within, where the soul is encloistered from sin; and this religious house the true followers of Christ carry about with them; who exempt not themselves from the conversation of the world, though they keep themselves from the evil of the world in their conversation . . . True godliness don't turn men out of the world, but enables them to live better in it and excites their endeavours to mend it."[8] This was an ethics of fight, not flight, of transformation, not evasion.

Not only the Puritans, but also the Baptists and Quakers expected genuine, if undramatic, conversion of life on the part of their religious societies. All called for what the Puritans termed "visible sainthood" by reliance upon the sanctifying power of the Holy Spirit.

Not surprisingly, then, the worship of the Baptists and Quakers shared common features. Both groups were iconoclasts, rejecting infant Baptism. Both groups considered forms as a hindering and hampering of the Spirit of God. Smyth, the Se-Baptist, took this conviction to the extreme: he insisted upon translating the Scriptures himself from the original tongues, and refused to allow a Bible in the hand of the preacher, or a Psalm book in the hand of the solitary singer of God's praise, for, as he explained it, "the worship of the new testament properly so-called is spirituall proceeding from the hart."[9] Both spiritual communities sought the supreme liturgical virtues of simplicity, freedom, spontaneity, and intimacy, avoiding pomp, coercion, formality, and distant superiority.

Each of the religious groups bears the marks of the Puritanism which it inherited and from which it partly dissents. It has even been suggested recently by a Quaker historian, Hugh Barbour,[10] that Quaker worship itself evolved by stages from the Puritan

[8] William Penn, *The Witness of William Penn* (eds. F. B. Tolles and E. G. Alderfer, New York, 1957), p. 48.
[9] *The Differences of the Churches of the Separation* (1605), p. v.
[10] *The Quakers in Puritan England* (New Haven, Conn., 1964), p. 8.

Bible-study sessions of "prophesyings" which were the weekday gatherings of pastors and laymen meeting to expound and discuss Scripture as God's marching orders to his covenanted people.

The closest similarity of Baptists and Quakers is found in their earliest meeting-houses. It is most significant that in these scrubbed domestic dwellings a bench for seniors and elders has replaced the Anglican altar, and even the central pulpit and Communion table of the Puritan meeting-house.

Radical Puritanism might well prove to be, however, the matrix from which Quakerism was formed. The ancestors of the Quakers have often been sought in the mystics and spiritual reformers of the left-wing Continental Reformation, but they might more easily be found among the so-called Spiritual Puritans among whom were those charismatic chaplains of Cromwell who depended on the Holy Spirit's direct guidance in worship and conduct.[11] They included John Saltmarsh, William Dell, Peter Sterry, and Walter Cradock. These anticipated Fox in their condemnation of worship attained through human gifts and which exhibited only the outward form of godliness without the inner reality. This demand for a Spirit-endowed, utterly sincere, interior, and heart-deep worship is already over half-way towards Quakerism. It stops short only by retaining the "ordinances"—preaching and the two Gospel sacraments, with the primacy of the Scriptures to which the Spirit bears witness. The Baptists stand on the thin Puritan line of demarcation from the Quakers.

If the outline of iconoclasm may be regarded, only for diagrammatic purposes, as a declivity, with Roman Catholicism at the top of the hill and Quakerism at the bottom, then the Baptists are on the foothill. To limit the process of reductionism and stripping the Christian religion to what are believed to be its essentials in England, it began with the lopping off of the Pope, the liturgy in Latin, images, and five of the sacraments, thus forming the Church of England. The Presbyterians subtracted the rule of bishops and established the parity of ministers, assisted by lay elders. The Independents, like the Presbyterians, exalted preaching and celebrated the sacraments of Baptism and Holy Communion, while decentralising church government even further to the extent of local autonomy. The Baptists followed the Independents, but eliminated Paedobaptism in favour of believers' Baptism by submersion, and

11 See Geoffrey F. Nuttall, *The Holy Spirit in Puritan Faith and Experience* (Oxford, 1946).

made church membership depend upon conversion and the gift of the Spirit. Finally, the Quakers completed the process of interiorisation by eliminating all the sacraments, claiming that they had the experience of sanctification without the ritual that had usually accompanied it,[12] and doing away with a professional ministry. In the latter respect many Baptist congregations had led the way by having laymen with spiritual gifts, but without formal theological training, minister to them. Both Baptists and Quakers emphasised the importance of charismatic "leadings" of the Spirit in prayer and in witness. If the Spirit was identified by the Cambridge Platonists as reason operative in the soul of man, and by Cromwell with God's providential ordering of history, the radical Puritans, Baptists, and Quakers interpreted it as a sudden insight, or the recollection of a singularly relevant Biblical verse.

Thus Baptists and Quakers were united in the intensity of their Christian commitment, their willingness to suffer for the faith, their total dependence upon divine providence, their theocratic concern, their democratic belief in the possibilities of ordinary folk, their abhorrence of a merely nominal membership of the church, their intramundane asceticism, and their emphasis on conversion of life. In worship, they were iconoclasts, stripping ritual and ceremonial away to the bare essentials, rejecting liturgies and all set forms, and seeking the virtues of simplicity, freedom, spontaneity, and intimacy in their approach to God, and recognising the need for dependence upon the leading of the Holy Spirit. The same characteristics are reflected in their simple meeting-houses, which are as unsacerdotal and unecclesiastical as it is possible to be.

So far we have considered the ideas and practices they had in common, but were there any historical links between them such as will prove or make highly probable direct dependence of the Society of Friends on the Baptists? The following considerations will bear out the close links between these two religious communities.[13]

It was, says W. C. Braithwaite, the Quaker historian, "a 'shattered' Baptist Society" at Mansfield in 1648 which first supplied George Fox with congenial fellowship and under his guidance it became the earliest congregation of the Religious Society

[12] Howard H. Brinton, *Friends for 300 Years* (New York, 1953), pp. 12-13 shows this process illustrated from the journal of John Gratton, a very searching Quaker.

[13] See Sir William Collins, "The General Baptists and the Friends" in *Transactions of the Baptist Historical Society*, Vol. v (1916-1917), pp. 65-73.

of Friends.[14] The very concept of the "inner light" had been expounded by the General Baptist minister, Henry Denne, in his *Drag-net* published in 1646 before Fox had begun his public witness.

Furthermore, it is most probable that the General Baptists mediated to the early Quakers those concepts and practices which were common to the Mennonites of Holland and the Quakers, and it is known that Fox and Barclay were in contact with the Collegiants, Dutch Baptists, several of whom were the first converts of Quakerism. The Mennonites, it should be recalled, were averse to war, refused to take oaths, and would not limit salvation to the elect. They were, moreover, the first Protestants to practise silent prayer in public worship.[15] They rejected creeds, sacerdotalism, and forms of worship. They believed in guidance through the inner light and in immediate conversion.[16] The very same attitudes characterized John Smyth and the first group of Baptists who had sought refuge in Holland and brought these convictions back to England. These "spiritualising" tendencies are made explicit in the following citation from the statement of faith made by the remnant of Smyth's church in their *Propositions and Conclusions* of 1612: "That the new creature which is begotten of God, needeth not the outward scriptures, creatures, or ordinances of the Church to support or help them . . . seeing he hath three witnesses in himself, the Father, the Word, and the Holy Ghost: which are better than all scriptures or creatures whatsoever" (Proposition 61). Proposition 73 of the same Confession of Faith states "That the outward baptism and supper do not confer, and convey grace and regeneration to the participants or communicants: but as the word preached, they serve only to support and stir up the repentance and faith of the communicants till Christ come, till the day dawn, and the day-star arise in our hearts."

The fact that proves the closeness of the Baptists and Quakers, however, is that three or four of the most ardent apostles of Quakerism in northwest England, namely, Francis Howgill, Thomas Taylor, John Wilkinson, and John Audland had been Baptist ministers in that area, and in some instances they had brought their congregations with them into the Religious Society of Friends.

[14] *The Beginnings of Quakerism* (2nd edn., Cambridge, 1955), p. 12.
[15] Robert Barclay, *The Inner Life of the Religious Societies of the Commonwealth* (3rd edn., 1879), p. 86. Some even rejected the sacraments. See reference in footnote 13 above, pp. 67-68.
[16] *Ibid.*, p. 73.

Our conclusion must be that while the Presbyterian and Independent Puritans were included in Cromwell's state church, the Arminian Baptists, Mennonites, and Quakers were pioneering a more charismatic type of Christian life and worship.[17]

Nonetheless there were differences between the Baptists and Quaker contributions to the worship of the English Free churches, and to these distinctives we now turn.

2. *Four Types of Baptists*[18]

There have been four types of Baptists on the English scene. The earliest to emerge were closely linked to the Dutch Anabaptists, and since 1608 when they can be traced in England leaving for Holland have been distinguished for their Arminianism. They are known by the designation of General Baptists. "General," because they refused to restrict salvation to the elect with the Calvinists. They did not associate with the Particular or Calvinistic Baptists who eventually came greatly to outnumber them. They did, however, as has been indicated, contribute some distinctive and interesting ordinances to English worship. Their leaders were John Smyth, Henry Denne, Thomas Grantham, and Joseph Wright. They were strongest in Lincolnshire, Northamptonshire, Buckinghamshire, Kent, Sussex, and London. From 1642 they practised Baptism by total immersion, thinking it as important as restricting it to believers and making redemption generally available.[19] They claimed to have twenty thousand adherents by 1661.

A second important group can be designated Calvinistic Baptists, but with open membership. They evolved from the Calvinist Separatists and were occasionally led by former clergymen of the national church, such as the learned John Tombes and Henry Jessey. They would not refuse admission to their membership to true believers who differed from them only in practising the rite of infant Baptism, and so they formed open membership churches. In practise they were autonomous religious communities of Independents and Baptists, and they were particularly strong in Bed-

---

[17] Henry W. Clark, *History of English Nonconformity*, 2 Vols. (1911-1913), I, pp. 374-75.

[18] Information on the four divisions of Baptists was derived from an anonymous article, "Baptist Literature till 1688" in *Transactions of the Baptist Historical Society*, I, pp. 114-20, probably written by W. T. Whitley, the denominational historian, and editor of the *Transactions* at the time.

[19] C. E. Whiting, *Studies in English Puritanism from the Restoration to the Revolution, 1660-1688* (1931), p. 83.

fordshire. John Bunyan[20] was the most distinguished minister of this ecumenical group. Eventually most of these local churches became Baptist or Independent.

The third group of Baptists were convinced that the fourth commandment retained its original force, and so they became known as Seventh Day Baptists. These have now practically died out, and were never strong, but they included in their number Joseph Stennett the elder, "the earliest English Baptist hymnwriter whose hymns are now in common use,"[21] and which were composed for use at the Lord's Supper.

The great majority of Baptist churches, however, belong to a fourth classification, namely, the closed Communion Particular Baptists. They derive from a split in the English Independents whom they resemble theologically and in church polity. In 1633 the first congregation under Spilsbury formally separated from the London Independent congregation meeting at Blackfriars and built a meeting-house at Broad Street near Coal Harbour.[22] This body has the distinction of first bringing hymns into English worship as distinct from metrical psalmody in the person of Benjamin Keach who in 1673, in imitation of Christ and His Apostles, composed a hymn to be sung at the close of the Lord's Supper.[23] The other leaders of the Particular Baptists included William Kiffin and Hanserd Knollys. It is estimated that at the end of the Commonwealth period there were in England 115 General Baptist congregations, and 131 Particular Baptist congregations.[24]

3. *The Worship of the General Baptists*

As we have seen, the first group of English General Baptists under the leadership of Smyth and Helwys had contacts with the Mennonites, and like them they baptized believers by the mode of sprinkling. It was the Dutch Collegiants who first practised immersion in 1620,[25] but Helwys and his company had left Holland long before then. What a Baptism by sprinkling was like may be pictured from the vivid account of Mennonite Baptism in Holland described by Bernard Picart in 1736.

---

20 See *The Baptist Quarterly*, Vol. III, No. 7 (July 1927), p. 316.

21 John Julian, *A Dictionary of Hymnology* (2nd edn., 1907), p. 1091a.

22 *Transactions of the Baptist Historical Society*, Vol. I, p. 180.

23 Julian, *op. cit.*, p. 111a.

24 *Transactions of the Baptist Historical Society*, Vol. II, p. 236.

25 Supplement to *Transactions of the Baptist Historical Society*, Vol. II, No. 3 (1910-1911), article by Gould, "The Origins of the Modern Baptist Denomination."

The ceremony of Baptism takes place after the sermon. Those who are to be baptised approach the minister (or teacher) who descends from his pulpit for this purpose. Then addressing them, he asks whether they desire to be baptised, to which they reply by an inclination of the body signifying approval. Then they kneel and the minister prays, like them, on his knees. The prayer concluded, the lector or leader of praise in the church approaches with a basin full of water, following the minister as he passes from one to another of these neophytes who continue kneeling. While pouring water on the top of the head of each, the minister says these words, "N.N., I baptise you with water; may Our Lord Jesus Christ baptise you with the Holy Spirit." After all are baptised, the same minister causes each to rise one after another, offers them Christian congratulations, and, on their entering into the Church of the faithful, salutes them with the kiss of peace.[26]

The Christological orthodoxy of the Mennonites may be suspected because they do not use the customary Trinitarian baptismal formula, but there can be no doubt as to the sincerity or warmth of the ceremony.

The sacraments for the General Baptists seem to have had an almost exclusively didactic value. The remnant of Smyth's Arminian Baptist congregation in Holland affirmed in 1612 in the seventy-fourth of their *Propositions and Conclusions* "that the sacraments have the same use that the word hath; that they are a visible word, and that they teach to the eye of them that understand as the word teacheth the ears of them that have ears to hear (Proverbs 10: 12) and therefore as the word pertaineth not to infants, no more to the sacraments."[27]

The regular service of the General Baptists was very like the "prophesyings" which Zwingli had begun in the Reformed Minister at Zurich as an important pedagogical device. It is comprehensively described in the Smyth-Helwys Church at Amsterdam in 1608: "The order of the worshippe and government of oure church

---

[26] My translation of Picart, *Cérémonies et Coûtumes Religieuses de tous les peuples du monde* (Amsterdam, 1736), IV, pp. 207-208. It should be noted that Robert Barclay (*op. cit.*, p. 73) asserts "we may conclude that the first Arminian Baptist Churches in England were really Mennonite." The Arminian Baptist churches in England agreed to refer their differences to the decision of the Dutch Mennonite church, and in 1626 there were churches in London, Lincoln, Sarum, Coventry, and Tiverton corresponding with the Waterlander Mennonites of Amsterdam.

[27] W. L. Lumpkin, *Baptist Confessions of Faith* (Philadelphia, 1959), p. 138.

is 1. we begynne with a prayer, after reade some one or two chapters of the bible gyve the sence thereof, and confer upon the same, that done we lay aside oure bookes, and after a solemne prayer made by the 1. speaker, he propoundeth some text out of the Scripture, and prophecieth owt of the same, by the space of one hower, or three Quarters of an hower. After him standeth up a 2. speaker and prophecieth owt of the said text the like time and space, some tyme more some tyme lesse. After him the 3. the 4. the 5.&c as the tyme will geve leave, Then the 1. speaker concludeth with prayer as he began wth prayer, wth an exhortation to contribute to the poore, wch collection being made is also concluded wth prayer. This morning exercise begynes at eight of the clock and continueth unto twelve of the clocke the like unto 5. or 6. of the Clocke. last of all the execution of the government of the church is handled."[28] What is, however, surprising is that, while "prophesying" was a device for weekday instruction of the pastors in Zurich and in Elizabethan England for training Puritan preachers, it is now the regular mode of instructing the entire congregation in the hands of the General Baptists. Even more striking is that it was used *twice* every Sunday and could have taken up as many as eight hours of the day. Two other features of this description are worthy of note. One is the importance of the offertory for the poor, prefaced by an exhortation, and concluded with a dedicatory prayer. The other novel characteristic of this Sunday service is the pneumatic emphasis on the importance of laying aside of books (even of the Bible) for the entire dependence upon the leading of the Holy Spirit.[29] Furthermore, this spiritual worship disapproved of unison singing of the Psalms, but encouraged an individual when inspired by the Spirit to do so. Edward Draper in *Gospel-Glory proclaimed before the Sonnes of Men* affirms in the most positive terms that "To singe Psalmes in the Gospel is a speciall gift given to some particular member in the church, whereby he doth blesse, praise, or magnifie the Lord through the mighty operation of the spirit." Ephesians 5:18 and 19 are given as the Biblical sanction,

[28] Letter of the Bromheedes to Sir William Hammerton, Harleian Ms. 360 fol. 71 *recto* in the British Museum.

[29] Helwys, Smyth's successor as minister of this congregation, in a letter of September 20, 1608 (cited Champlin Burrage, *The Early English Dissenters in the light of recent Research*, Cambridge, 1912, II, p. 166) explains that "we suppose yt will prove the truth that All bookes even the originalles themselves must be layed aside in the tyme of spirituall worshipp, yet still retayninge the readinge & interpretinge of the Scriptures in the Churche for the preparing to worshipp, Iudging of doctrine, deciding of Controversies as the grounde of or faithe & of or whole profession."

and the manner is suggested as requiring "to be performed I say, by one alone, at one time to the edification one of another and therefore it is an ordinance flowing from a cheerfulle heart. . . ."[30] Under the influence of the Mennonites, the English General Baptists were already half way on the road to the Quakerism of the future.

There appear to be no early accounts of General Baptist celebrations of the Lord's Supper. For this reason it will not be amiss to assume that this was like the Communion of the Waterlander Mennonites, a description of which is supplied, about a century later, by Bernard Picart.

The Supper is also in the same way administered after the sermon. The minister takes from one of the three baskets on the Communion-table, loaves which he breaks and distributes first to his colleagues, while saying these words, *Do this in memory of Our Saviour Jesus Christ.* After this distribution, two of his colleagues joining with him, and all three followed by three deacons, each of which holds a basket, they go from row to row communicating all the faithful in the congregation. But when the communication of the bread is complete, the minister who has been the preacher of the day, returns alone to the Communion-table; the others retire with the three deacons. Two things are worthy of remark in this ceremony: one, that the minister who is in front of the table asks in a loud voice whether all have been communicated, and supposing one of the faithful has not received communion, he must rise and make a sign, in which case the minister will come back to him and communicate him. The other point is, that the communicants do not eat the bread immediately after receiving it. They wait until the minister returns to the table, where, after a short prayer and communicating himself, he invites the faithful to communicate, to participate like him in the same Communion. Before partaking, they hold the bread in their hands, or fold it in a handkerchief, or simply place it in their pocket. The wine is distributed to the same faithful, after it has been blessed or consecrated by the minister, who partakes first himself with his colleagues; immediately afterwards some deacons go to present it from one of the faithful to another, until the entire congregation shall have

[30] *Op. cit.* (edn. of 1649), p. 163.

communicated. A prayer and the singing of a psalm, mark for them, as for other Protestants, the conclusion of this religious act.[31]

This very simple service is no more than a memorial of the great sacrificial love of Christ, and a means of unity among the faithful gathered to honour His memory. It does not convey grace. A Midland Association of General Baptists produced a Confession of Faith in 1651, largely to distinguish themselves from the Quakers who were then making inroads on them. Article 53 makes the Memorialist interpretation of the Lord's Supper very clear: "That Jesus Christ took Bread, and the juice of the Vine, and brake, and gave to his Disciples, to eat and drink with thanksgiving; which practice is left upon record as a memorial of his suffering, to continue in the Church until he come again."[32]

The most that can be said for the General Baptist interpretation of the Lord's Supper is that it stirs up faith, so that the worshipper can mount up on wings of faith to God and there receive His spiritual gifts. Thus, John Smyth taught in *A Short Confession* of 1610 that "the whole dealing in the outward visible supper setteth before ye eye witnesseth and signifieth, y^t Christes holy body was broken uppon ye crosse & his holy blood spilt for ye remission of our synnes: That he being glorifyed in his heavenly being, is the alive-making bread meate & drinck of our soules: it setteth before our eyes Christes office & ministery in glory & majesty by houlding his spirituall supper with ye believing soule, feeding & meating ye soule with spirituall food: it teacheth us by y^t outward handling to mount upwards with ye hart in holy prayer to begg at Christes hands ye true signified good: and it admonisheth us of thankfullnes to god, & of unity & love of one another."[33] The Sacrament is already becoming a materialistic superfluity, an extra that can be dispensed with, as long as the experience it channels is obtainable elsewhere.

It is interesting that the five General Baptist churches which in 1626 wrote to the Waterlanders seeking their advice on several points, were unable to commit themselves to weekly celebrations of the Lord's Supper. Hans Ries, the leader of the Waterlanders

---

[31] Picart, *op. cit.*, IV, p. 208, my translation.

[32] *The Faith and Practice of Thirty Congregations gathered according to the Primitive Pattern*, reprinted in W. L. Lumpkin, *op. cit.*, p. 183.

[33] John Smyth, *Works*, ed. W. T. Whitley, II, p. 196; see also Lumpkin, *op. cit.*, p. 110.

to whom was brought the letter of the churches in London, Salisbury, Coventry, Lincoln, and Tiverton, asked the two representatives who accompanied it, several questions. To one of them the two General Baptists replied that "there was not a full minister at each of the five churches, and that made it impossible to observe the Lord's Supper at each on each Lord's Day."[34] It would appear that celebration at these churches was dependent upon the visit of a travelling "episcopus." At the same time the spiritualising or dematerialising tendencies would seem to make the Sacrament less important and lead one to expect infrequent celebration.

Perhaps the most innovative practice of at least some, if not all of the General Baptists, was to precede the ordinance of the Lord's Supper with a love-feast.[35] This common meal was eaten according to the Pauline precedent of the "cup after supper" (I Corinthians 11:25) and may well have taken place in the evening on Sundays. The Church Record of the Warboys congregation has this entry for the year 1655: "The order of love-feast agreed upon, to be before the Lord's Supper; because the ancient churches did practise it, and for unity with other churches near to us."[36]

Another ordinance which appears to have been used exclusively by the Baptists, and particularly by the General Baptists, was that of feet-washing. The warrant for it was the practise of Christ prior to the Last Supper in washing the feet of His disciples to inculcate humility in them, as recorded in the Fourth Gospel. It was not, however, obligatory since it was not included in Hebrews 6. The Assembly of General Baptists left the practice optional, but were fully aware that it had been urged in Lincolnshire by Robert Wright in 1653, and in Kent by William Jeffrey in 1659.[37]

A very full contemporary account of the General Baptist marriage service exists, probably because it was required by the civil authorities. The reporter is Thomas Grantham, the leader of the entire group of churches. "The parties to be married, being qualified for that state of life, according to the law of God, and the law of the land, as to the degrees, &c. therein limited, they call together a competent number of their relations and friends; and having

---

[34] W. T. Whitley, *A History of British Baptists* (1923), pp. 51f.

[35] Robert Barclay, *The Inner Life of the Religious Societies of the Commonwealth* (3rd edn., 1879), pp. 374-75.

[36] *Fenstanton, Warboys, and Hexham Records* (ed. by E. B. Underhill, 1854), p. 272.

[37] "Original Sin, Feet washing and the New Connexion," *Transactions of the Baptist Historical Society*, Vol. I, No. 2 (1908-1909), pp. 129ff.

usually some of our ministry present with them, the parties concerned declare their contract formerly made between themselves, and the advice of their friends, if occasion require it; and then, taking each other by the hand, declare, That they from that day forward during their natural lives together, do enter into the state of marriage, using the words of marriage in the service book [Book of Common Prayer], acknowledging the words to be very fit for that purpose. And then a writing is signed by the parties married to keep in memory the contract and covenant of their marriage." Grantham then gives specimens of the writings, with signatures of the witnesses, and concludes, "after these things, some suitable counsel or instruction is given to the parties, and then prayer is made to God for his blessing on the parties married, &c."[38] Marriage was sanctioned only if the contracting parties were of the same faith, for if this rule were broken it usually led immediately to excommunication. Smyth's *Short Confession of Faith* of 1610 states categorically, "We permit none of our communion to marry godless, unbelieving, fleshly persons out of the church; but we censure such (as other sinners) according to the disposition and desert of the cause."[39]

All these ordinances of the General Baptists seem, if rather uncommon, yet hardly revolutionary. Moreover, they were practised in the quietude of the meeting-houses, so that it seems difficult to account for the persecution to which the Baptists were subject in the seventeenth century. One factor, however, has been omitted, and that is that the most striking difference between the General Baptists and the rest of Christendom—their Baptism of believers at first by sprinkling or pouring, but later by immersion in rivers and ponds—was a *public* act of iconoclasm, a challenge to both Anglican and Puritan practice.

The most notable, even notorious act of public immersion in the century was performed by a member of a family noted for courting opprobrium, Samuel, father of Titus Oates, and a "messenger" of the General Baptists. According to the polemicist, Thomas Edwards, the author of *Gangraena* (1646), in the cold weather of March of the previous year he had baptized an Ann Martin

[38] "Marriages before 1754," *Transactions of the Baptist Historical Society*, Vol. I, No. 2 (1908-1909), pp. 122-23. It should be noted that Grantham originally published this information in "Of the Manner of Marriages among the Baptized Believers" from which John Rippon who published a *Baptist Annual Register* from 1790-1802 took it and included it in the third volume, p. 452.

[39] *Op. cit.*, Lumpkin, p. 112.

who died a fortnight after the event to the great scandal of the neighbourhood.[40] In consequence, a famous ballad circulated, ridiculing this event all over England. Its title was *The Anabaptist out of order, Or, [T]he Relation of Samuel Oates, who lately Seduced divers people in the County of Essex, where he rebaptiz'd thirty-nine and drowned the fortieth for which offence he now lies imprisoned at Colchester, till his tryall.*[41]

The ballad suggests that the scandal was not so much believers' Baptism, as the nudity of the females that he baptized. The chorus asks:

> Shall Maidens then before young men,
> Their garments to be striping?
> No; Separatists take heed of this
> There's danger in your diping.

The implication is that charismatic religion is all too convenient, requiring neither theological learning nor discipline:

> Both Besse and Nan with this young man,
>   Desire to be acquainted;
> Which to the River after ran,
>   Thinking they should be Sainted;
> For why, quoth they, if that he pray,
>   According to the Spirit;
> All faults shall all be washt away,
>   He is so full of merit.

His sincerity is impugned, as a trickster:

> Thus thirty-nine being over past,
>   As he hath them deluded;
> The fortieth coming at the last,
>   With whom he then concluded;
> His Argument he made so strong,
>   Where on her hope she grounded,
> At last he held her in so long,
>   That she poore heart was drownded.

As verse this is sorry doggerel, but it is potent propaganda. It helped to bring the Baptists into general contempt in England.

[40] *Op. cit.*, pp. 121-22.
[41] The ballad is reprinted in full in *Cavalier and Puritan* (ed. Hyder E. Rollins, New York, 1923).

506

Even so generous a proponent of comprehension as Richard Baxter is violently opposed to Believers' Baptism and by immersion. This attitude was in part caused by the way that Baptist leaders would goad parish ministers into debate, and Baxter had an unpleasant encounter with the most learned exponent of the Baptist viewpoint of the age, one John Tombes in 1650. In a whole series of arguments, Baxter's sixth is against their manner of Baptism "by dipping over head in a river, or other cold water." He ludicrously claims it is a breach of the Sixth Commandment, forbidding murder. He thinks covetous landlords can get rid of their tenants and make them die rapidly by encouraging them to become Baptists, and that this should appeal to grasping physicians. Dipping will increase catarrhs, apoplexies, palsies, cephalalgies phthises, dysenteries, colics, convulsions, and so forth. "In a word, it is good for nothing but to dispatch men out of the world that are burdensome, and to ranken churchyards. . . ."[42] His seventh argument against outdoor Baptism, apart from the danger to the minister's health, is its immodesty. He asks: "Would not vain young men come to a baptising to see the nakedness of maids, and make a mere jest and sport of it?" It is plain that the General Baptists had shocked the sensibilities of the English and would pay the penalty of ridicule and persecution.

4. The Worship of the Particular Baptists

The Particular Baptists, as Calvinists, were not as far outside the pale of orthodox churchmanship as their Arminian brethren, the General Baptists. In fact, Baptism apart, it would be difficult to distinguish their worship from that of the Independents, for the latter were Calvinists in doctrine, demanded Scriptural warrants for all their ordinances, believed in extemporaneous prayer, and insisted upon the local autonomy of each gathered church. For this reason their worship will be treated with a brevity which is no index of its importance, because in the long run the Particular Baptists had an honourable history and impact in England and the New World across the Atlantic, while the General Baptists eventually withered away.

Their chief difference from the two major Puritan bodies (Presbyterians and Independents) was the restriction of Baptism to

[42] Baxter's *Plain Scripture Proof*, pp. 134-37, cited Neal's *History of the Puritans* (1822), Supplement to Vol. v, pp. 148-49.

believers and the method of immersion. It was the church of Baptists which had seceded from Henry Jacob's Independent congregation at Southwark which first practised Baptism by immersion in 1641, and by 1642 its pastor, Henry Jessey, accepted immersion as the only legitimate mode of Baptism, though he was for the time being prepared to administer it to infants. In 1645 Jessey was himself immersed by Hansert Knollys and he introduced believers' Baptism by immersion into his own church.[43]

The first Baptist statement of faith pronouncing in favour of immersion was the famous *London Confession* of 1644, representing the convictions of the seven Particular Baptist Churches in London. Article 40 of this document begins: "The way and manner of the dispensing of this Ordinance the Scripture holds out to be dipping or plunging the whole body under water." It continues by explaining the Sacrament as signifying "first, the washing of the whole soule in the blood of Christ: Secondly, that interest the Saints have in the death, buriall, and resurrection; thirdly, together with a confirmation of our faith, that as certainly as the body is buried under water, and riseth againe, so certainly shall the bodies of the Saints be raised by the power of Christ, in the day of the resurrection, to reigne with Christ."[44]

A marginal note in the Confession meets the kinds of criticisms of adult Baptism current at this time, by insisting that *Baptizo*, the word, signifies to dip under water "yet so as with convenient garments both upon the administrator and subject with all modestie." The editions of 1651 and 1652 add: "which is also our practice, as many eye witnesses can testifie."[45]

The fullest statement of the teaching of the Particular Baptists on the Lord's Supper is contained in their *Second London Confession* of 1677 which was confirmed by the First General Assembly of the Particular Baptists with representatives of 107 Churches meeting from September 3 to 12, 1689. This long section warrants a summary. It begins by affirming that the Lord's Supper was instituted by Christ for the perpetual remembrance of Christ's death, confirmation of the believers' faith in its benefits, their spiritual nourishment, and their deeper engagement in the duties they owe to Christ, and as a bond and pledge of their union with Christ and with each other. It is denied that Christ is offered up to God

---

[43] *Transactions of the Baptist Historical Society*, Vol. I, p. 238.
[44] Lumpkin, *op. cit.*, p. 167.   [45] *Ibid.*

the Father, or that any sacrifice is made; rather this is a memorial of Christ's efficacious sacrifice made upon the Cross the "alone propitiation for all the sins of the elect." Transubstantiation is totally rejected, and the denial of the cup to the people and the elevation or adoration of the elements are repudiated.

The mode of celebration is as follows: "The Lord Jesus Christ hath in this Ordinance, appointed his Ministers to Pray, and bless the Elements of Bread and Wine, and thereby to set them apart from a common to an holy use, and to take and break the Bread; to take the Cup, and (they communicating also themselves) to give both to the Communicants."[46]

According to the same Confession, the elements are to be received "inwardly by faith, really and indeed, yet not carnally and corporally" but "spiritually" and with them all the benefits of Christ's death.

The greatest contribution made by the Particular Baptists to the worship of this century is, however, in the realm of praise, and only after a gruelling controversy between the pioneer, Benjamin Keach, and his congregation at Horsleydown, and his literary antagonist, Isaac Marlow. Keach, a leading minister of the Particular Baptists, made the daring transition from metrical psalmody to genuine hymns of Christian experience. Although the Continental Anabaptists were well known for their hymnody, the English Baptists were slow to compose or adopt hymns. This may have been due to their desire in times of persecution not to betray their secret conventicles by singing. Possibly, also, they were out of sympathy with the formal music and praise of the established church, with its organs, choirs, and anthems. Furthermore, there were subtle distinctions current among the Baptists in general about allowable or disapproved forms of praise which threatened to disrupt the unity of the local churches, and such divisions ought not to be encouraged to develop further. For example, some persons approved the singing of psalmody (as Scriptural), and even approved the metrical paraphrases of Psalms, but rejected hymns of modern composition as merely human productions. Yet others objected to hymns being sung in a "mixed" congregation of church members and non-members, especially when the latter stayed to observe though not to communicate at the Lord's Supper. Such difficulties were tolerated for years with exemplary patience by

[46] *Ibid.*, p. 292.

Benjamin Keach, who composed hymns which deservedly fell into a rapid oblivion for their literary crudity which was only compensated for in part by their religious sincerity.[47]

In 1675 in *War with the Devil*, Keach had published a small collection of hymns and spiritual songs. His *magnum opus*, however, appeared in 1691. This was *The Breach Repaired in God's Worship: Or, Singing of Psalms, Hymns and Spiritual Songs, proved to be an Holy Ordinance of Jesus Christ*, which recounts the tale of his fiery combat. He argued that there was no more reason against compiling sacred hymns to be sung out of the Word of Christ, than there is to object to pre-composed sermons. He then provided hymns for public worship in the same year, in which there appeared *Spiritual Melody containing near Three Hundred Sacred Hymns*. This is the first Baptist hymnal worthy of the name to appear in the English language.

One does not know whether to admire more Keach's persistence or his prudent gradualism during fourteen years. He first gained the consent of his flock to sing a hymn at the end of the Sacrament of the Lord's Supper, and only two members opposed him. After six years of this practice, it was agreed to extend it to days of public thanksgiving, and this lasted for fourteen years. Then it was decided to sing hymns every Sunday, with the exception of about six persons who absented themselves out of several hundreds. Keach even tried to meet their scruples of conscience, by arranging that the single hymn in each service should be sung at the conclusion of the prayer after the sermon, when the dissidents could quietly and conveniently leave.[48]

The spread and defence of Baptist principles was widely disseminated by the verse of Bunyan, particularly his great "Pilgrim hymn" ("Who would true valous see, let him come hither"), and the hymns of Keach. There would be an even more impressive flowering of Free church praise in the next century in the hymnody of Isaac Watts and Charles Wesley, which would be as skilled technically as Marot's *chansonettes* (metrical Psalms) were for the French, no less Scriptural in context, but suffused with the incandescence of Christian experience, perhaps less solemn, but certainly more joyful.

---

[47] J. C. Foster, "Early Baptist Writers of Verse," *Transactions of the Baptist Historical Society*, Vol. III, No. 2, p. 108.

[48] Crosby, *History of the English Baptists*, 4 Vols. (1738-1740), II, pp. 373-75.

5. Quaker Worship: Its Characteristics

Because Quaker worship is so extremely undramatic externally, so deliberately inward, and so profoundly simple, it has seemed wise to me to use as many contemporary citations as possible to enable non-Quakers to try to enter into its silent worship of waiting, accepting and experiencing the uniting and tendering divine spirit or "Inner Light" communicating God's power and love.

This is the most radical type of worship to have taken firm root in the Commonwealth and Protectorate. Its classical description is provided by its leading theologian, Robert Barclay: "All true and acceptable worship to God is offered in the inward and immediate moving and drawing of His own Spirit, which is neither limited to places, times, or persons: for though we be to worship always, in that we are to fear before him; yet as to the outward signification thereof in prayers, praises, and preaching, we ought not to do it when and where we will, but when and where we are moved thereunto by the secret inspiration of the Spirit in our hearts. . . ."[49]

This definition emphasises two important aspects of Quaker worship. The first is its spirituality and inwardness. It is the Spirit of God alone that must inspire, direct, and control worship for, as the Fourth Gospel insists, the Spirit is sovereign in its absolute freedom and cannot be trapped: "The wind blows where it wills, and you hear the sound of it, but you do not know whence it comes or whither it goes, so is everyone born of the Spirit."[50] The freedom of the Holy Spirit was proclaimed by the Quakers as fervently as any Puritan, with its correlate of the futility and presumption of trying to direct it. One awaits, one cannot command the Spirit of God which is "not limited to places, times, or persons."

A second characteristic is emphasis on the inwardness of true worship. This was, if not the most distinctive characteristic of Quaker worship, yet an emphasis carried by the Quakers to great extremes. All mere convention and custom, all formality and externalism, and all forms of worship lead to hypocrisy and pretence, according to the Quaker conviction, and are utterly to be refused. For them insincerity is the major sin against God and the Friends. Barclay's definition of worship makes this its second point:

All other worship then, both praises, prayers, and preaching, which man sets about in his own will, and at his own appoint-

---

[49] *Apology for the True Christian Divinity* (1678), Chap. XI.
[50] John 3:8.

ment, which he can both begin and end at his pleasure, do or leave undone as he himself sees meet; whether they be prescribed form, as a liturgy, or prayers conceived extemporarily, by the natural strength and faculty of the mind; they are all but superstitious, will-worship, and abominable idolatry in the sight of God; which are to be denied, rejected and separated from in the day of His spiritual arising.[51]

Behind apparent Quaker iconoclasm, there was a desperate and diligent desire for a first-hand knowledge of the living God not in notions but as empowerment. George Fox, Quakerism's founder, is the supreme exemplar of this unwearied quest to be a "possessor" (not a "professor") of the inward knowledge of God. He wrote of how this seeker became a finder and of the joy that it brought him: "When all my hopes in them and all men were gone, so that I had nothing outwardly to help me, nor could I tell what to do; then O! then I heard a voice which said, 'There is one, even Christ Jesus who can speak to thy condition'; and when I heard it my heart did leap for joy. When God doth work, who shall hinder it? and this I knew experimentally. My desires after the Lord grew stronger, and zeal in the pure knowledge of God and of Christ alone, without the help of any man, book, or writing."[52] Now such a rejection of all outside assistance, whether advice from persons or aid from books, seems like arrogant Philistinism, at first blush. This judgment, however, overlooks the crucial fact that Fox was exhausted after testing out almost every variety of faith that England had to offer in the time of its most prolific sectarianism, and that he found much outward protestation and little inward integrity. The result was that he was driven to direct experiment in mysticism after rejecting all the traditions. This experience of direct communication with God even meant bypassing the Scriptures, except as checks on an independent experience of God, an attitude most offensive to most Puritans. Yet the over-riding aim was to attain that union with God that the Scriptures witnessed to. Margaret Fell (whose home at Swarthmore Hall became the early northern headquarters of the Religious Society of Friends) was attracted to Fox precisely because he knew what experimental religion was at first hand. She testified that the Ulverstone congregation had been questioned by Fox thus: "You will say, Christ saith this, and the apostles say this,

[51] Barclay, *op. cit.*, Chap. XI.
[52] *Journal* (ed. N. Penney, 1902), pp. 11-12.

but what canst thou say? Art thou a Child of Light, and hast walked in the Light, and what thou speakest is it inwardly from God, etc.?" Her own comment was: "This opened me so it cut me to the heart, and then I saw clearly we were all wrong, So I sat me down in my pew again, and cried bitterly: and I cried in my spirit to the Lord, 'We are all thieves, we are all thieves, we have taken the scriptures in words, and know nothing of them in ourselves.' "[53] This was, in short, an experience of moving behind the words to the Word of God. It was vividly expressed by Isaac Pennington, thus: "The scriptures are words, whose chief end and service is to bring men to the Word."[54]

If simplicity (or inwardness) and spirituality are two primary marks of Quaker worship, so also are silence and unity. William Britten, formerly a Baptist pastor, wrote in 1660 an interesting pamphlet on silent worship, entitled, "Silent Meeting, A Wonder to the World." It gives an invaluable analysis of silence as a help to self-criticism and solid spiritual judgment, whereas when speech is permitted there is almost always the tendency to reply in immediate self-justification. Silence for Britten is golden, especially for objective meditation on existential issues. He writes: "He is not a true minister of Jesus Christ but [he] who is led forth by His Spirit; and such we rejoice to hear declaring the things of God. Otherwise, upon meeting, we sit silent in the tongue, yet having a heart full of praises, where we worship God in Spirit and truth, Who makes our bodies temples for the same Spirit, not speaking of hearsay and human arts, but lay all that down, when earthy thoughts, earthy deeds and earthy works are all laid aside and the temple within us is ready, the light of Christ shining in it, and the Lord with a further manifestation of His love enters it by His eternal power, whereupon we can truly say that the Lord's presence is amongst us, feeding His flock and making us feel the power of an endless life."[55]

Important as silent worship was, it should however be made clear that there was no absolute requirement of silence. Isaac Pennington makes this point: "In absolutely silent meetings (wherein there is a resolution not to speak) we know not, but we wait on the Lord, either to feel Him in words or in silence of spirit without words, as he pleaseth. And that which we aim at, and are instructed

[53] *Journal* (Bicentenary edn. of 1891), II, p. 512.
[54] Isaac Pennington, *Works* (3rd edn., 1784), IV, p. 57.
[55] Cited by W. C. Braithwaite, *op. cit.*, p. 510.

by the Spirit of the Lord as to silent meetings, is that the flesh in every one be kept silent, and that there be no building up [edification] but in the Spirit and power of the Lord."[56]

The other remarkable characteristic of the first Quaker meetings was their striking unity, a unity created in the silence of waiting upon God and sealed in their sufferings for their religion. Just in passing, it might be recalled that in ten and one-half years of witnessing as a Quaker, Isaac Pennington spent four and three-quarter years in prison, and that when William Williams, a Cambridgeshire Quaker, who was a poor man with a large family of small children was imprisoned in 1662, when his wife appealed to a justice, he told her "to fry her children for steaks, and eat them, if she wanted food."[57] That was the cost of Quaker witness!

The sense of unity developed in Quaker worship is most movingly described by Robert Barclay: "As iron sharpeneth iron, the seeing of the faces of one of another, when both are inwardly gathered into the life, giveth occasion for the life secretly to rise and pass from vessel to vessel. And as many candles lighted and put into one place to greatly augment the light and make it more to shine forth, so when many are gathered together into the same life, there is more of the glory of God and his power appears, to the refreshment of each individual, for that he partakes not only of the Light and life raised in himself, but in all the rest."[58]

A fine modern account of the experience of silent group mysticism in the Society of Friends is given by the novelist, Christopher Isherwood, in *The World in the Evening* (1954). Since the locale of the experience is the contemporary bustling metropolis of Philadelphia, the description's evocation of an ancient peace is all the more significant. The context of the experience is the white walls of the meeting-house, the hard and plain old benches, and the elders seated on the low facing gallery, as part of a community of inclined heads in prayer and contemplation. This is the experience: "Nevertheless, the Silence in its odd way, was coming to life. Was steadily filling up the bare white room, like water rising in a tank. [N. B. Isherwood employs the very same image as Barclay.] Every one of us contributed to it, simply by being present. Togetherness grew and tightly enclosed us, until it seemed that we must all be breath-

[56] Pennington, *Works* (3rd edn., 1784), IV, p. 59, cited in *Isaac Pennington, The Hidden Life. A Series of Extracts from the Writings of Isaac Pennington* (ed. Robert Davis, 1951), p. 31.
[57] C. E. Whiting, *op. cit.*, pp. 205f.
[58] Barclay, *Apology for the True Christian Divinity* (1678), p. 383.

ing in unison, and keeping time with our heart-beats. It was massively alive, and somehow, unimaginably ancient, like the togetherness of Man in the primitive caves."[59]

The recognition that true unity is the fruit of reconciliation has been central in Quaker belief and practice and is, of course, exemplified in the witness for peace so characteristic of the Friends. Their conviction is that unity is achieved in the sphere of the inner light. This light is "the Word of Life, the Word of Peace, the Word of Reconciliation which makes of twain one new man, and if ye do abide there, there is no division but unity in the life. . . ." The consequence is "Therefore in the Light wait where the Unity is, where the Peace is, where the Oneness with the Father and the Son is, where there is no Rent nor Division."[60] One cannot understand the emphasis on reconciliation unless one appreciates the historical circumstances, with the bitter divisions caused in English society by the Civil War. Reconciliation was England's most pressing need, as spiritual interiority was religion's primary current demand, both of which were met by Quakerism.

Thus the leading characteristics of Quaker worship are its simplicity and inwardness, its spirituality, its silent character, and its healing understanding of reconciliation and unity between God and men. The rigour with which these characteristics of worship were maintained led to some fascinating practical consequences, often innovative and iconoclastic.

6. Consequences for Quaker Life

The most striking simplification of Quaker worship and religious life was the disavowal and rejection of all set forms of prayer and of the sacraments. For this iconoclasm there are at least four reasons, the first and last of which are specially influential. The first and the most frequent reason given was the belief that no external rite can guarantee internal sincerity. The second is that the Quakers were profoundly aware of the many manifestations of God's providence and power in the world, and that, believing in such a sacramental universe, they refused to restrict the sacraments to seven, like Roman Catholics and Eastern Orthodox, or to two, like the Protestant churches. Thirdly, they refused to celebrate sacraments because in other religious groups these had been dependent on a specially ordained priesthood or ministry, and this was to deny the priesthood of all believers. This was an emphasis in line with

[59] *Op. cit.*, p. 51. [60] *Epistle* 115 of 1656.

their thoroughgoing democratic insistence on the right of prophet-esses as well as prophets to be the publishers of truth. A fourth and significant reason against set prayers and sacraments was the conviction that God was not transcendent and remote, but imma-nent and near. This view was admirably expounded by Jacob Bauthumley in 1650: "And truly, I find by experience, the grand reason why I have, and many others do now use set times of prayer, and run to formal duties, and other outward and low services of God: the reason hath been and is because men look upon God as being without [i.e. outside] them and remote from them at a great distance, as if He were locally in Heaven, and sitting there only, and would not let down any blessing or good things, but by such and such a way and means."[61]

The Quaker claim was that they experienced mystical union with God and that this was not channelled through the sacraments, but was independent of them, rendering them unnecessary. The Quakers questioned by Bernard Picart before 1736 insisted that "the true Baptism of Christ was the ablution of the soul, which alone saves men."[62] He states also that their opinion of Holy Com-munion was not less scandalous to orthodox Christians, since they declared that the only Communion they knew was that of hearts.[63] Barclay, the Quaker apologist, claimed that Quakers knew the experiences which the sacraments were supposed to convey. Bap-tism, so he held, was "a pure and spiritual thing, to wit, the Bap-tism of the Spirit and fire, by which we are buried with him, that being washed and purged from our sins, we may walk in newness of life."[64] One cannot help feeling that Barclay has, in this way, reduced sacraments to the status of mere metaphors. Similarly, he asserts that "the Communion of the Body and Blood of Christ is inward and spiritual . . . by which the inward man is daily nour-ished in the hearts of those in whom Christ dwells."[65]

The positive side of this iconoclasm was that it made the Quak-ers practise the art of meditation more thoroughly, and enabled them to listen openly and attentively to the various messages God delivered through male and female human agency. Furthermore, religion was—in the absence of sacraments—a delight rather than a prescribed set of rules.

[61] *The Light and Dark Side of God*, p. 4.
[62] *Op. cit.*, IV, p. 135 in my translation.
[63] *Ibid.*   [64] Barclay, *Apology*, Chap. XII.
[65] *Ibid.*, Chap. XIII.

Too much must not be made of the importance of silent worship. Certainly this was not invented by Quakers, since their contemporaries, the Trappists, practised it even more rigorously, and they had been anticipated by the Mennonites in their gatherings for public worship. Nor is it entirely true to characterize most seventeenth-century Quaker meetings as silent, for more time was spent in listening to speeches than was spent in quietness, where statistics are available. The nineteenth-century historian of Quakerism and allied religious groups, who also is named Robert Barclay, claims after the careful perusal of minutes of Quaker meetings for worship in London "that silence to any large extent was the exception rather than the rule."[66]

The Quaker conviction that the truth will vindicate itself in a free and open encounter (a belief shared by Milton in the *Areopagitica* and memorably expressed), can be seen in their frequent interruption of services held in the "steeple-houses" and challenging of the ministers to debate with them. This conviction was most dramatically exhibited in the large-scale testimony and apologetical gatherings they convened in London. Early in 1655 part of a vast old house in Aldersgate Street (an address to be associated in less than a century with another popular movement in religion, Methodism) was taken by the Quakers as a meeting-place. It was called the Bull and Mouth Meeting, so named for the inn sign that adorned another part of the old mansion. In this "new hired great tavern chapel" (as the critics of the Quakers termed it), a thousand people could stand up. What transpired there under the leadership of Edward Burrough is recalled by William Crouch:

> I have beheld him filled with power by the Spirit of the Lord . . . when the room hath been filled with people, many of whom have been in uproars, contending one with another, some exclaiming against the Quakers, accusing and charging them with heresy, blasphemy, sedition, and what not . . . others vehemently endeavouring to vindicate them and speaking of them more favourably. In the midst of all which noise and contention, this servant of the Lord hath stood upon a bench, with his Bible in his hand . . . speaking to the people with great authority from the words of John vii.12; "And there was much murmuring among the people concerning

[66] R. Barclay, *The Inner Life of the Religious Societies of the Commonwealth* (3rd edn., 1879), p. 401.

517

Him": to wit, Jesus, "for some said, He is a good man: others say, Nay; but He deceiveth the people." And so suitable to the present debate amongst them, that the whole multitude was overcome thereby, and became exceedingly calm and attentive, and departed peaceably, and with seeming satisfaction.[67]

Such meetings were held "to thresh among the world" to winnow and win future Quakers from the chaff of the masses, a work in which Burrough and Howgill were especially proficient.

Perhaps the most dramatic manifestation of early Quakerism was in its appropriation of prophetic symbolism by its prophets and prophetesses on the precedents provided by the Old Testament prophets. Individual Quakers, chiefly men, would go naked as a sign of the way God was uncovering sins. As early as 1652 George Fox writes approvingly of this custom to the people of Ulverstone: "the Lord made one go naked among you, a figure of thy nakedness, and of your nakedness, and as a sign amongst you before your destruction cometh, that you might see that you were naked and not covered with the truth."[68] William Simpson frequently offered this type of testimony. Fox also mentions that Simpson "went three years naked and in sackcloth in the days of Oliver and his Parliament, as a sign to them and to the priests showing how God would strip them of their power, and that they should be naked as he was, and stripped of their benefices."[69] Such dramatic gestures would seem merely extravagant eccentricities on the part of those who believed themselves to be merely publicity-mongers for a new sect; but were entirely appropriate acts for those conceiving themselves to be prophets of a new dispensation of the Spirit, as the Quakers did. Moreover, the Quakers knew these "signs" were often a cause of their sufferings, yet they felt it essential to continue the witness made by such signs. In a document addressed to the King and both Houses of Parliament in 1664 concerning the sufferings of over six hundred Quakers in prison, they include this among the reasons for their ill-treatment: "because we speak in the Synagogues and Temples, or Steeple-houses, as we are commanded and moved of the Lord, and sometimes moved to go as signes amongst them, which was the practise of the prophets

[67] *Posthuma Christiana* (edn. of 1712), p. 26.
[68] *Journal* (Bicentenary edn.), I, p. 153.
[69] *The First Publishers of Truth* (ed. N. Penney, 1907), p. 365.

of old and the apostles in primitive times."[70] The most unfortunate example of a sign that embarrassed the Quakers was Nayler's quasi-messianic entry into the city of Bristol, which was intended to be a demonstration of the divine immanence and of the inner light shining through Nayler, yet was interpreted as a claim that Nayler thought himself to be the light of the world. It is a short step from the inner light to the outer darkness.

The most impressive witness of the Quakers, however, was their ability to irradiate the whole of their life from day to day with their religious convictions. Fox saw the correlation between the convincing power of Quakerism and the integrity of the ethics of its members. He paid it a handsome tribute in the *Journal*:

At the first convincement when Friends could not put off their hats to people, nor say you to a particular, but thee and thou; and could not bow, nor use the world's salutations nor fashions nor customs—and many Friends being tradesmen of several sorts—they lost their custom at the first, for the people could not trade with them nor trust them. And for a time people that were tradesmen could hardly get money enough to buy bread, but afterwards, when people came to see Friends' honesty and truthfulness and yea and nay at a word in their dealing, and their lives and conversations did preach and reach to the witness of God in all people, and they knew and saw that they would not cozen and cheat them for conscience' sake towards God:—and that at last they might send any child and be as well used as themselves at any of their shops, so then the things altered so that the inquiry was where was a draper or shopkeeper or tailor or shoemaker or any other tradesman that was a Quaker: then that was all the cry, insomuch that Friends had double the trade beyond any of their neighbours: and if there was any trading they had it, insomuch that the cry was of all the professors and others, If we let these people alone they will take the trading of the nation out of our hands. . . And this was from the years 1652 to 1656 and since.[71]

The historian must be impressed by the boldness and originality of the witness of the early Quakers, the costliness of their suffer-

[70] [To the?] *King and both Houses of Parliament, Being a Declaration of the present Suffering and imprisonment of above 600 of the people of God in scorn called Quakers, who now suffer in England for Conscience Sake* (1664), p. 5.
[71] *Journal*, I, p. 185.

ings for the truth, their close correlation of profession and practice, and their obedience to the voice of the Holy Spirit, even when it contradicted the values of the age, questioned society's hypocritical courtesies and titles, condemned war in the age of the Thirty Years War, and demanded of its publishers of truth that they give up the comforts of home life to accept itinerating and even imprisonment. The spiritual power-house and dynamo of all these activities was the Quaker meeting convened for worship which was charged with the energy of the enabling spirit.

7. Developments in Quaker Worship

A movement so dynamic in its origins, coming into being in a time of political and religious revolution, was bound to change. And change it did.

At the very beginning there was not only much speech in the silent meeting, but even singing to the Lord. Fox and Hubberthorne wrote in 1658: "Those who are moved to sing with understanding, making melody to the Lord in their hearts we own; if it be in meeter we own it."[72] Psalms, even metrical Psalms, were permitted as solos and almost certainly not as conjoint exercises, since it was not until 1690 that congregational singing was approved by the Baptists. Furthermore, the Quakers suspected those who sang words or recited prayers they did not believe. They ridiculed those who were "singing David's Psalms with Saul's Spirit, in such Meeter. . . as Q. Elizabeth's Fiddlers have moulded them into, and . . . as some Priest, Clark or Saxton saves them *lineatim*."[73] Yet Thomas and Elizabeth Holme ministered movingly to the Quakers by their singing.[74]

Also at the very beginning, it seems that the Friends kept lovefeasts. Fox's earliest tract make references to such, affirming "we have the Lord's Supper" or "the Table and Supper of the Lord we own" with the accompanying denial that the mode in which it was celebrated by others was according to the practice either of the Sacrament itself or the common meal that preceded it in the apostolic church which bore relation to it.[75] It is likelier that this was a love-feast than the Lord's Supper, precisely because the former was not imbued with the sacerdotalism of a sacrament. The

[72] *Truth's Defence against the Serpent*, p. 21.
[73] Samuel Fisher, *The Testimony of Truth Exalted* (1679), p. 92.
[74] The *Cambridge Journal of Fox*, I, p. 245.
[75] R. Barclay, *The Inner Life* (3rd edn., 1879), pp. 374-75.

increasing iconoclasm of the Society of Friends led to the abolition of this ordinance, whether Communion or love-feast.

A third development was the provision of a simple Marriage Service for Friends entering into matrimony. This simple exchanging of vows owed much to the Puritan simplification of the Anglican service as provided in the Westminster or Parliamentary *Directory*. The couple repeated their mutual vows of fidelity in the silent meeting convened for this purpose, then signed a certificate which was read aloud and also signed by the Friends present after the meeting concluded.[76]

Inevitably as the Society's numbers increased, and as persecution diminished, and a new haven was established for the expression of a gentler theocracy of the Friends in Pennsylvania, the more dramatic public witnessing of the Quakers, whether in "threshing Meetings" or in prophetical signs, or in challenges in the local parish churches, lessened. During the years of persecution the Friends had turned inward at their meetings for worship, instead of attacking their detractors or competitors as in the exciting polemics of earlier days. The serenity, security, and compassion of the silent meetings grew as the outward lot of Quakers worsened in days of "durance vile" and duress. This was the permanent legacy of Quakerism, which seems only more relevant in our cacophonous age.

[76] Ruth C. Burtt, "The Quaker Marriage Declaration," *Journal of the Friends Historical Society*, Vol. 46 (1954), pp. 53-59.

CHAPTER XV

CONCLUDING SURVEY
AND CRITIQUE

HITHERTO OUR exclusive interest has been to try to understand by the way of empathy the most varied rites and ceremonies whether complexly grandiose or severely simple. Our concluding concern will be to survey the developments in worship of the entire century and to attempt to evaluate them.

1. New Developments

The seventeenth century produced some fascinating new developments in worship. The English people were offered a choice of no less than four alternative modes of public prayer. The oldest and the most familiar was the use of a liturgy. The Roman Catholics used a venerable international liturgy in Latin. The Anglicans used a national liturgy in the English vernacular, which combined Catholic traditions and Reformed insights. In its revised form of 1662 their Prayer Book contained two superb new prayers, the General Thanksgiving and the General Confession. The second type of public prayer was the substitute for the Book of Common Prayer, the *Westminster Directory* of 1644, which provided an order of worship and proposed themes for prayers without prescribing their wording, thus combining fixity and freedom. It was almost certainly the first and only time that a manual of worship rather than a liturgy has been devised for the Christian worship of three kingdoms. The third type of public prayer was "conceived" prayer, either free or extemporary, the former giving the minister the right to prepare a prayer of his own composition and take it with him into the pulpit, and the latter an immediate and spontaneous creation under the inspiration of the Holy Spirit. The fourth and last option was taken by very few: it was the most radical of all types of public prayer, the silent unitive prayer of the Religious Society of Friends.

A second very significant development (with much greater promise for the eighteenth century in the gifted pens of Isaac Watts and Charles Wesley) was the transition made from prose psalm to metrical Psalm and eventually to hymnody. This provided the lyrical element so badly needed in worship, which without the element of adoration dries up in a dreary didacticism; but there were few oases in this seventeenth-century desert of hymnody. The efflorescence of the cacti of metrical psalmody among the Puritans and of the more luxuriant orchids of verse anthems in cathedrals and abbeys was another feature of the period.

A third characteristic, particularly strong in the Church of England, was a high evaluation of the doctrine and act of the Incarnation, and of its consequence, the continuing presence of Christ in the Eucharist, and the conviction that this was the church member's greatest privilege. (The Puritans, by contrast, felt the presence of Christ more potently in the audible than the visible World.) This sense of the "real presence" gave Anglicanism a great impetus to high ceremonial, to symbolical ornaments, and to the recognition that the sanctuary was the presence chamber of the King of Kings, and the altar was Christ's throne. Not until the advent of the Oxford and Cambridge[1] Movements of the mid-nineteenth century would the Church of England again have as splendid and beautiful a setting for the liturgy. This was the legacy of Hooker, Andrewes, and Laud and their trustees were Bishops Cosin and Wren.

A fourth feature of the age was the high level (abating some controversial cantankerousness) of the defences offered for the different types and styles of worship. The chief Anglican liturgical apologists were Henry Hammond and Herbert Thorndike, Bishops Jeremy Taylor and William Beveridge, and Archbishop Bramhall. The stalwart Puritan defenders of their type of worship were Perkins, Owen, and Richard Baxter. The single outstanding Quaker apologist was Barclay. These men penetrated to the core of the matter in their descriptions and defences of their own type of worship, but were generally myopic (with the probable exception of Baxter) in their views of other liturgical styles than their own. It is in this century that a new and important genre of ecclesiastical writing was born, namely, the Prayer Book commentary. It provided an analysis of the contents of the Anglican liturgy with historical notes in a devotional spirit. It aimed to enable loyal Anglicans to offer worship as "their reasonable service." The deep antagonisms of the ecclesiastical parties often produced an "either/or" demand where an unpolarised experience might have preferred

---

[1] See James F. White, *The Cambridge Movement: The Ecclesiologists and the Gothic Revival* (Cambridge, 1962).

"both/and" as more comprehensive and wiser. The century did, however, see sharply stated alternatives argued with conviction, historical lore, and enthusiasm.

Nor should it be forgotten in the confusion of controversy about the cultus that this was the golden age of English preaching. Dean Donne and Bishop Lancelot Andrewes were spectacular practitioners of the brilliant and daring art of metaphysical preaching. Bishop Jeremy Taylor dazzled his congregation with his ornate oratory, as freighted with golden metaphors and figures of speech as a captured Spanish galleon with ingots. Richard Baxter exemplified the plain, direct, yet emotionally charged, Puritan style seeking for a verdict from his congregation, and Tillotson preached modest, rational, pragmatic sermons as a Latitudinarian should. Here, indeed, was God's plenty in quality, quantity, and variety.

A minor but significant change was the recognition on the part of John Archer, the revolutionary Independent minister, that sitting at the Communion table was not the careless gesture that a later age might dub "the Congregational crouch," but a profoundly democratic and radical protest. It declared that the seventeenth-century disciples of Christ need not kneel in subservience to him as to an earthly king, as Roman Catholics and Anglicans did. It recognised that Christ had called the "visible saints" his friends and that they were to share in the political Christocracy to be established in this world.

In major ways the seventeenth-century developments in worship were to have effects that would last for centuries to come. Presbyterianism, which had hitherto followed Calvin and Knox in preferring a Biblically based liturgy and a set form of worship, now used a *Directory* or manual. This became the pattern of worship for all those in the Puritan-Pietist tradition for three centuries in England and New England, in the British Commonwealth of nations and in the United States. Free prayer would become characteristic of the worship of not only Independents and Baptists, but also of Presbyterians and Methodists. Even Lutherans, who began with liturgies, would go through a period of having free prayers and finally reappropriate liturgical forms.

Similarly, the long-range influence of the Caroline divines was great on the Anglican Communion throughout the English-speaking world. They established the characteristic ethos of Anglican worship: a reverence for the Sacrament of Holy Communion as an incentive to holiness, a dignified and beautiful ceremonial and setting for the liturgy as the expression of the holiness of beauty, and a conviction (with the Church of the Fathers) that the Incarnation (and its annual remembrance in the calendar of the Christian year) is the lever for the raising of humanity to the service of God and neighbour. The great Anglican monastic recovery in the nineteenth century is foreshadowed in the seventeenth century at Little Gidding, where the family of the Ferrars and their friends offered a round of praise and prayers to God through the day and the night.

Furthermore, the Quaker emphasis on the group waiting for the guidance of the inner light in silence has become not less, but more relevant with the passage of the frenetic years, and the arrival of our own cacophonic age, and is now providing extraordinary experimental opportunities for Quakers and Buddhist and Hindu contemplatives to meet in colloquia in depth.[2]

2. The Strengths and Weaknesses of Liturgical Worship

The necessity for Roman Catholics, except those in the highest places, to practise a cryptic cultus in our period, while their European co-religionists were worshipping in a setting of Baroque theatrical magnificence, forced their ceremonial and ornaments to approximate those of the Anglican liturgy. It is therefore appropriate to consider them together, despite their differences, because they both are strongly committed to liturgical worship.

It will probably be generally conceded that a cultus fulfils three major functions. First, it provides an ordered rite that enables a religious community to worship God together. Secondly, its structure and contents are designed to consecrate (and hopefully transform) the whole of life as an offering to God. Thirdly, its ritual and ceremonial provide an outward visible and audible expression for the inner devotion of the personality.

The first function—that of providing a structure for the common corporate expression of divine worship—is the chief benefit of a liturgy. It is a historical fact that no liturgy has ever united a larger group of Christians than the Roman Catholic liturgy, whether in its simple and early Roman form, in its medieval allegorical form, in its post-Tridentine rubrical uniformity, or in its modern, vernacular, alternative forms since Vatican II.[3] It has unified the devotions of countless millions in the Mass, as of count-

---

[2] See Douglas V. Steere, *On Being Present Where You Are* (Pendle Hill Pamphlet No. 151, Pendle Hill, Pennsylvania, 1967), pp. 20-27.

[3] See Hermanus A. P. Schmidt, *Introductio in Liturgiam Occidentalem* (Rome, Freiburg, Barcelona, 1960), passim.

less thousands of the religious in the Breviary and the Daily Office. Unquestionably, its venerable age and widespread tradition strengthened the loyalty of persecuted Roman Catholics in seventeenth-century England.

Similarly, the Anglican Book of Common Prayer proved an admirably suitable medium for expressing religious unity, though it was not comprehensive enough to include either the seventeenth-century Puritans after 1662 or the Methodists after 1795. It was unique in being both a priest's book and a people's book of worship in the vernacular, and in combining Catholic tradition with Reformation insight. We have, however, seen that the underside of the uniformity it claimed to provide was that it developed into an engine of "soul control" bringing persecution in its train [4]

Furthermore, it is only fair to recognise that both the Roman and Anglican liturgies are considerably more flexible than the mystical liturgies (for example) of the Eastern Orthodox churches. Their lections, their collects, and their prefaces in the Eucharistic Prayer of Consecration, change according to the Christian year. (Puritan worship can hardly be accused of invariability; its weaknesses are casualness and anarchy.)

If a second function of corporate worship is to consecrate and transform the whole of life, then much will depend on how prominently the concept of sacrifice is kept before the worshippers, or how strongly the emphasis on sanctification is maintained. On both scores it would be impossible to fault the Roman rite. If the worship of Eastern Orthodoxy can be characterized as the rehearsal of a mystery drama, and Puritan worship as listening to the oracles of God, Roman worship is unquestionably the representation of Christ's sacrifice. Furthermore, Rome is rightly known as the mother of saints, and the sanctoral round in the Roman Catholic calendar is its remembrance. At the very heart of the Mass there is sacrifice, primarily Christ's own eternally efficacious sacrifice offered to God the Father for the reconciliation of the world, and subordinately, the sacrifice of the people of God united to Christ.[5] It is this central sacrifice that provides the Mass with its great

[4] There is an extended consideration of this charge in Davies, *op. cit.*, I, pp. 219f.

[5] The sacrificial language of the Mass may be illustrated from the following citations from its prayers: in the Offertory the terms *oblatio, sacrificium, hostia* and *calix salutaris* are used; and the great prayer, *Te igitur* pleads that God will accept and bless *haec dona, haec munera, haec sancta sacrificia illibata, quae tibi offerimus pro ecclesia tua sancta catholica.*

objectivity in its transcendent reference, its independence of psychological moods. It is the awesome sense of Christ's corporal presence on the altar that makes the event renewed at Mass so numinous, so important, so life-changing.

Has the Anglican liturgy proved able to transform life? (This question has already been answered positively in our chapter on spirituality.) But *how* was this done? Clearly, Anglican worship had a strong sense of the "real presence" of the sacrificial Christ in its services of Holy Communion, though Anglican theologians of the seventeenth century insisted that this was a spiritual, not a corporal, presence. It cannot be claimed that the sense of sacrifice is as dominant as in the Roman Mass, but it is there and it is too frequently expressed to be ignored. The actual term "sacrifice" is rather carefully kept for the original sacrifice of Christ upon his Cross to avoid any possibility of misinterpreting this as the renewal of this unique act. The Prayer of Consecration most cautiously stresses that Christ made at the Cross "his one oblation of himself *once offered.*" The term sacrifice is also used for the congregation's responsive "sacrifice of praise" (and a post-Communion Prayer of Thanksgiving affirms that "we offer and present unto thee, O Lord, ourselves to be a reasonable, holy, and living sacrifice to thee").

On the other hand, the Church of England's Eucharistic rite is conceived primarily as a commemoration of a sacrifice and a spiritual banquet. At the heart of the Prayer of Consecration is the reminder that Christ made "a full, perfect, and sufficient sacrifice for the sins of the whole world, and did institute and in his holy Gospel command us to continue a perpetual memory of that his precious death until his coming again." Nonetheless, along with the images of "holy mysteries" and spiritual banquet, that of sacrifice is unquestionably important. And, although the sanctoral cycle is diminished, compared with the Roman calendar, the sense of spiritual transformation or sanctification is to be found in the exhortation that in warning against unworthy reception is, in effect, a "fencing" of the table. The same emphasis is also present in both alternative post-Communion prayers, the second of which asks God "so assist us with thy grace that we may continue in that holy fellowship, and do all such good works as thou hast prepared for us to walk in."

The third function of a cultus, namely, to provide an outward form for the expression of inner devotion, is admirably fulfilled by both Roman and Anglican liturgies in their ceremonial and words. Both take the Incarnation seriously and recognise the impor-

527

tance of that divine accommodation to the mixed psycho-physical nature of man. They both supply in processions, in varied gestures of reverence, in the use of "eye-gate" as well as "ear-gate," in arrow-like prayers that catch the attention and in responses, and in architectural symbolism and music, aids to assist worshippers. Moreover, the very forms of worship themselves inculcate the appropriate response to the living God whose mercy is as his majesty. (By contrast, Puritan worship made fewer concessions to human psychology and to the five senses. It almost eliminated ceremonial, and in the intensity of concentration required for its long prayers and longer sermons strained the attention of the elect.) Above all, it cannot be too strongly stressed that the Catholic and Anglican traditions of worship recognised the importance of the concept of an offering being made by the congregation as Christ's flock. Here, again, the contrast with the Puritan and later Free church tradition is glaring. In the course of time, as the Baptist exponent of worship, Stephen Winward reminds us, in the Free church tradition "getting a blessing" came to replace "making an offering" to the depreciation of worship.[6] Here at once is the greatest strength of the Catholic and Anglican tradition, and the greatest weakness of Nonconformist worship. Puritans and their successors seem to be unaware that habitually performed acts not only evoke the appropriate emotions, but even strengthen them. So even if one does not feel a sense of gratitude to God at the beginning of worship, it may be created by the experience of worship.[7] Worship is not only expressive as the devotees of sincerity insist, it is also (which the same coterie ignores) instrumental in creating emotions that ought to be felt.

Puritanism was far from doing justice to the strengths of Roman Catholic and Anglican worship—their uniformity (universality in

---

[6] See *The Reformation of our Worship* (1964), p. 3. Winward suggests the following cluster of reasons for the absence of the idea of offering in the Puritan and Free church tradition of worship: since Christ has made the perfect offering no other is needed; a prophetic criticism of Israel's cultus is misinterpreted to mean the prophets were against all sacrifices; there is a false pitting of prophet against priest; the strong and exclusive Puritan stress on the downward or revelational movement from God to man led to the exclusion of the upward response or the offering of man to God.

François Mauriac, the Catholic novelist, in *La Pharisienne*, makes his priest comment on the fact that a tragedy of Calvinism is that human acts of sacrifice seem to count for nothing, for they cannot add anything to Christ's complete and perfect sacrifice.

[7] Baron Von Hügel in his *Selected Letters* criticizes the Puritan viewpoint in the following citation: "What a curious psychology which allows me to kiss my child because I love it, but strictly forbids me to kiss it in order to love it."

the case of the Mass), transcendental reference and objectivity, the responsive element in the prayers, the variety in the Christological and sanctoral cycle, and the multi-medial aesthetic approach. In the Puritan criticisms of the superstition, formalism, impersonality, and rigidity of the Roman and Anglican rites, the Puritans ignored the large Biblical element in the lections, as in the actual wording of the prayers (especially strong in Anglican prayers which are often Biblical mosaics, and the Book of Common Prayer rejected legendary sanctoral material), and the strong Christological focus. The Puritans were unreasonably iconoclastic in their attitude towards the Book of Common Prayer because of its "guilt by association" in the retention of certain noxious ceremonies also used by Roman Catholics, and failed utterly to do justice to the centrality of Christ in lections, collects, and calendar.

For all this, the gravamen of the Puritan objection is the recognition that a liturgy can become exceedingly formal, mechanical, and artificial. It can project an idea of God as a remote and utterly transcendent sovereign "King of Kings and Lord of Lords" and not "the God and Father of our Lord Jesus Christ." Its spirit can be exceedingly sober, dignified, even stuffy. It can be singularly lacking in adoration and joy. Familiarity can breed contempt or indifference for its repetitiousness. Above all, the incantatory magic of the words of the Prayer Book and the medieval beauty of the setting may transform worship into a reverie rather than prepare the Christian for a re-entry into life transformed into a deeper commitment to serve God and humanity. Puritan worship may be a cold shower and bracing, but Anglican worship is likelier to be a soothing and possibly enervating bath.

3. The Strengths and Weaknesses of Puritan Worship

Had the criticisms of liturgical worship which we have just listed been entirely without substance, Puritans would not have gone to the enormous effort of creating an alternative cultus, least of all one which offered so few incentives to the natural man and was about as colourful as an etching.

What were the strengths of Puritan worship? Its greatest strength was its bracing Biblical authority. The Word of God, the authority of God's own appointing in Scripture, is its sanction, whether for the primacy of preaching as an exposition of the oracles of the living God (prepared for by a prayer for the illumination of the Holy Spirit), or for every other "ordinance" (as it was characteristically called, being a mandate from the Mediator). The lections are entire chapters of Scripture; no apocopated "pistling" or "gospelling" for them. Baptism and the Lord's Supper are prefaced as ordinances by reading their Biblical warrants and the formulae for the act of Baptism as for the reception of the consecrated elements in the Lord's Supper are directly from the New Testament. The curious Independent double Consecration, successively, of bread and wine, is justified not by reason, or custom, but only by fidelity to the New Testament narrative of its institution. The same submission to Scripture accounts for the unusual Independent order of having prayers of intercession and petition before prayers of confession, because it is thus given as the order in I Timothy. The songs were not human compositions, but the divinely inspired Psalms of David made into English poetry by translation into rhyme and metre. To worship God as he had commanded, rather than to be determined by reason, custom, beauty, convenience, or human psychology, was the commanding and demanding authority of Puritan worship, and it made vertebral Christians, supported by such a conviction into spiritual Ironsides. Their daily private and family prayers made the Puritans approach the worship of each Lord's Day with the expectation of a miniature Pentecost.

A second characteristic of Puritan worship was its utter simplicity and sincerity. This unostentatious and modest form of worship found its appropriate domestic setting in meeting-houses, scrubbed and whitewashed (not in ecclesiastical palaces or throne-rooms). It rejected all "storied windows richly dight, casting a dim religious light" to allow the sun to shine through unstained windows as the natural illumination of the Creator. The Puritans refused to

> let the pealing organ blow
> To the full-voiced quire below
> In service high and anthems clear . . .[8]

in favour of the pedestrian metres of the Psalms so that all could memorize them and sing them in unison. Their meeting-houses were, in fact, large homes, made spiritually so by the invisible presence of their Heavenly Father, whom they approached with a natural respect, and in the unaffected simplicity and spontaneity of free prayer that resembled a conversation. This simplicity did

---

[8] Milton's *Il Penseroso*, ll. 15-55.

not mean that they lacked all sense of the numinous. On the contrary, their sense of holiness in approaching God was so strong that they could do without any theatrical or adventitious aids which would make tawdry the splendour of the Creator's covenant mercies to his own. What could be more numinous than to hear the voice that thundered at Sinai or whispered the promises beside Galilee?

A third characteristic of Puritan worship was its interiority (which was, of course, carried to the furthest extreme by the Quakers). Negatively, it was an attempt to prevent all formalism and hypocrisy by recognising that the Spirit of God searches the heart and can unmask all pretences and disguises. Negatively also it is expressed as iconoclasm in the rejection of ecclesiastical vestments, of all ceremonial except the divinely donated signs of the Gospel sacraments, of set prayers, and set sermons (such as the homilies), and set creeds. Positively, it was an affirmation of the dominating role of the Holy Spirit in untrammelled freedom and sovereignty— and here again the Quakers carried this conviction to its logical conclusion, insisting that the Spirit must not be imprisoned in times, places, or sacraments.[9]

The gradual Puritan depreciation of the sacraments through infrequency and a memorialist doctrine, and the Quaker rejection of all sacraments was a serious defect. It left both Puritans and Quakers naked to the arrows of subjectivism, for once the august authority of the inerrant Scripture was lost, they were stripped of their defences. Indeed, the Quakers had already chosen the inner spirit over the exterior Word of God as their authority.

In the radical Puritan sects such as the Fifth Monarchists or the Seekers, the dependence upon the Holy Spirit uncontrolled by Scripture led to charismatic worship in which spontaneous witnessing and singing produced ecstasy. Within central Puritanism, however, the Holy Spirit generated illumination more obviously than warmth, although even here the Christ mysticism of Thomas Goodwin, Preston, Rous, and Sterry must not be forgotten. The point is that Scripture and the Spirit were conjoint authorities in

---

[9] Douglas V. Steere expresses the Quaker conviction in *The Hardest Journey* (The West Coast Quaker Lecture of 1968, published in the *Whittier College Bulletin*, Whittier, California, p. 4): "For Friends who know no outward Sacraments, this tendering action of the Holy Spirit is the baptism; it is the communion; it is the hallower of all facets of life. It is the revealer of injustice and the dissolver of men's dikes of reservation to the costly correction of those wrongs; it is the great magnet to draw men here and now from their enmities, their violence, their wars—into the peaceable Kingdom. . . ."

Puritanism, while in Quakerism the Spirit had precedence over Scripture which was used only for the confirmation of experience.

In the fourth place, in both Puritanism and Quakerism there was a profound concern for sanctification and integrity of life. Externally, this was visible in the Puritan fencing of the Communion table against all scandalous persons who dishonoured the holy community, in the "holy discipline" which cut off the dead limbs on the trunk of the church by excommunication, and, upon public repentance, re-grafted them. It is also evidenced in the deep concern of both Puritans and Quakers to live as children of the light, eagerly listening to God's Word as heard from the pulpit or in the heart, and (at least in the case of the Puritans) keeping a ledger book of the soul recording one's covenant promises to God and one's melancholy failures and resolutions to improve. The same procedure on a local, regional, or national scale was seen in the Puritan recognition of God's providence in criticism or in comfort, respectively in days of humiliation and days of thanksgiving. Puritans occasionally looked grim in their tenseness and censoriousness. They were never trivial with God and they were hard on themselves. They allowed neither the favour nor the flattery of men to divert them from offering to God the supreme homage of the obedience of faith issuing in sanctification.

The worship of the Puritans certainly strained after sanctification, for they wished to establish the rule of God in all the affairs of life. As a medium for the expression of unity, however, it was not as successful as a liturgy. If the Roman Catholics and the Anglicans stressed Catholicity and Apostolicity in the hope of attaining unity, the Puritans counted all else well lost for the sake of holiness. The conception of the "gathered church" necessarily meant separation from the world, and the Puritans considered compromise too great a price to pay for unity.

Nor was Puritan worship able to minister to the mixed spiritual-physical nature of man. Its worshippers were expected to live as angels, as bodiless spirits, using their ears, but neglecting the senses of touch, of scent, of taste, and above all, of sight. Its prolix prayers and marathon preaching left congregations edified and often even elated, but also exhausted. Catholics and Anglicans acknowledged with St. Thomas Aquinas that *natura non tollit sed perfecit naturam*, that grace does not trample on but raises nature. The Puritans seemed to think that heaven and earth, grace and nature, form and spirit, structure and freedom were antithetical and not complementary. Gerard Manley Hopkins, the Jesuit poet, knew the delights and dangers of beauty as well as any Puritan, but he recognised that it was a gift from the Creator. His poem, "To what serves Mortal Beauty?" is both the statement of the problem and the answer. He admits that beauty is

> —dangerous; does set danc-
> ing blood—the O-seal-that-so- feature, flung prouder form
> Than Purcell tune lets treat to? See: it does this: keeps warm
> Men's wits to the things that are; What good means

And "how meet beauty?" His answer is,

> Merely meet it; own,
> Home at heart, heaven's sweet gift; then leave, let that alone.
> Yea, wish that though, wish all, God's better beauty, grace.[10]

Moreover, Puritan worship had another defect arising from its concentration—over-didacticism. It was forgotten that symbols may teach more powerfully, if quietly, than scolding sermons, and that "where reason fails with all her powers, there faith prevails and love adores." There seemed to be, at least before 1662, so much argumentation and controversy in Puritan preaching, and so much frenetic experimentation in prayer, that it must have been difficult to attain to the serenity of contemplation or even to the lower levels of contentment, which Roman Catholics and Anglicans found in their familiar forms. The nemesis of didacticism was reported by Increase Mather, the New England Puritan divine, who was unconscionably fond of jeremiads, in the words: "We may here take notice that the nature of man is woefully corrupted and depraved, else they would not be so apt to sleep when the precious Truths of God are dispensed in his Name, Yea, and men are more apt to sleep then, than at another time. Some woful Creatures have been so wicked as to profess they have gone to hear Sermons on purpose, that they might sleep, finding themselves at such times much disposed that way."[11]

While Puritan worship was admirable in its concentration on the divine revelation in the audible and visible Word (in preaching and the Gospel sacraments), as the means for transforming the

---

[10] *Poems of Gerard Manley Hopkins* (2nd edn., with critical intro. by Charles Williams, 1930, p. 60).
[11] Perry Miller and T. H. Johnson, *The Puritans* (New York, 1938), p. 374.

human will, it left much to be desired as a medium for common worship. It had few responses for the people who became (except for the metrical Psalms they sang) attuned to the tyranny of the single ministerial voice. As we have seen, it had virtually no place for the offering by the people of their weekly work and witness. It lacked the radiant joy of discipleship, and expressed rather the desperate seriousness of duty. Puritanism is a resistance movement, and its worship provided the iron-rations. It was not a religion or a form of worship that would flourish, except in times of danger.

4. Complementarity

In the last analysis, Catholic styles of worship (whether Roman or Anglican) provide order, unity, dignity, historical continuity and popular participation, and they resemble the etiquette of a court and are appropriate for large traditional assemblies. The Puritan and Quaker styles of worship are rather an informal domestic gathering of Christian households of faith valuing sincerity, simplicity, spontaneity, and friendliness, as well as humility. Roman Catholics and Anglicans run the risk of formalism and hypocrisy; Puritans and Quakers run the risks of anarchy and subjectivity, especially when Scripture no longer speaks with unchallenged authority as it did in the middle seventeenth century before the advent of deism. Possibly even more significant for an age of increasing secularity is the fact that Puritan and Quaker modes of worship with their flexibility, experimental nature, and simplicity are able to operate in turbulent and uncertain times as expressions of a spiritual resistance movement. This may be their distinctive contribution to the history of worship.

In normal times, however, worshippers need a form of cultus which transmits the great tradition in the way that liturgies do, provided they also leave room for the contemporary expression of devotion. A genuine sense of the creativity of variety in worship might result in a lessened desire for competitiveness and a greater longing for complementarity. Just as one might hope for the inclusion of many present denominations as "religious orders" under the overarching aegis of One Holy, Catholic and Apostolic church, so one also might wish to see the creation of a liturgy comprehensive enough to include a place for free prayer and for silent prayer. Such a view was beyond the gaze of even so ecumenical a theologian and pastor as that self-styled "meer Catholick," Richard

Baxter. It may even be beyond the possibility of general acceptance in the late twentieth century.

It is worth recalling that those members whom we in this age would have elected to the *communio sanctorum*, Lancelot Andrewes, John Donne, Jeremy Taylor, Augustine Baker, the Benedictine, George Fox, the Baptist, John Bunyan, and the Puritan, Richard Baxter, would have found it impossible to worship together, for Roman Catholics, Anglicans, Puritans, Baptists, and Quakers unchurched one another at the least provocation. It may be, therefore, more realistic to recognise that pluralism in worship is likely to remain with us for many years. It might even have the advantage of giving a wider set of options to the people of God and lead to greater creativity in the attempt to produce a worthier worship.

BIBLIOGRAPHY

1. Liturgical Texts
2. Manuscripts
3. Periodicals and Publications
4. Sources in English Literature
5. Books

1. SELECTED LITURGICAL TEXTS

(Arranged Chronologically by Denomination)

ANGLICAN

Grisbrooke, W. Jardine. *Anglican Liturgies of the Seventeenth and Eighteenth Centuries.* Alcuin Club Collections, No. XL, 1958. This contains the so-called Laudian or Scottish Liturgy of 1637, the major liturgies of the Non-Jurors, and the liturgical compilation of Jeremy Taylor, *A Collection of Offices*, but in each case it is limited to the Order for Holy Communion. The latter is also to be found in Jeremy Taylor's *Works*, Ed. R. Heber. 15 Vols. 1822. xv, pp. 237-389.

Sanderson's *A Liturgy in Time of Rebellion*, an adaptation of the Prayer Book rite, can be found in *Fragmentary Illustrations of the History of the Book of Common Prayer.* Ed. W. K. Jacobson. 1874. Pp. 1-40.

Cuming, G. J., *The Durham Book, Being the First Draft of the Revision of the Book of Common Prayer in 1661.* Oxford, 1961.

The Book of Common Prayer. 1662.

Legg, J. Wickham, ed. *English Orders for Consecrating Churches in the Seventeenth Century.* Henry Bradshaw Society, Vol. XLI, 1911.

PURITAN AND REFORMED

John Knox's Genevan Service Book, 1556. Ed. William D. Maxwell. Edinburgh, 1931.

The Book of Common Order. Eds. G. W. Sprott and J. Leishman. Edinburgh, 1868.

A Booke of the Forme of Common Prayers, Administration of the Sacraments, &c. agreable to Gods Worde, and the Use of the Reformed Churches. Published in 1584 and 1586, respectively, as the Waldegrave and Middelburg Puritan liturgies; reprinted, *Fragmenta Liturgica.* Ed. Peter Hall. Vol. 1. Bath, 1848; and *Reliquiae Liturgicae.* Vol. 1. Bath, 1847.

The Parliamentary Directory, originally entitled, *A Directory for Publique Worship in the Three Kingdoms* (1644), issued by the dominantly Presbyterian Westminster Assembly of Divines. *Reliquiae Liturgicae,* reprinted; ed. Peter Hall. Vol. III. Bath, 1847. Also *The Westminster Directory.* Ed. T. Leishman. Edinburgh and London, 1901.

A Supply of Prayer for the Ships that want Ministers to pray with them agreeable to the Directory established by Parliament, published by authority. 1645.

Richard Baxter's *The Reformation of the Liturgy* (1661), sometimes known as the *Reformed Liturgy* or the *Savoy Liturgy* (the latter because it was prepared with the approval of the Presbyterian ministers for submission to the Anglicans, both parties meeting in the Savoy, an attempt at a possible comprehensive liturgy in 1661). *Reliquiae Liturgicae.* Ed. Peter Hall. Vol. IV. Bath, 1847.

ROMAN CATHOLIC

*Sacra Institutio Baptizandi, Matrimonium Celebrandi, Infirmos Un-
gendi, Mortuos Sepelandi, ac alii nonnulli ritus ecclesiastici juxta
usum insignis Ecclesiae Sarisburiensis.* Douai, 1604.

*Missae aliquot pro sacerdotibus itinerantibus in Anglia, Ex Missale
Romano reformata.* St. Omer, English College Press. 1615.

*Missale parvum pro sacerdotibus in Anglia itinerantibus, Ordo etiam
baptizandi & rituale . . . extractus.* 1623.

*Missale parvum pro sacerdotibus in Anglia, Scotia, & Ibernia itineran-
tibus.* 1626.

2. MANUSCRIPTS

In the Ampleforth Abbey Library: Inscription on blank leaf of an Antwerp Missal owned by the Middleton family.

In the Bodleian Library, Oxford: Rawlinson Ms. A. 441. f. 28; Rawlinson Ms. D. 85. f. 198; Tanner Ms. 59. II. 560 (transcript).

In the Dr. Williams's Library, London: Baxter Ms. 360. f. 71; Harleian
Ms. 3795. f. 23.

In the Dr. Williams's Library, London: Baxter Ms. 3. 156; Baxter Ms.
5. 9; A Parte of a Register.

In the Edinburgh University Library: Ms. of Robert Kirk's Commonplace Book.

3. PERIODICALS AND PUBLICATIONS

DENOMINATIONAL

ANGLICAN
Theology

BAPTIST
The Baptist Quarterly
Transactions of the Baptist Historical Society

CONGREGATIONALIST (INDEPENDENT)
The Congregational Quarterly
Transactions of the Congregational Historical Society

QUAKER (FRIENDS)
Journal of the Friends' Historical Society

ROMAN CATHOLICS
The Downside Review (Benedictine Abbey of Downside, near Bath,
England)
The Month (London)
Recusant History
Worship (The Benedictine Abbey and University, St. John's, College-
ville, Minnesota, U.S.A.)

UNITARIAN
Transactions of the Unitarian Historical History

INTERDENOMINATIONAL
Church History (published by the American Society of Church History, Chicago)
Journal of Ecclesiastical History (London)
Journal of Theological Studies (Oxford)
Studia Liturgica (Rotterdam, Holland)

SECULAR
Devonshire Association Transactions
History
The Library
The Listener
The Manchester Quarterly
Proceedings of the British Academy
Transactions of the Royal Historical Society

4. SOURCES IN ENGLISH LITERATURE

Since this is the Golden Century of the English Pulpit, considerable use was made of the sermons of Lancelot Andrewes, John Donne, and Jeremy Taylor, distinguished as literature as well as sacred oratory. It so happens that the greatest poets of the seventeenth century were also men of religion. The poetry they wrote is therefore invaluable as an index of their spirituality. For this reason much use was made of the sacred poetry of John Donne, George Herbert, Richard Crashaw, Henry Vaughan, and Thomas Traherne, and occasional use of John Milton's poetry and prose. Dekker, Davenant, Herrick, Marvell, and Dryden were also cited but only incidentally. Reference was also made to Bunyan's *Pilgrim's Progress* as well as to his autobiography, *Grace Abounding*.

Invaluable contributions to the period were made by those vivid and distinguished diarists, Samuel Pepys and John Evelyn, and by a minor figure, Ralph Josselin.

The *Lives* of leading Caroline divines by Izaak Walton were also important.

From other periods use was made of an Addison essay from the *Spectator*, Sir Walter Scott's novel, *Woodstock*, and Gerard Manley Hopkins's poems.

5. BOOKS

(Except where otherwise indicated, all books were published in London)

Adams, Thomas. *Works*. Folio edn., 1630.
Adams, William Seth. "William Palmer of Worcester, 1803-1885, the only learned man among them." Ph.D. Princeton University, 1973.

Addison, W. *The English Country Parson.* 1948.

Addleshaw, G.W.O. *The High Church Tradition: A Study in the Liturgical Thought of the Seventeenth Century.* Alcuin Club, 1963.

Addleshaw, G.W.O. and Frederick Etchells. *The Architectural Setting of Anglican Worship.* 1948.

A Kempis, Thomas. *Imitation of Christ.* Tr. Thomas Rogers, 1580.

————. *The sole-talke of the Soule.* . . . A trans. of *Soliloquium Animae* by Thomas Rogers, 1580.

Alexander, H. G. *Religion in England, 1558-1662.* 1968.

Alleine, Joseph. *Christian Letters full of Spirituall Instructions, tending to the Promotion of the Power of Godliness, both in Persons and Families.* 1672.

Alleine, Theodosia. *The Life and Death of Mr. Joseph Alleine, Late Teacher of the Church at Taunton, in Somersetshire, Assistant to Mr. Newton.* 1672.

Allison, A. F. and D. M. Rogers. *A Catalogue of Catholic Books in English printed abroad or secretly in England 1558-1640.* Bognor Regis, 1956.

Allison, C. F. *The Rise of Moralism; The Proclamation of the Gospel from Hooker to Baxter.* New York, 1966.

Ames, William. *The Marrow of Theology.* Tr. and intro. by J. D. Eusden. Boston and Philadelphia, 1968.

Andrewes, Lancelot. *A Manual of the Private Devotions and Meditations of the Right Reverend Father in God, Lancelot Andrewes.* Tr. R. Drake, 1648.

————. *Ninety-Six Sermons.* 5 Vols. Oxford, 1841-1843.

————. *A Pattern of Catechistical Doctrine and other Minor Works.* Oxford, 1843.

————. *Preces Privatae.* Ed. F. E. Brightman. 1903.

————. *Works.* Eds. J. P. Wilson and J. Bliss in Library of Anglo-Catholic Theology. 11 Vols. Oxford, 1841-1854.

Andrews, Nicholas. *The First Century of Scandalous Malignant Priests.* 1643.

Annesley, Samuel, ed. *A Continuation of Morning Exercise Sermons.* 1683.

[Anon.]. *The Arminian Nunnery, or, A Brief Description and Relation of the late Erected Monasticall Place called the Arminian Nunnery at Little Gidding in Huntingdonshire.* 1641.

————. *A Collection of Prayers and Thanksgivings used in His Majesties Chappell and in His Armies.* Oxford, 1643.

————. *A Dialogue between Mr. Prejudice . . . and Mr. Reason, a Student in the University.* 1682.

————. *Eikon Basilike, the Portraiture of His Sacred Majesty in His Solitudes and Sufferings.* 1648.

————. *A Free and Impartial Inquiry into the causes of that very great Esteem and Honour that the Nonconforming Preachers are generally in with their followers.* 1673.

————. *From What has been, may be again, or an instance of London's Loyalty in 1640, Etc.* 1710.

————. *A Manuall of prayers newly gathered out of many and famous divers authors as well aūcient as of the tyme present.* [Rouen], 1583.

————. *A New View of London.* 2 Vols. 1708.

————. *The Presbyterian Pater Noster.* A broadsheet of 1681.

————. *A Survey of the Book of Common Prayer.* 1606.

————. *Two Prayers, One for the Safety of His Majesties Person; The Other For the Preservation of this University and City of Oxford to be used in all Churches and Chappels.* Oxford, 1644.

————. *The Whole Duty of Man, laid down in a plain and familiar way for the use of all, but especially the meanest reader; divided into seventeen chapters, one whereof being read every Lord's Day, the whole may be read over thrice in the year; necessary for all families. With private devotions for several occasions.* 1692.

————. *The Whole Duty of Prayer containing devotions for every day of the week, and for several occasions ordinary and extraordinary.* . . . 1692.

Anstruther, Godfrey. *Vaux of Harrowden, A Recusant Family.* Newport, Monmouthshire, 1953.

Archer, John. *The Personal Reigne of Christ upon Earth, in a treatise wherein is fully and largely laid open and proved, that Jesus Christ, together with the Saints, shall visibly possesse a Monarchicall State and Kingdome in this World.* 1642.

Arderne, James. *Directions Concerning the Matter and Stile of Sermons.* 1671. Reissued, ed. John Mackay. Oxford, 1952.

Aubrey, John. *Brief Lives.* Ed. Andrew Clark. 1898.

[Augustine, Saint, of Hippo]. *S. Austin's Rule . . . together with the Constitutions of the English Canonesse regulars of our B. Ladyes of Sion in Paris.* Ed. and Tr. Miles Pinkney. 1636.

Aveling, Hugh. *The Catholic Recusants of the West Riding of Yorkshire, 1558-1790.* Leeds, 1963.

Babbage, Stuart Barton. *Puritanism and Richard Bancroft.* 1962.

[Baillie, Robert]. *A Dissuasive from the Errours of the Time.* . . . 1646.

————. *The Letters and Journals of Robert Baillie.* Ed. David Laing. 3 Vols. Edinburgh, 1841.

[Baker, Augustine]. *Augustine Baker's The Inner Life of Dame Gertrude More.* Ed. Benedict Weld. Blundell, 1911.

————. *Memorials of Father Augustine Baker and other Documents relating to the English Benedictines.* Eds. J. McCann and [R.] H. Connolly. Catholic Record Society. Vol. 33. 1933.

————. *Sancta Sophia, or Directions for the Prayer of Contemplation . . . Extracted out of more than Forty Treatises written by Augustine Baker. And Methodically digested by . . . Serenus Cressy.* Douai, 1657.

Ball, Frank E. "A Liturgical Colloquy: An Examination of the Savoy Conference, 1661." B. Litt. Oxford University, 1958.

Bampfield, Francis. *A name, an after-one, or Ὄνομα καινοῦ, a name, a new one, in the latter-day glory.* 1681.

Barbour, Hugh. *The Quakers in Puritan England.* New Haven, Conn., 1964.

Barclay, Alexander. *The Protestant Doctrine of the Lord's Supper.* 1927.

Barclay, Robert. *The Inner Life of the Religious Societies of the Commonwealth.* 3rd edn., 1879.

Barclay, Robert [Quaker apologist]. *Apology for the True Christian Divinity.* 1678.

Barnard, John. *A Short View of the Prelatical Church of England.* 1641. Reissued 1661.

————. *First Booke of Selected Church Musick.* . . . 1641.

Barrow, Isaac. *Works.* Ed. J. Tillotson. 4 Vols. 1683-1687.

Barrowe, Henry. *A Brief Discoverie of the False Church.* Dordrecht, 1590-1591.

Barry, A., ed. *Masters of English Theology* 1877

Baruzi, Jean. *Saint Jean de la Croix et le problème de l'expérience.* Paris, 1924.

Bates, William. *Harmony of the Divine Attributes.* 1674.

Bauthumley, Jacob. *The Light and Dark Side of God.* 1650.

Baxter, Richard. *An Apology for the Nonconformists' Ministry.* 1681.

[Baxter, R.]. *Autobiography of Richard Baxter.* Ed. J. M. Lloyd Thomas. Everyman Library, 1931.

Baxter, R. *Call to the Unconverted.* 1658.

————. *Catholic Communion Defended against both Extreams.* 1684.

————. *A Christian Directory, a Summe of Practical Theologie and Cases of Conscience.* 1673.

————. *Five Disputations of Church Government and Worship.* 1659.

————. *Now or Never.* 1671.

————. *Poetical Fragments.* 1683.

[Baxter, R.]. *The Practical Works of the Rev. Richard Baxter.* Ed. William Orme. 23 Vols. 1830.

Baxter, R. *The Reformed Pastor.* Edn. of 1860.

[Baxter, R.]. *Reliquiae Baxterianae.* Ed. M. Sylvester. 1696.

————. *The Safe Religion.* 1657.

Baxter, R. *The Saints Everlasting Rest.* 3rd edn., 1652.

————. *A Third Defence of the Cause of Peace.* 1681.

[Bayly, Lewis]. *The Practice of Piety, Directing a Christian how to walk with God.* 1612.

Bayne, Peter, ed. *Puritan Documents.* . . . 1862.

Bede, John. *The Right and Prerogative of Kings, Against Cardinal Bellarmine and other Jesuits.* 1612.

Bellarmine, Robert. *An ample declaration of the Christian Doctrine.* English trans., 1604.

————. *Short Catechisme of Cardinall Bellarmine illustrated with Images.* 1614.

Benson, Louis F. *The English Hymn: Its Development & Use in Worship.* New York, 1915. Reprinted Richmond, Va., 1962.

[Bernard, John]. *The Anatomie of the Service Book.* 1641.

544

Bernard, St. of Clairvaux. *The Golden Treatise, Joy in Tribulation, and the forme of an honest life.* 1613.

———. *A Hive of Sacred Honie—Combes Containing most Sweet and Heavenly Counsel.* [Douai], 1631.

[Bernard, St. of Clairvaux]. *St. Bernard His Meditations: or Sighes, Sobbes and Teares, upon our Saviour's Passion. . . .* Ed. and Tr. "W.P.," ca. 1610.

Besse, Joseph. *A Collection of the Sufferings of the People called Quakers.* 2 Vols. 1753.

Besse, Thomas. *A Rationale on Cathedral Worship.* 1720.

Bethell, Samuel L. *The Cultural Revolution of the Seventeenth Century.* 1951.

Betjeman, John. *First and Last Loves.* 1952.

Beveridge, William. *A Sermon on the Excellency and Usefulness of the Book of Common Prayer.* 1682.

[Beveridge, William]. *Works.* Ed. J. Bliss. 12 Vols. 1843-1848.

Biéler, André. *Architecture in Worship.* Edinburgh and London, 1965.

Blackstone, B. *The Ferrar Papers.* 1938.

Blanfield, R. *A History of Renaissance Architecture in England, 1500-1800.* 2 Vols. 1897.

Blunt, J. H. *Annotated Book of Common Prayer.* 1866.

Bolton, Robert. *Certain Devout Prayers of Mr. Bolton. . . .* 1638.

———. *Some Generall Directions for a Comfortable Walking With God.* 1625.

Bosher, R. S. *The Making of the Restoration Settlement.* New York, 1951.

Bourne, E.C.E. *The Anglicanism of William Laud.* 1947.

Bouyer, Louis. *Orthodox Spirituality and Anglican Spirituality.* Tr. Barbara Wall. 1969.

Bownde, Nicholas. *The doctrine of the Sabbath, plainely layde forth, and sundly proved.* 1595.

Boyes, John. *An Exposition of the Dominical Epistles and Gospels used in our English Liturgy throughout the whole yeare.* 1609.

Boyle, Robert. *The Excellency of Theology Compared with Natural Philosophy.* 1673.

Braithwaite, W. C. *The Beginnings of Quakerism.* 2nd edn. Cambridge, 1955.

———. *The Second Period of Quakerism.* Ed. H. J. Cadbury. 2nd edn. Cambridge, 1961.

Bramhall, John. *Works.* Ed. A. W. Haddam in Library of Anglo-Catholic Theology. 5 Vols. Oxford, 1842-1845.

Brémond, Henri. *Histoirè littéraire du Sentiment Religieux en France.* 11 Vols. Paris, 1915-1932.

Briggs, Martin S. *Puritan Architecture and its Future.* 1946.

———. *Wren the Incomparable.* 1953.

Brightman, F. E. *The English Rite, a Synopsis of the Sources and Revisions of the Book of Common Prayer.* 2 Vols. 1915.

Brinton, Howard H. *Creative Worship.* Swarthmore Lecture. 1931.

Brinton, Howard H. *Friends for 300 Years*. New York, 1953.

Brockett, Allen. *Nonconformity in Exeter, 1650-1875*. Manchester, 1962.

Browne, Robert. *A Booke which sheweth the life and manners of all true Christians*. Middelburg, 1582.

————. *A True and Short Declaration*. . . . 1583.

————. *The Writings of Robert Harrison and Robert Browne*. Eds. A. Peel and L. H. Carlson. 1953.

Bruggink, J. and Carl H. Droppers. *Christ and Architecture: Building Presbyterian/Reformed Churches*. Grand Rapids, Mich., 1965.

Buck, Fellowes, Ramsbotham and Warner, eds. *Tudor Church Music*: Vol. IV: *Orlando Gibbons*. 1925.

Bukofzer, Manfred. *Music in the Baroque Era, from Monteverdi to Bach*. New York, 1947.

Bull, George. *The Corruptions of the Church of Rome*. 1705.

————. *Works*. Ed. E. Burton. 6 Vols. Oxford, 1827.

Bunyan, John. *Grace Abounding to the Chief of Sinners*. 1666.

————. *The Holy War*. 1682.

————. *Pilgrim's Progress*. 1678.

————. *The Whole Works*. Ed. George Offor. 3 Vols. Glasgow, 1862.

Burnet, Gilbert. *Discourse of Pastoral Care*. 1692.

————. *History of My Own Time*. 2 Vols. 1723-1724. Republished. 6 Vols. Oxford, 1833.

————. *The Life and Death of Sir Matthew Hale*. 1682.

Burrage, Champlin. *The Church Covenant Idea*. Philadelphia, 1904.

————. *The early English Dissenters in the light of recent research, 1550-1641*. 2 Vols. Cambridge, 1912.

Burroughes, Jeremiah. *Gospel-Worship or the Right Manner of Sanctifying the name of God in generall*. 1648.

Burton, E. H. *The Life and Times of Bishop Challoner*. 2 Vols. 1909.

[Burton, Henry]. *A Divine Tragedy Lately Enacted*. Amsterdam, 1636.

————. *A Tryall of Private Devotion, or a Diall for the Houres of Prayer*. 1628.

Bury, A. *The Constant Communicant, a Diatribe proving that Constancy in Receiving the Lord's Supper is the Indispensable Duty*. Oxford, 1681.

Byfield, Richard. *The Doctrine of the Sabbath Vindicated*. 1631.

Calamy, Edmund. *Continuation of the Ejected Ministers*. 2 Vols. 1727.

————. *Historical Account of my Own Life*. Ed. J. T. Rutt. 2 Vols. 1829.

Calder, I. M. *Activities of the Puritan Faction of the Church of England, 1625-1633*. 1957.

Capp, B. S. *The Fifth Monarchy Men*. 1972.

Caraman, Philip. *Henry Morse: Priest of the Plague*. 1957.

Cardwell, E. *Documentary Annals of the Reformed Church of England, 1546-1716*. 2 Vols. Oxford, 1844.

————. *A History of Conferences and other Proceedings*. Oxford, 1841.

————. *Synodalia*. 2 Vols. Oxford, 1842.

Carpenter, E. *The Life and Times of Thomas Tenison, Archbishop of Canterbury*. 1948.

Carpenter, S. C. *The Church in England, 597-1688*. 1954.

Carritt, E. F. *A Calendar of British Taste, From 1600 to 1800*. 1948.

Carruthers, S. W. *The Everyday Work of the Westminster Assembly*. Philadelphia, 1943.

Carter, T. T. *Nicholas Ferrar, his Household and his Friends*. 1892.

Cartwright, Thomas. *A Treatise of the Christian Religion, Or, The Whole Bodie and Substance of Divinitie*. 1616.

Cary, Lucius (Lord Falkland). *The Discourse; The Answer*; and *The Reply*. Published in one vol. 1651.

Cawdrey, Robert. *A Treasurie or Store-House of Similies*. 1600.

Chamberlain, R. *Conceits, Clinches, Flashes and Whimsies newly studied*. 1639.

Chambers, Sabine. *The Garden of our B. Lady. Or a devout manner, how to serve her in her Rosary*. [St. Omer?], 1619.

Charnock, S. *Complete Works*. 5 Vols. Edinburgh, 1864-1866.

Chillingworth, William. *The Religion of Protestants, a Safe Way of Salvation*. 1637.

Chute, Marchette. *Two Gentle Men: The Lives of George Herbert and Robert Herrick*. New York, 1959.

Clagett, William. *An Answer to the Dissenters Objections against the Common Prayers and some other parts of Divine-Service prescribed in the Liturgie of the Church of England*. 1683.

Clarendon, Earl of. (See Hyde, E., 1st Earl of Clarendon.)

Clark, George N. *The Later Stuarts, 1660-1714*. Oxford, 1934. 2nd edn., 1955.

————. *The Seventeenth Century*. Oxford, 1929. 2nd edn., 1947.

Clark, Henry W. *History of English Nonconformity*. 2 Vols. 1911.

Clarke, Samuel. *A Collection of the Lives of Ten Eminent Divines*. 1661.

Clay, W. K., ed. *Liturgies and Occasional Forms of Prayer set forth in the Reign of Queen Elizabeth*. Cambridge: Parker Society, 1851.

Clifford, James. *Divine Services and Anthems*. 1663.

Cobb, Gerald. *The Old Churches of London*. 1942.

Cocceius, Johannes. *Summa doctrinae de Foedere et Testamento Dei*. 1648.

Cocks, H. F. Lovell. *The Religious Life of Oliver Cromwell*. 1960.

Coleridge, J. T. *Memoir of John Keble*. Oxford, 1870.

Collier, Jeremy. *An Ecclesiastical History of Great Britain*. 1708.

Collinson, Patrick. *The Elizabethan Puritan Movement*. Berkeley, Calif., 1967.

[Comber, Thomas]. *The Autobiography and Letters of Thomas Comber*. Ed. C. E. Whiting. Vols. CLVI-CLVII. Surtees Society, 1941-1942.

Comber, Thomas. *A Companion to the Altar*. 4th edn., 1685.

————. *A Companion to the Temple*. 7 Vols. 1672. Reissued Oxford, 1841.

Comber, Thomas. *A Discourse Concerning the daily frequenting the Common Prayer.* 1687.

Connolly, R. H. and Justin McCann, eds. *Memorials of Father Baker.* Vol. XXXIII. Catholic Record Society, 1933.

Coomer, Duncan. *English Dissent.* 1947.

[Cosin, John]. *A Collection of Private Devotions in the practise of the Antient Church, called, The Hours of Prayers.* 1627. Reissued; ed. P. G. Stanwood, Oxford, 1967.

———. *The Correspondence of John Cosin, Lord Bishop of Durham.* Vols. LII and LV. Surtees Society, 1869, 1872.

———. *Historia Transubstantiationis Papalis.* 1675.

———. *Works.* Ed. G. Ornsby. 5 Vols. Library of Anglo-Catholic Theology, Oxford, 1843-1855.

Cotton, John. *The Keyes of the Kingdome of Heaven.* 1644.

———. *A Modest and Cleare Answer to Mr. Balls Discourse of set formes of Prayer.* 1642.

———. *The Way of the Churches of Christ in New England.* 1645.

Cox, Harvey. *The Feast of Fools.* Cambridge, Mass., 1969.

Cragg, Gerald R. *The Church and the Age of Reason, 1648-1789.* 1960.

———. *From Puritanism to the Age of Reason.* Cambridge, 1950.

———. *Puritanism in the Period of the Great Persecution.* Cambridge, 1957.

Crashaw, Richard. *Poems* in *Complete Works.* Ed. A. B. Grosart. 2 Vols. 1872-1873.

Crashaw, William. *The Complaint or Dialogue Betwixt the Soul and the Bodie of a damned man.* 1632.

[Cromwell, Oliver]. *The Letters and Speeches of Oliver Cromwell.* Ed. Thomas Carlyle. 2 Vols. 1845.

Crosby, T. *The History of the English Baptists.* 4 Vols. 1738-1740.

Cross, F. L., ed. *The Oxford Dictionary of the Christian Church.* Corrected impression of 1963.

Crouch, William. *Posthuma Christiana.* Edn. of 1712.

Cudworth, Ralph. *The Works of Ralph Cudworth.* Ed. T. Birch. 4 Vols. Oxford, 1829.

Cuming, G. J., ed. *The Durham Book, Being the First Draft of the Revision of the Book of Common Prayer in 1661.* Oxford, 1961.

———. *A History of Anglican Liturgy.* 1969.

Curnock, Nehemiah, ed. *The Journal of John Wesley.* 8 Vols. 1909.

Curwen, Spencer. *Studies in Music and Worship.* 5 Vols. 1880-1885.

Danvers, H. *Theopolis.* 1672.

Davenant, William. *Gondibert.* 1650.

Davies, Godfrey. *The Early Stuarts, 1603-1660.* 2nd edn. Oxford, 1959.

Davies, Horton. *The Worship of the English Puritans.* 1948.

———. *From Cranmer to Hooker, 1534-1603, From Watts and Wesley to Maurice, 1690-1850, From Newman to Martineau, 1850-*

1900, The Ecumenical Century, 1900-1965. Worship and Theology in England. Vols. 1, 3-5. Princeton, 1961-1970.

Davies, J. Gordon, ed. *A Dictionary of Liturgy and Worship.* 1972.

Dearnley, Christopher. *English Church Music 1650-1750 in Royal Chapel, Cathedral and Parish Church.* 1970.

Dekker, Thomas. *The Shoemaker's Holiday.* 1599.

Denne, Henry. *The drag-net of the Kingdome of Heaven.* Republished as Part III of *Anti-Christ unmasked* in three treatises, 1646.

Dent, Arthur. *The Plaine Man's Path-way to Heaven.* 1601.

———. *Sermon of Repentance.* 1637.

Dewey, Meredith, Ratcliff, and Sykes. *The Anglican Tradition.* Sermons delivered in Chichester Cathedral, July 1958.

Dexter, H. M. *The Congregationalism of the Last Three Hundred Years.* 1880.

Dix, Gregory. *The Shape of the Liturgy.* 1945.

Dod, John. *A briefe dialogue concerning preparation for the Lord's Supper.* 1627.

Donaldson, Gordon. *The Making of the Scottish Prayer Book of 1637.* Edinburgh, 1954.

Donne, John. *The Divine Poems.* Ed. Helen Gardner. 1952.

———. *The Sermons of John Donne.* Eds. George R. Potter and Evelyn M. Simpson. 10 Vols. Berkeley and Los Angeles, Calif., 1953-1962.

[Doughty, John]. Phil-Iren-Alethius, I. D., pseud. *Velitationes Polemicae or Polemicall short Discussions of certain particular and select Questions.* 1651.

Dowden, Edward. *Puritan and Anglican: Studies in Literature.* 1900.

Downame, John. *The Christian Warfare.* 1604.

———. *Guide to Godliness.* 1622.

[Dowsing, William]. *The Journal of William Dowsing.* Ed. A. C. Moule. Cambridge, 1926.

———. *Journal of William Dowsing.* Ed. E. H. Evelyn White. 1885.

Drummond, A. L. *The Church Architecture of Protestantism.* Edinburgh, 1934.

Drysdale, A. H. *History of the Presbyterians in England, their Rise, Decline and Revival.* 1889.

Dugmore, C. W. *Eucharistic Doctrine in England from Hooker to Waterland.* 1942.

——— and Charles Duggan, eds. *Studies in Church History.* Vol. I. 1964.

Duppa, Bryan. *Private Formes of Prayer.* 1645.

Eachard, John. *Grounds and Occasions of the Contempt of the Clergy.* 1671.

Edwards, Thomas. *Gangraena.* 1646.

Elborow, T. *An Exposition of the Book of Common Prayer.* 1663.

Eliot, T. S. *For Lancelot Andrewes, Essays on Style and Order.* 1928.

Emerson, Everett H., ed. *English Puritanism from John Hooper to John Milton.* Durham, N.C., 1968.

Eusden, John D., ed. *The Marrow of Theology, William Ames, 1576-1663.* Boston and Philadelphia, 1968.
Evelyn, John. *Devotionarie Book.* Intro. W. H. Frere. 1936.
————. *Diary.* Ed. E. S. de Beer. 6 Vols. Oxford, 1955.
Evennett, H. O. *The Spirit of the Counter-Reformation.* 1963.
Every, George. *The High Church Party, 1688-1718.* 1956.

Fallow, T. M. and H. B. McCall. *Yorkshire Church Plate.* Leeds, 1912.
Farnworth, Richard. *Christian Religious Meetings.* 1664.
Fellowes, E. H. *English Cathedral Music.* 5th edn. Ed. J. A. Westrup. 1969.
Field, Richard. *Of the Church.* 1606. Reissued in 4 Vols. 1847-1852.
Firth, Charles H. *The Last Days of the Protectorate.* 2 Vols. 1909.
Fisher, Samuel. *The Testimony of Truth Exalted.* 1679.
FitzSimon, Henry. *The Iustification and Exposition of the Divine Sacrifice of the Masse and of al Rites and Ceremonies.* 1611. Reprinted Menstone, Yorkshire, 1972.
Flecknoe, R. *Enigmatical Characters.* 1665.
[Flinton, George]. *A Manuall of prayers newly gathered out of many and famous divers authors as well auncient as of the tyme present.* [Rouen ?], 1583.
Floyd, John. *A Plea for the Reall-Presence.* 1624.
Foley, Henry. *Records of the English Province of the Society of Jesus.* 7 Vols. in 8. 1875-1883.
Fox, George. *Journal.* Ed. N. Penney. 1902.
————. *The journal of George Fox.* Revised; ed. J. L. Nickalls. Cambridge, 1952.
Fox, George and Hubberthorne, Richard. *Truths Defence against the Serpent.* 1658.
Francis, St., of Assisi. *The rule and testament of the seraphical father S. Francis.* Tr. Richard Mason. Douai, 1635.
————. *The rule of the religious of the third order of Saint Francis . . . living together in communitie and cloyster.* Tr. Arthur Bell. Brussels, 1624.
Frankel, P. *Gothic Architecture: Literary sources and interpretations through eight centuries.* Princeton, N.J., 1960.
Frere, W. H. and C. E. Douglas. *Puritan Manifestoes.* 1907. Ed. N. Sykes. 2nd edn., 1954.
Frost, Maurice. *English and Scottish Psalm and Hymn Tunes c. 1543-1677.* 1953.
————. *Historical Companion to Hymns Ancient and Modern.* Rev. edn. of Frere's "Historical Edition," 1962.
[Fuller, Robert]. *Missale Romanum Vindicatum, or the Mass Vindicated from D. Daniel Brevent's calumnious and scandalous Tract.* 1674.
Fuller, Thomas. *The Church History of Britain.* Ed. J. S. Brewer. 6 Vols. Oxford, 1845.
————. *The Worthies of England.* Ed. J. Freeman. 1952.
Fürst, V. *The Architecture of Sir Christopher Wren.* 1956.

Gardiner, S. R. *The Constitutional Documents of the Puritan Revolution*. 1889.

————. *The Personal Government of Charles I, 1628-1637*. 1877.

Garey, Samuel. *Great Britaine's litle Calendar or triple Diary in remembrance of three dayes, viz. the 24 of March the day of his Maiesties proclamation, The fift of August the day of Gowries Conspiracy; The fift of November the day of our deliverance from the Gun powder treason, whereunto is annexed, a short dissuasive from Popery*. 1618.

Gataker, Thomas. *A Discussion of the Papist Doctrine of Transubstantiation*. 1624.

Gauden, J. *Considerations touching the Liturgy of the Church of England*. 1661.

————. *Ecclesiae Anglicanae Suspiria, the Tears, Sighs, Complaints and Prayers of the Church of England, setting forth her former Constitution compared with her Present Condition*. 1659.

Gee, H. and W. J. Hardy. *Documents Illustrative of English Church History*. 1914.

Gee, John. *The Foot out of the Snare. . . .* 1624.

George, Katherine and Charles. *The Protestant Mind of the English Reformation*. Princeton, N.J., 1961.

[Gerard, John]. *The Autobiography of John Gerard, S.J.* Edn. 1881. Tr. Philip Caraman of edn. of 1951.

Geree, John. *The Character of an old English Puritane or Nonconformist*. 1646.

G. F. *The Liturgical Considerator Considered*. 1661.

[Gibbons, Orlando]. *Tudor Church Music, vol. IV: Orlando Gibbons*. Eds. P. C. Buck, E. H. Fellowes, A. Ramsbotham, and T. Warner. 1925.

Gilchrist, James. *Anglican Church Plate*. 1967.

Gill, Harry and E. L. Guilford. *The Rector's Book, Clayworth, Notts*. Nottingham, 1910.

Gillespie, George. *Dispute Against the English Popish Ceremonies*. 1660.

Glanvill, Joseph. *Essays on several important subjects in Philosophy and Religion*. 1676.

————. *Philosophia Pia*. 1671.

Goodwin, Thomas. *The Heart of Christ in Heaven towards Sinners on Earth*. 1651.

————. *Works*. Ed. J. Miller. 12 Vols. 1861-1866.

Gosse, Edmund. *The Life and Letters of John Donne*. 2 Vols. 1899.

Gotch, J. A. *Early Renaissance Architecture in England*. 2nd edn., 1914.

————. *Inigo Jones*. 1928.

Gouge, William. *Workes*. 1627.

Gough, John. *History of the people called Quakers*. 4 Vols. Dublin, 1789-1790.

Gould, G., ed. *Documents relating to the Settlement of the Church of England by the Act of Uniformity of 1662*. 1862.

Graeff, Hilda. *The Story of Mysticism*. 1966.

Granada, Luis de. *Libro de la Oracion.* 1553.

————. *A Memoriall of a Christian Life.* 1586.

————. *The Sinners Guide.* Tr. F. Meres. 1598.

Grantham, Thomas. *Christianismus Primitivus.* 1678.

[Granville, Denis]. *The Remains of Denis Granville.* Surtees Society. Vol. XLVII. 1865.

Greaves, Richard L. *John Bunyan.* Grand Rapids, Mich., 1969.

Green, V.H.H. *Religion at Oxford and Cambridge.* 1964.

Greenham, Richard. *A Treatise of the Sabbath.* 1592.

————. *Works.* 1601.

Grisbrooke, W. Jardine. *Anglican Liturgies of the Seventeenth and Eighteenth Centuries.* Alcuin Club Collections. No. XL. 1958.

[Grove, George]. *Grove's Dictionary of Music and Musicians.* Ed. E. Blom. 9 Vols. 5th edn., 1954.

Guilday, Peter. *The English Catholic refugees on the Continent, 1558-1795.* Vol. I: *The English Colleges and Convents in the Low Countries.* 1914.

Hagedorn, Maria. *Reformation und Spanische Andachsliteratur.* Leipzig, 1934.

Hageman, Howard. *Pulpit and Table.* London and Richmond, Va., 1962.

[Hales, John]. *The Golden Remains of the Ever Memorable Mr John Hales.* Ed. John Pearson. 1659.

Hall, Joseph. *The Arte of Divine Meditation.* 1606.

————. *Works.* Ed. Peter Hall. 1837.

Hall, Peter, ed. *Fragmenta Liturgica.* Vol. I: *Puritan.* Bath, 1847.

————, ed. *Reliquiae Liturgicae.* Vol. I: *Middleburgh*; Vol. III: *Directory* [Westminster]; Vol. IV: *Savoy* [Baxter's]. All published in Bath, 1848.

Haller, William. *Foxe's Book of Martyrs and the Elect Nation.* New York, 1963.

————. *Liberty and Reformation in the Puritan Revolution.* New York, 1955.

————. *The Rise of Puritanism, 1570-1643.* New York, 1938.

[Hammond, Henry]. *The Miscellaneous Theological Works of Henry Hammond.* Ed. N. Pocock in the Library of Anglo-Catholic Theology. 3 Vols. in 4. Oxford, 1847-1850.

————. *A Practical Catechism.* 1644, 1646, etc.

————. *A View of the New Directory and a Vindication of the Antient Liturgy of the Church of England.* 1645.

————. *Works.* Ed. William Fulman. 4 Vols. 1684-1689.

Hanbury, Benjamin. *Nonconformist Memorials.* 3 Vols. 1839-1844.

Happ, Howard. "Calendary Conflicts in Renaissance England." Ph.D., Princeton University, 1974.

Hardwick, William. *Gods Holy House and Service according to the primitive and most Christian forme thereof.* 1639.

Harley, John. *Music in Purcell's London.* 1968.

[Harrison, William]. *A Brief Discourse of the Christian Life and Death of Mistris Katherin Brettergh . . . who departed this world the last of May, 1601.* 1612.

Hart, A. Tindal. *The Country Clergy in Elizabethan and Stuart Times, 1558-1660.* 1958.

————. *The Man in the Pew, 1558-1660.* 1966.

Havran, Martin J. *The Catholics in Caroline England.* Palo Alto, Calif., 1962.

H.D.M.A. *A Sober and Temperate Discourse concerning the Interest of Words in Prayer.* 1661.

Heber, R., ed. *The Whole Works of Bishop Jeremy Taylor.* 15 Vols. 1822.

Henry, Matthew. *The Communicant's Companion.* 1704.

[Henry, Philip]. *Diaries and Letters of Philip Henry, M.A.* Ed. M. H. Lee. 1882.

Henson, H. Hensley. *Studies in English Religion in the XVII Century.* 1903.

[Herbert, George]. *The English Works of George Herbert.* Ed. G. H. Palmer. 3 Vols. Boston and New York, 1905.

————. *Herbert's Remains.* 1652.

————. *The Works of George Herbert.* Ed. F. E. Hutchinson. 2nd edn. Oxford, 1945.

Hetherington, W. M. *History of the Westminster Assembly of Divines.* 1843.

Heylyn, Peter. *Cyprianus Anglicus; History of the Life and Death of that most Reverend and Renowned Prelate William* [Laud]. 1668.

————. *Aerius Redivivus, or, the History of the Presbyterians.* 1670.

————. *Ecclesia Restaurata, the History of the Reformation of the Church of England.* 1661.

[Heywood, Oliver]. *The Reverend Oliver Heywood, His Autobiography, Diaries, Anecdote and Event Books.* Vols. i and ii: Brighouse, 1882. Vol. iii: Bingley, 1883.

————. *Works.* 2 Vols. Idle, Yorkshire, 1837.

Hickeringill, Edmund. *The Ceremony Monger.* 1689.

Higham, Florence. *Catholic and Reformed: a study of the Anglican Church, 1559-1662.* 1962.

————. *Lancelot Andrewes.* 1952.

Higham, John. *A Devout Exposition of the Holie Masse with an ample Declaration of all the Rites and Ceremonies belonging to the same.* Douai, 1614; enlarged edn., 1622.

Hill, Christopher. *The Century of Revolution, 1603-1714.* 1962.

————. *Economic Problems of the Church from Archbishop Whitgift to the Long Parliament.* Oxford, 1956.

————, ed. *The English Revolution; Three Essays.* New edn., 1949.

————. *Intellectual Origins of the English Revolution.* Oxford, 1965.

————. *Puritanism and Revolution; Studies in Interpretation.* 1958.

————. *The World Turned Upside Down.* 1972.

Hinchliff, Peter B. *The South African Liturgy.* Cape Town, 1959.

Holden, William P. *Anti-Puritan Satire, 1572-1642.* New Haven, Conn., 1954.

[Homilies]. *The* [Second] *Book of Homilies*. 1571.

Hooker, Richard. *The Ecclesiastical Polity and other Works of Richard Hooker*. Ed. Benjamin Hanbury. 3 Vols. 1830.

Horton, R. F. *John Howe*. 1894.

Howe, John. *The Living Temple*. Intro. T. Chalmers. 2nd edn. Glasgow, 1839.

———. *Works*. Ed. J. Hunt. 8 Vols. 1810-1822.

Howell, W. S. *Logic and Rhetoric in England, 1500-1700*. Princeton, N.J., 1956.

Howgill, Francis. *Mistery Babylon the Mother of Harlots discovered . . . in answer to a Book tituled the Directory for the Publick Worship of God*. 1659.

Hügel, Baron Friedrich Von. *Selected Letters, 1896-1924*. Ed. Bernard Holland. 1927.

Hughes, H. T. *The Piety of Jeremy Taylor*. 1960.

Hughes, Philip. *Rome and the Counter-Reformation in England*. 1944.

Hutchinson, F. E., ed. *The Works of George Herbert*. Oxford, 1941.

Hutchinson, Lucy. *Memoirs of the Life of Colonel Hutchinson*. Ed. C. H. Firth. 1906.

Hyde, A. G. *George Herbert and His Times*. 1906.

Hyde, E. 1st Earl of Clarendon. *Calendar of the Clarendon State Papers*. Ed. O. Ogle. 1872.

———. *History of the Great Rebellion*. 6 Vols. Oxford, 1807.

———. *Life and Continuation*. 2 Vols. Oxford, 1857.

I. D. Phil-Iren-Alethius. *Velitationes Polemicae or Polemicall short Discussions of certain particular and select Questions*. 1651.

Isaacson, Henry, ed. *Institutiones Piae*. 1630.

Isherwood, Christopher. *The World in the Evening*. 1954.

Jackson, Thomas. *The Raging Tempest stilled*. 1623.

Jacobson, W. K. *Fragmentary Illustrations of the History of the Book of Common Prayer*. 1874.

James I, King. *The Book of Sports*. 1618. Reissued by Charles I in 1633.

Janson, H. W. *History of Art*. New York, 1962.

Jasper, Ronald C. D. *Prayer Book Revision in England, 1800-1900*. 1954.

Jeavons, Sidney. *The Church Plate of Nottinghamshire*. 1965.

Jenkins, David. *A Scourge for the Directorie and the Revolting Synod which hath sitten this 5 Yeares, more for foure shillings a Day then for Conscience sake*. 1647.

Jessop, Augustus. *One Generation of a Norfolk House*. 1879.

[Jolly, Thomas]. *The Note-Book of the Revd. Thomas Jolly, 1671-1693*. Manchester: Chetham Society, 1895.

Jones, Richard Foster. *The Seventeenth Century: Studies in the History of English Thought and Literature from Bacon to Pope*. Palo Alto, Calif., 1951.

Jones, Ronald F. *Nonconformist Church Architecture.* 1914.
Jones, Rufus M. *Spiritual Reformers in the Sixteenth and Seventeenth Centuries.* 1914.
———. *Studies in Mystical Religion.* 1909.
Jordan, Wilbur K. *The Development of Religious Toleration in England.* 4 Vols. 1932-1940.
[Josselin, Ralph]. *The Diary of the Rev. Ralph Josselin, 1616-1683.* Ed. E. Hockcliffe. 3rd series, Vol. xv. Camden Society, 1908.
Julian, John. *A Dictionary of Hymnology.* 1925.

Kaufmann, E. *Architecture in the Age of Reason; Baroque and Post-Baroque in England, Italy, and France.* 1955.
Kaufmann, U. Milo. *The Pilgrim's Progress and Traditions in Puritan Meditation.* New Haven, Conn., 1966.
Keach, Benjamin. *The Breach Repair'd in God's Worship.* 1691.
———. *The Spiritual Melody containing near Three Hundred Sacred Hymns.* 1691.
———. *War with the Devil.* 1675.
Kellam, Laurence. *Manuell of Praiers.* Douai, 1624.
[Ken, Thomas]. *Prose Works.* Ed. J. T. Round. 1838.
Ken, Thomas. *A Sermon Preached at the King's Chapel at Whitehall in the year, 1685.*
King, Henry. *An Exposition upon the Lords Prayer.* 1628.
Kinloch, T. F. *The Life and Works of Joseph Hall.* 1951.
Knappen, M. M. *Tudor Puritanism; A Chapter in the History of Idealism.* Chicago, 1939.
———, ed. *Two Elizabethan Puritan Diaries by Richard Rogers and Samuel Ward.* 1930.
Knowles, David, O.S.B. *The English Mystical Tradition.* 1961.

Lancicius, Michael. *The glory of the B. father S. Ignatius of Loyola, founder of the Society of Jesus.* Ghent, 1628.
[Laud, William]. *The Works of the Most Reverend Father in God, William Laud, D.D., Sometime Lord Archbishop of Canterbury.* Eds. W. Scott and J. Bliss. 7 Vols. in 9. Oxford, 1847-1860.
Lees-Milne, James. *The Age of Inigo Jones.* 1953.
Legg, J. Wickham. *English Church Life from the Restoration to the Tractarian Movement considered in some of its neglected or forgotten features.* 1914.
———. *English Orders for Consecrating Churches in the Seventeenth Century.* Henry Bradshaw Society. Vol. xli. 1911.
Le Huray, Peter. *Music and the Reformation in England, 1549-1660.* 1967.
L'Estrange, Hamon. *The Alliance of Divine Offices exhibiting all the Liturgies of the Church of England since the Reformation.* 1659. Reprinted Library of Anglo-Catholic Theology. Oxford, 1846.
Ley, John. *A Patterne of Pietie, Or, the Religious life and death of that Grave and Gracious Matron, Mrs. Jane Ratcliffe, Widow and Citizen of Chester.* 1640.

Leys, M.D.R. *The Catholics in England: 1559-1829, a Social History.* 1961.

Lichtenstein, Aharon. *Henry More, the Rational Theology of a Cambridge Platonist.* Cambridge, Mass., 1962.

[Lightfoot, John]. *Works.* Ed. J. R. Pitman. 13 Vols. 1825. Vol. XIII contains "The Journal of the Proceedings of the Assembly of Divines" from January 1, 1643 to December 31, 1644.

Little, Bryan. *Catholic Churches since 1623.* 1966.

Loarte, Gaspar. *The Exercise of a Christian Life.* 1579.

———. *Instructions and Advertisements, How to meditate the Misteries of the Rosarie.* Ca. 1579.

Long, Kenneth. *The Music of the English Church.* 1971.

"Lovekin, Philonax" [pseudonym for J. Wilson]. *Andronicus.* 1646.

Lowe, Edward. *Short Directions for the Performance of Cathedrall Service.* 1661.

Lowrie, Walter. *Action in the Liturgy.* New York, 1953.

———. *Art in the Early Church.* New York, 1947.

Lumpkin, William L. *Baptist Confessions of Faith.* Philadelphia, 1959.

Macaulay, Thomas Babington. *A History of England.* 1848.

Maclean, Donald. *London at Worship.* Presbyterian Historical Society of England. Manchester, 1928.

Maclure, Millar. *The St. Paul's Cross Sermons, 1534-1642.* Toronto, 1958.

Mager, Alois. *Mystik als seelische Wirklichkeit.* Salzburg, 1945.

Mahood, M. M. *Poetry and Humanism.* 1950.

Manton, Thomas. *The Complete Works.* 12 Vols. 1870-1873.

Marchant, Ronald A. *The Puritans and the Church Courts in the Diocese of York, 1560-1642.* 1960.

Marlow, Isaac. *Preliminting Forms of praising God, Vocally Sung by all the Church together, Proved to be no Gospel-Ordinance.* 1691.

Martin, Hugh. *Puritanism and Richard Baxter.* 1954.

Martz, Louis L. *The Poetry of Meditation.* New Haven, Conn., 1954.

Marvell, Andrew. *The Poems and Letters of Andrew Marvell.* Ed. H. M. Margoliouth. 2 Vols. Oxford, 1927.

Mascall, E. L. *Corpus Christi, Essays on the Church and the Eucharist.* 1953.

———. *Toward A Church Architecture.* 1962.

Mather, Cotton. *Magnalia Christi Americana.* 1702.

Matthews, A. G. *Calamy Revised.* 1934.

———. *Mr. Pepys and Nonconformity.* 1954.

———, ed. *The Savoy Declaration of Faith and Order, 1658.* 1959.

———. *Walker Revised.* 1948.

Maxwell, William D. *A History of Worship in the Church of Scotland.* 1955.

———. *John Knox's Genevan Service Book.* Edinburgh, 1931. 2nd edn., 1965.

Maycock, A. L. *Nicholas Ferrar of Little Gidding.* 1938.

Mayor, Stephen. *The Lord's Supper in Early English Dissent.* 1972.

McAdoo, H. R. *The Spirit of Anglicanism.* 1965.

McLachlan, H. J. *Socinianism in XVII Century England.* 1951.

McMillan, William. *The Worship of the Scottish Reformed Church, 1550-1638.* 1931.

Mede, Joseph. *Churches, that is, appropriate Places for Christian Worship both in and ever since the Apostles Times.* 1638.

Mercer, Eric. *English Art, 1553-1625.* Oxford, 1962.

Meres, Francis. *The Sinners Guide.* 1598.

Micklem, Nathaniel, ed. *Christian Worship.* Oxford, 1936.

Miller, Perry. *Errand into the Wilderness.* Cambridge, Mass., 1956.

———. *The New England Mind: From Colony to Province.* Boston, 1960.

———. *The New England Mind: The Seventeenth Century.* Boston, 1961.

———. *Orthodoxy in Massachusetts, 1630-1650.* Boston, 1959.

——— and T. H. Johnson. *The Puritans.* New York, 1938.

Milton, John. *Prose Works.* Yale edn. New Haven, Conn., 1953.

———. *Works.* Columbia edn. 13 Vols. New York, 1931-1938.

Mitchell, A. F. and John Struthers, eds. *Minutes of the Westminster Assembly of Divines . . . Nov. 1644 to March 1649.* Edinburgh and London, 1874.

Mitchell, W. Fraser. *English Pulpit Oratory from Andrewes to Tillotson.* 1932.

Montagu, Henry. *Appello Caesarem.* 1625.

[More, Gertrude]. *Augustine Baker's The Inner Life of Dame Gertrude More.* Ed. Benedict Weld-Blundell. 1911.

———. *The Holy Practises of a Divine Lover.* Paris, 1657.

More, Henry. *Philosophical Poems.* Ed. G. Bullough. Manchester, 1931.

More, P. E. and F. L. Cross, eds. *Anglicanism, the Thought and Practice of the Church of England.* 1935. 2nd edn., 1957.

Morgan, Edmund S. *Visible Saints, the History of a Puritan Idea.* New York, 1963.

Morgan, Irvonwy. *The Nonconformity of Richard Baxter.* 1946.

Morris, John. *The troubles of our Catholic forefathers.* 3 Vols. 1872-1877.

Morton, A. L. *The World of the Ranters.* 1970.

Mueller, William R. *John Donne: Preacher.* Princeton, N.J., 1962.

Neal, Daniel. *The History of the Puritans.* 5 Vols. 1822.

Nelson, R. *Life of Dr. George Bull.* 1713.

New, John F. H. *Anglican and Puritan, The Bases of Their Opposition, 1558-1640.* Palo Alto, Calif., 1964.

Newcome, Henry. *The Autobiography of Henry Newcome.* 2 Vols. Chetham Society, 1852.

———. *The Diary of the Revd. Henry Newcome.* Chetham Society, 1849.

Newton, Eric and William Neill. *2000 Years of Christian Art.* 1966.

Nichols, J. H. *Corporate Worship in the Reformed Church*. Philadelphia, 1968.

———. *A History of Christianity, 1650-1950*. New York, 1956.

Nicholson, William. *Plain but Full Exposition of the Church of England*. 1654.

———. *Works*. 2nd edn., reprint in Library of Anglo-Catholic Theology. Oxford, 1844.

Northbrooke, John. *A Treatise Wherein Dicing, Dauncing, etc. Are Reproved*. 1577. Reprinted by the Shakespeare Society, ed. Collier, 1843.

Notestein, Wallace. *English Folk; a Book of Characters*. New York, 1938.

Nuttall, G. F. *The Holy Spirit in Puritan Faith and Experience*. Oxford, 1946.

——— *Richard Baxter*. 1965.

———. *Visible Saints; the Congregational Way, 1640-1660*. Oxford, 1957.

———. *The Welsh Saints, 1640-1660*. Cardiff, 1957.

——— and Owen Chadwick, eds. *From Uniformity to Unity, 1662-1962*. 1962.

Nye, Philip. *Beams of Former Light; Discovering how Evil it is to impose Doubtful and Disputable Forms or Practices upon Ministers*. 1660.

Oechslin, Louis, O.P. *L'Intuition mystique de sainte Thérèse*. Paris, 1946.

Ogg, David. *England in the Reign of Charles II*. 2 Vols. Oxford, 1955.

Oman, Charles. *English Church Plate, 1597-1830*. 1957.

Orme, William. *Life and Times of Richard Baxter, with a Critical Examination of his Writings*. 1830.

———. *Memoirs of the Life, Writings and Religious Connexions of John Owen, D.D.* 1820.

Osmond, Percy. *A Life of John Cosin*. 1913.

Overton, J. H. *Life in the English Church* (1660-1714). 1885.

———. *The Non-jurors, their Lives, Principles and Writings*. 1902.

Owen, John. *A Brief Instruction in Worship*. 1667.

———. *A Discourse concerning Liturgies and their Imposition*. 1662.

———. *A Discourse of The Holy Spirit in Prayer*. 1662.

———. *Eschol, or Rules of Direction*. 1648.

———. *An Inquiry into the Origin, Order, and Communion of Evangelical Churches*. 1681.

———. *Works*. Ed. W. H. Goold. 16 Vols. Edinburgh, 1850-1853.

Packer, John William. *The Transformation of Anglicanism 1643-1660, with special reference to Henry Hammond*. Manchester, 1969.

Page, William. *A Treatise of Justification of Bowing at the Name of Jesus*. 1631.

Palmer, William. *Origines Liturgicae*. 1832.

Parker, J. *An Introduction to the History of the Successive Revisions of the Book of Common Prayer.* Oxford, 1879.

Passmore, J. A. *Ralph Cudworth.* Cambridge, 1951.

Patrick, Simon. *A brief account of the New Sect of Latitude Men.* 1662.

———. *A Continuation of the Friendly Debate.* 1669.

———. *A Friendly Debate between a Conformist and a Non-Conformist.* 1668.

Paul, Robert S., ed. *An Apologeticall Narration.* Boston and Philadelphia, 1963.

———. *The Lord Protector, Religion and Politics in the Life of Oliver Cromwell.* 1955.

Pearsall, J. S. *The Rise of Congregationalism at Andover.* 1844.

Peaston, A. Elliott. *The Prayer Book Tradition in the Free Churches.* 1964.

Peers, E. Allison. *Studies of the Spanish Mystics.* 2 Vols. 1927-1930.

[Penn, William]. *The Witness of William Penn.* Eds. F. B. Tolles and E. G. Alderfer. New York, 1957.

[Pennington, Isaac]. *The Hidden Life; A Series of Extracts from the Writings of Isaac Pennington.* Ed. Robert Davis. 1951.

———. *Works.* 4 Vols. 3rd edn., 1784.

Percival, A. P., ed. *The Original Services for the State Holidays.* 1838.

Perkins, Jocelyn. *Westminster Abbey: Its Worship and Ornaments.* 1952.

Perkins, William. *Arte of Prophesying.* Cambridge, 1607.

———. *A Reformed Catholike.* 1603.

———. *A Treatise of Mans Imaginations.* Cambridge, 1607.

———. *Works.* Edn. of 1631.

Persons, Robert, S.J. *The First Booke of the Christian Exercise appertayning to resolution.* 1592.

Peter, Saint, of Alcantara. *Golden Treatise of Mental Prayer.* A translation, Brussels, 1632.

———. *Treatise on Prayer and Meditation.* Ca. 1558.

[Peters, Hugh]. *Tales and Jests of Mr. Hugh Peters.* 1807.

Pettit, Norman. *The Heart Prepared: Grace and Conversion in Puritan Spiritual Life.* New Haven, Conn., 1966.

Phillips, C. S. *Hymnody Past and Present.* 1937.

Phillips, John. *The Reformation of Images . . . 1535-1660.* Berkeley, Calif., 1973.

Picart, Bernard. *Cérémonies et Coutumes Religieuses de tous les Peuples du Monde.* 4 Vols. Amsterdam, 1736.

Pinto, V. da Sola. *Peter Sterry Platonist and Puritan.* Cambridge, 1934.

Playfere, Thomas. *The Whole Sermons of that Eloquent Divine of Famous Memory: Thomas Playfere, Doctor of Divinitie.* 1623.

Playford, Henry. *Harmonia Sacra.* 1688.

Playford, John. *English Dancing Master.* 1650.

Pocklington, John. *Altare Christianum or the Dead Vicars Plea.* 1637.

Pope, Alexander. *An Essay on Man.* 1733-1734.

———. *Works.* Ed. W. Elwin and W. J. Courthope. 1871-1889.

Potter, G. R. and E. M. Simpson, eds. *The Sermons of John Donne.* 10 Vols. Berkeley and Los Angeles, Calif., 1953-1962.

Pourrat, Pierre. *Christian Spirituality.* Tr. W. H. Mitchell and S. P. Jacques. 3 Vols. Paris, 1922-1927.

Powell, Vavasor. *The Bird and the Cage.* 2nd edn., 1662.

———. *Common Prayer Book no Divine Service.* 1660.

Powicke, F. J. *The Cambridge Platonists.* 1926.

———. *The life of the Reverend Richard Baxter.* 2 Vols. 1924.

Preston, John. *The Cuppe of Blessing.* 3 sermons. 1633.

———. *Five Sermons on the Divine Love.* 1640.

———. *The Golden Sceptre held forth to the Humble, with the Churches Dignitie by her Marriage, and the Churches Dutie in her Carriage.* 1638.

———. *A Heavenly Treatise of the Divine Love of Christ.* 1640.

———. *The Soliloquy of a Devout Soul to Christ, Panting after the Love of the Lord Jesus.* 1640.

Prideaux, John. *A Sermon preached on the 5 Oct. 1624 on the Consecration of St. James Chappell at Exceter Colledge.* 1624.

Prothero, R. E. [Lord Ernle]. *The Psalms in Human Life.* 1903.

Prynne, William. *A Brief Survay and Censure of Mr. Cozens His Couzening Devotions. . . .* 1628.

———. *Canterburies Doome.* 1646.

[Quakers, The]. *The First Publishers of Truth.* Ed. N. Penney. 1907.

———. *[To the?] King and both Houses of Parliament, Being a Declaration of the present Suffering and imprisonment of above 600 of the people of God in scorn called Quakers, who now suffer in England for Conscience Sake.* 1664.

Ramsey, Arthur Michael. *Durham Essays and Addresses.* 1956.

Ramsey, Mary P. *Les Doctrines Mediévales chez Donne. . . .* Oxford, 1917.

Rapin. *Reflexions sur l'Eloquence de la Chaire.* Paris, 1672.

Ratcliff, E. C. *The Booke of Common Prayer of the Churche of England: its Making and Revisions, 1549-1661.* Alcuin Club Collections. 1949.

Ravenscroft, Thomas. *Whole Book of Psalmes.* 1621.

Reynolds, Edward. *Meditations on the Holy Sacrament of the Lord's Last Supper.* 1638.

Rice, H.A.L. *Thomas Ken: Bishop and Non-Juror.* 1965.

Richards, Michael. *The Liturgy in England.* 1966.

Richardson, Caroline F. *English Preachers and Preaching, 1640-1670.* New York, 1928.

Risbrooke, W. Jardine. *Anglican Liturgies of the Seventeenth and Eighteenth Centuries.* Alcuin Club. 1958.

Robarts, Foulke. *Gods Holy House and Service according to the primitive and most Christian forme thereof.* 1639.

[Robinson, John]. *The Works of John Robinson.* Ed. J. Ashton. 3 Vols. 1852.

Rogers, Richard. *Seven Treatises . . . leading and guiding to true happiness both in this life and in the life to come.* 1603.

Rollins, Hyder E., ed. *Cavalier and Puritan.* New York, 1923.

Rous, Francis. *The Mysticall Marriage.* 1635.

Routley, Erik R. *Hymns and Human Life.* 1952.

———. *The Music of Christian Hymnody.* 1957.

[Royal Commission on Historical Monuments Report]. *City of Oxford.* 1939.

Rugoff, Milton Allan. *Donne's Imagery: A Study in Creative Sources.* New York, 1939.

Russell, Elbert. *The History of Quakerism.* New York, 1942.

Sales, St. Francis de. *An Introduction to the Devout Life. . . .* Tr. T. Y. [Yakesley]. 3rd edn. [Rouen], 1614.

———. *Delicious Entertainments of the Soule. . . .* Douai, 1632.

———. *Of the Love of God.* Tr. Thomas Carre. 1630.

Sanderson, Robert. *The Case of the Liturgy Stated in the Late Times.* Ca. 1652.

———. *A Sovereign Antidote against Sabbatarian Errors.* 1636.

———. *Works.* Ed. W. Jacobson. 6 Vols. Oxford, 1859.

Sandys, Edwin. *Europae Speculum.* 1673.

Schaff, Philip. *The Creeds of the Evangelical Protestant Churches.* New York, 1877.

Schenk, W. *The Concern for Social Justice in the Puritan Revolution.* 1948.

Schmidt, Hermanus A. P. *Introductio in Liturgiam Occidentalem.* Rome, Freiburg, Barcelona, 1960.

Schmidt-Klausing, F. *Zwingli als Liturgiker.* Göttingen, 1952.

Schnorrenburg, John M. "Anglican Architecture, 1558-1662: Its Theological Implications and Its Relation to the Continental Background." Ph.D., Princeton University, 1964.

Scholes, Percy A. *The Oxford Companion to Music.* 3rd edn., 1941.

———. *The Puritans and Music.* 1934. Reissued 1970.

Seaver, Paul S. *The Puritan Lectureships: the Politics of Religious Dissent, 1560-1662.* Palo Alto, Calif., 1970.

Sedding, J. D. *Art and Handicraft.* 1893.

Sekler, E. F. *Wren and his Place in European Architecture.* 1956.

Sewel, William. *History of the Rise, Increase, and Progress of the Christian People called Quakers.* 1722.

Sharrock, Roger. *John Bunyan.* 1954.

Shaw, William A. *A History of the English Church during the Civil Wars and under the Commonwealth, 1640-1660.* 2 Vols. 1900.

Shepherd, Massey H., Jr. *The Oxford American Prayer Book Commentary.* New York, 1950.

Simpson, Alan. *Puritanism in Old and New England.* Chicago, 1955.

Skipton, H.P.K. *The Life and Times of Nicholas Ferrar.* 1907.

Slatyer, William. *Psalmes or Songs of Sion turned into the language and set to the tunes of a strange land.* 1635.

Smith, Henry. *Sermons and other Treatises.* 1675.

Smith, John. *Select Discourses*. Ed. John Worthington. 1660.

Smith, J. W. Ashley. *The Birth of Modern Education: the Contribution of the Dissenting Academies, 1660-1800*. 1954.

Smith, Thomas. *A Sermon about Frequent Communion, Preached before the University of Oxford, August the 17th, 1679*. 1685.

Smyth, Charles. *The Art of Preaching*. . . . 1952.

Smyth, John. *The Differences of the Churches of the Separation*. 1605.

———. *Works*. Ed. W. T. Whitley. 2 Vols. Cambridge, 1915.

South, Robert. *False Foundations removed*. 1661.

———. *The Scribe instructed to the Kingdom of Heaven*. 1660.

———. *Works*. 7 Vols. Oxford, 1823.

Southey, Robert. *The Life of Wesley and the Rise and Progress of Methodism*. 1846.

Sparke, Michael. *The Crums of Comfort to Groans of the Spirit*. 1652.

Sparrow, A. *Rationale or Practical Exposition of the Book of Common Prayer*. 1657. Reissued by J. H. Newman. Oxford, 1839.

Sprat, Thomas. *The History of the Royal-Society of London, For the Improving of Natural Knowledge*. 1667.

Sprott, G. W. and J. Leishman, eds. *The Book of Common Order*. Edinburgh, 1868.

Staley, Vernon. *Hierurgia Anglicana, Documents and Extracts Illustrative of the Ceremonies of the Anglican Church after the Reformation*. 3 Vols. New edn., 1903.

Stearns, Raymond P. *Congregationalism in the Dutch Netherlands*. Chicago, 1940.

Steere, Douglas V. *The Hardest Journey*. Whittier College Bulletin, Whittier, Calif., 1968.

———. *On Being Present Where You Are*. Pendle Hill Pamphlet. No. 151. Pendle Hill, Pa., 1967.

Stephens, Edward. *The Liturgy of the Ancients Represented, As near as well may be, In English Forms*. . . . 1696.

Stephens, W.R.W. and W. Hunt. *History of the English Church*. 9 Vols. 1901-1910.

Sterry, Peter. *The Rise, Race, and Royalty of the Kingdom of God in the Soul of Man*. 1683.

Stillingfleet, Edward. *Origines Sacrae*. 1662.

———. *The Unreasonableness of Separation*. 1680.

Stinton, George. *A Sermon . . . in the time of Pestilence . . . Nov. 27, 1636*. 1637.

Stock, Richard. *The Church's Lamentation for the Loss of the Godly*. 1614.

Stone, Darwell. *History of the Doctrine of the Holy Eucharist*. 2 Vols. 1909.

Stone, Lawrence. *The Causes of the English Revolution, 1529-1642*. London and New York, 1972.

———. *The Crisis of the Aristocracy, 1558-1641*. Oxford, 1965.

Stonor, R. J. *Stonor: a Catholic Sanctuary in the Chilterns*. Newport, Monmouthshire. 2nd edn., 1952.

Stoughton, John. *History of Religion in England*. 5 Vols. 1867-1874.

————. *Religion in England from 1800 to 1850.* 2 Vols. 1884.

Stranks, C. J. *Anglican Devotion.* 1961.

————. *The Life and Writings of Jeremy Taylor.* 1952.

Streatfield, Frank. *The State Prayers and Other Variations in the Book of Common Prayer.* 1950.

Summers, Joseph H. *George Herbert: His Religion and Art.* 1954.

Summerson, John. *Architecture in Britain, 1530 to 1830.* Harmondsworth and Baltimore, 1954.

Sutherland, James. *English Literature of the Late Seventeenth Century.* Oxford History of English Literature, Vol. V. Oxford, 1969.

Sykes, Norman. *Church and State in England in the XVIII Century.* Cambridge, 1934.

————. *The Church of England and Non-Episcopal Churches in the Sixteenth & Seventeenth Centuries.* 1948.

————. *Old Priest and New Presbyter.* 1956.

Talbot, Peter. *A Treatise of the Nature of Catholick Faith and Heresie.* Rouen, 1657.

Talon, Henri. *John Bunyan: The Man and his Work.* (English trans. of *John Bunyan, l'Homme et l'Oeuvre,* by Barbara Wall, 1951.)

Tate and Brady. *A New Version of the Psalms of David, Fitted to the Tunes used in Churches.* 1696.

Tatham, G. B. *The Puritans in Power, The English Church from 1640 to 1660.* Cambridge, 1913.

Taylor, Jeremy. *An Apology for Authorised and Set Forms of Liturgies against the Presence of the Spirit. 1. For ex Tempore Prayer, 2. Formes of Private Composition.* 1649.

————. *A Collection of Offices, or Forms of Prayer in Cases Ordinary and Extraordinary; Taken out of the Scriptures and the ancient Liturgies of Several Churches, especially the Greek, Together with A Large Preface in Vindication of the Liturgy of the Church of England.* 1658.

————. *Eniautos, or A Course of Sermons for all the Sundays of the Year, fitted to the great necessities and for Supplying the wants of preaching in many parts of this nation.* 1651.

————. *The Liberty of Prophesying.* 1647.

————. *The Rule and Exercises of Holy Living.* Ed. A. R. Waller. 1901.

————. *XXVII Sermons.* 1651.

————. *The Whole Works of The Right Rev. Jeremy Taylor, D.D., Lord Bishop of Down, Connor and Dromore.* Ed. Reginald Heber, revised by Charles Page. 10 Vols. 1847-1852.

Taylor, John. *A Swarme of Sectaries.* 1641.

Taylor, John, ed. *The Revised Liturgy of 1689.* Dublin, 1855.

Tenison, Thomas. *A Discourse of Idolatry.* 1678.

Teresa, Saint, of Avila. *The lyf of the Mother Teresa of Jesus foundresse of the Monasteries of descalced or bare-footed Carmelite nunnes and fryers.* Tr. "W.M. of the Society of Jesus." Antwerp, 1611.

Terry, Richard R. *Calvin's First Psalter* [1539]. Facsimile edn., 1932.

Thompson, Bard, ed. *Liturgies of the Western Church*. Cleveland and New York, 1961.

Thorndike, Herbert. *The Due Way of Composing Differences*. 1660.

————. *of Religious Assemblies and the Publick Service of God: A Discourse according to Apostolic Rule and Practice*. Cambridge, 1642.

————. *Works*. Ed. A. W. Haddan in Library of Anglo-Catholic Theology. 6 Vols. bound in 9. Oxford, 1844-1854.

[Tillotson, John]. *The Golden Book of Tillotson*. Ed. James Moffatt. 1926.

————. *Sermons*. Ed. R. Barker. 14 Vols. 1695-1704.

————. *Works*. Ed. T. Birch. 10 Vols. 1820.

Tindall, William York. *John Bunyan Mechanick Preacher*. New York, 1934.

Todd, II. J. *Bishop Gauden, Author of* εἰκὼν βασιλική. 1829.

Traherne, Philip. *The Soul's Communion with her Saviour*. 1685.

Traherne, Thomas. *Centuries of Meditations*. 1653.

Trevelyan, G. M. *England under the Stuarts*. 1933.

Trevor-Roper, Hugh R. *Archbishop Laud, 1573-1645*. 2nd edn., 1962.

Tulloch, John. *Rational Theology and Christian Philosophy in England in the Seventeenth Century*. 2 Vols. 1872.

Turner, G. Lyon. *Original Records of Early Nonconformity*. 3 Vols. 1911-1914.

Underhill, E. B., ed. *Broadmead Records*. 1847.

————, ed. *Fenstanton, Warboys and Hexham Records*. 1847.

Underwood, A. C. *A History of the English Baptists*. 1947.

Usher, Roland G. *The Reconstruction of the English Church*. 2 Vols. New York, 1910.

Ussher, James. *The Reduction of Episcopacy unto the form of Synodical Government received in the Ancient Church*. 1656.

————. *Works*. Eds. C. R. Elrington and J. H. Todd. 17 Vols. Dublin and London, 1847-1864.

Vann, Richard T. *The Social Development of English Quakerism, 1655-1755*. Cambridge, Mass., 1969.

Victoria County History of Somerset. Vol. 8. 1968.

Villacastin, Tomás. *A Manuall of devout Meditations and Exercises, instructing how to pray mentally*. Tr. H. More. St. Omer, 1618.

Wace, Henry. *The Classic Preachers of the Church*. 1877.

Wakefield, Gordon S. *Puritan Devotion, its place in the development of Christian Piety*. 1958.

Walker, Williston. *The Creeds and Platforms of Congregationalism*. New York, 1893.

Wallace, Ronald S. *Calvin's Doctrine of the Word and Sacraments*. Edinburgh, 1953.

Walton, Isaak. *The Lives of John Donne, Sir Henry Wotton, Richard Hooker, George Herbert and Robert Sanderson.* World's Classics edn., 1927.

Walzer, Michael L. *The Revolution of the Saints: A Study in the Origin of Radical Politics.* Cambridge, Mass., 1965.

Wand, J.W.C. *The High Church Schism.* 1951.

Warner, John. *A brief discourse of right worship.* 1684.

Warwickshire Parish Registers. 1904.

Waterhouse, Ellis. *Painting in Britain, 1530-1790.* Harmondsworth and Baltimore, 1953.

Waterland, D. *Works.* Ed. W. Van Mildert. 6 Vols. 2nd edn., Oxford, 1843.

Watkin, E. I. *Poets and Mystics.* 1953.

Watkins, Owen C. *The Puritan Experience; Studies in Spiritual Autobiography.* New York, 1972.

Watts, Isaac. *Guide to Prayer.* 1716.

————. *The Psalms of David imitated in the language of the New Testament and applied to the Christian State and Worship.* 1719.

————. *Works.* Ed. G. Burder. 6 Vols. 1810-1811.

Weber, Max. *The Protestant Ethic and the Spirit of Capitalism.* Tr. Talcott Parsons. 1930.

Wedgwood, C. Y. *The King's Peace, 1637-1641.* 1955.

Welsby, Paul A. *George Abbot: The Unwanted Archbishop.* 1962.

————. *Lancelot Andrewes, 1555-1626.* 1958.

[Wesley, John]. *The Journal of John Wesley.* Ed. Nehemiah Curnock. 8 Vols. 1909.

West, F. W. *Rude Forefathers.* 1949.

Whiffen, Marcus. *Stuart and Georgian Churches.* 1947.

Whinney, Margaret. *Christopher Wren.* 1971.

———— and Oliver Millar. *English Art, 1625-1714.* 1957.

Whitaker, Wilfrid Barnett. *Sunday in Tudor and Stuart Times.* 1933.

White, Helen. *English Devotional Literature, 1600-1640.* Madison, Wisc., 1931.

White, James F. *The Cambridge Movement: The Ecclesiologists and the Gothic Revival.* Cambridge, 1962.

White, John. *The First Century of Scandalous, Malignant Priests.* 1643.

Whitelock, Bulstrode. *Memorials of the English Affairs; or An Historical Account of what passed from the Beginning of The Reign of King Charles the First, to King Charles the Second His Happy Restauration.* Edn. of 1682.

Whiting, C. E. *Studies in English Puritanism from the Restoration to the Revolution, 1660-88.* Cambridge, 1931.

Whitley, W. T. *A History of the British Baptists.* 1923.

————, ed. *Minutes of the General Assembly of the General Baptists, 1654-1728.* 1909.

[Whittingham, William]. *The Forme of Prayers . . . used in the English Congregation at Geneva; and approved by the famous and godly learned man, John Calvyn.* 1556.

Whyte, Alexander. *The Spiritual Life; The Teaching of Thomas Good-win as received and reissued.* Edinburgh, 1917.

[Whytford, Richard]. *Certaine devout and Godly Petitions, commonly called Iesus Psalter.* 1575.

Wigan, B. J., ed. *The Liturgy in English.* 2nd edn., 1964.

Wilkins, John. *Discourse concerning the Gift of Prayer.* 1649.

———. *Ecclesiastes; or a Discourse concerning the Gift of Preaching.* 1646.

———. *On the Principles and Duties of Natural Religion.* Edn. of 1675.

———. *Sermons.* 1682.

Willey, Basil. *The Seventeenth Century Background.* 1934.

Williams, Peter. *The European Organ, 1450-1850.* 1966.

Wilson, John. *Cultus Evangelicus, Or, a brief Discourse concerning the Spirituality and Simplicity of New Testament Worship.* 1667.

Wilson, John F. *Pulpit in Parliament.* Princeton, N.J., 1969.

Winward, Stephen. *The Reformation of our Worship.* 1964.

Wither, George. *Hymns and Songs of the Church.* 1623.

Wittkower, Rudolph. *Gian Lorenzo Bernini, Roman Baroque Sculptor.* 2nd edn., 1966.

[Wood, Anthony A.]. *The Life and Times of Anthony à Wood.* Abridged from A. Clark's edn. by L. Powys, 1961.

Wood, Thomas. *English Casuistical Divinity during the Seventeenth Century.* 1952.

———, ed. *Five Pastorals: Selections from the Caroline Divines.* 1961.

Woodfill, Walter. *Musicians in English Society from Elizabeth to Charles I.* Princeton, N.J., 1953.

Woodforde, Christopher. *English Stained and Painted Glass.* Oxford, 1954.

Woodhead, Abraham. *Two Discourses concerning the Adoration of our B. Saviour in the H. Eucharist.* Oxford, 1687.

Woodhouse, A.S.P. *Puritanism and Liberty.* 1938.

Wordsworth, Christopher. *Ecclesiastical Biography.* 6 Vols. 2nd edn., 1818.

———. *Who wrote* ΕΙΚΩΝ ΒΑΣΙΛΙΚΗ? 1824.

Wormald, B.H.G. *Clarendon.* Cambridge, 1951.

Worthington, Thomas. *The Rosarie of our Ladie.* Antwerp, 1600.

Wren, Stephen. *Parentalia, or Memoirs of the Family of the Wrens.* 1750.

Wright, Abraham. *Five Several Sermons in Five several Styles or Waies of Preaching.* 1656.

Yarwood, Doreen. *The Architecture of England.* 1963.

Yule, George. *The Independents in the Civil War.* Cambridge, 1958.

Zimmerman, Franklin B. *Henry Purcell, 1659-1695: His Life and Times.* 1967.

INDEX

I. INDEX OF PERSONS

James II, King, 3, 22f, 28, 53, 56-60, 117, 231f, 266f, 337, 392, 394, 400, 459, 466, 488
James, St., 346, 364n
Janson, H.W., 55n
Jasper, R.C.D., 117n, 387n
Jeavons, Sidney, 308n
Jeffrey, William, 504
Jeffreys, Judge George, 171
Jenkins, 309
Jenkins, David, 421f
Jeremiah, 312
Jessey, Henry, 498, 508
Jessopp, Augustus, 479n
Joab, 170n
John, St. of the Cross, 70, 84, 89, 130, 485
John, St., of Damascus, 289
Johnson, James, T., 410n
Johnson, Robert, 210
Johnson, Samuel, 184
Johnson, T.H., 532n
Jolly, Thomas, 448, 452n
Jonah, 12, 37n
Jones, Inigo, 10, 23, 31, 33f, 49, 51, 57, 466
Jones, R.F., 31
Jonson, Ben, 250n
Jordan, W.K., 352
Josaphat, King, 238
Joseph of Arimathea, 463
Joseph, St., 165
Joshua, 231
Josselin, Ralph, 210, 301
Joyce, James, 83
Julian, John, 278n, 285n, 398n, 499
Justin, martyr, 364n
Juvenal, 159, 182
Juxon, Bp., 347n

Keach, Benjamin, 276, 283f, 499, 509f
Keble, John, 110, 157, 293n
Kellam, Laurence, 96
à Kempis, Thomas, 80, 91f
Kempster, William, 52
Ken, Bp. Thomas, 226, 283, 394, 397f
Kersheys, Joshua, 127
Kidder, Bp. Richard, 400
Kierkegaard, Søren, 104, 421n
Kiffin, William, 499
King, Bp. John, 142
Kirk, Robert, 456f
Knappen, M.M., 119n, 124n, 242
Knollys, Hansard, 499
Knox, John, 27, 97, 189, 208, 322, 336, 344, 367, 405, 408, 450, 524
Knox, Ronald, 129

Laing, David, 408n
Lake, Bp. John, 394

Lambert, 274, 448
Lancicius, Michael, 82
Langley, A.S., 170n
Laud, Abp. William, xviii, 12f, 16f, 23n, 32, 34-41, 43, 55, 93f, 120n, 133, 138, 154, 159, 161, 170, 191, 203, 205, 210f, 222, 232, 245, 280, 286, 291f, 304f, 308, 323, 336-344, 354f, 363, 375, 379, 389n, 397, 410, 463, 523
Laurence, St. Justinian, 83
Lawes, 258, 277
Lee-Milne, James, 466n
Legg, J. Wickham, 17n, 205n, 301n, 304n, 308, 389f
Le Huray, Peter, 278n, 280n
Leishman, J., 407n, 410, 412n, 413n, 419n
Leishman, T., 407n
Lemercier, 44n
Lennox, Duke of, 40
Leslie, 270
L'Estrange, H., 117n, 351f, 362, 364
Le Sueur, 35n
Ley, John, 128
Lightfoot, 172, 248
Little, Bryan, 57n, 59n
Lloyd, Bp. William, 384, 394
Loarte, Gaspar, 69, 82n
Locke, John, 137, 439
Long, Kenneth R., 258, 261n, 281n
Louis XIV, King, 264
Louis, St., 219
Lowe, Edward, 261-263
Lowrie, Walter, 306n, 421n
Loyola, St. Ignatius, 23n, 69, 82f, 102, 120n, 122, 485f
Lumpkin, W.L., 500n, 503n, 505n
Luther, Martin, 74, 104, 259, 281, 310, 425, 450

Macaulay, Lord, 250, 254, 398
Mackie, John, 178n
Maclean, Donald, 456n, 457n
Mahood, M.M., 151
Magdalen, Lady, 102
Mager, Alois, 70n
Maine, Jonathan, 52, 135
Malvolio, 217, 250n
Manchester, Lord, 249
Manners, Sir Oliver, 92
Manning, Bernard L., 20, 203
Mansart, 43, 44n, 50
Manton, Thomas, xx, 165, 437, 439, 450n
Marchant, Ronald A., 210n
Marin, Jean, 402
Marlowe, 79
Marlowe, Isaac, 274, 276, 509f
Marot, Clément, 270, 510
Marshall, Stephen, 409

Sherlock, William, 94n
Short, H.L., 11n, 31n, 61f, 64
Shorthouse, J.H., 105
Sibbes, Richard, 169, 225n
Sidney, Sir Philip, 102
Simons, Menno, 425
Simpson, Alan, 132n
Simpson, William, 518
Skinner, Bp. Robert, 379
Slayter, William, 280
Smart, Peter, 38n, 188, 203
Smith, Humphrey, 204
Smith, J.W.A., 454n
Smith, Thomas, 301n
Smith, Charles, 147n
Smyth, John, 272, 497-501, 503, 505
da Sola Pinto, V., 78n
de Solo, Alexis, 91n
Sophocles, 97, 181
South, Robert, 173-175, 180f
Southey, R., 110n
Southwell, 83, 91
Southworth, John, 473
Sparke, Michael, 72, 74f
Sparrow, Anthony, 116, 141n, 350, 352, 364
Spencer, 254
Spilsbury, 499
Sprat, Bp. Thomas, 177
Sprott, G.W., 407n, 410n, 412f, 419n
Staley, Vernon, 213n, 338n
Stanhope, 69n,
Stanton, 173, 248
Steere, Douglas V., 526n, 531n
Stennett, Joseph, Sr., 499
Stephens, Edward, 393, 394-397, 403
Sternhold, Thomas, 275, 277f
Sterry, Peter, 76, 78, 88, 131, 229n, 495, 531
Stillingfleet, Bp. Edward, 133, 135f, 399, 402, 456
Stockton, Richard, 124f
Stone, Darwell, 292n
Stonor, Robert J., 57n, 462n
Stoughton, John, 60n, 66f
Stranks, C.J., 95, 110n, 158-160
Stratford, Bp. Nicholas, 399
Streatfield, 231n-236n
Suso, 89
Sykes, Norman, 183, 387n
Sylvester, Matthew, 132n, 171, 243n, 369n, 371n, 372n, 426n

Tailour, Robert, 279, 281
Talbot, Peter, 383
Tallis, 253
Talon, Henri, 120n
Tamerlane, 150
Tate and Brady, 281
Tauler, 89
Taylor, Bp. Jeremy, xix, xxii, 70, 92n,

100, 106-11, 132, 134, 154, 157-162, 178, 180, 184, 194, 292n, 295, 299, 301, 333, 339, 348-350, 352, 353, 355, 359-362, 400f, 523, 524, 535
Taylor, John, 399n, 493n
Taylor, Thomas, 497
Tenison, Abp. Thomas, 390n, 399, 400
Teresa of Avila, St., 39n, 55, 56, 70, 84, 88, 460, 485
Tertullian, 153n, 191, 306, 364n
Theodoret, 16
Theophrastus, 156
Thomas, Bp. William, 83, 153n, 394
Thomas, J.M.L., 160n, 243n, 440n, 443, 453
Thomson, 448
Thompson, Bard, 307n, 310n
Thorndike, Herbert, 135, 140, 205f, 211, 292, 298, 364, 523
Thurston, Herbert, 82n, 467n, 475n, 477n, 487n
Thynne, Sir John, 63
Tijou, Jean, 53
Tillotson, Abp. John, 133, 136, 142, 176, 178, 180-184, 300, 395, 399, 402, 524
Timothy, 132n
Tindall, W.Y., 493n
Todd, H.J., 347n
Tolles, F.B., 494n
Tombes, John, 490, 498, 507
Tompkins, 258
Traherne, Philip, 78, 102n, 105, 283
Traps, 209
Travers, 369
Trevor-Roper, H.R., 112n
Trinterud, L.J., 6n
Troeltsch, Ernst, 494
Trosse, George, 165, 444
Turner, Bp. Francis, 394
Turner, G. Lyon, 491n
Turner, J. Horsfall, 126n, 172
Turner, Madam, 437
Twisse, 173
Tyndale, William, 6n
Tyrwhit, 464

Underhill, E.B., 274n, 448n, 449n, 504n
Ussher, Abp. James, 156, 294, 297, 343, 367n

Vandyke, 12n, 36n
Valentine, 249
Van Linge, Abraham, 37n
Van Linge, Bernard, 36
Vaughan, 102n, 105, 283
Venables, Edmund, 120n
Verrio, 22, 23n, 58-61

577

II. INDEX OF PLACES (AND CHURCHES)

(Churches are assumed to be Anglican unless otherwise identified.)